HENRY I

Also in the Yale English Monarchs series

Edward the Confessor by Frank Barlow*
William the Conqueror by David C. Douglas*
William Rufus by Frank Barlow
Henry II by W. L. Warren*
Richard I by John Gillingham
King John by W. L. Warren*
Edward I by Michael Prestwich
Richard II by Nigel Saul
Henry V by Christopher Allmand*
Henry VI by Bertram Wolffe
Edward IV by Charles Ross
Richard III by Charles Ross*
Henry VII by S. B. Chrimes
Henry VIII by J. J. Scarisbrick*
Edward VI by Jennifer Loach
James II by John Miller
George I by Ragnhild Hatton
George IV by E. A. Smith

*Available in the U.S. from University of California Press

HENRY I

C. Warren Hollister

Edited and completed by Amanda Clark Frost

YALE UNIVERSITY PRESS
NEW HAVEN AND LONDON

For information about this and other Yale University Press publications,
please contact:
U.S. Office: sales.press@yale.edu   yalebooks.com
Europe Office: sales@yaleup.co.uk   www.yaleup.co.uk

Set in New Baskerville by Best-set Typesetter Ltd, Hong Kong
Printed in Great Britain by St Edmundsbury Press, Suffolk

A catalogue record for this book is available from the
Library of Congress and the British Library.

ISBN 0-300-08858-2 (hbk.)
ISBN 0-300-09829-4 (pbk.)

1 3 5 7 9 10 8 6 4 2

For Edith

CONTENTS

ILLUSTRATIONS

FOREWORD

At last the definitive account of the reign of Henry I (1100–1135) appears in the English Monarchs Series published by Yale University Press. Its author, C. Warren Hollister (1930–1997), began working on the project in 1962, when the eminent Anglo-Norman historian Professor David Douglas recommended him as Henry's biographer for the series. Long in the making, the book was delayed by the great Santa Barbara fire of 1990, in which, as Hollister wrote to his editor, "among our losses were the hard and floppy disks and the printout of my Henry I MS, my entire research library, and all my research note cards." Discouraged only briefly, Hollister resumed writing a final draft of the book during a leave of absence in Brittany in 1994. He had completed a provisional draft of eight and a half chapters together with an outline for the remainder by 1997, and it had been his hope and intention to complete all eleven chapters soon afterward. His death sadly intervened, but not (if I may be permitted) fatally, for Hollister's former student in the field of Anglo-Norman church history and later an editor for the University of California Press, Dr Amanda Clark Frost, undertook the completion of the work at his request. She painstakingly edited the completed chapters and proceeded to finish the remaining chapters according to Hollister's outline. Dr Frost's knowledge, skill, perseverance, patience, accuracy, thoroughness, and clear style have made the book as close as humanly possible to what Professor Hollister would have wanted. It would not exist without her.

Hollister's lifework on Henry I has altered our perceptions of that king. The year before he died, he published an article in *Peritia* 10 (1996): "The Rouen Riot and Conan's Leap." It typifies his vigorous style, penchant for entertaining while instructing, and ability to tease out varieties of meaning from a peculiar event. Why did the future King Henry I cause a fellow named Conan to be hurled out the window to his death during the Rouen riot of 1090? Because, Hollister convinces the reader, Henry was a capable, responsible ruler devoted to making peace both in Normandy (as the date suggests) and in England after becoming king in 1100. Long remembered for his unrestrained sexuality and his cruelty, Henry will now be understood (despite his undeniable faults) chiefly as a great peacemaker on both sides of the Channel. In some thirty articles Hollister proved over and again that

Henry's administrative sophistication was unmatched in early twelfth-century Europe.

Hollister not only set out a new view of Henry I but also advanced the concept of administrative kingship: government through standard bureaucratic forms, professional administrators, and a series of institutions linking localities to the center. Even more important, Hollister bridged not only the Conquest but also the Channel. He became internationally famous for studies that emphasized the interrelationship of England and Normandy, two fields usually treated as separate subjects. Out of English history and French history, he made the field of Anglo-Norman history, now established and recognized everywhere.

Before devoting himself to the study of Henry I, Professor Hollister wrote extensively on Anglo-Saxon and Anglo-Norman military institutions. His books *Anglo-Saxon Military Institutions on the Eve of the Norman Conquest* (Oxford, 1962), which won the Triennial Book Prize of the Conference on British Studies, and *The Military Organization of Norman England* (Oxford, 1965) established the young scholar as a brilliant and precocious student of both sides of the Anglo-Norman divide. His choice of subjects was courageous, as English historians had been debating the nature of military, governmental, and administrative institutions for more than a century. His first book, about the fyrd, was a brave piece of scholarship by a young, unknown American, challenging the previous work of some eminent British scholars. The good sense of Hollister's arguments and the clarity of his prose won him and his theories admirers and then friends. By the mid-1960s, he was one of the few American historians of medieval Britain treated as an equal by English academics.

Professor Hollister was a Fellow of the Medieval Academy, of the Royal Historical Society, and of the Medieval Academy of Ireland; he was President of the North American Conference on British Studies, of the International Charles Homer Haskins Society, and of many other organizations. His fellowships and grants included two Fulbrights, a Guggenheim, two ACLS fellowships, and a Borchard Research Fellowship to Brittany. He received the Triennial Prize and the Walter D. Love Memorial Prize, and he was the youngest person ever (to date) to be named Faculty Research Lecturer at the University of California, Santa Barbara—the highest award that University of California faculty can bestow upon their peers.

Hollister graduated with honors from Harvard in 1951, served in the United States Air Force during the Korean War, and earned his Ph.D. at the University of California, Los Angeles, in 1958. He went on immediately to teach at the University of California at Santa Barbara, his one and only home institution, first as an Instructor ("a rank," he wrote once with typical ironic humor, "that has since been abolished on humanitarian grounds"), and then up to, and beyond, the top of the University of California's arcane merit system. At the time of his official (though hardly actual) retirement in 1994 he was the most respected and highest ranked professor in the Humanities at UCSB.

Hollister was also one of the best medieval generalists in the world. His textbooks, *The Making of England*, currently in its seventh edition, and *Medieval Europe*, in its eighth, are the most frequently used undergraduate textbooks in America on medieval history and have been translated into a variety of languages. Hollister presented invited lectures on four continents and was an energizing power at innumerable meetings.

None of this quite conveys the sense of what one of his colleagues called "The Hollister Touch." Hollister wrote, and spoke, with an easy clarity that all writers know is the hardest of all things to achieve, with a sure touch for just the right way to put what needs to be said, and without a trace of condescension. Hollister's teaching was as effective as his research. As a teacher of undergraduates he packed the largest auditoriums, and his classes were known as being tough but direct, incisive, and deceptively entertaining. He exercised his talents as a lyricist by setting historical events to well-known tunes. His devotion to teaching won him the Vice Presidency for Teaching of the American Historical Association, a National Teaching Award from the Danforth Foundation, and the UCSB Outstanding Faculty Teaching Award.

As a teacher of graduate students Hollister made a mark that will be indelible for a century or more. During his career he directed three dozen doctoral students in rigorous and often exhausting seminars, and (*mirabile dictu*) in a difficult job market he placed all his doctoral students who completed their degrees and sought academic positions. Among his graduate students (a "UCSB School" was centered on him), many have written or are writing prosopographical and other studies of the Anglo-Norman realm that promise to change scholarly views of how medieval government functioned, providing an understanding of how family interests and connections played out. Hollister taught his students a new appreciation for the rich charter evidence of the realm. Where this evidence had traditionally been mined for constitutional and legal information, he taught them to look also at their lists of signatories and witnesses and to construct from these an intimate knowledge of Anglo-Norman administration.

Hollister was one of the first to professionalize the work of medieval graduate students in America. His students were the first to give papers regularly at conferences across America and the first to give invited papers in England. And they were the first to assume that publishing before getting their degrees was a matter of course: another way that Hollister permanently changed the field intellectually and pedagogically.

One of Hollister's dearest achievements was the flourishing of the Haskins Society that he founded; it serves as a forum for colleagues and graduate students in America to meet scholars from Britain and Europe and to present their work to an appreciative scholarly audience that can provide them with criticism to help develop and refine their ideas. Hollister will be remembered as one of the most influential American medieval historians since the foundation of medieval studies in the United States.

Professor Hollister's other talents should also be mentioned. He was a lyricist and musician who produced two shows, a devotee of the Oz books to the extent of forming one of the two best collections on Oz in the world, and a connoisseur of music of all kinds and all periods, perhaps with a special fondness for the musical theatre of Andrew Lloyd Webber. He was a great friend to me, and I am pleased for myself as well as for him, for his widow Edith, and for Amanda Clark Frost that the book has at last appeared.

Amanda Clark Frost and I are convinced that Warren Hollister would have dedicated his completed book to his companion in life and work, Edith Hollister, and so it is.

University of California, Santa Barbara
September 2000

EDITOR'S PREFACE

Like Henry I, Warren Hollister died unexpectedly, in the prime of life and at the height of his powers, leaving his life's work unfinished. A week before his death, in September 1997, Hollister had told Jeffrey Burton Russell, his colleague and friend, that he expected to finish his biography of Henry I by Christmas. It was an optimistic prediction but an understandable one given his astonishing progress in reconstituting the manuscript after his entire first draft was consumed in a summer wildfire in 1990. Speaking with Russell, Hollister was particularly enthusiastic about the research for chapter 10, "King and Church," for which he was gathering information on Henry's benefactions to the regular clergy, a recent interest that had developed from his study of the king's widespread network of patronage. Barely a week later, in the intensive care unit of UCLA Medical Center, Hollister removed his oxygen mask and dictated to his wife, Edith, a plan for the completion of the manuscript, specifying the books he was currently using and selecting the colleagues and friends whom he counted on to help finish the book. He was then midway through chapter 9 ("Law and Governance"), with the research for chapters 10 ("King and Church") and 11 ("Final Years and Conclusion") in progress.

Entrusted with the task of finishing *Henry I*, I began work by carefully studying the first eight chapters. I was impressed as always with Hollister's graceful, lucid style, his persuasive argument, his humanity, and his wit. Optimistic as I was, it never occurred to me that the project would take three years to complete. Hollister would have written fewer words and offered less detail. But then he knew exactly what he was going to say. The guidance and instructions he left were brief, listing only topics, ideas to be developed, and research to be considered. Hollister had not had the opportunity to go over the notes, update primary sources after the appearance of new editions or translations, select the illustrations, draw up genealogies, reformat tables, compile a bibliography, nor pare, tighten, and regularize his text.

The first chapter of *Henry I* introduces the setting and the sources. The following six chapters offer a narrative of the king's life, from his landless youth to his ultimate triumph over pugnacious neighbors and fractious Norman nobles. Hollister's vivid account of the challenges that faced the Conqueror's third son reveals a command of the evi-

dence and an astuteness of interpretation that reflect the long gesta-
tion of this work. Chapters 8, 9, and 10 were designed as analytical
studies of topics that Hollister felt deserved careful explication.
Chapter 11 deals with Henry's final years, mostly spent in Normandy,
when the king and the realm were at peace, and concludes with
Hollister's overall assessment of the man and the reign.

My aim was to complete the book as Warren Hollister had envisioned
it. I have followed his outlines and researched the topics he intended
to cover. He proposed to his wife that chapter 9 be completed by
drawing on his previously published work on the royal administration,
and this I have done. It is therefore not his final word: we can never
know how Hollister would have responded to recent interpretations in
legal and administrative history.

Chapter 10 presented the greatest challenge, for Hollister's only
published work on the Church consisted of two articles, one dealing
with the investiture controversy and the other with the treatment that
William Rufus and Henry I accorded the archbishop of Canterbury in
particular and the Church in general. I have incorporated an important section from "William II, Henry I, and the Anglo-Norman Church"
in order to use Hollister's own words where it was appropriate to do so.
The further topics he proposed were many, making this chapter the
longest in the book. For this reason I have divided the chapter into sections, with pertinent quotes by Henry's contemporaries as headings.
Because I was trying to flesh out the topics that interested Hollister—
especially Henry's benefactions and his interest in the abbey of Cluny—
and because most of this material has not been previously published, I
have chosen to let the evidence speak for itself.

Chapter 11, the conclusion, shows Henry at his best, in his final years,
peacefully attending to affairs of the realm, basking in international
recognition, enjoying his grandsons—at least until 1135 when Geoffrey
of Anjou began to grow greedy on Normandy's southern frontier. The
overall assessment of the king presented here derives from Hollister's
narrative in chapters 2–7 and from his outlines and notes. The portrait
is both sensible and sensitive: one can see why, thirty years ago, the
young California professor was drawn to study this intelligent and
complex individual whom William of Malmesbury called "the greatest
of all kings in the memory of either ourselves or our fathers" and whose
reign John Horace Round described as the most tantalizing in European history. How could these favorable assessments and those of contemporary chroniclers be reconciled with the harsh twentieth-century
portrait of the man and his reign? What Hollister discovered (and, from
the 1970s, published in a flood of articles) permits a more nuanced
assessment of the king, revealing political astuteness tempered with
generosity, good humor, and human feeling. The dark and dated
stereotype of the cold, cruel, avaricious manipulator of men is now

replaced with a clear picture of a savvy political realist with a talent for administration, the strength to enforce peace, and the heart to win men's praise for both his pragmatism and his piety. Scrupulously detailing the reign, Hollister uncovered the man.

I could not have completed this book alone. Jeffrey Burton Russell read and critiqued every word I have written. Without his help and encouragement I would never have reached these final lines. The kindness and generosity of Marjorie Chibnall, doyenne of the field and longtime friend of Warren and Edith Hollister, can never be repaid. Deborah Gerish, Hollister's last graduate student, undertook the tedious task of compiling a bibliography from the footnotes (while struggling to complete her dissertation and interviewing for an academic job). I thank Robert Baldock of Yale University Press, London, for his confidence and patience. My husband, Frank J. Frost, cheerfully assumed the unaccustomed task of research assistant, in the process learning more about Henry I than a historian of ancient Greece might care to know. And a word of gratitude to the Interlibrary Loan Office of the Library of the University of California, Santa Barbara, for their efficiency and courtesy.

Amanda Clark Frost
Santa Barbara, California
September 2000

NOTE ON ABBREVIATIONS
AND REFERENCES

Full bibliographical details of all sources are given in the bibliography on pp. 507–534. References throughout the footnotes are by abbreviated title, with authors' or editors' names, where relevant.

The following abbreviations are also used to refer to sources:

Ann. Wint.	"Annales monasterii de Wintona". In *Annales monastici*, vol. 36, part 1
AO	*Anselmi opera: S. Anselmi Cantuariensis Archiepiscopi opera omnia*. Ed. Francis S. Schmitt. 6 vols. Stuttgart, 1946–1961. Repr. 1968
ASC	*Anglo-Saxon Chronicle*. Ed. Dorothy Whitelock. New Jersey, 1961
Bayeux, *Livre noir*	*Antiquus cartularius baiocensis (Livre noir)*. Ed. F. Liebermann. Strasbourg, 1879
BL	British Library
CDF	*Calendar of Documents Preserved in France, Illustrative of the History of Great Britain and Ireland*. Ed. J. H. Round. Vol. 1, AD 918–1206. London, 1889
Chron. Ab.	*Chronicon monasterii de Abingdon*. Ed. Joseph Stevenson. Rolls Series, vol. 2. London, 1858
Chron. Battle	*Chronicle of Battle Abbey*. Ed. Eleanor Searle. Oxford, 1980
CMH	*Cambridge Medieval History*. Vol. 5: *The Contest of Empire and Papacy*. Ed. J. R. Tanner, C. W. Previté-Orton, Z. N. Brooke. Cambridge, 1929–1967
CP	*Complete Peerage of England, Scotland, Ireland, Great Britain and the United Kingdom*. New edn, rev. and enl. Ed. Vicary Gibbs. 13 vols in 14. London, 1910–1959
CUL	Cambridge University Library
DB	*Domesday Book*. Ed. and trans. John Morris. 38 vols. Chichester, 1975–1992
DNB	*Dictionary of National Biography*. London, 1891
Eadmer, *HN*	Eadmer, *Historia novorum in Anglia*. Ed. Martin Rule. Rolls Series, vol. 81. London, 1884
EHD	*English Historical Documents*. Ed. and trans. David C. Douglas and George Greenway. Vol. 2: 1066–1189. 2nd edn, New York, 1981
ep./epp.	epistle/epistles
EYC	*Early Yorkshire Charters*. Ed. William Farrer and C. T. Clay. 12 vols. Edinburgh, 1914–1965
EYF	*Early Yorkshire Families*. Ed. Charles Travis Clay. Leeds, 1973
Farrer, *Itin.*	*Outline Itinerary of King Henry the First*. Ed. William Farrer. Oxford, 1920
FW	Florence of Worcester, *Chronicon ex chronicis*. Ed. B. Thorpe. 2 vols. London, 1848–1849

GC	*Gallia Christiana in provincias ecclesiasticas distributa; qua series et historia archiepiscoporum, episcoporum, et abbatum Franciae vicinarumque ditionum ab origine ecclesiarum ad nostra tempora, deducitur et probatur ex authenticis documentis ad calcem appositis.* 16 vols. Paris, 1715–1865. Reprint 1970
GND	*Gesta normannorum ducum of William of Jumièges, Orderic Vitalis and Robert of Torigni.* Ed. and trans. Elisabeth M. C. van Houts. 2 vols. Oxford, 1992–1995
GP	*see* William of Malmesbury
GR	*see* William of Malmesbury
HF	*Recueil des historiens des Gaules et de la France.* Ed. Martin Bouquet. 24 vols in 25. Vol. 15: *Reigns of Philip I, Louis VI, Louis VII.* Repr. Farnborough, 1967–1968
HH	Henry of Huntingdon, *Historia Anglorum.* Ed. Diana Greenway. Oxford, 1996
HN	*see* Eadmer and William of Malmesbury
JW	John of Worcester, *Chronicle.* Ed. J. R. H. Weaver. Oxford, 1908
Liber de Hyda	*Liber monasterii de Hyda.* Ed. Edward Edwards. Rolls Series, vol. 45. London, 1866
MGH	*Monumenta Germaniae historica. Scriptores rerum Germanicarum.* 13 vols. Berlin, 1955–1980
MMI	C. Warren Hollister, *Monarchy, Magnates, and Institutions in the Anglo-Norman World.* London, 1986
NI	C. H. Haskins. *Norman Institutions.* Cambridge, Mass., 1918
OV	Orderic Vitalis, *Historia ecclesiastica/Ecclesiastical History.* Ed. and trans. Marjorie Chibnall. 6 vols. Oxford, 1969–1980
PL	*Patrologia cursus completus. Series latina.* Ed. J-P. Migne. 221 vols. Paris, 1844–1864. Repr. 1958—
PR 31 Henry I	*Pipe Roll of Henry I, Michaelmas 1130.* Ed. Joseph Hunter. Rev. edn, London, 1929
RBE	*Red Book of the Exchequer.* Ed. Hubert Hall. Rolls Series, vol. 99. London, 1896
RRAN	*Regesta regum anglo-normannorum.* Vol. 1: *Regesta Willelmi Rufi,* ed. H. W. C. Davis. Vol. 2: *Regesta Henrici Primi,* ed. C. Johnson and H. A. Cronne. Vol. 3: *Regesta Regis Stephani ac Mathildis imperatricis ac Gaufredi et Henrici ducum normannorum, 1135–1154,* ed. H. A. Cronne and R. H. C. Davis. Oxford, 1913–1969
RS	Rolls Series: *Rerum Britannicarum medii aevi scriptores.* 99 vols. London, 1858–1911. Reprint, 1964–1965
RT, *Chron.*	Robert of Torigni, *Chronique.* Ed. Léopold Delisle. 2 vols. Rouen, 1872–1873
SD	Symeon of Durham, *Historia ecclesiae dunelmensis,* in *Symeonis monachi opera omnia.* Ed. Thomas Arnold. Rolls Series, vol. 75, part 1. London, 1882–1885
VCH	*Victoria County History*
WM	William of Malmesbury
WM, *GP*	William of Malmesbury, *Gestis pontificum anglorum.* Ed. N. E. S. A. Hamilton. Rolls Series, vol. 52. London, 1870
WM, *GR*	William of Malmesbury, *Gesta regum anglorum.* Ed. and trans. R. A. B. Mynors; completed by R. M. Thomson and M. Winterbottom. Oxford and New York, 1998
WM, *HN*	William of Malmesbury, *Historia novella.* Ed. and trans. K. R. Potter. London, 1955

The Norman Empire

The Pagi (pays)

I	P. Pontivus, le Pontieu.
II	P. Viminaus, le Vimeu.
III	P. Ambianensis, l'Amiénois (Amiens).
IV	P. Tellaus, le Talou.
V	P. Bellovacensis, le Beauvaisis (Beauvais).
VI	P. Caletus, le Pays de Caux.
VII	P. Rodomensis, le Roumois (Rouen).
VIII	P. Vilcassinus, le Vexin.
IX	P. Parisiacus, le Parisis (Paris).
X	P. Lexovinus, le Lieuvin (Lisieux).
XI	P. Ebroicinus, l'Évrecin (Évreux).
XII	P. Madriacensis, le Méresais (Mérey).
XIII	P. Pinciacensis, le Pincerais (Poissy).
XIV	P. Durocassinus, le Drouais (Dreux).
XV	P. Carnotenus, le Chartrain (Chartres).
XVI	Otlinga Saxonia.
XVII	P. Oximensis, l'Hiémois (Exmes).
XVIII	P. Sagensis, le Séois (Séez).
XIX	P. Corbonensis, le Corbonnais (Corbon).
XX	P. Bajocassinus, le Bessin (Bayeux).
XXI	P. Cenomanicus, le Maine (Le Mans).
XXII	P. Coriovallensis (Coriallum, Cherbourg).
XXIII	P. Constantinus, le Cotentin (Coutances).
XXIV	P. Abrincatinus, l'Avranchin (Avranches).
XXV	P. Redonicus (Rennes).
XXVI	P. Aleti, le Poulet (Alet, Saint-Malo).
XXVII	P. Racter (?) (Dol).

Boundaries of the *pagi*
Boundaries of the dioceses
Boundaries of the *coutume*
Pagus and diocese boundaries coinciding
Pagus and *coutume* boundaries coinciding
Diocese and *coutume* boundaries coinciding
Pagus, diocese, and *coutume* boundaries coinciding
Approximate limit of 'Conquêts Hue de Gournay'
Archbishop's, bishop's cathedral city
Religious houses (names of those founded before 1066 printed in italic)
Castle
Battlefields with dates
Other places named

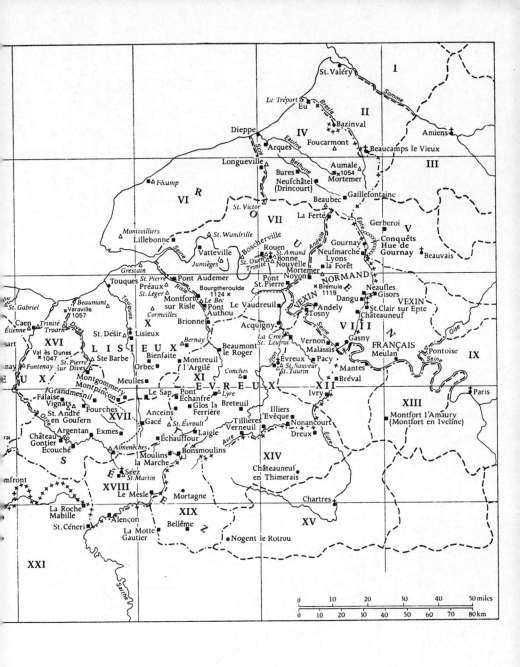

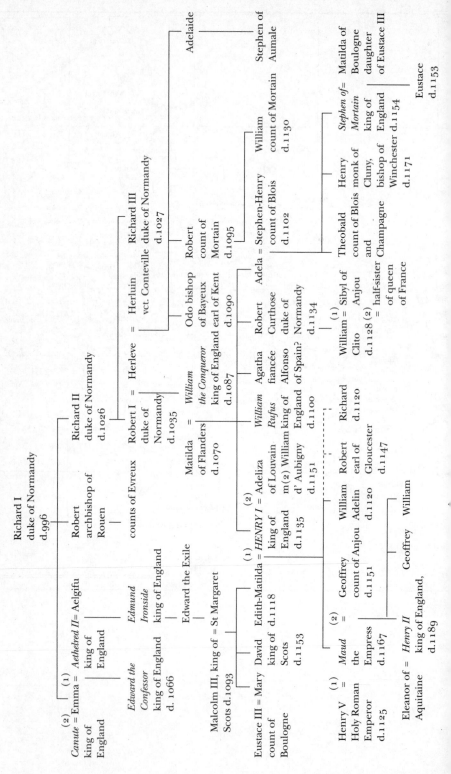

THE ANGLO-NORMAN FAMILY

Chapter 1

SETTING AND SOURCES

Henry I, in the words of the old Chinese curse, lived in interesting times. The youngest son of William the Conqueror and his royal wife, Matilda of Flanders, Henry was born in England roughly two years after his father's victory at Hastings, at a time when the Norman grip on the English realm was still far from secure.[1] By the time of his death in his later sixties, after a reign of some thirty-five years (1100–1135), the Anglo-Norman monarchy and aristocracy had become deeply rooted in England,[2] while, in the larger framework of medieval civilization, the great intellectual and cultural process known as the twelfth-century renaissance had reached full blossom.

Henry's lifetime thus witnessed fundamental changes in the Anglo-Norman world and, indeed, throughout Western Europe. Some of these changes were products of Henry's own governance; most were not. But Henry, whether by choice or necessity, adapted to them all. He left the Anglo-Norman government far better organized than he had found it, so much so that he has plausibly been credited with the building of an administrative "machine" of unprecedented effectiveness—the most sophisticated government in transalpine Europe since the days of the Roman Empire.[3] He and his ministers reconstituted and tamed the itinerant royal court along rational lines, reformed the exchequer and treasury, introduced the systematic use of itinerant justices on a kingdomwide scale, developed royal patronage into a science, and presided over a long generation of peace and prosperity in England and, to a lesser but very significant degree, in Normandy.[4] The prosperity of Henry's reign was propelled by a great wave of economic growth, resulting in an intensification of international trade—most notably the wool trade with Flanders—

[1] WM, *GR*, 2:467 [all references are to Rolls Series edition, unless otherwise noted]; Douglas, *William the Conqueror*, pp. 211–218; Bates, *William the Conqueror*, pp. 75–81.
[2] *MMI*, pp. 171–189; Southern, *Medieval Humanism*, p. 233. The civil war that followed Henry's death, pitting a grandson of the Conqueror against a grand-daughter, was obviously not a threat to the Norman settlement.
[3] Richardson and Sayles, *Governance*, pp. 159, 172.
[4] *MMI*, pp. 223–245, 303–304.

and in the expansion of towns and the proliferation of markets. Henry granted London its first charter of liberties (for a stiff but manageable price), and his wife, Queen Matilda II, gave the city its first "public convenience." Moreover, Henry sold or confirmed important privileges to the citizens of such burgeoning urban centers as Lincoln and Newcastle, York and Beverley. He and his associates founded numerous priories of the newly popular Augustinian order and substantial numbers of hospitals as well.[5] He was a lavish benefactor of the venerable international congregation of Cluny and a vastly generous contributor to its mother church, and when he established his great monastic foundation at Reading he filled it with monks bound to the Cluniac rule. But he and members of his court also supported the establishment of Britain's earliest Cistercian abbeys: Waverley, Tintern, Fountains, and Rievaulx. Henry's reign was marked by unbroken peace and amity with the kings of Scots and relative stability along the Welsh frontiers,[6] and it concluded with more than a decade of peace with France, ending two generations of intermittent warfare across the years following the Conquest.

Among Henry's contemporaries were some of the foremost intellectual and spiritual luminaries of the twelfth-century renaissance, and he had dealings with several of them. During the early years of his reign he was a close associate, friend, and sometime antagonist of St Anselm, archbishop of Canterbury, to whom he consigned the care of his family and kingdom during a royal absence overseas shortly before Anselm's death.[7] He was also a friend of Suger of Saint-Denis and met secretly with him on more than one occasion to negotiate peace with Suger's lord, King Louis VI.[8] Two pioneers in the emergence of Western science, Petrus Alfonsus and (probably) Adelard of Bath, worked for a time in Henry's service.[9] He and his two successive queens, Matilda and Adeliza, engaged in correspondence with such notable figures as the poet-prelate Hildebert of Lavardin, the great canonist Ivo bishop of Chartres, Peter the Venerable, abbot of Cluny,

[5] Ibid., pp. 191–208; *EHD*, 2:1012–1013, 1030–1032; *Select Charters*, ed. Stubbs and Davis, pp. 129–131; Tait, *The Medieval English Borough*, pp. 154–161; Dickinson, *Origins of the Austin Canons*, pp. 125–130, and see below, pp. 397–399.

[6] Knowles, *Monastic Order*, pp. 226–245, 281–282; Duncan, *Scotland: The Making of the Kingdom*, pp. 126–137; Davies, *The Age of Conquest*, pp. 34–45; Henry I owed his peace with Scotland in part to William II's policies: Barlow, *Rufus*, pp. 371, 399.

[7] Southern, *Anselm and His Biographer*, pp. 163–180; Vaughn, *Anselm of Bec and Robert of Meulan*, pp. 214–346; Southern, *Anselm: A Portrait*, pp. 289–307; *AO*, ep. 461.

[8] *MMI*, pp. 287–289.

[9] Ibid., p. 312; Poole, *Exchequer*, pp. 56–57; Haskins, *Studies in the History of Medieval Science*, pp. 113–120; Green, *Government*, p. 162.

who came to England in 1130 with Henry's authorization, and St Bernard of Clairvaux who, in the company of Abbot Suger, Pope Innocent II, and others, visited Henry's court at Rouen in 1131.[10]

As Sir Richard Southern has cogently observed, the renaissance of the twelfth century was not limited to learning and the arts but extended as well to the realm of governance.[11] In this sense, Henry I was both a child of the Norman Conquest and, in the context of the twelfth century, a renaissance prince. Not only did he consort with leading figures among the first and perhaps greatest generation of twelfth-century writers; he also absorbed and exemplified their passion for reason and order and applied it to the administration of his realm, to diplomacy, and even to military strategy and tactics. Henry was no philosopher, but contemporaries were struck by his openness to new ideas and his seemingly boundless curiosity, traits he shared with intellectuals of his era.[12]

Still another facet of the twelfth-century renaissance, as Sir Richard Southern aptly pointed out, was the writing of history, and this too was reflected in Henry's reign. His activities were recorded by an unprecedented number of historians and annalists, including some of the most talented writers since Bede.[13] Foremost among them was William of Malmesbury (ca. 1095–ca. 1143), a gifted historical scholar and an omnivorous reader, impressively well versed in the literature of classical, patristic, and earlier medieval times as well as in the writings of his own contemporaries. Indeed, William may well have been the most learned man in twelfth-century Western Europe.[14] A monk of the Benedictine community of Malmesbury, William was of mixed Anglo-Norman parentage. Although by no means a court historian or royal panegyrist, he was deeply sympathetic toward Henry I and enjoyed the patronage of Henry's *curia* through his contacts with the king's first wife, Queen Matilda II. The queen's financial support was generous but, as Malmesbury hinted, could have been more so toward English writers such as himself: "The disposition came upon the queen to

[10] *RRAN* 2, no. 1691 n.; *MMI*, pp. 287–288.

[11] Southern, *Medieval Humanism*, pp. 174–179. Southern is referring only to *writings* on governance; I am extending the idea to the subject of these writings: innovations in government itself that gave rise to such treatises as the *Dialogus de scaccario* and "Glanvill" (Ranulf de Glanvill, *Tractatus de legibus et consuetudinibus Anglie*, ed. and trans. G. D. G. Hall [London, 1965]).

[12] See, for example, OV, 6:100.

[13] Southern, *Medieval Humanism*, pp. 160–162, concluding that the Anglo-Norman historians displayed "a much wider historical curiosity than had been seen in England, or perhaps anywhere else in Europe, since the time of Bede."

[14] Thomson, *Malmesbury*, pp. 11–75; the evidence shows that Malmesbury knew at first hand at least some 400 works of 200 authors: ibid., pp. 7, 197–207. See in general Farmer, "William of Malmesbury's Life and Works."

reward all the foreigners she could, while keeping the others in suspense, sometimes with effectual promises but more often with empty ones."[15] Despite William of Malmesbury's veiled complaint, the queen may well have contributed financially to his far-flung travels throughout England, reflected most directly in his *Gesta pontificum Anglorum*.[16] This great work is a vividly descriptive history of the bishoprics and abbeys of England from the early Anglo-Saxon era to the time of its completion in 1125. It dwells on the lives of Anglo-Saxon saint-prelates, especially St Aldhelm, the learned, wonder-working abbot of seventh-century Malmesbury, but it also casts valuable light on the post-Conquest Church and, less directly, on the Norman kings.

William of Malmesbury's wide reading, extensive travels, and keen interpretive talents contributed similarly to the writing of his best known work, the *Gesta regum Anglorum*, which he also completed in 1125.[17] The *Gesta regum*, consciously patterned on Bede, relates the history of the English monarchy (with occasional intriguing digressions) from early Anglo-Saxon times to about 1120. These two parallel historical works, ecclesiastical and secular, provide a valuable portrait of Henry I's reign, enlivened by William's wit and his striking descriptive portrayals of places and persons (including Henry I himself) and deepened by his perceptive historical judgment.

In his later years William of Malmesbury revised his two *gesta* several times, disclosing in his second thoughts the mellowing effect of age. Around 1140 he began the writing of his third and last major historical work, the *Historia novella*, in which he rushed through the final years of Henry I to dwell less hurriedly on the early years of Stephen's reign and, in particular, the deeds of King Henry's favorite bastard son and Malmesbury's hero, Robert earl of Gloucester.[18] The *Historia novella* ends abruptly in 1142, halted presumably by its author's final illness.[19] William of Malmesbury also wrote saints' lives, a history of Glastonbury abbey, and much else; but it is, above all, his three great historical works that illuminate most clearly the life and reign of Henry I.

A second major historian of Henry's generation, Orderic Vitalis (1075–ca. 1142), admired the king no less than did William of Malmesbury.[20] Like William, Orderic was a student of the classics (although he

---

[15] WM, *GR*, 2:494–495; cf. Thomson, *Malmesbury*, pp. 15, 34–35.

[16] WM, *GP*, Thomson, *Malmesbury*, p. 15.

[17] See n. 1, this chapter; Thomson, *Malmesbury*, p. 3; Gransden, *Historical Writing*, p. 168.

[18] WM, *HN*; Gransden, *Historical Writing*, pp. 182–183.

[19] Thomson, *Malmesbury*, p. 3.

[20] See Marjorie Chibnall's introductions to the six volumes of Orderic's *Ecclesiastical History*; also Chibnall, *The World of Orderic*, pp. 188–190, 196, 198–200 and *passim*.

lacked William's deep erudition). Like William, too, he was of mixed, Anglo-French parentage. His mother was English; his father was a priest from Orleans who served as a chaplain to Roger of Montgomery, earl of Shrewsbury. Orderic's parents sent him from his Shropshire home as a child of ten to live out his remaining fifty-seven years at the distinguished abbey of Saint-Evroul in southern Normandy. As his life progressed, Orderic's perspective became increasingly Norman, but he retained his contacts with his native Shropshire and identified himself in his writings as an Englishman, "Ordricus angligena."[21]

Orderic did his historical apprenticeship during the first decade of the twelfth century as a continuer of William of Jumièges' *Gesta normannorum ducum*, a sweeping history of the Normans and their dukes from the founding of Normandy about 911 through the Norman Conquest and early settlement in England.[22] Picking up the story, Orderic carried it into the early twelfth century. But by 1110/1115 he had taken up a far more arduous task, the writing of his *magnum opus*, the *Historia ecclesiastica*.[23] This great rambling work, with its marvelous vignettes and fearlessly long digressions, occupies six volumes in its magisterial edition-translation by Dr Marjorie Chibnall. Orderic's *Historia ecclesiastica*, despite its title, is concerned with the Anglo-Norman monarchy and aristocracy no less than with the Church. Aptly described as the greatest social history of the Middle Ages, it provides what is by far our fullest, most detailed account of the life of Henry I. Orderic drew on numerous sources including his own notes of current events, many of which he must have gleaned from the visitors who were constantly drifting in and out of Saint-Evroul (in 1113 Henry I himself visited the abbey).[24] Orderic derived some of his information from the writings of other historians, past and present, and he seems to have learned much from his occasional travels, which carried him to such places as the Ile de France, Flanders, Burgundy, and England.[25] Like all historians, Orderic could lapse now and then into careless errors—as when, writing some

---

[21] Ibid., p. 3 and n. 2: the letter *e* was inserted into "Ordricus" long afterward; the monks of Saint-Evroul added the name "Vitalis" shortly after Orderic's arrival as an oblate: OV, 6:554.

[22] *GND*, ed. Jean Marx (Rouen/Paris, 1914); ed. van Houts [all references hereafter are to the van Houts edition, unless otherwise noted]; van Houts, "The *Gesta Normannorum ducum*: A History without an End."

[23] OV, 1:45–63; Classen, "*Res gestae*, Universal History, Apocalypse," pp. 388–390; Smalley, *Historians in the Middle Ages*, pp. 86–91; Chibnall, *World of Orderic*, pp. 177–203 and *passim*; Gransden, *Historical Writing*, pp. 152–165.

[24] OV, 6:174–176; *RRAN* 2, no. 1019.

[25] On Orderic's travels see Chibnall, *World of Orderic*, pp. 35–37, 76, 107, 222 (map of places visited by Orderic); OV, 1:25–26; 2:186–188, 324, 338; 3:182–184; 6:xix–xxi, 74 and n. 2, 424–426, 438.

years after the event and confusing his notes, he conflates Henry
I's two crucial military expeditions into Normandy in 1105 and
1106 into a single campaign. But he is on the whole an honest and
trustworthy guide to the history of his times. He continued writing
his history, by stages, across the long generation from 1110/1115
until 1141, when the approach of death, along with the daunting
tumults of King Stephen's anarchy and Geoffrey of Anjou's Norman
campaigning, stilled his pen at last.

Contemporary with the works of Malmesbury and Orderic are
an impressive number of other historical sources bearing on Henry
I and his era. The most complex of these sources, the *Anglo-Saxon
Chronicle*, consists of a number of semi-independent year-by-year annals,
in which the year and its events are often mismatched. Working
over many generations at various monastic houses, the anonymous compilers of these texts appended their diverging versions
to copies of a single original, dating from Alfred's reign, that ran
from the Incarnation through to AD 891.[26] Because some of these
texts have perished, the relationships among the remainder can
never be fully untangled. Fortunately for our purposes, by the time
of Henry I's reign the extant manuscripts had dwindled to one,
MS E, generally known as the Peterborough Chronicle.[27] This manuscript is largely the product of a single scribe, who copied an earlier
version of the chronicle through the year 1121 in one stretch and
continued it at intervals from 1122 through 1131, after which it
proceeds in other hands, sporadically and often carelessly, until
the accession of Henry II.[28] A preoccupation with events at Peterborough abbey in the annals of 1122–1131 identifies their author
as a Peterborough monk, and internal evidence of a similar sort
shows that the earlier manuscript that he copied (now lost) had
been written at St Augustine's, Canterbury, for some years prior to
1062. But it is impossible to locate with certainty the author of
the annals for the years 1062–1121. The suggestion that the
manuscript continued to be compiled at Canterbury during these
years[29] seems unlikely not only because its author provides an incorrect
date for Archbishop Anselm's death but also because of its silence
on such matters as the investiture settlement (AD 1105–1107),
Anselm's return from exile in 1106, and his consecration of an

---

[26] *ASC; Two of the Saxon Chronicles Parallel*, ed. Earle and Plummer; *The Anglo-
Saxon Chronicle: A Collaborative Edition*, ed. Dumville and Keynes; *ASC*, ed. Dorothy
Whitelock.

[27] Two other MS fragments survive for the period of Henry I: MS H for
1113–1114, paralleling E, and MS D for 1130, a brief notice of the death in battle
of Angus earl of Moray.

[28] *ASC*, ed. Whitelock, pp. xvi–xvii; Gransden, *Historical Writing*, pp. 143–145.

[29] *EHD*, 2:103.

unprecedented number of prelates-elect in 1107 (the consecrations are mentioned but Anselm is not).[30] It seems unlikely too that the year entries prior to the 1122 copy were compiled at Peterborough, for although the earlier annals include several pointed references to local Peterborough events, these were clearly interpolated by the 1122 copyist.[31] But despite its multiple authorship, the portions of the E manuscript relating to Henry I do convey the impression of a relatively cohesive narrative running across the 1121–1122 break. Its tone is pessimistic throughout, reaching depths of despair when describing the reigns of William Rufus and Stephen but continuing intermittently during Henry I's reign to deplore the ravages of bad weather, high taxes, cattle plagues, and abusive royal officials.[32] This pessimism was doubtless shared by many post-Conquest Anglo-Saxons throughout England and need not be identified with a single author or abbey.

Despite the attention that the E text devotes to local events and natural disasters, its authors were also capable of a wider perspective. They express serious interest in the affairs of the Anglo-Norman realm and its neighbors and thereby provide valuable information on the domestic and international politics of the Norman kings. The E text is, for example, our earliest witness to the significant information that Helias count of Maine (d. 1110) had rendered fealty to Henry I and that in 1126 the empress Maud persuaded Henry to transfer his captive brother Robert Curthose from Roger of Salisbury's custody to that of her political ally, Robert earl of Gloucester. And notwithstanding its chronic complaints, the E text describes Henry I in retrospect as "a good man" who "made peace for man and beast."[33]

Another major chronicle of Saxon and Norman England was compiled during the Anglo-Norman period at Worcester Cathedral priory. Its authorship used to be attributed to the monk Florence of Worcester up to AD 1118 and to a fellow monk, John of Worcester, from 1118 to 1140. Although it is almost certain that John of Worcester wrote a large section of the chronicle preceding 1140, the

---

[30] It could be argued that the author was writing at St Augustine's at a time when his abbey was in conflict with Anselm and the Christ Church community (AD 1106–1108: Eadmer, *HN*, pp. 188–191) and therefore neglected Anselm deliberately, but this argument seems too elaborate to be likely; Cecily Clark suggested very tentatively a London-Westminster provenance: *Peterborough Chronicle*, pp. xxi–xxiii.

[31] The Waverly annals for 1000–1121 constitute a Latin rendering of a text closely similar to E but omitting all references to events at Peterborough: *Annales monastici*, 2:170–218; *ASC*, ed. Whitelock, pp. xvii, xix; *Peterborough Chronicle*, pp. xix–xx.

[32] See Gransden, *Historical Writing*, p. 143, where the Anglo-Saxon chroniclers' complaints are described as "the grumbles typical of farmers of all ages."

[33] *ASC, s.a.* 1135.

authorship of the annals prior to 1118 is still disputed. That a Worcester monk named Florence contributed significantly to these annals is made clear by a notice in the annal for 1118 which reports his death and adds, "This chronicle of chronicles excels all others because of his deep knowledge and studious application."[34] But other evidence raises serious doubts about the traditional interpretation. Orderic Vitalis, who visited Worcester at some uncertain date, reports John as saying that he himself undertook the chronicle at the request of Bishop Wulfstan, who died in 1095. If so, then John would have written the entire chronicle, beginning it in his youth *ante* 1096 and completing it in 1140 as a person of unusual but not impossible longevity. Perhaps Florence served as John's assistant; perhaps, alternatively, Orderic erred. A further problem with the traditional assumption, however, is that no perceptible break in either the style or the manuscript tradition of the chronicle occurs with the annal for 1118. The likeliest solution to the riddle is that several Worcester monks, including Florence, contributed to the project up to 1118 and perhaps beyond. The earliest manuscript of the *Worcester Chronicle*, Corpus Christi College, Oxford, MS 157, is written in several hands; a single hand has entered numerous corrections and annotations from the beginning of the manuscript to AD 1124, and this same hand, very probably John of Worcester's, produced the text from 1128 to 1140. The evidence from the Corpus Christi manuscript suggests therefore that John of Worcester, as corrector-annotator of the earlier part and as author of the later part, is probably responsible for the whole of the chronicle in its present form.[35] But in deference to the accolade to Florence in the annal for 1118, I will follow tradition and cite the chronicle as "FW."

The *Worcester Chronicle* owes much to earlier writings, two in particular: the *Anglo-Saxon Chronicle*, and a "universal" chronicle running from the Creation to AD 1082 written by Marianus Scotus, a monk of Fulda who had migrated from Ireland. Like both these sources, the *Worcester Chronicle* is annalistic in format. It derives substantial amounts of information about pre-Conquest England from texts of the *Anglo-Saxon Chronicle* that are now lost, and it is therefore a source of considerable value for students of early English history. But it differs from the *Anglo-Saxon Chronicle* both in language (Latin rather than Old English) and in its high standards of chronological accuracy. For

[34] FW, 2:72; JW, p. 13.
[35] OV, 2:xxi, 186–188 and nn; on Florence's earlier sources see Darlington and McGurk, "The *Chronicon ex Chronicis* of 'Florence' of Worcester"; for comments on the authorship see JW, pp. 4–10; Brett, "John of Worcester," pp. 104–110; Darlington, *Anglo-Norman Historians*, p. 14; *Vita Wulfstani of William of Malmesbury*, pp. x–xviii; Flint, "The Date of the Chronicle of 'Florence' of Worcester."

most of the Norman period it is a contemporary source of information, and it is an indispensable guide to the history of Henry I's reign. It supplies important and otherwise unknown details, for example, on Henry's decisive military campaign of 1102 against Robert of Bellême; it provides the only comprehensive account of the 1126 Christmas court at which the magnates and prelates of England swore their solemn oaths to support the empress Maud as Henry's successor; and it may perhaps have inspired Charles Dickens by reporting (and vividly illustrating in line drawings) three nightmares suffered by Henry I during a single restless night in 1130.[36]

Another invaluable source for Henry I's life and reign is Henry of Huntingdon's *Historia Anglorum*.[37] Unlike the *Anglo-Saxon Chronicle* and the *Worcester Chronicle*, this work was written entirely and indubitably by a single author, Henry archdeacon of Huntingdon, the most important Anglo-Norman historian to emerge from the secular clergy. But although Henry's authorship is not in doubt, he did manage to leave a daunting trail for future scholars by putting his history through several editions and, like William of Malmesbury, softening earlier judgments in later revisions.[38] In one of the most significant of these revisions (unnoticed by his Rolls Series editor but meticulously recorded in the recent edition of Diana Greenway), he recast his original, rather ambiguous assessment of Henry I's character—a mixture of three virtues and three vices—by justifying the first of Henry's supposed vices, avarice, as necessary to effective governance, and deleting the other two (cruelty and lust).[39]

Henry of Huntingdon's grand design, like William of Malmesbury's, was the writing of a history of the English kings and people from early Anglo-Saxon times to his own. Both these historians reflect the inclination of contemporary Anglo-Normans to bring the history of the English securely within the compass of the new Norman monarchy—much as King Henry I himself had endeavored to graft the Norman ducal house to that of the Old English kings by marrying a young woman of the West Saxon royal line. Henry of Huntingdon

[36] FW, 2:49–50; JW, frontispiece and pp. 22–23, 26–28.
[37] HH, pp. xxiii–clxxii and *passim*; Partner, *Serious Entertainments*, pp. 11–48; Gillingham, "Henry of Huntingdon and the Twelfth-Century Revival of the English Nation"; Gransden, *Historical Writing*, pp. 193–199.
[38] Greenway, "Henry of Huntingdon."
[39] Ibid., pp. 119–121, 126; HH, pp. 698–701. The revised version, overlooked by Thomas Arnold in his Rolls Series edition of 1879 (see ibid., pp. 104–105), is to be found in CUL MS li.ii.3 and BL Royal MS 13.B.vi, the latter having been translated in *The Chronicle of Henry of Huntingdon*, trans. Thomas Forester (London, 1853), p. 261 and n. 2, some twenty-six years before the Rolls Series edition was published!

was clearly inspired by William of Malmesbury, and of course by Bede, but unlike them he cast his history in the annalistic format of the *Anglo-Saxon Chronicle*. Born around 1080, Henry of Huntingdon was a contemporary witness to most of the events of Henry I's reign. The first draft of his *Historia Anglorum* ran through 1129, and he subsequently extended it, in several stages during his long lifetime, to Henry II's accession in 1154. Necessarily, he drew heavily on both Bede and the *Anglo-Saxon Chronicle* for much of his earlier history, and he continued to consult the E text of the *Chronicle*, or a version much like it, until 1133. But Henry of Huntingdon added his own distinctive and entertaining touches to the sources he used, sometimes drawing from picturesque legends, sometimes from his own fertile imagination. It is to him that we owe such stories as King Cnut's unsuccessful attempt to turn back the tide and Henry I's fatal decision in 1135 to ignore his physician's order and dine on lampreys.[40] The inclusion of memorable incidents such as these contributed to Henry of Huntingdon's popularity among his contemporaries,[41] but he seldom related a story without drawing a Christian moral from it, usually about the vanity of earthly things and the downfall of the rich and mighty. King Cnut discovered from his foolishness that the power of kings is trivial when compared with the power of God, and Henry I learned (on his deathbed and thus too late) that men must not seek forbidden things. The disdain of worldly vanities—a commonplace among medieval writers—was an obsession with Henry of Huntingdon. It permeates his *Historia Anglorum* and becomes the dominating theme of a related treatise, *De contemptu mundi*, that Henry cast in the form of a letter to a certain Archdeacon Walter and appended to the final edition of his *Historia*.[42] In this joyless work, the only men to avoid plunges from the heights and sorrowful deaths are Henry of Huntingdon's literary patron and ecclesiastical superior, Alexander bishop of Lincoln, and a few of Henry's compatriots among the Lincoln clergy. Even Alexander's predecessor Bishop Robert Bloet, who had raised Henry to his archdeaconry, is made to fall from the royal favor (by a dexterous manipulation of the evidence), while kings and nobles are shown to have become victims, in the end, of divine retribution for their immoderate wealth and power, their hollow fame, and their sins.

By the standards of ecclesiastical reform that were sweeping across Europe just then, Henry of Huntingdon was himself a sinner, a married archdeacon whose father Nicholas had apparently occupied

---

[40] HH, pp. 189, 254: Henry of Huntingdon may well be correct about the cause of Henry I's death.

[41] Gransden, *Historical Writing*, p. 194: some twenty-five manuscripts of the *Historia Anglorum* survive from the Middle Ages.

[42] HH, pp. 295–320; Partner, *Serious Entertainments*, pp. 35–40.

the same archdeaconry before him, and whose son—bearing the memorable name Aristotle—carried on the family's clerical tradition. One must bear these facts in mind when reading Henry's slighting remarks about English church councils that banned clerical marriage.[43] He tells a spirited tale of Cardinal John of Crema, papal legate to England in 1125, being caught in bed with a young woman and publicly shamed, after having earlier presided at a council in London at which all married clergy were ordered to renounce their wives. The story was probably based on wishful rumor and was doubtless embroidered, but Henry can perhaps be forgiven for his delight in telling it.

Henry of Huntingdon's *Historia* proved a rich mine of information for his younger contemporary, the Norman historian Robert of Torigny, monk and later prior of Bec, who became abbot of Mont-Saint-Michel in 1154.[44] In the course of his long ecclesiastical career, running from 1128 when he entered Bec to his death in 1186, Robert wrote two major works of history: a further continuation of William of Jumièges' *Gesta normannorum ducum* (following Orderic's) and later a vast chronicle running from Roman times to 1186.[45] Robert's *Chronicle* was a continuation of a "world" chronicle by Sigebert monk of Gembloux which ran to AD 1112 and itself rested on the historical works of Eusebius and St Jerome. Robert continued the chronicle in stages during his years at Mont-Saint-Michel, long after Henry I's death, and although it is a valuable source for the reign of Henry II, virtually all its information on the Anglo-Norman era is derived from Henry of Huntingdon and others. Robert's continuation of William of Jumièges' *Gesta*, however, devotes many pages to the life of Henry I and is largely original. Written at Bec during the 1140s, it is a frustrating work, from which a large internal section is missing from all extant manuscripts. The surviving chapters, in which Robert indulges himself in long genealogical digressions and chronological leaps, illustrate his wisdom in subjecting himself later in life to the discipline of an annalistic framework. Nevertheless, his contribution to the *Gesta normannorum ducum*,

[43] HH, pp. 234, 245–246.

[44] Ibid., pp. xx–xxi; RT, *Chron.*, in *Chronicles of the Reign of Stephen, Henry II, and Richard I*, pp. vii–xxiv; RT, *Chronique*, ed. Delisle, pp. lix–lxi [all references hereafter to Delisle edition unless otherwise noted]; while visiting Bec en route to Rome in 1139, Henry of Huntingdon gave Robert of Torigny a copy of the 1135 edition of his *Historia Anglorum*; Robert, in turn, gave Henry a copy of Geoffrey of Monmouth's recently completed work of historical fantasy, the *Historia regum Britanniae*, which both Robert and Henry accepted unsuspectingly as authentic history and subsequently used in their own works.

[45] GND, 1:8, 2:289; RT, *Chron.*, in *Chronicles of the Reign of Stephen, Henry II, and Richard I*; RT, *Chronique*, ed. Delisle; see Gibson, "History at Bec in the Twelfth Century," pp. 175–180.

jumbled though it is, provides valuable commentaries on such diverse subjects as Henry I's measures to defend Normandy (castle building, in particular), his gifts to religious houses as far removed as Chartres and Cluny, the use of mounted archers by his military household, and the joy he took in his grandsons.

A far more informative and strictly contemporary view of Henry I's policies is provided by the English monk Eadmer of Canterbury.[46] In his two most notable works, the *Vita Anselmi* and the *Historia novorum in Anglia*, Eadmer provides a profoundly sympathetic portrayal of his archbishop, companion, and hero, St Anselm.[47] The *Vita* concentrates on Anselm's private, spiritual life, the *Historia* on his public life in which Anselm, as archbishop of Canterbury, is obliged to contend with two powerful Anglo-Norman kings in succession: William Rufus and Henry I. It is in his *Historia novorum* that Eadmer provides a unique if biased account of Henry I's policies toward the archbishopric of Canterbury, the English Church, and the papacy. The light that Eadmer casts on Henry is indirect, refracted through the prism of Anselm's own perspectives and ideals, yet Henry emerges from the pages of the *Historia novorum* as a much more sympathetic figure than his royal predecessor. Henry is firm to the point of stubbornness in his defense of the traditional royal position on investiture, while Anselm is equally unyielding in his devout adherence to the new papal policy. And yet the two antagonists maintain throughout their struggle a degree of civility and mutual restraint that is almost courtly.

Like Bede, who enriched his *Historia ecclesiastica* with verbatim copies of relevant letters from popes and English prelates,[48] Eadmer inserted into his *Historia novorum* a considerable number of illustrative letters written or received by St Anselm. These letters can be supplemented by others from Anselm's voluminous correspondence, much of which has survived in various manuscript collections. Two manuscripts of paramount value, one containing correspondence from Anselm's years at Bec and the other covering his archiepiscopal career, were compiled by contemporary scribes working under Anselm's direction.[49] These

---

[46] Southern, *Anselm and His Biographer*, pp. 229–354; *Anselm: A Portrait*, pp. 404–436.

[47] Southern, *Anselm: A Portrait*, 404–428; Eadmer, *Vita Anselmi*; Eadmer, *HN*.

[48] Gransden, *Historical Writing*, p. 26.

[49] Fröhlich, "The Genesis of the Collection of Anselm's Letters," and Fröhlich, *The Letters of Saint Anselm*, 1:5–65; Vaughn, *Anselm of Bec and Robert of Meulan*, pp. 132–133, 137–141; for a contrary view, to the effect that Anselm differed from other letter writers of his times in not overseeing the collection of his archiepiscopal correspondence, see Southern, *Anselm and His Biographer*, pp. 67–68 n. 2, and *Anselm: A Portrait*, pp. 459–481; see further Southern, "Sally Vaughn's Anselm," and Vaughn, "Anselm: Saint and Statesman." For the Bec letters: London BL MS Cotton Nero A. vii; for the Canterbury letters: London Lambeth Palace MS 59.

manuscripts exemplify a centuries-old genre that reached its culmination in Anselm's time and the generation just following, during which such eminent prelates as Peter the Venerable, Hildebert of Lavardin, Ivo of Chartres, Geoffrey of Vendôme, and Bernard of Clairvaux oversaw the collection and editing of their own correspondence.[50] Drawing on the Bec and Canterbury manuscripts of Anselm's letters, on Eadmer, and on a variety of other sources, Anselm's modern editor, Dom F. S. Schmitt, has published a body of correspondence consisting of no fewer than 472 letters written by or to Anselm.[51]

Evidence from these letters and from the *Historia novorum* makes it clear that the political issue of supreme importance to both Anselm and Eadmer, overshadowing the investiture controversy, was the primatial power of Canterbury. Even more sharply than their predecessors, the Anglo-Norman archbishops of Canterbury viewed themselves as primates of all Britain, and the chief impediment to the full realization of that status was the archbishopric of York. The conflict between the primacy of Canterbury and the independence of York narrowed down to the defining question of whether an archbishop-elect of York was obliged by tradition to render a profession of obedience in writing to the archbishop of Canterbury before being consecrated. It was this issue more than any other that engrossed the monastic community of Christ Church, Canterbury, and its post-Conquest archbishops, Lanfranc, Anselm, and their successors. It prompted Anselm, in a letter of 1108 to Thomas archbishop-elect of York, to make the peremptory statement: "You can be very certain that I shall exert myself in every possible way to see that the church of Canterbury does not lose one scrap of prestige in my time."[52] And it became the dominating theme of Eadmer's *Historia novorum*. On the successful defense of the Canterbury primacy, so Eadmer and his community believed, depended the proper, divinely sanctioned ordering of the English Church.

Eadmer's contemporary Hugh the Chanter of the cathedral chapter of York thought otherwise. In his *History of the Church of York,*

---

[50] *The Letters of Peter the Venerable*, ed. Constable; for an excellent discussion of twelfth-century letter writing and collecting, see ibid., 2:1–44. For Hildebert see *PL* 17; Dieudonné, *Hildebert de Lavardin*, pp. 115–239; Von Moos, *Hildebert von Lavardin*. For Ivo, Leclercq, "La Collection des lettres d'Yves de Chartres"; *PL* 162 (1854), and Yves de Chartres, *Correspondance, 1090–1098*, ed. Leclercq; note that the letters of lesser prelates were sometimes collected as well: e.g. Alexander, "Herbert of Norwich, 1091–1119"; *Herberti de Losinga primi episcopi norwicensis epistolae*, ed. Anstruther; *The Life, Letters and Sermons of Bishop Herbert de Losinga*, ed. Gouldburn and Symonds.

[51] Published in *AO*, vols 3–6. The letters have been skillfully translated and annotated by Walter Fröhlich, *The Letters of Saint Anselm of Canterbury*.

[52] *AO*, ep. 455.

Hugh voiced his opposition to the Canterbury primacy just as vehemently as Eadmer supported it. Hugh's hero was Archbishop Thurstan of York (1119–1140), whose adamant refusal to profess obedience to Canterbury had resulted in the archbishop of Canterbury's equally adamant refusal to consecrate Thurstan to his archbishopric. Thurstan eventually cut the Gordian knot, to Hugh the Chanter's glee, by obtaining consecration directly from the pope. As a consequence of Thurstan's success in winning papal support for York's independence, Hugh was able to end his history triumphantly, whereas Eadmer's closing pages are correspondingly bleak.[53]

Reverberations from the Canterbury–York battle echoed among a number of English religious houses, prompting several other Anglo-Norman historians to take sides in accordance with their allegiances and interests. Thus the *Worcester Chronicle* provides unstinted support to Canterbury, depicting Thurstan of York as a scoundrel.[54] William of Malmesbury, borrowing heavily from Eadmer, backs Canterbury with equal ardor in his lengthy discussion of the controversy in the *Gesta pontificum*.[55] And the Anglo-Saxon chronicler, although briefly and in passing, expresses a similar view. Hugh the Chanter's opposition to the Canterbury primacy is endorsed by only one major historian outside York, a monk commonly identified as "Symeon," whose monastic cathedral of Durham constituted York's only suffragan bishopric in England.

Whether written by "Symeon" or not, the Durham work entitled the *Historia regum* is an historical narrative of considerable importance.[56] Like Malmesbury's *Gesta regum* and Henry of Huntingdon's *Historia Anglorum*, the *Historia regum* attempts to trace the history of the English kings far back into Anglo-Saxon times. To do so, Symeon (or another Durham monk before him) cobbled together a miscellany of early sources, some of them otherwise unknown. From 848 to 1118 he depends primarily on the *Worcester Chronicle*, but he also draws on

[53] Hugh the Chanter, pp. 220–222; Eadmer, *HN*, pp. 255–289; below.

[54] FW, 2:69; JW, pp. 14–15, 17, 19–20, 22–23.

[55] WM, *GP*, pp. 39–132 *passim.*

[56] SD (RS). The *Historia regum* is one of several historical sources emanating from Durham during the Anglo-Norman period; another work of major importance, the *Historia dunelmensis ecclesiae*, is included along with the *Historia regum* in Thomas Arnold's Rolls Series edition of *Symeonis monachi opera omnia*, but, *pace* Arnold, internal evidence makes it unlikely that the two works were written by the same author. See Gransden, *Historical Writing*, pp. 114–123, 148–151; Brett, "John of Worcester," pp. 119–122; Offler, *Medieval Historians of Durham*, "Red Book of Durham," and "Hexham and the *Historia Regum*," commenting on Hunter Blair, "Some Observations on the *Historia Regum*"; see most recently, Rollason, ed., *Simeon of Durham, Historian of Durham and the North.*

Eadmer's *Historia novorum*, William of Jumièges' *Gesta normannorum ducum*, and Malmesbury's *Gesta regum*. From 1119 to 1129 (the last year that "Symeon" recorded), the *Historia regum* is a useful contemporary account, providing, for example, verbatim reports of several ecclesiastical councils, a number of references to the activities of Archbishop Thurstan (all of them laudatory), and independent information on relations between Henry I and Count Fulk V of Anjou culminating in the fateful marriage of Geoffrey le Bel and the empress Maud.[57]

Two further histories bearing on Henry I which scholars have tended to neglect until recently are the *Brevis relatio* and the *Hyde Chronicle*, both of which run through the first two decades of the reign.[58] The *Brevis relatio* is a difficult text that seems to have been patched together from several otherwise unknown sources. It includes an intriguing passage that provides a strongly pro-Norman interpretation of the feudal relationship between the dukes of Normandy and the kings of France—a passage that Robert of Torigny repeats almost verbatim in his mid-twelfth-century continuation of the *Gesta normannorum ducum*.[59] The *Hyde Chronicle*, an independent account of the first importance, provides fresh information on two of the foremost Anglo-Norman tenants-in-chief, William count of Mortain and, most particularly, William II of Warenne earl of Surrey. The chronicler's intense interest in the Warennes suggests that, despite the manuscript tradition associating him with the abbey of Hyde, Winchester, he was more likely a monk of the Cluniac priory of Lewes, Sussex, founded and patronized by the Warennes.[60] Whatever his provenance, the "Hyde" chronicler devotes much of his attention to Henry I's diplomacy and warfare on the Continent, on some aspects of which he is our only source. And he alone subsumes England and Normandy under the composite phrase *regnum Norman-Anglorum* or *Norm-Anglorum*.[61]

---

[57] Symeon's *Historia* was continued past 1129 by John prior of Hexham (ca. 1160–ca. 1200: SD, 2:284–332), who derived most of his account before 1139 from his predecessor, Richard prior of Hexham (1141–ca. 1160): *Historia de gestis Regis Stephani et de bello de standardo*, in *Chronicles of the Reigns of Stephen, Henry II, and Richard I*, 3:139–178, and from John of Worcester; neither of the Hexham canons provides independent information of more than local interest on Henry I's closing years.

[58] *Brevis relatio de Willelmo noblissimo comite Normannorum*, pp. 1–23; "Chronica monasterii de Hida juxta Wintoniam," in *Liber de Hyda*, pp. 283–321; the *Brevis relatio* is a text of considerable complexity, to which its editor, J. A. Giles, has failed to do justice: see *MMI*, p. 45 n. 155. A new edition-translation of the *Brevis relatio* by Elisabeth van Houts appeared in the Camden Miscellany, 5th ser., vol. 10 (1997). Thanks to Marjorie Chibnall for this information (ACF).

[59] *Scriptores*, ed. Giles, p. 19; *GND*, 2:286–287; *MMI*, pp. 44–45.

[60] *MMI*, pp. 46–47 and n. 160.

[61] Ibid.; Bates, "Normandy and England after 1066," pp. 877–880.

The abbey of Bec, the most influential monastery in the Anglo-Norman world, produced a series of biographies of its early abbots that was unique for its time. Because of the abbey's widespread cross-Channel connections, these *vitae* sometimes disclose historical information of more than local importance. In the 1130s the Bec monk Milo Crispin, in his *Vitae abbatum*, brought together lives of the first four abbots of Bec, taking the first two from earlier works and writing the last two himself. He began with a life of the founding abbot, Herluin (1037–1078), by Gilbert Crispin abbot of Westminster (d. 1117/1118), a former Bec monk and a lifelong friend of St Anselm.[62] Gilbert's *Vita Herluini* was probably a source of inspiration for Eadmer's *Vita Anselmi*, the opening sections of which contain a full account of Anselm's years as prior and abbot of Bec (1063–1093).[63] Milo incorporated the *Vita Anselmi* into his series as the second biography and followed it by his own *vitae* of Abbots William of Beaumont (1093–1124) and Boso (1124–1136). Associated with the lives of these four abbots are brief, anonymous accounts of their immediate successors, Abbots Theobald (1136–1138) and Letard (1139–1149), and a life of Lanfranc, prior of Bec before becoming abbot of Caen in 1063, written by a monk of Bec in the late 1130s.[64] Of considerably greater value than these last works is an anonymous contemporary life of the Bec monk Gundulf, a close friend and ally of St Anselm, who became prior of Caen under Lanfranc and then bishop of Rochester (1077–1108).[65]

Although such biographies were limited largely to Bec and its immediate circle, almost all major Anglo-Norman religious houses, including Bec itself, produced their own local chronicles or annals. Many of these narratives were compiled at too late a date to be useful for the reign of Henry I, but several of them are contemporary or nearly contemporary accounts. Some are hybrid works, part chronicle and part cartulary, in which historical passages serve primarily as introductions to records of benefactions. Two of the most communicative of these hybrids are the *Liber eliensis* and the *Abingdon Chronicle*, the former from a house of extraordinary wealth

---

[62] The *Vita Herluini* is printed in Robinson, *Gilbert Crispin*, pp. 87–110.

[63] Eadmer was also influenced, perhaps more directly, by Anglo-Saxon saints' lives: see Gransden, *Historical Writing*, pp. 132–133.

[64] *PL* 150, cols 29–58, 713–732; for translations and commentaries on the Bec *vitae*, and on the related text, "De libertate beccensis monasterii," see Vaughn, *The Abbey of Bec*. See also Margaret Gibson's important discussion: "History at Bec in the Twelfth Century," pp. 167–186.

[65] *Vita Gundulfi*, ed. Thomson; Gundulf's advancement to Rochester, a see that was strictly subordinated to Canterbury, was arranged by Lanfranc after his own advancement to the archbishopric: Eadmer, *HN*, p. 15; WM, *GP*, pp. 136–137.

that Henry I had elevated from an abbey to a bishopric, the latter from an abbey that for a time enjoyed intimate connections with the royal court and was richly favored by the king and his close associates.[66] Another eminent monastic house, the abbey of Ramsey, produced a chronicle and a lengthy cartulary as separate works.[67] Particularly illuminating are the chronicles from the cathedral priory of Winchester and the Conqueror's great foundation at Battle.[68] The *Winchester Annals* provide independent contemporary testimony, relating chiefly to the English Church, from the early years of Henry I's reign to AD 1125, after which, through the end of the reign and well beyond, the annals were written by a much later and less competent compiler. The *Chronicle of Battle* is of comparable significance, particularly in the way its accounts of the abbey's legal disputes cast light on the nature and evolution of English law.

Such, in brief, are the major Anglo-Norman narrative sources bearing on the reign of Henry I. From beyond the frontiers of England and Normandy, a handful of interrelated sources cast a glimmer of light on Henry I's activities in Wales.[69] Other, more communicative narratives extend our knowledge of Henry's relations, particularly his diplomatic and military relations, with Flanders, Anjou, and the French royal domain. From the neighborhood of Paris, Suger abbot of Saint-Denis contributed a revealing biography of his hero and benefactor, King Louis VI (1108–1137), Henry I's most persistent rival.[70] Despite its panegyrical celebration of the deeds of King Louis, Suger's biography presents Henry in a surprisingly favorable light, owing in part perhaps to Henry's generous treatment of Saint-Denis' Norman dependency of Berneval, which Suger had once ruled as prior. Henry's stormy relations with Flanders are treated by several contemporary Flemish writers—most significantly by Galbert of Bruges, whose vivid,

---

[66] *Liber eliensis; Chron. Ab.*

[67] *Chronicon abbatiae rameseiensis*, ed. Macray; *Cartularium monasterii de Rameseia*, ed. Hart and Lyons.

[68] *Ann. Wint.*, 2:3–125; *Chron. Battle.*

[69] *Brut y Tywysogyon or the Chronicle of the Princes, Peniarth MS 20 Version*, trans. Thomas Jones (Cardiff, 1952); *Brut y Tywysogyon, Red Book of Hergest Version*, ed. Thomas Jones (Cardiff, 1955; 2nd edn, 1973); *Brenhinedd y Saesson*, in *Myvrian Archaeology of Wales*, ed. Jones et al., pp. 652–684; *Annales Cambriae*; see in general Lloyd, *The Welsh Chronicles*, pp. 369–391. For Scottish sources *temp.* Henry I see Anderson, *Early Sources of Scottish History*, 2:119–185.

[70] Suger, *Louis le Gros*; Suger, *The Deeds of Louis the Fat*, trans. Cusimano and Moorhead; cf. Spiegel, *The Chronicle Tradition of Saint-Denis*; further material on Henry's relations with France is provided by Clarius of Sens, "Chronicon S. Petri Vivi Senonensis," [incl.] 281; by the *Chronique de Morigny*; and by Guibert of Nogent, *Histoire de sa vie*; see Guibert of Nogent, *Self and Society in Medieval France: The Memoirs of Abbot Guibert of Nogent*, trans. Benton.

day-by-day account of the great Flemish succession crisis of 1127–1128 is unique in medieval historical writing.[71] The chronicles of contemporary Anjou, although indispensable sources for Henry I's crucially important relations with the Angevin counts, are largely products of later writers looking backward and must therefore be used with caution. Among the most informative of them for our purposes are the *Gesta consulum andegavorum*, John of Marmoutier's *Historia Gaufredi ducis*, and the *Annales de Saint-Aubin*.[72]

Nowhere else in twelfth-century Europe does one encounter a configuration of historical sources comparable in quality and scope to the narratives of the Anglo-Norman realm. Collectively they illuminate the era of Henry I with a clarity and definition unmatched elsewhere. Although not even the foremost of the Anglo-Norman historians can be credited with surpassing Bede, their achievement as a group was unprecedented in England and, indeed, in medieval Western Christendom. It is not unreasonable to regard at least the more important among them as contributing to a single interrelated enterprise.

Martin Brett, in an illuminating and characteristically meticulous paper, has brought to light an intricate web of connections between the great English Benedictine centers of historical writing during the Anglo-Norman period: "Historical research at Durham, Worcester, Malmesbury, and Canterbury," he concludes, "was accompanied by a frequent and elaborate exchange of its results as the work progressed."[73] In demonstrating these connections, Brett is elaborating on Sir Richard Southern's stimulating suggestion that the outpouring of historical writing from these and other Benedictine houses during the generations after the Norman Conquest constituted a singularly English contribution to the twelfth-century renaissance.[74] The movement was energized, Southern maintains, by the deadly threat posed by the new Norman order to the lands, rituals, feasts, relics, and patron saints of the Old English abbeys: their very corporate survival depended on the spirited pursuit of historical research and writing, in the form of cartularies, saints' lives, and

---

[71] Galbert, *Histoire du meurtre de Charles le Bon*, ed. Pirenne; trans. Ross, *The Murder of Charles the Good, Count of Flanders*, rev. edn; Galbert's testimony is supplemented by that of Walter of Thérouanne, "Vita Caroli," pp. 531–561, and Hermann of Tournai, "Liber de restauratione monasterii S. Martini tornacensis," pp. 284–289.

[72] See *Chroniques des comtes d'Anjou et des seigneurs d'Amboise*, ed. Halphen and Poupardin, pp. 25–73, 172–231; and *Recueil d'annales angevines et vendômoises*, pp. 3–49.

[73] Brett, "John of Worcester," p. 125; see more generally ibid., pp. 101–126 *passim*.

[74] Southern, "The Place of England in the Twelfth-Century Renaissance," *Medieval Humanism*, pp. 160–162; above, this chapter, p. 3.

histories, as part of an effort to ensure the survival of the Anglo-Saxon past.[75]

These observations, cogent though they are, require certain modifications. First, one should be cautious not to misinterpret the surge of English historical writing in the reigns of Henry I and Stephen as a monastic expression of Anglo-Saxon patriotism in the face of an oppressive Norman regime. Professor Susan Ridyard has effectively rebutted the myth that post-Conquest Norman prelates of English abbeys were scornful of their houses' Old English saints. From the immediate post-Conquest era onward, most Norman prelates of English abbeys had the good sense to champion the general welfare and indigenous saints' cults of their newly acquired houses,[76] and the devotion of such abbots to the traditions of their monastic communities tends to deepen as one moves forward from the Conquest to the great age of English historical writing. At Christ Church, Canterbury, in Eadmer's time, for example, some monks were Anglo-Saxon while others were Norman (in what proportion it cannot be discerned), but their writings suggest much less concern with their ethnic differences than with their shared devotion to Saints Dunstan and Alphege and their collective hostility toward York. In the time of William of Malmesbury and Symeon of Durham (neither of whom was wholly Anglo-Saxon), the Benedictine abbeys were not Old English vestiges but established centers of the Anglo-Norman order.

It seems doubtful, moreover, that the burgeoning of historical writing in the Anglo-Norman world can be limited to English Benedictines or that their interactions were altogether distinctive. Insofar as there was an Anglo-Norman historical community, it should include such secular clergy as Henry of Huntingdon, Hugh the Chanter, and perhaps even Geoffrey of Monmouth. It should include, as well, Benedictine writers from houses in Normandy—Orderic Vitalis, Robert of Torigny, and the biographers of the Bec abbots. Indeed, the difficulty of dissociating Englishmen from Normans in these generations is exemplified not only by the mixed parentage of Orderic and William of Malmesbury (and the unknown ancestry of such persons as Henry of Huntingdon and John of Worcester) but also by the career of Gilbert Crispin, the product of an important Norman aristocratic family who became a monk of Bec and biographer of Bec's founding abbot and who spent the later decades of his life serving with great

---

[75] Ibid.; Southern, "Aspects of the European Tradition of Historical Writing," pp. 246–256; cf. Brett, "John of Worcester," p. 125.

[76] Ridyard, "*Condigna Veneratio*: Post-Conquest Attitudes to the Saints of the Anglo-Saxons."

distinction as abbot of Westminster. Events such as Orderic Vitalis'
visit with John at Worcester and Henry of Huntingdon's stimulating
encounter with Robert of Torigny at Bec provide further testimony
to the existence of this wider world.

The Anglo-Norman historians tended to derive their information
from a common pool of sources. Thus, William of Malmesbury
drew from Eadmer, from a manuscript of the *Anglo-Saxon Chronicle*
resembling the Peterborough E text (but not identical to it), from
William of Jumièges' *Gesta normannorum ducum*, and from Gilbert
Crispin's *Life of Herluin*. It is also clear that Malmesbury and John
of Worcester were using common source materials.[77] Henry of
Huntingdon's sources were at least as diverse: the E text of the
Anglo-Saxon Chronicle, William of Jumièges' *Gesta normannorum
ducum*, the *Worcester Chronicle*, and perhaps indirectly William of
Malmesbury and Orderic Vitalis.[78] Robert of Torigny, having added
a continuation to the *Gesta normannorum ducum*, based much of
his *Chronicle* (before 1147) on Henry of Huntingdon.[79] Symeon of
Durham, as we have seen, borrowed from the *Worcester Chronicle*,
Eadmer of Canterbury, William of Malmesbury, and the *Gesta normannorum ducum*.[80] Orderic was indebted to the two foremost historians of the Conquest generation, William of Jumièges and William of
Poitiers, to the *Worcester Chronicle*, and perhaps, indirectly, to the
writings of other contemporaries.[81] And the writings of the pseudo-
historian Geoffrey of Monmouth were used by Robert of Torigny,
Henry of Huntingdon, Orderic Vitalis, and even Suger of Saint-Denis.[82]
Since Geoffrey was endeavoring to fabricate for the ancient Britons
the kind of history that his contemporaries William of Malmesbury
and Henry of Huntingdon had provided for the English, it hardly
seems a coincidence that among Geoffrey's several dedicatees were
Henry of Huntingdon's patron, Alexander bishop of Lincoln, and
William of Malmesbury's patron, Robert earl of Gloucester.[83]

---

[77] Brett, "John of Worcester," pp. 113–117; Stubbs, in WM, *GR*, 2:cxxviii–cxxxii;
Thomson, *Malmesbury*, pp. 69–70, 202–203, 205–207.

[78] Gransden, *Historical Writing*, pp. 198–199; HH, p. liv.

[79] RT, *Chron.*, in *Chronicles of the Reigns of Stephen, Henry II, and Richard I*, pp. 7–153
passim; Gransden, *Historical Writing*, p. 200.

[80] See above, pp. 14–15.

[81] OV, 2:xxiii–xxv.

[82] RT, *Chron.*, in *Chronicles of the Reigns of Stephen, Henry II, and Richard I*, pp. 64,
75; HH, pp. xx–xxiv; OV, 5:292 and n. 1; 6:xviii, 380–388; Suger, *Louis le Gros*, pp.
99–103; Suger and Orderic used only the *Prophecies of Merlin*, which Geoffrey completed shortly before Henry I's death and later incorporated into his *Historia regum
Britanniae*.

[83] *The "Historia Regum Britanniae" of Geoffrey of Monmouth*, ed. Griscom. See in
general Tatlock, *The Legendary History of Britain*.

The stimulus resulting from these connections and interactions must not be exaggerated. There is no clear evidence, for example, that the two foremost historians of the age, William of Malmesbury and Orderic Vitalis, used each other's work—although as nearly exact contemporaries they would surely have been aware of each other's existence.[84] Similarly, Eadmer and the Peterborough chronicler worked in relative isolation from their fellow historians, drawing primarily on their own experiences and observations. And even when one historian can be shown to have borrowed from another, the borrower may well have acquired nothing more stimulating than a body of factual data. Accordingly, contacts between contemporary authors cannot entirely explain this eruption of interest in historical writing within a single society and generation.

The influences that prompted these men to take up history were manifold and complex and therefore difficult to encompass. They built, of course, on the deep-rooted historical and hagiographical traditions of the Anglo-Saxons and, in the case of Orderic and Robert of Torigny, on William of Jumièges' *Gesta* of the Norman dukes and the Conquest narratives of William of Poitiers and Guy of Amiens. The "universal histories" of the continental writers Marianus Scotus and Sigebert of Gembloux served as foundations for the chronicles of Florence of Worcester and Robert of Torigny respectively and were also known to Orderic.[85] The Norman Conquest itself, and the revolutionary changes that it brought to English aristocratic society, doubtless served as a further incentive to historical writing, as did the subsequent challenge of linking the new Norman elite in England with the Anglo-Saxon past (and with the heroic Norman past as well).[86] But there was still another stimulus at work in Henry I's generation—elusive yet deeply significant—which leads us back to the subject of the twelfth-century renaissance.

The art historian Kenneth Clark once suggested, metaphorically, that in the years after 1100 the atmosphere of Western Europe suddenly became "more radioactive."[87] Without succumbing altogether to such anachronistic and perhaps alarming figures of speech, one can nevertheless observe that Henry I's generation witnessed a great surge of intellectual and cultural activity at all levels throughout Europe. The French monk Guibert of Nogent, writing circa 1115, remarked that the schoolmasters of his youth could not compare

---

[84] OV, 2:xxiv–xxv.
[85] Gransden, *Historical Writing*, pp. 136, 155, 162, 200.
[86] Davis, *The Normans and Their Myth*; Loud, "The 'Gens Normannorum'—Myth or Reality?"; Bliese, "The Battle Rhetoric of Aelred of Rievaulx."
[87] Clark, *Civilisation: A Personal View*, p. 33.

in competence or number with those of the present day.[88] And with
the proliferation of competent teachers came a vast increase in the
numbers of schools. At the level of higher education, schools rose
to great prominence not only at Paris and Chartres but also at the
northern French hilltop town of Laon. The faculty of the Laon schools
during the early decades of the twelfth century included distinguished scholars such as the theologian Anselm of Laon and his
brother Richard, an expert on the theory of the abacus.[89] Among
the students who flocked to Laon from far and wide were men
who themselves would later achieve scholarly eminence: William of
Champeaux, Gilbert de la Porrée, and the brilliant egotist Peter
Abelard, who came to regard Master Anselm of Laon as a fool and
subsequently departed for Paris, where his instructors proved equally
unsatisfactory to him.

The new ideas of reason and order propelled some of the best
minds in Europe toward the systematic investigation of theology, law,
and human experience. Inevitably they influenced the discipline of
history, inducing the most thoughtful historians of the generation
to place less emphasis on divine intervention and more emphasis on
natural explanations of events.[90] Thus, while many people attributed
the collapse of the Winchester Cathedral tower in 1107 to the fact that
the wicked blasphemer King William Rufus was entombed beneath it,
William of Malmesbury dismissed such a notion as credulous, asserting
that "the building might have fallen because of faulty construction,
even though he had never been buried there." And when an arrow
fired from ambush struck the head of Henry I, Malmesbury ascribed
the king's survival to both the aid of Providence and the good mail
of the king's hauberk.[91] In a similar vein, Orderic describes the sinking
of the White Ship as God's retribution for the sins of the young
nobles aboard, but he also explains that the ship struck a submerged
rock because the crew was drunk and was rowing too fast.[92] Malmesbury begins his description of the same shipwreck with a perfunctory
reference to the working of God's will and then goes on to provide
a graphic account of the drunken crew, urged on by the equally

[88] Guibert, *Histoire de sa vie*, ed. Bourgin, pp. 12–13; Guibert, *Self and Society*, trans.
Benton, p. 45.
[89] Flint, "The 'School of Laon.'"
[90] When natural explanations failed, historians sometimes attributed events simply
to chance: the turning of fortune's wheel became a favorite cliché: Mason, "Magnates, Curiales, and the Wheel of Fortune."
[91] WM, *GR*, 2:379, 477; the attribution of such events to both the divine will and
natural agencies was anticipated by Bede: see Gransden, *Historical Writing*, pp.
21–22 with references.
[92] OV, 6:298–302.

inebriated aristocratic youths aboard, propelling the speeding ship
into the submerged rock. This is followed by a striking description of
the passengers struggling desperately but vainly to stay afloat as the
ship broke to pieces beneath them.[93] This new and growing interest
in naturalistic cause and effect may well have made the writing of
history a much more intriguing enterprise than before.

These novel currents and crosscurrents of thought had a significant effect on the records of royal government no less than on the
historical narratives of the time. The relationship between administrative advances and the new learning is suggested by the close
links between the scholarly center at Laon and the court of Henry I. The
connection first comes to light in 1106 when Henry I somehow arranged
the appointment of his chancellor Gaudry to the bishopric of Laon,
despite the fact that the city lay far beyond the frontiers of his own dominions. Subsequently Ranulf the Chancellor, Gaudry's successor in the
office, sent both his sons to Laon for their education.[94] Roger bishop of
Salisbury, the foremost figure in Henry's English government, sent his
nephews, Alexander and Nigel, to study there as well. After their return,
Alexander was advanced to the wealthy bishopric of Lincoln and also
played a major role in the royal entourage and administration. Nigel
became the first royal treasurer with responsibilities in both England and
Normandy, and although he was elevated to the bishopric of Ely in 1133,
he remained active in royal governance.[95] Roger of Salisbury's connections with Laon are further exemplified by Master Guy d'Etampes,
another Laon student, who became the master of Roger's school at Salisbury. It is not surprising that a group of canons from among the Laon
cathedral clergy, arriving at Salisbury in the course of a fund-raising tour
of England in 1113, received the warmest of welcomes from Bishop
Roger.[96]

---

[93] WM, *GR*, 2:496–497; compare Henry of Huntingdon's prose and poetic
accounts of the White Ship disaster (HH, pp. 242–243), which he attributes, in the
more traditional manner, solely to God's vengeance.

[94] Poole, *Exchequer*, pp. 53–56; Richardson and Sayles, *Governance*, pp. 270–271;
the sons of Ranulf studied at Laon under William of Corbeil, the future archbishop
of Canterbury. Note that Gaudry came to a bad end: Guibert, *Self and Society*, trans.
Benton, pp. 167–177.

[95] Kealey, *Roger of Salisbury*, pp. 48–50; Green, *Government*, pp. 159–160; *MMI*,
pp. 218–219.

[96] Kealey, *Roger of Salisbury*, pp. 48–49; Tatlock, "The English Journey of the
Laon Canons"; Martinet, "Le Voyage des Laonnais"; Hermann of Tournai, *De
miraculis S. Mariae laudunensis*, cols 961 ff. Other Anglo-Normans who studied
at Laon included Robert Bethune bishop of Hereford, Algar bishop of Coutances,
Robert of Chichester bishop of Exeter, and Hugh of Amiens, whom Henry I chose
as the first abbot of his great foundation at Reading and later advanced to the
archbishopric of Rouen: Richardson and Sayles, *Governance*, pp. 270–271; Kealey,
Roger of Salisbury, pp. 48–49.

A highly literate government such as Henry I's, directed by officials who were in close touch with one of Europe's foremost centers of learning, could well be expected to produce administrative documents unprecedented in their abundance and originality. And Henry's government more than met such expectations—with elaborate records of the newly constituted exchequer (the *Pipe Roll of 31 Henry I*) and reformed royal household (the *Constitutio domus regis*), the first treatise on English law (the *Leges Henrici Primi*, an unofficial document written by an anonymous royal administrator), and an avalanche of royal charters. But notwithstanding this outpouring, the most comprehensive record bearing on the condition of Norman England was produced some fourteen years before Henry I's accession by the government of William the Conqueror.

Domesday Book is the record of a vast royal survey of lands and landholders unparalleled in the history of medieval and early modern Europe. The scholarly literature on Domesday Book is so copious that further comment on its contents and purpose would be superfluous.[97] If used with caution, it can provide the historian of Henry I's reign with invaluable data on such matters as the relative wealth of the king and his lay and ecclesiastical tenants-in-chief in 1086, the locations and geld assessments (in hides or carucates) of their manors, and the identities, holdings, and geld assessments of their feudal subtenants. Although the Domesday survey was never repeated, it was supplemented under Henry I and shortly after the reign by a handful of regional and local surveys conducted in Leicestershire, Northamptonshire, Lindsey (Lincolnshire), Herefordshire, Worcestershire, and the town of Winchester, which Domesday Book omits.[98] These surveys cover only a small percentage of the lands surveyed in Domesday Book, but they do demonstrate both continuity in landholding and tenurial change, resulting not only from the rise and fall of great magnates but also from a variety of local negotiations—purchases, exchanges, divided inheritances, and religious benefactions—that would otherwise have gone unnoticed.

Just as the Domesday survey provides data on royal and aristocratic wealth, the charters of Henry I, of which more than 1,500 survive, furnish an abundance of information on the activities and personnel of the royal government.[99] The earliest of these charters

---

[97] Bates, *A Bibliography of Domesday Book*; for a brief overview see Darby, *Domesday England* and *Domesday Book: Studies.*

[98] *The Leicestershire Survey*, ed. Slade; *Herefordshire Domesday*, ed. Galbraith and Tait; *Winchester in the Early Middle Ages*, ed. Biddle, pp. 1–68; *The Lincolnshire Domesday and the Lindsey Survey*, ed. Foster and Longley, pp. xliv–xlv, 237–260; Round, *Feudal England*, pp. 169–224; *VCH, Northampton, Worcester.*

[99] I am using "charter" (*carta*) in the broad sense in which it was used at the time, to include the various sorts of documents issued by the royal chancery in the

announces the king's promises to his subjects at his coronation. Although based on the coronation oaths of previous kings, Henry's was much more detailed than its prototypes and was the first to be expressed in writing.[100] Toward the close of King John's reign Henry's coronation charter achieved posthumous fame when Archbishop Stephen Langton put it forward as a precedent for Magna Carta, and it has since found a place in all constitutional histories of England. Its original authors, however, unaware that they were enriching the English constitution, were simply endeavoring to cope with the immediate problem of bolstering Henry's disputed claim to the throne.

The address clauses and witness lists of Henry's charters provide important information on the royal government by identifying the officials responsible for carrying out the king's business in the shires and by disclosing the names and titles of persons regularly or occasionally present at the royal court. Most of Henry I's surviving charters were calendared (with complete lists of addressees and witnesses) by Charles Johnson and H. A. Cronne and published in 1956 as volume 2 of a series entitled by its modern editors *Regesta regum anglo-normannorum*. This *Regesta 2* (as we will call it) can be augmented to a degree by consulting an unpublished collection unknown to Johnson and Cronne consisting chiefly of Henry I's Norman charters, compiled in 1932 by Dr Henri Chanteux and deposited since 1966 in the Archives de Calvados, Caen.[101] A number of other charters of Henry I, overlooked by the editors of *Regesta 2*, have been published since 1956 in a variety of cartularies and other collections,[102] and some remain unpublished to this day.[103] But the matters with which they deal and the names in their witness lists and address clauses echo those of the charters previously published. The 1,500 charters calendared in *Regesta 2* constitute well over 95

---

king's name: solemn diplomas and other formal *acta* conveying title to property, and writs conveying royal orders or otherwise expressing the royal will: mandates, warrants, precepts, notifications, etc.

[100] *RRAN* 2, no. 488; *Gesetze*, ed. Liebermann, 1:521.

[101] Chanteux, "Recueil des actes de Henri Ier Beauclerc duc de Normandie," Archives de Calvados, unclassified. The Chanteux collection includes only a handful of charters overlooked by Johnson and Cronne; it occasionally provides better texts, but it does not add substantially to the *RRAN* 2 collection.

[102] E.g., "An Interim List of *Errata* and *Addenda* to Davis's *Regesta regum anglo-normannorum*, Volumes I and II," *University of Birmingham Historical Journal* 6 (1958): 176–196; *The Cartulary of Worcester Cathedral Priory*; *English Lawsuits*, ed. Van Caenegem, vol. 1.

[103] E.g., The Red Book of Thorney, CUL Add. MS 3020, 3021; Archives départementales de la Seine-Maritime, G 3666 (Rouen, 1124), parts of which have been published in *English Lawsuits*, ed. Van Caenegem.

percent of the total known today and, as one might expect from a database of that magnitude, are consistent with those that have been published since.[104] It therefore seems unlikely that any major surprises will be encountered in the charters of Henry I still awaiting discovery.[105]

Among the other major sources bearing on law and governance under Henry I, perhaps the most notable emanated from the exchequer, an institution based on the recently introduced abacus system of reckoning in which sheriffs presented their annual accounts to a royal court of audit by moving counters on a checkered table. The first surviving record of this new auditing process is the *Pipe Roll of 31 Henry I* or, more informally, the Pipe Roll of 1130.[106] As the earliest surviving comprehensive account of royal income in European history, this remarkable document provides a unique view of the workings of Henry I's precocious government. It is the record of transactions at the exchequer court meeting at Winchester in Michaelmas 1130 to review the collection of royal revenues over the previous year. Proceeding on a shire-by-shire basis, like the Domesday survey, the Pipe Roll of 1130 discloses not only the sources of royal income—such as sheriffs' farms, gelds, fines, reliefs, and payments for royal privileges—but also the scope and patterns of royal patronage and the mechanisms of royal administration. We know from internal evidence that the Pipe Roll of 1130 is one of a series of such records produced annually by Henry I's exchequer court, the remainder of which has perished. The series may have commenced as early as 1110, at about the time the exchequer system was itself taking shape, and it is not unlikely that the rolls evolved only gradually into the elaborate form that we encounter in 1130.[107] The series doubtless extended forward into the reign of Stephen, but the first roll to survive after 1130 is that of 1156, the second year of Henry II's reign, and it is much more diminutive than the earlier surviving pipe roll. Thereafter the series of pipe rolls continues year by year into the future, but not until almost a quarter-century into Henry II's reign (1177) does total pipe-roll income exceed the level of 1130—and it does so only twice thereafter before Henry

---

[104] Two charters absent from *RRAN* 2, published in the Worcester cartulary, add measurably, however, to our knowledge of Queen Matilda II's entourage: *Cartulary of Worcester Cathedral Priory*, nos 40, 262; *MMI*, p. 229 and n. 19; another document not fully published in *RRAN* 2 provides a further rare glimpse of Henry I's regency court functioning in the king's absence: see Stenton, *English Justice*, p. 62 n. 46.

[105] See appendix.

[106] *PR 31 Henry I*, below, pp. 356–360.

[107] See the allusion to Henry I's pipe rolls in the *Dialogus de scaccario*, p. 42, and the discussions in Clanchy, *From Memory to Written Record*, pp. 136–181, and Green, *Government*, pp. 41, 54.

II's death in 1189. Most of the pipe rolls of Henry II and his immediate successors have been published by the Pipe Roll Society, in meticulous editions, but the roll of 1130 and the first three rolls of Henry II were published much earlier, in the 1830s, by the Record Commissioners.[108] Judith Green has subjected the roll of 1130 to computer analysis, and the resulting information is now conveniently summarized in an appendix to her valuable book *The Government of England under Henry I*.[109] As analyzed and interpreted by Dr Green and other modern historians, Henry I's pipe roll reveals an administrative system far more sophisticated than one could possibly have suspected had this precious record not survived.

Like the exchequer, the household of Henry I functioned for many years in the historical shadows before springing into view fully mature, bathed in the light of a unique administrative text. Just as unprecedented as the Pipe Roll of 1130, the *Constitutio domus regis* records the emoluments of an elaborate and complex hierarchy of officials in a functioning royal household.[110] The document is likely to have been derived from one or more earlier exemplars, now lost. In its surviving form it dates from about 1136 and was presumably intended as an aid to King Stephen's fledgling regime in perpetuating King Henry's household organization. Although royal households have existed in one form or another ever since there have been kings, it is clear from the independent testimony of William of Malmesbury and Eadmer that sometime between about 1108 and 1110 the obstreperous and predatory household of the Norman kings was thoroughly reformed by Henry I, who prohibited courtiers from plundering or molesting villagers on pain of mutilation or death and established a schedule of prices that all courtiers must pay when purchasing goods from local residents.[111] It was probably in conjunction with this prohibition on pillaging that Henry undertook to provide his household staff with fixed stipends from the royal treasury. The *Constitutio* lists the stipends (wages, food, wines, horses, even candles and candle-ends) pertaining to a considerable multitude of household officials from the greatest and best rewarded—chancellor, master chamberlain, stewards, master butler, constables, and treasurer—down to lowly functionaries in the hunting staff and the kitchen. Several

[108] *PR 31 Henry I, Great Roll of the Pipe*, ed. Hunter; despite the excellence of the Record Commissioners' edition, a number of corrections were incorporated into a revised edition of the *Pipe Roll of 1130*, ed. Hunter, and Judith Green has provided further corrections: *Government*, p. 222 n. 6.

[109] Green, *Government*, pp. 220–225; see also ibid., pp. 38–94, and Mooers, "Patronage and the Pipe Roll of 1130."

[110] *Dialogus de scaccario*, pp. 128–135.

[111] Eadmer, *HN*, pp. 192–193; WM, *GR*, 2:487.

historians have analyzed much or all of this body of data with results
that are illuminating, particularly so if the writer resists the temptation
to linger over every detail down to the last candle-end.[112] For emerging
from its wealth of details is an ordered overall structure with clear
gradations of rewards and coherent lines of command, further exem-
plifying the impulse in Anglo-Norman government toward rational
organization and dependence on the written word.

   Other texts from Henry I's reign, most notably the *Quadripartitus* and
the *Leges Henrici Primi*, reflect a powerful renewal of interest in royal
law.[113] Neither is an official document, but both display familiarity with
the law such as to suggest that their authors, or author, may have been
associated with the royal administration. Henry had promised in his
coronation charter to restore the laws of Edward the Confessor (as
emended by William I), and both the *Quadripartitus* and *Leges* reflect
this commitment.[114] Since the Confessor issued no collection of laws,
the meaning of Henry's promise was that he would abide by the laws
in effect during Edward's reign, embodied chiefly in the several law
codes of Cnut, preceded by those of Ethelred and his royal predecessors back through Alfred to King Ine of Wessex. Thus the *Quadripartitus* (ca. 1108–1118), whose author lauded Henry I as a veritable
fountain of justice, sought to encompass in a single work (of which the
textual history is heartbreakingly tangled) all the laws promulgated
by the Anglo-Saxon kings along with some tenth-century treaties with
the Danes and a decree of William I. The second and final volume of
the *Quadripartitus*[115] is a collection of diverse materials, legislative and
otherwise, associated with Henry I: the coronation charter, some correspondence with the pope, the decrees of primatial synods, and the royal
ordinance on hundred and shire courts. Saxon and Norman England
are thus linked in this ambitious, complex work.

   The Anglo-Saxon legal tradition is of similar importance in the *Leges
Henrici Primi* (ca. 1115–1118), which is not simply a compilation of laws
but an effort to integrate them into a legal treatise.[116] Indeed it is the

---

[112] See in particular the illuminating studies of White, "The Household of the
Norman Kings"; Green, *Government*, pp. 26–37; and Barlow, *Rufus*, pp. 134–155.

[113] *Quadripartitus*, ed. Liebermann; *Leges Henrici Primi*.

[114] E.g. Sharpe, ed. and trans., "The Prefaces of 'Quadripartitus,'" p. 167: "Not
only has he [Henry I] given us back the law of King Edward, which we received
with every delight of rejoicing, but strengthened as it was by the improvements
introduced by his blessed father, he has improved it with his own laws."

[115] The remaining two volumes of the *Quadripartitus*, promised in its introduction
and implied in its title, do not exist and probably never did; see Richardson and
Sayles, *Law and Legislation*, pp. 41–43; and, now most important, Patrick Wormald,
"Quadripartitus," pp. 111–147.

[116] *Leges Henrici Primi*, pp. 1–78; cf. the brief but valuable comment by John
Hudson, "Administration, Family and Perceptions of the Past in Late Twelfth-
Century England," p. 76.

first such effort in the history of England. As such, it has the flaws and confusions that are apt to result from an absence of prototypes. The literal English translation of its Latin title, "The Laws of Henry I," can be misleading, for neither Henry I nor any other post-Conquest king issued a law code; like the laws of Edward the Confessor, those of Henry I were simply the body of laws in effect during his reign. The modern editor of the *Leges*, Professor Leslie Downer, devoted his expert attention to tracing a great many of its provisions back to specific clauses in the laws of Cnut and other, earlier Anglo-Saxon codes. Numerous Old English precedents underlay the law administered in Henry I's tribunals, but it is not always clear to what extent the author of the *Leges* is describing laws currently in effect and to what extent he is engaging in anachronism, perhaps digging studiously into the past for royal laws that no longer applied. Still, there is much of value in this perplexing text. The *Leges Henrici Primi* reminds us, for example, that besides the administrative division of Henry's dominions between England and Normandy there remained the older divisions and distinctions between the laws of Wessex, Mercia, and the Danelaw, and that beneath the layer of new procedures exemplified by the emerging system of itinerant justices emanating from an increasingly centralized court a far older substratum of legal custom and practice endured. The *Leges Henrici Primi* is a blend of the old and the new: a body of ancient legal traditions, rooted in the dooms of Anglo-Saxon kings, modified by the Anglo-Normans, and now integrated into England's first treatise on law. Most interestingly, its anonymous author is very likely to have been the author of the *Quadripartitus* as well. The most recent and satisfactory interpretation of the two texts views them as products of a single enterprise—the most successful of several contemporary endeavors to make explicit the "laws of Edward the Confessor" which Henry I had undertaken to restore.[117] Like the histories of William of Malmesbury, Henry of Huntingdon, and "Symeon" of Durham—like the Norman monarchy itself—the *Quadripartitus* and the *Laws of Henry I* rest on deep Anglo-Saxon foundations.

---

[117] Wormald, "Quadripartitus," pp. 111–147. Wormald plausibly suggests that the author deliberately abandoned his initial idea of a "Quadripartitus" of four books of laws in favor of a legal treatise, the *Leges Henrici Primi*, for which the "Quadripartitus" provided raw materials. Another such endeavor to provide an Anglo-Saxon foundation to Anglo-Norman law was the *Textus roffensis*, ed. Thomas Hearne; facsimile edn, ed. Sawyer, 2 vols; Wormald, "*Laga Eadwardi*." Other compilations of early English law, most or all dating from Henry I's reign and some of them related, are the *Instituta Cnuti*, the *Consiliatio Cnuti*, the so called "Ten Articles of William the Conqueror," the *Leis Willelme* or *Leges Willelmi*, and the *Leges Edwardi Confessoris: Gesetze*, ed. Liebermann, 1:486–488, 612–619, 627–672; 3:283–292, 330–335, 339–350; cf. Richardson and Sayles, *Law and Legislation*, pp. 176–179.

Chapter 2

CHILDHOOD AND YOUTH

It has been said that the honest historian affirms what is true, avoids what is false, and respects the uncertain. And despite the exceptional wealth of documentation, many aspects of Henry I's life and reign remain stubbornly uncertain. Indeed, the uncertainties commence with the place and date of his birth.

There can be no doubt that Henry was born in England. William of Malmesbury's clear statement to that effect is corroborated by Orderic, Henry of Huntingdon, Robert of Torigny, and the Winchester annalist and is nowhere contradicted.[1] A local tradition places his birth at Selby,[2] but no contemporary writer confirms that belief or, indeed, provides so much as a hint as to Henry's exact birthplace. As for the date, historians have been virtually unanimous in placing Henry's birth in 1068,[3] on the grounds of William of Malmesbury's statement that Henry was born in the third year after his father's arrival in England.[4] Bishop Stubbs, in his Rolls Series edition of the *Gesta regum*, epitomized Malmesbury's statement with the marginal annotation, "Henry was born in 1068."[5] But the import of the passage is more ambiguous than Stubbs' annotation suggests. To begin with, we cannot be certain that Malmesbury is beginning his year on 1 January. Just as regnal years are calculated from the date of a king's coronation, Malmesbury could well be calculating the years after William's arrival in England from the arrival date itself, 28 September 1066, a date that was etched in William of Malmesbury's memory when he reported that Henry I's victory at Tinchebray on 28 September 1106 occurred exactly forty years after the Conqueror's arrival in England.[6] If so, then Malmesbury is placing

---

[1] WM, *GR* (RS) 2:467; OV, 5:292; HH, p. 255; *GND*, 2:216–217; *Ann. Wint.*, p. 27.

[2] *Monasticon*, 3:485.

[3] E.g., *Handbook of British Chronology*, p. 35.

[4] WM, *GR*, 2:467: "anno tertio postquam pater eam adierat."

[5] Ibid.

[6] WM, *GR*, 2:475: "Idem dies ante quadraginta circiter annos fuerat, cum Willelmus Hastingas primus appulit." Malmesbury has William land at Hastings rather than Pevensey (perhaps from reading the E version of the *Anglo-Saxon Chronicle*), but the date is correct.

Henry's birth no earlier than 28 September 1068 and opening the possibility that he was born in 1069. A second complication is that Malmesbury might well be following the not uncommon procedure of including in his calculation only one terminal date rather than both, in which case William the Conqueror's third year would be 1069, not 1068. Henry of Huntingdon follows this practice throughout his *Historia Anglorum*, identifying AD 1069, for example, as *Willelmi regis anno tertio*.[7] A final difficulty is that Malmesbury, writing half a century after the event, may simply have erred in his calculation, just as he erred a paragraph later by having Henry knighted in the twenty-first rather than the twentieth year of William I's reign.[8]

We are on firmer ground in dating Henry's birth at some point subsequent to his mother's coronation at Westminster on Whitsunday, 11 May 1068, shortly after her arrival from Normandy.[9] The Winchester annalist reports that the birth occurred "not many days" after her coronation,[10] whereas Orderic allows the possibility of a considerably longer interval when, having reported Matilda's coronation on 11 May, he adds that she give birth to Henry "within a year" or "within the year."[11] Henry would thus have been born between about mid-May 1068 and 10 May 1069. The time frame can be narrowed by considering the period during which Henry could have been conceived: before 6 December 1067, when both William and Matilda were in Normandy, or after April 1068, when both were in England. Henry must therefore have been born between either mid-May and early September 1068 or early February and early May 1069. In the light of all contemporary evidence, particularly the testimony of the usually reliable Winchester annalist, the earlier date range is much the more likely, but 1069 remains a bare possibility.

---

[7] HH, p. 204; Orderic is inconsistent in this regard: OV, 4:xxiii.

[8] WM, *GR*, 2:468; cf. WM, *HN*, p. 11, where Malmesbury mistakenly describes 5 August 1133 as beginning the thirty-third year of the reign—in a paragraph that abounds in dating errors.

[9] OV, 2:214, providing the coronation date of 11 May and implying that Matilda arrived in England at some point after Easter (23 March) 1068.

[10] *Ann. Wint.*, p. 27: ". . . et post non multos dies"; Matilda's coronation date is confirmed by FW, ed. Thorpe, 2:2; and *ASC*, D, *s.a.* 1067 (for 1068); see also *RRAN* 1, nos 22 and 23, both dated Whitsunday 1068 and signed by William I, "Queen Matilda," and a large assembly of notables.

[11] OV, 2:214: "Decorata regio diademate matrona priusquam annus perficeretur filium nomine Henricum peperit." "Within a year" is Chibnall's translation; William Farrer, with equal justification, has translated the phrase "within *the* year," but he further assumes that Orderic, perhaps following the lost conclusion of William of Poitiers' *Gesta Guillelmi*, has the year commence with Easter (thus beginning AD 1069 on 12 April): *EYC*, 1:362–363; cf. OV, 2:xviii–xxi, 214 n. 5.

The outside chance that Henry's birth occurred during the later of the two date ranges has prompted at least one historian to give some credence to the tradition that he was born in Selby. The argument centers on the Conqueror's northward march of February or early March 1069 to relieve a Norman garrison besieged in York Castle. Having crushed the besiegers, slaughtering those who could not escape, William ravaged the city of York and then spent a further eight days strengthening its defenses before returning to Winchester in time to celebrate Easter on 12 April.[12] This itinerary raises the interesting possibility that Queen Matilda might have traveled northward in March to join her husband after he had quelled the rebellion and that if so she might well have given birth to Henry either on her way north or on her return with William.[13] If the birth occurred at Selby, a sizable town on the usual route northward from the Midlands, one could then comprehend the otherwise inexplicable fact that about 1069, for the first and last time in their careers, William I and Queen Matilda collaborated in founding a Benedictine abbey and that they did so at Selby, far to the north of their normal circuit of activities.[14] That Henry I was born around March 1069 at Selby is thus a possibility, albeit a remote one.

William and Matilda derived the name Henry not from the Norman ducal family but from the royal line of France. The name was introduced into the Conqueror's lineage by his wife, whose mother, Adela countess of Flanders, was the daughter of the Capetian king Robert II and the sister of Robert's son and heir King Henry I (d. 1060). The infant Henry was thus, like the other offspring of William I and Matilda,

[12] OV, 2:222; at approximately this time Queen Matilda returned to Normandy, but Orderic does not say precisely when. See also ASC, D and E, s.a. 1068 (1069); FW, 2:2; Douglas, William the Conqueror, pp. 217 and n. 7, 218 and nn. 1–3.

[13] See William Farrer in EYC, 1:362–363. William had previously traveled to the north in summer 1068, building castles at Warwick and Nottingham as he progressed, and that journey too might have provided the occasion for Henry's birth at Selby: ASC, D, s.a. 1067 (for 1068); OV, 2:216–218.

[14] The founding date of Selby is usually given as 1069 × 1070: Knowles and Hadcock, Medieval Religious Houses, pp. 57, 76; Knowles et al., Heads of Religious Houses, p. 69; the date is narrowed to 1069 in SD, 2:186. See Coucher Book of Selby, 1:v–viii, [3]–[16]: Benedict, the first abbot, was a holy man from Auxerre who settled at Selby ca. 1068, having been called to England, so it was later said, by a divine vision; the (much later) Selby account of Benedict's foundation (again dated 1069) declares that he was introduced to William I by a certain Hugh sheriff of Yorkshire, who can be identified independently as Hugh fitz Baldric, sheriff of Yorkshire (RRAN 1, no. 130). If, as seems probable, William I and Queen Matilda conferred with Benedict before founding the abbey, they are likely to have done so at Selby. Their role as cofounders is made clear by Coucher Book of Selby, 1:23–24 (RRAN 2, no. 850); see further VCH, Yorkshire, 3:95. See also Regesta regum anglonormannorum, ed. Bates, pp. 818–823.

a direct and immediate descendant of the Capetian kings no less than of the dukes of Normandy and the counts of Flanders.[15] But despite his lineage and royal name, the child was well removed from his father's inheritance by three older brothers: Robert, the later Robert II, "Curthose," duke of the Normans; Richard, who as a youth suffered a fatal hunting accident in the New Forest;[16] and William, the later William II, "Rufus," king of the English. Although the rules governing royal successions were as yet quite fluid, Henry must nevertheless have grown up with only modest expectations. That he received an education has suggested to some historians, plausibly but without explicit evidence, that he was being groomed for a career in the Church.[17]

Henry's education has been a subject of much dispute. He was once thought to have acquired a formidable degree of learning in the course of his youth. Writers from the later fourteenth century onward awarded him the sobriquet "Beauclerc,"[18] and historians subsequently came to regard him as an author, a poet, and a translator fluent in Latin, Old English, and even Greek; the fifteenth-century writer Thomas Rudborne went so far as to credit Henry with an M.A. from the University of Cambridge (an institution that emerged more than a century after Henry had completed his schooling).[19] But Henry's reputation for deep erudition began to fade in the course of the nineteenth century, and in 1929 it was damaged beyond repair by Charles W. David, whose aptly titled paper "The Claim of King Henry I to Be Called Learned" dispelled the myth.[20] David argued persuasively that Henry's education must be stripped of all its later legendary accretions and that even the comments on his learning by contemporary writers cannot be swallowed whole. William of Malmesbury is obviously indulging in rhetorical exaggeration when he associates Henry with the philosopher kings of Plato's Republic, and in the light of William I's illiteracy and shortness of temper, one cannot seriously believe Malmesbury's account of young, bookish Henry remarking in his father's hearing that an illiterate king is a crowned ass.[21]

But setting aside such embellishments, there remains William of Malmesbury's clear testimony that in his youth Henry received formal instruction in letters and in other subjects as well.[22] Only occasionally,

---

[15] The name also passed down through Henry I of England to the son of his brother-in-law and admirer, David king of Scots, and of course to seven future kings of England.

[16] OV, 3:114; 5:282; FW, 2:45; WM, *GR*, 2:333.

[17] Matthew Paris, *Chronica majora*, 1:102, 2:130.

[18] David, "Claim of King Henry I," p. 48.

[19] Ibid., pp. 48–53.

[20] Ibid., pp. 45–56.

[21] WM, *GR*, 2:467: "Rex illiteratus, asinus coronatus."

[22] Ibid.: Malmesbury uses the phrase "Philosophia non adeo exiliter informatus."

Malmesbury concedes, did Henry read openly, and he displayed his scholarly attainments sparingly, but we are left with the unmistakable impression that he had some acquaintance with the liberal arts, that he could read Latin, and that, most important, he put his learning to effective use.[23] These conclusions are consistent with Henry I's warm friendship in later life with the learned churchman Boso abbot of Bec. And they are decisively corroborated by the independent testimony of Orderic, who states that Henry was well instructed in Latin letters, natural philosophy, and the study of doctrine.[24] This evidence should be neither exaggerated nor dismissed. Having set aside the myth of the Cambridge-educated poet-king, one must not leap to the conclusion that he was illiterate. Such an assumption recklessly disregards the clear testimony of Malmesbury and Orderic and the judicious words of C. W. David himself, who concluded that Henry was undoubtedly schooled in Latin and "did acquire a considerable, though by no means a complete, mastery of the language."[25]

Professor V. H. Galbraith added another dimension to the argument by observing that the importance of Henry I's education extended far beyond such unfathomable questions as the level of his competence in Latin or the scope of his training in the liberal arts. Much more important was his repute among his associates and contemporaries as the first lettered king in recent memory. "He was an intellectual," Galbraith wrote, "an educated man in a sense that his predecessors, always excepting Alfred, were not."[26] And he possessed the intelligence to apply his learning effectively to the tasks of governance.[27] There are hints in the sources that, in his youth, Henry's analytical turn of mind could be annoying to carefree young nobles of a less studious disposition and could even provoke their ridicule.[28] If so, it stands to reason that, as Malmesbury points out, he would have learned to refrain from a lavish display of his scholarly attainments. Yet Galbraith correctly insists that to more thoughtful contemporaries "Henry was a portent and a

[23] Ibid.

[24] RT, *Chron.*, p. 110; "De libertate beccensis monasterii," p. 605, trans. Vaughn, *Abbey of Bec*, p. 143; OV, 2:214, 4:120; cf. 6:50; Suger of Saint-Denis also regarded Henry as a man of learning: *Louis le Gros*, p. 14: "Henricus, cujus tam admiranda quam predicanda animi et corporis strenuitas et scientia gratam offerrent materiam."

[25] David, "Claim of King Henry I," p. 56.

[26] Galbraith, "Literacy of Medieval English Kings," p. 90. See, in a similar vein, Thompson, *Literacy of the Laity*, pp. 168–170.

[27] WM, *GR*, 2:467, stating that Henry's learning was of great help to him *ad regnandum scientiae*; even Henry of Huntingdon, in his rather mixed review of Henry I's attributes, remarks on his keen intelligence: "sapientia summa, nam et consilio profundissimus, et providentia conspicuus, et eloquentia clarus habebatur:" HH, p. 255.

[28] *MMI*, p. 315; cf. WM, *GR*, 2:471.

wonder."[29] From Galbraith's perspective, <u>Henry's learning was more sig-</u>
<u>nificant than Alfred's because it marked an enduring change in the</u>
<u>quality of royal governance and the standards that came to be expected</u>
of kings. The metaphor of an illiterate king being a crowned ass, which
William of Malmesbury had attributed to young Henry, was repeated
by writers of the next generation—John of Salisbury, Gerald of Wales,
Breton d'Amboise—until it became a cliché and a growing embarrassment to unlettered monarchs.[30] Thus Henry I's grandson Henry II and
all subsequent English kings received education as a matter of course.[31]
In Henry I's own reign it was becoming common not only for leading
administrators to send their young kinsmen abroad for advanced
schooling but also for great barons to arrange for the education of their
sons. Henry's closest baronial adviser in the early years of his reign,
Robert of Beaumont count of Meulan, placed his twin sons Waleran
and Robert under the tutelage of the learned Italian scholar Faritius
abbot of Abingdon, and two of the wealthiest barons of Henry's later
reign, Brian fitz Count lord of Wallingford and Henry's own natural
son Robert earl of Gloucester, are both known to have been well educated.[32] Henry I was by no means the cause of this surge of political
literacy—its origins are elusive and widespread—but as Galbraith
concludes, he "accurately dates the change."[33]

   That Henry spent his early years and received his education in
England is suggested by the evidence of his early charter attestations
and confirmed by the direct testimony of both Robert of Torigny and
the *Brevis relatio*.[34] As a child Henry visited Normandy on occasion.
Queen Matilda must have taken him with her as an infant when she
returned to the duchy in 1069, and his charter attestations disclose that
he was in Normandy in 1080 and again in 1082.[35] Orderic places him
with his two older brothers in a house in Laigle (south-central Normandy) in late 1077 or early 1078 where the siblings had a serious
falling out. William Rufus and Henry, "deeming their strength equal to
that of their brother Robert," infuriated him by directing fetid water
(urine?) down upon him from the upper gallery, shaming him in the
presence of his numerous followers.[36] Orderic describes William and

[29] Galbraith, "Literacy of Medieval English Kings," p. 90.
[30] Ibid., pp. 90–91.
[31] Ibid., pp. 91–95.
[32] *Chron. Ab.*, 2:229; *MMI*, p. 312 and nn.
[33] Galbraith, "Literacy of Medieval English Kings," p. 91.
[34] *RRAN* 1, nos 135, 136*, 137*, 147, 149, 220, 232; *RRAN* 2, nos 393–394, no.
136a; *GND*, 2:216: ". . . natum et nutritum in Anglia"; *Scriptores*, ed. Giles, p. 12,
confirming that Henry was *nutritus in Anglia*.
[35] OV, 2:222, above, p. 32; *RRAN* 1, nos 125 (Caen, 14 July 1080), 150 (Normandy, 1082), 168, 170–171 (all Normandy, 1080–1082): cf. *RRAN* 2, no. 394.
[36] OV, 2:356–358.

Henry on this occasion as having been casting dice "as was the custom of soldiers" before setting about to moisten Robert. Since Henry cannot have been more than eight or nine years old at the time, one is inclined to doubt that he actually took part in an event that, although memorable, occurred several decades before Orderic wrote.[37]

Henry spent most of his time in England from later childhood until after Pentecost (24 May) 1086, when the Conqueror recognized his coming of age by making him a knight.[38] There is little evidence of Henry's exact whereabouts during these early years, apart from the infrequent occasions on which he witnessed royal charters and a notice in the *Abingdon Chronicle* that he spent the Easter feast days of 1084 at Abingdon Abbey while his father and brothers were in Normandy.[39] Nor is there any clear indication of the circumstances of his schooling. It is not unlikely, however, that his education, like that of the Beaumont twins in the next generation, was entrusted to some learned prelate and that Henry spent some of his childhood in a monastic or episcopal community.

One possibility is that Henry was reared for some years at Salisbury Cathedral under the tutelage of Bishop Osmund (1078–1099), a sainted prelate of great learning who was also one of the Conqueror's trusted administrators and was reputed (by a very late source) to be his nephew.[40] St Osmund had served as William I's chancellor before being advanced to the newly relocated bishopric of Salisbury, where he built a cathedral church atop the hill at Old Sarum. An avid book collector, Osmund set his scribes not only to copying theological and exegetical manuscripts in great number but also, in all probability, to producing portions of the Wiltshire Geld Accounts and the Exon Domesday.[41] Osmund was thus exactly the sort of scholar-administrator whom the

[37] David Bates expresses similar doubts about this episode: *William the Conqueror*, pp. 160–161.

[38] *ASC, s.a.* 1086 and WM, *GR*, 2:468, both reporting that the Conqueror dubbed Henry a knight at Westminster at Pentecost, 1086; OV, 4:120, asserts that Henry was knighted by Archbishop Lanfranc, who may indeed have participated in the ceremony.

[39] *Chron. Ab.*, 2:12.

[40] *Charters and Documents Illustrating the History of the Cathedral, City and Diocese of Salisbury in the Twelfth and Thirteenth Centuries*, p. 373; *Vetus registrum sarisbereiense*, 2:xxi–xxiii.

[41] Osmund was royal chancellor between ca. 1070 and 1078: Douglas, *William the Conqueror*, p. 293; *RRAN* 1, pp. xvi–xvii, corrected by *RRAN* 2, p. ix.; *DNB*, 14:1207–1209; Wootten, "A Study of Henry I, King of England"; Chaplais, "William of Saint-Calais and the Domesday Survey," pp. 67–68; Ker, "The Beginnings of Salisbury Cathedral Library," pp. 35, 49; Webber, *Scribes and Scholars at Salisbury Cathedral, ca. 1075–ca. 1125*, pp. 4, 6–7, 10, 16–17, 24, 80–81; WM, *GP*, pp. 183–184, reports that Osmund himself participated in the copying and binding of books for his cathedral library.

Conqueror might have chosen to tutor his youngest son, and it may well be significant that during the years 1080–1086 Henry was often in the bishop's company. During the Easter season of 1084, for example, Osmund accompanied Henry on his aforementioned visit to Abingdon Abbey (which was in Osmund's diocese) along with Milo Crispin, the lord of nearby Wallingford.[42] Beyond that, Osmund's attestation accompanies Henry's on most of the royal charters that Henry witnessed from England during these years (ca. 1080–1086) and even a charter from Normandy.[43] One of these charters was issued from Salisbury (1081), and two more are from other towns in Wiltshire: Downton (1082) and Laycock (1086).[44] The hypothesis that Henry was reared at Salisbury is therefore altogether plausible, but it is also entirely circumstantial. The charters on which it is based, both genuine and spurious, are all attested by a number of witnesses besides Henry and Osmund, including in each instance several other bishops.[45] Accordingly, the circumstances of Henry's education, like most other facets of his childhood, must remain uncertain.[46]

At Westminster on 24 May 1086 Henry left his schooling and childhood behind him when his father dubbed him a knight. Afterward he probably accompanied the royal entourage to Salisbury where on 1 August, at a celebrated ceremony, William received the homage and fealty of the major landholders of England. Malmesbury alleges that Henry accompanied his father on his final crossing to Normandy toward the end of the year,[47] but we are not told whether he participated in the Vexin campaign of summer 1087 on which William was

---

[42] *Chron. Ab.*, 2:12: Robert d'Oilli, royal constable and custodian of Oxford Castle, handled arrangements for their stay at the abbey. The visit occurred at the command of William I.

[43] *RRAN* 1, nos 125 (Caen, 1080), 135, 136*, 137*, 147, 220, 232, and 136a (ibid., pp. 393–394); of the English charters witnessed by Henry before his knighting in 1086, only *RRAN* 1, no. 149 (1082) and perhaps no. 247 (1080–1087, probably from England) lack Bishop Osmund's attestation. If, as seems likely, no. 149 is concurrent with no. 147 (they have nine witnesses in common), then Osmund may have been present on every occasion that Henry is known to have attested in England through May 1086.

[44] Salisbury: *RRAN* 2, nos 393–394, no. 136a; Downton: *RRAN* 1, no. 147 (and possibly 149); Laycock: no. 220 (see *RRAN* 2, no. 396).

[45] Nos 136a and 232 (4 bishops each); nos 135 and 136* (6 bishops each); nos 125 and 220 (10 bishops each); no. 137* (15 bishops).

[46] *RRAN* 2, no. 1134 (1107–1116), announces that Henry I has granted a knights fee of five manors in Berkshire to Robert Achard, *magistro meo* (see ibid., xvii, xx, and no. 833, mentioning a certain Achard as lord of Spratton, Northants.); but this may well be the "A(r)chard" (*Harcherius*) who conveyed the offer of the lordship of Domfront to Henry in 1092 (OV, 4:256–258 and nn.) rather than a childhood tutor: see below, pp. 87–88.

[47] WM, *GR*, 2:468.

mortally injured.[48] We know only that Henry was among the group at his dying father's side at Saint-Gervais outside Rouen in September.[49]

At the Conqueror's entombment ritual at his foundation at Saint-Etienne, Caen, Henry is reported to have rendered him one final service. A local townsman named Ascelin son of Arthur created an embarrassing and long-remembered scene by protesting vehemently that the dead king must not be entombed on land that, so Ascelin perhaps correctly claimed, the late king had unjustly seized from his father for the building of the abbey church. The uproar was quieted, William of Malmesbury declares, when Henry arranged to have Ascelin's claim settled by paying him a hundred pounds of silver.[50]

The reasons underlying the Conqueror's deathbed bequests to his sons have given rise to much controversy,[51] but the broad outlines are well known. Having provided generously for the Church and pardoned his prisoners, William granted Normandy to Robert Curthose, England to William Rufus, and "incalculable treasures" to Henry.[52] The implications of this tripartite settlement, however, are more complex than they might at first appear, and the customs and thought processes underlying the division of William's dominions have been much debated.[53] In my own view, which is largely consistent with those of John Le Patourel and Frank Barlow, William I was guided by the long-standing Norman practice in which all the lands of the dying duke—inherited, conquered, or however else obtained—passed intact to his eldest son (or in the absence of sons, as in 1027, to the eldest brother). This practice, although sometimes challenged by pretenders, governed the Norman succession

---

[48] Or fell mortally ill: Douglas, *William the Conqueror*, pp. 356–358.

[49] OV, 4:80, 94–96.

[50] WM, *GR*, 2:337–338; Orderic tells the same story with different details, omitting Henry's role in it: OV, 4:106 and n. 1; see further Eadmer, *HN*, p. 25, and *Actes de Guillaume le Conquérant et de la reine Mathilde pour les abbayes caennaises*, pp. 45–46, confirming Ascelin's right to the land in question.

[51] E.g., *De obitu Willelmi* (*GND*, 2:184–195), a narrative of William's last days, once accepted as an eyewitness account but now known to be largely a conflation of Einhard's *Vita Karoli Magni* and the Astronomer's description of Louis the Pious' death in his *Vita Hludowici imperatoris*; see Engles, "*De obitu Willelmi ducis Normannorum*, pp. 209–255; see also OV, 4:80–94, quoting William's lengthy and imaginary deathbed speech, which, in Orderic's optimistic view, "deserves to be remembered for all time."

[52] *ASC*, s.a. 1087.

[53] E.g., Le Patourel, "The Norman Succession, 996–1135," pp. 225–234; Holt, "Politics and Property," p. 45 ff.; Beckerman, "Succession in Normandy, 1087, and in England, 1066," p. 258; Barlow, *Rufus*, pp. 40–50; Davis, "William of Jumièges, Robert Curthose, and the Norman Succession"; Tabuteau, "The Role of Law in the Succession to Normandy and England, 1087"; English, "William the Conqueror and the Anglo-Norman Succession."

throughout the century between William Longsword and William the Conqueror, and there seems little doubt that the Conqueror too had originally intended to leave his dominions, including England, to his eldest son. Before the Conquest he had invested Robert Curthose with Normandy, and on several occasions, before and after the Conquest, Robert had received oaths of homage and fealty from the Norman aristocracy, including most of the greatest landholders in England.[54] But as William lay dying Curthose was far away in Ponthieu, engaged in rebellion against his father for the second time, and the Conqueror, furious at the betrayals by his eldest son, and heedless of such niceties as bygone oaths of allegiance and distinctions between inheritances and acquisitions, was evidently on the point of disinheriting him altogether.[55] He was persuaded otherwise by Curthose's friends and *fideles.* "Reluctantly and by compulsion," Malmesbury writes, "he gave Normandy to Robert."[56] But he felt free to give England, which he had won through such bitter strife and subjugated with such cruel bloodshed, to the one son who was both loyal and mature enough to rule.[57]

The details of Henry's inheritance are similarly complex. He is usually reported to have been bequeathed a large quantity of money but no land—five thousand pounds of silver, so Orderic reports; three thousand silver marks, according to William of Malmesbury.[58] It has often been taken as a sign of Henry's budding avarice that, after failing to cajole his father into endowing him more generously, he had his treasure weighed and put into a strong treasure house for safekeeping "among trustworthy friends."[59] But there can be no doubt that Henry's inheritance was also supposed to have included his mother's lands in England. On this matter Orderic and William of Malmesbury are in agreement.[60] These lands, concentrated in

---

[54] OV, 4:92 and n. 5; David, *Curthose,* pp. 12, 15, 19, 29, 40.

[55] WM, *GR,* 2:460.

[56] WM, *GR,* 2:337; Le Patourel's argument (see "The Norman Succession, 996–1135," and *Norman Empire,* pp. 182–183, esp. 183 n. 1), to much the same effect, has been criticized for its dependence on the evidence, since discredited, of *De obitu Willelmi* (above, this chapter, n. 51), but Malmesbury's testimony cannot as easily be dismissed. If the succession to Normandy in 1087 had been controlled by Norman custom and not open to dispute, Malmesbury would surely have been aware of the fact.

[57] OV, 4:94; Lanfranc's role in Rufus' accession (see English, "William the Conqueror and the Anglo-Norman Succession") was significant but probably exaggerated by Eadmer and the *Acta Lanfranci.* Henry was about eighteen at the time; see above, p. 30 ff.

[58] OV, 4:94, supported by Wace, *Roman de Rou,* 2, ll. 9182–9183; WM, *GR,* 2:468.

[59] OV, 4:94–96.

[60] OV, 2:214; 4:148; WM, *GR,* 2:337: "... possessiones maternas Henrico delegavit."

Gloucestershire and Buckinghamshire, were worth roughly £260–£320
a year. They had passed to Matilda from their pre-Conquest holder, the
thegn Brictric son of Algar, and had evidently been willed to Henry
by Matilda herself at some point before her death on 2 November
1083—probably at the time of Henry's birth in 1068/1069.[61] It was
evidently Matilda rather than her husband who chose their youngest
son's name. The Conqueror roundly disliked King Henry I of France,[62]
whereas Queen Matilda took great pride in her kinship with him,
styling herself "daughter of Baldwin duke of the Flemings, and niece
of Henry, most illustrious king of the French."[63] The epitaph on her
tombstone, which stands to this day before the high altar of her great
monastic foundation of Holy Trinity, Caen, describes her as she would
have wished, not only as the wife of the illustrious King William but
also as a woman who was herself of royal blood, whose mother
Adela was the daughter of King Robert of France and "sister of King
Henry."[64] It is reasonable to suppose that Queen Matilda had a special
fondness for her young son who bore her uncle's royal name and
quite understandable that she chose to leave him her English estates.
He would not have taken possession of them at her death in
1083 because he was not yet of age. But had William I lived, Henry
might well have received them on their next crossing to England.
This supposition is consistent with Orderic's statement that in the
year after the Conqueror's death, Henry journeyed to England to
ask William Rufus to grant him custody of his mother's lands.[65] As
it turned out, however, Henry never took possession of them because
William Rufus did not permit him to do so. The sequestration of
his maternal inheritance is the first of a series of instances in which
Henry was victimized by one or both of his older brothers.

---

[61] *MMI*, p. 82; *CP*, 5:682–683; the lands were in Gloucestershire, Buckinghamshire, Cornwall, and possibly Wiltshire and Somerset: DB, 1, fos 73b, 98b, 99,
120, 152b, 163b, 164, 170b; OV (2:214) reports that Matilda gave birth to a son
named Henry, "quem totius terrae suae in Anglia haeredem constituit."

[62] OV, 4:86: Orderic has William complain that the Capetian Henry I "hostiumque
meorum derogationibus admodum stimulatus, sepe nisus est me uelut inermem
conculcare, multisque modis proterere, et indebita michi iura imponere."

[63] *RRAN* 1, no. 149 and p. 122, XV: ". . . Balduini Flandrensium ducis filia
neptisque Henrici Francorum illustrissimi regis."

[64] Quoted in OV, 4:44: Dr Chibnall's exact translation is "Sister of Henry, Robert's
royal son," which, for the sake of meter, takes minor and justifiable liberties with
the Latin; see 4:46 n. 1.

[65] Ibid., 4:148: "Henricus . . . in Angliam transfretauit, et a fratre suo terram
matris suae requisiuit." Frank Barlow raises the possibility that the money that
Henry received on William's death might have been a redemption for part of her
English dower lands: *Rufus*, p. 49. This seems most unlikely, however, since the Conqueror seemingly intended to provide all three sons with substantial monetary
wealth; Henry's portion is singled out because, unlike his brothers, he did not stand
to inherit the contents of a royal or ducal treasury.

By chance, the reigns of the first three Norman kings correspond closely to three significant phases in Henry's life: his childhood and adolescence (up to the knighting ceremony); his youth (from knighting to marriage); and his adulthood when he himself ruled. As a youth, a *juvenis*, Henry experienced some of the vicissitudes that Georges Duby, in a classic paper, has shown to have typified the lives of contemporary aristocratic youths.[66] Although Henry's princely pedigree and immense monetary inheritance set him apart from the throng of less exalted *juvenes*, he followed their pattern in other ways. Like them, he wandered (briefly) as a landless bachelor, sowed his wild oats, and pursued as his principal goal the acquisition of an appropriate lordship.[67]

Henry's wild oats, many of which were doubtless sown in this period of his life, produced more than twenty known bastards, a greater number than that of any other English king.[68] Some contemporary cleric-historians deplored his licentiousness, although usually rather offhandedly. Orderic regretted that during his entire life Henry was enslaved by the sin of lust and had many sons and daughters by his mistresses, but the regret lies buried in the midst of a long passage devoted primarily to the celebration of Henry's merits.[69] William of Malmesbury went so far as to credit Henry with sexual restraint!

> Throughout his life he was altogether free of lewd desires, for, as we have learned from those who know the matter well, he cast himself into the embraces of women not for the gratification of carnal

[66] Duby, "Youth in Aristocratic Society," in *The Chivalrous Society*, pp. 112–122.

[67] On wild oats sown by the aristocratic youths of Henry's era see ibid., p. 115 and n. 19, citing as examples "of the depraved habits of the *juvenes*" OV, 3:228–230, and Guibert, *Histoire*, pp. 57, 220. On their pursuit of lordships (usually obtained by winning the hand of an heiress), ibid., pp. 117–119, 121.

[68] *CP*, 11, app., pp. 112–120, listing most of Henry I's bastards. One can perhaps add to this list a daughter who married Fergus earl of Galloway (Barrow, *Robert Bruce*, p. 36 n. 2) and another who married Guy IV of Laval: *MMI*, p. 283. The *Complete Peerage* overlooks the episode in which the intended marriage of an unnamed bastard daughter of Henry's to Hugh II of Châteauneuf-en-Thymerais ca. 1113 was blocked by Ivo bishop of Chartres on the grounds of consanguinity (*MMI*, pp. 283–284, 288); but she may well be identical to some other daughter on the *Complete Peerage* list. As I calculate it, the total number of Henry's known bastards is 24, including probables. I have profited greatly from an as yet untitled paper prepared for my 1993–1994 graduate research seminar at the University of California, Santa Barbara, by Laura Wertheimer on the subject of aristocratic bastards in Anglo-Norman society.

[69] OV, 6:98; similarly, *Gesta Stephani*, p. 26; and HH, pp. 255–256, where the author compares Henry I's "enslavement by female seductions" with that of Solomon. After second thoughts, Henry of Huntingdon withdrew his criticism in a later manuscript of the *Historia Anglorum*: Greenway, "Henry of Huntingdon," pp. 119–121, 126.

pleasure but to beget offspring, nor did he assent to sexual intercourse except when it could bring about the spreading of the royal
seed. He was thus the master of his libido, not its servant.[70]

Malmesbury's apologia has struck many readers as tortuous, even
ludicrous. But Professor Eleanor Searle, who takes it more seriously
than most, has argued cogently that Henry's bastards did in fact turn
out to be significant political assets to him in subsequent years. His
two eldest sons, Robert of Gloucester and Richard, provided him
with invaluable and absolutely dependable administrative and military
support, while his daughters, through their marriages, cemented
alliances with a number of princes whose lands bordered and
often shielded Henry's Anglo-Norman dominion—lords of such importance as Alexander king of Scots, Conan duke of Brittany, and
Rotrou count of Perche.[71] Henry's flock of bastard daughters, in short,
offered a uniquely effective means of sealing valuable alliances with
princes just below the level of a count of Anjou or a German emperor,
for whom a legitimate daughter was the appropriate mate.[72] And his
bastard sons could be entrusted with vast lands and power such as to
make them highly effective and loyal supporters, bound by gratitude
to their father and his policies and likely to support rather than challenge the succession of a legitimate heir.[73] But even so, it is difficult
to believe that such calculations dominated Henry's mind during the

[70] WM, GR, 2:488.
[71] Searle, "Women and the Succession," p. 169; MMI, p. 251 and n. 17:
as king, Henry arranged the marriages of at least eight and probably nine of
his daughters to princes or great nobles, all of whom ruled lands of strategic
importance to him.
[72] The power and status of the counts of Anjou were comparable to those of
the dukes of Normandy: see Bachrach, "The Idea of the Angevin Empire," and
Fulk Nerra, pp. 1–21 and passim. The Angevin counts, hereditary seneschals of
the kings of France, had extended their lordship over Touraine and, from AD 1110,
Maine.
[73] The eldest of Henry's bastard sons, Robert, became first earl of Gloucester; the
second son, Richard, was about to acquire the vast Norman honor of Breteuil
through marriage when he drowned in the White Ship. Two others, Reginald of
Dunstanville and Robert "fitz Edith," received lands from Henry (despite GND,
2:248–249) but on a far less lavish scale: see PR 31 Henry I, pp. 22, 51, 152; RBE,
1:43, 248; after Henry's death they followed his wishes and, like Robert of Gloucester, provided faithful support to their half-sister the empress Maud: RRAN 3, passim;
Gesta Stephani, pp. 100–102, 186; OV, 6:510; John of Hexham, p. 19; Davis, King
Stephen, pp. 51, 57; Chibnall, Empress Matilda, pp. 74, 121. It was by no means
uncommon for princes to use their bastard sons and daughters in these ways,
although on a much smaller scale: for Louis VI see OV, 6:248 and n. 1; for Robert
Curthose, ibid., 93; for others, ibid., 202–203; GND, 2:250–251. I am indebted for
many of these references to the 1994 graduate seminar paper by Laura Wertheimer
(above, this chapter, n. 68).

moments he was conceiving these offspring. If so, then Henry was an even more devious schemer than some modern historians have accused him of being.

To view the matter in its larger context, several points must be considered. First, young noblemen of this era frequently spent a great many years between puberty and marriage. Some relished the bachelor life and postponed marriage accordingly. For others, an available bride with the proper lineage and landed endowment might prove so difficult to find that the search could stretch on for many years.[74] Whether by choice or necessity or a little of both, aristocratic *juvenes* might postpone marriage until well into their thirties or beyond. Such was the case of such prominent contemporaries of Henry's as Louis VI of France, who married in his middle thirties, Robert Curthose, who was well into his forties when he married, and William Rufus, who died unmarried at about forty or forty-one.[75] Thus although nearly fifteen years elapsed between Henry's knighting in May 1086 and his marriage in November 1100 at about the age of thirty-one, his "youth" was not abnormally protracted by contemporary standards. The period of fifteen years did, however, provide ample time for Henry to sire his bastards at leisure, at a rate of well under two per year.

One must further bear in mind the blatantly promiscuous environments of the royal, ducal, and comital courts to which *juvenes* of Henry's generation flocked. Contemporary monk-historians provide scathing condemnations of the courts of William Rufus and Robert Curthose, to each of which Henry belonged at one time or another. Young men at these courts (as doubtless at others) found themselves consorting with swarms of prostitutes and camp followers.[76] Many young courtiers seized the further opportunity of seducing or ravishing wives and daughters from the villages through which the court was constantly passing. The Anglo-Saxon chronicler complains repeatedly of the depredations inflicted on villagers when the ducal or royal courts passed through; Orderic describes the itinerant court of Hugh earl of Chester as an undisciplined mob, "noisy with swarms of boys of high and low birth," and charges Hugh himself with being altogether devoted to carnal lusts and siring "a multitude of bastards by his concubines."[77] In a similar vein, Eadmer charges William Rufus' courtiers

[74] Duby, *Chivalrous Society*, pp. 118–120, describing the adventures of wandering *juvenes* as "quests for wives perhaps first and foremost."
[75] Luchaire, *Louis VI*, pp. 3, 97; David, *Curthose*, pp. 4–5, 123; Barlow, *Rufus*, pp. 1, 8; WM, *GR*, 2: 379, stating that Rufus was "major quadragenario" when he died.
[76] Freeman, *Rufus*, 1:154; 2:176–177, 491–494, 498–503; Barlow, *Rufus*, p. 109; OV, 5:26, 300–302, 308; 6:62; WM, *GP*, pp. 79, 84.
[77] *ASC*, s.a. 1097 (Rufus), 1101 (Curthose), 1104 (Henry I, before he reformed his court ca. 1108); OV, 4:114; 6:62; HH, pp. 232–233.

with pillaging the goods of defenseless village households and molesting village women.[78]

Whether Henry participated in these horrors we cannot know. But the combination of ebullient bachelor knights, crowds of harlots, and young women of the countryside—whether compliant or not—must have resulted in a plethora of aristocratic bastards. The great majority of them must have been unknown to their fathers and their aristocratic roots would have gone unrecorded amidst their peasant upbringing. Others may well have been known to their fathers but deliberately ignored. The children in both these groups are to be distinguished sharply from the more fortunate bastards, doubtless very much fewer in number, whose fathers chose to grant them formal recognition. This distinction is reflected clearly in the *Leges Henrici Primi*, in which fathers of unrecognized bastards are prohibited from collecting their wergeld.[79]

The recognition by an aristocratic father of his illegitimate progeny normally carried the moral obligation to support them and see to their rearing and well-being. The mother of a recognized bastard would usually have been a woman of at least minimal social status and was likely to have been the father's mistress for at least a moderate period of time—not a prostitute or peasant villager or companion for a night. Orderic tells of the beautiful concubine of an old priest who became the mistress of Robert Curthose during his youthful wanderings and who, unbeknownst to him, bore him two sons. How Robert could have overlooked these births is difficult to fathom (although he is known to have been a singularly inattentive person), but Orderic assures us that he did. Many years thereafter, when the sons were grown, their mother presented them to Duke Robert and requested that he accord them recognition. Robert was suspicious of her claim at first and demanded that she prove it by the ordeal of the hot iron. Once she had done so, he conferred recognition on them and took them under his protection.[80]

The same distinction between recognition and nonrecognition is evident in the household of the earl of Chester. Despite Orderic's aforementioned statement that Earl Hugh sired "a multitude of bas-

---

[78] Eadmer, *HN*, pp. 192–193.

[79] *Leges Henrici Primi*, 78.4; cf. 78.5. On the process of recognizing natural offspring in late antiquity and the early Middle Ages see Bachrach, *Anatomy of a Little War*, p. 5 and n. 26.

[80] OV, 5:282. The two young men, Robert and William, both died young, Robert from a hunting accident in the New Forest while attached to Rufus' court (presumably while Curthose was off crusading), William in the Holy Land after his father's capture in 1106.

tards by his concubines," only two of them are named and identified.[81] These fortunate two had been recognized, whereas the remainder of the multitude had apparently not been. We know that Earl Hugh's two known bastards were set up very well indeed: one became abbot of Bury St Edmunds while the other acquired a substantial estate and custody of the Tower of London.[82]

Like most of his fellow *juvenes*, Henry was serially unchaste. But we will never have any idea just how many bastards he actually begat, or how his total compared with that of others, or whether he really does hold the English royal record. Unlike his brothers, who are described as spending their youthful years consorting with prostitutes of all kinds,[83] Henry may have preferred more lasting arrangements with women of higher status, even though he entered a goodly number of such relationships. It may also be that Henry, unlike many *juvenes*, lacked the taste for bisexuality and limited himself to heterosexual relationships.[84] Whatever the elusive truth of the matter, we cannot say with confidence that Henry exceeded his brothers and royal successors in siring bastards, only in recognizing them. Perhaps there is a kernel of truth in Malmesbury's apologia after all; for only by recognizing his bastards could Henry later employ them, with such decisive effect, in the advancement of his interests (and of course theirs). What point is there in spreading the royal seed, Henry may have reflected, if it is to remain invisible?

During these unsettled years Henry's primary goal, like that of most *juvenes*, was to acquire and retain an honor befitting his status. As the son of a king, Henry's status was, next to that of his brothers, the highest in the entire Anglo-Norman nobility. He appears to have been well aware of this fact, attesting charters of both his

---

[81] OV, 5:296–298; 6:304 and n. 1.

[82] Hugh's son Robert, appointed abbot of Bury in 1100 as a very young man, was roundly hated by his monks and was deposed for incompetence at Archbishop Anselm's synod of 1102: OV, 5:296–298 and 298 n. 1; Eadmer, *HN*, p. 142; *AO*, epp. 251–252, 266, 271; *Councils and Synods*, 1: part 2, p. 669; Brett, *English Church*, p. 78. To have been appointed to a prelacy of which he was so blatantly unworthy is eloquent testimony to the advantages, sometimes unmerited, of being the recognized bastard son of an earl. Hugh of Chester died, incidentally, in 1101, after Robert's appointment but before his deposition. The other high-rising son, Othuer, died in the White Ship: see *MMI*, pp. 120–127.

[83] OV, 5:202; HH, pp. 232–233; Barlow, *Rufus*, p. 109.

[84] On bisexuality among Anglo-Norman *juvenes* see the valuable discussion in Barlow, *Rufus*, pp. 108–109; Professor Barlow is inclined to regard William Rufus as bisexual. For evidence in contemporary narrative sources see, *inter alia*, HH, p. 242; Eadmer, *HN*, pp. 48–49. See also Boswell, *Christianity, Social Tolerance, and Homosexuality*, pp. 228–232.

brothers as "Henry the king's son."[85] He also attested on occasion as "Henry the king's brother," but he was tactful enough to do so on Rufus' charters only.[86]

It must have seemed unfitting to many, surely to Henry himself, that such status was not accompanied by the lordship of a princely honor. At the time of the Conqueror's death Henry appears to have had no land at all. He had been promised his mother's holdings in England but had not yet obtained possession of them. They were, in any event, quite modest in size—far down the list of important Domesday honors and only about a tenth the value of the greatest of them.[87] And Henry is not known to have held so much as a village in Normandy. While William I was announcing on his deathbed the division of his dominions between his two eldest sons, Orderic quotes Henry as asking:

"And what, Father, do you give to me?" The king answered him, "I give you five thousand pounds of silver from my treasure." To which Henry said, "What shall I do with treasure if I have no place to make my home?"[88]

Whether Henry actually uttered such words is less important than the fact that Orderic believed them to be an appropriate reproach. The Conqueror is supposed to have answered, "Patiently allow your elder brothers to take precedence over you . . . You in your own time will have all the dominions that I have acquired and be greater than your brothers in wealth and power."[89] But not knowing what Orderic knew when

---

[85] *RRAN* 1, nos 320, 324. Similarly, Curthose could style himself "Roberti Willelmi regis Anglorum filii ducis Normanniae" or "Roberti comitis Normannorum filii Willelmi regis Anglorum": Haskins, *NI*, pp. 67 n. 19, 286; cf. *RRAN* 1, no. 299.

[86] *RRAN* 1, nos 301, 318*, 398; *RRAN* 2, p. 405, no. 414a; he also attests on two known occasions, just following his ascent to the countship of the Cotentin, as "Henrici comitis": *RRAN* 1, no. 297 (= Haskins, *NI*, pp. 288–289); Haskins, *NI*, p. 291.

[87] Queen Matilda's Domesday honor was worth roughly £300 a year, whereas Odo of Bayeux's earldom of Kent was valued at £3,050: Bates, "Character and Career of Odo," p. 10. The honors of Roger of Montgomery and Robert of Mortain were each worth about £2,100 a year; that of the tenth wealthiest Domesday tenant-in-chief, Eustace of Boulogne, had an annual value of £770—more than twice the value of Matilda's: *MMI*, p. 99. It is likely that Matilda had held lands in Normandy as well, but the bequest to Henry is reported to have been limited to her English lands: OV, 2:214.

[88] OV, 4:94; in a similar vein, Robert of Torigny chides Henry's brothers for failing to make provision for him such as would have enabled him to live respectably in keeping with his status as their brother and a king's son: *GND*, 2:204–207. The same thought occurs in WM, *GR*, 2:470.

[89] OV, 4:94–96; the entire conversation is repeated in RT, *Chron.*, *s.a.* 1106; Malmesbury records a similar prophecy by the Conqueror to Henry: "Ne fleas, fili, quoniam et tu rex eris": WM, *GR*, 2:468.

he wrote these suspiciously prophetic words, King William of course said no such thing.

Yet the reproach remains, and there is much force in it. Younger sons and bastard sons in the Norman ducal line had traditionally received counties, along with appropriate comital titles.[90] Indeed, up to the Conqueror's death, every count in Norman history—of Evreux, Eu, Mortain, Arques, Ivry, and Brionne—had been a cadet, bastard son, or half-brother of a duke or the direct descendant of such a person. Other noninheriting members of the ducal family were raised to wealthy bishoprics—Robert archbishop of Rouen, Hugh bishop of Lisieux, Hugh and Odo successive bishops of Bayeux—or to great lordships such as were conferred on the offspring of the duchess Gunnor's siblings and nieces—Montgomery, Longueville, Warenne, Breteuil, Beaumont (probably), and others.[91] William the Conqueror's two half-brothers Robert count of Mortain and Odo bishop of Bayeux, even though not in the direct ducal line, were prodigiously enriched: Robert received the wealthiest county in Normandy and one of the two or three wealthiest honors in Domesday England, whereas Odo acquired the richest bishopric in Normandy and the greatest of all Domesday honors.[92]

In providing so handsomely for their younger offspring and relatives, the Norman dukes were addressing the problem of arranging appropriate endowments for noninheriting kinsmen, a problem that became acute with the emergence of primogeniture after the turn of the millennium.[93] Other princely houses responded in similar ways: the Capetians with their appanages, the kings of England with their policy, evident from the reign of Henry I to the present day, of advancing younger sons to counties and duchies.[94] In short, Henry's aspiration for a great honor was altogether consistent with the traditions of his dynasty

[90] Douglas, "The Earliest Norman Counts"; Le Patourel, *Norman Empire*, p. 258; Yver, "Les Premières institutions du duché de Normandie," pp. 323–325. A reproach similar to Orderic's occurs in the pages of Robert of Torigny's interpolations: *GND*, 2:206–207: "fratrem suum Henricum debuissent adjuvare, eique providere, ut sicut frater eorum et filius regis honorabiliter posset vivere."

[91] Hollister, "Greater Domesday Tenants-in-Chief," pp. 230–235; van Houts, "Robert of Torigny as Genealogist," pp. 215–233; Searle, *Predatory Kinship*, pp. 100–105; Douglas, *William the Conqueror*, pp. 89–90; *GND*, 2:268–275.

[92] *MMI*, p. 99; Hollister, "Greater Domesday Tenants-in-Chief," pp. 220–226, 242–247.

[93] Bates, *Normandy before 1066*, pp. 111–116.

[94] On Capetian policy see Wood, *The French Appanages*; on Henry I's enrichment of his eldest bastard sons see above, this chapter, n. 73. King Stephen's first son became count of Mortain and Boulogne; his second became earl of Surrey; Henry II's younger sons acquired the principalities of Aquitaine and Brittany and the lordship of Ireland; thereafter the granting of countships and dukedoms to the noninheriting sons of English kings became conventional.

and his era, and his complaint to his dying father is quite understandable, whether he actually uttered it or not.

At William the Conqueror's death, William Rufus was en route to England to claim his crown while Robert Curthose was encamped near Abbeville in Ponthieu. From there Robert and his entourage of young Norman nobles had been raiding and plundering across Normandy's northeastern frontier. At the news of his father's death Robert hastened unopposed to Rouen and assumed the lordship of the duchy. Rufus in the meantime, having been consecrated and crowned by Archbishop Lanfranc, succeeded to the English throne. Robert Curthose, who had expected to acquire both Normandy and England without opposition, first responded to the news of Rufus' coronation with disbelief. Afterward, as Robert of Torigny put it, "serious disagreement arose between Robert and his brother William."[95]

Henry chose to remain in Normandy for the time being. To have crossed to England would probably have seemed an act of defiance against Curthose, who may well have been urging Henry to join his court. Henry may even have been daunted by the logistical problem of shipping five thousand pounds—1.2 million silver pennies—out of the dominions of a potentially hostile duke. Whatever his reasons, Henry did frequent the ducal court and seems to have been warmly welcomed there. In fact, the charter evidence suggests that during the initial months of Curthose's rule, Henry, not yet twenty, enjoyed the status of chief ducal counselor. In a ducal charter of fall 1087 confirming a manor to Saint-Etienne, Caen, which had been granted by the Conqueror in his last illness, Curthose consummates the transaction with his own hand "and that of my brother Henry and of my aforesaid faithful men [unnamed]."[96] Again, in July 1088 Curthose restored to Fécamp lands that his father had taken from the abbey, "with the council and assent of Henry my brother and others among my *optimates* who have signed this charter."[97] In another charter of this period Curthose seems solicitous of the welfare of Henry's immortal soul when he donates gifts to Mont-Saint-Michel "for my own salvation and

---

[95] *GND*, 2:204–205. A miracle story from Fécamp indicates that Curthose planned from the beginning to seize Rufus' throne: R. N. Sauvage, "Des Miracles advenus en l'église de Fécamp," pp. 29 ff. (no. 21). A rebellion in England in Curthose's behalf broke out in March 1088: Barlow, *Rufus*, pp. 74 ff.

[96] Haskins, *NI*, p. 285 (shortly after September 1087).

[97] *RRAN* 1, no. 297 (7 July 1088); Haskins, *NI*, pp. 287–289: ". . . consilio et nutu Heinrici fratris mei aliorumque optimatum meorum quorum subscriptione presens carta roboratur," followed by four *signa*: Henry's and Duke Robert's along with those of Gilbert bishop of Evreux and William of Arques monk of Molesme (whom Orderic describes as a principal ducal adviser: OV, 4:186, 224; David, *Curthose*, pp. 48–49; Haskins, *NI*, pp. 76–77).

that of my father and mother and of my brother Henry"—but not of William Rufus.[98]

The omission of Rufus' name should be no surprise, since Curthose continued to covet England and, during the first half of 1088, was organizing an expedition to conquer it. As in other matters, however, Curthose did not manage his undertaking well. Orderic and William of Malmesbury both comment that he was far too lavish in spending his wealth on mercenary soldiers and greedy young knights.[99] In March a major rebellion broke out in England in the duke's behalf, led by his powerful uncles Odo of Bayeux and Robert of Mortain and backed by many of the greatest magnates in the kingdom.[100] The expectation was that Robert Curthose would join them with an invasion fleet, but he evidently ran out of money before he could launch it. Knowing that Henry had a large fortune, Curthose asked him for a loan and Henry wisely refused, declining to throw his money away, as E. A. Freeman colorfully expressed it, "into the bottomless pit of Robert's extravagance." The duke then offered to sell Henry a portion of Normandy. The brothers struck a bargain in which Henry gave Robert three thousand pounds—more than half his inheritance—and acquired in return the greater part of western Normandy along with a comital title.[101]

Henry had thus realized his great hope, and he had done so at the age of nineteen, within half a year of his father's death. He had become a count—"count of the Cotentin," Orderic titled him.[102] His *signum*, "Henrici comitis," occurs on a ducal charter for Jumièges dated 30 March 1088 and on another, for Fécamp, dated 7 July.[103] His continuing predominance at the ducal court is suggested by the parallel forms of his and Curthose's *signa* on these two charters: "Signum Rotberti

---

[98] *RRAN* 1, no. 299 (1088).

[99] OV, 4:118; WM, *GR*, 2:468: a somewhat garbled account; on the origins of the conspiracy see David, *Curthose*, pp. 45–47 and n. 17.

[100] See Barlow, *Rufus*, pp. 74–82; cf. *MMI*, pp. 99–101.

[101] Chesnel, *Le Cotentin*, pp. 21–24. For the quote from Freeman see his *Rufus*, 1:196. On the details of the transaction see OV, 4:120. The chroniclers differ as to the details of this business arrangement, its place in the sequence of events, and its consequences, but Orderic's narrative is by far the most coherent and is corroborated, as will be seen, by charter evidence (*RRAN* 1, nos 297, 301). It has, understandably, been followed by almost all modern authorities: Freeman, *Rufus*, 2:510–516; Barlow, *Rufus*, pp. 69–70; David, *Curthose*, pp. 48–49; cf. *GND*, 2:202–205; WM, *GR*, 2:468–469 (where Henry's payment to Robert is recorded as 3,000 marks rather than the £3,000 reported by Orderic); Wace's account is fanciful and best ignored.

[102] OV, 4:148; Robert of Torigny describes him shortly afterward as "comes Henricus": *GND*, 2:206–207.

[103] Haskins, *NI*, pp. 69, 287–289, 290–291; *RRAN* 1, no. 297; see below, this chapter, n. 104.

comitis Normanniae + Signum Hen+rici comitis, fratris ejus . . ." on the first; "Si+gnum Rotberti comitis . . . Si+gnum Henrici comitis" on the charter of 7 July.[104]

At the time that he issued this last charter, Curthose had assembled a large army and fleet for his invasion of England. He had already managed to send off a smaller advance force with the object of reinforcing Odo of Bayeux and the other rebels, but many of Curthose's knights were killed or captured when an English coastal fleet decimated their ships.[105] And now Curthose's main invasion armada failed to set sail, whether because of bad winds, declining funds, or flagging spirits. Perhaps Curthose had already delayed so long that his supporters in England were on the verge of capitulating.[106] Whatever the case, Curthose had left them stranded. The dating clause of Duke Robert's charter includes his cryptic, regretful phrase, "on the day I ought to have left for England."[107]

The collapse of the pro-ducal uprising was costly to many of its backers. Rufus forgave some of them but others suffered forfeiture and banishment.[108] Robert Curthose had lost his chance at the throne, and Odo of Bayeux, perhaps the heaviest loser of all, was compelled to relin-

---

[104] Haskins, *NI*, p. 291: "Signum Rotberti comitis Normannie+ Signum Hen+rici comitis fratris eius Signum Vuillelmi comitis Ebroicensis+"; p. 289: "[Si+gnum Rotberti comitis Signum+ Gisleberti episcopi Ebroicensis] Si+gnum Henrici comitis +Signum [Willelmi monachi de Archis]"; the princes of Normandy were only gradually coming to use the title "dux Normannorum" in place of "comes Normannorum."

[105] *ASC, s.a.* 1088, echoed by FW, 2:22, HH, p. 215, and SD, 2:216. WM, *GR*, 2:362–363, reports that the English made a joke of the ducal fiasco. The best modern authorities are Barlow, *Rufus*, p. 81; David, *Curthose*, pp. 49–52; and, in greatest detail, Freeman, *Rufus*, 2:481–483.

[106] The rebellion was essentially brought to an end with the surrender of Rochester Castle, which cannot be dated more closely than summer 1088: Barlow, *Rufus*, p. 81: "It is likely that Rochester surrendered in July." Cf. ibid., p. 449. Robert of Torigny observes that while the rebels in England were awaiting the arrival of Curthose, he was amusing himself with sensual delights in Normandy: *GND*, 2:204–205.

[107] David, *Curthose*, p. 51 n. 52: ". . . quando in Angliam transire debui." I have followed Barlow's translation (*Rufus*, p. 81 and n. 139), which is slightly more accurate than those of Haskins (*NI*, p. 287) and H. W. C. Davis (*RRAN* 1, no. 297).

[108] OV, 4:128–134, 5:210, reporting that as a consequence of the surrender of Rochester Bishop Odo, Eustace count of Boulogne (a great Domesday landholder), Robert of Bellême (who possessed no Domesday lands but held the vast Bellême lands on the Continent and would soon inherit the Montgomery lands in Normandy as well), "et insigni phalange armatorum" were disinherited and had to leave England. See also *ASC, s.a.* 1088; HH, p. 215. Many, but not Bishop Odo, were reseised when Rufus and Curthose came to terms in February 1091: Le Patourel, *Norman Empire*, p. 198; Barlow, *Rufus*, pp. 281–282.

quish his earldom of Kent and to abandon England.[109] Henry, however, was one of the great winners in the affair. He had risen from a condition of landlessness to become a count with territories comparable to those of previous ducal kinsmen. Orderic described his newly acquired countship as encompassing a third of Normandy.[110] Although Robert of Torigny expresses a degree of uncertainty as to whether Henry received his lands as a gift or, "as some say," only as a pledge, Orderic and William of Malmesbury are doubtless correct in describing it as an outright grant.[111] Henry is unlikely to have claimed a comital title on the basis of a lordship that was merely temporary or to have been so rash as to attest ducal charters as *Comes Henricus* on such flimsy grounds. Nonetheless, the grant was undoubtedly an enfeoffment, to be held under Duke Robert's overlordship, and it was probably on the occasion of receiving it that Henry performed the act of homage, unrecorded at the time, that Robert is described as relinquishing some thirteen years later.[112]

Of what lands and rights did Henry's grant consist? What, precisely, was encompassed by the countship of the Cotentin? The answer is clouded by the fact that, except for two brief and ill-recorded intervals, there had previously been no such countship. The former Carolingian *pagus* of the Cotentin had long been administered as a *vicomté* by successive members of the deeply rooted vicecomital family of Saint-Sauveur.[113] An addendum to a charter of *Vicomte* Nigel of Saint-

[109] See, in addition to the sources cited in n. 105, *MMI*, pp. 99–101. Bishop Odo had earlier been imprisoned by the Conqueror in 1082, purportedly for undertaking to raise himself to the papacy with the support of Anglo-Norman troops, and was released only on William I's death: Bates, "Character and Career of Odo," pp. 15–16.

[110] OV, 4:120. That Henry was titled "count of the Cotentin" does not mean that his authority was limited to that *pagus*; Anglo-Norman *comites*, in Normandy and even more commonly in England, might have lordships extending over a number of counties.

[111] *GND*, 2:204–205; Robert of Torigny, overlooking Henry's payment for the county, asserts that Curthose simply gave it to him ("dedit illi comitatum") or, "ut alii dicunt, invadiavit"; cf. OV, 4:120; WM, *GR*, 2:468.

[112] David, *Curthose*, p. 134; *MMI*, p. 92; Le Patourel, *Norman Empire*, pp. 343–344; Barlow, *Rufus*, p. 70.

[113] On the evidence for earlier countships of the Cotentin see Chesnel, *Le Cotentin*, pp. 22–23: in 1126–1127, shortly before his death, Duke Richard III had granted his wife Adela, daughter of the Capetian King Robert the Pious, the countship of the Cotentin along with Coutances, Caen, Ver, Valognes, the castles of Cherbourg, Holme, Brix, and a number of other properties: *Recueil des actes des ducs de Normandie*, no. 58. On the vicomital family of Saint-Sauveur see ibid., pp. 7–14, 107–122; Delisle, *Histoire . . . de Saint-Sauveur*, pp. 1–28. For a reference to the activity of an early member of this family, bearing the family name Nigel and exercising military responsibility in the Cotentin ca. AD 1000, see *GND*, 2:10–11; cf. Delisle, *Histoire . . . de Saint-Sauveur*, p. 2, and Chesnel, *Le Cotentin*, p. 8.

Sauveur records grants to the family abbey of Saint-Sauveur by Nigel's brother and successor, "Eudo vicecomes, concessu Henrici comitis," thus verifying that Henry had interposed his comital authority in the Cotentin between the duke's authority and that of the *vicomte*.[114] Orderic observes that Henry was punctilious in discharging his co-mital responsibilities, governing the Cotentin "effectively" (*strenue*) and fortifying his castles "resolutely" (*constanter*).[115] These observations are confirmed, less flatteringly, in the cartulary of Holy Trinity, Caen, wherein *Comes Henricus* turns up seventeenth on a list of some thirty lords who had misused abbey property. The nuns complain that "Count Henry took toll from Quettehou and from all the Cotentin, and made the men of Holy Trinity in that vill and county work on the castles of his men."[116]

But Henry's power in western Normandy extended well beyond the Cotentin. Orderic declares that Duke Robert's grant included not only the *pagus* of Coutances but that of Avranches as well, along with the adjacent abbey of Mont-Saint-Michel and the entire Norman *feudum* of Hugh, earl of Chester and *vicomte* of the Avranchin.[117] It is indicative of the authority that Henry exercised throughout these two *pagi* that he took direct control not only of the vicecomital castles of Coutances, Gavray, and Cherbourg in the Cotentin but also of Avranches, "and other castles as well."[118] Evidently the vicecomital castle at Avranches passed to him with the willing assent of his powerful new *fidelis*, Viscount Hugh, who remained always on the friendliest of terms with him. To Hugh of Chester's name can be added those of Roger of Mande-ville and Richard of Redvers, both of whom held lordships in the Cotentin and are reported by Robert of Torigny to have joined Earl Hugh in helping restore Henry's power there after his expulsion in 1091.[119] Master Wace tells the not unlikely story of Curthose consent-ing, evidently in 1088, to Henry's request that Richard of Redvers be permitted to become his vassal. And Orderic includes Richard among Henry's supporters in the period prior to the 1091 expulsion, adding

---

[114] Delisle, *Histoire . . . de Saint-Sauveur*, p. 27, and *Preuves*, p. 53.

[115] OV, 4:120, 220.

[116] Haskins, *NI*, pp. 62–64; the abbess of Caen at the time was Henry's own sister, Cecilia. The abbey's little list includes such other notables as William count of Evreux, Richard of Courcy, Nigel of Oilli, Robert of Mowbray earl of Northumbria, Fulk d'Aunou, and the treasurer of Odo bishop of Bayeux (Adelulf *camerarius*). Quettehou lies south of Barfleur on the Cotentin peninsula.

[117] OV, 4:120; Malmesbury has a somewhat garbled reference to Henry's occu-pancy of Avranches: WM, *GR*, 2:469.

[118] OV, 4:220.

[119] *GND*, 2:206–207. Roger's family seat was Magneville in the Cotentin, only a brisk walk from the Redvers manor of Nehou.

that all the major barons of the Cotentin had joined Henry's cause with the exception of Robert of Mowbray.[120]

The extent of Henry's authority in western Normandy is further illuminated by a passage in the tract "De statu constantiensis ecclesie," an annal of some value in providing a localized perspective on these events. The tract reports that Robert's grant to Henry in 1088 included the entire *pagi* of Coutances and Avranches and authority over the bishoprics of both counties, adding that while Michael bishop of Avranches submitted amicably to these terms, Geoffrey bishop of Coutances, the great Domesday tenant-in-chief, did not.[121] Geoffrey strenuously resisted having his status lowered by deferring to any lesser lord than the duke of Normandy, so he and Count Henry were often at odds until the proud old bishop fell ill in August 1091 (he died early in 1093). This information nicely confirms Orderic's aforementioned statement that the only Cotentin baron to oppose Henry was Robert of Mowbray, earl of Northumberland, Bishop Geoffrey's nephew and heir.[122]

But it is unsatisfactory, for several reasons, to limit Henry's authority even to these named counties and bishoprics. First of all, Henry's overlordship over magnates such as Hugh earl of Chester and Richard of Redvers and over the abbey of Mont-Saint-Michel would have extended to their lands throughout the duchy, wherever they might be.[123] We know from the research of Dom J. Dubois that the vast lands of Mont-Saint-Michel stretched across western Normandy and from that of Lucien Musset that the *vicomtes* of the Avranchin had widespread holdings as well.[124] Earl Hugh's grandfather, Thurstan Goz, had been *vicomte* of the Hiémois in south-central Normandy between about 1017 and 1025 and had appropriated extensive lands in that *pagus*. Thurstan's

---

[120] Wace, *Roman de Rou*, 2:235–236; OV, 4:220.

[121] *GC*, 11, *Instrumenta*, cols 221–223; Le Patourel, "Geoffrey of Montbray," pp. 130–132, 147–148. Recall, however, that Henry's garrison occupied Coutances Castle: OV, 4:220. Haskins pointed out that Michael bishop of Avranches never attested a surviving charter of Robert Curthose and that Geoffrey of Coutances very seldom did: *NI*, p. 76; I find no instances of either bishop attesting for Curthose, although Geoffrey of Coutances and Curthose both attested a charter of William archbishop of Rouen, perhaps issued at the council of Rouen in June 1091: *RRAN* 2:400, no. 317b; Bishop Geoffrey's attestations for William Rufus suggest that he was often in England during the early years of Rufus' reign: *RRAN* 1, nos 306, 315, 320, 323, 345, and 346 (no. 348 is a forgery: *Facsimiles of English Royal Writs*, ed. Bishop and Chaplais, p. xxii); Le Patourel, "Geoffrey of Montbray," pp. 146–148.

[122] Ibid.; *CP*, 9:705–706; Loyd, *Anglo-Norman Families*, p. 71.

[123] See Le Patourel's valuable discussion of this point in *Norman Empire*, pp. 341–347, arguing that Henry may have been building a kind of pan-Norman coalition for future use.

[124] Dubois, "Les Dépendances de l'abbaye du Mont-Saint-Michel et la vie monastique dans les prieurés," p. 623 (map); Musset, "Les Origines et le patrimoine," pp. 357–367.

son Richard Goz became *vicomte* of Avranches about 1055/1056 and later passed his office and lands to his son Hugh, the future earl of Chester. The family not only kept its lands in the Hiémois and acquired many more in the Avranchin but also procured substantial holdings in the neighboring *pagus* of the Bessin, where its influence was furthered by the politically significant marriage of Earl Hugh's sister Margaret to Ranulf *vicomte* of the Bessin. Ranulf's son and heir, Ranulf le Meschin ("Junior")—nephew of Earl Hugh—succeeded to his father's vice-comital office during the years when Henry was count of the Cotentin.[125] The lands of Henry's *fidelis* Richard of Redvers, although much less extensive, were even more widely scattered: he held the fief of Nehou in the Cotentin, but he also possessed a holding at the other end of Normandy, at Vernon in the Norman Vexin, while the vill from which his family drew its name was at Reviers in the Bessin between Bayeux and Caen.[126] Henry would presumably have had the overlord-ship of all the Redvers lands.

One must always try, of course, to distinguish between comital authority and seigneurial authority, but the two could sometimes blur and overlap to a greater degree than legal and administrative histori-ans might wish. Henry enjoyed overlordship—seigneurial authority—over a number of holdings in the Bessin, including those of the Redvers and the vicecomital family of Avranches among others. Robert of Torigny states that in 1096, when Curthose went on crusade and William Rufus acquired Normandy in pawn, Henry received from Rufus *ex integro* "the county of Coutances and Bayeux, with the excep-tion of the city of Bayeux and the town of Caen."[127] It is reasonable to suppose that Robert of Torigny understood Rufus' grant to Henry as a renewal—a restoration of lands that had been granted to Henry as early as 1088. That Henry exercised some sort of authority over the Bessin from the first is suggested by the fact that Curthose is not known to have so much as set foot in that *vicomté* or ventured into western Nor-mandy at all, except on two extraordinary occasions. The first was in 1091, in the company of William Rufus, when the two princes, briefly in alliance, marched against Henry at Mont-Saint-Michel, drove him temporarily out of Normandy, and then conducted a joint inquest at Caen on the subject of ducal rights. The second occasion was in May

---

[125] Musset, "Les Origines et le patrimoine"; *GND*, 2:176–177; Hollister, "Greater Domesday Tenants-in-Chief," pp. 236–237; *CP*, 3:166, 4:310; Loyd, *Anglo-Norman Families*, p. 85; *Magni rotuli*, ed. Stapleton, 2:cclxxi.

[126] *CP*, 4 309–311; Loyd, *Anglo-Norman Families*, p. 85. At Vernon on 24 April 1089, Richard of Redvers provided his only known attestation of a charter of Duke Robert's: *RRAN* 1, no. 308, in favor of Bayeux Cathedral. See below, p. 57.

[127] *GND*, 2:210–213.

1096 when the duke visited Bayeux in the company of the papal legate Jarento abbot of Saint-Bénigne, Dijon, who had come to make the arrangements for Curthose to pawn Normandy to Rufus and join the crusade, thus ending all hostilities between the three brothers. Despite Caen's being a great center of ducal administration under William the Conqueror and again under Henry I, Curthose cannot be shown ever to have entered the city during the eight years between the time he sold western Normandy to Henry and his departure for the Holy Land, except on the abovementioned occasion.[128]

This oddity can perhaps be explained in part by the extremely disheveled state of the ducal government under Curthose, whose incessant need of funds may have resulted less from his personal extravagances (on which the chroniclers dwell) than on a general breakdown of ducal control over the *vicomtes* and, through them, the financial system of the duchy.[129] The virtual independence of the Bessin from ducal authority is further suggested by the persistent failure of the *vicomte,* Ranulf, and his son and successor, Ranulf le Meschin, to attend the ducal court over the nine years between the duke's accession and his departure on crusade: their names occur, together, on but a single ducal charter of spring 1089.[130] And on that one occasion they may well have been visiting the ducal court, as will be seen, on a mission relating to Henry.

---

[128] The events of Robert Curthose's career are well recounted in David, *Curthose, passim.* Barlow (*Rufus,* p. 281 and n. 77) has argued persuasively that the treaty of February 1091 between Rufus and Curthose was executed at Rouen, not Caen (as Robert of Torigny alleges, *GND,* 2:206–207). The two princes were in Caen on 18 July 1091 when the *Consuetudines et iusticie,* summarizing the results of an inquest into ducal rights, was issued under their joint authority after Henry had been expelled temporarily from Normandy: Haskins, *NI,* pp. 277–284. Curthose's charters, calendared in Haskins, *NI,* pp. 66–70, often lack places and dates; this is true of all seven of Curthose's charters favoring Saint-Etienne, Caen, three of which were probably issued at Caen during the 1091 venture (one of them, no. 15, was issued jointly with William Rufus, and nos 14 and 16 are probably concurrent with it). Of the four in favor of Bayeux, two were issued from eastern Normandy in 1089 and two from Bayeux, both on 24 May 1096; the first of the May 1096 pair is a charter of Bishop Odo, attested by Duke Robert, granting the important local church of Saint-Vigor to Saint-Bénigne, Dijon; the second is Robert's confirmation of the same gift in a concurrent charter written by Abbot Jarento's companion, the author Hugh of Flavigny, monk of Dijon (Haskins, *NI,* p. 67, no. 4 = *RRAN* 1, no. 376).

[129] See in general David, *Curthose, passim;* Haskins, *NI,* pp. 62–84.

[130] *RRAN* 1, no. 308; Bayeux, *Livre noir,* no. 4: Viscount Ranulf le Meschin's name is also absent from ducal charters between Duke Robert's return from crusade in autumn 1100 and his defeat and capture in autumn 1106; indeed, Ranulf was one of Henry's commanders at Tinchebray.

Lacking authority over the bishop and episcopal city of Bayeux and the ducal center at Caen, Henry's power in the Bessin cannot be regarded as fully comital. Bishop Odo would surely have raised decisive objections to Henry's administrative presence in the cathedral city, and Caen was too closely associated with the great ducal monastic foundations and castle of the Conqueror's regime to be lightly granted away. Nevertheless, the autonomy of Bayeux and Caen does not seem to have extended into their immediate surroundings. A charter of Robert Curthose suggests very strongly that at an early date Henry's jurisdiction ran up to the very walls of Caen, on the eastern reaches of the Bessin. The charter conveys to the Conqueror's daughter Abbess Cecilia and the nuns of Holy Trinity, Caen, certain lands just outside the town and a market at the nearby port of Ouistreham.[131] Duke Robert deemed it necessary to transfer these privileges "with the consent of his brother Henry." More than that, Henry participated in the issuing of the charter not merely as one of its signatories but also, more significantly, by supplying his own witnesses alongside Robert's: "On the part of Henry, the king's son: Ranulf fitz Ulger; Odo the Chamberlain."[132] Haskins dates the charter 1087–1091 on the grounds that Henry attested no ducal charters after his expulsion from Mont-Saint-Michel early in the latter year; since Henry is not known to have exercised any authority in the west before 1088 or to have attested ducal charters after July of that year, the charter probably dates from early to mid-1088. Even if slightly later, it surely looks back to the conditions of Curthose's original grant. Historians have impugned Orderic's statement that Henry acquired a third of Normandy in 1088, pointing out that the Cotentin and Avranchin by no means constitute so large a portion of the duchy. But when one adds the Bessin, the fraction does reach approximately one-third, suggesting not only that Henry struck a most advantageous bargain for his three thousand pounds but also that one should think twice before questioning Orderic's grasp of Norman geography.

Robert Curthose, having spent the money that Henry gave him, twice endeavored to renege on his transaction and to reappropriate western Normandy by main force. But however arrantly the duke might disregard his original commitment, Henry's power in the west quickly acquired a stability that proved largely immune to the ducal whim. Only a few months elapsed between Henry's assumption of the position of count and his departure for England—marking the beginning of a time

---

[131] *RRAN* 1, no. 324; Haskins, *NI*, p. 69, no. 19; *CDF*, no. 423.
[132] A Ralph fitz Olger attests a charter of Henry I of 1108–1118 but cannot otherwise be identified; Odo the Chamberlain is altogether unknown.

of violent ups and downs for the nineteen-year-old prince. But during these initial months Henry was establishing a web of loyalties with the families of western Normandy that proved remarkably resilient, a friendship network that endured for the remaining forty-seven years of his life.

Orderic states that while ducal misgovernment was permitting anarchy to spread through much of Normandy, Henry "shrewdly won over many of his father's nobles to the support of his cause."[133] As matters turned out, support for Henry at this early stage in his career could pay large dividends indeed—a point that has been discussed by several major scholars. It was John Horace Round who first observed that a number of families from lands under Henry's influence in western Normandy and eastern Brittany would later flourish exceedingly under Henry's regime in England, and the point has been expanded by John Le Patourel, G. W. S. Barrow, K. S. B. Keats-Rohan, and others.[134]

Of those of his early supporters named explicitly in the narrative sources, King Henry granted Roger of Mandeville (from Magneville in the Cotentin) the barony of Erlestoke, Wiltshire, while Roger's brother Geoffrey, who attested a number of King Henry's charters and served him as sheriff of Devon, acquired the barony of Marshwood, Dorset, within a few years of Henry's coronation.[135] Richard of Redvers, who became one of the principal royal counselors on Henry's coronation, was far more lavishly enriched—so much so that the immense stretches of *terra regis* that Henry granted him in Devon, Hampshire, and the Isle of Wight became, in the time of his son Baldwin, the basis of the earldom of Devon.[136] And although Hugh earl of Chester died soon after Henry's accession, his young son and heir Earl Richard basked in the royal favor and was granted a bride of the very highest distinction: Henry's own niece Matilda of Blois, sister of Count Theobald and granddaughter of William the Conqueror.[137]

---

[133] OV, 4:220.

[134] Round, *Studies in Peerage and Family History*, pp. 115–125; Le Patourel, *Norman Empire*, pp. 341–348; Barrow, *The Kingdom of the Scots*, pp. 320–327; Keats-Rohan, "The Bretons and Normans of England," and "North French Prosopography," pp. 34–35; Green, *Government*, pp. 146–149.

[135] Sanders, *Baronies*, pp. 42, 64; *RRAN* 2, *passim*; Green, "Sheriffs," p. 35; *Book of Fees*, pp. 85, 96, 99. Geoffrey de Mandeville of Marshwood, Devon, is not to be confused with the great Domesday tenant-in-chief of the same name (but an altogether different family) whose grandson and namesake became the first earl of Essex.

[136] *Charters of the Redvers Family and the Earldom of Devon, 1090–1217*, pp. 1–5 and nos 1–5; OV, 5:298, 314; WM, *GR*, 2:471; Green, *Government*, p. 61; Loyd, *Anglo-Norman Families*, p. 85; *CP*, 4:310; Sanders, *Baronies*, p. 137.

[137] *CP*, 3:164–170; OV, 6:304; WM, *GR*, 2:474. Richard and Matilda both drowned in the wreck of the White Ship in 1120.

Other landholders from western Normandy and the Breton border-lands, who may well have been among the unnamed lords whom Orderic describes as having joined Henry's cause, prospered similarly in England after his accession. Round, Le Patourel, Barrow, and Keats-Rohan have called attention to a number of them: the Bretons Wigan the Marshal and Alan fitz Flaald, founder of the house of Stewart, both came from the region of Dol-de-Bretagne near Mont-Saint-Michel; the family of de la Haye from Haye-du-Puits in the Cotentin acquired from Henry I the honor of Halnaker (Sussex) and substantial lands in Lincolnshire and played an important role in Henry's government; William and Nigel of Aubigny (or Albini) from Saint-Martin d'Aubigny near Coutances became major figures in Henry's royal administration and very wealthy landholders; the brothers John and Thomas of Saint-Jean-le-Thomas (near Avranches) acquired estates in Oxfordshire and Sussex and served King Henry in both his military *familia* and his administration; the great administrative family of de Vere, future earls of Oxford, probably originated at Ver south of Coutances; and a group of three Cotentin families—Brus, Moreville, and de Sules—prospered in England under Henry I and then made their fortunes in Scotland under his brother-in-law, King David.[138] To them must by all means be added Roger priest of Avranches, the head of Henry's house-hold in the years before his accession, who became bishop of Salisbury, chief of the English administration, and one of the very wealthiest men in the realm.[139]

The likelihood that Curthose had granted Henry authority over the Bessin (apart from its two urban centers) suggests the addition of other names to what Le Patourel has called "Henry's gang." One such person is Robert fitz Hamon, a *familiaris* of William Rufus to whom that king had granted the English lands of the late Queen Matilda which she had intended for Henry. It has been something of a puzzle to historians that this diversion of Henry's maternal inheritance did not estrange him from Robert fitz Hamon,[140] yet the two men give every appearance of being close friends, and fitz Hamon was one

---

[138] Round, *Studies in Peerage and Family History*, pp. 124–125 (fitz Flaald); Keats-Rohan, "North French Prosopography," pp. 26–29, 34–35 (Wigan the Marshal); Le Patourel, *Feudal Empires*, pp. vii, 34–35, and Green, *Government*, p. 258 (de la Haye); ibid., p. 276 (Vere); Le Patourel, *Norman Empire*, p. 341 nn. 6 (Aubigny) and 7 (Saint-Jean-le-Thomas); Prestwich, "The Military Household of the Norman Kings," pp. 24–26 (Aubigny); Barrow, *Kingdom of the Scots*, pp. 320–327, and *Anglo-Norman Era of Scottish History*, pp. 70–77 (Brus, Moreville, and de Sules).

[139] Kealey, *Roger of Salisbury*, pp. 4–5, 96–98; WM, *HN*, p. 37.

[140] E.g., Le Patourel, *Norman Empire*, p. 345 n. 2, on Rufus' diversion of Queen Matilda's lands: "It is remarkable that this did not estrange Henry from Robert fitz Hamon."

of Henry's most steadfast supporters from the onset of his reign.[141] The problem can be largely resolved if we recall that Robert fitz Hamon's two major holdings in Normandy were in the Bessin, at Torigny and Creully—the former on the western bank of the Vire dividing the Bessin from the Cotentin, the latter some distance to the northeast, between Bayeux and Caen.[142] It is probable, therefore, that Robert fitz Hamon was not only a *familiaris* of King William's but a *fidelis* of Count Henry's as well. During the final seven or eight years of Rufus' reign, when he and Henry were on excellent terms, fitz Hamon could comfortably serve both masters.

So too could Roger Bigod, a steward and *familiaris* of William Rufus whose Norman roots were in the Bocage, the wooded country of the southern Bessin. At Henry's accession Roger became a principal royal adviser, and some time before his death in 1107 he appears to have acquired the manor of Framlingham from Henry.[143] Although Roger Bigod had been only a middling, "class B" Domesday landholder, the family prospered thereafter to such a degree that Hugh Bigod, Roger's son, became earl of Norfolk under King Stephen and accounted to Henry II for an honor of some 150 knights fees.[144] Still another of Rufus' stewards and *familiares*, Eudo *Dapifer*, also came from the Bessin—where he continued to hold lands centering on the family seat at Ryes just northeast of Bayeux, near Robert fitz Hamon's holding at Creully.[145] Like Robert fitz Hamon and Roger Bigod, Eudo was loyal to Henry from the time of his accession, and he was later enriched, by royal mandate, with the city of Colchester, the manor of Witham, and

---

[141] OV, 4:220; on fitz Hamon's friendship with Rufus see WM, *GR*, 2:377; with Henry I, ibid., 471; *MMI*, pp. 81, 110, 113–114. Robert fitz Hamon was the son of the royal steward Hamo *Dapifer*, and the brother of Hamo's heir and namesake, who was another firm supporter of both William II and Henry I: *MMI*, pp. 81, 110; *CP*, 5:683; *Domesday Monachorum*, ed. Douglas, pp. 55–56.

[142] *CP*, 5:683; *GND*, 2:248–249; Robert fitz Hamon would have been touched to know that one of the newer residential streets in modern Creully has been named "rue de Robert fitz Haimon." (Another bears the name of his grandfather, Haimo aux Dents.)

[143] OV, 5:298, reports that Henry's principal counselors at the beginning of his reign were Roger Bigod, Richard of Redvers, Hugh earl of Chester, and the senior member of the Beaumont family, Robert count of Meulan; WM, *GR*, 2:471, provides names of Henry's adherents in 1100–1101: Roger Bigod, Richard of Redvers, Robert fitz Hamon, and the Beaumont brothers Robert of Meulan and Henry earl of Warwick; Florence of Worcester (2:57), when noticing the deaths of Robert fitz Hamon, Roger Bigod, and Richard of Redvers in 1107, identifies them all as royal counselors. On Roger Bigod's Norman origins see Loyd, *Anglo-Norman Families*, pp. 14–15; on his acquisition of Framlingham, Sanders, *Baronies*, pp. 46–47.

[144] *CP*, 9:568–596; *RBE*, 1:395–397; Sanders, *Baronies*, p. 47 n. 1; *MMI*, p. 185.

[145] Sanders, *Baronies*, p. 92; *MMI*, pp. 81, 200; Loyd, *Anglo-Norman Families*, p. 40.

three valuable manors held previously by his kinsmen, the Mandevilles of Essex (worth altogether about £165 a year in 1086).[146]

Perhaps the most powerful family in the Bessin (excluding Bishop Odo's) was that of its *vicomtes*, Ranulf "de Briquessart," who was connected by marriage to the ducal house, and his son and successor, Ranulf le Meschin. Despite their vicecomital responsibilities, the two Ranulfs had virtually no known contact with Robert Curthose and, unlike the three men just discussed, none with William Rufus. This is perhaps noteworthy because Ranulf le Meschin, having succeeded his father as *vicomte* of the Bessin sometime after spring 1089, had become a great landholder in Lincolnshire through his marriage to the twice-widowed heiress Lucy of Bolingbroke. Ranulf's connections during these years seem to have been with Henry rather than with either of his brothers. After Henry's accession, Ranulf's name turns up repeatedly in the address clauses of royal charters as justiciar in Lincoln, and he received further, extensive lands in Cumberland. He became one of Henry's principal military commanders, leading the first wing of the royal army at Tinchebray, serving Henry devotedly during the great Norman rebellion of 1118–1119, and successfully overseeing the defense of Normandy during the uprising of 1123–1124. By that time Henry had permitted him to succeed, by an agile sideways step, to the earldom of Chester.[147] He was

---

[146] *MMI*, pp. 105 n. 29, 117–127. Other families from western Normandy who were active in Henry I's reign but were well established in England beforehand include the Ports (from Port-en-Bessin north of Bayeux) and the Valognes (from the Cotentin southeast of Cherbourg). I have passed over several important figures from western Normandy or Brittany who rose to prominence only later in Henry's reign and are unlikely to have supported him before his accession: e.g., Geoffrey of Clinton (from Semilly, near Saint-Lô), the brothers Payn and Eustace fitz John (with family lands at Caen and in the Avranchin), and the Bretons Brian fitz Count and William of Albany *Brito*.

[147] On Ranulf le Meschin's succession to the *vicomté* of the Bessin see Douglas, *William the Conqueror*, p. 93; *RRAN* 1, no. 308, Bayeux, *Livre noir*, no. 4; on his enrichment and that of his family see Le Patourel, *Norman Empire*, pp. 192–193, 345–346; Le Patourel, *Feudal Empires*, pp. iv, 444–445; *CP*, 3:166; *EYC*, 7:4–6 (William le Meschin); Holt, "Politics and Property," pp. 51–52; before his advancement to the earldom of Chester in 1120/1121, Ranulf attests for Henry I: *RRAN* 2, nos 533 [1100–1101], 829, 941, 981, 1043, 1077, 1098, 1102, and 1128; he appears as a member of special judicial commissions in nos 796 [1106] and 1116 [1105–1115], and he is addressed, apparently in his capacity as justiciar of Lincolnshire, in nos 531 [1101], 534–535, 727, 746, 781, 818, 821, 968, 1043, and 1118; no. 1130, dated 1116? [1114–1121], is the earliest royal charter to bear on Ranulf's holdings in Cumberland; we do not know when he received these lands, but his lack of any known contact with Rufus (who took control of Cumbria in 1092) makes it likely that his benefactor was Henry I: see Le Patourel, *Norman Empire*, p. 69.

thus at least as highly favored as any of the better known Norman friends of Henry's youth.

Such were some of the men and families of western Normandy, later enriched by Henry I, who may well have been his *fideles* during his tenure as count. The evidence is largely circumstantial, yet since Orderic tells us, without providing names, that Henry won over many of his father's nobles, there seems no good reason to doubt that most of the above-mentioned people, perhaps all of them, were participants in the web of loyalties that Henry wove so dexterously while count of the Cotentin.

Shortly after attesting Robert Curthose's charter of 7 July 1088, Henry crossed the Channel to England with the hope of taking possession of his maternal inheritance. He had wisely delayed his departure, Orderic explains, until news had reached Normandy of the surrender of the rebels in Rochester Castle.[148] Only then could he safely enter England without becoming involved in the armed struggle between the king and the duke's baronial supporters. Henry left behind him his network of friends and, one can safely assume, most of his remaining treasure of several hundred thousand silver pennies under the guard of some trusted supporter—someone such as Hugh of Chester, Richard of Redvers, *Vicomte* Ranulf, Michael bishop of Avranches, or perhaps the monks of Caen or Mont-Saint-Michel. Orderic reports that Rufus received Henry cordially, and his name appears as a signatory on Rufus' charter granting the manors of Hadnam (Bucks.) and Lambeth (Surrey) to the bishop and monks of Rochester, "to repair the damage which the king did to the [cathedral] church of St Andrew when he obtained a victory over his enemies who had unjustly gathered against him in the city of Rochester."[149] But although Orderic puts a good face

---

[148] OV, 4:148; on Henry's decision to remain in Normandy during the period of uncertainty following his father's death see also *GND*, 2:202–205; *Brevis relatio*, p. 11.

[149] *RRAN* 1, no. 301: "Henry the king's brother" is one of fourteen signatories including Archbishop Lanfranc; we lack a firm date for the surrender of Rochester, and the charter is undated, but its subject and Lanfranc's attestation limit it to summer 1088–28 May 1089; Henry's *signum* further narrows it to summer (post 7 July) or autumn 1088; Henry attested another royal charter during the same visit: ibid., no. 320, which the editor wrongly dates ca. 1091; having left England in autumn 1088, Henry almost certainly did not return until 31 October 1094; Roger of Montgomery, who also attests the charter, died on 27 July 1094.

on the visit, Henry almost certainly did not get his mother's lands. In all likelihood, Rufus had already granted them to Robert fitz Hamon during the rebellion, perhaps to hold the Clares in check at Tonbridge, as Barlow suggests, or more generally to stiffen resistance at the heart of the rebellion around Rochester, where Robert fitz Hamon's father, as sheriff of Kent, may well have been responsible for leading some of the English that Rufus had summoned to his cause.[150] Rufus might of course have compensated Henry with lands elsewhere in England. Perhaps, as Barlow implies, he decided against such a course out of fear that Henry might be a danger to him—although nothing in Henry's behavior during these years suggests that he had any designs on the English crown.[151] More likely, Rufus was deterred by his accustomed reluctance to grant substantial amounts of land to anyone except during military crises.[152] Whatever the case, Henry crossed back to Normandy in the autumn with his mission apparently unaccomplished.

Henry sailed in the company of Robert of Bellême, one of the rebels of Rochester who had surrendered to Rufus along with the others and afterward had been forgiven.[153] Henry and Robert were an odd couple: they were both bachelors—although Robert was the older by some years—and whatever the camaraderie they may (or may not) have

---

[150] Barlow, *Rufus*, pp. 73, 93; *ASC, s.a.* 1088; FW, 2:22–23; Orderic (4:148) states, literally, that when Henry asked for his mother's lands Rufus "fraternally granted his petition." The chronicler later states, in connection with events of early 1091, that Rufus had disseised Henry of his mother's lands and given them to Robert fitz Hamon ("... pro terra matris suae qua rex eundem in Anglia dissaisiuerat, et Roberto Haimonis filio dederat"): 4:220. The two passages together could be taken to mean that Rufus granted Henry the lands on his visit in 1088 and afterward, at some point before early 1091, seized them back and gave them to fitz Hamon—conceivably while Henry was in prison and therefore helpless, or when in late 1090 Henry helped suppress a rebellion in Rufus' behalf in Rouen. But if so, the king's motives in passing the lands on to Robert fitz Hamon in time of peace are not easy to fathom. Conversely, Orderic's statements could mean simply that Rufus lulled Henry with cheerful but empty promises (although for Henry to be lulled in this way seems out of character). Whatever the case, as Orderic's editor Marjorie Chibnall points out, "There is no record that Henry ever received any of his mother's land" (OV, 4:148 n. 2).

[151] Although one cannot prove a negative, it is worth recalling that of the two rebellions in Rufus' reign, neither aimed at placing Henry on the throne or had his support. The first, led by Bishop Odo, supported Curthose's claim; the second, in favor of Stephen of Aumale, had as its most conspicuous participant Robert of Mowbray, Henry's adversary in the Cotentin. The idea that Henry was involved in an assassination plot that resulted in Rufus' death has been thoroughly discredited: *MMI*, pp. 59–75; Barlow, *Rufus*, pp. 425–426; below, pp. 102–104.

[152] *MMI*, pp. 105–111.

[153] OV, 4:148.

THE BELLÊME FAMILY

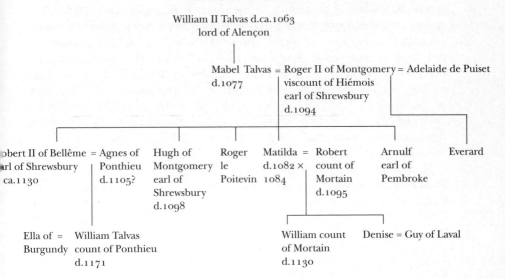

William II Talvas d.ca.1063
lord of Alençon

Mabel Talvas = Roger II of Montgomery = Adelaide de Puiset
d.1077 | viscount of Hiémois
earl of Shrewsbury
d.1094

obert II of Bellême = Agnes of   Hugh of   Roger   Matilda = Robert   Arnulf   Everard
rl of Shrewsbury | Ponthieu   Montgomery le   d.1082 × count of   earl of
ca.1130   d.1105?   earl of   Poitevin 1084 | Mortain   Pembroke
Shrewsbury   d.1095
d.1098

Ella of = William Talvas   William count   Denise = Guy of Laval
Burgundy count of Ponthieu   of Mortain
d.1171   d.1130

enjoyed aboard ship, they were destined to become mortal enemies. Robert of Bellême was the eldest son of the immensely wealthy cross-Channel magnate Roger II of Montgomery and his wife, the great heiress Mabel of Bellême, whose family's lands stretched across the southern frontier of Normandy toward Maine. Mabel's marriage to Roger had, in short, united two great aristocratic dynasties and two family fortunes, and Robert of Bellême stood to be the chief beneficiary of the union. The Bellême lands had already passed to Robert on his mother's death in the late 1070s, although the Conqueror, exercising an established ducal right, had taken the precaution of placing his own garrisons in the Bellême castles. At the news of William I's death Robert of Bellême had immediately driven the ducal garrisons out and replaced them with his own, thereby ascending to a dominating position along the southern frontier of Normandy. His father Roger, who still lived, was a kinsman and companion of the Conqueror and one of the greatest landholders in post-Conquest England—lord of the rape of Arundel in Sussex and earl of Shropshire. Roger's English lands were reserved for his second son, Hugh of Montgomery, but Robert of Bellême stood to inherit the extensive Montgomery estates in the Hiémois and Séois in southern Normandy, adjacent to the Bellême lands that he already possessed. On his father's death, therefore, Robert was destined to become a truly formidable power in the south.[154]

---

[154] The best study of the Bellême family and its holdings is Gérard Louise, *Seigneurie de Bellême*. See also Boussard, "Seigneurie de Bellême," 1:43–54; Dupont,

Roger of Montgomery seems to have been well regarded by his fellow Normans, but Mabel of Bellême had a generally bad reputation and their son Robert developed an even worse one. Although evidently a person of keen intellect—a gifted military commander and a superlative castle architect—he was noteworthy among his contemporaries for his extraordinary cruelty, which he is said to have expressed in part by torturing his prisoners.[155] Having title to no land in England, Robert had lost nothing by the rebellion's collapse. Henry, however, had gained nothing and was doubtless disappointed as he returned from his amicable but fruitless visit to the royal court.

Henry's mood cannot have been nearly as dark as that of his uncle Odo of Bayeux, now disseised of his earldom of Kent and exiled from England. Having crossed to Normandy ahead of Henry, Odo now

"Nouvelles recherches sur la famille de Bellême (I)"; Musset, "Administration et justice"; Thompson, "Family and Influence." That Robert possessed his mother's lands in 1088 but not yet his father's lands is clear from OV, 4:132 and n. 4, 158, 302. On the Montgomerys: Mason, "Montgomery and His Sons"; Bates, Normandy before 1066, pp. 79–81, 112–113; Hollister, "Greater Domesday Tenants-in-Chief," pp. 231–233. On Robert's recovery of the Bellême castles in 1087 see OV, 4:112–114.

[155] OV, 6:30, and HH, p. 310; both attest to Robert's fondness for torturing his prisoners to death. OV, 3:134–136, discusses his mother's penchant for poisoning her enemies; on Mabel of Bellême see further Chibnall, "Women in Orderic Vitalis," pp. 107–108. Efforts to rehabilitate Robert of Bellême's character by blaming his bad image on Orderic's bias do not successfully account for the largely independent corroborative testimony of William of Malmesbury, Robert of Torigny, and Henry of Huntingdon: OV, 4:xxxiv; 5:214, 216, 226, 238; 6:46, 144; WM, GR, 2:475–476; GND, 2:206–207; HH, pp. 234, 310: in this last passage, which has been cited (without being quoted) as less critical of him than Orderic's biased accounts, Henry of Huntingdon describes Robert of Bellême as "a very Pluto, Megaera, Cerberus, or anything you can conceive still more horrible"; the chronicler adds: "Nec curabat captos redimere, sed interimere . . . homines utriusque sexus ab ano usque in ora palis transforabat. Erat ei caedes horribilis hominum cibus jucundus animae," etc. The somber portrait depicted by these writers is reflected in Louise, Seigneurie de Bellême, 2:168–174. The most ardent effort to redeem Robert was undertaken by Le Vicomte du Motey, Robert II de Bellême et son temps; more measured is Thompson, "Robert of Bellême Reconsidered," and "Orderic Vitalis and Robert of Bellême" (which, however, while arguing that Orderic was biased, ignores Robert's other contemporary critics). Robert's abiding interest in human pain and torture (a not uncommon pathology, as studies in abnormal psychology make clear) is widely reported to have been shared by certain other lords of his era, e.g., Thomas of Marle and Arnau of Perella: see Thomas N. Bisson's cogent discussion in "The 'Feudal Revolution,'" p. 31. Robert of Bellême can also usefully be viewed as a great frontier lord caught unwillingly in the tightening coils of the Anglo-Norman administration (he once attempted to transfer the overlordship of Bellême to the king of France: Recueil des actes de Philippe Ier, ed. Prou, no. 129). Other such frontier lords, evidently unafflicted by sadism—Henry's friend Robert count of Meulan and his enemy Amaury de Montfort—had much better contemporary reputations and happier careers.

prowled the duchy "like a fire-breathing dragon."[156] There is nothing to suggest that Odo had previously disliked Henry or had given him much thought at all until now. But it cannot have pleased the "vanquished" and "very angry" bishop[157] that a youth of scarcely twenty years had come to be accepted as the duke's principal adviser and, far worse, had established his authority across the Bessin up to the ramparts of Odo's own episcopal city. Not only would Henry have seemed to have a stranglehold on Bayeux; he would have been overlord of almost the entirety of Odo's vast episcopal lands stretching across western Normandy.[158]

Next to Henry on Odo's little list was his shipmate, Robert of Bellême. For Odo, having burned his bridges in England, could well have predicted that Rufus would soon be seeking revenge for Curthose's abortive attempt on the crown. It was clearly in Odo's interest, therefore, that Curthose be sufficiently strong to safeguard Normandy from any military threat by Rufus. And the bolstering of ducal power in Normandy, so Odo evidently reasoned, depended on purging the duchy of the dangerous and violent Robert of Bellême, heir to the continental dominions of two great families, whose first act on hearing of the Conqueror's death had been to purge of ducal garrisons the Bellême castles along the frontier and whose potential for further mischief made him a menace to the stability of the duchy.[159]

That Henry and Robert of Bellême were about to land in Normandy in a single ship, unprepared for trouble, was an opportunity not to be missed. The bishop seems to have had little difficulty convincing Robert Curthose, "who stood in great fear of Odo,"[160] that Henry and Robert of Bellême had formed a conspiracy with Rufus against the duke. According to Orderic, when this unlikely rumor was conveyed to Curthose by "hostile mischief-makers" (who must have crossed the Channel about the same time that Odo did), the duke took counsel with the bishop of Bayeux and then had Henry and Robert seized and taken captive as they were disembarking. Having been consigned to the bishop's custody, Robert of Bellême was incarcerated in an episcopal prison at Neuilly-l'Evêque (now Neuilly-la-Forêt), about thirty kilometers due west of Bayeux near the River Vire, whereas Henry was imprisoned in Bayeux itself.[161] Curthose took advantage of

---

[156] OV, 4:148.
[157] Ibid.
[158] Hollister, "Greater Domesday Tenants-in-Chief," pp. 225–256.
[159] OV, 4:150–152.
[160] Ibid., p. 148.
[161] OV (ibid.) is clearly more reliable than Malmesbury's garbled account reporting that Henry was imprisoned at Rouen: WM, *GR*, 2:468; but Malmesbury's statement that Henry remained in captivity for half a year (ibid.) is not inconsistent with Orderic's brief report of Henry's release: cf. David, *Curthose*, pp. 52–53; Barlow, *Rufus*, p. 268 n. 22.

Henry's predicament by extorting from him his county of western Normandy.[162]

Curthose had by now fallen strongly under Bishop Odo's influence. And Odo was bent on reinforcing ducal power by rousing the lethargic Curthose to action. He urged the duke to reestablish his control of the neighboring province of Maine, long disputed between Normandy and Anjou, and then to break the power of the Montgomery-Bellême family by seizing their castles.[163] Odo even undertook to serve as one of the commanders of the ducal army—as he had once done at Hastings. Curthose consented to some of Odo's proposals but not to all: the duke succeeded in restoring his authority in Le Mans and recovering the allegiance, at least temporarily, of most of the nobility of Maine. He then took the Bellême castle of Saint-Céneri near Alençon—punctuating his victory by blinding its castellan and mutilating its garrison. (So much for the historical myth of Robert Curthose's kindliness.) But afterward, Curthose apparently grew tired of such activities; he halted the campaign, came to terms with Roger of Montgomery, and ordered the release of his son from Bishop Odo's prison. This may have been a mistake, for Robert of Bellême, once freed, "took vengeance daily in every way he could."

Henry remained for a time incarcerated at Bayeux. But eventually, Orderic reports, Robert Curthose yielded to the supplications of his great men (*optimates*) and had Henry set free.[164] The exact date of his release is nowhere mentioned, but Orderic's statement that he had crossed from England in autumn 1088 and was immediately taken captive, combined with Malmesbury's assertion that he was held in captivity for half a year, suggests that he was released sometime in spring 1089.[165] A ducal charter of 24 April 1089 in favor of the see of Bayeux could well be a diplomatic footprint of the event.[166] Duke Robert issued the charter at Vernon on the Seine, near the eastern frontier of Normandy, as he was about to set off for France *in expeditionem*.[167] Of the twelve signatories besides the duke himself, six are frequent or occasional ducal companions: William Bonne-Ame archbishop of Rouen,

[162] *GND*, 2:204–205.

[163] For this and what follows: OV, 4:150–158; on Bishop Odo's influence on Robert Curthose see, very briefly, Bates, "Character and Career of Odo," pp. 18–19.

[164] OV, 4:164: Orderic dates the event simply as "tunc."

[165] See David, *Curthose*, p. 53 n. 57; on the basis of this same evidence, David guesses late winter or spring 1089.

[166] *RRAN* 1, no. 308; Bayeux, *Livre noir*, 1, no. 4.

[167] The exact circumstances of this expedition are unrecorded; Curthose, as we have seen, had recently been conducting military operations against Bellême strongholds and would shortly afterward be fighting in alliance with King Philip I against barons of northeastern Normandy: David, *Curthose*, pp. 55–56, 58–59; Barlow, *Rufus*, pp. 272–273.

William of Saint-Calais bishop of Durham (exiled from England after 1088 and employed by Curthose in the administration of the duchy),[168] Roger of Ivry the ducal butler, the ducal *familiares* Enguerran fitz Ilbert and William Bertran,[169] and the ducal counselor William of Arques, monk of Molesme.[170] The six remaining signatories were rarely if ever in the duke's company. Gilbert abbot of Caen attests only one other surviving ducal charter, at the single known meeting of Robert Curthose's *curia*, at Bonneville-sur-Touques in 1093.[171] The names of the other five occur nowhere else in the ducal records. Their appearance in the ducal entourage on this occasion is apparently unique. Three of these five have already been mentioned as friends or probable friends of Count Henry from western Normandy: Richard of Redvers (of whose lands Vernon was the eastern outpost), Ranulf *vicomte* of the Bessin, and his son Ranulf le Meschin, nephew of Hugh d'Avranches and future lord of Cumberland and earl of Chester. Two other westerners are in their company—the otherwise obscure Aigell "of the Cotentin" and the aforementioned Gilbert abbot of Saint-Etienne, Caen, who must have known Henry well since his town seems to have been encircled by Henry's authority. Gilbert would have had a close friendship with another of the charter's attesters, Archbishop William Bonne-Ame, his fellow monk in the Bec–Caen circle and immediate predecessor as abbot of Caen.[172] Still another attester, Enguerran fitz Ilbert, had roots in Caen, and although he is known to have been strictly loyal to Robert Curthose in later years, he might well have joined with others in urging Henry's release in 1089. It looks very much as though these men, or most of them, were among the *optimates* mentioned by Orderic whose supplications in Henry's behalf won him his freedom. If so, one might see in this witness list (with a little imagination) the remote origins of the Redvers earldom of Devon and the

---

[168] "De iniusta vexatione Willelmi," SD, 1:194; Haskins, *NI*, p. 76 and n. 35; but Symeon says the same thing of Odo of Bayeux: SD, 2:216.

[169] Haskins, *NI*, pp. 76–77: this is Roger of Ivry's last known attestation of a ducal charter. On Enguerran fitz Ilbert see OV, 6:78 and n. 4: he was a western Norman, a tenant of the bishopric of Bayeux, and was serving Duke Robert in 1105 as castellan of Caen.

[170] On the monk William of Arques see OV, 4:186 and n. 1, 224. One remaining signatory, Hugh fitz Baldric, cannot be shown to have been either ducal or Henrician; on him see Le Patourel, *Norman Empire*, p. 34 and n. 6; Stenton, *English Feudalism*, p. 137 n. 1; *RRAN* 2, no. 844.

[171] *RRAN* 1, no. 342; Abbot Gilbert and Duke Robert were both among the magnates and prelates present at Archbishop William Bonne-Ame's council of Rouen in June 1091: *RRAN* 2, p. 400, no. 317b; and both are signatories to an agreement of 1096 between Abbot Gilbert and Jarento abbot of Saint-Bénigne of Dijon: Haskins, *NI*, pp. 285–286 (no. 2).

[172] Hollister, "St Anselm on Lay Investiture," pp. 153–154.

Bessin dynasty of earls of Chester. If these men did petition successfully
for Henry's release, he would have been, to say the least, very much
obliged to them.

One great lord of western Normandy, Odo of Bayeux, Henry's jailer,
cannot have been pleased at his release. It was perhaps to placate Odo
that the charter witnessed by Henry's friends granted and confirmed
lands to the cathedral church of Bayeux. The charter concludes with
the daunting threat that anyone who meddles with these episcopal
properties will be anathematized personally by Archbishop William
Bonne-Ame. Perhaps Odo was indeed placated; perhaps not. Whatever
the case, the years just following saw the bishop drifting away from the
duke's inner circle.

Henry's activities during the year and a half after his release are ill-
recorded. Malmesbury reports that he crossed to England at the
invitation of Rufus, who again put him off with empty promises, and
then, at Curthose's invitation, returned to Normandy where the duke's
enmity had once more been aroused against him by poisoned
tongues.[173] But Malmesbury is here simply recycling previous events
and is not to be believed. In reality Henry kept his distance from both
his brothers. By all indications, Curthose did not act to restore Henry's
comital title or his authority in western Normandy; indeed, the two
brothers probably did not meet at all when Henry was released from
Bayeux. He seems to have remained in western Normandy and, with
the backing of his friends and *fideles*, resumed his comital authority
without reference to Curthose.[174] Robert of Torigny, who is our source
for Curthose's withdrawal of Henry's countship in autumn 1088, refers
to him as "comes Henricus" in 1091.[175] During Henry's imprisonment
Curthose had been occupied, as we have seen, with military campaigns
in the south and east—and with his own pleasures. He simply did
not concern himself with western Normandy.[176] In the meantime, as
Curthose permitted the remainder of the duchy to slide more and
more deeply into anarchy, letting lands and castles drift from ducal
control—Brionne, Alençon, Exmes, Evreux, Ivry—and failing to curb
the private wars ignited by local feuds, Henry strengthened the
defenses of his castles in the west and extended his network of
baronial supporters. Once again Orderic includes Richard of Redvers
and Hugh of Chester among Henry's *fideles* and suggests that there
were a great many more.[177]

Meanwhile William Rufus, who had not forgiven Curthose for his

[173] WM, *GR*, 2:468–469.
[174] Such is the implication of Orderic (4:220), corroborated by Robert of Torigny
(*GND*, 2:208–209).
[175] *GND*, 2:271.
[176] Barlow, *Rufus*, pp. 268–273.
[177] OV, 4:220, 250.

attempt on the English crown, seized the opportunity arising from ducal misrule by purchasing baronial allies in upper Normandy and the neighboring county of Ponthieu.[178] Most of these men held lands on both sides of the Channel and were therefore vassals of both duke and king. Among those whom Rufus bribed to join his cause were Reginald of Saint-Valery (from whose harbor at the mouth of the Somme the Conqueror had embarked for England in 1066), Stephen of Aumale (on the Bresle), Robert count of Eu (who controlled the mouth of the Bresle and was also lord of Hastings), Gerard of Gournay (with three castles near the Epte frontier), Walter II Giffard (with a castle at Longueville controlling the River Scie and substantial estates in Buckinghamshire soon to become an earldom), and Ralph of Mortemer (lord of Wigmore in Herefordshire). Rufus also drew into his burgeoning alliance system Ralph of Tosny, a great baron of the Evreçin in east-central Normandy with castles at Tosny on the Seine and Conches to the southwest, who had obtained Rufus' military aid in a feud with his neighbor and half-brother, William count of Evreux.[179]

The king remained in England for the time being, but he garrisoned the castles of his allies with knights in his pay who ravaged and burned enemy lands round about.[180] Rufus' grip on the northeast was tightening through most of 1090, but it remained less than complete. Duke Robert made a dependable ally of one important upper Norman baron, Helias of Saint-Saens, by giving him an illegitimate daughter in marriage, with the lordship of nearby Bures-en-Bray and the county of Arques as her *maritagium*. Helias reciprocated with a lifelong devotion to the duke and, in later years, to his son.[181] Curthose also gained the support of his overlord, King Philip I, but only for a time. The French king was by now nearing forty and growing increasingly fat. William of Malmesbury, in a memorable passage, describes him as coming hiccuping to Curthose's aid, "belching from his daily surfeit of food; but as he was making great boasts, the king of England's money met him along the way and overcame his resolution, whereupon he unbuckled his armor and returned to his gourmandizing."[182]

---

[178] For what follows see Barlow, *Rufus*, pp. 273–274.

[179] OV, 4:212–214; cf. 3:126–128: the feud was stimulated, so Orderic relates, by a rivalry between the lively wives of the two barons, Isabel of Conches (of the great frontier family of Montfort l'Amaury) and Helwise of Evreux (of the comital family of Nevers): Chibnall, "Women in Orderic Vitalis," pp. 115–116. As recently as 1088 Ralph had served under Curthose's command: Barlow, *Rufus*, pp. 268–269. On the Tosny family see Musset, "Aux origines d'une classe dirigeante."

[180] *ASC, s.a.* 1090.

[181] OV, 4:182; 6:92, 162–164, 286–288, 368.

[182] WM, *GR*, 2:363; see also *ASC, s.a.* 1090. Philip was, however, by no means incapacitated by gluttony; he was soon to create an international scandal by abandoning his wife, Bertha of Holland, for a younger woman, the beautiful Bertrade de Montfort countess of Anjou: Fliche, *Philippe Ier*, pp. 41–46.

Rufus, still in England, raised the stakes in Normandy still higher by winning over a faction of townsmen in the ducal capital of Rouen through his bribes and promises. The leader of the faction was the wealthiest and most influential burgher in the city, Conan son of Gilbert Pilatus, whose followers were known as "Pilatenses."[183] In the view of Orderic and William of Malmesbury, both of whose writings often reflect aristocratic values, Conan was far wealthier and more powerful than any burgher deserved to be. He "arrogantly maintained against the duke," Orderic complains, "a huge permanent household of knights and dependants."[184] Far worse, he had made a secret pact with Rufus to hand over the city to him. Conan and his crowd of followers were thus committing treason against their rightful lord (to whom they had sworn allegiance in some form) and would have been reviled by many nobles for their breach of faith, regardless of whether it had been against Curthose or Rufus. Orderic, although no admirer of "the slumbering duke," condemns Conan for his "vile treachery," and Malmesbury, writing independently of Orderic, denounces "the treachery of the citizens" whom Conan led.[185]

With a following that included the majority of Rouen's citizens, Conan seems to have been confident of victory. Late in October 1090 he sent messages to the king's forces in their castles in upper Normandy telling them to move immediately on Rouen to join forces with his own men, who were ready to take up arms on their arrival.[186] Curthose, by an enormous stroke of good fortune, somehow got wind of the plot and was able to act in time to thwart it. He summoned to Rouen several of his trusted barons of southeastern Normandy: Orderic names William count of Evreux, his nephew William of Breteuil, and Gilbert of Laigle, of whom the first two had served the duke the previous year as military commanders in his campaigns against Maine and Saint-Céneri.[187] They answered his summons quickly, prompted not only by loyalty to their lord but also perhaps by outright shock at the effrontery of the ignoble citizens of Rouen (the era of the great communal riots had as yet scarcely begun) and by the hope of extracting immense

---

[183] OV, 4:220 and 221 n. 5; Haskins, *NI*, p. 92, recording a later judgment that refers back to the "gravis dissentio" in 1090 "in urbe Rothomagensi" between the "partes Pilatensium . . . et Calloensium." For another later reference back to the riot see *RRAN* 2, no. 1002. See, in general, David, *Curthose*, pp. 56–58.

[184] OV, 4:220.

[185] Ibid.; WM, *GR*, 2:469, where Conan himself is condemned as one who turned traitor after having done homage to Duke Robert ("qui tibi juratus fecerit hominium").

[186] OV, 4:220.

[187] Ibid., pp. 154–156, 222; Barlow, *Rufus*, pp. 268–269, 274–275; it is uncertain whether the Gilbert of Laigle who came to Duke Robert's assistance in 1090 is Gilbert son of Richer or his uncle Gilbert son of Engenulf: see OV, 4:224 n. 3.

ransoms from them. Curthose even had the temerity to seek help from his two recent victims, Count Henry and Robert of Bellême, and both of them, impelled perhaps by similar motives of outrage and greed, brought their contingents to Rouen to fight in the duke's behalf. Henry's willingness to come to the rescue and his leadership in the subsequent melee may well have saved Curthose's regime, for without Rouen the duke's prospects would have been dim indeed.[188]

Henry was the first to arrive, joining Curthose in Rouen Castle around the beginning of November, well in advance of the outbreak of fighting.[189] Hostilities commenced on the morning of 3 November, a Sunday, and lasted for several hours.[190] They were set off by the arrival of a ducal contingent and a company of royalists, approaching the city from opposite directions. The duke's *fidelis* Gilbert of Laigle led his knights across the Seine bridge up to the south gate of the city, while Reginald of Warenne, an ally of William Rufus, approached the west gate, known as the Cauchoise gate, to join forces with Conan.[191] At this news, Conan urged his men to unbar the west gate to admit Reginald and his knights into the city while resisting the entrance of Gilbert of Laigle's contingent through the south gate. Conan's forces were supported by a number of retainers in the king's pay who had filtered secretly into the city, while a minority of citizens fought against Conan in behalf of the duke.[192]

The conflict that followed was violent, chaotic, and lethal. The streets of Rouen echoed with an appalling din as citizen fought citizen until it became uncertain who was on which side. Amidst this savage melee, Robert Curthose and Henry burst out of the ducal castle—the "tower of Rouen"—accompanied by their knights.[193] Orderic credits Curthose

---

[188] Frank Barlow offers this plausible opinion: *Rufus*, p. 274.

[189] For this and what follows we must again depend primarily on Orderic: see OV, 4:222–226.

[190] Dr Chibnall observes that the precision of Orderic's date of 3 November suggests that he derived it from a written source, perhaps an obit (OV, 4:222 n. 1); the obit of Queen Matilda, Henry's mother, was celebrated on 3 November at Saint-Evroul (ibid., p. 45 n. 3).

[191] The Cauchoise gate was so called because it opened to the road into the district of Caux, northwest of Rouen. Reginald of Warenne, younger brother of William II of Warenne, earl of Surrey, held lands in Flanders but was probably based at this time in one or the other of the two Warenne castles in upper Normandy, Bellencombre and Mortemer-sur-Eaulne: *MMI*, pp. 140–141; *EYC*, 8:1–12, 40–46; *CP*, 12, i:491–496.

[192] The pro-ducal citizens were, presumably, the "Calloenses" of n. 183 (above, this chapter).

[193] No trace of the tower has survived. It stood next to the Seine, due south of the cathedral, at the southeast corner of the square city walls of Roman and medieval times. Its site is now denoted by the place de la Haute-Vieille-Tour: OV, 4:225 n. 4.

with the intention of aiding his supporters among the townspeople, but the violence and confusion were so great that the duke appears to have lost his nerve. Described as being "much alarmed," he yielded to the advice of his friends to flee the tumult and avoid risking an ignoble death at the hands of some berserk townsman. Slipping off with a small following, he made his way through the east gate into the suburb of Malpalu, just outside the city wall to the south of the cathedral. From there he was ferried across the Seine to the more distant and safer suburb of Emendreville (the present industrial district of Saint-Sever, across the Pont Jeanne d'Arc). The escape may well have been planned in advance, because when Curthose arrived at Emendreville his close adviser, the monk William of Arques, was awaiting him. They took refuge there during the remainder of the rebellion at the church of Notre-Dame du Pré—a Bec priory as yet unfinished that Curthose subsequently rewarded with the tithe of the hay from his hunting park outside Rouen.[194]

Henry remained in the city with his knights and continued to fight in behalf of his absent brother, rallying pro-ducal citizens to his side. Now Gilbert of Laigle, with the aid of ducal supporters inside the walls, captured the south gate and led his knights into the city where they joined forces with Henry and his men and engaged the rebel townsmen in furious hand-to-hand fighting. The tide now turned against Conan and his rebels as the ducal party grew larger and more assured. Citizens on both sides continued to fight murderously, resulting in a ferocious slaughter "as men struggled and fought and fled and women wept and wailed."[195] The royalist knights, sensing defeat, panicked and fled into the nearby woods where they sought out hiding places. And the ducal allies, now including such latecomers as William count of Evreux and Robert of Bellême, began snatching up the wealthy prisoners whom they had been hoping to find. Conan himself was taken captive and led to the ducal castle, where he was placed in Henry's custody.[196]

---

[194] OV, 4:222–224 and 224 n. 2; Haskins, *NI*, p. 68; *RRAN* 1, no. 327; for several reasons the charter must be February 1091, not February 1092 as it is dated internally and by Haskins and H. W. C. Davis. By 1092 Rufus, whose rights are reserved in the charter, was again at odds with Curthose (*ASC, s.a.* 1091), and William bishop of Durham, who attests the charter for the duke, was in England: *RRAN* 1, nos 330, 332, *RRAN* 2:400, no. 319a. Notre-Dame du Pré (or "de Bonne-Nouvelle") was founded by the Conqueror and his wife Matilda and completed by Henry I: *Neustria Pia*, p. 611; *RRAN* 2, no. 1290.

[195] OV, 4 224: Orderic seems to ascribe the ferocious slaughter of townspeople less to Gilbert or Henry or their knights than to other townspeople: "Ciuibus ut prelibatum est uicissim dissidentibus et tristis infortunii procellis periclitantibus."

[196] William of Malmesbury evidently errs in stating that Conan was first a prisoner of the duke, who then granted Henry's request for custody of the rebel leader: WM,

There followed one of the most striking episodes in Henry's life. The young prince, now twenty-one or twenty-two years old and probably accompanied by some of his knights, led Conan up the spiral stairway of the great tower to the topmost room. According to Orderic, Henry was deeply angered by Conan's treason against the duke. The chronicler "quotes" Henry as addressing Conan in these bitter, mocking words:

> Admire, Conan, the beauty of the country you tried to conquer. Away to the south there is a delightful hunting region, wooded and well stocked with beasts of the chase. See how the River Seine, full of fishes, laps the wall of Rouen and daily brings in ships laden with merchandise of many kinds. On the other side see the fair and populous city, with its ramparts and churches and town buildings, which has rightly been the capital of all Normandy from the earliest days.[197]

Pale with dread, Conan begged for mercy:

> My lord, I deserve condemnation for my own guilt, but now I ask mercy for the sake of God who created all things. For my ransom I will give my lord all the gold and silver that I can find in my own and my kinsmen's treasure-stores, and in compensation for my treachery I will give you faithful service until I die.

Henry answered with an oath that meant much to him: "By my mother's soul, there shall be no ransom for a traitor, only swifter infliction of the death he deserves." Then Conan cried out, "For the love of God, allow me to confess my sins." But Henry, trembling with anger, thrust him out the tower window to his death. The men on the ground below tied Conan's lifeless body to a horse's tail and had him dragged like Hector through all the streets of the city as a warning to traitors. For many decades thereafter, the tower of Rouen was known as "Conan's Leap."[198]

GR, 2:469; Orderic, whose account is much more detailed and credible, has Curthose lingering in his church at Emendreville while Henry disposed of Conan: OV, 4:224.

[197] Orderic's "quotations" of Henry's words, while obviously not verbatim transcripts, may be substantially authentic; they are more or less consistent with William of Malmesbury's narrative of the event, in which Henry addresses Conan with similar irony on the beauty of Rouen (WM, *GR*, 2:69). I have taken the liberty of using Marjorie Chibnall's skillful translation of Orderic: OV, 4:225–227.

[198] OV, 4:224–226; Orderic, writing in the mid-1130s (4:xix), reports that the tower "is called 'Conan's Leap' to this day." William of Malmesbury tells the same story much more briefly and vaguely, adding to Henry's oration on the beauties of Rouen the ironic statement that it should all belong to Conan—perhaps evoking the biblical account of Jesus' temptation: WM, *GR*, 2:469. For a detailed comparison of the two accounts see Freeman, *Rufus*, 2:516–518.

The defenestration of Conan has been regarded by many historians as an act of blatant cruelty on Henry's part. By modern Western ethical standards it certainly was. But since it is the historian's responsibility to understand how such acts were viewed at the time, it must be observed that contemporaries would have applauded Henry's spirited response to the treason of an overweening commoner. Orderic clearly admires Henry for his eloquence and high spirits and for his determination to inflict just and summary punishment on an evildoer. Malmesbury's account of the episode places even more emphasis on the importance of punishing treason, ascribing to Henry such words as "No respite is due a traitor" and "The punishment of a man who turned traitor after swearing loyalty and doing homage ought never to be deferred."[199] Suger of Saint-Denis and Galbert of Bruges display similar attitudes when they describe with unabashed admiration the summary punishments in 1127 of the *nouveaux riches* murderers of Count Charles the Good of Flanders and their (presumably innocent) followers, a great many of whom were put to death by being pushed from the tops of ramparts or by other, less forthright means.[200] John Gillingham has correctly pointed out that in Anglo-Norman times punishments for treason were becoming gentler, with imprisonment and ransoming replacing death or mutilation, but only within the charmed circle of the aristocracy.[201] Understood in this way, Gillingham can convincingly describe William the Conqueror as "chivalrous" despite the mass atrocities that he inflicted on the citizens of Alençon and later on the inhabitants of Yorkshire and Cheshire.[202] As Gillingham states with regard to Henry's deed in 1090, "Conan was a bourgeois and different rules clearly applied."[203]

The significance of the Rouen riot and its outcome can only be discerned if one understands that Henry's behavior throughout the affair

[199] WM, *GR*, 2:469.

[200] Galbert, *Histoire*, pp. 92, 125–126, 128–129, and *passim*. The chief participants in Count Charles' murder were kinsmen of Erembald castellan of Bruges, who was suspected of having risen from villein ancestry; the family dominated the towns of Flanders much as the *Pilatenses* had dominated Rouen. For an alternative punishment see Suger, *Louis le Gros*, pp. 246–248, where Suger writes approvingly of King Louis VI's having a Flemish rebel suspended from a gallows alongside a mad dog and eaten alive.

[201] Gillingham, "1066 and the Introduction of Chivalry," pp. 31–55.

[202] In the early 1050s Duke William punished the townsmen who had defended Alençon against him by having their hands and feet cut off: Douglas, *William the Conqueror*, p. 60; *GND*, 2:122–125. On his wasting of Yorkshire and Cheshire in 1069 see Douglas, *William the Conqueror*, pp. 219–221, and Hollister, "The Aristocracy," pp. 52–53, and "Magnates of Stephen's Reign," pp. 82–83. Several years later he blinded many of the men who rebelled against him in the uprising of 1075: HH, p. 206.

[203] Gillingham, "1066 and the Introduction of Chivalry," p. 45.

would have been widely regarded as heroic, particularly so in contrast with the timidity of the duke.[204] Henry, as Orderic stresses, was the first to come to his brother's aid; it was he, Malmesbury asserts, who almost single-handedly expelled the king's party from Rouen; and it was he, Orderic concludes, who took proper vengeance on the chief traitor.[205] The killing of Conan would have been seen as the act of a dauntless, high-spirited young man; it constituted a memorable climax to a day of gallant warfare on Henry's part in defense of the ducal capital against the vile treachery of low-born townsmen. And for years to come the name "Conan's Leap" would have evoked the memory of an upstart traitor on whom a valiant prince, refusing to be bought off, had inflicted the summary justice that was so clearly appropriate and richly deserved. Such, at least, were the views of Orderic and William of Malmesbury, of those who had Conan's corpse dragged through Rouen "as a warning to traitors," and, very likely, of those who renamed the tower.

When Curthose returned from Notre-Dame du Pré to the castle after the rebellion had been quelled, he is said to have been moved by compassion for the suffering of the citizens. He asked his barons to act gently toward them, but Orderic regretfully reports that they ignored his plea altogether. Robert of Bellême, Gilbert of Laigle, and William of Breteuil, "like foreign raiders," carried off inhabitants of Rouen en masse. They were imprisoned in dungeons until they could pay the highest ransoms and pitilessly abused as though they were foreign enemies. William of Breteuil kept one especially wealthy citizen, William fitz Ansgar, in a foul dungeon until, after a long period of suffering, he was permitted to ransom himself for three thousand pounds (the exact sum that Henry had given Curthose for western Normandy).[206] Orderic does not include Henry among the captive-takers.

The utter futility of Curthose's request for clemency toward the citizens is perhaps indicative of the depth to which his prestige had plunged. Just as Henry emerged from the Rouen riot as a hero, Curthose emerged with a severely damaged knightly reputation. In the

---

[204] The uprising in Rouen was not the only occasion when Duke Robert's timidity evoked comment: see, for example, OV, 5:26, writing generally of Curthose: "plus prouinciales subditos timens quam ab illis timebatur"; and WM, *GR*, 2:363, in reference to the duke's response to the allies that Rufus acquired during 1090 in upper Normandy: "Nec fuit animus comiti ut resisteret."

[205] OV, 4:222; WM, *GR*, 2:469.

[206] OV, 4:226. A William fitz Ansger, probably the same person, later served as a justice for Henry I in Normandy: ibid., p. 227 n. 2; Haskins, *NI*, p. 98. William of Breteuil had recently paid an identical ransom for his own release after being captured in the course of a private war with his uncle, Ralph of Conches (Tosny): OV, 4:214–216.

face of grave danger to his principal city, the duke of Normandy had retired to the safety of a suburban church while a brother some fifteen years his junior had fought energetically to save his duchy. The spectacular execution of Conan and the renaming of the tower doubtless added salt to the wounded ducal psyche. His own principal residence, looking down on his capital city, would thenceforth bear a nickname that rekindled embarrassing memories. Seen in this light, it is comprehensible that the duke's gratitude toward Henry was both grudging and short-lived. In Malmesbury's disapproving words, Curthose immediately became ungrateful and, being a man of changeable disposition, compelled his deserving brother to leave the city.[207] Perhaps Henry had requested and been denied a de jure restoration of his de facto countship, but the sources are silent on any such matter. Whatever the case, the grave damage to Duke Robert's military reputation may have contributed to his otherwise surprising decision shortly afterward to combine forces with Rufus to drive Henry from Normandy. It could also have been a factor in impelling the duke to seek the restoration of his fortunes and self-respect by joining the First Crusade.

Apart from quarreling with Henry, Duke Robert's first recorded act after the Rouen riot was to lend his military backing to Robert of Bellême. The latter was striving to expand his power to the northeast of the River Orne into the lands of the Bellêmes' traditional enemies, the Giroie family, represented in the persons of Hugh of Grandmesnil and his kinsman by marriage, Richard of Courcy.[208] Robert of Bellême had been among Curthose's rescuers at Rouen, and now Curthose reciprocated by leading a ducal force to support Robert's siege of Courcy. The siege accomplished nothing, however, except to make ducal enemies of the Grandmesnils and Courcys.[209] After about a month Curthose and Robert of Bellême suddenly abandoned the project at the alarming news that William Rufus had crossed to Normandy with a large fleet and great treasure.[210]

On 2 February 1091, having failed to topple Curthose by encouraging rebellion from afar, Rufus arrived in the duchy in person. He established his headquarters at Eu in upper Normandy, where he assembled a formidable military force. With the men he had brought with him,

---

[207] WM, *GR*, 2:469.

[208] OV, 1:6–8; 2: chart opposite p. 370. On the siege see Barlow, *Rufus*, p. 276; Freeman, *Rufus*, 1:274; 2:519–522; Hugh of Grandmesnil's daughter was married to Richard of Courcy's son.

[209] Orderic (5:26) lists Richard of Courcy among Rufus' supporters against Curthose in the mid-1090s; both he and Hugh of Grandmesnil were at William II's court between 1091 and 1094: *RRAN* 1, nos 334, 349, 361.

[210] OV, 4:250.

his allies already on the scene, and the mercenaries attracted by his countless barrels of silver pennies, he commanded what Robert of Torigny described as "an immense army of English and Normans."[211] Curthose and his advisers, clearly overawed, were persuaded to negotiate a peace with Rufus, and the terms of the resulting treaty were sufficiently favorable to induce the king to accept them. Executed at Rouen, the scene of the recent uprising, the treaty provided for the sharing out of Normandy between the two older brothers, to the total exclusion and disinheritance of Henry.[212]

The treaty does not survive as an independent document, but the Anglo-Saxon chronicler, who is likely to have had a copy at hand, reports its terms (or most of them) in meticulous detail. Duke Robert granted Rufus title to the abbey of Fécamp—the venerable ducal foundation on the coast of upper Normandy—along with the entire county of Eu, the city of Cherbourg, and all other castles in Normandy whose lords had gone over to the king. Rufus in return promised to help restore to Curthose the county of Maine—which had once again rebelled successfully against Norman ducal authority—and to help him recover all the lands in Normandy that their father had held, except those that the duke ceded to Rufus. It was also agreed that all former landholders in England who had been disseised for supporting Curthose should have their lands restored and that Curthose should himself receive a quantity of land in England as well. Finally, the treaty stipulated that if Curthose predeceased Rufus and left no legitimate son Rufus should inherit all of Normandy, whereas if Rufus should be the first to die Curthose would inherit England. The agreement was then confirmed by the oaths of twelve chief men from each side.[213]

Other chroniclers add or clarify a few points. Orderic includes among the lands that passed to Rufus not only the county of Eu but also the lordships of Stephen of Aumale and Gerard of Gournay in upper Normandy and the holdings of Ralph of Conches/Tosny in the southeast, and he adds that Rufus acquired these lands in return for

---

[211] *GND*, 2:204–205.

[212] Almost surely Rouen, not Caen: above, this chapter, n. 128. I must respectfully disagree with Rufus' major biographers, Barlow (*Rufus*, p. 276 n. 55) and Freeman (*Rufus*, 2:522–523), both of whom give some credence to Robert of Torigny's assertion that King Philip of France was present at the accord; Torigny's account is very brief, not altogether trustworthy, and, with regard to Philip's presence in Normandy in 1091, contradicted by both William of Malmesbury (WM, *GR*, 2:363) and the Anglo-Saxon chronicler (*s.a.* 1090). See further David, *Curthose*, pp. 55–60; Fliche, *Philippe Ier*, pp. 292 ff.; and Chibnall in OV, 4:236–237 n. 3.

[213] ASC, *s.a.* 1091. The absence of any reference to the possibility of Rufus having a son has been taken by some as an indication of his homosexuality, but it is surely not conclusive evidence.

large gifts.[214] Robert of Torigny lists Fécamp, the strongholds of William count of Eu and Stephen of Aumale, and all other lands that Rufus had seized in Normandy "owing to the infidelity of the duke's retainers, who had handed over to the king the fortifications which the duke had entrusted to them."[215] Florence of Worcester adds to Rufus' acquisitions the abbey of Mont-Saint-Michel.[216]

Certain provisions of the treaty were never implemented and, indeed, may not have been negotiated in good faith. In agreeing to restore the lands of Curthose's supporters in 1088, Rufus was prepared to admit William of Saint-Calais not only to his bishopric of Durham but to the royal inner council as well; but Rufus and his exiled prelate had already become reconciled shortly before the treaty, and Bishop William would thus have been restored under any circumstances.[217] Odo of Bayeux, in contrast, was to stay out of England whatever the treaty might provide, and Eustace count of Boulogne, another of the 1088 exiles, also failed to recover his English lands.[218] Moreover, despite Rufus' promise Robert Curthose never received so much as a scrap of land in England.

The great victim of the treaty was of course Henry. It was clearly with the aim of seizing Henry's countship that Curthose obtained Rufus' pledge to help restore ducal power throughout Normandy except in lands ceded to the king. In recompense for this service Rufus was to receive, as a kind of commission, Henry's town of Cherbourg and abbey of Mont-Saint-Michel. As a final touch, the treaty disinherited Henry so long as either of his brothers should live.

The provision regarding the recovery of Maine was never executed. It may be that Rufus and Curthose did intend to undertake such a

---

[214] OV, 4:236. For a fuller list of the lordships under Rufus' control in 1090–1091 see above, p. 69.

[215] GND, 2:206–207.

[216] FW, 2:27; Florence, who is closely following the Anglo-Saxon chronicler, lists the county of Eu, the abbey of Fécamp, the abbey of Mont-Saint-Michel, and Cherbourg. Barlow suggests the possibility that the chronicler may have added Mont-Saint-Michel to the list because he subsequently reported Henry's ejection from it: Rufus, p. 282 and n. 84. But the Worcester chronicler seems sure of his information, reporting that Henry, when besieged atop Mont-Saint-Michel, conducted raids against the king's land (presumably in the immediate vicinity): "regisque terram vastavit, et ejus homines quosdam captivavit, quosdam exspoliavit . . ." (FW, 2:27).

[217] SD, 1:128: in late 1090 or early 1091 Bishop William negotiated the withdrawal of a ducal force that was about to capture a castle garrisoned by knights in the king's pay, an act that prompted Rufus to readmit William to England and restore all his episcopal lands.

[218] On Odo see OV, 5:220; on the count of Boulogne's enormous Domesday holdings (worth £770 a year) see MMI, pp. 98–99; Eustace II (sometimes numbered III), son of the Domesday Eustace, having joined the rebellion in 1088, recovered his lands only in 1101: ASC, s.a. 1101.

campaign, on the mistaken assumption that Henry had no spies in Rouen. But they were preempted by Henry's public challenge to their treaty and his preparations for the defense of western Normandy against them. Henry expressed strenuous objections to his brothers' "covetousness" in dividing the Conqueror's possessions between themselves with the intention of leaving him destitute.[219] He raised a force of Norman and Breton mercenaries and put Coutances, Avranches, and his other castles in a state of readiness.[220] But the threat of a full-scale attack by the king of England created a grave problem that had not troubled Henry before: the disintegration of his network of friends and *fideles* in western Normandy. Some of them yielded their castles to Rufus because they were intimidated and overawed by his vast military resources. Others, being vassals and *familiares* of both Henry and Rufus, had little choice but to side with their royal master against the young count. Among these last was Henry's usually stalwart friend, Hugh of Avranches, whose allegiance to Henry was attenuated by the homage and fealty he had rendered to Rufus for the earldom of Chester. More than that, Hugh was Rufus' friend too. He was frequently in attendance at Rufus' court and in fact had just crossed from England to Normandy in Rufus' invasion fleet. Rufus was also accompanied across the Channel by other major cross-Channel landholders with interests in the Norman west: Robert fitz Hamon, Geoffrey bishop of Coutances (never a friend of Henry's), and perhaps others unnamed. All three were in Rufus' Norman entourage in 1091, and Bishop Geoffrey may have played some role in encouraging the campaign against Count Henry.[221]

Thus as Rufus and Curthose led their armies westward, Henry's support dissolved. Hugh of Chester and other friends, as Orderic indignantly puts it, "deserted the noble prince in his military need and handed over their castles to the king."[222] Leaving garrisons in some of his own castles, Henry withdrew with most of his mercenary troops and military household to his westernmost and most formidable bastion, the hilltop monastery of Mont-Saint-Michel, where, so the Worcester

[219] WM, *GR*, 2:363–364; OV, 4:250; *GND*, 2:206–207.
[220] OV, 4:250.
[221] Of several royal charters from England attested by Earl Hugh which might well have been issued on the eve of Rufus' crossing to Normandy, the conclusive ones are *RRAN* 1, nos 315 (Dover, 27 January 1091) and 319 (Hastings, 1091). Attesters to the former include others in Rufus' circle who held lands in western Normandy: Robert fitz Hamon, Geoffrey bishop of Coutances, Hamo *Dapifer*, and Eudo *Dapifer*. *RRAN* 2:400, no. 317a, demonstrates that both Earl Hugh and Robert fitz Hamon were in the royal entourage in Normandy sometime between February and August 1091; on Bishop Geoffrey see Le Patourel, "Geoffrey of Montbray," pp. 147–148.
[222] OV, 4:250.

chronicler reports, some of the monks assisted him in installing his knights.[223] His brothers pursued him there, probably arriving in the earlier part of March 1091, and proceeded to lay siege to the abbey.[224] Wace relates, plausibly, that Rufus established his headquarters at Avranches (with *Vicomte* Hugh perhaps offering hospitality), that another body of knights was based at Ardevon, much closer to the abbey, and that Curthose based himself at the village of Genets, some ten kilometers westward from Avranches along the north shore of the Baie de Mont-Saint-Michel and well out of harm's way.[225] Perhaps, as has been suggested, the king and duke stationed themselves on the north shore of the bay in order to cut Henry off from the Cotentin. But Avranches, with its vicecomital castle, would always have been the most reasonable royal headquarters, whereas it is difficult to see how Curthose's base at Genets—a small coastal village set amidst quicksand, beset by hazardous tides, and well off the beaten track—could have been of any strategic importance at all.[226]

Mont-Saint-Michel was superbly defensible, set high atop an immense rock jutting up out of a vast flat plain and bay, where the tides are among the most treacherous in the world. At high tide the Mount is an island, and at most other times its north and northwest sides, where the village of Mont-Saint-Michel used to rise before the Bretons burned it

[223] FW, 2:27. There is no record of the role played in the siege by the abbot of Mont-Saint-Michel, Roger, who was a ducal appointee and unpopular with the monks: "Annales du Mont-Saint-Michel," *s.a.* 1085 (on Roger), 1090 (on the siege).

[224] Florence of Worcester (2:27) states that the siege lasted through the entire Lenten season (26 February to 12 April 1091), whereas Orderic (4:250) has the siege commence in mid-Lent. The Worcester chronicler was farther removed from the scene than Orderic but was very good at chronology. Nevertheless, since Rufus had only arrived in Normandy on 2 February and had in the meantime established himself at Eu, organized his forces, negotiated with the duke, executed their treaty, deliberated an attack on Maine, and then, with Curthose, led a combined royal-ducal army into the far west of Normandy, it seems unwise to take the Worcester chronicler literally and begin the siege in February.

[225] Wace, *Roman de Rou*, 2:240.

[226] For the suggestion see Barlow, *Rufus*, p. 284, where it is further proposed (as a possibility) that the two headquarters were located so as to allow Henry to escape to Brittany if he chose; but such an escape would have been hindered by the general blockade, which was preventing adequate supplies of water from reaching the abbey, and by the base at Ardevon—for which we also depend on the local lore available to Wace (*Roman de Rou*, 2:240), born on Jersey and educated at Caen, but writing between 1160 and 1174.

In the months before his death, Prof. Hollister and Marjorie Chibnall were discussing by mail the importance of the village of Genets. She argued that Genets was an important estate and priory of the abbey of Mont-Saint-Michel as well as a principal supply harbor that had to be occupied to make a siege effective. It is possible that Hollister intended to alter this section in the light of this informed opinion (ACF).

down in 1204, continue to face the sea. Crowning the rock even then was an impressive complex of monastic buildings, vividly illustrated in the Bayeux Tapestry. Then as now they were of stone, and apart from the spire on the Romanesque tower of the abbey church, the late Gothic choir, and the two celebrated thirteenth-century buildings known as the Merveille, they are recognizably the same today as in the eleventh century. The nave and transept, the crossing tower, the convent buildings, and of course the crypt and the subterranean Carolingian church of Notre-Dame sous Terre are essentially unchanged. Considering the ease with which a large stone church could be converted to a fortress simply by providing a garrison, Mont-Saint-Michel was virtually impregnable.

Wisely, Rufus and Curthose did not attempt to storm the citadel. They simply blockaded it, with the object of exploiting its one great weakness: the lack of a dependable internal supply of fresh water. Henry responded by harassing the besiegers with constant sallies, taking captives, killing men and horses, and ravaging the surrounding lands—now evidently expropriated by King William in accordance with the treaty of the previous month.[227]

William of Malmesbury illustrates Rufus' "magnanimity" in the course of the siege with the story, perhaps legendary, of Rufus impetuously galloping off alone against a band of Henry's knights. His splendid horse was fatally wounded beneath him and dragged the king about by the foot until the knight who had unhorsed him drew his sword and prepared to strike. "Hold, wretch," Rufus cried out in alarm. "I am the king of England!" The soldiers all trembled at the sound of Rufus' well-known voice and quickly brought him another horse. Leaping astride it Rufus shouted, "Who unhorsed me?" "It was I," the knight boldly replied, "who took you not for a king but for a knight." In a sudden change of mood, the king exclaimed, "By the face of Lucca" (for such was his usual oath, Malmesbury explains), "from now on you shall be my man and, being placed on my muster list, you shall be well rewarded for your gallant deed."[228]

Malmesbury tells a related story about Curthose's conduct at Mont-Saint-Michel, which purports to equate the duke's "compassion" with the king's "magnanimity." After the siege had dragged on for some time and the blockade was causing a growing water shortage among the defenders, Henry is said to have sent messengers to Duke Robert to complain of the thirst he endured. Intending perhaps to strike a raw nerve, Henry reminded his brother that water was the common right

[227] FW, 2:27–28; above, this chapter, n. 216; WM, *GR*, 2:364.
[228] WM, *GR*, 2:364–365. On Rufus' oath, "By the (holy) face of Lucca," see Barlow, *Rufus*, pp. 116–118.

of all people and suggested that he show his courage not through the force of the elements but through the valor of a knight. Strongly affected by Henry's remonstrance, Curthose ordered his knights to relax their guard and let Henry's men bring water through the blockade, so that his brother should not go thirsty. When Rufus heard of this he was furious at the duke: "This is a fine way indeed to run a war, allowing the enemy all the water they need! How shall we ever conquer them if we indulge them with food and drink?" Robert replied, smiling, "Indeed, should I condemn my own brother to die of thirst? And if we lose him, where shall we find another?" At this, Rufus scoffed at Duke Robert's mild temper and broke off the war.[229] Malmesbury's testimony finds confirmation of sorts in Wace, a well-placed but dangerously late source, who improves on the story by having Duke Robert send his thirsty brother a cask of the finest wine.[230] The story is consistent with the Worcester chronicler's statement that Rufus grew tired of the long siege and departed without achieving his ends.[231] Robert of Torigny seems at first sight to support this view, stating that when their long campaign appeared fruitless the duke and king quarreled, enabling Henry to depart from the Mount unchallenged.[232]

Robert of Torigny does not explain, however, why Henry chose to leave Mont-Saint-Michel at all, or why (as Torigny reports) he should later have found it necessary to win back possession of his county of Coutances.[233] The king and duke may well have quarreled, Rufus may have tired of the siege and relinquished some of his goals, and Curthose may even have permitted water to leak through the lines, but the siege unquestionably succeeded in driving Henry from Normandy.

As before, Orderic provides the most coherent narrative. He states that the siege ended when Henry, with his water running short and his strategic position hopeless, decided to save himself for better days and negotiated the surrender of the Mount on honorable terms. Perhaps if Rufus had not grown tired of the conflict he would not have permitted Henry to depart in freedom. The king must have tired quickly, however, if Orderic is correct in stating that the siege lasted only fifteen days. The Worcester chronicler, more plausibly, puts it at about six weeks.[234] Whatever the case, it was probably in early April 1091 that Henry handed over his remaining castles to his brothers and left the

---

[229] WM, *GR*, 2:365.

[230] Wace, *Roman de Rou*, 2:241–243. In this version of the tale Duke Robert permits Henry's men to bring water through the lines as well as sending him wine.

[231] FW, 2:27.

[232] *GND*, 2:206–207.

[233] Ibid., p. 271.

[234] OV, 4:250 ("fere xv diebus"); FW, 2:27 ("per totam Quadragesimum"); see above, this chapter, n. 224. The Worcester writer's chronological data are usually reliable, and fifteen days seems rather too short an interval of time for the siege, as described, to have run its course.

Mount. He departed under a safe conduct, accompanied by his companions and all his baggage—possibly including the remnants of his treasure. He traveled southwestward into neighboring Brittany, which, with the exception of Normandy, offered the only land route out of Mont-Saint-Michel. Having paid off his Breton followers, he thanked them for the assistance they had rendered him in his need, when his allies in western Normandy had deserted him.[235] He then crossed the frontier into France, landless once more.[236]

Now for the first time Henry's life closely resembled those of the wandering aristocratic *juvenes* of his era.[237] For more than a year he lived in the *Vexin français* in a state of poverty (so Orderic alleges), seeking lodging where he could find it, accompanied by only five companions: a knight, a clerk, and three attendants.[238] It is tempting to speculate that the clerk might have been Roger, future bishop of Salisbury and chief royal minister, who is reported to have been in Henry's entourage before he became king,[239] but one can never know. Orderic observes that Henry's poverty in this phase of his life taught him to be compassionate toward the poor and humble in later years, but the chronicler is obviously spinning a moral tale. Apart from these few edifying

[235] OV, 4:250; see Malmesbury's reference to Henry's policy of purchasing Breton support during his days at Mont-Saint-Michel (and subsequently at Domfront): WM, *GR*, 2:478; on Henry's later advancement of Bretons to high positions in England see above, pp. 58, 60 n.–146.

[236] OV, 4:258. One can now relegate to a footnote the alternative, oft-told narrative of Henry becoming reconciled with his brothers after the siege and accompanying them to England (Freeman, *Rufus*, 1:293–295, 305–306; 2:535–536; David, *Curthose*, p. 65; cf. Barlow, *Rufus*, pp. 285–288). The story is based on WM, *GR*, 2:365, and is allegedly confirmed by *RRAN* 1, no. 318, a charter of William bishop of Durham to his prior and monks, dated by an analysis of the attesters to September–December 1091, and carrying the *signa* of King William II, Duke Robert, and Henry "brother of the king." H. S. Offler (*Durham Episcopal Charters*, pp. 48–53) has demonstrated conclusively that the charter is a forgery (perhaps of the late twelfth century). And as has been seen, William of Malmesbury's information on the sequence of Henry's youthful travels is quite unreliable; in this instance his testimony follows on his incorrect report that Rufus and Curthose abandoned their siege of Mont-Saint-Michel. Since their campaign was in fact successful in depriving Henry of all his lands, the notion that he immediately afterward and without recompense became reconciled with his brothers is inconceivable. The *Consuetudines et iusticie*, issued by Rufus and Curthose in July 1091, several months after the siege and shortly before their Channel crossing, continues to exclude Henry absolutely from any role in the governance of Normandy: Haskins, *NI*, pp. 277–284.

[237] Above, pp. 41–45 and n. 66.

[238] OV, 4:250–252; Orderic here states that Henry's Vexin exile lasted "rather less than two years," but see below, this chapter, n. 245.

[239] WM, *GR*, 2:483.

reflections, Orderic tells us nothing more about Henry's experiences during his exile, nor does anyone else. He simply vanishes.

We are also told very little about the activities of Rufus and Curthose after the siege. One result, Orderic states, was that Curthose granted a great part of Normandy to Rufus, doubtless in accordance with the provisions of the brothers' agreement the previous February in Rouen.[240] Although Rufus remained with Curthose in Normandy for several months, they undertook no campaign to recover Maine, nor are they known to have made any effort to curb the private wars then raging in Normandy—between Ralph of Tosny and William of Evreux in the southeast or between Robert of Bellême and his neighbors in the south. Curthose's appeasement of Rufus by no means quieted the duchy.

Rufus did, however, collaborate with Duke Robert in undertaking a joint inquest of the jurisdictional rights that William the Conqueror had exercised in Normandy and that his ducal successors were entitled to enjoy. The inquest occurred on 18 July at Caen, and the findings of the inquest jurors (bishops and magnates) were recorded in an extraordinarily valuable document known as the *Consuetudines et iusticie*.[241] Its contents bear witness not only to the considerable powers of jurisdiction wielded by the Conqueror but also, by implication, to their disintegration under Curthose. The jurors affirmed, for example, that in the Conqueror's regime private war was carefully restricted, private castles could be built only with ducal license and could be occupied at will by ducal garrisons, the taking and ransoming of prisoners in private wars was forbidden, the duke enjoyed a monopoly on coining money, and the peace of the duchy was strongly enforced in a variety of specific ways. In these and other respects the jurors strongly affirmed ducal authority.

The energizing force behind this remarkable inquest was of course William Rufus, who could claim and exercise his father's rights throughout the portions of the duchy under his control. It is perhaps of some importance that the inquest provided the occasion of Curthose's single recorded appearance in the city that had risen under his father to become the administrative and spiritual center of western Normandy and the family's necropolis.[242] The very fact of his

---

[240] OV, 4:252.

[241] Haskins, *NI*, pp. 277–284; *RRAN* 1, no. 316; discussed in David, *Curthose*, pp. 65–66.

[242] This is not to say that Curthose made no other visits to Caen, but only that he visited it rarely—and perhaps never during Henry's countship. Curthose did issue charters favoring the Caen monasteries (none with places and dates), but all of them seem to have been issued either in 1087–1088 with Henry, in 1091 during his visit to the city with Rufus, in 1096 with the papal legate Abbot Jarento of Dijon, or, in one instance, after his return from the crusade: Haskins, *NI*, p. 69 (above, nn. 128, 131 and pp. 54–56); *RRAN* 2, no. 621.

visiting Caen constituted a reassertion of ducal power, if a faint one. But the confident pronouncements on ducal authority in the *Consuetudines et iusticie* had no perceptible effect on Robert Curthose's governance. Shortly afterward, in late July or the beginning of August, he accompanied Rufus to England, surprising many of his Norman subjects by his sudden, unannounced departure.[243] The king and duke traveled north together through England and into Scotland, where Curthose was helpful in negotiating a truce between Rufus and Malcolm king of Scots. But despite the duke's territorial concessions to Rufus in Normandy and his help in Scotland, Rufus declined to honor the remaining terms of the Rouen treaty. The English lands that he had promised to Curthose, like the lands that their mother had promised to Henry, he kept out of reach. Curthose remained at his brother's court through part of the 1091 Christmas season but at last became so angry that he departed abruptly. Finding little to rely on in their agreement, the Anglo-Saxon chronicler asserts, he left his brother's court two days before Christmas and returned empty-handed to Normandy.[244]

The rupture of the alliance between Rufus and Curthose and the concomitant scrapping of the treaty of Rouen were to Henry's advantage. For the time being his rootlessness and relative impoverishment prevented him from exploiting the situation. But some months later, perhaps around mid-1092, his luck turned dramatically with the coming of an unexpected opportunity. "With the help of God and the support of his friends," Orderic writes, Henry gained possession of the fortified hilltop town of Domfront in southwestern Normandy.[245]

Domfront had long been a key stronghold of the Bellême-Talvas family. Toward the beginning of the eleventh century William I of Bellême, Robert of Bellême's great-grandfather, had built a wooden keep on a prominent headland that juts out from the town to the

[243] OV, 4:252–254, suggesting late July despite Orderic's earlier statement that the brothers departed in August: ibid., 4:250; corroborated by FW, 2:28; see Barlow, *Rufus*, p. 287 and n. 104.

[244] *ASC, s.a.* 1091; FW, 2:28; HH, p. 216; SD, 2:219.

[245] OV, 4:256; Orderic dates Henry's acquisition of Domfront to 1092, and he earlier stated that Henry remained in exile for rather less than two years after leaving Mont-Saint-Michel (in early April 1091). This would suggest that he gained Domfront late in 1092; but in a subsequent account Orderic places Henry in Domfront "at the beginning of the month of July," in a year that Dr Chibnall plausibly calculates to be 1092 (4:292 and n. 3), based on the fact that Orderic's narrative strongly implies that Henry was at Domfront in July shortly after the siege of Bréval in spring 1092: 4:288 and n. 6. Assuming that Orderic's sequence of events is correct, Henry's exile is shortened to fifteen months at most. Elsewhere and in another context, Dr Chibnall comments that Orderic sometimes "counted a fraction of a year as a whole year" (4:xix).

west.[246] Looking out over large stretches of the Passais bocage countryside, the castle was of great strategic importance, and its superb location on a rocky sandstone promontory, from which a precipice drops
some two hundred feet to the gorge of the Varenne river, made it most
difficult to take by assault.[247] Count Geoffrey Martel of Anjou had occupied it around the mid-eleventh century, probably with the assent of
the Domfront townspeople and garrison, and William the Conqueror
had captured it from Count Geoffrey while in the course of advancing
Norman ducal authority southward into Maine.[248] The Bellêmes had
thereupon become ducal vassals, opening the way to the marriage
uniting the Bellême heiress Mabel and the Conqueror's great *fidelis*,
Roger II of Montgomery.[249] Their eldest son, Robert of Bellême, having
acquired the Bellême inheritance on his mother's death, had counted
Domfront as the western bastion of his far-flung possessions and had
defended it strenuously against all enemies until its inhabitants, weary
of his abusive rule, invited Henry to be their lord.[250]

The details of this astonishing bloodless coup have remained less
than clear. What became of Robert of Bellême's castle garrison? Did he
have no supporters at all in the town? Does Orderic's allusion to the
help of Henry's friends suggest the operation of larger forces? From
the information provided by our sources—largely Robert of Torigny
and Orderic—the impetus behind the coup seems to have been chiefly
internal. Some of Henry's west Norman friends may have put in a good
word, but there appears to have been no major conspiracy in his behalf.
Indeed, the most powerful of his friends, Earl Hugh, was far away in

---

[246] Louise, *Seigneurie de Bellême*, 2:69; Boussard, "Seigneurie de Bellême," pp.
43–54; Thompson, "Family and Influence," pp. 215–226; Chibnall, in OV,
2:362–365 (appendix 1); *GND*, 2:134–135, 2:264–267; see above, this chapter, n.
154.

[247] E. A. Freeman provided a vivid description of Domfront based on his own keen
observations but outdated archaeology: *Rufus*, 1:319–320.

[248] Douglas, *William the Conqueror*, pp. 59–60; William of Poitiers, *Histoire de Guillaume le Conquérant/Gesta Guillelmi*, pp. 40–44; *GND*, 2:122–127.

[249] See above, pp. 62–64 and n. 154.

[250] Strictly speaking, Robert of Bellême had acquired possession of the castle of
Domfront only after the Conqueror's death in September 1087, at the news of
which Robert hastened to drive out the ducal garrisons that had occupied the
Bellême family castles at Alençon, Bellême, "et omnibus aliis castellis suis": OV,
4:112–114; (on the right of Norman dukes to occupy baronial castles see above,
p. 84). He had then defended it against the claims and attacks of the count of
Perche: OV, 4:160–162. But Robert of Bellême had held Domfront for only five
years when, as Robert of Torigny reports, its inhabitants became indignant at the
treatment they experienced at the hands of their lord, "homo ferox et mentis inhu-
manae . . .": *GND*, 2:206–207. Orderic states that Robert had sorely oppressed the
townspeople "for many years": 4:258. On Robert of Bellême's style of lordship see
above, this chapter, n. 155.

Chester during the summer of 1092 suffering from a serious illness—
or at least complaining of one.[251]

The only person besides Henry himself whose name occurs in
connection with the coup is an inhabitant of Domfront named
"Harecherius" or "Archard." The men of Domfront, Orderic states,
took pity on Henry's misfortunes and sending for him from France "per
Harecherium" they received him with honor.[252] Robert of Torigny
provides a further grain of information about what must surely be the
same individual, an unnamed inhabitant of Domfront—"vir nobilis et
dives"—whose skillful arrangements enabled Henry to take possession
of the stronghold.[253] Since "Archard" is a relatively uncommon name,
Henry's benefactor is very likely to have been a descendant and namesake of a certain Archard Dives (or "the Rich"), whose attestation
as "Achardus dives, miles de Donnifronte" occurs on the witness list
of William I of Bellême's foundation charter of circa 1015–1025 for
Lonlay Abbey near Domfront.[254] Although *milites* were not ipso facto
members of the nobility at this early date, it nevertheless seems more
than a coincidence that Henry's benefactor in Domfront in 1092,
whom Orderic identifies by a variant form of the same name, should
also be, according to Robert of Torigny, both noble and rich. Gérard
Louise, in a brief but valuable archive-based study of this family, has
identified as son and heir of the original Archard Dives a certain
Gervais of Domfront, an occasional attester for William the Conqueror,
who was sufficiently important to have his own steward and who occurs
in a Jumièges charter of 1086 as a "baro laicus" of Robert of Bellême.[255]
The family's importance is further indicated by the abundance of
its property scattered throughout the extensive Bellême lordship—
at Bellême itself, at Condé-sur-Sarthe, at Saint-Loup-du-Gast, and of
course at Domfront. Although one cannot specify the precise relationship connecting Archard Dives, *miles* of Domfront, and his son Gervais,
to Archard of Domfront, the *vir nobilis et dives* who aided Henry, Louise
does show that a brother of the 1092 Archard—Henry's Archard—bore
the family name Gervais of Domfront. The family had thus been afflu-
ent and widely influential for at least three generations when Archard
admitted Henry into Domfront. Louise regards it as all but certain that
Henry's benefactor and his forebears—as *milites*, *nobiles*, and *barones* of

---

[251] Eadmer, *HN*, pp. 27–29; Eadmer, *Vita Anselmi*, p. 63.
[252] OV, 4:256–258.
[253] *GND*, 2:206–207; Henry's friend in Domfront appears again in Wace, *Roman de Rou*, 2:244, as "Haschier." Henry is not known, incidentally, to have voiced any complaint to Archard about townsmen betraying their lord by opening their gates to a rival, as he had done to Conan in the tower of Rouen.
[254] *Neustria Pia*, p. 424; OV, ed. Le Prevost, 3:384 n. 2.
[255] Louise, "Châteaux et pouvoirs."

the Bellêmes—were hereditary castellans of Domfront. If this was indeed the case, it would explain Archard's ability to deliver the keep to Henry along with the walled town, especially if, as Orderic and Robert of Torigny indicate, he enjoyed widespread support. The peaceful coup that conferred Domfront on Henry evidently occurred when the scion of the town's leading castellan family chose to repudiate his allegiance to the lord of Bellême and managed to win the backing of the disaffected townspeople for his act of defiance.[256]

When the people of Domfront opened their gates to Henry, he pledged to them by oath that he would never allow his lordship over them to pass to another person, nor would he ever change their laws or customs.[257] It would not be the last time that Henry promised good governance after the rule of a heavy-handed predecessor. From the time that he assumed the lordship of Domfront his cause prospered. His power spread as he and his knights descended from their well-protected fortress town to make war on the two men who had become his chief enemies, Robert of Bellême and Robert Curthose, avenging his banishment from Normandy with ravaging and plunder and the taking of many captives.[258] He joined forces with Robert of Bellême's traditional foes, the Giroies, to plunder Bellême lands and do battle with Bellême knights.[259] As Frank Barlow vividly expresses it, "Henry was living like a robber baron in the southern marches of Normandy."[260]

But Henry's hopes and opportunities stretched far beyond those of a robber baron. And with Rufus out of the duchy and once again at

[256] The Archard active in 1092 had a nephew named Henry of Domfront (ibid., p. 16), a name that occurs in *PR* 31 *Henry I*, p. 42, under the honor of Arundel, as the recipient of a small payment *per breve regis*. The name Archard occurs in a charter of Henry I of 1107–1116 (*RRAN* 2, pp. xvii, xx, and no. 1134) granting five Berkshire manors in fee to Robert Achard "magistro meo," which if taken literally would identify the recipient as a former tutor of Henry's. It seems doubtful that Henry, who was approaching his mid-twenties in 1092, would have required any tutoring at that time. If, however, this Robert Archard was by any chance the person who delivered Domfront to the homeless prince, one hopes that the Berkshire manors were not his only reward. The charter is discussed in Stenton, *English Feudalism*, p. 102 n. 1, and Southern, "The Place of Henry I," p. 163.

[257] OV, 5:318; Henry recalls these pledges during negotiations with Curthose at Alton in 1101 to justify his retention of Domfront.

[258] OV, 4:258, 292; the ravaging and plundering of enemy lands was by far the most common activity in medieval warfare: Hollister, "Magnates of Stephen's Reign," pp. 84–86. One of Henry's captives was a certain Ruald from the territory of Saint-Evroul who, Orderic delights to tell us, effected a miraculous escape from the castle of Domfront (ibid., pp. 258–260).

[259] OV, 4:292–294.

[260] Barlow, *Rufus*, p. 288.

odds with the duke, Henry's network of friends and *fideles* in western Normandy came back into play. Consequently, over the years between about mid-1092 and 1094 Henry's authority spread once again through western Normandy.[261] Robert of Torigny singles out as Henry's baronial supporters at this time his long-standing associates Richard of Redvers and Hugh of Avranches, along with Richard of Redvers' neighbor in the Cotentin, Roger of Mandeville.[262] Earl Hugh had recovered his health and was back in Normandy, where Henry, in gratitude for his faithful support (and doubtless to cement it even more firmly after Hugh's lapse at Mont-Saint-Michel), granted him the lordship of Saint-James le Beuvron, an important castle on the frontier between the Avranchin and Brittany.[263] Saint-James had previously been a ducal castle, built by the Conqueror during a campaign against Conan duke of Brittany. Hugh, as *vicomte* of Avranches, had provided the garrison in the duke's behalf, but now Henry gave him the castle as a fief, to be passed down in his family from father to son.

This grant illustrates the extent to which Henry's power had grown. He was acting as a duke of Normandy in the Avranchin, granting a ducal castle in fee to a *vicomte*—a castle situated at a considerable distance from Domfront (but at no great distance from Mont-Saint-Michel). Robert of Torigny asserts that Henry regained most of the county of Coutances, "which had previously been deceitfully taken away from him," while Orderic credits Henry with extending his authority over a great part of Normandy "either by influence or by arms."[264] He was aided not only by his friends but also by the illness or death of his enemies. Geoffrey bishop of Coutances, the Conqueror's friend and companion who had resisted Henry's lordship over his cathedral city, had fallen mortally ill by early 1092 and died on 2 February 1093.[265] His successor Bishop Ralph (1093–1113), lacking Geoffrey's immense cross-Channel wealth, was a far less formidable figure and is not known to have quarreled with Henry. Geoffrey's nephew and heir, Robert of Mowbray, who had also opposed Henry in the Cotentin, was by then preoccupied with his earldom of Northumberland: in November 1093 he ambushed and killed Malcolm III king of Scots; by early 1095 he was plotting rebellion against Rufus; and in late summer of that year his lifelong imprisonment commenced.[266] The spread of Henry's

[261] *GND*, 2:208–209.

[262] Ibid.; above, this chapter, n. 119.

[263] Ibid.; *ASC*, *s.a.* 1094, reports Hugh's presence in Normandy; on his recovery, Eadmer, *HN*, p. 29.

[264] *GND*, 2:208–209; OV, 5:26.

[265] *GC*, 11, *Instrumenta*, cols 222–224; Le Patourel, "Geoffrey of Montbray," pp. 157–158.

[266] *CP*, 9:705–706; Barlow, *Rufus*, pp. 316, 338, 346–359; *GC*, 11, col. 873, on Ralph bishop of Coutances.

authority was doubtless aided too by the death in 1090 of Robert count
of Mortain, Bishop Odo's vastly wealthy but unassertive older brother.
The county of Mortain, centered in the southeastern quadrant of the
Avranchin, lay astride the routes between Domfront and Avranches and
extended eastward almost to Domfront itself.[267] The inheritance of
Robert's son William was delayed for several years until he came of age,
leaving a power vacuum that is likely to have been filled by *Vicomte* Hugh
and his lord, Count Henry.[268]

Perhaps surprisingly, the most powerful of all Henry's friends was
William Rufus, whom Robert of Torigny describes as giving his
"consent" to Henry's reestablishing himself in western Normandy.[269]
Rufus' break with Robert Curthose at the 1091 Christmas court,
together with the growth of Henry's strength at Domfront, activated a
diplomatic revolution in which Rufus now aligned himself with Henry
against Curthose. Since Henry was already waging war against the duke
and Rufus was determined once again to conquer all of Normandy, the
interests of the two younger brothers coalesced. To Rufus, the count
of the Cotentin could be an even more valuable client than the count
of Eu. We know that by early 1095 Rufus was providing Henry with
generous financial backing for his campaign against Curthose, and it
is possible that some such backing had been flowing into Domfront
at an earlier date as an accompaniment to the king's "consent."[270]
Thenceforth, for the remainder of William Rufus' life he and his
younger brother remained staunch allies.

Henry's sworn determination never to relinquish Domfront, nourished perhaps by the outpouring from the royal treasury, seems to
have resulted in a significant building boom on the hilltop citadel
and its environs. In Domfront today stand the substantial ruins of a
rectangular stone keep some eighty feet in height, almost certainly
built by Henry and largely destroyed in 1608 on the orders of the

---

[267] Boussard, "Le Comte de Mortain," p. 273; see also *CP*, 3:427–428; and
Golding, "Robert of Mortain."

[268] William of Mortain attests as early as 1082 in the company of his father and
mother, probably as a child or perhaps an infant: *RRAN* 1, nos 145–146, 159*
(genuine in Boussard's view: "Le Comte de Mortain," pp. 267–268). But he attests
no known charters of William Rufus or Robert Curthose. The fact that a royal
judicial eyre could hold pleas of the crown throughout the Mortain earldom
of Cornwall in 1096 suggests that William of Mortain was still in wardship at the
time: *RRAN* 1, no. 378; *Monasticon*, 2:497; Barlow, *Rufus*, pp. 208–209. Later, as a
young adult, Count William was a source of serious trouble for Henry: below,
pp. 171, 182–184.

[269] *GND*, 2:208–209: "consensu Willelmi."

[270] *ASC, s.a.* 1095.

duc de Sully.[271] The ruins—large portions of the northern and western sides of the keep along with remnants of the surrounding stone curtain walls—rise amidst the lawns and flowers of a lovely public garden on the promontory where William of Bellême had earlier erected his wooden keep. Just below the garden, some hundred feet to the north of the keep and still within the perimeter of the former curtain walls, are the impressive stone ruins of the castle priory of Saint-Symphorien, now being excavated and partially reconstructed. The priory was originally established by William of Bellême early in the eleventh century near his wooden keep, but archaeological evidence makes it clear that the present priory ruins are coeval with those of Henry's rebuilt castle, and the archaeologists involved in the excavations believe that both structures date approximately from the period 1092–1100, that is, the period between Henry's arrival at Domfront and his coronation.[272]

Looking southward from the castle, one can see far below, on a bend in the River Varenne, the beautiful Norman Romanesque church of Notre-Dame-sur-l'Eau dating from about the same period.[273] It remains to this day a functioning parish church despite the savage demolition of its side aisles and four of the six bays of its nave in 1836. This atrocity was perpetrated by a barbarian tribe known as the "Ponts et Chaussées," who determined to construct a more direct road between Domfront and Mortain via the nave of Notre-Dame-sur-l'Eau.[274] The much foreshortened church was further damaged by warfare in 1944 but has since been restored with commendable taste, and even without its aisles and four west bays it remains a gem of Norman architecture. The fact that it is distinctively Norman in style, with recognizable similarities to contemporary churches in the Bessin, provides another possible link with Henry and his entourage.[275] Both Saint-Symphorien and Notre-Dame-sur-l'Eau had originally been

[271] See *Guide historique . . . de Domfront*, pp. 16–27.

[272] Ibid., pp. 2–3, 23; Bayle, "La Priorale Saint-Symphorien (Domfront)"; Jaubert, "Fouilles archéologiques": Mme Jaubert, who is directing the excavation at Saint-Symphorien, has concluded that the present ruined priory was built very swiftly, perhaps in about five years; see further, Redelius, "Observations architecturales sur Saint-Symphorien."

[273] *Guide historique . . . de Domfront*, pp. 18–19, 28–33; Susong, "Notre-Dame-sur-l'Eau à Domfront," dating its construction to the end of the eleventh century and the beginning of the twelfth (p. 9).

[274] Musset, *Normandie romane*, vol. 1: *La Basse-Normandie*, pp. 211–213.

[275] Ibid., p. 213: Professor Musset finds architectural points in common with "certaines églises de la région caennaise" and cites the example of Rots, a similarly admirable specimen of Norman architecture located a few kilometers west-north-west of Caen, toward Bayeux.

priories of the nearby abbey of Lonlay, which itself had been rebuilt about 1100.[276] On the basis of the archaeological evidence it is possible to credit Henry with the construction of all four of these impressive stone structures—the castle, the two priories, and the abbey—during the years just following 1092.

But it would be hazardous to conclude too quickly that Henry was the Pericles of late eleventh-century Domfront. There is first of all the possibility that Henry may have had little directly to do with the rebuilding of Lonlay Abbey or even Notre-Dame-sur-l'Eau. The surviving Romanesque portions of Lonlay disclose the architectural influence not of Normandy but of the Loire Valley, and the impetus for rebuilding may have come less from Henry than from the abbot and monks themselves—assisted of course by the economic vitality that Henry's activities would have brought to the region. It is possible too that the impetus for the rebuilding of Notre-Dame-sur-l'Eau came primarily from the mother house at Lonlay rather than the lord of Domfront.[277] Second, one must bear in mind the extreme difficulty of providing precise dates for ruined and excavated monuments in the absence of relevant documentary information. Because of the absence of historical texts from this period bearing on the monuments of Domfront, the interval of 1092–1100 is too small a keyhole in which to fit them. Historians and archaeologists differ as to the years of construction. Whereas the specialists working on the current excavations lean toward the years 1092–1100, they are too experienced to insist on them and would certainly allow the possibility of an early twelfth-century date. Lucien Musset doubts that the surviving Romanesque portions of Lonlay Abbey could antedate 1100; most specialists would share his view that the elegant choir of Notre-Dame-sur-l'Eau rose toward the beginning of the twelfth century even if, as seems likely, the less elaborate nave was built in the late eleventh.[278] And whereas Mme Jaubert, director of excavations at Saint-Symphorien, believes that it is concurrent with the keep and dates from about 1100, Dr Louise has recently suggested that the keep may date from as late as the 1120s.[279] It must be remembered that

---

[276] Ibid., p. 34: the former Benedictine abbey of Notre-Dame de Lonlay, founded by William I of Bellême (above, this chapter, n. 254) and colonized by monks of Fleury-sur-Loire, is now the parish church of the town of Lonlay l'Abbaye, some five miles north-northwest of Domfront. The abbey's nave was destroyed altogether by unidentified culprits of the fifteenth or sixteenth century; the choir was rebuilt in the Gothic style, leaving only the transepts to exemplify the Romanesque building of ca. 1100.

[277] Ibid., pp. 34, 213.

[278] Ibid., pp. 34, 212–213.

[279] Louise, "Châteaux et pouvoirs," pp. 21–22; Jaubert, "Fouilles archéologiques,"

Domfront remained a very special place for Henry long after his coronation,[280] and rather than limiting its building program to 1092–1100 one should view it as progressing as Henry advanced from robber baron to count and finally to king, and quite likely continuing through his reign. Henry's impact on Domfront during the forty-three years of his lordship was, as Louise aptly puts it, "spectaculaire." Domfront under Henry, he adds, became "un vaste chantier," a boom town vitalized directly or indirectly by the wealth of the English monarchy.[281]

While Henry was recovering his power in western Normandy, Robert Curthose continued to harbor a deep grudge toward Rufus for violating their treaty of 1091. The duke sent messengers to the king's 1093 Christmas court at Gloucester with the angry ultimatum that unless the king carried out the terms of the treaty (presumably with regard to the promise of English lands), Curthose would repudiate it utterly. The duke accused his royal brother of being "forsworn and faithless" unless he would either honor the treaty immediately or journey to Rouen where it had been made and submit to the formal judgment of the twelve jurors from each side who had confirmed it by their oaths. Whether goaded by the duke's challenge or—more likely—eager for a second try at conquering Normandy, Rufus crossed the Channel on 19 March 1094.[282] Over the previous months he had scoured England for money, so that even though he was willing to confer with the duke, he also brought with him a substantial war chest.[283]

The negotiations went badly. When the jurors concluded that Rufus was entirely responsible for the violations, he rejected their judgment and refused to honor the treaty further. The brothers thereupon parted "with much dissension," and Rufus headed northeastward to his previous military base at Eu to prepare for war. He is said to have drawn

pp. 5–13. Louise's date, suggested by the many similar rectangular keeps built by Henry I ca. 1120–1135 and enumerated by Robert of Torigny, is perhaps weakened by the fact that Domfront is not on Robert's list; but Robert warns his readers that the list is incomplete (*GND*, 2:250–251). Similarly, the notion that Henry's benefactions to Saint-Symphorien and (if any) Lonlay and Notre-Dame-sur-l'Eau antedated his coronation finds qualified support in the fact that no such benefactions are recorded in the very considerable charter evidence surviving from his reign.

[280] OV, 5:318.

[281] Louise, "Châteaux et pouvoirs," p. 21.

[282] On the campaign of 1094 and its background the best source is *ASC, s.a.* 1094; much the same information, but with a few additions and variations, is to be found in FW, 2:33–35, and HH, pp. 217–218. Barlow provides an expert summary (*Rufus,* pp. 331–336): in analyzing Rufus' motives, Barlow may perhaps be too reluctant to include among them the conquest of Normandy.

[283] References to the king's unbridled fund raising are to be be found in Eadmer, *HN,* pp. 43–45, 50–52, 74–75; FW, 2:35; HH, pp. 216–217; WM, *GR,* 2:376.

knights to his cause from far and wide by a lavish distribution of gold, silver, and promises.[284] But although he captured Helias of Saint-Saens' castle of Bures-en-Bray and was able as before to bribe some lesser lords of upper Normandy to defect from the duke, his campaign seems gradually to have bogged down. Eadmer of Canterbury believed that its lack of success resulted from the king's having quarreled with Archbishop Anselm and refused his blessing as the royal fleet was about to embark for Normandy: "As to his blessings and prayers," Eadmer quotes Rufus as saying on that occasion, "I utterly abominate them and spew them from me!"[285] Whatever the damage that farewell quarrel may have done to the morale of Rufus' men, his campaign was also hindered by the duke's qualified success in winning the military support of King Philip I—who obtained the surrender of Alençon without bloodshed but afterward proved vulnerable once again to the lure of silver.[286] Although Rufus conducted the usual plundering and captive-taking expeditions against the duke's lands and Curthose succeeded in recapturing one of the king's castles, there was never any serious military confrontation between the two.[287] Rufus stayed in the northeast, Curthose by and large in the southeast. And Henry, in Domfront and western Normandy, remained well clear of the action.[288]

While the war of sieges and pillaging dragged on inconclusively, changes of major significance to Anglo-Norman politics were occurring in the fortunes of two great baronial families: Montgomery and Beaumont. On the death of Roger of Montgomery on 27 July 1094 his earldom of Shropshire passed, as expected, to his second son, Hugh of Montgomery, while all the Montgomery lands in Normandy passed to Robert of Bellême.[289] Combined with the Bellême lands just to the

---

[284] FW, 2:34.

[285] Eadmer, HN, pp. 47–52.

[286] Philip took hundreds of captives at Alençon, ransomed them, and returned home; afterward he joined Curthose in what was to be an attack on Eu, but the campaign collapsed "when the king was turned away from his purpose by intrigue": ASC, s.a. 1094.

[287] Ibid. (and above, this chapter, n. 258); FW, 2:34–35: Curthose besieged a castle called "Hulme" (ASC) or "Holm" (FW) until its custodian William Peverel, who was defending it for the king, surrendered the stronghold with its garrison of (allegedly) 800 men. Barlow (Rufus, p. 333 and n. 293) seems correct in placing the castle somewhere in the pagus Holmensis, in the Hiémois south of Falaise, and rejecting Freeman's contention that it was the castle of Le Homme in the northern Cotentin, which is improbably distant from the main theaters of military operations: Freeman, Rufus, 1:462, following Magni rotuli, ed. Stapleton, 2:xxv, xxviii.

[288] Such is the unmistakable implication of ASC, s.a. 1094.

[289] CP, 11:683–692; Louise, Seigneurie de Bellême, 1(2):387 ff.; Mason, "Montgomery and His Sons." Barlow suspects that the succession to the Norman Montgomery lands may have been disputed very briefly by Robert's younger brother, Roger the Poitevin, but the evidence is far from conclusive: Rufus, pp. 332–333.

south of them, which Robert had inherited from his mother, they brought him immense wealth and power in Normandy, Maine, and the surrounding marches.[290] Although Robert is not known to have participated in the warfare of 1094, his vastly increased strength posed an ominous threat to his enemies—who included not only baronial neighbors such as the Giroies and Grandmesnils and the counts of Perche but also King William II himself, and of course Henry.

Still another of Normandy's foremost families, the Beaumonts, underwent a change as well. The year 1094 also marked the death of the aged paterfamilias Roger of Beaumont, close friend and kinsman of the Conqueror and one of the duchy's wealthiest magnates.[291] But the political significance of Roger of Beaumont's death was relatively slight because he had been inactive for some years before he retired to die in the family abbey of Préaux. Well before his retirement, Roger had left all his lands to his eldest son, Robert count of Meulan, who had also acquired his mother's county of Meulan in the *Vexin français*. These two great inheritances raised Robert of Meulan to a position of power in the Risle Valley (southwest of Rouen) and across the eastern frontier of Normandy comparable to that of Robert of Bellême in the south. Roger of Beaumont had possessed relatively few lands in England, but William Rufus had elevated a second Beaumont son, Henry, to the earldom of Warwick in return for his loyalty in the rebellion of 1088.[292] Henry of Warwick held a lordship in Normandy as well, consisting of family lands around Le Neubourg not far from his brother's lands along the Risle. The two brothers were close friends and often collaborated to advance their interests, even though they differed in personal style: Henry of Warwick was quiet and retiring; Robert of Meulan, although always exhibiting a mild exterior, was gifted with extraordinary political astuteness and was widely believed to possess the most powerful intelligence among the Anglo-Norman nobility.[293] Both Beaumont brothers were to become friends and admirers of the future Henry I.[294] But with respect to the Anglo-Norman world of the 1090s,

---

[290] On Robert of Bellême's nine castles and many fortified houses in Maine see OV, 5:234 and n. 1; Latouche, *Maine*, pp. 61–62. By the early twelfth century he is said to have held a total of thirty-four castles on the Continent: OV, 6:32.

[291] *CP*, 7:522–526; Vaughn, *Anselm of Bec and Robert of Meulan*, pp. 78–105; Hollister, "Greater Domesday Tenants-in-Chief," pp. 234–235.

[292] *CP*, 12,2:357–360; Le Patourel, *Feudal Empires*, pp. vi, 14–15; Vaughn, *Anselm of Bec and Robert of Meulan*, pp. 103–104 and n. 108: on the occasion of Henry of Warwick's promotion to the countship, Robert of Meulan gave all his own Domesday lands to his brother, retaining only his father's modest lands in Dorset.

[293] Several contemporary writers comment on Robert of Meulan's keen mind: cited and quoted in Vaughn, *Anselm of Bec and Robert of Meulan*, pp. 6–9.

[294] WM, *GR*, 2:470 (reporting Henry of Warwick's friendship and support at the point of Henry's being elected king); OV, 5:294, naming Robert of Meulan (and him alone) as Henry's companion as he rode from Winchester to London for his coronation.

the great shift in the family's political orientation occurred when Robert of Meulan decided to abandon Duke Robert's court for that of King William. The shift was not abrupt: but whereas one finds Robert of Meulan attesting ducal charters regularly during the late 1080s and early 1090s, by 1093 he is in England attesting royal charters and advising Rufus in his heated conflict with Archbishop Anselm.[295] It was characteristic of Robert of Meulan's political style that he continued to visit the ducal court, although rarely.[296] The change was not so much a matter of burning one's bridges as of shifting one's balance. But as a consequence, Curthose could no longer depend on the allegiance of the Beaumont castles along the Risle, dangerously close to Rouen.

It was probably in the early autumn of 1094 that William Rufus, his military campaign having stalled, sent a message to Henry at Domfront asking for his help.[297] The king promised to send ships to bring both Henry and Hugh earl of Chester from western Normandy to the royal headquarters at Eu, "because they could not go through Normandy in peace."[298] The continuing strength of Curthose and his adherents around Rouen and in central Normandy would have impeded an overland journey. Henry and Hugh responded to the royal summons, but once having embarked, probably from the port of Barfleur in the Cotentin,[299] they sailed not to Eu but to Southampton, arriving on 31 October and traveling on to London. This change in destination, which the Anglo-Saxon chronicler does not explain, was doubtless the result of a second message from Rufus, perhaps to Henry and Hugh's embarkation port in the Cotentin. As autumn progressed and the king's campaign continued to go badly, he decided to abandon the war for a time and return to England. He may also have been drawn homeward by reports of renewed military activity by the Welsh, against whom the king led an expedition shortly after his return, with mediocre results. Having decided to leave Normandy, Rufus would doubtless have made every effort to inform Henry of his change of plan. Indeed, Henry of Huntingdon, when repeating the Anglo-Saxon chronicler's story, amends it to state that Rufus had asked Henry to meet him in England

---

[295] Vaughn, *Anselm of Bec and Robert of Meulan*, pp. 101–105, 164; Haskins, *NI*, pp. 68, 70, 76, 285, 292; Eadmer, *HN*, pp. 40, 86; OV, 5:26, where Robert of Meulan's name occurs on a list of Rufus' supporters against Curthose around the mid-1090s.

[296] *Lives of William and Boso*, PL 150, col. 717 (trans. Vaughn, *Abbey of Bec*, pp. 120–121), placing Robert of Meulan at Robert Curthose's court in autumn or early winter 1093.

[297] *ASC*, s.a. 1094.

[298] Ibid.; cf. *Ann. Wint.*, p. 38.

[299] Barfleur is the only port in western Normandy known to have been used by Anglo-Norman kings for their crossings to England: Le Patourel, *Norman Empire*, pp. 163–164, 175–176.

to spend Christmas in London.[300] Henry was indeed in London at Christmas, but Rufus was still awaiting his crossing at the port of Wissant in Boulogne. The king crossed to Dover on 29 December and presumably conferred with Henry soon afterward. The visit is probably marked by the attestation of "Henry the king's brother" on a royal charter granting the priory of Bermondsey, London, to La Charité-sur-Loire. The charter also bears the *signa* of three bishops, several royal *curiales*, and a number of others and could well have emanated from a rump Christmas court.[301] Henry lingered in England until spring 1095, when, as the Anglo-Saxon chronicler expresses it, "he crossed back to Normandy with great treasures, in fealty to the king against their brother." Thereafter, the chronicler adds, he fought often against the duke "and did him much damage both in land and men."[302]

That same fall, while Henry was harassing Curthose's territories, there occurred an event that would transform the Anglo-Norman world and all of Western Christendom: the calling of the First Crusade by Pope Urban II at the Council of Clermont in November 1095. Among the throng of churchmen and laymen attending the council was Henry's old nemesis, Odo bishop of Bayeux. Also at Clermont were two other Norman bishops, Gilbert of Evreux (known as "the crane" because of his extraordinary height) and Serlo of Sées, former abbot of Orderic's Saint-Evroul.[303] On their return to Normandy all three, along with many other Norman prelates, participated in a provincial synod at Rouen in February 1096 summoned by Archbishop William Bonne-Ame at which the decrees of Clermont were promulgated.[304] Shortly thereafter Robert Curthose resolved to join the crusade, and among the Normans who chose to accompany him was Bishop Odo.[305]

Orderic is doubtless correct in suggesting that by 1096 Robert

[300] HH, pp. 217–218.
[301] On William II's arrival date see FW, 2:35; cf. *ASC, s.a.* 1095 (beginning the year at Christmas). The royal charter, *RRAN* 1, no. 398, is dated 1093–1097 by the editor; it is all but impossible that Rufus and Henry were together in peace at any time during this interval other than during Henry's visit to England in 1094–1095 (with Rufus arriving on 29 December and Henry departing in the spring), or, just possibly, 1097, when Rufus returned from Normandy during Lent (Easter: 5 April: FW, 2:40–41); Henry is not mentioned by any source as being in England during 1097 but might conceivably have accompanied the king nonetheless; one of the charter's attesters, Walchelin bishop of Worcester, died on 3 January 1098.
[302] *ASC, s.a.* 1095; HH, p. 218; *Ann. Wint.*, p. 38.
[303] OV, 5:18.
[304] Ibid., 5:18–24; *Concilia rotomagensis provinciae*, ed. Bessin, 1:77–79; Foreville, "The Synod of the Province of Rouen," p. 31.
[305] David, *Curthose*, pp. 89–96, 221–229.

Curthose had fallen on hard times. Henry was once again a dominating force in the west, having "gained control of a large part of Normandy either by influence or by arms," while Rufus' power, despite the disappointing outcome of the 1094 campaign, remained formidable in the central and eastern parts of the duchy. Among the Norman magnates whom Orderic names as now supporting the king were his longtime allies in the northeast—Robert count of Eu, Stephen of Aumale, Walter Giffard, and Gerard of Gournay—along with Ralph of Conches in the Evreçin and, more recently, Robert count of Meulan, with his powerful string of Beaumont castles in the Risle Valley.[306] In the absence of firm ducal authority the peace of Normandy was shattered by feuds and private warfare, and Curthose, "distressed at the sight of such misery and fearing still worse to come since almost everyone had abandoned him, resolved on the advice of certain men of religion to relinquish the governance of the duchy to his brother" and take up the Cross.[307] Needing money as usual, Curthose arranged, through the intervention of the papal envoy Jarento abbot of Saint-Bénigne, Dijon, to make peace with Rufus and to grant him Normandy in pawn for ten thousand marks of silver.[308] It was slightly more than double the amount that Henry had given Curthose for western Normandy, and although the arrangement in 1096 was a pledge rather than a sale, envisioning a resumption of ducal authority by Curthose after a period of three to five years, it seems most unlikely that Rufus ever intended to relinquish the duchy he had struggled so long to possess.[309] Bishop Odo, who also faced joyless prospects in a principality now to be dominated by Rufus and Henry,[310] may well have been engaging in fund raising for his journey when on 24 May 1096 he granted the important church of Saint-Vigor, Bayeux, to Abbot Jarento and Saint-Bénigne, Dijon.[311]

In September 1096 Rufus personally conveyed the ten thousand marks to Curthose in Normandy and the duke set off for Constantinople and the Holy Land. Bishop Odo died en route in Norman Italy and was entombed at Palermo Cathedral, where he still lies. And with Odo conveniently out of the picture, William Rufus for-

---

[306] OV, 5:26; above, pp. 95–96. To this list Orderic adds Philip of Briouze, Richard of Courcy, "and many others."

[307] OV, 5:26.

[308] For discussions of the terms see Barlow, *Rufus*, p. 363 and n. 104; David, *Curthose*, pp. 91–92.

[309] *MMI*, pp. 66–67; OV, 5:280. (Barlow disagrees: *Rufus*, pp. 414–415.)

[310] OV, 5:208–210: Odo seems to have been unable to effect a reconciliation with either Henry or Rufus.

[311] *RRAN* 1, no. 376; Haskins, *NI*, pp. 67 and n. 19, 75–76.

mally regranted to Henry the countship of the Cotentin with authority over all western Normandy including the Bessin, apart from Bayeux and Caen.[312]

For the next four years Henry stayed out of the limelight. Robert of Torigny states that after joining Rufus in Normandy in 1096 Henry thereafter remained at the king's side, and Orderic includes him along with William count of Evreux, Hugh earl of Chester, and Walter Giffard as one of the leaders of Rufus' army during his Vexin campaigns of 1097–1098.[313] But we are told nothing more of his participation in Rufus' military activities, either in the Vexin or in Maine. Since Robert of Bellême served as Rufus' chief commander in both regions, it may be that Henry found it more comfortable to attend to his own affairs in western Normandy or Domfront.[314]

We do know that Henry was present at the royal court in England on at least two occasions during the last fifteen months of Rufus' reign. He was with the king in London on Pentecost (29 May) 1099 where, as "Henry brother of the king," he witnessed a charter in which Rufus announced the appointment of his ubiquitous and widely loathed henchman Ranulf Flambard to the bishopric of Durham. It was, as the Anglo-Saxon chronicler pointed out, the first occasion on which a royal court assembled at William Rufus' stunning new palace at Westminster.[315] The palace stands to this day some 240 feet in length, perhaps the largest stone hall of its time in all of Europe. When Rufus' courtiers commented on its size, the king is said to have responded, with characteristic overstatement, that it wasn't half big enough for him.[316] More than a year later, Henry was reported to have been a member of William Rufus' fateful hunting party on 2 August 1100.[317]

On this, the final day of his life, William Rufus was at the pinnacle of his power. Still only forty or forty-one years old, he was master of England and Normandy alike. He had every expectation of extending his authority—at least for a time—to Poitou and probably all Aquitaine, having accepted a proposal by Duke William IX to mortgage his dominions and go on crusade, just as Curthose had done. In Orderic's words, Rufus "snatched at the opportunity to add the duke's wide possessions

[312] GND, 2:210–213; Hugh of Flavigny, Chronicon, MGH, SS, 8:474–475; OV, 5:32–34, 208.
[313] GND, 2:210–213; OV, 5:214.
[314] OV, 5:214, 242.
[315] RRAN 2:415 (no. 414a); ASC, s.a. 1099; FW, 2:44.
[316] HH, p. 231; Barlow, Rufus, pp. 372, 400.
[317] OV, 5:290; ASC, s.a. 1100.

to his father's duchy and kingdom."[318] Indeed, rumors were circulating that Rufus aspired to the throne of France itself.[319] He had amassed a huge treasure with which to consummate the agreement with William IX, and at the time of his death he was on the point of leading a formidable army across the Channel. "Like a lion ready to pounce on its prey," as Orderic colorfully expressed it, William Rufus intended to "offer battle to prevent his brother from entering Normandy, purchase the duchy of Aquitaine with great sums of silver, and, conquering all who resisted him, extend the limits of his empire [*imperium*] to the River Garonne."[320]

In the light of these hopes and plans, the impact of Rufus' sudden and unexpected death was jolting, and accounts of the event quickly became entangled in a thicket of legend. There were stories of prophecies and forewarnings—usual to the ex post facto narratives of great historical discontinuities in the Middle Ages.[321] Since Rufus suffered a notorious reputation as a plunderer of the Church[322] and had therefore been roundly despised by most of the English clergy (with the exception of his hand-picked bench of curial bishops), it is perhaps understandable that churchmen might dream wishfully of his death. William of Malmesbury reports (retrospectively, of course) that on the morning of the shooting in the New Forest a certain foreign monk came to the royal court and reported dreaming that Rufus had been gnawing on the arms and legs of a crucifix. At length the crucifix kicked the king, who fell backward and began breathing out flames and smoke that rose into the heavens. According to Orderic, a monk of Gloucester had a vision of a young virgin—representing the Church—begging Jesus in heaven to strike out in vengeance against her royal oppressor. Jesus replied that the virgin should bear her oppression patiently for she would soon be avenged. On 1 August, we are told, Fulchered abbot of Shrewsbury, preaching at the same abbey of Gloucester, prophesied

---

[318] OV, 5:280 and n. 2: "Is nimirum decreuit Guillelmo Rufo regi Anglorum Aquitaniae ducatum totamque terram suam inuadiare"; WM, *GR*, 2:379, less specifically: "comes Pictavensis Jerosolimam ire gestiens, ei terram suam pro pecunia invadaturus dicebatur." Orderic's identification of the pledged territories as the duchy of Aquitaine and all the lands of its duke is entirely consistent with Malmesbury's identification of them as the land of the count of Poitou. The troubadour prince William IX duke of Aquitaine (= William VII count of Poitou) had served in Rufus' Vexin campaign of 1098; the arrangement to pawn Aquitaine was aborted on Rufus' death, but William IX managed his crusade nevertheless, departing in 1101: OV, 5:324; Riley-Smith, *The First Crusade and the Idea of Crusading*, pp. 126, 128–131.

[319] Suger, *Louis le Gros*, p. 10; *MMI*, p. 67.

[320] OV, 5:280; *MMI*, p. 67.

[321] On these prophecies see *MMI*, pp. 62–64 with references.

[322] Jared, "English Ecclesiastical Vacancies"; Hollister, "William II, Henry I, and the Anglo-Norman Church."

a sudden change in affairs that would soon free England from iniquity: "The blow of divine vengeance is bent on the sinner, and the swift arrow is out of its quiver ready to wound. The blow will quickly be struck." On the following morning Rufus is reported to have received a message from Serlo abbot of Gloucester warning him of these premonitions. Exploding with mirth, so Orderic tells us, the king told his companions (among whom, very probably, was Henry) that he had more important things to do than listen to the dreams of snoring monks.[323]

Other writers attributed similar prophecies of Rufus' death to such diverse persons as St Hugh abbot of Cluny, St Anselm in his French exile, and Merlin the Magician from his remote perspective back in the sixth century.[324] But if any such stories were conveyed to the king and his companions on that August morning, one can well believe Orderic's report that Rufus laughed them off as the idle dreams of monks. The king himself is likelier to have been dreaming of Christmas in Poitiers, or perhaps even April in Paris, as he set off on his final hunt.

[323] OV, 5:284–288.
[324] *MMI*, p. 63.

Chapter 3

KINGSHIP AND DEFENSE

"The death of William Rufus," E. A. Freeman asserted, "is one of those events in English history which are familiar to every memory and come readily to every mouth."[1] Like the constructing of Stonehenge, Hitler's suicide, and the assassination of John F. Kennedy, it is the kind of striking historical event that has evoked an abundance of tenuous speculations and intricate hypotheses. But with regard to Rufus' death, elaborate theories of this sort were late in developing. Until well into the modern era, explanations of the shooting were relatively straightforward: a misaimed arrow, guided no doubt by the avenging hand of God.

The several and varying contemporary reports of the event have been subjected to meticulous historical analysis, most notably and skillfully by E. A. Freeman and Frank Barlow.[2] But despite the differences one encounters in contemporary accounts—by the Anglo-Saxon and Worcester chroniclers, William of Malmesbury, Orderic Vitalis, and others—it is clear, as Barlow shrewdly concludes, that "there is only one story."[3] On Thursday, 2 August 1100, William Rufus and his hunting party fanned out into the New Forest at an unusually late hour—after the midday meal instead of early morning, as was customary. The king may have been delayed by pressing royal business, or by mild alarm at prophecies of danger ahead, or—as Barlow speculates—by a royal hangover.

Whatever the reason, Rufus set out for the hunt in the afternoon, accompanied by his huntsmen and a number of notable men of his entourage. Reliable sources indicate that among these companions were Count Henry, the Beaumont brothers Henry earl of Warwick and

---

[1] Freeman, *Rufus*, 2:336; I have borrowed this splendid quote from Freeman, along with other materials and ideas in these pages, from my "Strange Death of William Rufus," in *MMI*, pp. 59–75, where the various conspiracy theories bearing on the death of Rufus are analyzed and dismissed.

[2] Freeman, *Rufus*, 2:310–343, 667–676; Barlow, *Rufus*, pp. 408–432. Other modern accounts, briefer and more speculative, are Warren, "The Death of William Rufus"; Brooke, *Saxon and Norman Kings*, pp. 164–172; and Poole, *Domesday Book to Magna Carta*, pp. 113–114.

[3] Barlow, *Rufus*, p. 425; similarly, Freeman, *Rufus*, 2:658.

Robert count of Meulan, Robert fitz Hamon, William of Breteuil (son and Norman heir of the great Conquest magnate William fitz Osbern), and the French magnate Walter Tirel, lord of Poix in Ponthieu and castellan of Pontoise in the French Vexin—who was both a boon companion of William Rufus' and a friend of St Anselm's.[4]

The rest of the story is simple and brief. One of Rufus' huntsmen or companions, allegedly Walter Tirel, stood opposite him in the woods and fired an arrow that (perhaps grazing a stag) pierced the king's chest. Malmesbury reports that Rufus fell forward onto the ground, driving the arrow through his body. All agree that the king died almost immediately, unable to evade hell by confessing his many sins. Walter Tirel, whom William of Malmesbury and Orderic both accused of firing the arrow (which Walter later vehemently denied), fled immediately for his lordship in France. The accusation alone would have sent him dashing off to safety whether he actually fired the arrow or not. The other barons in the hunt, on hearing of the king's death, galloped off to safeguard their own interests—to secure their fortresses or to engage in plunder, or both. The intervals between the death of a king and the crowning of his successor were typically anarchic. Some of the humbler royal attendants threw a rough cloth over Rufus' body and carried him off to nearby Winchester, "like a wild boar stuck with spears."[5] As a consequence of Rufus' policy of sequestering bishoprics and abbacies and draining off their revenues, Winchester was without a bishop. The royal funeral and burial were supervised by the cathedral prior, Geoffrey of Cambray, an accomplished poet and a person of notable sanctity, who would doubtless have seen to it that the obsequies for the anticlerical blasphemer were austere.

Among those magnates who rushed off to secure their interests was Count Henry, who immediately dashed to Winchester to take possession of the royal treasure, probably accompanied by the two Beaumont brothers. There is nothing in Henry's actions or the Beaumonts' to suggest foreknowledge of the event. At the news of Rufus' death the options would have been obvious, and Henry and the Beaumonts were by no means dull-witted. Neither Henry's prompt response nor any other aspects of the momentous event suggest an assassination conspiracy involving either Henry, an Anglo-Norman baronial faction, or (as has recently been proposed) the French royal house. Nor was Rufus affiliated with a witchcraft cult through which he contrived

---

[4] Eadmer, *Vita Anselmi*, pp. 27–28; OV, 5:288. Geoffrey Gaimar adds the names of Gilbert of Laigle and Gilbert and Roger of Clare, and while he could well be correct, his account of Rufus' death and burial is so grossly error-ridden as to be altogether unreliable: *L'Estoire des Engleis*, ll. 6348 ff.; cf. *MMI*, pp. 68–70.

[5] OV, 5:292; WM, *GR*, 2:378.

his own death.[6] By far the likeliest explanation for the killing is simply, as everyone supposed at the time, that it was a hunting accident.

This explanation seemed reasonable enough to contemporaries because such accidents were by no means uncommon. They had already accounted for the deaths of two members of the Norman ducal family: Richard son of William the Conqueror and, earlier in 1100, Richard natural son of Robert Curthose (both in the New Forest). In 1143 Miles of Gloucester earl of Hereford, while hunting deer on Christmas Eve, "was pierced through the breast by a knight, who shot an arrow wildly at a stag, and died wretchedly without profit from repentance."[7] At about the same time Malcolm of Morville perished in a hunting accident in Scotland, the victim of Adulf of St Martin's poor aim.[8] There is no evidence that these deaths were anything but accidental, nor is there any evidence that Rufus' was. Theories of witchcraft, conspiracy, and murder only demonstrate how a fortuitous chain of events involving a person of great eminence can acquire a misleading aura of premeditation when viewed in retrospect.

Having galloped to nearby Winchester to obtain control of the castle and royal treasure and to gain baronial assent to his accession as king of the English, Henry was challenged by William of Breteuil, also recently arrived at Winchester, who reminded Henry and the barons that they had all sworn homage to Robert Curthose. Regardless of his capricious reputation in earlier years, Curthose was now a respected crusader, and he was reported to be on his way home from Apulia. Henry, drawing his sword, declared that he would suffer no upstart to cause "ill founded delay in seizing his father's sceptre before he could."[9] With the support of other barons led by Henry earl of Warwick, "with whom he had long been in the strictest intimacy," Henry assumed control of the royal castle with its treasure and was acclaimed king of the English by the barons who happened to be present.[10] This show of

---

[6] For conspiracy or cultist theories alleged to explain the killing of William Rufus see Murray, *God of the Witches*; Williamson, *Arrow and the Sword*, pp. 105–119; and Grinnell-Milne, *The Killing of William Rufus*. Emma Mason ("William Rufus and the Historians," pp. 17–20) advances the surprising idea that Rufus was the victim of an international, French-inspired assassination plot directed by the future Louis VI.

[7] *Gesta Stephani*, p. 160; cf. ibid., pp. 24, 148; John of Hexham, in SD, 2:315.

[8] *Liber S. Marie de Dryburgh*, pp. 68–69.

[9] OV, 5:290. Robert Curthose's behavior on the crusade was in fact less than heroic: David, *Curthose*, pp. 89–119.

[10] On Henry of Warwick, WM, *GR*, 2:470; on the probability that in 1100 the Winchester treasury was located in the Conqueror's castle rather than the pre-Conquest central palace, see *Winchester in the Early Middle Ages*, ed. Barlow et al., pp. 291, 295, 304–305.

baronial support was regarded, not unreasonably, as an "election" by the "people," which was a traditional prerequisite for accession to the English throne—along with anointing and coronation. Baronial "elections" of new kings were often highly informal and unrepresentative affairs, and Henry's was neither better nor worse than most. Having made good his claim to the royal treasure and having obtained a sufficient measure of baronial assent, he then turned to the matter of his coronation. In the company of Robert count of Meulan, the older and shrewder of the Beaumont brothers, Henry set off for Westminster.[11]

Henry's claim on the kingship of England cannot be regarded as a "usurpation." The Conqueror's eldest son, Robert Curthose, had already been passed over once for the royal succession, at his father's command. It has been alleged that the succession had been decided by a formal agreement between Curthose and Rufus in 1091, but this is incorrect. In the words of the Anglo-Saxon chronicler, the agreement of 1091 "lasted only a little while"; Curthose repudiated it at Christmas 1093 and it is not known to have been renewed.[12] Henry justified his claim to the throne, in part, by the theory of "porphyrogeniture," the right of having been the only one of the Conqueror's sons to have been born of a reigning king and queen—born "in the purple."[13] This theory, which has Persian, late Roman, and (especially) Byzantine precedents, is inconclusive, but perhaps little more so than primogeniture, which, as of AD 1100, had very rarely determined the English royal succession. Kin-right was a crucial principle in determining a claim to the English throne, but being the *eldest* son of the previous king did not ensure succession, as illustrated not only in the case of William Rufus in 1087 but also in such instances as that of Alfred the Great in 871. Primogeniture had played a more important role in succession to the dukedom of Normandy, but Henry was not at the moment claiming that office. His title to the English crown was, in short, by no means fraudulent.

---

[11] OV, 5:294. On Henry's election, see his coronation charter, clause 1, *Select Charters*, ed. Stubbs and Davis, p. 117: "Sciatis me Dei misericordia et communi consilio baronum totius Angliae ejusdem regni regem coronatum esse"; *ASC, s.a.* 1100; HH, p. 233; RT, *Chron., s.a.* 1100; WM, *GR*, 2:470. The Hyde chronicler (*Liber de Hyda*, p. 304) and RT, *GND*, 2:216, place the election at Westminster at the coronation.

[12] For the idea of an arrangement between Curthose and Rufus that each was the other's heir: Brooke, *Saxon and Norman Kings*, p. 165; but see *ASC, s.a.* 1093; *MMI*, p. 66.

[13] Lintzel, "Heinricus natus in aula regali," pp. 86–95; Kern, *Gottesgnadentum und Widerstandsrecht*, pp. 27–28 (= *Kingship and Law*, p. 18); Dagron, "Nés dans le Pourpre"; cf. Brooke, *Saxon and Norman Kings*, pp. 171–172.

It was, however, debatable, and that fact presented grave difficulties to Henry during the initial year of his reign. The greatest impediment to his acceptance as king was not that he was a younger son but that he and most of the Anglo-Norman barons were already homage-bound to Curthose.

Determined to avert the anarchic conditions that a long royal vacancy invited and to forestall Curthose and other possible rivals, Henry moved as swiftly as possible to secure the throne. Departing Winchester shortly after his "election," in the company of Robert count of Meulan, he probably made the seventy-mile journey to Westminster on Saturday, 4 August, and, traveling light, could have completed it in a day.[14] He would thus have spent Saturday evening at Westminster, in ample time for a traditional Sunday coronation. The formalities took place on Sunday, 5 August, in Edward the Confessor's majestic Westminster Abbey, the site of the two previous Anglo-Norman coronations.[15] The ceremony was performed neither by Anselm archbishop of Canterbury, whose conflicts with Rufus had propelled him into exile in France, nor by the second in line, the aged and infirm Thomas I archbishop of York, who was at Ripon when Rufus died and thus too far away to make the long journey to Westminster in time for the hurried coronation. Henry was crowned instead by Maurice bishop of London, formerly an archdeacon of Le Mans and afterward the royal chancellor. Maurice was *ex officio* vicar and senior suffragan bishop of the archbishop of Canterbury and thus the highest ranking prelate available.[16] He is unlikely to have received the news of Rufus' death before 4 August, and during the hours just following he must have been the busiest prelate in Christendom, preparing for a complex ceremony and coronation *ordo* of decisive importance to the English realm, and one that he had never before performed. Henry knew only too well

[14] *MMI*, pp. 64–65.

[15] Edward the Confessor's Westminster Abbey was replaced in the thirteenth century by Henry III's great French Gothic structure, which stands to this day. The Confessor's abbey church, in which Henry I was crowned, resembled the nearly concurrent church of Jumièges Abbey on the lower Seine, which survives today as a magnificently impressive ruin: *Normandie romane: La Haute-Normandie*, pp. 61–126; Gem, "Romanesque Rebuilding of Westminster Abbey," where it is plausibly argued that Jumièges may well have been modeled on Westminster rather than the reverse.

[16] *ASC, s.a.* 1100; OV, 5:294; Thomas of York (who himself died on 18 November 1100) rushed to Westminster on hearing the news but arrived too late for the coronation: Hugh the Chanter, pp. 16–18. Henry's coronation by a bishop of London (who was *ex officio* vicar of Canterbury) would of course have been enormously less offensive to Anselm than a coronation by an archbishop of York. The officiating by Bishop Maurice was thus a convenience in more ways than one.

that the circumstances of his coronation constituted a drastic departure from precedent and, in a letter to Anselm shortly afterward, he went to some length to explain the need for haste. Keenly aware of Canterbury's reluctance to forgo traditional privileges, he made all the appropriate apologies, and Anselm subsequently accepted them without recorded objection.[17]

Because the ceremony had necessarily been arranged in frantic haste and could not safely be postponed, Bishop Maurice is likely to have used the coronation *ordo* most readily at hand, the rite known as the *Third English Ordo*, which seems to have been the work of Archbishop Ealdred of York adapted from a German imperial *ordo* that Ealdred had encountered while visiting Cologne in the 1050s. Archbishop Ealdred evidently utilized this *ordo* in the coronations of both Harold Godwineson and William the Conqueror in 1066, and Archbishop Lanfranc probably used it when he crowned William Rufus in 1087.[18] Historians have argued heatedly over the issue of which *ordo* was employed at which English coronation and for what reasons, but for Henry, as for most kings-elect, the words and structure of the *ordo* were of drastically less importance than the acts of anointment and coronation themselves. Once a person was properly anointed and crowned, he was transformed from a mere mortal into a consecrated *rex*, God's anointed one—a symbol, as many believed, of Christ on earth—and it was extraordinarily difficult to dislodge such a person from his royal office.[19] Hence the tendency for news of a royal death to send an aspirant to the throne dashing to Westminster to be crowned.

---

[17] *AO*, ep. 212; Eadmer, *HN*, pp. 118–120. On the Anglo-Norman custom of archbishops of Canterbury crowning kings see ibid., pp. 292–293, and Gilbert of Limerick, *Liber de statu ecclesiae*, col. 1003.

[18] See especially Nelson, "Rites of the Conqueror" (reprinted in Nelson, *Politics and Ritual in Early Medieval Europe*, pp. 371–401); cf. Lapidge, "The Origin of CCCC 163," and "Ealdred of York"; Bruckmann, "The *Ordines* of the Third Recension of the Medieval English Coronation Order," pp. 99–115; on Rufus' coronation, Barlow, *Rufus*, pp. 57–58.

[19] E.g., Kantorowicz, *The King's Two Bodies*, p. 47: "Christ was king and *Christus* by his very nature, whereas his deputy on earth was king and *christus* by grace only. For . . . the spirit 'leaped' into the terrestrial king at the moment of his consecration to make him 'another man' (*alius vir*)." See further, Kern, *Kingship and Law*, pp. 27–68; the Norman Anonymous, *Die Texte des Normannischen Anonymus*, ed. Pellens, especially texts J 2 (pp. 7–18), J 4 (pp. 35–45), J 12 (pp. 84–90), J 23 (pp. 125–128), J 28 (pp. 214–225), J 29 (pp. 226–230). On the indelible nature of the royal anointing (William Shakespeare, *Richard II*, II, ii):

> Not all the water in the rough rude sea
> Can wash the balm off an anointed king.

The *Third English Ordo*[20] commences with an antiphon, after which the candidate for coronation prostrates himself. After a litany, he stands before the altar and publicly declares the "threefold promise": to keep the peace, to prohibit all rapaciousness and iniquities, and to maintain just laws as well as any king before him has done. Henry, emending tradition (as kings-elect sometimes did), elaborated on the second promise by vowing to put right all the injustices of his brother's reign.[21] After the recitation of these promises, Bishop Maurice asked the magnates, prelates, and officials assembled in the abbey whether they would accept Henry as their king, upon which, as the *ordo* dictated, they proceeded to acclaim him—thus firmly seconding the rather casual election at Winchester. After further prayers, the bishop anointed the upper parts of Henry's body with the blessed oil—his hands, breast, shoulders, elbows, and head—and then anointed his head, for a second time, with sacred chrism. Bishop Maurice next presented Henry with the royal sword, armlet, and pallium. Finally, as the climax of the great liturgical ritual, the bishop blessed the royal crown and, with a prayer, placed it on Henry's head. He then invested Henry with the royal ring, staff, and scepter, and the ceremony concluded with benedictions, the kiss of peace, a *Te Deum*, and Henry's enthronement. As Henry sat upon his throne, the Mass was celebrated, at the conclusion of which the new king received the Holy Eucharist. Afterward, so the Anglo-Saxon chronicler reports, "all in this country submitted to him and swore oaths and became his men."[22]

Eadmer, commenting on Henry's coronation promises of good laws and the repudiation of past oppressions, adds that the new king ordered these promises confirmed by a sacred oath to be published throughout the kingdom in a written document authenticated by the royal seal.[23] It was probably in the course of the journey from Winchester to Westminster that Henry framed this coronation charter, a relatively brief document of fourteen clauses. Concerned primarily

---

Earlier studies of English coronations and their *ordos* include Schramm, *A History of the English Coronation*, and Richardson, "Coronation," pp. 161–180; see further the skeptical and sensible observations of Warren: *Henry II*, p. 244.

[20] *The Pontifical of Magdalen College*, pp. xiii–xxxi, 89–95.

[21] Foreville, "Le Sacre des rois anglo-normands et angevins"; Richardson, "Coronation," pp. 161–180; *ASC, s.a.* 1100; HH, p. 233; Eadmer, *HN*, p. 119; *Select Charters*, ed. Stubbs and Davis, p. 116.

[22] *ASC, s.a.* 1100; *Pontifical of Magdalen College*, pp. 89–95; Nelson, "Rites of the Conqueror," p. 120; Richardson, "Coronation," pp. 177–180. The first English coronation to be described in detail is Richard I's, by Roger of Hoveden, *Gesta Regis Henrici Secundi Benedicti Abbatis*, 2:80; Henry I's coronation was probably similar to it but less well rehearsed.

[23] *ASC, s.a.* 1100; FW, 2:46–47; WM, *GR*, 2:470.

with rectifying abuses alleged to have been committed by the previous regime, it was doubtless contrived with the help of Henry's traveling companion, Robert count of Meulan who, as an intimate counselor of Rufus, had been at his side when many of these policies were formulated. The coronation charter was based on the spoken coronation oaths of Henry and his royal predecessors. But going beyond the oaths of previous kings, it was more elaborate, much longer, and, for the first time, expressed in writing.[24]

Henry I's coronation charter was evidently issued on the day of the crowning.[25] It was evoked in subsequent generations as a guarantee of the rights of free English men and women against the crown: in 1135 or 1136 by King Stephen, in 1154 by Henry II, and perhaps most important in 1215 when Archbishop Stephen Langton cited it as a precedent and model for Magna Carta. But although the coronation charter later became enshrined as a milestone, even the foundation stone, in the long development of the English constitution, it was surely not regarded as such by Henry I or his advisers. For them it was merely one of several expedients to announce his intention to correct the wrongful policies of Rufus' reign and thus to strengthen his own precarious hold on the throne.

The first clause addressed Rufus' widely criticized oppression of the Church. Rufus, on his death, had left vacancies in two bishoprics, including one of the wealthiest (Winchester), and eleven or twelve abbeys, including five of the six wealthiest (Glastonbury, Ely, Bury St Edmunds, St Augustine's, Canterbury, and Abingdon).[26] Nor is there anything to suggest that Rufus was planning to fill any of these prelacies in the foreseeable future. Henry promised to

> make free the Church of God, so that I will neither sell nor lease its property, nor will I, on the death of an archbishop or bishop or abbot, take anything from the demesne of a church or from

---

[24] *Gesetze*, ed. Liebermann, 1:521; *Select Charters*, ed. Stubbs and Davis, pp. 116–119; the best translation is in *EHD*, 2:432–434; the documents are summarized in *RRAN* 2, no. 488.

[25] The date of 5 August is confirmed by the Worcester chronicle, which reports that Henry promulgated the liberties enumerated in his charter "consecrationis suae die": FW, 2:46–47; the date is also implied by Eadmer, *HN*, p. 119, and fixed by the coronation charter itself, which concludes: "Apud Westmonasterium quando coronatus fui": *Select Charters*, ed. Stubbs and Davis, p. 119.

[26] ASC, *s.a.* 1100; WM, *GR*, 2:380; Hollister, "William II, Henry I, and the Anglo-Norman Church," pp. 197–200 and references. Canterbury was also in the hands of the king because of the exile of Archbishop Anselm. Gilbert Crispin had been ruling the sixth abbey, Westminster, since the Conqueror's reign, thereby denying Rufus the opportunity to hold the abbey vacant.

its vassals during the period that elapses until a successor is installed.[27]

Although some scholars have doubted that Henry kept these promises, most authorities on Anglo-Norman church history now agree that he did respect most of them.[28] Henry never in fact relinquished the traditional regalian right to sequester the revenues of churches during vacancies, and it is most unlikely that he intended the above clause as a promise to do so. Rather, he was renouncing the extraordinary measures of which Rufus had been accused: harassing monks or their tenants or reducing the value of their lands by taking reliefs from vacant churches, driving monks from their abbeys, seizing properties whose revenues had been intended for the sustenance of monks, granting new knights fees on the estates of vacant bishoprics, and selling off capital resources through such measures as chopping down orchards and marketing the lumber.[29] There is evidence from the Pipe Roll of 1130 of temporarily vacant and sequestered churches being "farmed"—by other churchmen, royal officials, or tenants of the vacated church, and in one instance military tenants were assessed a knights aid. But although Henry's administration exploited ecclesiastical wealth to a degree and continued the traditional royal practice of diverting normal ecclesiastical revenues into the royal treasury during vacancies, there were no more complaints about new knights fees being created, monks harassed, or orchards cut down. And although vacancies could occasionally stretch on for several years—especially years of military crisis when Henry was overseas—there was no repetition of the scandalous accumulation of vacancies that marked the closing years of Rufus' reign. As a result, the complaints of churchmen were relatively muted under Henry I.[30]

The next eight clauses of the charter undertake to rectify various oppressions suffered by lay subjects, especially aristocratic men and women, during previous regimes. In part, these provisions repudiate abuses inflicted by William Rufus, and in part they reject legal

[27] *Gesetze*, ed. Liebermann, 1:521; translation in *EHD*, 2:433.
[28] *Councils and Synods*, 1: part 2, p. 653; Howell, *Regalian Right*, pp. 21–24: "It is certain that Henry I continued to exercise a claim to the issues of vacant sees and abbeys; it seems a likely hypothesis that he never renounced it."
[29] *Gesta abbatum monasterii S. Albani*, 1:65; Eadmer, *HN*, pp. 26–27; cf. *AO*, epp. 203, 210; *Chron. Ab.*, 2:42, 285; Hollister, "William II, Henry I, and the Anglo-Norman Church," pp. 192–193 with references.
[30] Hollister, "William II, Henry I, and the Anglo-Norman Church," pp. 183–205; for a less optimistic appraisal see Green, *Government*, p. 79, echoed by *Gesta Stephani*, pp. 17–18.

innovations of both Henry's Norman predecessors, returning to what
were seen as the rightful customs of Edward the Confessor. In clause 2,
Henry vows to assess only just and lawful reliefs, not arbitrary sums "as
in the time of my brother." His promise would have had the effect of
stabilizing aristocratic inheritance by assuring families that their lands
would pass to heirs on the payment of a reasonable relief to the king.
Clause 5 seems to reject a policy of both William II and William I by
prohibiting *monetagium*—a general levy imposed by the Conqueror on
the coining of silver pennies—"since it was not levied in the time of
King Edward."[31] Similarly, clause 8 stipulates that pledges of chattels to
cover forfeitures should not be unlimited in amount, as "in the time of
my father and brother," but only to the amount of the forfeiture itself,
as "before the time of my father." Again, clause 9 provides that murder
fines be assessed justly "according to the law of King Edward." In one
instance (clause 11) Henry struck out on his own, granting for the first
time that those who render knights service in return for their lands
shall hold their demesnes free of all gelds and obligations, "so that they
may furnish themselves so well with horses and arms that they may be
properly equipped and ready to discharge my service and defend my
kingdom." But for the most part the coronation charter restored the
good laws of the past. In a statement of general principle (clause 13),
Henry pledged to restore to his subjects "the law of King Edward
together with such emendations to it as my father made with the
council of his barons." This last clause should probably not be taken
to imply that Henry knew precisely which of the Conqueror's laws
were issued with the council of his barons and which were not, but
it was a principle that could at least in theory bridge the chasm, inherent in the charter, between the laws of Edward the Confessor and
the emendations of William the Conqueror. And it left space for
the retention of the Conqueror's laws on matters of major importance
to Henry, for example (clause 10): "By the common council of my
barons I have retained the forests in my own hands as my father did
before me."

In the thirty-five years of his reign, Henry failed to keep all his
coronation promises, as is made clear in the Pipe Roll of 1130. But
the campaign promises of many other regimes have proved fragile
as well. Similarly, Henry promised in 1100 not to give a widow in
marriage without her consent (clause 4), yet in 1130 he collected a
substantial sum from Countess Lucy for the privilege of not having to

---

[31] On *monetagium* see Blackburn, "Coinage and Currency," p. 50; Grierson,
"Domesday Book"; Metcalf, "Taxation of Moneyers." On Henry I's policy on reliefs
in subsequent years see *MMI*, pp. 183–184, as against Stenton, *English Feudalism*,
pp. 219–220. No aristocratic honor is known to have failed to pass to an heir under
Henry I because of an excessive relief.

remarry for five years.[32] Over a generation, promises tend to fade from memory.

Underlying the coronation charter are several basic principles that remained significant, if not always observed, throughout Henry I's reign. The limitation of relief payments committed the new regime to safeguarding the rights of inheritance of loyal tenants-in-chief, and the commitment, whether by conscious royal policy or the deepening of aristocratic roots in the English soil, became increasingly effective as the reign progressed. At Henry's accession, tenure in great estates was fragile; at his death, inheritances were largely secure. Clause 12, arguably a political cliché, became the central aim of Henry's regime and, ultimately, its crowning glory: "I establish a firm peace in all my kingdom, and I order that this peace shall henceforth be kept." The final clause, clause 14, focuses this last statement of principle on an immediate problem, namely, the brief anarchy engendered by the vacant throne: all property seized during the interregnum, whether owned by the king or by others, shall be swiftly returned. If it is returned, no penalty will be exacted; if not, whoever seized it "shall, when discovered, pay a heavy penalty to me." Thus, in a potentially violent and larcenous society, did Henry intend to keep the peace.

"I restore to you," Henry wrote, "the law of King Edward." This was doubtless the fundamental principle underlying the coronation charter, just as the idea of continuity with the Anglo-Saxon royal line and the Anglo-Saxon past was a major theme of Henry's reign. There was of course, literally speaking, no "law of King Edward." Unlike a number of his Old English predecessors, Edward the Confessor issued no dooms. But as is made clear in legal treatises written during Henry I's reign—the *Quadripartitus* and the *Leges Henrici Primi*—the "law of King Edward" was taken to summarize the entire Anglo-Saxon past; it constituted the totality of earlier Anglo-Saxon laws that remained in effect during Edward's reign. The new regime of Henry I would put an end to violent land seizures, arbitrary reliefs, and emergency regulations such as the post-Conquest *murdrum* fine redirected to the problem of English desperadoes assassinating Normans. Such measures would give way to the norms of a more settled, peaceful society such as the Anglo-Saxon era was remembered, wrongly, to have been: hereafter, *murdrum* fines "shall be paid justly, according to the laws of King Edward." And it became one of the dominating goals of legal scholars under the new regime to bring to light and make explicit the laws of Edward the Confessor under which, with cautious Anglo-Norman emendations, the English would thenceforth live.

[32] *PR 31 Henry I*, p. 110.

So far as our sources disclose, the *Laudes regiae* were not chanted at Henry I's coronation. These litany-like acclamations, although employed to exhibit and enhance the prestige of secular rulers, were intended primarily to glorify Christ—as is emphasized by their opening and repeated phrase: *Christus vincit, Christus regnat, Christus imperat.*[33] The first certain occasion on which the *Laudes* were chanted in Norman England was the coronation of Queen Matilda I at the Conqueror's Westminster court of Pentecost 1068.[34] Then and afterward, their use was customarily limited to the great ecclesiastical festivals of Easter, Christmas, and Pentecost, which were also the usual occasions for Anglo-Norman crown-wearings.[35] The *Laudes* may have been omitted from the coronation of 1100 because Henry could not safely postpone the ceremony until Michaelmas or Christmas.

Nevertheless, it was important to the survival of the new regime that Henry should embellish his kingly status with every possible token and display of royalty, and immediately after the coronation he began preparing the way for future crown-wearings at the three great liturgical feasts. The Anglo-Saxon chronicler reports that William the Conqueror

> wore his crown three times a year when he was in England: at Easter at Winchester, at Pentecost at Westminster, and at Christmas at Gloucester, accompanied by all the great men of England: archbishops and bishops, abbots and earls, thegns and knights.[36]

A closer analysis of the English itineraries of William I and William II shows that although their crown-wearings sometimes conformed to this sequence they sometimes did not. Throughout the Anglo-Norman era, crown-wearings were determined as much by royal convenience as by a prescribed cycle of itineration.[37] Nevertheless, Henry issued a writ granting that the traditional coronation abbeys—Winchester, Westminster, and Gloucester—receive full livery and that their chanters receive an

---

[33] See in general Cowdrey, "Anglo-Norman *Laudes regiae*," especially pp. 42–43, 46–47, 65–66. The fundamental study, outdated at points, is Kantorowicz, *Laudes Regiae.*

[34] Shortly before the birth of Henry I: above, p. 31; Cowdrey, "Anglo-Norman *Laudes regiae*," pp. 50–58, where the author also discusses, and finds unlikely, the possibility that the *Laudes* were chanted at William I's coronation at Christmas 1066.

[35] *ASC, s.a.* 1087; Biddle, "Seasonal Festivals."

[36] *ASC, s.a.* 1087 (the translation here, as elsewhere unless otherwise acknowledged, is the author's own); Malmesbury (*GR*, 2:335), elaborating on the chronicler's testimony, dwells at length on the Conqueror's lavish banquets on these three occasions and on the great numbers and distinction of the men whom his great courts attracted from England and abroad.

[37] Biddle, "Seasonal Festivals," *passim.*

ounce of gold "at all feasts when the king wears his crown in their churches." Maurice bishop of London had testified, the writ adds, that these had been the customary allowances under Henry's predecessors.[38]

In the initial, troubled year of his reign Henry was scrupulous about crown-wearings at the great religious festivals. He arranged to be crowned at Christmas 1100, although the ceremony took place not at Gloucester but at the more convenient Westminster. He "wore his crown" again in 1101, at his Easter court at Winchester and at Pentecost (9 June) at St Albans. Afterward, although the chronicles regularly report the convening of great courts, they are silent on the matter of crown-wearings until Eadmer discloses that Henry was crowned at his Christmas court at Westminster in 1109 and again at Windsor in January 1121 at the coronation of his new queen, Adeliza of Louvain. Henry of Huntingdon adds that the king and his new queen were again crowned later in the same year at King Henry's Whitsun court at Westminster.[39] The H fragment of the *Anglo-Saxon Chronicle* reports that Henry wore his crown at his Christmas court of 1113 in Windsor, while the E text of the *Chronicle*, in its notice of the same Windsor court, does not mention a crown-wearing. This discrepancy illustrates the peril of assuming from the silence of chroniclers that Henry remained uncrowned at other great courts. The crownings of 1109 and January 1121 appear in Eadmer only because Canterbury prerogatives were challenged, and it could be that on other occasions the crown-wearings were simply not regarded as news-worthy. Nevertheless, it seems likely that Henry's interest in such display may have become less urgent after Robert Curthose formally relinquished his claim to the throne in August 1101. In any case, Gloucester removed itself decisively from the royal festival list when, in June 1101, the town and abbey were consumed by fire, and it did not return to Henry's circuit of festival councils.[40] Throughout his reign,

[38] *RRAN* 2, no. 490; Round, *The King's Serjeants and Officers of State*, pp. 321–323, where "full livery" is identified as 100 simnels (bread loaves), a third of a tun of wine, and fish in an amount left to the king's discretion. The allusion to Bishop Maurice, who crowned Henry, and the attestation of William bishop elect of Winchester (the chancellor) who also attested the coronation charter, makes 5 August the most likely date. Gilbert Crispin abbot of Westminster, whose interests are well served in this writ and whose church witnessed the royal crowning, attests one version of the coronation charter: *RRAN* 2, no. 488.

[39] *Ann. Wint.*, p. 41; *ASC, s.a.* 1101; Eadmer, *HN*, pp. 212, 292–293; HH, p. 468.

[40] Gloucester was, however, the site of a great council at Candlemas (2 February) 1123; *ASC, s.a.* The sequence of royal crown-wearings in 1100–1101, and the relative silence of the chroniclers thereafter, can be deduced by comparing Biddle's convenient chart of Henry I's whereabouts at the great feasts ("Seasonal Festivals," p. 67) with Farrer's *Outline Itinerary*, the *Anglo-Saxon Chronicle*, the Winchester annals, and the other standard narrative sources. On the 1101 Whitsun court at St Albans and the sequence of Robert Curthose's invasion and subsequent truce, see

Henry continued to use Winchester and Westminster as sites for great councils, on the three major feasts and at other times as well, but he also sometimes convened great councils elsewhere—at such places as Salisbury, St Albans, Dunstable, his hunting park at Woodstock (more often as his reign progressed), and, with increasing frequency, Windsor. It was at Windsor, in September 1101, that Henry and Robert Curthose celebrated their recent peace treaty before a great assemblage of magnates and prelates along with two papal legates. Henry held his court at Windsor again at Pentecost 1103 and at Christmas 1104.[41] His fondness for Windsor became particularly marked from 1110, when he first held his court at New Windsor, which he himself had built on the Thames a short distance from the former castle built by his father. Between 1110 and his final departure from England in 1133, Henry presided over at least seven great courts at New Windsor, substantially more than at any other royal residence.[42]

While attending to such exalted matters as great courts and ceremonial crown-wearings, Henry was also addressing himself to the challenge of building a loyal following. Having been so successful in creating a party of supporters in western Normandy during his youth, he now endeavored to generate similar support for his claim to the English throne. He already enjoyed, from his Norman years, the friendship of major cross-Channel landholders such as the Beaumont

MMI, pp. 85–91; on the Gloucester fire of 6 June 1101, FW, 2:48; Henry would perhaps have been reluctant to risk further offending Archbishop Anselm by engaging in crown-wearings during Anselm's absence on the Continent (April 1103–1107) or at Pentecost 1107 when Anselm was absent because of illness. Nonetheless, Eadmer states that Henry was crowned at his Christmas court of 1109 at Westminster, after Anselm's death, by Richard bishop of London, filling in as vicar of Canterbury and deflecting an assault on the prerogative by the archbishop of York (*HN*, p. 212). The narrative sources state explicitly that Henry did not wear his crown or preside over a great court while in England at Pentecost 1106, Christmas 1110, Easter 1111, Pentecost 1111, Easter 1114, and Pentecost 1114 (*ASC, s.a.*; Biddle, "Seasonal Festivals," p. 67), and Malmesbury makes the general comment that Henry I permitted the custom of great royal festivals to decline: WM, *GR*, 2:335; *Vita Wulfstani*, p. 34. A passage in Eadmer makes clear, however, that in the absence of a watchful primate the king might crown himself: *HN*, pp. 292–293.

[41] For the 1101 and 1103 councils, *RRAN* 2, nos 544–550, 648; for the Windsor council of Christmas 1104, *ASC, s.a.* 1105.

[42] Henry's "New Windsor" occupied the site of the present Windsor Castle, the extensive structures of which have obliterated Henry I's buildings. Among the seven great councils that Henry convened at New Windsor was the council of April 1114 whose deliberations resulted in Ralph d'Escures' elevation to the archbishopric of Canterbury, the "council of all England" in late January 1121 that witnessed the wedding and double coronation of Henry and Adeliza of Louvain, and the Christmas council of 1126 at which David king of Scots "and all the chief men, both clerics and laymen, that there were in England" took oaths to support the empress Maud's succession to the English throne: Eadmer, *HN*, pp. 222, 293; SD,

brothers and Hugh of Avranches earl of Chester (all three of whom had also been close to Rufus), Richard of Redvers (on whom Henry now showered estates in southern England), and probably Ranulf *vicomte* of the Bessin. He now undertook to win to his cause most of the leading members of the late king's household and *curia*. One of his first acts, while still at Winchester before the coronation, was to nominate Rufus' chancellor, William Giffard, to the singularly wealthy bishopric of Winchester. Other men of the late king's inner circle also became frequent attesters of Henry I's early charters: Urse of Abitôt sheriff of Worcester, Roger Bigod *Dapifer* (and sheriff of Norfolk), Eudo *Dapifer*, Hamo *Dapifer* (sheriff of Kent), and his brother Robert fitz Hamon (to whom Rufus had diverted the late Queen Matilda's lands in western England).[43]

The single significant exception to Henry's policy of curial continuity was Ranulf Flambard, bishop of Durham, William Rufus' vastly unpopular chief minister. Ranulf was a convenient and obvious culprit who was widely detested as a low-born, self-important, overmighty upstart and was particularly offensive to churchmen because of his ruthless exploitation of ecclesiastical vacancies and his extortionate fund raising. On 15 August 1100 Henry, on the advice of his court and in the hope of soliciting further lay and ecclesiastical support for his new regime, charged Ranulf with misappropriating funds relating to his administrative office. Thomas archbishop of York, tightening the noose, testified before the *curia* that Flambard had violated the promises that he had made at his consecration as bishop of Durham. Henry and his court commanded

---

2:259; *ASC, s.a.* 1127. In 1113, as we have seen, Henry "wore his crown" at the Windsor Christmas council, and *RRAN* 2, no. 1740, makes it clear that Henry's court of Christmas 1132 at Windsor constituted a great council as well. See again Biddle, "Seasonal Festivals," p. 67, which shows that New Windsor, from the time of its completion, was more often used than any other royal residence as the site of Henry's courts at the three great liturgical feasts (more often than Winchester and Westminster combined). The statement in local guidebooks and encyclopedias that Windsor Castle remained a wooden tower with wooden domestic buildings until Henry II built the present shell keep in the 1160s and 1170s can neither be proven by archaeological evidence nor even remotely sustained by the historical record: as one of his generation's foremost builders of great stone castles and halls—Portchester, Falaise, Domfront, Caen, Arques, Winchester, Vire, Argentan, Vernon, Evreux, Corfe, and many more—Henry would not (as one of my doctoral students perceptively observed) have wished to celebrate the double coronation and marriage to Adeliza of Louvain in a cabin. (Indeed, the royal justice Richard Bassett, who was by no means the wealthiest lord in Henry's England, found it possible to build a magnificent stone castle on his small fief in Normandy; OV, 6:468.) For both the archaeological and historical evidence see Brown et al., eds, *History of the King's Works, The Middle Ages,* 1:33–40 (on the castles of Henry I); 2:864–865 (on Windsor). On New Windsor see ibid., 1:47; *ASC, s.a.* 1110; HH, p. 237.

[43] *MMI,* pp. 10–14.

that Ranulf be held captive in the Tower of London, where he became the first known prisoner in the Tower's bloodstained history.[44] But the remaining notables in Rufus' administration, some of them very wealthy, all of them highly competent and less egregiously unpopular than Bishop Ranulf, remained in place.

The imprisonment of Ranulf Flambard was merely one of several acts undertaken by the newly crowned king to signify the advent of a new political order, more equitable than the last. Henry's coronation charter was perhaps the most evident expression of his policy of wielding a new broom. Another was his effort to accommodate the Church by appointing prelates to the many bishoprics and abbeys that Rufus had left vacant. On the day of his coronation, for example, Henry restored Chertsey to its former abbot Odo and nominated Robert, monk of Saint-Evroul and a natural son of his old friend Hugh earl of Chester, to the abbacy of Bury St Edmunds.[45] In a similar effort to win aristocratic support while filling ecclesiastical vacancies, Henry appointed to the abbacy of Ely a son of Richard fitz Gilbert of Clare, a monk of Bec named Richard (whose years as abbot of Ely turned out to be stormy).[46]

Henry's most significant effort at reconciliation with the Church was his invitation to St Anselm to return to England from his exile in Lyons:

> I ask you as a father, with all the people of England, to come as quickly as you can to give your advice to me, your son, and to that people the care of whose souls was committed to you. Indeed, I entrust myself and the people of the whole kingdom of England to your counsel and the counsel of those who ought to advise me with you. And I pray that you not be displeased that I received consecration as king in your absence, for, had it been possible, I would more willingly have received it from you than from any other . . .[47]

From the tenor of this letter, and from all that followed, it is clear that Henry really was prepared to abandon Rufus' policies on the Church

---

[44] SD, 1:138; *MMI*, pp. 85–86; Archbishop Anselm, on his return from exile in September 1100, appointed an ecclesiastical commission to hear Flambard's defense; the commission reported back to Anselm that Flambard had failed to clear himself. He did, however, endure his imprisonment in the Tower in considerable comfort and style: OV, 5:312.

[45] *Monasticon*, 3:155; *Ann. Wint.*, p. 40; OV, 5:296–298, where a number of Henry's other early ecclesiastical appointments are listed.

[46] *Liber eliensis*, pp. 224–236; OV, 5:296 and n. 8.

[47] *AO*, ep. 212; Eadmer, *HN*, pp. 118–119.

which had offended Anselm and many other ecclesiastics: he would end the abuses of regalian right, cease the practice (to which Anselm frequently objected) of undertaking to create new knights fees on ecclesiastical lands, fill the numerous vacant prelacies, and resume the convening of kingdomwide primatial councils, the abolition of which had been a primary factor in forcing Anselm into exile.[48] Henry's ensuing record shows that he did in fact support Church reform in all these respects. From the beginning, as we have seen, he moved vigorously to provide prelates for vacant churches. He backed Anselm's primatial councils of 1102 and 1108 and permitted further kingdomwide councils after Anselm's death (along with at least five provincewide councils during his twenty-nine-year rule in Normandy). And although Henry continued to exercise regalian right, he did not conspicuously abuse it.[49] In brief, Henry had every reason to anticipate a placid and fruitful relationship with Anselm on his return from exile.

Henry's letter to Anselm is not dated, but it must have been sent shortly after the coronation. When it reached him, the archbishop was already on the way from Lyons to Cluny en route to England, having heard the news of Rufus' death from two swiftly traveling monks, one from Canterbury, the other from Bec. He landed at Dover on 23 September and met the new king a few days later at Salisbury, where, as we learn from charter evidence, Henry presided at a great council at Michaelmas (29 September).[50] On receiving Anselm, the king apologized once again for being crowned in his absence, and Anselm accepted the king's explanation. To seal the reconciliation between crown and primate, Henry asked Anselm to render him the accustomed homage and to be restored to the long-confiscated archbishopric by undergoing the traditional ceremony of receiving the symbols of the office from the royal hand.[51] Anselm replied that he neither would nor could agree to either ceremony. It was at this point and on these grounds that the English investiture controversy commenced.

Henry must have been flabbergasted at Anselm's response. As archbishop under Rufus, Anselm had received investiture from the king, permitted him to invest other prelates without demur, rendered him homage, and accepted as routine the rendering of such homages by

---

[48] FW, 2:41.

[49] Hollister, "William II, Henry I and the Anglo-Norman Church," pp. 183–205 *passim.*

[50] Eadmer, *HN*, p. 119; *RRAN* 2, nos 494–495 (Salisbury, "in concilio"). Anselm does not figure among the small handful of witnesses, but the hypothesis that the archbishop attended the Michaelmas court is supported by Eadmer's statement that when Anselm and Henry had concluded their discussions and negotiations, Henry dismissed his *curia*: Eadmer, *HN*, p. 121.

[51] Eadmer, *HN*, pp. 119–120.

other prelates.[52] Henry had had no inkling that matters would be suddenly and joltingly reversed. Anselm, for his part, must have felt a sense of reluctance in announcing the new policies, for he took no pleasure in fighting with kings. On the contrary, he had long cherished the hope, traditional among Canterbury archbishops, of working with the monarchy in a relationship of close cooperation such as Archbishop Dunstan had enjoyed with King Edgar and Lanfranc with the Conqueror, and he was sensitive to Henry's willingness to renew such a relationship, as expressed in his letter welcoming Anselm as his adviser. But the Western Church was just then in the process of profound changes, and the circumstances of Anselm's exile had made the implication of some of these changes clear to him for the first time.

As Anselm proceeded to explain to Henry, Pope Urban II, at the council of Rome of Easter 1099, had condemned the practices of lay investiture of prelates and clerical homage to lay lords. The council of Rome coincided with the high tide of Gregorian reform, for although the papacy had been condemning lay investiture for nearly a quarter-century, the ban on clerical homage was much more recent, having first been proclaimed at Clermont in 1095.[53] Anselm must have been aware of the earlier ban on lay investiture and may also have known of the ban on homage since his envoy Boso of Bec had attended the Council of Clermont.[54] But because Anselm himself had never before been present at a council that had condemned these practices, he seems to have felt no pressing obligation to enforce the bans in England. It was never his wish to pick a quarrel with the king.

Anselm did, however, attend the Roman council of Easter 1099 in the course of his exile. Indeed, he was seated in a place of honor alongside the pope and cardinals around the apse of Old St Peter's directly behind the altar, while the remaining prelates of the council (mostly Italian and French) filled the choir and nave. Anselm cannot have overlooked or underestimated the force of the council's condemnations, which occurred in singularly dramatic circumstances. As the council was about to conclude, Pope Urban rose to his full height and, in the resonating voice that had launched the First Crusade, declared a series of anathemas that would shape the future relationship between Anselm and Henry I. One of his anathemas required the excommunication of all laymen who invested churchmen in their lands and offices, all churchmen who received such investitures, and all

---

[52] Southern, *Anselm: A Portrait*, pp. 291–292; Vaughn, *Anselm of Bec and Robert of Meulan*, pp. 219–220.
[53] Blumenthal, *The Investiture Controversy*, pp. 140, 157; Tellenbach, *Church in Western Europe*, p. 266 and references.
[54] *Vita Bosonis, PL* 150, col. 726.

bishops who consecrated invested clerics. A second anathema condemned all churchmen who rendered homage to laymen for their churches. Eadmer states that the pope pronounced these anathemas "with the concurrence of the whole council"; when he had concluded, according to Eadmer's firsthand report, everyone present endorsed the condemnations (as was customary) with cries of "Fiat! Fiat!"[55]

As a responsible Christian prelate profoundly devoted to Benedictine monastic obedience, Anselm found himself, for the first time in his long career, firmly pledged to important precepts of the Gregorian reform movement. After the Easter council of 1099, he returned to Lyons, where he had spent much of his exile with his friend Hugh archbishop of Lyons. Hugh had served some years as papal legate and had demonstrated a scrupulous devotion to Gregorian principles of ecclesiastical liberty. It is probable, as several historians have suggested, that the bans proclaimed at the council were reinforced in Anselm's mind by conversations with Archbishop Hugh. In any case, Anselm brought the papal prohibitions with him on his return to England.

Henry I could not easily submit to these radical reorderings of the relationship between Church and kingdom. Although willing to renounce the abuses of the previous reign, he would relinquish neither the traditional royal authority over churches and their prelates nor the symbols that had long made this authority manifest. "It seemed to him a terrible thing," Eadmer wrote, "to lose the investitures of churches and homage of prelates . . . as if he were losing half of his sovereignty." As Sir Richard Southern expresses it, with characteristic perceptiveness and brevity, "Under Rufus, the alliance of king and archbishop had been broken because the king was unmanageable; under Henry, it broke down because of Anselm's loyalty to the papal decree of 1099."[56]

Anselm of Aosta was sixty-six or sixty-seven years old when he stunned King Henry (then in his early thirties) at the Salisbury court of Michaelmas 1100. A man of deep piety and surpassing sanctity, Anselm was also one of medieval Europe's foremost philosopher-theologians, whose writings on the Incarnation and the Redemption, for example, revolutionized Christian theology and whose ontological proof of God worries some philosophers even today. He contributed decisively to the emergence of the abbey of Bec as one of the foremost centers of

---

[55] Eadmer, *HN*, pp. 112–114. On the custom of papal councils acclaiming decisions with the words "Fiat! Fiat!" see Robinson, *The Papacy*, pp. 125–126 with references (of which the reference at the conclusion of n. 21 should be to the council of Rome in 1099, not the council of Bari).

[56] Eadmer, *HN*, p. 120; Southern, *Anselm: A Portrait*, p. 344.

religious life and thought in Western Christendom, and at Canterbury he is still warmly remembered. In July 1979 Archbishop Michael Ramsey opened the Third Annual Anselm Conference, at Canterbury, with these eloquent words:

> We commemorate today the greatest of the archbishops of Canterbury, Anselm of Bec. He served God as a monk, as a man of contemplation who led many and still leads many in the way of prayer, as a loving pastor, as a profound thinker, and as a courageous statesman.[57]

Anselm was a polymath—a saint, a spiritual adviser, a theologian, an ecclesiastical statesman—and a formidable potential opponent of Henry I and his gifted baronial confidant, Robert of Meulan, if opponents they must become. For although some historians in recent generations have doubted the quality of Anselm's leadership, his skills were so highly regarded in his own time that when he was only three years into his monastic profession and not yet thirty, he was forced by his ecclesiastical superiors to become prior of Bec—which catapulted him over a flock of more senior monks, some of whom were left grumbling. For the next thirty years he served Bec as prior and abbot (about fifteen years in each office). Indeed, he occupied significant administrative offices—prior, abbot, archbishop—for forty-six of his forty-nine years in the monastic profession. And although he roundly disliked administration and was disinclined to immerse himself in its mundane details, his years as prior and especially as abbot of Bec were immensely fruitful with regard to its international prestige and spiritual influence, the growing numbers of its monks, the proliferation of its daughter houses, and its material well-being. The spectacular success of the abbey under Anselm's direction constitutes potent evidence of his remarkably effective leadership and statesmanship. By the end of his abbatiate Bec had become one of Europe's foremost intellectual and spiritual centers. With young men flocking in from far and near, its monastic congregation grew approximately threefold under Anselm's rule, and its more seasoned monks were being sent out to govern a growing number of dependent priories on both sides of the Channel.[58] Abbot Anselm, in the meantime, had won the devoted friendship of a number of the wealthiest magnates in the Anglo-Norman world—Hugh of Chester,

---

[57] *Anselm Studies*, 1:1, quoted in Vaughn, *Anselm of Bec and Robert of Meulan*, pp. 363–364.

[58] A contemporary list of Bec monks, ranked in order of their entry into the community, under chronological subdivisions corresponding to the tenure of successive abbots, discloses that 34 monks had entered at the time of Lanfranc's arrival

Arnulf of Montgomery, Richard fitz Gilbert of Clare—and of William the Conqueror himself, all of whom became friends and supporters of Bec.

As archbishop of Canterbury, Anselm demonstrated similar skills, assiduously safeguarding the rights of his archiepiscopal see and advancing its claims to primacy over all Britain more effectively than any previous or subsequent archbishop, despite a swelling tide of papal opposition to primacies.[59] The rights of the archiepiscopal see of Canterbury and the full realization of its claims to the primacy of all Britain and Ireland were of fundamental importance to Anselm, far overshadowing the issues of lay investiture and clerical homage. These latter policies Anselm supported because he had been ordered to do so by the pope; he had no personal convictions about them and, indeed, no particular taste for the Gregorian idea of a Church free of monarchical control. His preference was for teamwork between king and primate. As he expressed it to a Canterbury monk:

> They say that I forbid the king to grant investitures ... Tell them that they lie. I do not forbid the king to invest churches on my own authority, but because I heard the pope in a great council excommunicating laymen who grant investitures as well as churchmen who receive such investitures and those who consecrate the receivers.[60]

The inviolability and primacy of the see of Canterbury, in contrast, commanded Anselm's full devotion. Although he felt morally constrained to follow the papal decrees on investiture (unless the pope

---

circa 1042, 33 more had professed before Anselm's entry in 1060, 69 entered between Anselm's profession and his election to the abbatial office in 1078, and 160 professed during Anselm's fourteen or fifteen years as abbot. Allowing for deaths, these figures suggest that the number of Bec monks may have tripled under Anselm's rule as abbot: Porée, *Bec*, 1:629–631; Vaughn, *Anselm of Bec and Robert of Meulan*, pp. 69–70; on the growing fame of the school of Bec under Anselm: ibid., pp. 68–69; on the proliferation of dependent priories under Anselm, ibid., pp. 63–67; Chibnall, "Relations of St Anselm with the Abbey of Bec," pp. 521–530, demonstrating that Anselm made no fewer than three visits to England while abbot of Bec to supervise Bec property there; see Marjorie Morgan (Chibnall), *The English Lands of the Abbey of Bec*, pp. 1–37; in the meantime, Bec acquired five or six priories in France during Anselm's abbatiate (Porée, *Bec*, 1:384–444; Vaughn, *Anselm of Bec and Robert of Meulan*, p. 67). On Anselm's skill at organizing dependent priories, Southern, *Anselm: A Portrait*, p. 185.

[59] Southern, *Anselm: A Portrait*, pp. 330–364.

[60] *AO*, ep. 327. Similarly, ep. 280, Anselm to Paschal II: "Aut ergo, si sanctitate vestrae placet, hanc excommunicationem in Anglia absolvite, ut in ea possim manere sine animae meae periculo; aut eam vos servare velle, quidquid mihi inde contingat, vestris litteris significate."

should waive them), he was deeply suspicious of anything that savored of papal micromanagement of the English Church and, for that reason, he adamantly opposed the presence of papal legates in England. As primate of Britain he believed in accepting papal authority, but only if exercised in very general terms and from a distance.

As a person who disliked administration and had no taste for worldly grandeur, Anselm had sought to avoid acceptance of the archbishopric of Canterbury to begin with, and he had engaged in all the traditional acts of protest against accepting the office. But once convinced that God intended him for Canterbury he submitted to the divine will. The fact that he recoiled personally from serving as archbishop of Canterbury was irrelevant. To Anselm, the monastic vocation constituted above all an utter abandonment of self. It required that the monk become a new man, God's slave, absolutely obedient to the divine will— just as Jesus took up the Cross in obedience to the will of the Father. "When I professed myself a monk," Anselm wrote, "I surrendered myself in such a way that thereafter I could not live in accordance with my own will, but only in accordance with obedience [which ought to be accorded] either to God or to the Church of God."[61] And in accepting the archbishopric of Canterbury Anselm echoed Jesus' words in the garden of Gethsemane: after asking that the cup might pass him by, Anselm said, "Nevertheless, let it be not as I will but as you will."[62] To become a monk was to become God's slave; to become a monk-prelate, however unwillingly, was, for Anselm, to strive with all one's mind, heart, and soul to fulfill the responsibilities of one's prelacy. God demanded no less than that of his servants.

Bearing in mind this Benedictine commitment to obey God totally and Anselm's belief, following Lanfranc, that the archbishopric of Canterbury was a divinely commissioned stewardship, one must resist the familiar notion that Anselm sought opportunities to evade his archiepiscopal responsibilities and return to the ever-beckoning cloister. On the contrary, he would have regarded such dereliction of duty as a betrayal of God akin to Lucifer's.[63] His dedication to his stewardship of Canterbury was absolute. Toward the end of his life he expressed this dedication in a letter to archbishop-elect Thomas II of

[61] Ibid., ep. 156.

[62] Ibid., ep. 148, from Matthew, 26:39, quoted in Vaughn, *Anselm of Bec and Robert of Meulan*, p. 119; cf. Staunton, "Eadmer's *Vita Anselmi*."

[63] It is therefore hazardous to accept at face value the petitions of Anselm, and Lanfranc and Becket as well, to resign the episcopal office at moments when all were in good health if not good spirits. That all three offered their resignations without serious expectation that they would be accepted, see, on Lanfranc, Ruud, "Episcopal Reluctance"; on Anselm, Vaughn, *Anselm of Bec and Robert of Meulan*, pp. 204–208; on Becket, Barlow, *Becket*, p. 123.

York: "You can be very certain that I shall exert myself in every possible way to see that the church of Canterbury does not lose one scrap of her prestige in my time."[64]

Underlying the clash of wills between the archbishop and the king was Henry I's strikingly similar concept of stewardship with regard to the English monarchy. "Your Holiness should be aware," he wrote to Paschal II at the beginning of 1101, "that as long as I live, with God's help, the privileges and usages of the kingdom of England shall not be diminished."[65] Thus, the traditional concept of royal stewardship, demanding, as Anselm well understood, the safeguarding of customary rights, ceremonies, and privileges, had come into conflict with the Gregorian vision of a new and rightful order. As the Gregorians argued, Jesus had said not "I am custom" but "I am truth." This perception resonated scarcely at all with Anselm, but having heard and assented to the new provisions at the Easter council of 1099, he was constrained to enforce them until such time as they might be rescinded by the pope. Yet given not only Anselm's powerful intelligence but also the lesser but not inconsiderable intelligence of Henry I and Robert of Meulan, one suspects that the two sides understood each other better than in most such conflicts and that each, appreciating the constraints on the other, was more than ordinarily open to accommodation. Or even if accommodation should fail for the time being, there was an effort to be reasonable and, to a degree, courteous. The English investiture controversy was played out and resolved far more civilly than the conflict between Henry II and Becket, which involved hotter, less thoughtful heads.

Anselm accompanied his bombshell with a dangerous threat. If the king accepts the papal bans, he said, all will be well between us, but if not, "I cannot see that my remaining in England would be profitable or honorable."[66] Henry feared, so Eadmer suggests, that Anselm "might approach his brother Robert, who had just returned to Normandy from Jerusalem, and first induce him to return to the Apostolic See, which he

[64] AO, ep. 455.
[65] Ibid., ep. 215.
[66] Eadmer, HN, p. 120. In a letter of Anselm to Paschal II of late 1101, Anselm provides a contrary account of the episode, stating that when he first raised the issue of the papal prohibitions to Henry I, the king and his bishops and magnates threatened to banish him from England and repudiate papal authority. This account seems unlikely, however, because Anselm's three previous letters to Paschal II from England (epp. 214, 217, and 218), while mentioning Henry's objections to the papal bans, say nothing about being threatened with expulsion. After the resolution of Henry's conflict with Robert Curthose in mid-1101, the king did threaten Anselm with banishment if he continued to recognize the papal bans (Eadmer, HN, p. 131). By then Henry's throne was relatively secure, but in September 1100 it was not, and Henry is most unlikely to have threatened to expel

knew could easily be done, and then make him king of England."[67] It is all but certain that Anselm had no such intention, having endured many years of personal experience of Curthose's shortcomings as a ruler, but Henry and his *curia* could not be sure. Thinking quickly, they proposed a compromise: let there be a truce until the following Easter (21 April 1101), during which time all the sequestered Canterbury estates would be restored to Anselm and the English Church would remain in its current state, with the king granting no investitures and the archbishop performing no consecrations. In the meantime, a mission would be sent to Paschal "to enable representatives from both sides to have the papal decrees changed back to what was the former practice in the kingdom."[68] Anselm expressed doubts about the outcome of such a delegation, but he agreed to the truce and, in a letter to Paschal accompanying the envoys, urged him that "so far as your authority under God permits, you would yield to the aforesaid petition, which the messengers will explain to you."[69] Anselm is later quoted by Eadmer as saying that the envoys were sent to the pope "for the express purpose of having these decrees varied."[70]

Anselm's position was thus that he would welcome the waiving of the bans if the pope so agreed but that the decision was Paschal's. His own obligation to God was as steward of the see of Canterbury, and, as such, it was his duty to safeguard the archiepiscopal lands, rights, and primacy; the issues of investiture and clerical homage affected the entire Church and clearly pertained to the pope alone. Anselm could join Henry in appealing to Paschal to reconsider and exempt England from the bans, but in the end he could only abide by the pope's decision. Both king and primate were acting as circumstances required, and both were seeking a solution to their predicament. Some modern historians have described Anselm as "stiff necked" and uncompromising; they have even gone so far as to picture him as a kind of holy diehard preventing by his intransigence an arrangement that might otherwise have been worked out by the subtle and accommodating politicians of the royal and papal curias. This is incorrect: Anselm was always ready to compromise on the issues of investiture and homage; it was the papacy that proved intransigent. For the time being, however, the king and archbishop had agreed to a truce and, the royal court having been dissolved, Anselm returned to Canterbury in peace.

Anselm immediately on his arrival. Most likely Anselm's letter, written after September 1101, shifts Henry's expulsion threat from 1101 to 1100 in order to simplify the story.

[67] Eadmer, *HN*, p. 120.

[68] Ibid., pp. 120–121.

[69] *AO*, ep. 217.

[70] Eadmer, *HN*, p. 131.

In the fourth month of his reign, Orderic writes, Henry I, "not wishing to wallow in lasciviousness like any horse or mule . . . married with royal state a high-born maiden named Matilda."[71] His wife, originally named Edith (perhaps after St Edith of Wilton), had, at some unspecified point in her young life, adopted the name Matilda, which was much favored among aristocratic Norman women. It has been suggested that she may have taken the new name at her baptism in autumn 1080, when Duke Robert Curthose, who had just then completed a military expedition into Scotland and concluded a peace agreement, stood as her godfather. She was the daughter of the late king and queen of Scots, Malcolm Canmore and his wife, St Margaret, and she was twenty years old when she married Henry I (who would have been about thirty-one at the time).[72] Like Henry, she was the offspring of a reigning king and queen, "born in the purple." Moreover she was, through St Margaret, a kinswoman of Edward the Confessor, a great-granddaughter of the Anglo-Saxon king Edmund Ironside, and a direct descendant of King Alfred the Great (see the Anglo-Norman family genealogy, p. xxii). Edith-Matilda's brothers, Edmund, Alexander, and David, were successive kings of Scots throughout Henry's reign. Alexander married one of Henry's natural daughters, and David lived for some years at Henry's court. Henry's marriage to Matilda and his friendship with her brothers contributed much to the unbroken peace and warm relations with Scotland that prevailed throughout his reign.

The chief motivation for the marriage, however, was Matilda's Anglo-Saxon lineage. It could be argued that Henry was deliberately seeking to legitimize his dynasty by choosing a wife whose offspring would carry the blood of the Old English royal line, and such an argument has much to commend it. Henry may not, however, have been quite so calculating. It may simply have been natural for a king whose coronation charter placed such heavy emphasis on perpetuating the laws of Edward the Confessor to marry an Anglo-Saxon princess, joining Edward's lineage to his own. Henry's offspring would thus become members of the Anglo-Saxon royal line, and Henry himself would in some sense become an Anglo-Saxon king. In reporting the wedding, the Anglo-Saxon chronicler rejoiced that Matilda was "of the true royal family of England." The English monk Eadmer of Canterbury commented that she was "known to have been descended from the old kings of the English," and William of Malmesbury, himself

[71] OV, 5: 298; see ibid., 4:272; *ASC, s.a.* 1100; Eadmer, *HN*, pp. 121–126.
[72] WM, *GR*, 2:366, 462; David, *Curthose*, p. 131; SD, 2:211; Hermann of Tournai, "De restauratione," pp. 281–282. On Matilda II see, in general, Lois Huneycutt, "'Another Esther in Our Times'": this, the best work on the subject, has been of great help to me in the sections on Queen Edith-Matilda.

half-English, would later remark, in words that he attributed to Henry I himself, that Matilda's "royal lineage went back for many centuries—the reigns of fourteen kings, from Egbert king of Wessex [to] King Edward."[73]

Edward the Confessor was remembered to have uttered a deathbed prophecy that a green tree would be split down the middle of its trunk and the severed piece would be carried the space of three furlongs from the stock, after which it would be joined once more to the trunk and again produce leaves and fruit. Only then, Edward said, would England's ills cease.[74] Henry's marriage to Matilda and their offspring, by fusing the lines of the West Saxon kings and Norman dukes in the third post-Conquest generation, could thus be seen as fulfilling the Confessor's prophecy.

In attempting to weigh the various motivations for the marriage, it is important to consider not only those of Henry I and his counselors but those of Matilda as well. For as Eadmer stresses, it was Matilda who took the initiative in persuading Anselm to condone the marriage and perform the attendant ceremonies—marrying the couple and crowning the new queen.[75] She was by no means a passive victim of royal manipulation. It is doubtless true that most women would have had the same desire to become queens as most men to become kings. Beyond that, there is evidence that Matilda was genuinely attracted to Henry and that her feelings were reciprocated. Eadmer, Malmesbury, and Orderic all agree that in the period before the wedding Henry and Matilda had become extremely fond of each other, and Eadmer goes so far as to describe them as being "in love." Both may have welcomed the union for that reason among others.[76] Further, Matilda may have been just as interested as Henry was in regrafting the green tree. She was clearly proud of being, through her mother, a member of the West Saxon royal line, and she must have realized, as most people of her time did, that there was little chance of her line

---

[73] *ASC, s.a.* 1100; Eadmer, *HN*, p. 121; WM, *HN*, pp. 3–4.

[74] Barlow, ed., *The Life of King Edward Who Rests at Westminster*, p. 118. For later versions of the prophecy see Bloch, ed., "La Vie de S. Edouard le Confesseur par Osbert de Clare," pp. 107–109, and Aelred of Rievaulx, *Vita S. Edwardi regis et confessoris*, cols 771–774.

[75] Eadmer, *HN*, pp. 121–126.

[76] Ibid., p. 121, stating that Henry had fallen in love with Matilda, but that discretion "held back the two from embracing one another as they desired." Similarly, WM, *GR*, 2:470, describing the young Matilda as a woman "to whom Henry had long been greatly attached"; and Orderic, 5:300, stating that Matilda was a maiden "whose perfection of character he had long adored." Some modern historians, being certain that Henry I was both unlovable and unloved, would be inclined to reject these passages.

reascending the English throne except through a marriage such as was now contemplated.[77]

The great difficulty was that Matilda was suspected of having been a nun. Her royal parents had sent her as a child of about six or seven years to be educated at the convent of Romsey, a distinguished, venerable, and wealthy religious house with a large and impressive stone church.[78] At that time or shortly afterward they sent Matilda's younger sister Mary to Romsey as well. There the two sisters lived for several years under the care of their aunt Christina, who became a nun of that house in 1086. Some time before 1093, perhaps when Matilda was around eleven or twelve, she and Mary moved to the even wealthier convent of Wilton.[79] Both Romsey and Wilton were noted for their schools, and there is every reason to suppose that Matilda was well educated. One need not question her insistence that she never took religious vows and that she wore the veil only at the insistence of her aunt Christina, who sought to protect her "from the lust of the Normans" by covering her head with "a little black hood, and when I threw it off she would often make me smart with a good beating and a most horrible scolding." The high-born young woman was much sought after— by William Rufus himself (according to the error-prone Hermann of Tournai, writing much later), by William II of Warenne, earl of Surrey, whose proposal of marriage she rejected, and by Alan "the Red" lord of Richmond who, on visiting Wilton, chose to carry off another young woman, the former King Harold's daughter, Gunhilda.[80] Matilda seems to have been eager, however, to marry Henry I and appealed directly to Anselm for permission to do so. Anselm had previously written stern letters reprimanding Gunhilda for leaving her convent to marry Alan of Richmond, implying that the wearing of the religious habit bound a woman to the religious life regardless of whether or not she had taken vows. He had also written, early in 1094, to Osmund bishop of Salisbury on the subject of Matilda herself, "whom the devil caused to cast off the veil of religion and causes to persist shamelessly in wearing

---

[77] Huneycutt, "'Another Esther in Our Times,'" pp. 66–67, 88–90.

[78] Knowles, *Monastic Order*, pp. 138–139. The present church of Romsey, an impressive Norman Romanesque edifice built in late Anglo-Norman times, superseded an earlier Anglo-Saxon building, also of stone and of comparable size, parts of which have been uncovered by excavations during the 1980s and 1990s.

[79] The church of Wilton was likewise built of stone, resulting from a gift of Edward the Confessor's queen Edith: Barlow, *The Life of King Edward Who Rests at Westminster*, pp. 71–73. There is no specific evidence that Christina accompanied her nieces to Wilton or, indeed, that she ever occupied the office of abbess at either house. William of Malmesbury asserts that Christina grew old at Romsey: WM, *GR*, 1:278.

[80] *AO*, epp. 168–169, 177; Hermann of Tournai, "De restauratione," pp. 278–281; Searle, "Women and the Succession," pp. 165–169; Southern, *Anselm: A Portrait*, pp. 260–264.

secular clothing," exhorting Bishop Osmund to compel her to return "to the order which she arrogantly despised."[81] Matilda, whose intention to eschew the religious life was avidly backed by her father, had been removed from Wilton by King Malcolm in 1093, shortly before his death, and there is no evidence that she ever returned, despite Anselm's letter to Osmund a few months later.[82] In November 1100, however, Anselm, having been forced to pit himself against the new king by his indelible memory of the council of Rome in 1099, was anxious to cooperate with Henry in every other possible way. He did not include his letters to Gunhilda or his letter to St Osmund regarding Matilda in the standard collection of his correspondence, MS Lambeth 59; whether the exclusion of these letters was accidental, or whether, as has been suggested, it was an attempt on Anselm's part to craft a consistent record of his political and moral views for posterity, by late 1100 he had changed his mind.[83] Indeed, Eadmer's painfully elaborate account of the proceedings makes it clear that Anselm supported the marriage despite the criticism of many of the stricter clerics. It was Anselm who paved the way for the marriage, calling for a council of Anglo-Norman bishops, abbots, and magnates at Lambeth Palace to decide (in his absence) whether Matilda was indeed marriageable. He had earlier dispatched two envoys to Wilton to inquire whether Matilda had taken religious vows, and on their return the envoys reported to the council that she had not. Predictably, the council of curial prelates decided in Henry and Matilda's favor, resting its case on a letter of Lanfranc's to Gundulf bishop of Rochester to the effect that cloistered women "who have been neither professed nor presented at the altar are to be sent away at once without change of status" and that those who entered the convent not for love of the religious life but for fear of the French are to "be granted unrestricted leave to depart."[84] Anselm accepted the council's judgment, "with all the more confidence, as I am told that it is supported by the authority of so great a father."[85] That Anselm reversed his opinion on the

[81] AO, epp. 168, 169, 177.

[82] Hermann of Tournai, "De restauratione," p. 281; Southern, Anselm: A Portrait, pp. 260–262; Eadmer (HN, p. 121) speaks of Henry falling in love with Matilda, presumably in or before 1100, "long after she had discarded the veil."

[83] Fröhlich, "The Letters Omitted from Anselm's Collection of Letters," pp. 64–66.

[84] Eadmer, HN, pp. 121–125; Letters of Lanfranc, no. 53.

[85] Eadmer, HN, pp. 124–125; compare the less tendentious but much less reliable account by Hermann of Tournai "De restauratione," pp. 278–281. The issue of Matilda's religious vocation reemerged early in Stephen's reign when his representative in Rome, Arnulf of Lisieux, advanced the (ultimately unsuccessful) charge that because Matilda was a nun, her daughter, the empress Maud, was illegitimate:

matter—and that he did so in the face of criticism—shows the degree to which he was prepared to back the regime of Henry I. Had it not been for the council of Rome, the two men might always have been the best of friends.

On the completion of the council's deliberations, Anselm himself performed the marriage ceremony and crowned the new queen. On Sunday, 11 November 1100, the archbishop married the couple in Westminster Abbey "before all the nobility of the realm" and crowned Matilda II queen of the English.[86] On the same day Henry I issued a charter dated *in nuptiis meis* to Abingdon Abbey, which was to become Queen Matilda's favorite Benedictine foundation, and whose newly appointed abbot, the Italian monk Faritius of Malmesbury, was to become her personal physician and one of her dearest friends.[87]

Matilda was an impressive queen who, with better luck, might have become a royal saint.[88] Well educated, intelligent, "not despicable in point of beauty," she was an enthusiastic patron of literature and an effective, politically sagacious regent who, in Henry's absence, presided over the exchequer court during its formative era.[89] If, as Eadmer says, she was in love with Henry during the early years of their relationship, she managed to outgrow it and settled down at Westminster, living in leisure and luxury surrounded by poets, scholars, and musicians as Henry itinerated around the Anglo-Norman realm. She bore him two children: first Matilda (whom I shall call Maud), the future empress, born probably in early February 1102; then William "Adelin," heir to the throne, sometime in 1103. Matilda's death on 1 May 1118 was regarded as a major setback to the regime, and her successor, Queen Adeliza of Louvain, played a much less active role in government.[90]

Letters and Charters of Gilbert Foliot, p. 65; John of Salisbury, *Historia pontificalis*, pp. 83–86; Chibnall, *Empress Matilda*, pp. 75–76.

[86] The fact that St Anselm had married the couple and crowned Matilda dampened the effect of the charge. See Chibnall, *Empress Matilda*, p. 76.

[87] Eadmer, *HN*, p. 125; *RRAN* 2, nos 498, 499.

[88] Lois L. Huneycutt, in an unpublished paper, "The Rise and Fall of the Cult of Queen Matilda II", argues convincingly that Edith-Matilda's cult, which had a promising beginning, was weakened by rivalries between Westminster Abbey and St Paul's, London, and, later, by King Stephen's reluctance to support the canonization of his rival's mother, despite evidence that she kissed lepers: *PL* 195, col. 736; cf. *Liber de Hyda*, pp. 305–306, 311–313.

[89] WM, *GR*, 2:493–495; *RRAN* 2, no. 1000; a meticulous and illuminating biography of Matilda by Lois L. Huneycutt is forthcoming.

[90] I have counted at least seven Matildas who figure in this biography of Henry I. I have therefore chosen to identify Henry's legitimate daughter Matilda by the nineteenth-century appellation Maud. WM, *GR*, 2:493–495; OV, 6:188; Hermann of Tournai, "De restauratione," *MGH, SS*, 14:280, mistakenly reports the existence

At the Christmas season 1100 Henry held a great council at Westminster and, with Matilda, engaged in a crown-wearing ceremony.[91] His court was honored by the presence of the future king and *rex designatus* of France, Louis VI, accompanied by attendants "who were few in number but mature in judgment."[92] Louis dined at Henry's Christmas banquet seated between the king and Anselm. Sally Vaughn has made the interesting observation that Robert count of Meulan, who had accompanied Henry to Westminster in early August for his coronation and was one of the most frequent witnesses of his later charters, attested no surviving royal charters between August and Christmas 1100. Robert, whose estates in the Risle Valley suffered from the anarchic conditions that prevailed in Normandy after Rufus' death, was probably on the Continent during these months—in Normandy and the French Vexin—and could well have been responsible for bringing Louis to Henry's Christmas court.[93] Orderic relates an elaborate story of how Henry received a letter, purportedly from King Philip I of France but actually from his second wife, Bertrade de Montfort, asking that Henry arrest and imprison Louis. Bertrade was anxious, Orderic explains, that one of her own sons by the king, Philip or Florus, should succeed him. As Orderic reports, Henry took counsel and then tactfully warned Louis, through one of his advisers, to leave the court and return to France. Orderic goes on to report that Bertrade then sought to end Louis' life first through sorcery (the arts of the sorcerers in her pay had no discernible effect on him) and then through poison. But the young prince survived all her machinations—although the poison left him pale for the remainder of his life. Marjorie Chibnall, very reasonably, doubts Orderic's story, which, she says, "reads like epic invention." But Bertrade de Montfort was a most remarkable and inventive woman and, in the absence of any corroboration (or refutation) of the story, we are left to wonder.[94]

---

of a second legitimate son who allegedly died in the wreck of the White Ship in 1120, presumably confusing him with Henry's bastard son Richard who perished along with William Adelin. (Similarly, Hermann invented a nonexistent son for the childless couple Emperor Henry V and King Henry I's daughter Maud: ibid., 14:282.) On the date of Maud's birth (probably 7 February 1102): Chibnall, *Empress Matilda*, pp. 8–9; in view of the time required for messages to travel to and from Rome, a letter of Pope Paschal's dated 23 November 1103 congratulating Henry I on the birth of a son suggests that William Adelin was born before the beginning of October.

[91] *RRAN* 2, nos 501–509; *ASC, s.a.* 1101.
[92] OV, 6:50–52; SD, 2:232; Luchaire, *Louis VI*, nos 8–12.
[93] Vaughn, *Anselm of Bec and Robert of Meulan*, pp. 225–226.
[94] OV, 6:50–52 and n. 2.

Despite the coronation charter, the marriage to Matilda, and the Christmas council, Henry's regime remained unstable. In its early months, young barons were inclined to ridicule Henry, perhaps for his literacy and bookishness. He may have been too intelligent to consort easily with his unreflective aristocratic contemporaries. One of his barons, unnamed, taunted the couple with the Anglo-Saxon names Godric and Godiva. Writing many years later, Master Wace describes William II of Warenne, earl of Surrey, once a suitor of Matilda, as ridiculing the king some years before his accession for having studied hunting so thoroughly that he could tell the number of tines in a stag's antlers simply by examining his footprints. Earl William mockingly referred to Henry as "Stagfoot" for having turned a joyous, mindlessly athletic pastime into a science.[95] The *Liber eliensis* reports that the great magnate families of Clare and Giffard, recently united by marriage, showed up at Henry's court with large, unruly followings who bullied the king and his other courtiers.[96] Although many of his barons had done homage to Henry since his coronation, he could by no means rely on their support in a crisis. Hugh earl of Chester and Robert of Bellême earl of Shrewsbury, for example, had hastened to England in August 1100 on the news of Henry's coronation to do homage and fealty for their earldoms, but Robert of Bellême was utterly unreliable and by early 1101 Hugh was dying.[97] Robert Curthose had meanwhile returned to Normandy from the First Crusade in September with a Norman-Italian bride, Sibylla of Conversano, and a very large dowry. He had reclaimed his dukedom without having to fight for it, as he surely would have had to do if Rufus had lived, and without having to return so much as a farthing of the ten thousand marks that Rufus had loaned him.[98] Curthose clearly had every intention of challenging Henry's rule of England, and he could count on the support of not only Robert of Bellême and William of Warenne but most of the other Anglo-Norman magnates as well. All were homage-bound to Curthose, and most of them would have preferred the loose, happy-go-lucky governance of the Conqueror's eldest son to the keenly intelligent, centralizing policies of Henry I and the Beaumonts.

William of Malmesbury and Orderic Vitalis both identify Henry I's close lay advisers and supporters at this time: Orderic names Robert count of Meulan, Hugh earl of Chester (who died on 27 July 1101, leaving a seven-year-old heir), the very recently enriched Richard of

---

[95] WM, *GR*, 2:471; Wace, *Roman de Rou*, 2:275–276.
[96] *Liber eliensis*, p. 226.
[97] OV, 5:298; cf. Eadmer, *HN*, p.126; *RRAN* 2, no. 531.
[98] *MMI*, pp. 65, 78–79.

Redvers, and Roger Bigod, sometime sheriff of Norfolk and one of William Rufus' stewards. Malmesbury adds to the royalist group Robert fitz Hamon and Robert of Meulan's brother, Henry earl of Warwick.[99] To these names can be added Anselm archbishop of Canterbury and his friend, suffragan, and fellow Bec–Caen monk Gundulf bishop of Rochester, plus, more tepidly, most of the other English prelates, with the probable exception of Richard of Clare abbot of Ely. Also supporting Henry were several men who had been active in the court and household of William Rufus: Hamo *Dapifer* sheriff of Kent (brother of Robert fitz Hamon), Eudo *Dapifer*, and Urse of Abitôt sheriff of Worcestershire.[100] Virtually all the remaining barons—Robert of Bellême, William count of Mortain, William II of Warenne, Walter Giffard II, Arnulf of Montgomery, Gilbert of Clare, Eustace of Boulogne, and many others—were either clandestine supporters of Robert Curthose or fence-sitters ready to defect when the time was right. This latter group, openly or covertly hostile to Henry I, was much wealthier and more powerful than the handful of barons and churchmen on the king's side.[101]

On 2 or 3 February 1101 Ranulf Flambard escaped from the Tower of London.[102] Orderic's detailed account, corroborated to a degree by William of Malmesbury, reports that Henry I had granted Ranulf the very generous allowance of two shillings a day for food and beverages while imprisoned (at a time when common knights were paid threepence a day), and with this allowance and the help of friends "he made merry in prison, and every day ordered a fine feast to be set before him and his guards." It is a comfort to note that the first recorded prisoner in the history of the Tower, unlike later sufferers, had such a festive time in his captivity. Nevertheless, Ranulf evidently longed for freedom and formulated an elaborate plan for his escape. One day his butler smuggled a rope into his chamber inside a flagon of wine. The guards, feasting and drinking joyously with the bishop, "grew jolly" as they drained generous portions of wine. When they were thoroughly drunk and snoring, Ranulf made his move. He fastened the rope to a mullion in a tower window and, carrying his pastoral staff, slid down the rope. Being quite portly and not in the best of physical shape, he skinned his hands on the way down, and because the rope was too short he suffered a bad fall at the bottom, which "almost

---

[99] OV, 5:298; WM, *GR*, 2:471; cf. FW, 2:49, and *RRAN* 2, nos 534–536.

[100] *MMI*, p. 81 and n. 1.

[101] Ibid., pp. 79–83.

[102] *ASC, s.a.* 1101, dating the escape at Candlemas (2 February) 1101; the first continuer of Symeon's *Historia ecclesiae dunelmensis* (SD, 1:138) and MS Caligula A viii (*MMI*, p. 96) both give the date 3 February.

flattened him and made him groan with pain."[103] He was met at the foot of the tower by friends and followers who supplied him with horses. Galloping off toward the coast, Ranulf encountered other accomplices who brought him his treasure. With them he reached the Channel and sailed for Normandy.

Orderic goes on to report that Flambard's mother, "who was a sorceress and had often conversed with the devil, losing an eye through this infamous familiarity," carried her son's treasure toward Normandy in a separate ship. As they crossed, she appears to have irritated others on her ship by ceaselessly howling incantations. The ship was attacked by pirates who plundered the treasure, and Flambard's mother and her crew arrived in Normandy "naked and sorrowing." Her son, however, sought out Robert Curthose, joined his court, and became his chief adviser for the next half-year. With Ranulf's shrewd guidance, Curthose's policies for the first time acquired purpose and coherence.[104]

Robert Curthose had already been considering a move against Henry at the urging of prominent barons in England and had sent a complaint against Henry's seizure of the throne to Pope Paschal II.[105] But until Flambard's arrival one gets the impression of lethargy and lack of direction at the Norman court. Curthose's movements in these months seem unhurried and politically aimless. He went on a short pilgrimage to Mont-Saint-Michel, perhaps paid a visit to his sister Cecilia, abbess of Caen, and lavished money, strategic castles, and huge tracts of land on his favorites.[106] It is at this point that Orderic inserts his remarks about Curthose surrounding himself with harlots, buffoons, and idlers who consumed all his money and even stole his clothes.[107] Orderic's enthusiasm for Henry I doubtless prompted him to exaggerate the duke's shortcomings, yet as a monk of Normandy Orderic was obliged to suffer from these shortcomings. We are left with the impression that without Flambard's guidance Curthose would have had as much trouble mounting a cross-Channel invasion in 1101 as he had in 1088.

In the months following Flambard's arrival everything changed. By mid-July a sizable army and fleet had been assembled at Le Tréport in northwestern Normandy, ready to cross to England.[108] Flambard was

---

[103] OV, 5:312; William of Malmesbury also mentions that he strained his arms and hurt his hands: WM, *GR*, 2:471.

[104] OV, 5:312.

[105] *MMI*, p. 85; OV, 5:300, 306–308; David, *Curthose*, pp. 124–127.

[106] OV, 5:308.

[107] Ibid.

[108] FW, 2:48.

well informed on Henry's defensive arrangements and had an effective plan to circumvent them. Henry, in the meantime, was taking what measures he could to consolidate support and defend his realm. On 10 March 1101 he renewed a money-fief treaty with Robert II count of Flanders, an arrangement that dated back to before the Norman Conquest when William the Conqueror, as duke of Normandy, had undertaken to pay Baldwin V of Flanders three hundred silver marks a year in return for Count Baldwin's counsel and military assistance. Similar arrangements with the counts of Flanders had continued off and on after the Conquest between the Conqueror and Baldwin VI and between Rufus and Robert II.[109] On 10 March 1101, at Dover, Henry I renewed the money-fief with Robert II: Count Robert agreed to make a thousand knights available to Henry in Normandy or England, or five hundred in Maine, in return for an annuity of five hundred pounds.[110] Although the treaty was renewed in 1110 (on slightly altered terms), it appears to have contributed neither to Henry's defense against Curthose nor to his overall relations with Flanders, which remained stormy throughout much of the reign. It may, however, have been responsible for keeping Count Robert neutral during Henry's Norman campaigns of 1105 and 1106.[111]

At Easter (21 April) Henry held court and wore his crown at Winchester and at Pentecost (9 June) at St Albans.[112] By the time of this last court, rumors of Curthose's preparations had reached England, and the chronicles report that the allegiance of many of Henry's chief men was, to say the least, unreliable.[113] Eadmer reports that Henry again required their oaths of fidelity and that in return, under Anselm's mediation, he renewed his promise to rule the kingdom with just and righteous laws as long as he should live.[114]

It was also at the Whitsun court at St Albans that Henry struck out at his brother's new counselor. With Anselm's firm backing, Ranulf Flambard was disseised of the lands of the bishopric of Durham, and shortly afterward Gerard, the new archbishop of York and Ranulf's

---

[109] WM, *GR*, 2:478–479; Hollister, *Military Organization of Norman England*, pp. 187–188. Count Robert II issued a charter in 1094 when on the point of bringing help to the king of the English against the Normans: *CDF*, no. 1325.

[110] *RRAN* 2, no. 515; *Diplomatic Documents Preserved in the Public Record Office*, 1: no. 1.

[111] *Diplomatic Documents*, no. 2; *Liber de Hyda*, p. 320; Galbert, *Histoire*, p. 176; OV, 6:378 and n. 4. Henry did, however, enjoy cordial relations with the Flemish counts Charles the Good (1119–1127) and Thierry of Alsace (1128–1168), with both of whom he had money-fief treaties.

[112] *RRAN* 2, nos 518, 527; *ASC, s.a.* 1101; *Ann. Wint.*, p. 41; *Monasticon*, 1:242 n. 12.

[113] *ASC, s.a.* 1101; HH, p. 233; Eadmer, *HN*, p. 126.

[114] Eadmer, *HN*, p. 126.

ecclesiastical superior, deposed him from his bishopric.[115] These acts were the culmination of the series of sanctions, secular and ecclesiastical, that had been taken against Ranulf at Henry's instigation: the accusation of misappropriating funds relating to his royal administrative office, the testimony of the late Archbishop Thomas of York before the king's court of Flambard's malfeasance as bishop, and the finding of an ecclesiastical commission appointed by Anselm—who had suffered much under Rufus and was no friend of Flambard's[116]—that the bishop of Durham had failed to clear himself of the charges levied by the royal *curia*. Anselm had responded to Flambard's escape from the Tower and flight to Normandy by writing a letter to Paschal II summarizing the case against him and requesting papal support. He wrote that the bearer of the letter would provide Paschal with the details of the specific accusations of simony and other offenses that Flambard had committed before and after his elevation to the bishopric of Durham.[117] Paschal responded by granting Anselm power of decision in the case and wrote a firm letter to Flambard in Normandy ordering him to return to England and give satisfaction to Anselm or be defrocked by canonical sentence.[118] Having lost the bishopric of Durham, Flambard now found his whole ecclesiastical career placed in jeopardy. The key to his future in the European Church was Henry's own friend and archbishop, a man unlikely to be swayed even if Curthose should conquer England. Flambard's best hope clearly lay in reconciliation with the monarch whom he was preparing to attack.

Immediately after the Whitsun council, news arrived that Curthose's invasion was imminent. Henry responded by sending letters to his subjects reaffirming the promises in his coronation charter and requesting that they swear to defend the land against all men, and especially against Robert Curthose, until Christmas Day. The one letter in this group that has survived is addressed to Bishop Robert of Lincoln, Ranulf le Meschin, Osbert the Sheriff, Picot son of Colsuen, and all the men of Lincolnshire: they are to take the aforesaid oath from all the king's demesne tenants, both French and English, and the tenants-in-chief are to take the same oath from their own tenants.[119]

---

[115] Craster, "A Contemporary Record . . . Flambard," pp. 55–56; *MMI*, pp. 85–86; the archbishop is not named, but since Flambard's deposition must surely have postdated his disseisin, the archbishop in question must have been Gerard, who, on the death of Thomas I, was translated to York from Hereford on 6 January 1101.

[116] See especially Eadmer, *HN*, pp. 41–42; *AO*, ep. 214.

[117] *AO*, ep. 214.

[118] Craster, "A Contemporary Record . . . Flambard," pp. 41–42.

[119] *RRAN* 2, no. 531; Stevenson, "An Inedited Charter of King Henry I": Stevenson reaches the reasonable conclusion that the king sent similar letters to every shire. See *The Registrum antiquissimum of the Cathedral Church of Lincoln*, ed. Foster, for a facsimile of the letter.

Henry now sent word throughout England summoning his subjects to arms.[120] Many of his barons failed to respond despite their repeated oaths of fealty, and others joined him with faint enthusiasm. But the great ecclesiastical estates were strongly represented. Eadmer tells us proudly that Anselm camped with his own men in the field near Pevensey and, with his suffragan Gundulf of Rochester, he gave Henry stalwart backing.[121] From the Abingdon chronicle we learn that Henry demanded the full *servicium debitum* from his tenants-in-chief—or at least his ecclesiastical tenants-in-chief; when the holder of one of the abbey's knights fees refused service, the abbot had to find a substitute.[122] When thirty knights were required, twenty-nine would not do. Henry summoned the English, too, and large numbers of them responded.[123] As the army gathered, Henry sent a fleet out into the Channel, manned by English sailors, to guard the coast.[124]

On about 24 June, Midsummer's Day, Henry led his army to the Channel shore and encamped in the neighborhood of Pevensey bay to await his brother's armada.[125] The site of the Conqueror's landing in 1066 doubtless seemed a good place to guard, and Henry may have had specific intelligence that Curthose was planning to land there. Pevensey is on the section of the English coastline nearest Le Tréport, where Curthose was assembling his army, and Pevensey Castle belonged to the dangerous and immensely wealthy magnate William count of Mortain, earl of Cornwall and nephew of Robert of Bellême. William of Mortain was best not left unwatched.[126]

Eadmer writes at considerable length of Anselm's indispensable role in strengthening the wavering loyalties of Henry's barons. The archbishop persuaded them individually and preached to them collectively. Had it not been for Anselm's intervention, Eadmer writes, "King Henry would at that time have lost the English throne."[127] Eadmer describes

---

[120] Eadmer, *HN*, p. 126.

[121] Ibid., p. 127; *Vita Gundulfi*, ed. Thomson, p. 59.

[122] *Chron. Ab.*, 2:128–129.

[123] Hollister, *Military Organization of Norman England*, pp. 226–227, 252.

[124] On this obligation see Hollister, *Anglo-Saxon Military Institutions*, pp. 103–126; cf. *RRAN* 2, no. 1135.

[125] *ASC, s.a.* 1101; Some sources say Pevensey, others Hastings. If the editors of *RRAN* 2 are correct in their very plausible supposition that nos 529 and 530 (AD 1100–1116) are to be dated ca. 24 June 1101, the actual place of Henry's encampment may have been Wartling (Sussex), about eleven miles west of Hastings and three miles north of Pevensey Bay. On the likelihood of this hypothesis see Searle, *Lordship and Community*, pp. 211–212.

[126] *CP*, 3:426.

[127] Eadmer, *HN*, p. 127; WM, *GP*, pp. 104–106; the anonymous author of the *Vita Gundulfi* asserts that Bishop Gundulf also contributed to persuading the barons to support Henry I: *Vita Gundulfi*, ed. Thomson, p. 59.

the king as making extravagant promises to his archbishop on matters of ecclesiastical policy and governance and even as having agreed to relinquish investiture and clerical homage unless Paschal agreed to waive the prohibitions. Eadmer further reports that Henry had untrustworthy barons brought to Anselm for lectures on loyalty. But Henry was also busy with his troops, moving frequently through their ranks, emboldening the large force of English foot soldiers he had summoned, instructing them personally in the art of meeting a cavalry charge by holding their shields firmly and returning their enemies' strokes.[128] The situation was grave, but with a large army on the coast and a fleet in the Channel Henry was in a strong defensive position.

Henry was outwitted, however, by Flambard. Curthose, "advised by Bishop Ranulf," bribed a number of Henry's English sailors to join his side and, using some of them as pilots, sailed his fleet past Pevensey to Portsmouth. There Curthose and Flambard, with an army of horsemen, archers, and foot soldiers, landed unopposed on 20 July.[129] It was a far smaller army than the Conqueror's in 1066[130]— the Winchester annalist reports that it crossed in two hundred ships whereas the Conqueror's fleet may have numbered a thousand, and a Worcester annal reports that it included 260 knights.[131] But its numbers were quickly swelled by baronial forces in England: Robert of Bellême with his entourage, William of Warenne with his, and other "distinguished and wealthy men who had formed a conspiracy and were expecting him."[132] William of Malmesbury states that on Robert Curthose's landing "almost all the nobility of this country violated the fealty they had sworn to the king, some without cause, some feigning slight pretenses," and Eadmer concurs: "When it was reported that Duke Robert himself, with his allies, had crossed the Channel, the chief personages of the kingdom, as though they had forgotten their promises, at once prepared to desert the king and to join Robert."[133] Once safely ashore at Portsmouth, Curthose and his allies were ideally

---

[128] WM, *GR*, 2:472.

[129] FW, 2:48–49. The episode is mentioned in nearly all the chronicles. Anselm reported to Paschal in ca. February 1101 that Flambard, after his flight to Normandy, became a lord of "pirates" whom he sent out to sea (ep. 214), which could explain in part his means of contacting Henry's shipmen. On the date of Curthose's landing see *MMI*, pp. 88 and notes, 96.

[130] OV, 5:314.

[131] *Ann. Wint.*, p. 41; for the size of the 1066 armada, Douglas, *William the Conqueror*, p. 190 n.; for the Worcester evidence, BM Cotton MS Vespasian E 4: *Annales monastici*, 4:374. This would be somewhat under half the *servicium debitum* of Normandy as reported in the Inquest of 1172: *MMI*, p. 88 n. 3.

[132] OV, 5:314.

[133] WM, *GR*, 2:471; Eadmer, *HN*, p. 127.

poised to move on Winchester and the royal treasure, with Henry's army some eighty miles to the east.

Until the time of the Portsmouth landing Curthose's strategy bore the mark of skillful direction. But after 20 July his campaign bogged down. He advanced toward Winchester, encamped some miles outside it, and then evidently abandoned any plan to take the city by storm or stealth. He simply sat in his encampment until he was confronted by Henry I's army, which had raced westward on the news of Curthose's landing. Curthose then entered into a disadvantageous truce with the king.

What had gone wrong for Robert Curthose? One of two things must have happened: either Flambard's influence declined or Flambard was himself maneuvering for an accommodation with Henry and Anselm through which he might salvage his ecclesiastical career. The first alternative is suggested by Orderic's account of how Robert of Bellême, William of Warenne, and other baronial confederates met Curthose when he landed, conducted him toward Winchester, and then persuaded him to send a formal message to Henry challenging him to fight or abdicate.[134] Orderic seems to imply that Robert of Bellême and his allies were now the duke's chief counselors and that Flambard's voice was muted accordingly. To the extent that the decisions to turn from Winchester and to accept a truce were Curthose's own, they were probably muddied by considerations of chivalry and sentiment. Queen Matilda, Curthose's goddaughter, was evidently in residence in Winchester. But Flambard cannot have lost his influence altogether, and it is suggestive that the final outcome of the affair was very much to his personal advantage.[135]

Advancing north-northwestward from Portsmouth toward Winchester, the ducal army had pitched camp "on a suitable spot," which a contemporary Durham manuscript, Caligula A viii, identifies as *in rivaria de Walmsforde*.[136] The site in question may well be Warnford, Hampshire, on the River Meon, about nine and a half miles southeast of Winchester and two miles northwest of the ancient earthworks atop Old Winchester Hill.[137] Henry reacted swiftly. The moment he heard of his brother's landing, he led his army northwest into Surrey, then southwest into Hampshire, following a great arc that would shield the approach to London as he hastened toward Winchester.[138] According

---

[134] OV, 5:314.

[135] In the aftermath, Flambard not only had recovered his see of Durham but he also had a hold on the see of Lisieux in Normandy: ibid., pp. 320–322.

[136] FW, 2:49; *MMI*, pp. 89, 96.

[137] *RBE*, 3:1342; *MMI*, p. 89 and n. 4.

[138] *MMI*, p. 89.

to the later testimony of Wace (who cannot be altogether trusted), Curthose now turned from Winchester and began to march on London.[139]

Curthose had only moved fifteen miles from his original encampment when the two armies met.[140] The confrontation occurred at Alton in Hampshire, where, as often happened in medieval warfare, the two sides held back from pitched battle and negotiated. The English chroniclers report that the barons mediated a peace between the brothers, whereas Orderic attributes the initiative to the brothers themselves. The Durham-based manuscript account, which may reflect the eyewitness observations of Ranulf Flambard, reports the negotiations in these words: "With the barons of both sides mediating, the king and the count conversed with one another, and a concord was declared between them."[141] Wace names three of the baronial negotiators: Robert of Bellême and his nephew William of Mortain (presumably for the duke) and the royal counselor Robert fitz Hamon.[142]

By the agreement at Alton Curthose formally renounced his claim to the English throne, the prize that had drawn him to England. His exact motives for this astonishing decision are beyond recovery. His modern biographer approvingly quotes H. W. C. Davis as describing Curthose's concession as "the most ill-considered step in the whole of Robert's long career of folly."[143] Yet one should bear in mind that in this era of military maneuverings, raids, and siege warfare, a major pitched battle was a rare and terrifying thing, sufficiently so, perhaps, to daunt even a former crusader. The barons on both sides risked their lands and possibly their freedom if the battle should turn against them. The former crusader may have been further sobered by Anselm's threat to excommunicate him if he persisted in his campaign; and it may well be, as Eadmer suggests, that disloyalty within the royal ranks was less widespread than Curthose had originally been led to hope.[144] Finally, one must not discount the role of Flambard who, despite the silence of the chroniclers, was surely present and active at Alton. The first continuator of Symeon's history of the church of Durham implies that the agreement at Alton provided for Flambard's full reinstatement as bishop of Durham, and whether or not he had been mentioned by name in the general amnesty, he was evidently included in it. Flambard had

---

[139] Wace, *Roman de Rou*, 2:268.

[140] *MMI*, p. 90 and n. 1.

[141] *ASC*, s.a. 1101; WM, *GR*, 2:472; FW, 2:49; HH, p. 233; "Chron. de Hida," in *Liber de Hyda*, p. 306; OV, 5:316–318; MS Caligula A viii, in *MMI*, p. 96.

[142] Wace, *Roman de Rou*, 2:270–271.

[143] David, *Curthose*, p. 137, quoting Davis, *England under the Normans and Angevins*, p. 124.

[144] Eadmer, *HN*, pp. 127–128.

won what he came to England to seek: the salvation of his ecclesiastical career and the exchange of his not uncomfortable quarters in the Tower of London for a much more lavish life in his former episcopal palace. With all this at stake, Flambard would doubtless have urged the impressionable duke to reach an accommodation with Henry I.[145]

Having achieved a peaceful and eminently satisfactory resolution to the threatened war, Henry and his entourage traversed the fifteen miles from Alton to Winchester, arriving by 31 July. There, on 2 August—the first anniversary of William Rufus' death—the treaty was solemnly ratified by the oaths of twelve leading men from each side.[146] Traditionally known to historians as the "treaty of Alton," it might more accurately be identified as the "treaty of Winchester." But whatever one calls it, the agreement was a turning point in Henry's reign and a key to the long peace that afterward prevailed in England. The agreement assured Henry's right to the throne and spared his kingdom the seemingly endless civil strife that would darken the reign of Stephen.

The unusually complete narrative accounts of this pivotal event make it possible to trace step by step the process that produced the settlement of 1101: baronial negotiations, the meeting and agreement of the brothers on the field, and the subsequent ratification of the treaty, in more formal surroundings, by oaths and pledges of faith between the brothers, supported by the oaths of their chief barons. The procedure is reminiscent of other political settlements of the age. In 1052, for example, when the armies and fleets of King Edward the Confessor and Earl Godwine faced one another at London, intermediaries on both sides arranged the terms of a peace, and on the following day, perhaps at Westminster, the formal settlement was effected between king and earl, Godwine swearing to his and his sons' innocence and Edward

---

[145] It has been suggested, wrongly, that Henry I made a secret of his reinstatement of Ranulf Flambard to the bishopric of Durham in 1101 and that Ranulf subsequently acted as a secret agent for Henry I in Normandy. This supposition is shown to be incorrect in *MMI*, p. 95 and n. 5, citing royal charters publicly displaying Ranulf's restoration to the king's favor: Craster, "Flambard," nos x (Curthose attests Henry's safe-conduct for Flambard), xi–xiii (Robert of Bellême attests charters restoring to Flambard the customs and lands of Durham); *RRAN* 2, nos 544, 548 (Flambard as bishop of Durham attests charters of Henry I at Windsor, 3 September 1101, in the presence of Robert Curthose, Robert of Bellême, William of Warenne, William of Mortain, and a great company of magnates and prelates). In August 1104 Flambard acted publicly in his episcopal capacity as a central figure in a liturgical event of international prominence, the translation, at Durham, of the relics of St Cuthbert (which were found to be incorrupt): SD, 1:247–261, 316–317, 2:236; FW, 2:53.

[146] *RRAN* 2, nos 534–536, recording the presence at Winchester on 31 July of King Henry, Queen Matilda, Roger Bigod, Hamo *Dapifer*, Urse d'Abitôt, Henry earl of Warwick, and Eudo *Dapifer; MMI*, p. 96; *ASC, s.a.* 1101.

formally restoring them to favor.[147] In 1091 Rufus had invaded Normandy "for his brother's undoing," but subsequent negotiations brought Rufus and Curthose together, and their mutual promises were secured by the oaths of twelve chief men from each side.[148] In 1153, after the intervention of the leading men of each army, King Stephen and Duke Henry exchanged views across the river at Wallingford. The interview was unsuccessful, but some months later, after further negotiations, the two rivals met at Winchester and worked out their accord. Shortly afterward at Westminster, probably after final negotiations on details, they sealed their treaty with mutual oaths and published it in the form of a royal charter attested by men from both sides.[149]

The treaty of 1101 has not survived and must be reconstructed from chronicle accounts. The chroniclers agree that Curthose renounced his claim to England, recognized his brother's royal title, and released Henry from an oath of homage that he had once taken—probably in 1088 when Henry purchased the countship of the Cotentin from the duke.[150] Henry in return agreed to pay Curthose three thousand marks a year for life and to surrender his possessions in western Normandy and elsewhere on the Continent except for Domfront, whose inhabitants Henry had sworn years before never to abandon. A survivor clause provided that if either Henry or his brother should die without a lawful male heir, the other should inherit the entire Anglo-Norman state.[151] Since Queen Matilda was probably approaching her fourth month of pregnancy at the time and since Robert Curthose's newly wed duchess, Sibylla of Conversano, was not yet pregnant (so far as we know), the clause was slightly to the king's advantage.[152]

The treaty also provided that the barons who had been disseised for supporting either side in 1101 should have their lands restored.[153] This is a curious clause for several reasons. Henry began disseising ducal supporters before Curthose left England, at a time when the two brothers seemed on the best of terms.[154] Orderic adds the further information that the brothers swore to punish wicked sowers of discord and to render mutual aid in recovering their father's lands.[155] These

---

[147] *ASC, s.a.* 1052; Barlow, *Edward the Confessor,* pp. 123–124.
[148] *ASC, s.a.* 1091; David, *Curthose,* pp. 59–61.
[149] Davis, *King Stephen,* pp. 117–120; *RRAN* 3, no. 272.
[150] David, *Curthose,* pp. 134–136 with references.
[151] *MMI,* pp. 92 with references, 96.
[152] Ibid.
[153] MS Caligula A viii (*MMI,* p. 96); *ASC, s.a.* 1101; FW, 2:49.
[154] OV, 5:320.
[155] Ibid.

apparently contradictory provisions, for amnesty and the punishment of traitors, are both well corroborated. The former is described in the *Anglo-Saxon Chronicle*, related Latin chronicles, and the independent testimony of Caligula A viii, while the treason clause would become a fundamental issue in the diplomacy of 1103–1106.[156] The solution appears to be that the amnesty clause, as the chronicles make clear, applied to the past—to those disseised before Alton—whereas the treason clause applied to the future. Together they embodied the principle, vital to the peaceful functioning of the proposed condominium, that the brothers would follow a uniform policy toward their cross-Channel baronage.

But there is a further problem. If, as seems likely, nobody had been disseised before Alton except Ranulf Flambard, why was the amnesty expressed in such general terms? The inappropriateness of wording to circumstances probably arises from the fact that this was one of several clauses patched into the treaty of Winchester from the Norman treaty of 1091 between Curthose and Rufus. As the one previous effort to work out terms for an Anglo-Norman condominium, the 1091 agreement was an obvious model for negotiations in 1101. The two treaties, both ratified by twelve barons from each side, had parallel survivor agreements, parallel commitments to recover William the Conqueror's lands (virtually meaningless in 1101), and parallel amnesty provisions.[157] In 1091 the restoration of confiscated lands had benefited English barons disseised in the rebellion of 1088, but when the clause was copied into the Winchester treaty it was ambiguous toward all except Flambard. By implication it would bar subsequent action against barons simply for having cast with one side or the other in 1101, but it would not protect them against charges for other crimes, past or future.

Henry quickly began to exploit these loopholes. William of Warenne, still earl of Surrey in early September 1101, was disseised of all his English lands soon afterward, perhaps for acts of violence committed by his men in Norfolk,[158] and in time certain other ducal sympathizers were punished on charges other than that of following Curthose in 1101. It is true that Orderic exaggerates the speed and thoroughness with which Henry acted against such men. Several of them lost their lands for complex or obscure malfeasances or held them far longer

---

[156] OV, 6:46, 56–58; *GND*, 2:220–223.

[157] On the 1091 treaty see *ASC*, *s.a.*; David, *Curthose*, pp. 59–61; and above, pp. 77, 142.

[158] *RRAN* 2, no 542 and p. 306 (29 August 1101); William attests as earl at Henry's Windsor court of 3 September 1101 (ibid., nos 544, 548–549), and subsequently at Robert Curthose's court in Normandy, still styling himself *comes*: ibid., no. 621 (AD 1102): see OV, 5:320.

than Orderic implies. Robert de Lacy held until about 1113; Ivo of Grandmesnil, under extreme royal disfavor for waging private war in England and burning the crops of his neighbors, eluded the king's justice by pledging his lands to Robert of Meulan around 1102 and going on crusade.[159] William count of Mortain seems to have left England voluntarily about 1104 and forfeited his immense earldom of Cornwall only after declaring for Curthose in his struggle with Henry for Normandy. And Robert Malet never fell from Henry's favor at all. His heir, William Malet, whom Orderic confuses with Robert, was disseised in 1110 in connection with an entirely different military-diplomatic crisis.[160]

Henry's conduct toward baronial traitors and peace-breakers could be severe—although most contemporary historians praised such severity as essential to the maintenance of peace.[161] English supporters of Curthose were not easily forgiven. Robert of Meulan, counseling the king on the eve of Alton, excused any later retaliation against them as being appropriate to the responsibilities of the king and his associates, "who have been entrusted by God to provide for the common good." As quoted by Orderic, Count Robert went on to advise the king, "Soothe them all with promises, grant whatever they ask," even if it should be London or York, "and in this way draw all men assiduously to your cause." And when we have come safely to the end of this affair "we will suggest practical measures for recovering the lands appropriated by rash deserters in time of war."[162]

Henry's policy toward the baronage during the months and years following Alton was never aimed at crippling great magnates or even reducing the sizes of their estates. Rather, it was designed to eliminate particular magnates whose loyalties the king could not trust and to convert others into royalists. The creation of a loyal baronage that frequented the royal court (and behaved themselves there) was the essential step in bringing peace to England. Accordingly, the decade following Alton and Winchester witnessed a substantial reordering of

[159] OV, 6:18; *MMI*, p. 94 and n. 1.

[160] *MMI*, pp. 94, 129–136; Lewis, "The King and Eye," pp. 569–589; Keats-Rohan, "Domesday Book and the Malets."

[161] OV, 618; WM, *GR*, 2:486–487.

[162] OV, 5:314–316; Vaughn, *Anselm of Bec and Robert of Meulan*, pp. 231–232. Orderic probably obtained much of his information about Robert of Meulan from Richard of Leicester, a fellow monk of Saint-Evroul and subsequently abbot of that house who, before taking monastic vows, "had spent a long time in the court of Robert, count of Meulan, where he had been admitted to his most intimate counsels and had taken a leading part in judging cases and in carrying out business as his close adviser": OV, 6:488.

the English aristocracy, with the fall of such dominant eleventh-century families as the Montgomerys, the counts of Mortain, the Grandmesnils and Malets, to be replaced in time by great royalist landholders accustomed to serving the king and to rising and flourishing through his favor—men such as Roger bishop of Salisbury, Robert of Meulan, the Albinis (Aubigny), Brian fitz Count, Stephen of Blois, and Robert of Gloucester.

Robert Curthose lingered on in England for two or three months after the treaty of Winchester. He was at Henry's court in London sometime in August, and he attended a great royal council at Windsor on 3 September in company with a distinguished assemblage of magnates and prelates from both sides of the recent struggle including Queen Matilda, Archbishops Anselm and Gerard, Robert count of Meulan and Henry earl of Warwick, Robert of Bellême earl of Shrewsbury, William of Warenne earl of Surrey, William count of Mortain and earl of Cornwall, almost the entire bench of English bishops, a plethora of distinguished abbots, and many other notable figures.[163]

Curthose and his friends are said to have been instrumental in persuading Henry to take a hard line with Anselm at the Windsor council. They were "boiling with hatred," Eadmer explains, "because Anselm had caused them to lose the kingdom."[164] Henry's and Anselm's emissaries had by then returned from Rome with a letter from Paschal to the king refusing to yield on the issues of lay investiture and clerical homage but conveying the broadest of hints that if Henry agreed to obey the papal decrees, Paschal would support Henry's throne against the claim of Robert Curthose:

> If for God's sake you give up this practice . . . from then on anything you ask of us which we can do with God's approval we shall gladly grant; and willingly encourage for your dignity and majesty . . . You will then reign more powerfully, firmly, and honorably when divine authority reigns in your kingdom.[165]

The letter arrived too late for the offer to be attractive. Curthose had already renounced the English crown, and Henry therefore had no urgent need of the pope's political support.

---

[163] *RRAN* 2, nos 544–548.

[164] Eadmer, *HN*, p. 131.

[165] *AO*, ep. 216; for Paschal's awareness of Curthose's desire for the English crown, ep. 213. An exchange of letters between England and Rome might well have taken five or six months: about ten weeks each way (if all went well) and perhaps a couple of weeks of negotiation at the papal court: see Poole, *Studies in Chronology and History*, p. 264.

According to Eadmer, Henry, with the backing of his followers and
Curthose's, tried to intimidate Anselm. He ordered his archbishop to
submit on the issues of investiture and homage or else leave the
country. If Eadmer is correct in his reporting of events, Henry's ultimatum to Anselm in September 1101 was nearly the exact reverse of
Anselm's to Henry a year before, when Anselm threatened to leave the
country if Henry did not yield to the papal decrees.[166]

Anselm's meeting with Henry and Robert Curthose at Windsor
was clouded by other factors as well. Anselm took as a deliberate
insult—perhaps rightly so—the fact that Paschal's letter responding
to Henry's and Anselm's envoys was addressed to Henry but not to
Anselm. Anselm found his position on investitures becoming
increasingly awkward: he felt bound by God to enforce the papal
decrees that he had witnessed in such dramatic circumstances in
1099 unless the pope released him from them, yet he did not hear
from the pope.[167]

Paschal's reply to Anselm arrived at last in late spring 1102, in a letter
dated 15 April. The pope reiterated the prohibitions against homage
and investiture and then cast them in a broader, Gregorian context that
was foreign to Anselm's view of clerical and secular joint rulership: "The
reverend majesty of the holy Councils," Paschal said, "has decreed that
the power of secular princes must be altogether excluded from ecclesiastical elections."[168] Ignoring this dictum, Anselm at no point contested Henry's power to "elect" bishops but only to invest them. In
short, the investiture issue was enormously more important to Henry I
than to Anselm. To Anselm, investiture was a mere ritual, prohibited
by a papal decree that might be waived; to Henry the ceremony was
deeply ingrained in his concept of the sacred duties of kingship and
royal stewardship: "The usages of my predecessors I am not willing to

---

[166] Eadmer, *HN*, pp. 120, 131. Anselm, however, declined to either submit or
leave England, and after some further discussions and negotiations he departed,
unmolested, for Canterbury.

[167] "You replied to the king by letter," Anselm complained to Paschal, "but you
did not reply to me." Repeatedly Anselm explained to the pope that he had no
ethical or theological opposition to lay investiture or clerical homage but simply
felt conscience-bound to uphold the papal decrees: "For as it does not pertain to
me to loosen what you bind, so it is not up to me to bind what you loosen." Again,
"since I have not received a letter with your reply, once again I request in humble
entreaty definite advice in a written document from your sublimity through our
envoys." And still again, "for it is not for my humility to give advice to your wisdom
in this case but to expect it from you": *AO*, epp. 218, 219, 220, all late 1101 or
early 1102. Paschal may well have delayed his reply to avoid responding to Anselm's
claim that Canterbury was entitled to the papal legateship in England: below, pp.
147–148, 151, 308, 444.

[168] *AO*, ep. 222.

lose, nor to tolerate anyone in my kingdom who is not my man."[169] The strength of Henry's feelings on investiture can perhaps be understood by imagining Anselm being asked to relinquish his professions of obedience from the English episcopal bench. Anselm would sooner have died.[170]

For Anselm, the focus of his archbishopric was not the investiture ceremony but his guardianship of the rights and prerogatives of Canterbury. And on this point Anselm was much more directly at odds in 1101 with the pope than with the king. For Anselm, the most significant issue in the English Church during 1100–1101 was the actual or potential activities of papal legates. Anselm, like Lanfranc before him, believed with all his heart that the primate of England, the archbishop of Canterbury, ought to be papal legate *ex officio* and that no other legates ought ever to visit the kingdom. The issue turned on the authority of legates over primates, which included the custom that legates, rather than primates, were to preside at kingdomwide legatine synods. It was essential to the Canterbury primacy that the archbishop always be the foremost prelate in the land.

In his first letter to Paschal on returning to England, Anselm devoted only a few laconic lines to the investiture issue; they were followed by a long and fervently argued paragraph objecting to the legatine visit of Guy archbishop of Vienne (the future Pope Calixtus II). Anselm insisted that, "as everyone asserted," the church of Canterbury had held the Roman legation to the kingdom from ancient times. He went on to state that during his exile Pope Urban II had "not taken away" from Anselm this legation, and he objected in the most strenuous terms to Guy's usurpation of it.[171] Guy departed England quickly, apparently without encountering Anselm and probably before his return. But Paschal, in his very first letter to Anselm in fall 1100 before Anselm's first letter had arrived, provided the unwelcome news that he was dispatching two papal nuncios to help adjudicate the impending dispute between Henry and Curthose and also to promote church reform and assist in the collection of Peter's Pence. Paschal was perhaps hoping to appease Anselm when he selected as the chief nuncio a former monk of Bec, John of Telese, who had been advanced to the cardinalbishopric of Tusculum. Cardinal John was accompanied by Tiberius, the pope's chamberlain.[172] Both were present at the Windsor council of 3 September, to the acute discomfort of Anselm, and both attested

---

[169] Eadmer, *HN*, p. 131.
[170] E.g., *AO*, ep. 462. One might also try to imagine a modern American Congress being asked to abolish the no less ritualistic pledge of allegiance to the flag.
[171] *AO*, ep. 214.
[172] Vaughn, *Anselm of Bec and Robert of Meulan*, pp. 227–228.

charters issued on that occasion, usually as legates, although their appearance on these witness lists below rather than above the English archbishops and bishops suggests that they did not exercise full legatine authority.[173] Hugh of Flavigny mentions only that Cardinal John was in England to collect Peter's Pence, and both Anselm and Eadmer maintain a wintry silence about their visit. But, as Sally Vaughn plausibly observes, their presence at Windsor is very likely to have been the irritant that prompted Anselm, in a charter to Holy Trinity, Norwich, issued at the same council, to style himself, in uniquely exalted terms, "archbishop of Canterbury, primate of Great Britain and Ireland, and vicar of the supreme pontiff Paschal."[174]

After the return of the two nuncios to Italy, the papacy honored Anselm's assertion of the Canterbury legateship by sending no further legates to England for the remainder of his life. Anselm, declining exile, returned to Canterbury unreconciled with the king. Robert Curthose returned in peace to Normandy laden with gifts. He was accompanied by William of Warenne and others (unnamed) "who had been disinherited in his cause."[175] And Henry, rejoicing that his throne was secure at last, celebrated Christmas 1101 at a great court at Westminster: "the first Christmas after the concord between me and my brother, Count Robert."[176]

---

[173] *RRAN* 2, nos 544, 547–548; Vaughn, *Anselm of Bec and Robert of Meulan*, p. 236.

[174] *RRAN* 2, no. 548; Vaughn, *Anselm of Bec and Robert of Meulan*, p. 236; *The Charters of Norwich Cathedral Priory, Part One*, no. 260; see also Brett, *English Church*, pp. 48–49; *Councils and Synods*, 1: part 2, pp. 667–668.

[175] OV, 5:320; the *ASC*, s.a. 1101, reports that Curthose left England "after Michaelmas"; MS Caligula A viii *(MMI*, p. 96) states that he left on 1 November.

[176] *RRAN* 2, no. 552.

Chapter 4

THE LOSS OF INVESTITURE AND THE WINNING OF NORMANDY

Although Anselm had departed Windsor for Canterbury without the friendship of Henry I, both men must have realized the necessity of undertaking further efforts to resolve their differences. (See chronology of the investiture settlement below, p. 202.) It was King Henry who made the overture. He wrote to Anselm at Canterbury, probably in early October 1101, offering him unrestricted peace and inviting him in the friendliest of terms to attend his court at Winchester to consider a change in the king's position on the investiture issue and a new plan.

The king's proposal was this: under cover of another truce between them, new envoys, more distinguished than the last, should be sent to Rome by both sides to persuade the pope to waive his decrees on investiture and homage. If Paschal did not, they were to tell him, Henry would banish Anselm from England, renounce the kingdom's allegiance to the papacy, and abolish the payment of Peter's Pence.[1] Henry and Robert of Meulan would doubtless have reasoned that, without the threat of Robert Curthose, they were in a far stronger bargaining position than before and that the pope might be more pliant. The threat to banish Anselm was probably aimed more at the pope than at the primate, who had demonstrated repeatedly that he was absolutely fearless.

Anselm apparently took no offense at Henry's threat to exile him. Always ready to seek an accommodation with the king, he agreed to the plan at once. It was clearly Anselm's hope throughout this phase of the controversy to have the burden of the investiture stalemate removed by a papal waiver and thus to assume his proper role as primate of England under a supportive king. But, as before, he scrupulously avoided using language that might imply that he was lobbying the papacy. A decision on investitures was the pope's alone to make. The primate of Canterbury could only obey. Nevertheless, Anselm pointed out to Paschal in a letter to be carried by the new legation that he had already suffered a great deal, "continuously for nine years since the beginning of my episcopate, both in exile and in my diocese, because I have

---

[1] Eadmer, *HN*, p. 132.

adhered tenaciously to the submission and obedience due to the [Apostolic] See." Anselm concluded with a prayer that God "may direct your heart to the praise and glory of his name and the benefit of his church."[2]

The new royal delegation was headed by Gerard, who had served as chancellor under the Conqueror and Rufus, was subsequently elected bishop of Hereford, and had recently been translated to the archbishopric of York to succeed Thomas I.[3] Archbishop Gerard had the twofold mission of winning a papal waiver on investitures and obtaining the pallium for his own archiepiscopal office. He was accompanied by two other bishops, Robert of Limesey bishop of Chester, who sought papal permission to move his see to the well-endowed abbey of Coventry, and Herbert Losinga bishop of Thetford, a former monk of Fécamp who had obtained his bishopric under Rufus through simony (he had paid the king a thousand marks to obtain the abbey of Newminster, Winchester, for his father and the bishopric of Thetford for himself).[4] Herbert had subsequently confessed, been forgiven by the pope, and reformed. He was now striving to obtain papal sanction for moving his see from Thetford to the larger and more prosperous town of Norwich and to restore his episcopal authority over the wealthy East Anglian abbey of Bury St Edmunds.[5] Accompanying the three bishops were two representatives of the primate, the trusted Bec monk Baldwin of Tournai and Alexander, a monk of Canterbury, who were instructed to witness the proceedings and report back to Anselm.[6]

The mission was not without success. Gerard received his pallium and the envoys returned, sometime during the summer of 1102, with papal letters and privileges permitting Bishop Robert to establish his see at Coventry and Bishop Herbert to move his see from Thetford to Norwich (but not to exercise authority over Bury St Edmunds).[7] On the issue of investiture, however, Paschal would not budge. He wrote to Henry, in an otherwise genial letter, "The investiture of churches we utterly forbid," and he informed Anselm that the Lateran synod of Lent 1102 had renewed the bans on both lay investiture and clerical homage.[8] Responding to Anselm's veiled complaint that he had already

---

[2] *AO*, ep. 220.

[3] Barlow, *English Church, 1066–1154*, p. 72; Galbraith, "Gerard the Chancellor"; Hugh the Chanter, p. 12; Fröhlich, *Die bischoflichen Kollegen Anselms*, pp. 120–135.

[4] FW, 2:33; Fröhlich, *Die bischoflichen Kollegen Anselms*, pp. 69–72, 83–89.

[5] Eadmer, *HN*, pp. 132–133; Alexander, "Herbert of Norwich, 1091–1119," pp. 158–160.

[6] Eadmer, *HN*, p. 132; Southern, *Anselm: A Portrait*, pp. 241–242 (Baldwin), 244, 368, 389–390 (Alexander).

[7] Vaughn, *Anselm of Bec and Robert of Meulan*, p. 241.

[8] *AO*, epp. 224, 222; Blumenthal, *Early Councils of Paschal II*, pp. 11, 17–18.

suffered much for the papal cause, Paschal provided added weight to Canterbury's primatial claim—though less decisively than Anselm would have wished—confirming the primacy "to your fraternity as fully and undiminished as it is known to have been held by your predecessors." And responding at last to Anselm's vigorous protests over legates, Paschal conceded, "To you personally we grant this additional privilege: that as long as your worship is preserved by divine mercy for that kingdom, you are to be subject to our judgment alone and never to that of any legate."[9] Anselm would doubtless have preferred that the Canterbury primacy be defined more explicitly and not be limited to him alone and that the legateship be granted *ex officio* not only to himself but to his successors. Nevertheless, the concessions provided a degree of papal support with regard to matters dear to Anselm's heart, and the papacy's endorsement of the Canterbury primacy was expressed in stronger terms than Anselm's revered predecessor Lanfranc had ever been able to obtain from Rome. Perhaps most specifically the pope had assured Anselm that never again would he have to contend with papal legates.

On the issues of investiture and homage, the results of the legation were more ambiguous than Paschal's letters might indicate. First, as Sir Richard Southern has perceptively suggested, the papal position on clerical homage to laymen may have begun to soften. Paschal does not mention the homage ban in his letter to Henry, and although he mentions it to Anselm, he does so for the last time. Interestingly, in his transcription of Paschal's letter, Eadmer suppresses the pope's allusion to the prohibition of clerical homage at the Lateran Lenten synod of 1102, which suggests either that he and perhaps Anselm were coming to regard the homage ban as too harsh or that, after the fact and in retrospect, Eadmer preferred to downplay the issue on which the Church eventually yielded.[10]

The other ambiguity, more striking than the first, is that the three bishops testified on their return that Paschal had instructed them, verbally and confidentially, that if the king behaved as a good Christian prince he would have tacit papal permission to invest prelates without suffering ecclesiastical penalties. Paschal did not mention this waiver in his letters (which the royal *curia* attempted to keep secret—unsuccessfully) out of fear that other princes might learn of the concession and demand similar leniency. Anselm's chief envoy, Baldwin of Tournai, denied vehemently that the pope had made any such verbal exception. The bishops replied that the exception had been intended for their

[9] *AO*, ep. 222.
[10] Vaughn, *Anselm of Bec and Robert of Meulan*, pp. 240–241 with references; Southern, *Anselm: A Portrait*, pp. 295–296.

ears alone and that the word of bishops was worth more than that of simple monks. When the Canterbury party argued that the monks' report was corroborated by the papal letters, the curial party responded that the word of three bishops was to be preferred to mere ink scribblings on sheepskins. The Canterbury party replied that the Gospels themselves consisted of ink scribblings on sheepskins.[11]

Anselm himself was in a quandary. Henry I, continuing to cherish his ancestral rights, insisted that Anselm either accept the bishops' word and honor the customs of his royal predecessors or depart the kingdom. That the bishops were telling the truth is possible but unlikely. By all reports, the court of the reform papacy was corrupt. Herbert of Norwich's failure with regard to Bury St Edmunds may well have been the result of his having been robbed on his journey to Rome of money intended for bribes at the papal curia, and similar stories of the effects of bribery on papal decision making abound in contemporary records.[12] The bishops' allegation that the waiver had to be verbal in order to protect the papacy from a rash of similar demands from other princes is quite plausible. But against this view is the fact that Paschal did not communicate any such concession to Baldwin of Tournai or Alexander of Canterbury—and that his response to the bishops' story, when it later came to his attention, was to excommunicate all three of them.[13] The bishops were all devoted to the royal court, and their story could have been of great assistance to the king's position. It seems too good to be true.

For Anselm the situation was truly puzzling. As primate of Britain and a fellow bishop, he was conscience-bound to honor the testimony of three distinguished episcopal colleagues. But Baldwin of Tournai did not believe their story, and in all probability neither did Anselm.[14] Nevertheless Henry I, supported by his magnates and prelates, was now insisting "that he would take no refusal but that Anselm should do him homage and promise to consecrate those to whom he had said that he would give bishoprics, thereby maintaining unimpaired the customs of the king's predecessors." Anselm responded by declaring that he must consult the pope further on this question "rather than make a hasty decision on a matter that admits of so much doubt."[15] When the bishops insisted once again that Anselm trust their word, he proposed still another compromise: during the period when the archiepiscopal envoys were traveling to and from Rome, King Henry might invest

[11] Eadmer, *HN*, pp. 137–138.
[12] Ibid., pp. 132–133.
[13] *AO*, ep. 280.
[14] Eadmer, *HN*, pp. 137–139.
[15] Ibid., p. 140.

prelates without Anselm's excommunicating either the giver or receiver of the investitures. But Anselm would not *consecrate* any prelates until hearing from Rome.

Anselm wrote to Paschal almost imploringly, coming nearer than ever before to begging the pope to lift the investiture ban on England:

> Prostrate in spirit at your feet, I implore you with all the fervor that I can, placed in a desperate position, that I may experience apostolic pity toward my soul, and I imploringly invoke the love of the whole Roman Church to obtain this pity. I do not fear exile, poverty, torture, or death, for my heart, fortified by God, is prepared to bear all these for the sake of obedience to the Apostolic See and the liberty of my mother the Church of Christ. I only seek certainty so that I may know what I should maintain by your authority. . . . Grant absolution from this excommunication in England so that I can remain here without danger to my soul, or else instruct me by letter that you wish to retain it, cost me what it may.[16]

Henry, rejoicing in the outcome of his negotiation with Anselm, invested his chancellor Roger, his chaplain and companion in his youthful, wandering days, as bishop of Salisbury, and Roger, his larderer, as bishop of Hereford to replace Gerard. On Roger the larderer's early death, Henry appointed and invested as bishop of Hereford Reinhelm the chancellor of Queen Matilda. None of these prelates-elect, however, was consecrated.

This was how matters stood in the autumn of 1102. King and primate were still at peace, but circumstances had engendered an outright reversal of the Church–state conflict of the previous reign. Whereas Rufus had offended Anselm and scandalized the Church by keeping a shameful number of prelacies vacant, now Anselm, constrained by the papal directives, was preventing Henry I from filling them. Consequently, the English episcopal bench remained riddled with vacancies and unconsecrated prelates. And the issue of lay investiture was far from resolved.

In the meantime, Henry I faced the task of creating a loyal or at least manageable baronage out of a group of great landholders many of whom held on both sides of the Channel and were homage-bound to both Henry I and Robert Curthose. Henry had already demonstrated impressive skill in winning over landholders while count of the Cotentin, and he had managed to more than hold his own in the crisis

---

[16] *AO*, ep. 280.

of summer 1101. But in the years just following, his challenge was even greater. At the time of Curthose's invasion in July 1101, despite the sermons on loyalty by Anselm and Gundulf, William of Malmesbury describes almost all the nobility of England as violating the fealty they had sworn to the king, and Eadmer concurs.[17] Five years thereafter, on the eve of Henry I's great victory at Tinchebray in western Normandy in September 1106, the balance of power was completely reversed. Duke Robert had only a small handful of magnate supporters, whereas the vast majority of the Anglo-Norman baronage backed Henry.[18] How did this transformation come about? The king and his party accomplished it partly by generous and dexterous patronage and partly by using their growing power to weed out magnates whom they regarded as incorrigible troublemakers. Let us turn first to the weeding out.

Henry took his coronation promise to "establish a firm peace in all my kingdom" very seriously. He had banished William of Warenne, not simply because he sided with Curthose in 1101 but probably on the specific charge that his men had seized lands and men of the bishop of Norwich. Similarly, he had brought Ivo of Grandmesnil to trial and burdened him with a heavy fine for waging private war in England and burning his neighbors' crops.[19] Henry's next step was to rid his kingdom of Robert of Bellême and his brothers, Arnulf earl of Pembroke and Roger "the Poitevin," a great landholder in Lancashire and count of La Marche in Aquitaine *jure uxoris.*

Robert of Bellême was an old acquaintance of Henry's, and no love was lost between them. They had been shipmates during their Channel crossing of 1088, at the conclusion of which they had both unexpectedly been taken captive by Robert Curthose. The betrayal of the Bellême citadel of Domfront to the young Henry in 1092 cannot have endeared him to Robert of Bellême, and Henry appears to have spent a substantial amount of his time as lord of Domfront in armed conflict with Robert. They had fought on the same side, however, under Rufus in the French Vexin in 1097, and in autumn 1100 Robert had done homage to Henry for the earldom of Shrewsbury and the rape of Arundel. But Robert had betrayed Henry by joining Curthose's force in 1101, just as he had waged war against Rufus in 1088. And he was evidently guilty of compromising the peace of Henry's kingdom by building Bridgnorth Castle (Shropshire) without royal license. He was prodigiously wealthy, having inherited most of the estates of the two

---

[17] Ibid.

[18] Below, pp. 178, 200.

[19] *RRAN* 2, no. 542; OV, 6:8; William of Warenne and Ivo had both supported Curthose in the war of 1101: OV, 5:308.

great aristocratic houses of Montgomery and Bellême, with thirty-four castles (according to Orderic) and three family abbeys: Troarn, Sées, and Almenesches.[20] On the death in 1098 of Robert of Bellême's younger brother Hugh earl of Shrewsbury, Robert, on payment of a spectacular relief of three thousand pounds to Rufus, gained his father's far-flung English estates, consisting primarily of the earldom of Shrewsbury and the rape of Arundel in Sussex—and still another great Benedictine abbey, at Shrewsbury. In addition to these formidable Montgomery lordships, Robert of Bellême obtained from Rufus (after another large payment) the honor of Tickhill in Nottinghamshire and southern Yorkshire—either by inheritance from Tickhill's Domesday lord, Roger of Builli, or as guardian of Roger's son and heir.[21] In addition, Robert's marriage to the heiress Agnes of Ponthieu brought him that important county to the northeast of Normandy *jure uxoris*.[22] At the time of Henry I's accession, Robert of Bellême was the wealthiest and most powerful magnate in the Anglo-Norman world.[23]

Robert appears to have acquired the Montgomery lands in England to the disadvantage of his two surviving full brothers, Roger the Poitevin and Arnulf of Montgomery.[24] Neither brother, however, was left destitute. Roger was a major Domesday tenant-in-chief in Lancashire, Lincolnshire, Nottinghamshire, Essex, Yorkshire, and Suffolk, with lands worth more than three hundred pounds a year, and his marriage to a Poitevin heiress in 1091 brought him the countship of La Marche. Moreover, as C. P. Lewis has shown, he held the great Malet honor of Eye (£680 a year) during much or all of Rufus' reign, although it had reverted to Robert Malet by the early years of Henry I.[25] Arnulf, having received the lands in south Wales that his father had acquired by

---

[20] Much of what follows is based on my paper "The Campaign of 1102 against Robert of Bellême," pp. 193–202; see also Thompson, "Family and Influence," pp. 215–226; Mason, "Montgomery and His Sons," pp. 1–28; *CP*, 11:682–696; Le Patourel, *Feudal Empires*, pp. 17–21; Bates, *Normandy before 1066*, pp. 100, 115–116; Hollister, "Greater Domesday Tenants-in-Chief," pp. 220–226, 231–233; OV, 6:32. On Robert's building of Bridgnorth without the king's permission, see *Brut*, trans. Jones, p. 23.

[21] OV, 5:224–226; Chibnall, "Robert of Bellême and the Castle of Tickhill," pp. 151–156.

[22] OV, 4:300; *CP*, 11:695–696; Mason, "Montgomery and His Sons," p. 13.

[23] *MMI*, pp. 106–108; Hollister, "Greater Domesday Tenants-in-Chief," pp. 220–226; Mason, "Montgomery and His Sons," pp. 26–27.

[24] Mason, "Montgomery and His Sons," pp. 19–20.

[25] Ibid., pp. 14–17; Lewis, "The King and Eye," pp. 569–589. K. S. B. Keats-Rohan suggests that Robert Malet gave Eye to Roger the Poitevin voluntarily, or pledged it to him, in order to pursue interests in Poitou: "Domesday Book and the Malets," *passim*.

conquest, bore the title earl of Pembroke, and his wealth increased significantly when Rufus gave him the honor of Holderness in Yorkshire, forfeited by Odo of Champagne after the rebellion-conspiracy of 1095.[26] All three Montgomery brothers thus bore comital titles, and together they constituted a dangerously potent and refractory force in Anglo-Norman and French politics.

By 1102 members of the Montgomery family had on no fewer than three occasions lent their support to enemies of the kings of England. Roger of Montgomery, his son Robert of Bellême, and perhaps two of Robert's brothers participated in the unsuccessful rebellion against William Rufus in 1088. Hugh of Montgomery earl of Shropshire and his younger brother Philip of Montgomery (who perished on the First Crusade) were named as being involved in the baronial conspiracy against Rufus in 1095—their father Roger having died the previous year. And the three surviving brothers—Robert of Bellême, Roger the Poitevin, and Arnulf of Montgomery—all violated recent oaths of homage to the newly crowned Henry I by supporting Robert Curthose in his abortive effort to wrest England from Henry in 1101.[27] Robert of Bellême, with his vast ancestral lands occupying the limbo between Normandy, Maine, and the French royal domain, was an archetypal frontier baron, independent to the point of being wild, radically unlike another powerful frontier baron of his generation, Robert count of Meulan, who, following Beaumont family tradition, had consistently cast his lot with one or another of the great princes of his region. Thus, Robert of Meulan was Henry I's closest friend and Robert of Bellême his most implacable enemy.

Henry, who usually exhibited considerable finesse in his dealings with great magnates, drew the line at the Montgomery brothers. He seems to have regarded their continued presence in Britain as an unacceptable menace to the stability of his kingdom. If England was to enjoy peace, Robert of Bellême had to go. It is probable that from the time of the failure of Robert Curthose's invasion effort in July 1101, Henry had deliberately set about to drive him from England.

When the king moved against the Montgomerys he evidently had popular opinion on his side. Several contemporary historians comment on Robert of Bellême's wickedness and sadism—Orderic Vitalis, William of Malmesbury, Henry of Huntingdon, Robert of Torigny—and no one speaks well of his character.[28] He was a military architect of the first order, whose latest creation, the castle of Bridgnorth, sat

<hr />

[26] Mason, "Montgomery and His Sons," pp. 17–19; English, *A Study in Feudal Society*, pp. 13–14.
[27] *MMI*, pp. 100–113.
[28] Above, pp. 64 and n. 155, 86 and n. 250.

high on a hill overlooking the Severn. His reputation for savage cruelty seems to have cost him sympathy and support and was probably a factor contributing to Henry I's success in isolating him from his fellow nobles.[29] When Robert of Bellême was under attack, the only magnates to rally to him were his own brothers, Arnulf and Roger. Surprisingly, Henry managed even to keep Robert's nephew and sometime ally, William count of Mortain, out of the fray.

Orderic reports that during the months between mid-1101 and spring 1102 Henry's agents had been watching Robert of Bellême carefully and recording instances in which he violated the law "in deed or word." In spring 1102, probably at the Easter court at Winchester (6 April), Henry confronted Robert with a list of forty-five offenses that he had committed against the king and his brother Duke Robert. Having been permitted to withdraw briefly from the royal presence to consult with his vassals in private, Robert of Bellême managed to escape from Henry's court on horseback, and he proceeded to strengthen his castles against the king's inevitable response.[30] The Welsh author of the *Brut y Tywysogyon* adds that one of the charges against Robert was his erection of the castle at Bridgnorth without royal permission and that Arnulf of Montgomery was also summoned to answer the king's charges.[31] Henry, continuing to follow the letter of the law, publicly condemned Robert of Bellême as an outlaw, issued another summons to him to appear at court, and, when Robert ignored the summons, led an army against him—the last military operation that Henry would conduct in England during his reign.[32] The campaign was altogether successful, and its success was vital to the keeping of the peace in Henry's kingdom for the next generation. As Orderic said, "After Robert was exiled, the realm of Albion remained in peace, and King Henry reigned prosperously for thirty-three years, during which time no one again dared to rebel against him in England or hold any castle against him."[33]

Chronicle accounts of the 1102 campaign vary to such a degree that they cannot be reconciled. But one can reconstruct the campaign by correlating chronicle references to charter evidence and by placing the movements of Henry's army within the time frame indicated by the *Anglo-Saxon Chronicle*. The chronicler reports that Henry first moved against Robert of Bellême shortly after the Winchester Easter court of 6 April 1102 and that he had completed the campaign before

---

[29] OV, 6:20.
[30] Ibid.
[31] *Brut*, trans. Jones, pp. 22–23.
[32] OV, 6:20–22.
[33] Ibid., p. 30.

participating with Archbishop Anselm in the great reform council at Winchester beginning at Michaelmas (29 September).[34] All three modern itineraries of Henry I place him at Westminster at the 1102 Whitsun court of 25 May, but the contemporary record and narrative evidence show only that Queen Matilda was at Westminster on Whitsunday.[35] Where then were Henry I and his army between 6 April and 29 September?

The chroniclers differ markedly as to what transpired during this interval. Most of them agree that Henry's campaign consisted of obtaining the surrender of Robert of Bellême's castles of Arundel (Sussex), Tickhill (south Yorkshire), and, in Shropshire, Shrewsbury and the newly constructed Bridgnorth. But here agreement ceases. Florence of Worcester reports that the campaign began when, on hearing the news that he had been proclaimed a traitor, Robert of Bellême, supported by his brother Arnulf, led his Anglo-Norman followers and Welsh allies on a plundering expedition into Staffordshire. Next, Henry besieged Arundel, built counter-fortifications against it, and then, leaving a force to continue the siege and sending his *curialis* Robert Bloet bishop of Lincoln to besiege Tickhill, he led "nearly the whole military force of England" into Shropshire and laid siege to Bridgnorth. Winning over many of Robert's Welsh allies with lavish gifts, Henry took both Bridgnorth and Shrewsbury within thirty days and expelled Robert of Bellême from England.[36]

The Anglo-Saxon chronicler tells a simpler tale. Henry, quarreling with Robert of Bellême, besieged Arundel and constructed siege works against it. Then, leaving a force at Arundel, he led his army to Bridgnorth, took it by siege, and exiled Robert. William of Malmesbury reverses matters by having Henry begin his campaign by besieging Bridgnorth, Robert having meanwhile withdrawn to Arundel. Bridgnorth surrendered within a few days and the men of Shrewsbury followed suit, sending Henry the key to the castle by Ralph abbot of Sées (future archbishop of Canterbury). Finally, the men of Arundel mutinied against Robert and offered their castle to the king

---

[34] *ASC, s.a.* 1102.
[35] Farrer, *Itin.*, p. 14; *RRAN* 2:xxix; Christelow, "A Moveable Feast," appendix: "A Revised Outline Itinerary for Henry I of England, August 1100–December 1135," p. 213. The only indication that Henry may have been present at the Whitsun court of 1102 is *RRAN* 2, no. 570 (attested by Archbishop Anselm and William Peverel of Nottingham) which the editors date 1102 but which is more probably 1108: cf. nos 880–881, 885, testifying to Anselm's presence at the 1108 Whitsun court, after which he presided at a primatial council: *Councils and Synods*, 1: part 2, pp. 694–704.
[36] FW, 2:49–51.

on condition that Robert be permitted to depart unharmed for Normandy.[37]

The remaining detailed account of the campaign is provided by Orderic, who, although writing from Normandy, was a native of Shropshire and seems to have had trustworthy informants in his home county.[38] His account is the most plausible of all.[39] Orderic, like Florence of Worcester, reports that Henry responded to Robert of Bellême's flight from the royal court by summoning the army of all England. This force was surely the feudal levy based on the knights owed by each of his tenants-in-chief, along with the Old English *fyrd*, consisting of one armed foot soldier from every five hides, six carucates, or comparable units of land.[40] Henry's first military effort was against Arundel, where he built siege castles and left troops to continue the siege. The castle garrison surrendered, Orderic states, after three months, having first taken the customary step of asking their lord for either reinforcements or permission to capitulate.

Leaving the siege of Arundel to continue, Henry next led his army north to the castle of Tickhill, the garrison of which surrendered immediately on the king's arrival and acknowledged him as their natural lord. Henry then disbanded his army for a time, "allowing the people a short breathing space." He sent envoys to remind his brother Robert Curthose in Normandy that they had sworn to take common action against traitors and that Robert of Bellême had committed treason. Curthose responded by raising an army and laying siege to the Bellême castle of Vignats. But the siege failed because of the duke's characteristic lethargy and the treason of one of his magnates, Robert of Montfort. Robert of Bellême's followers in Normandy thereupon went on a rampage.

In autumn 1102, Orderic continues, Henry once again summoned the army of all England—feudal host and *fyrd*—and led it into Shropshire, where it occupied Bridgnorth after a siege of three weeks, Robert of Bellême having retreated to Shrewsbury. Henry had won the allegiance of the former Montgomery vassal and wealthy Shropshire landholder William Pantulf, to whom he gave the custody of Stafford Castle and the responsibility to restore order in that region. Through William Pantulf's mediation and Henry's generosity, important Welsh princes who had been Robert of Bellême's allies joined the royal cause.

---

[37] WM, *GR*, 2:472–473.
[38] Chibnall, *World of Orderic*, pp. 3–13.
[39] OV, 6:20–32.
[40] Ibid., p. 20 and n. 4; FW, 2:50. Hollister, *Anglo-Saxon Military Institutions*, pp. 38–102; Hollister, *Military Organization of Norman England*, pp. 72–135, 216–260; Abels, *Lordship and Military Obligation, passim*.

The *Brut* reports specifically that the preeminent Welsh prince, Iorwerth son of Bleddyn, entered Henry's service at that time, having been won over in large part by Henry's grant of dominion over most of south and central Wales, and that Iorwerth began to harry Robert of Bellême's lands.[41] On the surrender of Bridgnorth (by its enfeoffed knights and against the heated objections of its mercenary garrison), Henry advanced to Shrewsbury, cutting his way through the *Huvel hegen*—the "evil hedge" (perhaps the stretch between Harley and Cressage on the present A458). On the king's entry into the town, Robert of Bellême, convinced of the hopelessness of his situation, personally delivered to Henry the keys to the castle and submitted to the forfeiture of all his English lands and to exile from Henry's dominions.[42] His brothers, Arnulf and Roger the Poitevin, suffered the same punishments.

Orderic is the only source to state that Henry went personally to Tickhill and that he granted his army a summer vacation before reassembling it to march west into Shropshire. That Henry did indeed move northward from Arundel to Tickhill is demonstrated by a royal writ in favor of Aldwin abbot of Ramsey issued at Weybridge, Huntingdonshire, *in expeditione*.[43] The writ has a date range of 1100–1102 or 1107–1110 (determined in part by Aldwin's deposition at the Michaelmas council of 1102 and his reinstatement in 1107), but the only conceivable military expedition that Henry could have been leading through Huntingdonshire would have been in 1102, and the location of Henry's court at that time makes it clear that he was heading northward toward Tickhill, not westward toward Shropshire.

The dating of the Weybridge writ to mid-1102 makes it likely that other charters of Henry I issued from Huntingdonshire within a date range that includes 1102 are roughly contemporary with it and may have been issued on Henry's march to Tickhill. Let us suppose that Henry traveled from Arundel to London and then followed Ermine Street to Brampton (a favorite royal hunting lodge), Weybridge, Ramsey (just off Ermine Street), Stamford, Lincoln, and Tickhill. His path may have been marked by a group of ten writs issued from Brampton, or at least by most of the ten.[44] One of them is in favor of the bishop of Winchester, one in favor of Earl Simon of Huntingdon and Northampton, one in favor of St Albans, two in favor of Thorney, and five in favor of Ramsey. The identity of the beneficiaries suggests

---

[41] OV, 6:28; *Brut*, trans. Jones, pp. 23–24; Nelson, *Normans in South Wales*, pp. 120–121.

[42] OV, 6:28–30.

[43] *RRAN* 2, no. 574.

[44] Ibid., nos 558, 578–586.

the picture of a king traveling through a district on urgent business, being lobbied incessantly by local interests, largely ecclesiastical. Among the witnesses are Gérard of Caux (two writs favoring Earl Simon and Ramsey: his only two attestations of surviving charters of Henry I), Urse d'Abitôt (four: all in favor of Ramsey), and Roger Bigod (five: four in favor of Ramsey and one in favor of Thorney; Roger attests the four Ramsey writs with Urse d'Abitôt and no other witnesses). These three men—Gérard of Caux, Urse d'Abitôt, and Roger Bigod—witness seven of the ten Brampton charters likely to have been issued in mid-1102.[45]

Having stopped at Brampton, Henry next appears to have passed through Weybridge, now a farm near the town of Alconbury but then in the midst of a royal forest, where Henry issued his writ *in expeditione*. He probably also stopped off at nearby Ramsey Abbey, where he issued another writ, in favor of Ranulf bishop of Durham and attested by Eustace of Breteuil and Urse d'Abitôt.[46] The next surviving footprint on his mid-1102 itinerary is an act addressed to Roger Bigod and the sheriffs of Yorkshire and Nottinghamshire in favor of the Augustinian priory of St Mary's, Blyth, and issued from Blyth, near Tickhill.[47]

Following Orderic, we can take it that Tickhill surrendered immediately on Henry's arrival and that the king then returned south, perhaps toward Woodstock or Winchester, and disbanded his army. His return journey may well have been marked by royal writs issued from Brigstock (Northants.) and nearby Geddington, the latter dated *in die SS Petri et Pauli*, that is, 29 June 1102.[48] A final writ from this return itinerary may be Henry's notification issued from Northampton to his officials in Essex in favor of Colchester Abbey, whose founder, Eudo *Dapifer*, had apparently accompanied Henry on his expedition northward.[49]

The resumption of the campaign in late summer is probably marked by a writ in favor of Abingdon Abbey issued at Wolverhampton when the king was en route to Bridgnorth.[50] And Henry's return journey from his triumph in Shropshire seems to be memorialized in writs issued from Hereford (benefiting Ranulf bishop of Durham and attested by Urse d'Abitôt) and Newham on Severn (benefiting the abbeys of Gloucester—two writs—and Marmoutier—one writ).[51]

Florence of Worcester's report that Henry I sent Robert bishop of Lincoln northward from Arundel to besiege Tickhill receives some

[45] Ibid., nos 578–583, 585.
[46] Ibid., no. 575.
[47] Ibid., no. 588.
[48] Ibid., nos 587, 573.
[49] Ibid., no. 577, cf. no. 584.
[50] Ibid., no. 576.
[51] Ibid., nos 589, 592–594.

confirmation from the absence of attestations by Bishop Robert, an extremely frequent attester of Henry I's charters, for any of the writs that we have singled out as marking Henry's itinerary along Ermine Street to Tickhill, although the bishop of Lincoln does attest two of the three writs that seem to have been issued on Henry's journey southwestward after the fall of Tickhill as well as his charter from Wolverhampton en route to Bridgnorth.[52] The charter evidence thus supports the possibility suggested by conflating Florence's and Orderic's accounts that Henry first dispatched Robert Bloet to lead an army against Tickhill and then joined him with a larger army, prompting the garrison to surrender.

Combining the chronicle and charter evidence, it becomes possible to construct a plausible, if inexact chronology for the campaign. If we follow the Anglo-Saxon chronicler's assertion that the siege of Arundel began "soon after" Easter (6 April) and Orderic's report that the siege lasted three months, then we might suppose that it ran from (very approximately) mid-April to mid-July. The distance from Arundel to Tickhill is about two hundred miles, which could have been covered in the twelfth century by easy but steady travel in about four days (at eight to fifteen miles an hour). If Henry, for example, traveled directly from Arundel to Blyth, he might have departed Arundel on, say, the morning of 23 June and arrived at Westminster or Windsor that evening. He might then have traveled on to his hunting lodge at Brampton on 24 June, left it on the morning of 25 June, and arrived that evening at Newark or Lincoln via Weybridge and Ramsey. He could then have arrived at Blyth/Tickhill on the early afternoon of 26 June and immediately have received the capitulation of the garrison. Departing Tickhill on 28 June he might have arrived at Stamford that evening and traveled the following day to Northampton (or possibly on to Woodstock) via Brigstock and Geddington, where he is known to have issued a writ attested by Robert bishop of Lincoln and dated 29 June.[53] It would thus have been entirely possible for him to have been present (as Orderic reports that he was) at the surrender of the Arundel garrison around mid-July.[54] We would then have to date the beginning of Henry's campaign in Shropshire to not much later than mid-August, if we follow Florence's statement that the castles of Bridgnorth and Shrewsbury surrendered within thirty days—which is consistent with Orderic's statements that the siege of Bridgnorth lasted three weeks and that Shrewsbury surrendered on Henry's arrival. The king

---

[52] Ibid., nos 573, 576–577.
[53] Ibid., no. 573.
[54] OV, 6:22.

would then have returned to London, via Hereford and Newnham, in time for the Michaelmas councils at Westminster.

It is possible to resurrect one uncorroborated fact from William of Malmesbury's otherwise garbled account of the campaign. William reports that it was Ralph d'Escures abbot of Sées, not Robert of Bellême himself, who presented the keys of Shrewsbury Castle to Henry I. This statement may reflect an authentic memory that Abbot Ralph mediated the negotiations between the king and Earl Robert for the surrender of Shrewsbury.[55] We know that the abbey of Shrewsbury had been colonized by monks of Sées, as had other religious houses established on Montgomery lands in England.[56] That the abbot of Sées should be in England to visit these houses is by no means an unreasonable supposition, nor is it unlikely that he might offer his services to his patron, Robert of Bellême, in mediating the surrender of Shrewsbury. After his forfeiture and banishment, Robert returned to the Continent in an evil mood,[57] and Ralph, having become a victim of Robert's wrath, abandoned the abbey of Sées and fled to England where, with the support of Henry I and Archbishop Anselm, he pursued a distinguished ecclesiastical career.[58] But his break with Robert of Bellême occurred only *after* Robert's banishment from England.[59] If Ralph's presentation of the keys of Shrewsbury Castle to Henry I actually occurred, it may well have endeared Ralph to the king, but he was nevertheless acting at the time as a loyal agent of his patron, the lord of Bellême.

As a consequence of this, the last military campaign in England for a generation, Henry confiscated all the Montgomery lands in England—Robert's earldom of Shrewsbury and rape of Arundel, Arnulf's earldom of Pembroke and honor of Holderness, Count Roger the Poitevin's vast estates in Lancashire, Lincolnshire, and beyond, and other Montgomery estates spread across many shires. Henry granted the fallen Earl Robert a safe conduct to the Channel, and Robert crossed to Normandy sadder but perhaps no wiser. He was not mourned. As Orderic says, "All England rejoiced as the cruel tyrant went into exile, and many flatteringly congratulated King Henry, saying, 'Rejoice, King Henry, give thanks to the Lord God for you have begun to rule freely now that you have conquered Robert of Bellême and driven him out of the kingdom.' "[60]

---

[55] Clark, "Ralph d'Escures," pp. 51–54, 96.
[56] Ibid., pp. 52–53; Knowles and Hadcock, *Medieval Religious Houses*, p. 76.
[57] OV, 6:32–36.
[58] OV, 4:70, 6:46.
[59] OV, 6:46; WM, *GP*, p. 127; *Recueil des actes des comtes de Pontieu*, pp. 28–29, no. xv; Abbot Ralph attests a charter of Robert of Bellême at La Fourche (near Nogent-le-Rotrou in Maine) dated 5 November 1101.
[60] OV, 6:30.

Shortly before Michaelmas 1102, probably on 26 September, a great primatial council assembled at Westminster Abbey, the first such council since the reign of William the Conqueror. It is said by a later but well-informed source to have lasted only two days, and the record of its proceedings was prepared in such haste that Anselm seems to have planned another synod, perhaps in 1103 but prevented by his exile, to tidy up the conciliar legislation and provide an authoritative text.[61] Nevertheless, the achievements of the council were substantial; as Martin Brett observed, it acted "on a scale which not even the most impressive of Lanfranc's councils had achieved."[62] And it marked a conspicuous exercise of primatial authority and responsibility that had been forbidden to Anselm by Rufus, much to Anselm's consternation.

Hugh the Chanter of York endeavors to depict the council as a joint enterprise of the archbishops of York and Canterbury:

> Archbishops Anselm and Gerard afterwards decided to hold a council. When this assembled at Westminster, and the monks [of Canterbury] had prepared a seat higher than any of the others for their archbishop, Gerard felt himself insulted and, openly cursing the man who had done this, he kicked over the seat and would not sit down until his seat was made as high as the other archbishop's, plainly showing that he owed him no subjection.[63]

Anselm's own record of the council (as reported by Eadmer) is markedly different—and probably more reliable in its emphasis on his own central role. With the approval of Henry I,

> a Council was held at the church of St Peter on the western side of London. At this council, Anselm, archbishop of Canterbury and primate of all Britain, presided, and the following dignitaries of the Church sat with him: Gerard archbishop of York, Maurice bishop of London, William bishop elect of Winchester, and others, both bishops and abbots.

Archbishop Gerard is thus lowered from his high seat down into the episcopal throng, alongside bishops Maurice, William Giffard, and "others."

Also in attendance, as was customary at such councils, were many lay magnates and probably, intermittently, the king himself, who presided

---

[61] "Annals of Margan," in *Annales monastici*, 1:7; *Councils and Synods*, 1: part 2, pp. 668–688; Brett, *English Church*, pp. 76–79.

[62] Brett, *English Church*, p. 76.

[63] Hugh the Chanter, p. 22.

at a Michaelmas council of his own at Westminster. The inclusion of laymen in Anselm's synod served the purpose of having its canons affirmed and observed by each of the estates of the realm. "This was needed," Anselm explains, "because, the practice of holding synods having been in abeyance for many years past, and vices having sprung up like weeds, the ardour of Christianity in England had grown quite cold."[64]

The canons of the council addressed and condemned a variety of such vices: simony and sodomy, lax monastic discipline, assaults by unscrupulous laymen on the privileges of parish churches, clergymen's wearing of garish clothes and shoes with pointed toes or getting drunk at parties (or on other occasions). To the chagrin of many members of the clergy, clerical celibacy was to be enforced more strictly than ever before. Lanfranc, in a council of 1076, had forbidden priests to marry but had permitted those already married to keep their wives. But Anselm's council of 1102 presented all priests with the wrenching choice of abandoning their wives or their ecclesiastical careers. And although this canon was widely ignored, the seriousness of Anselm's efforts at reform is indicated by the council's deposition of no fewer than nine abbots and abbots-elect, six of them for simony and the remaining three for other reasons, the nature of which is not altogether clear.[65] At least three and perhaps more of the simoniac abbots seem to have bought their offices from Rufus. One of the "simoniacs," Godric of Peterborough, was an Anglo-Saxon whom the Peterborough monks had elected on payment of three hundred marks to "the king" (William II or Henry) for the right of electing a new abbot. (Their previous abbot, the Norman Turold appointed by William the Conqueror, had made himself enormously unpopular with his monks by alienating nearly half the abbey's lands to kinsmen and knights and building a castle for himself near the abbey church.) Anselm, who was intent on reforming English abbeys by installing abbots trained at Bec or at houses associated with Bec (Caen, Lessay, Canterbury, Rochester, Westminster), saw nothing to be gained by permitting a monastery inhabited predominantly by Anglo-Saxons to be ruled by an unreformed Anglo-Saxon abbot, and he took a hard line in interpreting the payment of the Peterborough monks as "simony." He was able to replace Godric with a Norman monk from Mont-Saint-Michel (which was then under a Caen-trained abbot), and by 1107 he had arranged for the abbacy of Peterborough to pass to his close associate Ernulf, former prior of Canterbury.[66] In the course of the reign, Peterborough

---

[64] Eadmer, *HN*, pp. 141–142, for both quotations.
[65] Ibid., pp. 141–144.
[66] Hollister, "St Anselm on Lay Investiture."

Abbey, a religious house of formidable wealth, built one of the largest and most impressive abbey churches of the age—a church that stands to this day as a noteworthy monument to the architectural genius of early twelfth-century England.

Another deposition, that of Richard of Clare abbot of Ely, was occasioned in part by Richard's failure to obey royal commands with sufficient punctuality, perhaps his failure to bring his knights to the army that Henry assembled against Robert Curthose in 1101.[67] Another of Henry's political appointees, Robert son of Earl Hugh of Chester, was vastly unpopular with the monks of Bury St Edmunds and was deposed, presumably for incompetence.[68]

The warm relations between Henry and Anselm chilled once again early in 1103 when a letter arrived from Paschal II dated 12 December 1102 vehemently denying having given Gerard of York and the other bishops a verbal waiver permitting lay investiture in England. Paschal excommunicated the three bishops and ordered Archbishop Gerard to humble himself and his chapter by providing a written profession of obedience to Canterbury.[69] Henry had earlier, in the months following the 1102 Westminster synod, maneuvered to obtain the consecrations of prelates whom he had invested—if not from Anselm then from some other bishop. He arranged to have the curial bishops Robert Bloet of Lincoln and Robert of Bath consecrate various abbots whom he had invested,[70] and he continued to press Anselm to consecrate the three bishops-elect: William Giffard of Winchester, Roger of Salisbury, and Reinhelm of Hereford. Anselm agreed to consecrate William of Winchester, whom he himself had invested, but Henry refused to permit the consecration of William without the others.[71] The king then threatened to humiliate Canterbury by having Gerard of York consecrate all three bishops-elect. This arrangement backfired, however, when first Reinhelm of Hereford and then William of Winchester refused consecration by

---

[67] *MMI*, p. 73; Richard was later restored: Knowles et al., *Heads of Religious Houses*, p. 45 with references.

[68] Knowles et al., *Heads of Religious Houses*, p. 32 with references; Eadmer, *HN*, p. 142.

[69] *AO*, epp. 281, 283; Eadmer, *HN*, p. 216: Eadmer highlights the letter by placing it at the end of his book 4, concluding his treatment of Anselm. The written profession of archbishops of York to Canterbury was one of the most hotly disputed issues in the post-Conquest English Church; the issue had earlier been settled between Gerard and Anselm by Gerard affirming the written profession that he had previously given to Canterbury as bishop of Hereford and, subsequently, professing verbally to Anselm: Eadmer, *HN*, pp. 186–187. Despite Paschal's letter, Gerard did not, as archbishop of York, profess in writing to Canterbury.

[70] Eadmer, *HN*, p. 148; *AO*, ep. 261.

[71] Eadmer, *HN*, pp. 144–145.

anyone except Anselm. Henry, furious at their disobedience, had them both expelled from England.[72]

By March 1103 both Anselm and Henry had received Pope Paschal's letters repudiating the allegation of the three bishops that he had waived the investiture ban for England. Henry now came to Canterbury, where he proceeded to negotiate with Anselm through intermediaries. Although the papal letters forcefully reasserted the investiture ban and excommunicated the three bishops, both king and archbishop avoided a political impasse by adopting the useful fiction that they had left their letters unopened and were unaware of their contents. Anselm was thus able to evade the wrath of the king and the English Church by ignoring the papal command to excommunicate the three bishops. (Henry's and Anselm's messengers would of course have reported the pope's position to them—and in much greater detail than the letters themselves did.[73]) Henry, asserting that his patience was becoming exhausted, asked Anselm to cease opposing the exercise of traditional royal prerogatives, and royal advisers began spreading rumors that the king intended to have Anselm exiled, or even mutilated (so Eadmer improbably asserts), if he did not yield on the issues of investiture and homage.[74] Anselm responded by suggesting that he and the king open their letters from Paschal. Henry is said to have refused, responding, "What business do I have with the pope about things that are mine? If anyone wishes to rob me of them, he is my enemy."[75]

The confrontation between Henry and Anselm at Canterbury in March 1103 was a standoff. As had been their custom, king and primate exchanged no angry ultimatums; the rumors of mutilation (if any) or exile were circulated by royal counselors, not by the king. Henry remained absolutely determined to retain the prerogatives that his father and other predecessors had exercised, but he kept his temper and avoided an irrevocable break. Indeed, a few days after the confrontation at Canterbury, Henry offered still another compromise proposal to Anselm: he urged that the archbishop himself travel to Rome to persuade the pope to waive the bans. To accompany Anselm, the king would send his seasoned envoy William Warelwast, whom Sir Richard Southern has perceptively described as the first clear example of a professional civil servant in English history.[76] Anselm, who doubted that Paschal would relent under any circumstances, asked that the issue be postponed until he could consult the great men of the realm at the

---

[72] Ibid., pp. 144–146; AO, epp. 265, 273–276.
[73] Vaughn, *Anselm of Bec and Robert of Meulan*, p. 254.
[74] Eadmer, *HN*, pp. 146–147.
[75] Ibid., p. 147.
[76] Southern, *Anselm and His Biographer*, p. 172.

coming Easter court at Winchester (29 March), and Henry agreed.
Once again they parted in peace.[77] At Easter the magnates and prelates
of the realm agreed unanimously with Henry that the only solution to
the impasse was for Anselm to journey to Rome and himself plead with
the pope for an exemption from the investiture ban. And Anselm,
although asserting that he was already feeling the infirmity of old age,
agreed to go (his papal letter still unopened).[78]

Anselm crossed the Channel and arrived at Wissant in Boulogne on
27 April 1103. Passing into Normandy, he arrived at Bec, to the great
joy of the monastic congregation. At Bec he at last opened Paschal's
letter, which reaffirmed the investiture ban and pronounced the
excommunication of the three "lying" bishops and of all prelates-
elect who had accepted investiture from the king.[79] Anselm must have
realized that the effect of the letter was to make it impossible for him
to return to England and function as primate. He moved on to Chartres
but was told there by his friend Ivo bishop of Chartres that the Italian
summer was singularly hot that year and deadly to foreigners. Anselm
therefore returned to Bec and spent some time in the congenial task
of providing instruction to the monks. In mid-August he set off again
for Rome.

Shortly after arriving at the papal court, Anselm met Paschal
and explained to him "the circumstances that had occasioned my
coming." The pope rejected Anselm's petition, replying "that he
refused absolutely to dissent from the decrees of his predecessors."[80]
Paschal did grant Anselm a privilege that might enable him to continue
functioning as primate in England: he was empowered to restore to
communion the erring bishops and the prelates who had accepted
investiture from the king, on their performance of whatever penance
the primate deemed appropriate. Much more important for Anselm,
Paschal granted him, "so that it may not be thought that you are leaving
the home of the shepherds of the church empty-handed," his request
for papal confirmation of the Canterbury primacy not only to Anselm
but to all his lawful successors, "as your predecessors have undoubtedly
held by the authority of the Apostolic See."[81] Although the precise
scope of Canterbury's primatial powers remained undefined, this privilege constituted the apogee of papal support for Canterbury's authority over the English Church. It was a much firmer endorsement than
Lanfranc had achieved or than any of Anselm's successors would

[77] Eadmer, HN, p. 147.
[78] Ibid., p. 148.
[79] AO, ep. 222.
[80] Ibid., ep. 308, Anselm to Henry.
[81] Ibid., ep. 303, dated 17 November 1103; Eadmer, HN, pp. 154–155.

achieve. As Richard Southern asserts, it was "the high-water mark in the Canterbury claim to primacy."[82]

Nevertheless, Paschal's intransigence on investitures, coupled with Henry's, left Anselm without room to negotiate further. In the firm conviction that the papacy was arbitrarily changing the rules, violating ancient custom, and endeavoring to rob him of his ancestral privileges, Henry had declared that he would "risk the loss of his kingdom rather than let himself be deprived of the right of investiture of churches." The pope had replied that "not even to save his life will Bishop Paschal ever let him have such a right with impunity."[83] Not only the eloquent arguments of the king's envoy, William Warelwast, but even the petition of Anselm himself had failed to dent the papal resolve. There could be no further truces while delegations journeyed between England and Rome. The king's claim, Eadmer writes, "was tried in Rome and finally decided."[84] The issue was now closed, and Anselm was trapped by the two conflicting powers, royal and papal.

Anselm departed Rome for England carrying his papal privilege for Canterbury and a letter, now lost, from Paschal to Henry that was presumably stern. The archbishop left ahead of William Warelwast, who evidently continued without avail to seek a papal waiver of the investiture ruling. He did manage to elicit from Paschal a more conciliatory letter to the king than the one that Anselm carried. William's party was joined by Anselm's at the Lombard town of Piacenza on the River Po. The two groups traveled together toward Lyons, where Anselm planned on celebrating Christmas with his friend and host in his previous exile, Archbishop Hugh of Lyons. William Warelwast chose not to enter the city but to move swiftly on toward England.

Before the parties separated, William spoke privately with Anselm and presented him with an ultimatum from Henry, cautiously worded and perhaps not unexpected. Eadmer quotes William as saying:

I was expecting that at Rome our case would turn out differently, so I refrained until now from acquainting you with the message that my lord the king told me to give to you. But now, since I plan to return to him in haste, I do not wish to keep back his message any longer. What he says is that if you return to him on the understanding that you will treat him in all respects as your predecessors are known to have treated his predecessors, then he will gladly approve of your returning to England and will welcome it.

[82] Southern, *Anselm: A Portrait*, p. 342.
[83] Eadmer, *HN*, p. 153.
[84] Ibid., p. 154.

Anselm replied, "Is that all you will say?" "To you," William answered, "a word is enough. There is no need in this matter to say anything more." William assumed that Anselm possessed the political acumen to understand Henry's guarded message, and he was not mistaken. "I note what you say," Anselm replied, "and I take your meaning." With these words they parted, and Anselm entered Lyons to greet Archbishop Hugh and begin his second exile as the archbishop's guest.[85]

In the months that followed, Anselm corresponded with both Henry and Queen Matilda. Henry repeatedly urged that Anselm return to be with him as Lanfranc, Anselm's revered predecessor, had been with Henry's father, William the Conqueror. In the meantime, however, since Anselm was no longer functioning as archbishop, Henry confiscated the very considerable Canterbury revenues—the largest of any English bishopric—and diverted them to the royal treasury. Anselm responded firmly, demanding the return of the revenues and arguing that the papal decrees made it impossible to return to the old days of William I and Lanfranc and lay investiture. At Queen Matilda's urging, Henry eventually restored half the Canterbury revenues to the archbishopric, but Anselm refused to be consoled until the king had restored them all. Nevertheless, the correspondence between Henry and Anselm at this time remained a model of civility. If only Anselm would consent to be with the king "like your predecessor Lanfranc was with my father for many years," Henry would grant him "all the honors and dignities and friendship that my father gave to your predecessor." In announcing the seizure of the Canterbury revenues, which Henry softened into a concession to permit Anselm to withdraw from the responsibility of the Canterbury archbishopric, he added that he did so most unwillingly, "because I would wish to have no mortal man with me in my kingdom more willingly than you."[86] Anselm replied with a gentle, point-by-point refutation of the royal position: "Neither at baptism nor at any of my ordinations did I promise to obey any law or customs of your father or Lanfranc, but only the laws of God." Nevertheless, thanking the king for his affectionate words, Anselm responded, "With no other king or prince would I so willingly live, no other so willingly serve."[87] In drastic contrast to other Church–state clashes of the High Middle Ages—Gregory VII and Henry IV, Henry II and Becket, Alexander III and Barbarossa, Philip the Fair and Boniface VIII—the conflict between Henry I and Anselm, with its courtesies and soft words, suggests not so much a fight to the death as a quarrel between like-minded men who respected each other.

---

[85] Ibid., p. 157.
[86] AO, ep. 318.
[87] Ibid., ep. 319.

As Henry I and Robert of Meulan shadow-boxed with Anselm, they were also engaged in winning over to Henry's side the majority of the Anglo-Norman barons, most of whom had backed Robert Curthose in 1101. It may be helpful to examine two tables suggesting the identities of the wealthiest magnates in both England and Normandy in AD 1100, based on Domesday statistics in England and on several less precise but not unreliable indices in Normandy.[88] In reconstructing the English baronial power structure in 1100, Domesday evidence must be used with caution, taking into account changes in the political fortunes of several Domesday holders and their families during the years since the original Norman settlement. Odo of Bayeux, the wealthiest landholder in Domesday England, had been disseised and imprisoned by his royal brother in 1082, restored in 1087, and disseised again by William Rufus in 1088. Still earlier, in 1075, the vast holdings of the Conqueror's steward, kinsman, and bosom friend William fitz Osbern had passed to the king on the failed rebellion of his son and heir, Roger earl of Hereford. Conversely, some men grew wealthier during the years between the Domesday survey and 1100—Robert fitz Hamon, Urse of Abitôt, Arnulf of Montgomery, Robert of Bellême, and others. Yet William Rufus does not appear to have created any new honors on the scale of the major Domesday configurations. With appropriate caution, one can therefore use Domesday statistics, modified by narrative and charter evidence, to reconstruct the upper baronial power structure that Henry I encountered at his accession. Table 4.1 shows its approximate shape.

The list of magnates in this table discloses with clarity the formidable baronial opposition that Henry had faced in 1101: The three wealthiest English magnates—Robert of Bellême, William of Mortain, and William of Warenne—either backed Curthose or leaned toward him; the fourth, Stephen of Richmond, was probably off in his Breton homeland and out of the picture. Henry's friend Hugh of Chester was dying; he became a monk at his abbey of St Werbergh, Chester, on 23 July 1101 and died four days later, leaving his seven-year-old son Richard as his heir. As for the remaining magnates on the list, Gilbert of Clare and his men had made it a habit of bullying King Henry at the royal court; William of Mandeville as constable of the Tower of London had, whether knowingly or not, allowed Flambard to escape;[89] Robert Malet, a friend of the king's, may not have been in possession of his lands in 1100;[90] and the loyalties of Henry of Ferrers and Philip of

[88] *MMI*, p. 106; Hollister, "Greater Domesday Tenants-in-Chief," pp. 242–248.
[89] *MMI*, pp. 73, 81, 118–119, 180 (cf. p. xv).
[90] Robert Malet's Domesday lands seem to have been in the possession of Robert of Bellême's brother Roger the Poitevin in 1100, although they reverted to Robert

Table 4.1. England: The Greater Domesday Families Holding in 1100

1100 Holder	Domesday Wealth/£ per Year
Robert of Bellême	£2,430
William count of Mortain	£2,100
William II of Warenne	£1,165
Stephen lord of Richmond	£1,100, plus waste
Hugh earl of Chester	£800
Gilbert of Clare	£780
William of Mandeville	£780
Robert Malet	£680
Henry of Ferrers	£545
Philip of Braose	£455, plus Welsh lands

Braose were far from certain. Henry of Ferrers' son, William, would fight on the ducal side at Tinchebray in 1106, and Philip of Braose would be arrested for treason in 1110.[91] In short, the dominating English magnates in 1100 constituted a group with which the king could hardly have felt safe.

By the end of 1102, however, Henry had begun to reshuffle his aristocracy—a continuation of the reshuffling that had been going on ever since the Conquest. Robert of Bellême and his brothers were disseised and in exile, as was William of Warenne. Another great landholder, Eustace count of Boulogne (£915 a year, which would have placed him fifth on the above list), had been disseised by Rufus in 1088 but restored by Henry in the settlement of 1101. He married Matilda II's sister Mary of Scotland and became a trusted royalist.[92]

Still another magnate who acquired very great wealth in England at about this time was King Henry's first counselor, Robert count of Meulan in the French Vexin and lord of the vast Beaumont lands in Normandy, whose English holdings had until then been relatively modest. Robert of Meulan responded to a plea for help by Ivo of Grandmesnil, a great landholder in and around Leicestershire who, as we have seen, ran afoul of Henry I by waging private war and burning his neighbors' crops—"which is an unheard-of crime in [England] and can be atoned for only by a very heavy fine."[93] King Henry imposed exactly such a fine and withdrew his friendship from Ivo, who sought refuge from the royal enmity by placing himself under the protection

Malet shortly thereafter: Lewis, "The King and Eye," *passim*; see also *MMI*, pp. 129–136.

[91] *AO*, ep. 401; *ASC*, *s.a.* 1110.

[92] FW, 2:51.

[93] For this and what follows, OV, 6:18–20; Vaughn, *Anselm of Bec and Robert of Meulan*, p. 238; *CP*, 7:524–525.

of Henry's closest associate, the count of Meulan. Ivo, who had earlier cut short his participation in the First Crusade by fleeing home in panic from the siege of Antioch, resolved to redeem at least a few shreds of his tattered military reputation by journeying again to the Holy Land. In return for Robert of Meulan's good offices with the king and a loan of five hundred marks, Ivo granted Robert all his English lands in pledge for fifteen years, at the end of which Robert promised to give the daughter of his brother Henry earl of Warwick in marriage to Ivo and restore his paternal inheritance. Neither the marriage nor the restoration ever occurred, owing at least in part to Ivo's death abroad and the death of his two sons in the wreck of the White Ship in 1120. Robert of Meulan, meanwhile, acquired most of the town of Leicester, its castellanship, and a new title, "earl of Leicester" (which he did not personally use, preferring the more prestigious title "count of Meulan"). With these extensive new lands, along with further gifts from the royal domain and, in or after 1104, chunks of the forfeited lands of William of Mortain in the rape of Pevensey and elsewhere, Robert of Meulan became one of the very wealthiest magnates in England.[94]

Further major alterations in the list of English magnates included the reinstatement of William of Warenne in 1103 and his conversion to the royalist cause, accompanied by the gradual taming of the Clares and the disseising of William count of Mortain in 1104.[95] It was probably in 1103 that Henry punished William of Mandeville for his carelessness (or worse) as keeper of the Tower two years before by depriving him of his three most valuable manors—Great Waltham and Saffron Walden (Essex) and Sawbridgeworth (Hertfordshire)—and placing them in the hands of Eudo *Dapifer*, a trusted, frequently attesting royal servant who also happened to be William of Mandeville's father-in-law.[96] The future history of these three manors is interesting to trace, but for now suffice it to say that they did not revert to the Mandeville male line until Stephen's reign. In the meantime, the Mandevilles played no significant role in the Anglo-Norman aristocratic power structure. Collectively, these changes resulted by late 1104 in

[94] Fox, "Honour and Earldom of Leicester," pp. 385–388; Mason, *William the First and the Sussex Rapes*, p. 20. The English lands acquired by Robert of Meulan, and held in 1166 by his son Robert earl of Leicester, contained some 157 knights fees in the later twelfth century: Keefe, *Feudal Assessments*, p. 162. A vestige of the old Grandmesnil claim to Leicester is probably reflected in the marriage, in the 1150s, of Robert of Meulan's grandson, Robert *Blanchemains* earl of Leicester to Ivo's granddaughter Petronilla, heiress of the Norman honor of Grandmesnil: *CP*, 7:532.

[95] Below, pp. 182–183, 236, 339–340.

[96] *MMI*, pp. 117–127; the three manors had a Domesday value, collectively, of £160, about a third of the Mandeville demesne revenues.

a much friendlier English baronage than Henry had confronted at his accession.

It is possible to compile a list of the greatest landholders in Normandy, comparable to the English list and only marginally less reliable. The Norman landholding elite can be identified by comparing (1) a list of persons identified by William of Poitiers as the outstanding Norman magnates of 1066 with (2) the leading baronial contributors on William the Conqueror's Ship List of circa 1066, (3) the Norman families that had founded Benedictine abbeys before and during the Conquest era, and (4) information on enfeoffment totals and *servicia debita* provided in the Norman *Infeudationes militum* of 1172 (see table 4.2).[97] None of these sources provides data of comparable precision to that of Domesday Book, but the correlation between them is remarkably tight, sufficiently so as to warrant confidence in their collective testimony. This testimony provides valuable context to the loosening of Robert Curthose's hold on Normandy, permitting us to go beyond mere anecdotal evidence to explore in deeper perspective the erosion of ducal support among the Norman baronage between 1101 and 1106.

William of Poitiers identifies seven men as the greatest Norman lay magnates in 1066—"shining like luminaries and ornaments and equal in wisdom to the entire Senate of the Roman Republic." These magnificent seven were the counts or lords of Mortain, Evreux, Beaumont, Eu, Montgomery, and Breteuil, and Hugh "the *Vicomte*."[98] This last person was almost certainly not Hugh *vicomte* of Avranches, whose *vicomté* was still held in 1066 by his father, Richard Goz, but Hugh II of Montfort, who had inherited his *vicomté* from his father, Hugh I, probably in the 1040s, and is identified in other pre-Conquest documents as *Vicomte* Hugh.[99] When we review the eight Norman laymen on the Ship List owing the most ships (fifty or more), they include all seven of William of Poitiers' luminaries. This striking parallel prompted one historian to suggest to me that William of Poitiers may have peeped at the Ship List before providing his seven names, but this seems highly unlikely—if only because the Ship List, at least in its present form (of which there is but a single manuscript), presents the names of the ship providers in considerable disorder. Indeed, one luckless nineteenth-century editor drastically mistranscribed the name of one of the

---

[97] Hollister, "Greater Domesday Tenants-in-Chief," pp. 221–248; van Houts, "Ship List"; Keefe, *Feudal Assessments*, pp. 141–153.

[98] William of Poitiers, *Histoire de Guillaume le Conquérant*, p. 148.

[99] Bates, *Normandy before 1066*, p. 142 n. 93; *Recueil des actes des ducs de Normandie*, no. 137, a ducal charter of 1055 signed by, among others, "Hugonis vicecomitis de Monteforti."

Table 4.2. Normandy: The Wealthiest Landholders, 1066–1172

Name [holder in 1100 in brackets]	1066 List Ship (ships/ knights)	Family abbeys	Knights 1172 (quota in parentheses)
*Robert count of Mortain [William count of Mortain]	120/__	Grestain	?? (29 2/3)
Odo bishop of Bayeux [Turold bishop of Bayeux]	100/__	—	120 (20)
*William count of Evreux [? same]	80/__	Saint-Sauveur, Evreux	58?
*Roger of Montgomery [Robert of Bellême]	60/__	Saint-Martin, Sées; Troarn; Almenesches	111 (20)
*William fitz Osbern [William of Breteuil]	60/__	Lyre; Cormeilles	98.5 (?)
Hugh earl of Chester [same]**	60/__	Saint-Sever	52 (10)
*Robert count of Eu [Henry count of Eu]	60/__	Saint-Pierre-sur-Dives; Notre-Dame du Pré, Lisieux; Le Tréport	? (?)
*Roger of Beaumont [Robert count of Meulan]	60/__	Saint-Pierre, Préaux; Saint-Léger, Préaux	78.6 (S-P) or 88.6 (S-L) (25)
*Hugh of Montfort [Robert of Montfort]	50/60	—	55.5 (?)
Fulk of Aunou [Fulk of Aunou]	40/__	—	34.5 (4)
Gerald *Dapifer* (lord of Roumare) [Robert or Roger fitz Gerald]	40/__	—	14 (3 or 4)
Walter Giffard [Walter II Giffard earl of Buckingham, son & heir]	30/100	(Cluniac priory at Longueville)	99 or 103 (?)
Ralph III of Conches/Tosny [same]	__/__	Conches	50 (?)
Hugh of Grandmesnil [Robert of Grandmesnil]	__/__	Saint-Evroul	40 (10)

* On William of Poitiers' list of seven leading magnates, 1066.
** These figures represent the *vicomtés* of both the Avranchin and the Bessin, which were separate in 1066 and 1100 but were joined in 1121 under Ranulf I earl of Chester.

foremost contributors of ships, thereby masking the significance of the list for the next 140 years.[100] In table 4.2 I have rearranged the order of names to correspond with the number of ships that each of them provided. I have ignored the quotas of knights, which are assigned to four of the fourteen men on the list, because our single surviving manuscript presents the knights quotas with hopeless inconsistency: the top eight names, responsible for six hundred ships, are not assigned any knights at all!

I have also omitted two churchmen on the Ship List, Nicholas abbot of Saint-Ouen and Remigius almoner of Fécamp (future bishop of Lincoln), because the numbers of their ships (fifteen and one, respectively) seem insufficient to rank them in the upper tier of the Norman aristocracy.[101] Conversely, I have added two lay magnates absent from the Ship List, Ralph of Conches/Tosny and Hugh of Grandmesnil, both of whose families are in the charmed circle of abbey founders and whose enfeoffments, as later recorded in the Norman *Infeudationes militum* of 1172, are substantial.[102]

About nineteen abbeys were founded by some twelve Norman aristocratic families between 1030 (when the process began) and the 1070s, when William of Poitiers was writing. Two of the nineteen abbeys were founded by a family that had died out by 1066, leaving seventeen abbeys founded by eleven families active at the time of William of Poitiers' list and the Ship List. The founding of a full-scale Benedictine abbey was at once pious, fashionable, and extremely expensive: families of less than formidable wealth had to settle for mere priories (with the exception of Cluniac priories, which were usually at least as elaborate and expensive to found as abbeys, the two Anglo-Norman

---

[100] The culprit, J. A. Giles (*Scriptores*, ed. Giles p. 5), compounded the error of the seventeenth-century editor Silas Taylor (*Gavel-kind with the Etymology Thereof* [London, 1663], p. 209), who had mistranscribed the largest donor of ships, Robert *de Morotein* (120 vessels) as "Robert de Mortemer." Giles, having evidently not consulted the original document, changed the name to "Roger of Mortemer"—presumably on the grounds that Roger of Mortemer was a well-known Conquest magnate whereas Robert of Mortemer was not. Elisabeth van Houts has at last made good sense of the list by providing a correct transcription, clarifying that the list's largest donor was Robert count of Mortain, the Conqueror's immensely wealthy half-brother: "Ship List," pp. 175–176; cf. Hollister, "Greater Domesday Tenants-in-Chief," pp. 221–223, 243. The names of the major donors on the list are those most prominent in the Conqueror's councils, but their order is badly garbled in the surviving manuscript: Robert count of Mortain, for example, although credited with more ships than anyone else, occurs next to last, with Odo of Bayeux, the second most generous provider (100 ships), immediately behind him.

[101] Nicholas of Saint-Ouen, however, is credited with providing 100 knights. He was William the Conqueror's first cousin and the most frequent abbatial attester of his pre-Conquest charters: Hollister, "Greater Domesday Tenants-in-Chief," p. 223.

[102] On abbey foundations see ibid., pp. 224–225, 244–245.

examples being the Giffard Cluniac priory at Longueville in upper Normandy and the Warenne Cluniac priory at Lewes in Sussex).[103] Table 4.2 discloses the high correlation between abbey-founding families and the persons on William of Poitiers' list and the Ship List: six of William of Poitiers' seven represent abbey-founding families, and these families were responsible for twelve of the seventeen abbeys in question. Similarly, the men on the Ship List (including every layman charged with sixty ships or more) represented eight of the eleven abbey-founding families and were responsible for thirteen of the seventeen abbeys.

Henry II's *Infeudationes militum* provides data, not always complete, on the military quotas to the duke and the total enfeoffments of some 185 lay and ecclesiastical honors. Since many Conquest honors survived more or less intact through the twelfth century, even when passing from one family to another, their military quotas and enfeoffments as recorded in 1172 do have some bearing on their wealth in 1066 or 1100. The relationship is of course not exact. As families rose and fell, honors might grow or crumble. Enfeoffment policies and quota assessments might also have been idiosyncratic. Worst of all, the survey of 1172 concludes with a list of twenty-three landholders, some from celebrated families, who, deplorably, neglected to provide any information at all. Occasionally one can fill in the missing information from other, slightly later sources; often, one cannot. But it is reassuring to find that when one rearranges the names in the 1172 inquest in descending order of quotas and enfeoffments, one finds familiar names at the top: the count of Mortain with the highest quota in Normandy and the bishop of Bayeux with the highest recorded enfeoffment total. Among the twelve men who had enfeoffed fifty knights or more (from the *Infeudationes* or later data), six represent families or honors included in William of Poitiers' magnificent seven (the return of the seventh man, the count of Eu, is absent altogether from the 1172 inquest), nine represent families or honors on the Ship List—including all providers of at least fifty ships except the missing count of Eu—and nine represent Conquest and pre-Conquest abbey-founding families.

A concordance of all these sources—William of Poitiers, the Ship List, family abbey foundations, and the inquest of 1172—can thus provide a reasonable approximation of the post-Conquest Norman upper aristocracy. A glance at table 4.2 will make clear that Robert

---

[103] The abbeys and their founders are tabulated ibid., pp 244–245; the table is based on Potts, "Les Ducs normands et leur nobles," and, more generally, Besse, *Abbayes et prieurés de l'ancienne France* 7, *Province écclésiastique de Rouen*. In my analysis of abbey-founding families, I include the Giffard Cluniac priory at Longueville.

Curthose's position in Normandy in 1102–1106 was far less stable than Henry's in England after his reshufflings. Curthose's relations with Robert of Bellême alternated between enmity and fragile friendship. Curthose had agreed to Henry's demand in 1102 that the duke honor the treaty of Winchester by declaring war against Bellême but, as so often before, Curthose's war went badly and he had to come to terms.

Several other major Norman landholders had substantial holdings in England as well: William of Mortain earl of Cornwall, Henry of Eu lord of the rape of Hastings, Walter Giffard II earl of Buckingham, Robert of Montfort lord of Haughley (Suffolk), and Stephen lord of the strategic lordship of Aumale in northeastern Normandy, to whom Henry had restored the lordship of Holderness on the fall of the Montgomerys in 1102. None of these lords could defy King Henry, now that his regime was stable, without risking their English lordships, and few of them chose to. The honor of Giffard was out of the picture on the death in mid-July 1102 of Walter II Giffard, whose son, heir, and namesake was still a minor. Nor could Curthose count on Robert of Montfort, whose defection from the ducal army at the siege of Vignats in 1102 had doomed the entire military operation and plunged the Hiémois into anarchy.[104] The bishopric of Bayeux, since the departure and death of Odo, had suffered great losses in land and prestige and, under its new and ineffective bishop, Turold of Envermeu, was for all practical purposes *hors de combat*.[105] And of course Robert of Meulan, with his vast and strategically situated lands dominating the Risle Valley in central Normandy (along with the county of Meulan to the east of the duchy), was Henry's confidant.

The years just following Robert of Bellême's expulsion from England witnessed a steady peeling off of Curthose's support among the Norman aristocracy. It began with the death of William of Breteuil on 12 January 1103 without a direct legitimate male heir, which resulted in a complex struggle for the succession to this immensely wealthy lordship that had once been the Norman patrimony of William fitz Osbern. While William of Breteuil was being buried at the family abbey of Lire, his natural son Eustace, who had earlier participated in the royal military expedition against Tickhill,[106] took possession of his lands and castles, against the claims of William of Breteuil's nephews, the Breton William of Gael and the Burgundian Reginald of Grancey.[107] The

[104] OV, 6:22–24; above, pp. 157, 159. On Henry count of Eu see Searle, *Lordship and Community*; on Stephen of Aumale, English, *A Study in Feudal Society*, pp. 14–16; on Walter II Giffard, below, pp. 257, 264, 339–340.
[105] Gleason, *Ecclesiastical Barony*, pp. 17–23.
[106] *RRAN* 2, no. 575.
[107] *GND*, 2:230; OV, 6:40.

former died shortly afterward, but Reginald of Grancey made war against Eustace and devastated the Evreçin, winning over several neighboring magnates who were traditional enemies of the lords of Breteuil—William count of Evreux, his nephew Amaury of Montfort (whose sister Bertrade was the former countess of Anjou and present queen of France), Ralph of Tosny, and Ascelin Goel lord of Ivry. Eustace sought the help of Henry I, who granted him his illegitimate daughter Juliana in marriage and promised him military support against his enemies.[108] At about the same time Henry I married another of his bastard daughters, bearing the fashionable name Matilda, to Rotrou count of the neighboring principality of Perche. The king took the further step of sending his trusted adviser Robert of Meulan to Normandy to intervene in the dispute and to urge Robert Curthose and the Norman barons to support his new son-in-law Eustace against the pretensions of the "foreigner" Reginald.

Gradually the tide turned in Eustace's favor and Reginald became increasingly desperate. Seizing a castle held by Eustace's supporters, Reginald personally plunged his sword into the entrails of each member of the garrison, but instead of intimidating Eustace's allies the act made Reginald "an object of general hatred."[109] Eustace thereupon occupied his father's entire honor, and Reginald returned empty-handed to Burgundy (where he met a bad end). Undeterred, Ascelin Goel continued to fight. He kidnapped one of Robert of Meulan's clients, a very wealthy burgher of the town of Meulan named John, who had evidently been providing loans to support Robert of Meulan's activities but was now confined for four months in Ascelin Goel's gaol. Having tried in vain to rescue him, Robert of Meulan, "being a cunning man," arranged a peace with all concerned parties, who now recognized the right of Eustace and Juliana to the lordship of Breteuil. A marriage was promised (but never took place) between Robert of Meulan's one-year-old daughter and William of Evreux's nephew, Amaury of Montfort; Ascelin Goel released John of Meulan; and the other contenders laid down their arms. As the dust cleared, King Henry had three formidable allies among the highest nobility of central and south-central Normandy: the lords of Beaumont and Breteuil and the count of Perche—the last two being royal in-laws. Beaumont and Breteuil, of course, were among the foremost Norman lordships on William of Poitiers' list and the Ship List; their lords had owed 120 ships, had founded no fewer than four Benedictine abbeys, and had enfeoffed, between them, some 180 knights. And by mid-1103 they were both staunch backers of Henry I.

---

[108] OV, 6:40; *CP*, 11, app. D, p. 187.
[109] OV, 6:44.

One noteworthy aspect of the Breteuil inheritance dispute is the absence of Robert Curthose from the conflict. His invisibility is typical of his very casual rule over Normandy and may also have been occasioned by the absorbing events that were then occurring in Curthose's personal life. On 25 October 1102 his duchess, Sibylla of Conversano, gave birth to his first and only legitimate son, William "Clito." Sibylla was much admired by the writers of her time, who praised her for her beauty and intelligence. Robert of Torigny observed that when she administered Normandy during Curthose's absences, she did so more successfully than her husband had done.[110] But not long after giving birth to William Clito, Sibylla died—of an illness, so William of Malmesbury reports, brought on by a midwife mistakenly binding her breasts too tightly, or as Robert of Torigny remarks, more darkly, "by a jealous cabal of some noblewomen."[111] Orderic, who similarly admired Sibylla, quotes the epitaph on her tomb at the cathedral of Rouen, which implies that she died on 18 March 1103. He tells of an adulterous relationship between Robert Curthose and Agnes Giffard, widow of Walter II Giffard (who died on 15 July 1102), explaining that Agnes, hoping to marry Duke Robert and rule Normandy for him, arranged to have Duchess Sibylla poisoned. But Normandy was by then lapsing into such a state of anarchy that Curthose, as Orderic explains, simply did not have the time or opportunity to marry Agnes.[112] Whatever the actual circumstances of Sibylla's death may have been, the absence of her counsel seems to have left Normandy more hopelessly adrift than ever.

In the months following the deaths of William of Breteuil and Sibylla of Conversano, Robert Curthose witnessed the total breakdown of his military campaign against Robert of Bellême. The duke had indeed made an effort to abide by the provision in the treaty of Winchester requiring each brother to wage war against anyone who betrayed the other. But Robert Curthose was simply no match for Robert of Bellême, who ravaged central Normandy with terrifying force. His brother Arnulf of Montgomery, angry that Robert of Bellême had seized the entire family inheritance to the disadvantage of his younger brothers, captured the Bellême castle of Almenesches and turned it over to Curthose. But Robert of Bellême responded by setting fire to the nunnery at Almenesches and burning it to the ground, and his forces overwhelmed the ducal garrison in the castle, subjecting some of the men to grotesque punishments and prompting Curthose to retire to Exmes. A number of magnates of the region were now in arms

---

[110] *GND*, 2:222.
[111] WM, *GR*, 2:461; *GND*, 2:222–224.
[112] OV, 6:38–40.

against Robert of Bellême—Rotrou count of Perche, William count of Evreux, and Robert of Grandmesnil—but they failed to overcome him. The conflict was resolved in a decisive battle between Robert of Bellême and Curthose and his allies, at a time and place that our sources do not disclose. Robert of Bellême directed a furious charge against the advancing ducal army and smashed it completely, making prisoners of the duke's brother-in-law, William of Conversano, and many others and moving on to seize the strategic castle of Exmes. Curthose had little choice then but to make peace with Robert of Bellême, regranting him official possession of his vast holdings throughout Normandy, which included the castle of Argentan, the bishopric of Sées, and the forest of Gouffern.[113] Having triumphed over all his enemies, Robert of Bellême harassed Serlo bishop of Sées and Ralph d'Escures abbot of Saint-Martin, Sées, demanding exorbitant taxes from the two prelates and their tenants. As a result, Bishop Serlo and Abbot Ralph both fled to England, where they obtained the protection of Henry I.[114]

One of Curthose's most powerful allies among the English baronage back in summer 1101 was William II of Warenne earl of Surrey, a former suitor of Queen Matilda. In Henry's youth Earl William is said to have ridiculed his bookish expertise in the science of hunting. Nevertheless, Henry tried during the initial year of his reign to win the friendship of the young earl, who was among the three wealthiest nobles in England. Henry sought to gain William's loyalty with the accustomed policy of offering him a royal bastard daughter to wed. The marriage was blocked, however, by Archbishop Anselm on the grounds of consanguinity. Earl William, having betrayed the king by backing Curthose in 1101 and having permitted his men to engage in private war, was disseised of all his English lands and exiled to Normandy.[115]

In summer 1103, at William of Warenne's urging and chiding, Robert Curthose made an impetuous, uninvited visit to England to seek the restoration of William's earldom of Surrey. The journey seems to have angered Henry, although it may be that he feigned anger in order to intimidate Curthose.[116] He sent some of his *familiares*—led by Robert of Meulan, according to Wace[117]—who warned Curthose of the king's anger and his threat to capture and imprison the duke for his effrontery in visiting England without a royal invitation and for the truce that

---

[113] Ibid., pp. 22–24, 32–36, 46; David, *Curthose*, pp. 143–144 and n. 23.

[114] OV, 6:46.

[115] *MMI*, pp. 137–144, with references.

[116] OV, 6:12–16. Malmesbury alleges that Henry invited Curthose to England, in a passage that also states that Pope Paschal urged Henry to conquer Normandy; both assertions are almost surely incorrect: WM, *GR*, 2:474.

[117] Wace, *Roman de Rou*, 2:277.

he had illicitly concluded with Robert of Bellême. In the end, however, Henry greeted his brother pleasantly, concealing his wrath under a smiling face, and Curthose "dissembled his fear with forced cheerfulness."[118] Henry agreed to restore the earldom of Surrey to William of Warenne, and in return, at the request of Curthose's goddaughter Queen Matilda, the duke agreed to relinquish the annuity of three thousand marks that Henry had granted him in 1101.[119] Since the annual Domesday income from the earldom of Surrey in 1086 was £1,165, slightly over half the annuity, the exchange was very much to Henry's advantage, as well as to William of Warenne's (but not, of course, to Curthose's). One aspect of the agreement seems to have been that William of Warenne undertook thenceforth to be a truly loyal vassal of Henry I, rendering the king his unmitigated allegiance. Duly chastened, Orderic writes, William of Warenne "served the king faithfully for the remaining thirty-three years that they both lived."[120] Despite the very expensive favor that Curthose had done him, once William was reinstated in his earldom of Surrey, the duke could no longer count on his support in Normandy.

Henry courted other members of the Anglo-Norman nobility in a similar fashion. He tried but failed to win over the hyperactive and immensely ambitious young earl of Cornwall, Robert of Bellême's nephew William count of Mortain. The most vivid accounts of William are to be found in the Hyde chronicle, which describes him as incorrigibly turbulent, and the judgment is supported by William of Malmesbury's allegation of William of Mortain's "shameless arrogance."[121] He does not appear to have been the sort of prudent, sensible person that Henry I preferred to welcome into his regime. Indeed, during the crisis of 1101 William of Mortain is said to have demanded his deceased uncle Odo of Bayeux's earldom of Kent. The integration of the earldoms of Cornwall and Kent would have resulted in an honor of prodigious wealth, producing some £4,530 a year in Domesday revenues. Had Henry yielded to this demand, William of Mortain would have loomed over England as an early twelfth-century Harold Godwineson or Thomas of Lancaster. The young count went so far as to announce that he would not put on his cloak until Henry granted him his uncle's earldom. (King Henry seems to have taken this dire threat in stride.) During the crisis months of the first half of 1101, the king put off William's demand "with the subtlety of an ambiguous answer" and instead offered him the hand of Queen Matilda's high-born sister

---

[118] OV, 6:14.
[119] Wace, *Roman de Rou*, 2:277–280; OV, 6:14.
[120] OV, 6:14.
[121] *Liber de Hyda*, p. 306; WM, *GR*, 2:473.

Mary.[122] William contemptuously rejected the offer (Mary being blue-blooded but landless), and after the 1101 settlement at Winchester, Henry gave Mary in marriage to Eustace of Boulogne. Nevertheless, he continued to keep William of Mortain at bay, somehow persuading him to refrain from joining forces with his uncle Robert of Bellême during the warfare of mid-1102.

William of Mortain never acquired Kent. After a time, with the Montgomerys safely out of England, Henry undertook legal action to recover lands in the vicinity of the earldom of Cornwall that the count had allegedly misappropriated. Furious, William of Mortain departed for Normandy in 1104, joined forces with Robert of Bellême, and declared for Robert Curthose. Henry proceeded to disseise him of his English lands and redirect the immense revenues of the earldom of Cornwall into the royal treasury.[123]

Although Curthose could now count on the loyalty of William of Mortain, King Henry continued to chip away at the duke's remaining support. He granted William of Mortain's forfeited rape of Pevensey in Sussex to Gilbert of Laigle, lord of an important honor in southeastern Normandy. In 1105 Gilbert reciprocated by making available to Henry his castle at Laigle as a site for the king's climactic negotiations with Archbishop Anselm.[124] An even more formidable Norman magnate, Ralph of Tosny, with strategic castles at Tosny on the Seine and Conches in southeastern Normandy (along with lesser castles in the region: Portes and Acquigny), crossed to England on his father's death in 1102 to claim his family's English lands. As the senior member of one of Normandy's wealthiest families, Ralph found Henry's welcome warm indeed. The king arranged an immensely lucrative marriage for him with Adeliza, younger daughter and co-heir of the late Earl Waltheof and his wife, Countess Judith, whose impressive holdings (£613 a year) are recorded in Domesday Book. "Other prudent magnates abandoned their foolish lord in the same way," Orderic adds, "and sought out the politic king to good purpose."[125]

In 1104, according to the *Anglo-Saxon Chronicle*, Robert Curthose was constrained to enter into a formal alliance with Robert of Bellême, "and through this agreement the king of England and the count of

---

[122] WM, *GR*, 2:473–474; *Liber de Hyda*, p. 306.

[123] *ASC*, s.a. 1104; WM, *GR*, 2:473.

[124] OV, 6:196 and n. 1; Sanders, *Baronies*, p. 136, where the date 1106 should be corrected to 1104; Eadmer, *HN*, pp. 165–166; Thompson, "Lords of Laigle"; Vaughn, *Anselm of Bec and Robert of Meulan*, pp. 289–295.

[125] OV, 6:54–56; 244; Le Prévost, *Notes . . . de l'Eure*, 1:89; Countess Judith's Domesday lands, which stretched across seven shires, were concentrated in Northamptonshire, Huntingdonshire, Lincolnshire, and Bedfordshire and were valued altogether at about £613 a year.

Normandy were set at enmity."[126] Orderic reports that Henry crossed
to Normandy in August 1104 with a large fleet and proceeded in great
state to visit Domfront "and other strongholds under his command."
He was joined by a plethora of Norman nobles, who accompanied the
king in a cavalcade through his brother's duchy, evidently unopposed.
Robert count of Meulan was of course a member of Henry's Norman
entourage, as were, among others, such royal friends and relations as
the young Richard earl of Chester (now about ten years old), who governed the Avranchin through his officials, Robert fitz Hamon, Ralph
of Tosny, Robert of Montfort, Henry count of Eu, Stephen of Aumale,
and the two royal in-laws Rotrou count of Perche and Eustace of
Breteuil. Orderic observes that all these magnates "held great estates
from Henry in England, had already gone over to his side in Normandy
with their vassals, and were ready and eager to fight with him against
all the world."[127] He reports that Henry's retinue even undertook to
adjudicate Robert Curthose's capacity to govern the duchy, in a kind
of court proceeding with Curthose himself apparently present. The
luckless duke was able to forestall the judgment only by granting Henry
the allegiance of still another immensely wealthy Norman magnate,
William count of Evreux, who thereupon transferred his homage from
Curthose in a public ceremony in which the duke placed William of
Evreux's hands between King Henry's.[128] On his return to England in
late autumn 1104, Henry thus enjoyed the support of the great majority of Norman magnates: the lords of Evreux, Breteuil, Avranches
(Chester), Eu, Beaumont, Montfort, and Tosny, to mention only those
families on our Norman chart. Among these same high-status families,
Robert Curthose was supported only by the lords of Mortain and
Bellême. As the Anglo-Saxon chronicler expressed it, the chief magnates of Normandy welcomed Henry's men "and, to the betrayal of
their liege lord, received them into their castles."[129]

In early April 1105 Henry launched a full-scale invasion of Robert
Curthose's duchy, impelled in part, Orderic explains, by "the tearful
laments of unhappy Normandy."[130] Another motive was the news that
two of Curthose's commanders—Gunter of Aunay who guarded
Bayeux, and Reginald of Warenne, brother of William earl of Surrey—
had captured Henry's good friend and *curialis* Robert fitz Hamon, lord

[126] *ASC, s.a.* 1104.
[127] OV, 6:56.
[128] Ibid., p. 58.
[129] *ASC, s.a.* 1104.
[130] OV, 6:60.

of Torigny and Creully in the Bessin and of a large barony in and around Gloucestershire.[131] Fitz Hamon, whom Wace accuses of harrying the Norman countryside, had taken refuge in the church tower at the village of Sequeville-en-Bessin, which Gunter and Reginald proceeded to burn. They seized fitz Hamon and made him a prisoner in Bayeux.[132]

Henry crossed the Channel with a large army, obviously intending to conquer the duchy from his brother in the course of the year. Henry and his advisers had prepared meticulously for the campaign. The Anglo-Saxon chronicler complains of unusually heavy taxes levied by the king in 1104 and 1105, and Florence of Worcester speaks of Norman nobles betraying their castles and towns to Henry as they grasped at "the gold and silver that the king had brought with him from England."[133] The distribution of bribes to win over potential Norman supporters was of course not a novel policy, but Henry—who distributed not only gold and silver but lands, heiresses, and bastard daughters as well—courted the Norman nobility with unprecedented finesse.

Moreover, Henry accompanied his enticements with a barrage of propaganda, the major theme of which was that he came to restore peace to strife-ridden Normandy. This theme was all the more effective because it was essentially true—as witnessed by an abundance of fleeing peasants, crops laid waste, endemic lawlessness, refugee prelates such as Serlo and Ralph of Sées, and churches burned down or converted into fortresses (for example, Tournay near Sées and Saint-Pierre sur Dives). Orderic is clearly reflecting both royal propaganda and vexatious fact when he dwells on the anarchy that afflicted Normandy at this time. Henry, like Rufus before him, assumed the role of savior of the Normans and their Church from the pillaging of evil men permitted by Curthose's incompetence.[134]

Still another important sign of the painstaking preparations underlying the campaign of 1105 was the skillful diplomacy that won Henry the active or tacit support of all the important neighboring princes. His army included a sizable contingent of Manceaux led by Helias count of Maine, a contingent of Angevin forces led by Geoffrey Martel (who

---

[131] Robert fitz Hamon's Gloucester estates included the lands that had once belonged to Henry I's mother; they would later become the nucleus of the earldom of Gloucester: above, pp. 39–40, 61–62; below, pp. 236, 311 n. 117; *CP*, 5:683.

[132] Ibid.; Wace, *Roman de Rou*, 2:296–297; the church at Sequeville, which Henry apparently caused to be rebuilt shortly afterward with a new tower, is a splendid example of Norman Romanesque architecture (and visitors would think so if its rector did not keep the door locked much of the time): Musset, ed., *Normandie romane*, 1:128–131 and plates 50–52.

[133] *ASC*, s.a.; FW, 2:54; OV, 6:60, 78, 86; David, *Curthose*, p. 161.

[134] OV, 4:178–180; 6:58–64.

was associated with his father Fulk IV in the governance of Anjou), and a force from Brittany.[135] Henry also sent envoys to the royal court of France who evidently persuaded King Philip and his son Louis, *rex designatus*, not to intervene in his Norman campaign.[136] And his money-fief with Robert count of Flanders, executed in 1101, may have been reconfirmed at least verbally at a meeting at Dover in 1103.[137] William of Malmesbury reports that as Henry's Norman campaign progressed, Curthose arranged a conference in Rouen with his lord King Philip and his kinsman Robert count of Flanders. He implored their assistance but obtained none.[138] Henry's diplomacy had covered all possibilities, and Curthose was left without allies.

Henry and his retinue landed unopposed at Barfleur, at the northern tip of the Cotentin peninsula, and then proceeded without trouble to Carentan at the base of the peninsula. The lack of ducal resistance doubtless resulted from the fact that western Normandy was largely controlled by Henry's friends. At Carentan the royal entourage encountered Bishop Serlo of Sées, a refugee from the oppressions of his lord of Bellême. Serlo conducted Easter services (on 9 April) for the king and his following in the village church, which was cluttered with chests, tools, and gear of all kinds that neighboring peasants had taken there for protection against thieves and bandits.

Orderic reports Bishop Serlo's sermon at Carentan in detail and no doubt improves the bishop's text as he proceeds—perhaps by a great deal. The sermon is divided into two parts: a plea to Henry and his men to rescue Normandy and a diatribe against the fashionable custom among aristocratic men of wearing long hair and beards. The entire performance has been viewed as simply a display of royalist propaganda, and to a degree it was.[139] Yet Serlo, self-exiled from his diocese by the excesses of Robert of Bellême, had good reason to complain about violence and chaos in the duchy, conditions from which he and some of his associates were suffering personally.

Bishop Serlo began by commenting on the piles of goods and equipment stored in the church and on how they testified to the breakdown of order in the Cotentin, "for lack of a just protector." He went on to observe that such conditions had become common to all Normandy under Robert Curthose. He spoke of the burning of churches and their

---

[135] Serlo of Bayeux, "De capta Bajocensium civitate," 2:244–245; "Annales de Saint-Aubin," p. 44; HH, p. 235; OV, 6:78 and n. 3.

[136] OV, 6:78; Suger, *Louis le Gros*, pp. 100, 106; once Henry had completed the conquest of Normandy, he purchased Louis' official sanction: *Chronique de Morigny*, p. 21; WM, *GR*, 2:480.

[137] Eadmer, *HN*, p. 146.

[138] WM, *GR*, 2:463.

[139] E.g., David, *Curthose*, pp. 161–164.

congregations within them and the general breakdown of civil order because of the lethargy and boundless extravagance of the duke: "Often he dares not rise from his bed . . . because he has no breeches, socks, or shoes. Indeed, the jesters and harlots who constantly accompany him steal his clothes while he lies snoring in drunken sleep." Recalling that Curthose's predecessors among the Norman dukes had been active and capable, he urged Henry to restore the great tradition by taking up arms "not for lust of earthly power but for the defense of your homeland [*pro defensione patriae*]." With the avid support of Robert count of Meulan and other nobles present in the church, Henry responded, "I will rise up and work for peace in the name of the Lord and will devote my utmost endeavours to procure, with your help, the tranquillity of the Church of God."[140] Having just crossed the Channel with a large army and war chest and having already arranged to be joined by allied forces from Maine, Anjou, and Brittany, Henry was only too easily induced to proceed. But although Serlo's sermon, and propaganda similar to it, obviously served the royal ambition, it also represented a genuine and widespread yearning for the return of peace and order.[141]

Serlo now turned to his second subject, that of cutting one's hair and trimming or shaving one's beard. These were vitally important, divisive issues in the Church of the early twelfth century. Long hair and beards were widely censured at ecclesiastical synods and in the writings of church reformers, often along with the wearing of flowing, extravagant clothes and shoes with pointed toes that curled up like scorpion tails. Most recently and immediately, such practices had been condemned at Anselm's primatial council of 1102 at Westminster as well as in the archbishop's correspondence.[142] At Carentan Serlo quoted St Paul's admonition, "If a man have long hair it is a shame unto him"; he went on to complain that long beards give men "the look of billy-goats, whose filthy viciousness is shamefully imitated by the degradations of fornicators and sodomites . . . and by growing their hair long they make themselves seem like imitators of women."[143]

The Easter Mass at Carentan reached its emotional crescendo when Serlo, having observed that Henry and all his court "wear [their] hair in woman's fashion," received the king's consent to correct the situation. The bishop pulled out a pair of shears that he had conveniently brought along in his bag and proceeded personally to cut King Henry's hair. He then cropped the count of Meulan and most of the magnates.

---

[140] OV, 6:62–64.

[141] E.g., *GND*, 2:220; WM, *GR*, 2:461–462, 474; Ivo of Chartres (letters to Henry I and Robert of Meulan): *PL* 162, epp. 154–155.

[142] *Councils and Synods*, 1: part 2, pp. 677–678 (cap. 24); *AO*, ep. 365.

[143] OV, 6:64–66; the Pauline passage is from 1 Corinthians 11:14–15.

Others followed the example, until the entire royal entourage was as closely shorn as their short-haired, all-conquering Norman predecessors of William the Conqueror's days. They must have made a striking sight as they rode east from Carentan toward Bayeux.[144]

Henry reached the walls of Bayeux a few days later, accompanied by Helias count of Maine with his military following and, probably, Geoffrey of Anjou with his men. Gunter d'Aunay, evidently intimidated, turned Robert fitz Hamon over to the king. Henry, receiving fitz Hamon, now demanded that Gunter surrender the town, and Gunter refused. Henry and his army thereupon undertook to besiege Bayeux and met with almost immediate success, setting it afire and driving its garrison and population out into Henry's arms. The entire episode is described by a local poet and canon of Bayeux Cathedral, Serlo, a protégé of the late Bishop Odo, and his sympathies are clearly with Curthose.[145] Serlo tells of how a high wind whipped the flames from rooftop to rooftop, consuming houses, churches, the magnificent cathedral of Notre-Dame that Odo had built, even Serlo's own house of cathedral canons, along with many of the town's inhabitants, some of them inside the cathedral, where they had fled for refuge from the fire. Henry took captive Gunter d'Aunay and many of his soldiers and permitted the Manceaux and Angevins to plunder what remained of the city. In later years Henry had the cathedral rebuilt in the same majestic proportions that Odo had originally achieved. But the burning of Bayeux was a horror not soon forgotten.[146]

It was a horror not lost on the inhabitants of Caen, Henry's next target, some fifteen miles to the east: "The townsmen of Caen, hearing of the massacre of those of Bayeux and fearing that they might suffer similarly, sent to the king, who was already hurrying against them in fierce array, and made peace with him on his own terms."[147] William of Malmesbury and Wace both assert, surprisingly, that Robert Curthose was himself in Caen at the time. Learning at the last minute that the citizens intended to betray the city to Henry, the duke fled precipitously through the Porte Milet and into the Hiémois, leaving his baggage to be rifled by guards.[148] The citizens expelled Curthose's castellan, Enguerrand son of Ilbert, along with his garrison, and turned the castle over to the king. Henry in return granted the four chief townsmen of the city the English manor of "Dallington," worth eighty pounds a year,

[144] OV, 6:66–68.

[145] *Anglo-Latin Satirical Poets*, 2:141–151.

[146] The sources for the burning of Bayeux and the 1105 campaign are conveniently and expertly summarized by Chibnall in OV, 6:78, n. 3. See especially Böhmer, "Der sogenannte Serlo von Bayeux."

[147] OV, 6:79.

[148] WM, *GR*, 2:463, and, in much greater detail, Wace, *Roman de Rou*, 2:303–305.

which, Orderic explains, had been called "Traitors' manor" ever since.[149] Once again, as in his youth, Henry controlled all of western Normandy—the Cotentin, Avranchin, and Bessin—and he had now added the two major west Norman cities, episcopal and ducal, that Rufus had reserved for himself back in 1096. At this moment Henry clearly aspired to nothing less than reuniting his father's entire Anglo-Norman dominions.

The king moved next against the formidable castle of Falaise—not the present majestic rectangular keep built by Henry I himself in the 1120s but its eleventh-century predecessor, also of stone and similarly difficult to assault.[150] In the course of the siege Henry lost at least two of his nobles: Roger of Gloucester was killed by a crossbow shaft from a member of the castle garrison and Robert fitz Hamon, having just been rescued from captivity at Bayeux, was struck in the head with a lance and rendered senseless. Robert lived on for another two years, "almost in a state of idiocy," and died in 1107.[151]

But for Henry there was much worse to come. At Falaise, astonishingly, his methodically planned, well-financed military offensive suddenly collapsed. Henry had intended to take the castle by storm but was prevented from doing so when Count Helias abruptly withdrew his strong Manceau contingent from the king's service. Eadmer indicates that Henry suffered other defections as well, perhaps many. Helias, for example, could well have been followed out of Henry's army by his friend Geoffrey of Anjou, whom he had earlier persuaded to join the expedition.[152] With his support diminishing, Henry was unable to take the castle and had to abandon the siege. Indeed, although it was still very early in the campaigning year (about mid-May), he called a halt to his entire 1105 military operation. During the week of Pentecost (28 May–3 June) Henry conducted peace negotiations with his brother for two days at the village of Cintheaux in Calvados, on neutral ground

[149] Enguerrand son of Ilbert was a frequent attester of Curthose's charters; "Dallington" cannot be positively identified, but Chibnall makes the very reasonable suggestion that it may be Deddington (Oxon.), previously a manor of Bishop Odo, worth £60 in 1086 (OV, 6:79 n. 6).

[150] Chatelan, *Donjons romans des pays d'ouest*, pp. 118–120 and pl. 23. A room at the top of Henry I's great keep of ca. 1123 is wrongly identified at its entrance as the very room from which ca. 1027 Duke Robert the Magnificent (Henry's grandfather) looked down on fair Herlève drawing water from a well and lost his heart to her.

[151] WM, *GR*, 2:474–475; Malmesbury associates Robert's injury with the 1105 campaign but not explicitly with the siege of Falaise, yet it is hard to imagine where else the blow might have fallen. See also OV, 6:78–80.

[152] Eadmer, *HN*, p. 166; "Annales de Saint-Aubin," p. 44; Helias fought at Geoffrey's side at the siege of Cande, north of the Loire, where Geoffrey was killed by an arrow on 19 May 1106: Chartrou, *L'Anjou*, p. 3; OV, 6:74–76.

between the ducal stronghold of Falaise and the royal city of Caen. But, "because seditious troublemakers interfered," the brothers separated without agreement.[153]

What can have been the reason for this jolting reversal of Henry's fortunes? The only explanation provided by the sources for the defection of Helias (who turned up again the following year as a commander in Henry's victorious force at Tinchebray) is Orderic's enigmatic statement that Helias withdrew from the campaign *a Normannis rogatus*, "at the request of the Normans."[154] Since the majority of men on both sides were Normans, the explanation makes no sense at all. Florence of Worcester implies that Henry's campaign rolled to a halt because he ran out of money and had to return to England to raise more. Florence, however, conveys the impression that the king was simply pausing for breath after a highly successful campaign that had made him the master of most of Normandy. Nothing is said about defections, or that Henry had to abandon his campaign in mid-spring, or that he failed to storm Falaise. Yet Orderic is surely correct in reporting that the siege was attempted and was unsuccessful. If so, it strains belief that, for all their elaborate preparations, Henry and his ministers could irresponsibly have permitted the royal coffers to run dry while in the midst of a serious military operation, after a single month's leisurely campaigning, or that Count Helias, an old and close friend of Henry I's who had a reputation for chivalry and honor, would desert the army of his lord and *amicus* at the height of a castle siege simply for lack of the latest installment of his wages.[155]

Eadmer provides a much more plausible reason for the campaign's collapse. He associates the debacle with Anselm's decision to journey northward from his refuge in Lyons with the announced intention of excommunicating Henry I. Excommunication by Anselm would obviously deal a devastating blow to Henry's self-image as savior of the Norman churches. As the rumor of Anselm's intention spread, Eadmer writes, "many mischiefs were being prepared which, it was thought, would be inflicted on him all the more effectively if he were excommunicated by a man of such eminence. The king himself was aware of this."[156] Eadmer does not identify the perpetrators of these mischiefs, but it may be suggestive that demonstrable ties of friendship linked Anselm to the one defector named by Orderic, Count Helias, a man of

---

[153] OV, 6:80.

[154] Ibid., p. 78.

[155] On Helias' character and reputation, OV, 5:232; on his close friendship with Henry, OV, 6:98, remarking on the *maxima familiaritas* that bound the king and count; see further, Richard E. Barton's unpublished paper, "Helias of Maine, Henry I, and the Importance of Friendship."

[156] Eadmer, *HN*, p. 166.

outstanding piety with qualities that would have been congenial to Anselm: Helias was zealous in prayers and almsgiving, he maintained a strict fast all day every Friday, and he wore his hair closely cropped.[157] A letter has survived (1100 × 1109) from Anselm to Helias, "his lord and dearly beloved friend in God," rejoicing that the count seeks his advice "about the path and way of life in which you can more certainly and effectively reach the kingdom of heaven and the blessed company of the angels."[158] Anselm's letter is clearly a reply to a letter from Helias (now lost) and suggests the possibility of a fuller correspondence. An obvious link between the two men is the eminent poet and correspondent Hildebert of Lavardin, bishop of Le Mans, a warm friend of Helias' who wrote an adulatory epitaph on the count's death in 1110.[159] Hildebert was also a correspondent and affectionate friend of Anselm; indeed, it was at Hildebert's request that Anselm wrote his last theological treatise, *De processione Spiritus Sancti*.[160] Although there is no direct evidence linking Helias' defection at Falaise with the rumors and defections generated by Anselm's northward journey at precisely the same time, a connection between the two events is at least plausible. There seems no other reasonable explanation for Helias' behavior. Let us turn back, then, to the events that precipitated Anselm's departure from Lyons.

By the time of Henry's peaceful and triumphant Norman sojourn of 1104, Anselm had been in unhappy exile in Lyons for seven or eight months. His correspondence makes it clear that he longed to return to Canterbury and resume his role as primate of Britain, but the impasse between king and pope over investitures made his return impossible. Henry had insisted that he would forfeit his kingdom rather than relinquish the right to invest prelates; Paschal, for his part, would forfeit his life rather than permit the king to do so. Henry continued to urge Anselm to return to England, to resume control of the vast Canterbury estates and to be with him as Lanfranc had been with Henry's father. Anselm could not, in good conscience, accept this offer while memories of the Roman synod of 1099 remained etched in his mind—and so he remained at Lyons. He could return only if Paschal or Henry relented.

---

[157] OV, 5:232.

[158] *AO*, ep. 466.

[159] Hildebert of Lavardin, *Carmina minora*, no. 29; it was through Hildebert's mediation that William Rufus released Count Helias from captivity at Bayeux in 1098: Latouche, *Maine*, p. 48.

[160] *AO*, epp. 239–241; *Chronicon beccense abbatiae*, PL 150, col. 650; Vaughn, *Anselm of Bec and Robert of Meulan*, p. 289.

Anselm continued to correspond with his most trusted friends among the English clergy—prelates such as Ernulf prior of Canterbury, who received Anselm's instructions for the care of the Canterbury community; Gundulf bishop of Rochester, former monk of Bec and Caen who served as Anselm's agent in affairs of larger scope and his mediator with the king; and William Giffard, Rufus' former chancellor now elected to the bishopric of Winchester.[161] Anselm also maintained his wide network of friendships with members of the Anglo-Norman aristocracy, most of whom had demonstrated their dedication to Benedictine monasticism by lavish benefactions to monastic houses and who, however worldly their behavior often was, regarded Anselm's sanctity with the most profound respect. Anselm was thus in a position, from his refuge in Lyons, to follow Anglo-Norman political affairs closely and to influence them. As he wrote to the monks of Canterbury from Lyons, he was fully aware of the troubles in England "by rumors flying in many directions."[162]

Anselm's interest in the fortunes of rival claimants to the kingdom and duchy is suggested by his earlier participation in the military affairs of England. In 1095 he had assumed responsibility for the defense of the southeast coast against the threat of an invasion in behalf of Count Stephen of Aumale.[163] In 1101 he had camped in the field with his Canterbury knights in Henry's army at Pevensey and had repeatedly urged Henry's unreliable magnates to stand firm with the king against Robert Curthose; he had even threatened the duke with excommunication if he persisted in his efforts to conquer England.[164] Conversely, Anselm had written to William Giffard from Lyons in 1104/1105 urging him not to betray a Norman castle to the king. Anselm maintained that holders of castles ought always to behave honorably and that William Giffard, regardless of provocation, should not betray Robert Curthose and deliver the stronghold to Henry's men.[165] It may also have occurred to Anselm that creating impediments to Henry's conquest of Normandy might impel the king to relax his position on investiture. But setting the investiture controversy aside, Anselm's position—as former prior and abbot of Bec—doubtless mirrored that of other Norman churchmen who supported Henry's campaign to conquer the duchy as a means of restoring peace to a land long tormented by civil strife. For Anselm, then, the ideal outcome would have been for Henry

---

[161] *AO*, epp. 293, 295, 299, 300, 306, 307, 310, 311, 314, 316, 322, 330, 331, 344, 349, 357, 359.

[162] Ibid., ep. 357, cf. ep. 355; Vaughn, *Anselm of Bec and Robert of Meulan*, pp. 280–281 and ff., from which much of the following analysis is derived.

[163] *AO*, epp. 191–192.

[164] Eadmer, *HN*, pp. 127–128.

[165] *AO*, ep. 322.

to relinquish investitures and then conquer Normandy. This, in fact, is exactly what occurred.

It was probably in November 1104, about the time that Henry was returning to England from his bloodless Norman sojourn, that Anselm dispatched his most trusted disciple, Baldwin of Tournai, on a mission to Rome. In his accompanying letter to Paschal, Anselm is silent as to the purpose of the mission except to say that it concerns the case between himself and King Henry, leaving it to Baldwin to convey the message verbally. But the depth of Anselm's feelings in imploring papal support is clear: "Due to my obedience to you and your predecessors, and for the freedom of the Church which I do not wish to disavow, I am in exile from my bishopric and despoiled of its possessions. In this matter your prudence has no need of my prayers or my advice."[166] The importance of the message is suggested by Anselm's concurrent letters to his closest friends in the papal curia, John cardinal bishop of Tusculum, his former student at Bec, and Cardinal John of Gaeta, the papal chancellor, asking them with the greatest urgency to support Baldwin's petition for papal action against Henry at the Roman curia. In all probability, Anselm also sent a letter to the same effect to his friend Matilda countess of Tuscany.[167]

The mission spurred Paschal to take action against the king, as Baldwin reported to Anselm on his return to Lyons.[168] After prolonged delay, the pope sent a courteous but firmly worded letter to Henry I, dated 23 December 1104 (his first known letter to the king in more than a year), wishing him "salvation, honor, and victory [*victoria*]," but also asking that his representatives answer for his intransigence in the investiture issue at the coming Roman Lenten synod (1105) and threatening that "otherwise it will be necessary for us to implement the decision of this synod . . . that those who do not wish to have the grace of Christ may feel the sword of Christ."[169]

Henry, adopting his characteristic policy of delay and clearly hoping to complete his conquest of Normandy before the pope could act, sent no envoys to the Lenten synod.[170] He himself spent most of the 1105 Lenten season at Romsey preparing for his large-scale Norman expedition, which he launched during the week before Easter. Since he and his men had been at Romsey *in transitu* from at least mid-February and since Anselm's friend William Giffard was among them, Anselm would

---

[166] Ibid., ep. 338.
[167] Ibid., epp. 338–339, 350; Vaughn, *Anselm of Bec and Robert of Meulan*, p. 283, with references.
[168] *AO*, ep. 349.
[169] Ibid., ep. 348.
[170] Ibid., ep. 353.

surely have received timely warnings of Henry's intention to conquer Normandy.[171] Paschal, meanwhile, was now acting with remarkable swiftness. In an undated letter to Henry of early 1105, he wrote: "Behold, for the third time we are forced to send you a letter of admonition." Commanding Henry to relinquish investitures and restore Anselm to his see, Paschal threatened to strike Henry and his advisers with the sword of anathema.[172] This third (and final) warning, coming only a few weeks after the second—but more than a year after the first— probably reached Henry at Romsey. Ignoring it, perhaps leaving it unopened, Henry proceeded with his Norman campaign. For although the pope was acting with unusual speed, the king was a step ahead of him. It must have occurred to Henry that once he possessed all of Normandy he would be in a far stronger position to bargain with Paschal, retain investitures, and, if necessary, even withstand the papal anathema for a time.

On 26 March 1105 Paschal responded to Henry's silence by sending him a letter, via Anselm, announcing that by the unanimous judgment of the Lenten synod, the sentence of excommunication had been passed against Robert of Meulan and other advisers (unnamed), along with all churchmen whom Henry had invested. "Sentence against the king himself, however, has been deferred because he must send his messengers to us at the coming feast of Easter."[173] If, as seems likely, the letter was sent immediately by couriers riding at express speed (say, fifty miles a day), Anselm would have received it at Lyons about two weeks later, around Easter (9 April), when King Henry was hearing Mass and having his hair cut at Carentan.[174] His army is very likely to have taken both Bayeux (around 13 April) and Caen (mid-April) before the letter caught up with him. Robert of Meulan's excommunication would have been an embarrassment, but a relatively slight one. So long as the king himself remained in good standing with the Church, his propaganda campaign would remain plausible and his coalition would hold firm.

Giving due respect to Anselm's acumen and statesmanship, and in view of his profound desire to see the investiture controversy resolved and to return to his primatial responsibilities at Canterbury, it is reasonable to suppose that he understood the situation and acted effectively. The motives underlying his actions on receiving the copy of

---

[171] *RRAN* 2, nos 682, 684; William Giffard accompanied Anselm to Rome in 1103: FW, 2:52.

[172] *AO*, ep. 351.

[173] Ibid., ep. 354.

[174] Poole, *Studies in Chronology and History*, p. 263; the journey from Rome to Lyons is about half the distance from Rome to Canterbury, which, including the Channel crossing, was accomplished by couriers in twenty-nine days in 1188.

Paschal's letter to Henry are obscured both by Eadmer's account of them and by Anselm's own explanation to the pope (which omits any reference to his excommunication threat). Eadmer has it that Anselm was gravely disappointed by the pope's letter: he saw "the uselessness of waiting any longer in Lyons for any help from Rome, especially since he had already repeatedly sent letters and messages to the pope . . . and thus far had received nothing from him except, from time to time, some kind of comforting promises. Further, he had for the third time written to the king of the English asking for the return of his property."[175] Eadmer's words, of course, make no sense. Papal excommunication of royal advisers was the traditional prelude to excommunication of the king. Moreover, Paschal had promised action on the case at his Easter synod, which would have been occurring in Rome at the very time Anselm received the letter at Lyons.[176]

Nevertheless, Anselm acted decisively—and on his own. After consulting with Archbishop Hugh of Lyons, he began a journey northward with the announced intention of personally excommunicating Henry I. Eadmer explains that Anselm had "for the third time written to the king asking for the return of his property" and now intended to anathematize him.[177] Anselm was aware, however, that Pope Paschal, after sending Henry three warnings, had excommunicated the royal advisers and was considering the possibility of excommunicating Henry himself at the Roman Easter synod. Henry's case was pending before the papal curia, and Anselm's threat to excommunicate the king was therefore a clear violation of canon law. Gregory VII had earlier chided Anselm's confidant Hugh of Lyons for excommunicating some men who had refused to pay tithes, "whereas we have, as a matter of prudence, postponed bringing men of this sort under the ban of anathema by synodal decision."[178]

Still, Anselm departed Lyons and journeyed northward. He was allegedly heading toward Reims when, while resting briefly at the Cluniac priory of La Charité-sur-Loire, he received a message from Adela countess of Blois, one of Anselm's spiritual daughters and Henry I's favorite sister, stating that she was seriously ill and needed Anselm's company. It was perhaps a "diplomatic" illness, for when

---

[175] Eadmer, *HN*, pp. 163–164.
[176] We have no record of what transpired at this Easter council: Blumenthal, *Early Councils of Paschal II*, pp. 31–32.
[177] Eadmer, *HN*, pp. 163–164.
[178] *Gregorii VII regestum*, 2, book 9, ep. 5, pp. 579–580; cf. ibid., book 1, ep. 60, p. 87: Gregory VII to Archbishop Siegfried of Mainz: "You are not to imagine that you, or indeed any of the patriarchs or primates, can take the liberty of retracting apostolic judgments."

Anselm proceeded to Blois he found Adela much recovered.[179] Despite her fine health, Anselm remained with her for the next several weeks, during which he not only provided her with his spiritual counsel but also disclosed to her, in answer to her pointed inquiries, that he intended to excommunicate her royal brother. Adela quickly sent messengers to Henry I, who, having endured a fruitless siege at Falaise and a fruitless conference with his brother at Cintheaux, invited Anselm to meet him at the castle of Laigle and promised important concessions on investitures if he did so.

Anselm and Henry met at Laigle, in southeastern Normandy, on 21 July 1105 and negotiated the settlement of the English investiture controversy.[180] Neither Eadmer nor Anselm, in his letter to Paschal reporting on the meeting, states the terms of the settlement. To Anselm, as we have seen, the issue of lay investiture was for the pope to resolve, not the primate of Canterbury. Nevertheless, without such a settlement Anselm could not return to his see, so he had to have been deeply concerned with the issue. His letter to Hugh of Lyons, concurrent with his letter to Paschal, shows that he was entirely familiar with the terms of the proposed settlement: Henry agreed to relinquish investitures, but he insisted on retaining the custom of receiving homage from his prelates.[181] Since the homage of prelates was a matter on which the pope had been silent for some time and is not reported to have raised in his negotiations with Anselm in Rome in 1103, Anselm must have had every hope that Paschal would find Henry's offer acceptable. Indeed, Anselm seems to have endorsed the offer, although cautiously because the issue was for the pope to decide. In a letter to Robert of Meulan, he described the compromise as an agreement "so badly needed and so clearly right,"[182] and he asked the monks of Canterbury to offer their prayers that the agreement between pope and king might be effected so that he could be reconciled with both.[183]

Anselm's letter to Paschal reporting on the Laigle conference contains no reference to his own excommunication threat against Henry I —which was in violation of canon law but, having never been implemented, could be overlooked. Anselm suggests that he journeyed northward to publicize the papal excommunication against Robert of Meulan, which he lifted at Laigle.[184] After his conference with Henry,

---

[179] Eadmer, *HN*, p. 164. Anselm had recently written to Paschal in Adela's behalf (*AO*, ep. 340) and had visited her on his trip to Rome in 1103: ibid., epp. 286–287.
[180] On the date, see *AO*, ep. 164, and Vaughn, *Anselm of Bec and Robert of Meulan*, p. 290 and n. 111.
[181] *AO*, ep. 389.
[182] Ibid., ep. 369.
[183] Ibid., ep. 376.
[184] Ibid., ep. 388.

Anselm returned to Bec, declining to resume his responsibilities at Canterbury until the settlement was ratified by the pope. Henry, in the meantime, returned to England in August and then entered again into his delay mode, postponing the dispatch of his envoys to Rome to convey the terms of the Laigle agreement to Paschal and doing everything possible to entice Anselm to return to England to display publicly his reconciliation with the king. Henry had conceded much for the opportunity to conquer Normandy, but he still hoped to lure Anselm home while putting off a formal concession on investitures to the pope.

There followed a series of letters between Anselm and various English prelates and members of the Canterbury community urging him to return and restore order to the English Church.[185] Anselm refused to budge from Bec until the envoys were dispatched to Rome and Paschal's reply was received, and he chided Henry for his fund-raising tactic of taxing priests with wives or concubines and, when that policy provided insufficient funds, taxing all priests, with or without female companions.[186] Henry replied with characteristic good cheer, promising Anselm "an explanation that will be so satisfactory to you that . . . you will not, I'm certain, blame me for what I have done."[187]

In December 1105 Henry's envoy, William Warelwast, departed for Rome at last, accompanied by Anselm's confidant, Baldwin of Tournai. Henry continued to tax his clergy and Anselm continued to complain of it. Henry eventually reduced the tax, on the advice of Robert of Meulan.[188] In the meantime, Robert Curthose's party engaged in desperate negotiations with Henry. Robert of Bellême crossed to England during the Christmas season, but his efforts were fruitless (perhaps he requested the restoration of his earldom in return for betraying Curthose), and he left for Normandy "in hostile fashion."[189] Robert Curthose too visited Henry about February at Northampton, evidently on Anselm's advice, to request the return of Henry's Norman holdings, but the king refused to accommodate him and Robert departed in anger.[190]

In spring 1106 William Warelwast and Baldwin of Tournai returned from Rome bearing a papal letter dated 23 March accepting the Laigle compromise. Henry had conceded much, having given in to the papacy on his right to invest prelates, but in return he had rid himself of

---

[185] Ibid., epp. 363, 365, 373, 386–387.
[186] ASC, s.a. 1105–1106; Eadmer, HN, pp. 171–172, 175.
[187] AO, ep. 392.
[188] WM, GP, p. 115.
[189] ASC, s.a. 1105–1106.
[190] Ibid., s.a. 1106; HH, p. 235; AO, ep. 396; RRAN 2, no. 737.

Anselm's excommunication threat and was free to resume his Norman campaign. On receiving the pope's answer, Henry was "greatly pleased" and sent William Warelwast back to Bec to invite Anselm to return to Canterbury.[191] Henry had originally planned to cross to Normandy on 3 May, but he was evidently postponing the resumption of his Norman campaign until he could effect a public reconciliation with Anselm in England. But when William Warelwast arrived at Bec he found that Anselm was too ill to cross to Canterbury. Whether his illness was actual (Anselm was now in his seventies) or "diplomatic," Anselm remained for the time being at Bec. He had earlier written to Ernulf prior of Canterbury that his refusal to cross to England was motivated by his insistence that Henry should abide by his undertakings "in such a way that I might without doubt have confidence that I would remain there in peace."[192]

The summer campaigning season was slipping by and Henry could await Anselm in England no longer. In late July he sailed for Normandy, and on 15 August he met with Anselm at Bec, sheltered against Robert Curthose by the surrounding lands and castles of the royalist magnates Robert of Meulan and Robert of Montfort. Anselm had been ill, and a number of Norman prelates had gathered at Bec in fear of his death. By the time of Henry's arrival, however, Anselm had recovered sufficiently to open the ceremonies with the celebration of a solemn high mass. Henry then made a series of promises. He pledged "that he would not thenceforth claim any privilege for himself or his heirs with regard to ecclesiastical investitures, and that in making elections he would demand nothing more than his mere consent, just as the judgment of the holy canons lays down."[193] Henry made further promises to Anselm: that he would restore all churches that Rufus had let out at rent, that he would take nothing from churches when they were without a pastor, that his taxes on churches would be abolished, and that all Canterbury lands and revenues would be fully restored. Henry also conceded that Anselm would serve as regent of England until the king returned. With these assurances, which Henry apparently made in the presence of a considerable assemblage of Norman prelates and therefore could not easily withdraw, Anselm crossed the Channel at last. At Dover Queen Matilda and many others greeted him joyously.[194] Henry and his entourage were now, after much delay, free to resume their campaign to conquer Normandy.

[191] Eadmer, *HN*, p. 181.
[192] *AO*, ep. 364.
[193] Ralph of Diceto, 1:227.
[194] Vaughn, *Anselm of Bec and Robert of Meulan*, p. 306; Eadmer, *HN*, p. 183; *AO*, ep. 407.

Henry moved first with a relatively small force against the fortified abbey of Saint-Pierre sur Dives, some dozen miles from the ducal stronghold of Falaise. In order to thwart a projected ambush, he traveled all night and seized the abbey in an early-morning surprise assault. The buildings were set ablaze, and the fire frightened off a ducal contingent coming from Falaise in the hope of seizing the king. Henry, instead, succeeded in capturing two leading ducal supporters, Reginald of Warenne (William II of Warenne's younger brother) and Robert of Stuteville the younger, who had sequestered them-selves with their troops inside the abbey in hopes of ambushing Henry.[195] Then, instead of turning on Falaise as he had done unsuc-cessfully the previous year, Henry moved southwestward against William of Mortain's castle of Tinchebray, situated on the hill rising from the town.

The king first dispatched a siege force under the command of Thomas of Saint-Jean, probably an old friend from Henry's youthful days as count of the Cotentin.[196] Thomas of Saint-Jean stationed his troops in a hastily built siege castle, but it quickly became clear that his force was too small to prevent William of Mortain from continuing to stock the castle with food and other supplies. Henry thereupon assem-bled a very large army before the walls of Tinchebray and sealed off the castle. William of Mortain, in turn, enlisted the help of his uncle Robert of Bellême and his cousin Robert Curthose and directed their combined forces against Henry's besieging troops. As sometimes occurs in a chess match, the opponents concentrated the bulk of both their forces on a single square; king and duke were poised to risk everything on the outcome of a pitched battle before the castle.

The duke is said to have had the greater number of foot soldiers, but Henry had the larger force overall. He placed it under the command of four *comites*: Robert count of Meulan, William count of Evreux, Helias count of Maine, and William of Warenne earl of Surrey, who was much pleased when his captive brother Reginald was released by the king.[197] The two armies faced off on 28 September 1106, forty years to

---

[195] OV, 6:72–74, 80–82; on Reginald of Warenne, *MMI*, 142; *EYC*, 8:6; on the Stutevilles, Robert I and II, see ibid., 9:1–5; *EYF*, pp. 85–86; *Charters of Mowbray*, xx–xxi. Henry later provided the funds to rebuild Saint-Pierre sur Dives: OV, 6:88 and n. 3; *RRAN* 2, no. 905 (Argentan, 1108); *GC*, 11, *Instrumenta*, col. 155.

[196] On Thomas of Saint-Jean (from Saint-Jean-le-Thomas, Manche, arr. Avranches) see above, chapter 2, p. 58, and Loyd, *Anglo-Norman Families*, pp. 89–90; also Chibnall's valuable commentary in OV, 6:84 n. 2. Thomas was sheriff of Oxford from circa 1110 to 1117, a benefactor of Mont-Saint-Michel, and a longtime officer in Henry I's military *familia* (see Chibnall, "Mercenaries and the *familia regis*"); he was held captive briefly by the Angevins about 1123–1124: *RRAN* 2, no. 1422.

[197] OV, 6:84.

the day after William the Conqueror's landing at Pevensey.[198] The celebrated hermit and holy man Vital of Savigny, standing between the two armies, implored the brothers to make peace, but to no avail.[199] Henry himself then offered Duke Robert the equivalent of all the revenues of Normandy with which to live in style while Henry undertook the labor of governing the duchy, but Robert, on the counsel of his advisers, declined these insulting terms.[200] Accordingly, the two armies prepared for battle.

In the king's force, in addition to the *comites* of Meulan, Surrey, Evreux, and Maine (and Duke Alan of Brittany), were Ranulf of Bayeux (a friend from Henry's youthful days in western Normandy), Ralph of Tosny, Robert of Montfort, Robert of Grandmesnil (whose family had long fought the Bellêmes), and many others.[201] Of the eight greatest Norman magnates active in 1106 (see table 4.2, above, p. 175), six were in Henry's army and only two in Curthose's, while the lesser magnates favored Henry overwhelmingly. As Henry of Huntingdon put it, King Henry had with him "almost all the chief men of Normandy and the best soldiers of England, Anjou, and Brittany. He was therefore not unprepared."[202]

The battle of Tinchebray is said to have lasted only an hour.[203] The troops of both the king and the duke dismounted "that they might make a more determined stand."[204] The royal army was arrayed in three columns, with Ranulf of Bayeux commanding the first, Robert count of Meulan the second, and William of Warenne the third. The king

---

[198] The date of 28 September is provided by most but not all of the sources. See Marjorie Chibnall's detailed discussion in OV, 6:89 n. 4; WM, *GR*, 2:475, dates the battle, similarly, on the day before Michaelmas (but provides the wrong day of the week), and adds: "idem dies ante quadraginta circiter annos fuerat, cum Willelmus Hastingas primas appulit" (cf. above, chap. 2, n. 6); the priest of Fécamp, however, reports the day as 29 September (Davis, 1910 "Correction to 'Contemporary Account,'" p. 296; original article, "Contemporary Account," appeared in 1909— see bibliography), and the Bec annalist, followed by Robert of Torigny, provides 27 September: *Chronique du Bec*, ed. Porée, p. 5; *GND*, 2:222.

[199] OV, 6:86; on Vital see OV, 4:330–332, and, in affectionate detail, Auvrey, *Histoire de la congrégation de Savigny*, 1:11–377.

[200] OV, 6:86–88.

[201] Ibid., p. 84; Davis, "Correction to 'Contemporary Account,'" p. 296; David, *Curthose*, p. 247.

[202] HH, p. 235.

[203] Davis, "Contemporary Account," p. 728; "Correction to 'Contemporary Account,'" p. 296.

[204] HH, p. 235; David, *Curthose*, pp. 171–176, 245–248; for recent descriptions of the battle, see Bradbury, "Battles in England and Normandy," pp. 6–7; Morillo, *Warfare*, pp. 169–170.

himself dismounted and led a force of Englishmen and Normans on foot, while positioning a force of mounted Bretons and Manceaux some distance away, out of sight, under the command of Helias count of Maine.

Although Henry of Huntingdon's account suggests that most of the men on both sides dismounted, the battle began with a mounted charge by ducal knights. They made some progress against Henry's army, but after a time the two forces became locked in a mass melee. "They were so closely crowded together and were brought to a halt with their weapons so closely locked that it was impossible for them to strike one another, and all in turn struggled to break the solid lines."[205]

Then suddenly Henry's reserve force, led by Helias count of Maine and supported by Alan duke of Brittany, charged against the flank of the ducal infantry, cutting down great numbers of them on the first onslaught and routing them completely. Robert of Bellême, who commanded the rear of Curthose's forces, panicked and fled with his troops, precipitating the collapse of the entire ducal army. Henry's chancellor, Waldric, captured Robert Curthose, and the Bretons seized William of Mortain, whom Henry took from them only with "the greatest difficulty."[206] The king had thus won the supreme victory of his career, reuniting the kingdom and duchy as a result of greatly superior diplomacy and more skillful military tactics. He had reconstructed his father's Anglo-Norman realm, and it must have occurred to him that the loss of investitures, though painful and subversive to his royal status, was a reasonable price to pay.

At Canterbury, Anselm rejoiced in Henry's great victory. He wrote:

To Henry, glorious king of the English and duke of the Normans, Archbishop Anselm sends faithful service with faithful prayers and wishing that he may always increase towards greater and better things and never decrease. I rejoice and give thanks with as much affection as I can to God, from whom all things come, for your prosperity and your successes. . . . I therefore pray to almighty God with heart and lips, as much as my spirit is capable of, both myself and through others, that in the mercy of his grace which he has begun to expend on you, he may unceasingly continue to lead you from earthly exultation after this life to the heavenly kingdom and eternal glory. Amen.[207]

[205] OV, 6:88.
[206] Ibid., p. 90.
[207] *AO*, ep. 402.

Chronology of the Investiture Settlement and the Conquest of Normandy

Henry I	Anselm/Papacy
	1103
	23 Nov.: first papal warning of excommunication to Henry I
1104	*1104*
Aug.–Oct./Nov.: Henry visits Norman castles unopposed	
	Nov.–Dec.: Baldwin of Tournai delivers Anselm's message to Paschal II
	23 Dec.: second papal warning to Henry I
1105	*1105*
Feb.–Mar.: Romsey, *in transitu*	Jan./Feb.: Paschal's third warning to Henry
	26 Mar.: Paschal sends letter to Anselm announcing excommunication of Robert of Meulan
2–8 Apr.: Henry lands at Barfleur	Early Apr.: Anselm receives Paschal's letter
9 Apr.: Easter at Carentan	9 Apr.: Henry's envoys absent from Roman Easter synod
Ca. 13 Apr.: Henry burns Bayeux	
Mid-Apr.: Caen capitulates	Mid-Apr.: Anselm departs for France to excommunicate Henry: rumors fly ahead
Later Apr./early May: Henry at Falaise; Helias defects; siege fails	Late Apr./May: Anselm visits Adela of Blois, tells her of excommunication plan
28 May–3 June: Cintheaux; fruitless meeting with Robert Curthose	
21 July: Laigle conference	21 July: Laigle conference
Aug.: Henry returns to England	

Aug.–Dec.: Henry delays mission to Rome

Aug.–Dec.: Anselm remains at Bec, complains of delay and church taxes

Early Dec.: William Warelwast leaves Henry's court for Bec and Rome

Early Dec.: Baldwin of Tournai leaves with Warelwast for Rome

1106
Ca. early May: Warelwast returns to Henry's court with papal letter

1106
Ca. early May: Warelwast brings papal letter to Anselm at Bec

Late July: Henry crosses to Normandy

15 Aug.: Henry comes to Bec; formal agreement on investiture

13 Aug.: Anselm receives Henry at Bec; final investiture settlement

Later Aug.: Anselm returns to Canterbury

28 Sept.: Henry defeats and captures Robert Curthose at Tinchebray

Early Oct.: Anselm sends letter to Henry congratulating him on his victory

Chapter 5

ADMINISTRATIVE REFORMS AND INTERNATIONAL TRIUMPHS

Henry's decisive victory at Tinchebray left many loose ends that occupied the king for months to come. Two surviving charters allude enigmatically, for example, to a military engagement that may have occurred shortly after Tinchebray: Henry issued them from northeastern Normandy, *in obsidione ante Archas*.[1] But since the narrative sources mention no such siege of Arques, we can safely conclude that it was not one of the preeminent military engagements of the era, and we cannot actually be certain of the year in which it took place. Still, the capture of the duke and most of his leading magnates at Tinchebray ensured that the remainder of the duchy would fall easily to Henry.

Besides the duke and William count of Mortain, Henry took captive four others whose names have passed down to us. One of them was Robert I of Stuteville, whose son and namesake, Robert II, had fallen into Henry's hands shortly before at Saint-Pierre sur Dives. A second was William of Ferrers, whose brother, Henry of Ferrers, was one of the wealthier magnates of England (see table 4.1, above, p. 172). A third was William II Crispin, whose kinsmen were great benefactors of Bec and whose brother Gilbert, a former Bec monk, was abbot of Westminster and a close friend of Anselm's. The fourth named prisoner was Edgar "the Aetheling," Queen Matilda's uncle, whose claim to the English royal succession had been advanced long ago—with singular futility—and whose luckless career had recently led him into Curthose's

---

[1] *RRAN* 2, nos 794–795: although these two charters, like most, are undated, the editors speculate that Henry may well have besieged the castle of Arques shortly after Tinchebray. But we cannot be certain, and the fact that Curthose's son-in-law Helias of Saint-Saens, with whom Henry at the time appears to have been on the best of terms, was count of Arques lends further mystery to the charter evidence. The editors date the two charters 1104–1106, but a siege of Arques ill fits the royal itinerary during any of these years. Since the single witness of both charters, Hugh of Envermeu, was still alive in 1111 (*RRAN* 2, no. 973) and could have lived on until 1117 or 1118 (ibid., no. 1085 n.), the siege might conceivably be associated with the attempted arrest of William Clito near Arques ca. 1110, or Baldwin VII's raid into northeastern Normandy ca. 1114, or subsequent hostilities in the region preceding the major outbreak of 1118: below, pp. 227, 234, 244 ff. Baldwin VII was fatally wounded near Arques in 1118: OV, 6:190; WM, *GR*, 2:479.

ill-starred following. King Henry had boasted in a letter to Anselm, doubtless exaggerating, that he had captured some four hundred knights and ten thousand foot soldiers at Tinchebray, adding that of those slain by the sword "there is no reckoning."[2]

King Henry released most of his prisoners. Of those named, Edgar the Aetheling, William Crispin, William of Ferrers, and Robert II of Stuteville were all set free, although Henry confiscated the Stuteville lands in England and gave most of them to his favorite, Nigel of Aubigny.[3] But Robert Curthose, William count of Mortain, and Robert I of Stuteville ("the elder") remained Henry's prisoners throughout their lives—or his. All were sent to England for perpetual confinement: Robert Curthose was incarcerated first at Wareham and then, under the care of Roger of Salisbury, at the bishop's great castle at Devizes, where he evidently dwelled in considerable luxury. William of Mortain replaced Ranulf Flambard as Henry's guest in the Tower of London, perhaps as a less festive inmate than the bishop of Durham.[4]

Once in Henry's hands, Robert Curthose cooperated fully and most obligingly. Explaining that the ducal garrison at Falaise was under oath to surrender to nobody except the duke himself or his faithful follower, William of Ferrers, Curthose suggested that Henry send William of Ferrers ahead to take possession of the castle in the king's behalf, so as to avert the possibility of Robert of Bellême seizing Falaise. Accordingly,

[2] OV, 6:90; *AO*, ep. 401; *ASC*, *s.a.* 1106. Robert of Torigny reports that the king's army suffered no fatalities at all at Tinchebray and estimates that no more than sixty men in the ducal army perished: *GND*, 2:222.

[3] *Charters of Mowbray*, pp. xx–xxi; *EYC*, 9:1–5; on Robert of Stuteville, ibid., 3–5 and OV, 6:88; on William Crispin, Robinson, *Gilbert Crispin*, pp. 16–17; Green, "Lords of the Norman Vexin," pp. 49–50, 54–56, 60–61; *ASC*, *s.a.* 1112; OV, 6:180, 198, 236–240; HH, p. 241; on William of Ferrers, *RRAN* 2, no. 1002.

[4] On Curthose's incarceration at Wareham, *Ann. Wint.*, p. 42; on his apparently very luxurious confinement at Devizes, and, much later, at Bristol, see David, *Curthose*, pp. 200–202, and Chibnall, in OV, 6:98 n. 2; on William of Mortain's imprisonment in the Tower, see *Ann. Wint.*, p. 42, and *PR 31 Henry I*, p. 143, reporting that William received an annual allowance while in the Tower of £15 17 s. 12 d., which amounts to about 10 or 11 pence per day, nearly twice the daily pay of a knight at the time: Hollister, *Military Organization of Norman England*, p. 206 and n. 1 (William's *servientes* received an additional £12 3 s. 4 d. annually); although this allowance is hardly worthy of William's former status as count and earl, it suggests a life far above the level of bread, water, and chains. Nevertheless, Henry of Huntingdon (pp. 255–256) asserts that King Henry had William of Mortain blinded; a grain of doubt is cast on the allegation by a (brief and very late) notice in the Bermondsey annals that William of Mortain became a monk of Bermondsey in 1140, after Henry I's death, on which occasion nothing is said about William's being blind: *Annales monastici*, 3:436; much later rumors that Henry had Curthose blinded are clearly false: David, *Curthose*, p. 179 n. 17; on Robert I of Stuteville's life imprisonment, at an unnamed stronghold, OV, 6:94.

Henry immediately sent William ahead to Falaise while the king and duke followed. At Curthose's command, the garrison and townsmen of Falaise swore fealty to Henry.[5]

At Falaise Henry encountered Duke Robert's son, William Clito, who was then a child not quite four years old. It has been said that Henry made the greatest mistake of his career in not placing the child in strict confinement then and there. But the deadly threats to Henry's rule that would be advanced in Clito's behalf in later years by the king of France and the counts of Flanders and Anjou were not yet discernible. Believing himself secure in his victory and trusting in the promise of the French monarchy to condone his reunification of England and Normandy, Henry chose to be compassionate.[6] Anxious that the child suffer no accidental injury while attending the royal court, Henry placed Clito in the custody of the Norman magnate Helias of Saint-Saens, who had wed an illegitimate daughter of Robert Curthose. Helias was devoted to the duke, who had previously raised him to the countship of Arques near the northwestern frontier of Normandy. In subsequent years, Helias became similarly devoted to William Clito.

As matters turned out, Henry's incarcerations of Robert Curthose and William of Mortain proved to be prudent acts, contributing decisively to the tranquillity of the realm and the reduction of suffering and death among his subjects, whereas his release of William Clito and William Crispin would later result in severe hazards to the peace of Normandy. William Clito became the focus of international threats and attacks against Henry's Anglo-Norman realm by France, Flanders, and Anjou in 1111–1113, 1117–1119, and 1123–1124, and in 1119 William Crispin attempted unsuccessfully to murder Henry. If anything, therefore, Henry I's treatment of his captives in 1106 was kind almost to the point of foolhardiness.

This point becomes all the more evident when one understands that in the aftermath of Tinchebray and the settlement with Anselm, Henry anticipated a peaceful reign. And to a considerable degree he achieved it, despite these external threats. In William of Malmesbury's words, "he preferred to contend by council rather than by the sword."[7] Henry ill fit the eleventh-century Norman image of the all-conquering warrior.

---

[5] OV, 6:92.

[6] John Gillingham ("1066 and the Introduction of Chivalry," pp. 31–55) on Henry's treatment of Clito: "Not even the ruthless Henry I had been able to bring himself to keep a child in prison, despite the eminently foreseeable problems which would—and did—arise when William Clito grew up. In the early twelfth century there were conventions of chivalrous conduct which prudent kings dared not flout" (p. 31).

[7] WM, GR, 2:488.

He disliked war, and having reunited his father's Anglo-Norman realm, he seems to have had no further territorial ambitions. Although he preferred that the principalities across his frontiers be ruled by friendly princes—and bound many of them to him by marriage ties—he required no tribute payments from his neighbors and displayed no taste for military expansion beyond the limits of his patrimony. "Peace he loved," wrote Hugh archbishop of Rouen on Henry's death, and all contemporaries agreed.[8]

Peace he loved, and peace he kept, perhaps more effectively than any previous prince in the annals of Western Christendom. It is well known that during all but the first two years of his thirty-five-year rule of England the kingdom was at peace. It has been less well appreciated that after 1106 Henry was also remarkably successful in keeping the peace in Normandy, where twenty-seven of his twenty-nine years were virtually free of domestic turmoil.[9] Notwithstanding successive international conspiracies in favor of William Clito, Normandy suffered warfare within its boundaries on only two occasions during Henry's reign. The first and most significant such occasion was 1118–1119, when hostilities, lasting for about eighteen months, were limited primarily to the Pays de Bray, the Norman Vexin, the county of Evreux, and the Maine frontier. Although Henry's control of the duchy was severely threatened during these months, most of central and western Normandy remained free of violence. There were, in addition, about five months of hostilities in 1123–1124, confined largely to the Risle Valley. Suger remarks that in 1118 Louis VI invaded a land long accustomed to peace; likewise, Orderic reports, relative to Count Geoffrey's invasion of Normandy after Henry I's death in 1135: "Provisions were abundant . . . after a long peace under a good prince"; and Malmesbury credits Henry with establishing such peace in Normandy as had never been known before.[10]

After delivering Falaise to Henry, Duke Robert accompanied him to Rouen and commanded the ducal vassal Hugh of Nonant to surrender the city to the king. Welcomed by the citizens of Rouen, Henry confirmed his father's laws and restored the city's traditional privileges. At Curthose's order, the other castellans of Normandy surrendered their fortresses to Henry and rendered him their homage.[11]

In mid-October, Orderic relates, Henry summoned the Norman magnates to a council in Lisieux. There he decreed "by royal authority" that peace should be securely enforced throughout the duchy, that robbery and plundering should cease, that the properties that churches

[8] WM, *HN*, p. 14.
[9] *MMI*, pp. 250–251.
[10] Suger, *Louis le Gros*, pp. 104–106; OV, 6:472; WM, *GR*, 2:476.
[11] OV, 6:92.

held at the time of the Conqueror's death should be returned to them, that secular lands as well should be restored to their lawful heirs, that all the ducal demesne lands held in the Conqueror's time should be restored to him, and that his brother's rash grants be nullified.[12] Thus Henry took all possible steps to restore to Normandy the conditions it had enjoyed under the Conqueror, much as he had undertaken to restore to England the laws of the Confessor. In both cases he was endeavoring to move his dominions backward past eras of violence and lawlessness to more placid, well-ordered times.

Henry next returned to Rouen where, on 7 November, he presided over a tribunal "in the chamber of William archbishop of Rouen" which settled a dispute between the abbeys of Fécamp and Saint-Taurin, Evreux. Present was a plethora of Norman and Anglo-Norman notables that included, besides the archbishop, a number of Norman bishops and abbots along with such familiar names as William Giffard bishop of Winchester, Ranulf bishop of Durham, Waldric the Chancellor, and two magnates from Henry's innermost circle, Richard of Redvers and Robert of Meulan.[13] On 30 November Henry issued another charter from Rouen, confirming an earlier grant by Robert fitz Hamon in favor of the nuns of St Mary of Malling.[14] In still another Rouen charter, issued some time before the end of 1106, William archbishop of Rouen, with Henry's assent, confirmed to the abbey of Bec the church of Notre-Dame du Pré in the Rouen suburb of Saint-Sever—the priory church in which Robert Curthose had taken refuge back in 1090 during the Rouen riot. Among the witnesses of this last document was Robert of Bellême, who had by then become reconciled once again with King Henry.[15]

Orderic gives an account of this surprising reconciliation. As he reports it, Robert of Bellême sought out Helias of Maine and requested his support in carrying on the struggle against Henry I. Orderic took this opportunity to provide Helias with a long speech, not unlike Bishop Serlo's at Carentan, defending Henry's claim to Normandy over that of an ineffective elder brother whose lethargy had allowed Norman monasteries to be plundered, poor people to be driven into exile, and churches throughout the duchy to be burned to the ground. Helias, refusing to betray his friend and lord King Henry, suggested that Robert of Bellême seek a reconciliation with the king and agreed to intercede with Henry on Robert's behalf. Henry, because of his affection for Helias, agreed to reinstate Robert of Bellême to his Norman inheritance, including the *vicomté* of Falaise, but required that Robert

[12] Ibid., pp. 92–94.
[13] *RRAN* 2, no. 790; Haskins, *NI*, p. 87.
[14] *RRAN* 2, no. 791.
[15] Ibid., no. 792.

surrender the strategic frontier stronghold of Argentan and all other ducal demesne possessions that he had usurped.[16]

In the weeks and months just following Tinchebray, Henry moved decisively to restore orderly government to Normandy. He held councils to that purpose at Falaise in January 1107 and at Lisieux (for the second time) in March.[17] Not only did he restore ducal demesne lands, church properties, and other estates misappropriated after the Conqueror's death; he is also reported to have imposed penalties for rape and counterfeiting and to have undertaken the destruction of unlicensed castles.[18] Another result of Henry's reforms was that the Norman ducal courts, which were somnolent under Curthose, now began once again to operate effectively.[19]

Suger of Saint-Denis, who as a young man in his twenties served between 1107 and 1109 as *prévôt* of the Saint-Denis priory of Berneval in the Pays de Caux near Dieppe, bears witness to the administrative transformation of the duchy. When he assumed his new responsibility at Berneval shortly after Tinchebray, he found the priory largely devastated and shorn of its lands and rights. After two years of strenuous efforts in the courts of Henry I, he had largely restored Berneval's losses. As he realized, his success resulted not only from his own vigorous pursuit of the priory's interests but also from the fairness and effectiveness of the newly reformed ducal courts. From this point Suger became a lifelong admirer of Henry I.[20]

During the Lenten season of 1107 (27 February–13 April) Henry returned to England. His most urgent item of business there was to conclude the final settlement of the English investiture controversy and thereby fill the abundance of episcopal and abbatial vacancies that had accumulated in recent years. The terms of the settlement had already been agreed on; it remained only to seal them with an appropriate ceremony. The ceremony was twice postponed, first at Easter by a papal order requiring that the chief English negotiators, Baldwin of Tournai and William Warelwast, attend a papal council at Troyes; second at

---

[16] OV, 6:94–98; either then or shortly afterward Robert of Bellême also became *vicomte* of Argentan and Exmes: ibid., p. 178; the administrations of all three *vicomtés*—Falaise, Argentan, and Exmes—were closely related throughout much of the twelfth century: Powicke, *Loss of Normandy*, pp. 72, 77.

[17] OV, 6:126–128.

[18] Haskins, *NI*, p. 86.

[19] Ibid., pp. 77 ("Once and once only do the charters mention a meeting of the ducal *curia*" under Robert Curthose), 86–122 (on Norman administration under Henry I).

[20] Bur, *Suger*, pp. 73–74; Suger, *Louis le Gros*, pp. 12–14: "vir prudentissimus Henricus, cujus tam admiranda quam predicanda animi et corporis strenuitas et scientia gratam offerrent materiam." See also Grant, *Abbot Suger of Saint-Denis*, p. 91.

Pentecost by a turn of bad health on Anselm's part.[21] Finally, on 1 August 1107 at the royal palace of Westminster, the council commenced.

Henry had summoned to Westminster Palace all the bishops, abbots, and nobles of the realm to ratify the agreements of Laigle and Bec.[22] For three days he conferred with the bishops—with Anselm absent but nearby. Some bishops continued to argue against Henry's concession on investitures, but it seems clear that the discussion was a mere formality and that Henry had no intention of reneging on his agreement with Anselm and Paschal. According to Anselm, the king's decision to renounce investitures was strongly backed by two of his closest lay advisers, Richard of Redvers and Robert of Meulan.[23] Afterward Henry summoned Anselm and the nobles and abbots to join the bishops and before the entire assemblage he announced his decision: no English prelate would thenceforth receive investiture from the king or any other layman. Anselm in turn, echoing the Laigle compromise, conceded that no one elected to any prelacy should be denied consecration because of his having rendered homage to the king. The English investiture controversy was thus formally and finally settled and the conflict between Henry and Anselm fully healed.

With the settlement officially confirmed, it became possible to fill the numerous vacancies in the English Church. "Now that these questions had been settled," Eadmer writes, "the king, on the advice of Anselm and the nobles of the realm, appointed fathers to nearly all the churches of England that had so long been widowed of their pastors ... but without any investiture with the pastoral staff or ring."[24] At Canterbury, on Sunday, 11 August 1107, Anselm and his suffragans consecrated a parade of bishops: Roger to Salisbury, Reinhelm to Hereford, William Giffard to Winchester, Urban to Llandaff, and the faithful royal envoy William Warelwast to Exeter. All rendered written professions of obedience to Canterbury; Urban of Llandaff's profession was especially significant in that it enhanced Canterbury's authority in Wales.[25] Anselm also consecrated abbots of Ramsey, Bury St Edmunds, Battle, Peterborough, and (probably) Cerne.

Anselm wrote subsequently to Pope Paschal reporting that "now the king, in choosing people for advancement, does not consult his own wishes at all but relies entirely on the advice of men of religion."[26] This

---

[21] Eadmer, *HN*, pp. 184–185.
[22] On the council of 1107 see ibid., pp. 186–187; *Councils and Synods*, 1: part 2, pp. 689–694.
[23] *AO*, ep. 430.
[24] Eadmer, *HN*, p. 186; *ASC, s.a.* 1107: Henry filled so many vacancies "that nobody could remember that so many had been given together before."
[25] *Canterbury Professions*, ed. Richter, nos 55–59.
[26] *AO*, ep. 430.

is surely what the pope wished to hear, but it is not altogether correct. Although the new dispensation discouraged the appointment of prelates of notorious reputation such as Ranulf Flambard, it remained possible to consecrate to bishoprics (other than Canterbury and Rochester) men of administrative capability but dubious sanctity— prelates such as Roger of Salisbury, who was known to have a mistress, or Richard bishop of London, consecrated in 1108, who likewise had a female companion, or the brilliant and crafty William Warelwast, whom Anselm knew well and cannot have entirely trusted. William Giffard of Winchester was a good friend of Anselm's, but he was also a seasoned administrator who had served as William Rufus' chancellor, and Reinhelm of Hereford had been Queen Matilda's chancellor.

The new abbots, in contrast, were of a different sort. Ralph, the incoming abbot of Battle, was precisely the kind of man whom Anselm needed to advance his reform program in the English Church: a monk of Bec, monk and prior of Caen (which had a close relationship with Bec), and prior of the Canterbury suffragan bishopric of Rochester. Ernulf, the new abbot of Peterborough, was also closely associated with the Bec–Caen–Canterbury reform configuration as prior of Canterbury and Anselm's friend and correspondent in exile. Indeed, in Anselm's later years as archbishop, a network of Bec–Caen–Canterbury prelates ruled a surprising number of Anglo-Norman religious houses. The Bec monk Gilbert Crispin presided at Westminster, the Caen monk William of Rots was abbot of Fécamp, another monk of Caen, Roger, was a (most controversial) abbot of Mont-Saint-Michel, and Richard of Aubigny abbot of St Albans had been a monk of the Bec colony of Lessay in the Cotentin.[27] The establishment in 1107 of Bec–Caen–Canterbury monks as abbots of Peterborough, Battle, Cerne, and Bury St Edmunds (where the new abbot had been a monk of Westminster under Gilbert Crispin), along with Anselm's consecration of a Bec monk to the abbacy of St Augustine's, Canterbury, in February 1108 resulted in a network of reform abbeys that blanketed the Anglo-Norman world.[28] The nature of these appointments, taken as a whole, suggests an unspoken agreement between Anselm and Henry I that bishops, under the new dispensation, would normally be expert administrators whose private lives, while outwardly respectable, need not be examined microscopically, whereas abbots would be men of serious spiritual commitment and, usually, Anselmian reformers in the Bec–Caen tradition. This arrangement hardly conformed to high Gregorian doctrine, but it did accurately reflect Anselm's belief in royal-primatial corule.

[27] Hollister, "St Anselm on Lay Investiture," p. 154.
[28] Ibid., p. 156.

In the aftermath of his conquest and rehabilitation of Normandy and his final settlement with Anselm, Henry turned energetically to the reforming of governance in England. Florence of Worcester, echoed by Symeon of Durham, reports for 1108 that Henry increased the penalties for various offenses, making theft and robbery capital crimes and decreeing that false moneyers thenceforth be punished by blinding and castration.[29] Eadmer asserts that these severe punishments were ordained on the advice of St Anselm and the nobles of the realm, and he offers the opinion that "great good resulted at once to the whole kingdom."[30] Eadmer (again, about 1108) and William of Malmesbury corroborate Florence's and Symeon's report that, on hearing that merchants refused to accept coins that were broken or bent, the king commanded that all pennies, halfpennies, and farthings should be incised.[31] Symeon and the Worcester chronicle add the further information that Henry also ordered that halfpennies should thenceforth be round (rather than semicircular—literally, pennies broken in half), and their report has been confirmed by the discovery of several round halfpennies from the period. Malmesbury adds that the measure of Henry's own arm was to become the standard throughout the kingdom for the length of the ell and that the new standard should be enforced on all tradesmen to replace the "false ell" that was too often used.[32]

In a much discussed writ of mid-1108, copies of which were sent to every shire, Henry ordered that all shire and hundred courts should meet at the times and places that they had traditionally met, "as in King Edward's days and not otherwise."[33] This measure confirmed and

[29] FW, 2:57; SD, 2:239. The adulteration of the king's coinage had traditionally been regarded as a felony of the most serious kind, akin to treason. In earlier law, running far back into Anglo-Saxon times, false moneyers suffered various forms of mutilation, or in some instances death: Richardson and Sayles, *Law and Legislation*, pp. 33–34; cf. *RRAN* 2, no. 501.

[30] Eadmer, *HN*, pp. 192–193.

[31] On the coinage reform see ibid., p. 193; WM, *GR*, 2:487; Eadmer is the earliest of these texts, and Malmesbury, Florence, and Symeon are clearly drawing from him. See further, Green, *Government*, pp. 89–91, and Blackburn, "Coinage and Currency," pp. 62–63: of Henry I's coins, a few of type 6 and all of types 7–12 "have a deliberate cut extending a quarter or third of the way across the coin," presumably to show that the coin was truly silver and not merely silver plated. On the ell see WM, *GR*, 2:487: the ell, a standard unit of length at the time, was equivalent to about 45 inches. Malmesbury does not date this measure, but he couples it with the coinage reform that Florence, Symeon, and Eadmer date to 1108.

[32] FW, 2:57; SD, 2:239; Blackburn, "Coinage and Currency," pp. 63–64; cf. Geoffrey of Monmouth's "Prophecies of Merlin," as reported in OV, 6:384, and Suger, *Louis le Gros*, p. 98.

[33] *RRAN* 2, no. 892; *Select Charters*, ed. Stubbs and Davis, p. 122; the writ also assigns land actions between tenants-in-chief to the king's court, between two tenants of the same lord to the lord's court, and between tenants of different lords to the shire court. Only the copy addressed to Worcestershire has survived.

perhaps rehabilitated a system of local justice that stretched far back into Anglo-Saxon times and had continued under the first two Norman kings. Although there is an abundance of evidence for the functioning of shire courts under the first two Williams, there are also indications that courts at all levels were subject to serious abuses during the years preceding Henry I's accession, when William Rufus granted Ranulf Flambard authority over sheriffs and other royal officials and made him manager of the king's justice. Flambard, "an incorrigible plunderer of his country," thereupon used this authority to vastly enrich the king and himself, "raking in riches from all sides . . . while the sorrowing people of the realm were stripped of their own property."[34] Indeed, the Anglo-Saxon chronicler states explicitly that Flambard had "driven and managed all the king's courts throughout England."[35] If one can accept these indications that local courts were devolving under Rufus and Flambard, Henry's writ should then be viewed as constituting a significant reform rather than a mere confirmation of existing practice, as yet another sign of the king's aspiration to restore the laws and practices of King Edward.

Eadmer gives particular praise to Henry for reforming the royal *curia regis*. Prior to 1108 the behavior of the Anglo-Norman *curia regis* had been notorious, and the problem did not cease with the death of William Rufus. As we have seen, Henry had great difficulty early in his reign controlling the behavior at his court of the Clares and Giffards and their boisterous followings, and the *Anglo-Saxon Chronicle*, echoing several complaints in previous reigns, reports under the year 1104 that "wherever the king went there was complete ravaging of his wretched people caused by his court."[36] Eadmer, commenting on the court of William Rufus, provides this grim account:

A great number of those who attended his court had made a practice of plundering and destroying everything. And because there was no discipline to restrain them, they laid waste all the territory through which the king passed. Not content with this, they took up another malevolent practice. When they could not consume all the provisions that they found in the homes that they invaded, many of them, intoxicated by their own wickedness, made the inhabitants take the remaining provisions to market

---

[34] OV, 4:170, 5:250, 310; FW, 2:46; see further, *Leges Henrici Primi*, pp. 98–100; *RRAN* 1, no. 393; the argument is particularly well expressed in Stubbs, *Constitutional History*, 1:393; see also Richardson and Sayles, *Law and Legislation*, pp. 33–34; Stenton, *English Justice*, p. 57.

[35] *ASC*, s.a. 1099: "the aeror ealle his gemot ofer eall Engleland draf and bewiste," using the corrected translation of Frank Barlow: *Rufus*, p. 200 and n. 168.

[36] *ASC*, s.a.; *Liber eliensis*, p. 226.

and sell them for the benefit of the invaders; or else they set fire to the goods and burned them up; or if it was drink, they washed their horses feet with it and then poured the rest on the ground. . . . It is shocking to contemplate the cruelties they inflicted on the fathers of families, the indecencies on their wives and daughters. As a result, whenever it became known that the king was coming, the inhabitants would all flee their homes, intent on doing the best they could for themselves and their families by hiding in the woods or seeking refuge elsewhere.[37]

In or around 1108, according to Eadmer, Henry subjected the royal court to a thoroughgoing reform. He issued strict regulations limiting the practice of requisitioning and he established fixed prices for local purchases. By forbidding his courtiers to plunder, extort, steal, or rape on penalty of blinding and castration, he brought these practices to an abrupt halt.[38] As a king who had put down two major rebellions and conquered Normandy, Henry was no longer a person to be trifled with. We hear no further complaints about rowdy courtiers for the remaining twenty-seven years of his reign.

Henry softened the impact of this reform by providing his household with a series of precisely stipulated allowances. The *Constitutio domus regis*, the earliest copy of which dates from about 1136, records a significant administrative reform that probably dated from this earlier time. The document describes in mind-numbing detail the precise allowances of every member of Henry I's household from chancellor and master chamberlain down to watchmen, ushers, and tent-keepers.[39] The royal clerk Walter Map, looking back nostalgically from the bustle and confusion of Henry II's court, reports very plausibly that Henry I had a register compiled of all his earls and barons and that he provided them too with set per diem allowances of bread, wine, and candles while they were in attendance at his court, thus compensating in part for the new rule against robbing villagers. Walter Map remarks further on the great precision with which Henry I arranged his court's itineraries, in edifying contrast to the impulsiveness and improvisation of Henry II's travel plans. Henry I, Map states, "gave full public notice of the days of his traveling and of his stays, with the number of days and the names of the vills," so that everyone—courtiers, merchants, litigants, and magnates—would know exactly where the royal court would be at any given time.

---

[37] *HN*, p. 192; above, chap. 2, pp. 43–44.
[38] Eadmer, *HN*, pp. 192–193; WM, *GR*, 2:487; Green, *Government*, p. 27.
[39] *Dialogus de scaccario*, pp. xlix–lii, 128–135; above, chap. 1, pp. 27–28.

"Nothing was done without preparation," Walter Map adds, "or without previous arrangement, or in a hurry; everything was managed as befitted a king, and with proper control." As a consequence, Henry I's court was always well supplied by merchants: "There was a veritable market following the king wherever he moved his court, so fixed were his journeyings and his welcome stays."[40]

By such means as these, Henry transformed his court from a gang of itinerant predators into a company of well-controlled courtiers who, despite the new constrictions and meticulous organization, evidently still managed to enjoy courtly life and to make it a nucleus of incipient chivalry. Geoffrey Gaimar, looking back on the court of Henry I perhaps two years after the king's death, speaks glowingly

> Of the feasts that the king held,
> Of the woods, of the banter,
> Of the gallantry and of the love,
> Showed by the best king
> Who ever was or ever would be.

One could write verses, Gaimar adds, about the fairest deeds,

> That is, about love and gallantry,
> And woodland sports and jests,
> Of feasts and splendour,
> Of lavish gifts and riches,
> And of the barons whom he led,
> And of the great gifts he gave.
> Of all this one well might sing![41]

One eminent historian, convinced that Henry's personality was unredeemably dour, rejected Geoffrey's testimony on the grounds that there can have been little to joke about at Henry's court, and another like-minded scholar has suggested that it may have been Geoffrey Gaimar himself who was joking. But Geoffrey's testimony, dating from about 1136–1137, provides by far the best near-contemporary account of Henry's court, and nothing in it implies that Geoffrey was writing with tongue in cheek. Moreover, his portrayal of gallantry and jesting is explicitly confirmed by Walter Map, who reports that while the mornings at Henry I's court were devoted to governance and the adjudication of disputes, the

---

[40] Walter Map, *De nugis curialium*, pp. 438, 470–472.
[41] Gaimar, *L'Estoire des Engleis*, p. 206; Hollister, "Courtly Culture and Courtly Style," p. 16.

afternoons, following the midday siesta, were given over to sports, hilarity, and decent mirth.[42]

Very shortly after the reform of Henry's court, the exchequer appears, perhaps as still another product of this outburst of administrative reform. The exchequer first passes into view around 1110 with Roger of Salisbury clearly in control. A royal writ of that year is addressed to *baronibus de scaccario* and is attested by Roger of Salisbury and Ranulf the Chancellor. It is the earliest document to refer to the exchequer by name, and it deals with a substantial aid taken by the king in 1110 for the betrothal of his daughter Maud to the emperor Henry V.[43] The origins of the exchequer remain obscure, but the *Dialogus de scaccario* from the end of the century implies that Roger of Salisbury did not invent the exchequer. He did, however, doubtless improve and modernize it, giving it the *form* we recognize. The impulse toward administrative reform following Tinchebray, combined with the need to raise a huge sum as dowry for Maud's betrothal in 1110, may have spurred the reforms that produced what we know as the English exchequer: abacus accounting procedure, court of audit, and pipe rolls recording receipts from the sheriffs and their shires.[44]

In 1108 Henry's daughter and eldest child, Maud, was still aged only six, but she was not too young to take a crucial role in international diplomacy. The Norman monarchy was as yet a very young dynasty that had occupied a royal throne for less than a half-century. A marriage alliance with the king of Germany and future Roman Emperor—the most eminent monarch in Western Christendom —would enhance the prestige of Henry I and his house immeasurably. Yet the evidence suggests that the initiative for the projected union was taken by Henry V, not Henry I. Such is the testimony of the Anglo-Norman writers Henry of Huntingdon and Robert of Torigny, and it is confirmed by a letter of Emperor Henry V to Queen Matilda of England offering her his most glowing thanks for speaking well

---

[42] Walter Map, *De nugis curialium*, pp. 438, 470; Walter Map and Geoffrey Gaimar, writing independently, provide our only twelfth-century evidence of life at Henry I's court. Their testimony is dismissed by Sir Richard Southern (*Medieval Humanism*, p. 230: "it is hard to see what there was to joke about. It was an unloveable reign") and by Professor John Gillingham ("Kingship, Chivalry and Love," pp. 57–58). On the lavish provisions provided by Henry I in 1130 for his court see Green, *Government*, p. 36.

[43] *RRAN* 2, no. 963. See ibid., no. 1000, AD 1111 (discussed below) recording a meeting of the exchequer court, under the name of the "Treasury," with Queen Matilda presiding as viceregent and Roger of Salisbury as first officer and first witness.

[44] *MMI*, pp. 231–232; Poole, *Exchequer*, pp. 36–50, 94–116, and *passim*; Kealey, *Roger of Salisbury*, pp. 45–46. See chapter 9 below for a thorough discussion of the king's administration.

of him to Henry I and expressing the hope that she will continue to assist him in the things that he requests of the king.[45] In a letter of March/April 1109 Henry reported from Rouen to Anselm, shortly before the archbishop's death, that "in the matter being discussed between me and the emperor of the Romans, we brought it to a good end by the grace of God."[46] Shortly after the king's return to England on 31 May/2 June, he held a great Whitsun court at Westminster (13 June) where he received envoys from the emperor and completed the formal arrangements for the betrothal, signing the necessary contracts and swearing the appropriate oaths. Henry of Huntingdon reports that Henry's Whitsun court was of unparalleled magnificence and that the imperial envoys, not to be outshone, were imposingly tall and splendidly dressed.[47]

Much of England's attraction for Emperor Henry V was its wealth, and Henry I demonstrated his avid interest in the connection with the empire by offering an immense dowry of ten thousand marks on Maud's betrothal and coronation. The empire, having endured years of civil war generated in part by the investiture controversy and possessing no central fiscal institutions remotely comparable to those of Norman England, was in poor financial shape. Henry V faced the further burden of having to undertake a large, ostentatious, and very expensive expedition to Rome to seek imperial coronation from Pope Paschal. So although Maud was a mere child, Henry V (himself about twenty-five) welcomed his new fiancée and her treasure.

But even the Anglo-Norman realm was hard pressed to raise such an immense sum. It was more than three times the annual stipend that Henry had promised Curthose in return for his relinquishing his claim to England in 1101, and it was the equivalent of the amount for which Curthose had pawned the duchy of Normandy before he left on crusade. Like Rufus in 1096, Henry was obliged to take extraordinary measures. He levied an "aid for the king's daughter" in the form of a geld of three shillings on the hide, half again as large as the normal danegeld. And although the rate was substantially less than some of the danegelds of Henry's Anglo-Norman and Anglo-Saxon predecessors, it was sufficiently high to evoke a shrill protest from the Anglo-Saxon chronicler: "This was a very severe year in this country because of taxes that the king took for the marriage of his daughter, and because of

[45] HH, p. 237; *GND*, 2:218; "Monumenta bambergensis", ed. Jaffé, pl. 259, no. 142; Leyser, *Medieval Germany and Its Neighbours*, p. 194.
[46] *AO*, ep. 461; the date is established by Henry's reference to his meeting with Louis VI at Neaufles on the Epte in March–April 1109 and by Anselm's death on 21 April 1109.
[47] HH, p. 237; Leyser, *Medieval Germany and Its Neighbours*, p. 193.

storms."[48] Several religious houses obtained writs for some of their properties that either stipulated that paying the aid would not set a precedent or provided an exemption from the aid altogether.[49] At a great council at Nottingham on 17 October 1109 the young bride-to-be, now seven years old, signed the royal diploma creating the see of Ely as *Mathildis sponsa regis Romanorum*—promised bride of the king of the Romans—and in late February 1110, having recently turned eight, she set off for Germany in the company of a distinguished party of imperial envoys and of Norman nobles bearing the munificent dowry.[50] Early in March they arrived in Liège, one of the more important cities of the empire, where Maud and her future husband met for the first time. The child was received "as befitted a king," so a German annalist reports.[51] The royal entourage traveled next to Utrecht for the Easter court of 10 April. There Maud and Henry were formally betrothed, and Henry granted Maud her dower, probably including lands in the neighborhood of Utrecht, from which she is later known to have made donations to a religious house in the region.[52] Finally, on St James Day, 25 July 1110, Maud was crowned queen of the Germans in the majestic early Romanesque cathedral of Mainz by Frederick archbishop of Cologne (the archbishopric of Mainz being vacant just then). Archbishop Frederick was assisted by Bruno archbishop of Trier, first counselor to Henry V and "vice-lord of the royal curia" (*vicedominus regiae curiae*), who held the eight-year-old child reverently in his arms as she received the royal crown.[53] Archbishop Bruno subsequently became Maud's guardian and assumed responsibility for her education, including her instruction in the German language.

Orderic reports that a number of great men in Maud's Norman escort, including Roger fitz Richard of Clare, hoped to win high rank for themselves in Germany. They aspired to achieve, through their daring and ruthlessness, the authority that their ancestors had won for

---

[48] *ASC*, s.a. 1110; on earler danegelds (looking only at the years following 1066) see Barlow, *Rufus*, pp. 200, 240–247: Malmesbury accuses Rufus and Flambard of often doubling the danegeld rate, and we know that they did so in the particularly demanding year of 1096 when it ran 4 shillings on the hide; in the mid-1080s the Conqueror levied a geld of 6 shillings on the hide: ibid., p. 240; Douglas, *William the Conqueror*, p. 302; *ASC*, s.a. 1083.

[49] *RRAN* 2, nos 946, 963–964.

[50] Ibid., no. 919; Chibnall, *Empress Matilda*, p. 16; SD, 2:241; OV, 5:200, 6:166–168; HH, p. 237; *Ann. Wint.*, p. 43, reporting (plausibly) that on the day of Maud's departure from England she was eight years and fifteen days old.

[51] Leyser, *Medieval Germany and Its Neighbours*, p. 193 with references; Chibnall, *Empress Matilda*, p. 22.

[52] Ibid., p. 24; Leyser, *Medieval Germany and Its Neighbours*, p. 193.

[53] *GND*, 2:218; Leyser, *Medieval Germany and Its Neighbours*, p. 193; Chibnall, *Empress Matilda*, pp. 21–22, 25 with references.

themselves in England and Apulia. But the wily emperor, "a man of great experience," gave presents to the Normans and sent them home.[54] Orderic exaggerates just slightly, for we know of one Norman in Maud's entourage, Henry archdeacon of Winchester, who remained behind and was later raised to the bishopric of Verdun.[55]

The ten-thousand-mark dowry was of decisive importance in subsidizing Henry V's expedition to Rome in 1110–1111. The enterprise was at once a grand procession and a military operation involving "perhaps the biggest army that had so far been raised by a German ruler."[56] Henry V's army proved so intimidating that after various complex disputes and the temporary arrest of the pope and his curia, Paschal not only crowned Henry Roman Emperor but even waived the ban on lay investiture. The result was a surge of protests by reform churchmen across Western Christendom and rebellion in Germany. But Henry V managed to suppress the rebellion for a time, and on 7 January 1114 the emperor and his eleven-year-old bride were formally married at Worms in a ceremony of great splendor. It is reported that among the vast crowd of notables attending the nuptials were five archbishops, thirty bishops, and five dukes, along with countless abbots, counts, and lesser nobles.[57]

After the wedding, anti-imperial rebellions resumed. Otto of Friesing even suggested that renewed rebellions were being hatched among the nobles who had assembled for the wedding festivities.[58] The reign of Henry V was therefore troubled in subsequent years, and perhaps the greatest disappointment of all to the imperial cause was Maud's childlessness.[59] It must also have disappointed Maud that although her husband had received the imperial crown from the pope, she herself had never been crowned empress of the Romans. She had been too young to accompany Henry V on his Roman expedition of 1110–1111, and Henry V's relations with the papacy were thereafter too stormy to permit an imperial coronation for his wife.[60] After Maud returned to the Anglo-Norman court on Henry V's death in 1125, she came to be referred to as *imperatrix augusta* by Anglo-Norman writers, courtiers, and (according to Robert of Torigny) the king himself, and in her

---

[54] OV, 6:168.

[55] Leyser, *Medieval Germany and Its Neighbours*, p. 195 n. 3.

[56] Morris, *The Papal Monarchy*, p. 158.

[57] Ibid., p. 161; Chibnall, *Empress Matilda*, pp. 26–27.

[58] Chibnall, *Empress Matilda*, p. 26, citing Otto of Freising, *The Two Cities*, trans. Mierow, p. 421.

[59] The blame for this misfortune must surely rest on Henry V, since Maud bore three sons by her second husband, Geoffrey of Anjou.

[60] On the issue of Maud's imperial coronation, or lack of it, see Leyser, *Medieval Germany and Its Neighbours*, pp. 197–200.

subsequent charters she routinely styled herself *Matildis imperatrix*. But on the emperor Henry V's charters, down to the end of his reign, she bears the more modest title, *Romanorum regina*.[61]

During the years between Henry I's accession and the betrothal of his daughter Maud, important changes occurred in the inner councils of his regime. Three men who had originally been among his chief advisers all died in 1107: Richard of Redvers, the friend of his youth from western Normandy; Robert fitz Hamon, severely disabled at the siege of Falaise; and Roger Bigod, from the Bocage in western Normandy, who served as *dapifer* to both Rufus and Henry I and to whom Henry had made a substantial grant at Framlingham, Suffolk.[62] But Henry's governance was more significantly altered by the death of Archbishop Anselm on 21 April 1109. Anselm had served as regent or coregent of England during Henry's absences from 1106 to the time of the archbishop's death, and his resolute governance of the English Church was firm and purposeful, if occasionally resented as being too harsh.[63]

The final months of Anselm's life were clouded by a fierce struggle precipitated by his demand for a written oath of obedience from Thomas II, archbishop-elect of York, whose refusal and evasions enjoyed the solid backing of the York Cathedral chapter. The conflict, involving frequent exchanges of messengers and intemperate letters, remained unsettled at Anselm's death. Even afterward the contradictory, highly partisan accounts of Hugh the Chanter of York and Eadmer of Canterbury muddied the exact terms of the final resolution supervised by the king—who was embroiled in a conflict with France at the time and would doubtless have preferred to avoid the whole business.[64] A resolute defender of Canterbury archiepiscopal prerogatives and a significant participant in the governance of King Henry's realm, Anselm had played a central role in the early years of the reign. His death modified the political landscape of

---

[61] Ibid., pp. 199–200; *GND*, 2:246; *RRAN* 3, *passim*.

[62] Orderic (*OV*, 5:298) names as Henry I's chief advisers ca.1101 Robert of Meulan, Hugh of Chester, Richard of Redvers, and Roger Bigod, of whom only Robert of Meulan was still alive in 1109; *CP*, 4:309–311, 5:683, 9:575–579; Sanders, *Baronies*, pp. 46–47.

[63] Vaughn, *Anselm of Bec and Robert of Meulan*, pp. 246–248, 319–322, 345–346.

[64] *AO*, epp. 443–445, 451, 453–456; 464–465, 471–472; Hugh the Chanter, pp. 30–50; Eadmer, *HN*, pp. 203–211: Hugh (p. 49) states that Thomas' profession to Canterbury included the crucial qualification, "saving the rights of the church of York," whereas Eadmer (p. 210), in "quoting" Thomas' profession, omits that qualification altogether.

England. And it left a vacancy in the see of Canterbury that would endure for the next five years.

The passing of this older generation did not immediately result in the emergence of new men but for the most part simply gave greater power to men who had long served the king and now became the most frequent attesters of his charters: the lay magnates Robert count of Meulan, Nigel of Aubigny, William of Warenne, and William of Tancarville chamberlain of Normandy and England, and the administrator-bishops Roger of Salisbury, Robert Bloet of Lincoln, William Giffard of Winchester, and Richard Beaumais of London.[65] Since the guiding force behind the regime remained Henry I himself, in close collaboration with Robert of Meulan (on general policy) and Roger of Salisbury (on the English administration), the overall direction of the royal government did not change appreciably.

Nevertheless, by 1109 conditions were changing drastically in the world beyond the Anglo-Norman frontiers. In his final letter to Anselm, announcing the successful conclusion of marriage negotiations with the empire, Henry also discusses a confrontation with the new French king, Louis VI. Henry had befriended Louis at his Christmas court of 1100 at Westminster, and Louis is reported to have acquiesced in Henry's conquest of Normandy.[66] But Louis, on his accession to the French throne in 1108, adopted a much more aggressive policy than his predecessors toward Normandy and the other French principalities. Elizabeth Hallam aptly remarks on the close connection between the growth of Capetian power over neighboring lordships and principalities and Louis VI's newly aggressive attitude with respect to his control of royal lands and the territories beyond them. And as Olivier Guillot has argued, Fulk V initiated a similarly aggressive centralizing policy on his accession to the countship of Anjou in 1109.[67]

Back at the time of his victory at Tinchebray in 1106, Henry had displayed an abundance of confidence. He released most of his captives and took pity on his three-year-old nephew William Clito by placing him under the protection of Helias of Saint-Saens, Curthose's devoted follower, whose chief castle was dangerously close to Normandy's northeastern frontier. It would have been difficult for Henry to foresee in 1106 the great shifts in European political history that lay just ahead: the surge of French royal authority that commenced in 1108 or the parallel surge that followed Fulk V's succession to Anjou in the following year. Although Henry's affectionate treatment of William Clito

---

[65] *MMI*, p. 241.

[66] OV, 6:50–52; *Chronique de Morigny*, p. 21; WM, *GR*, 2:480.

[67] Hallam, *Capetian France*, p. 95; Guillot, *Le Comte d'Anjou et son entourage*, 1: 433–434.

involved a risk, it would have seemed a small one at a time when the great powers of France smiled benignly while Henry reforged the cross-Channel Anglo-Norman dominions.

But Louis VI, immediately after his father's death, demanded Henry's homage for Normandy, along with the homage of other princes of France, and the neutralization of two of Henry's frontier castles on the Norman bank of the River Epte (the river that divided Normandy from the French Vexin): Bray-et-Lu and, more important, the great Norman stronghold of Gisors that had been designed by Robert of Bellême for William Rufus during the late king's Vexin war. According to Suger, Henry held both these strongholds in violation of an earlier agreement (otherwise unrecorded) in which he had also allegedly sworn to render homage to Louis for Normandy. Henry, in his final letter to Anselm, firmly denied these allegations. Because of his obvious self-interest, pitted against Suger's ardent bias toward the cause of his French royal hero (and the fact that he confused many of the details of the subsequent war), one cannot be certain which story is correct—or whether there had been a genuine misunderstanding between the two kings.[68] Although Gisors had been a ducal castle under Rufus, Robert Curthose seems to have granted it as a fief to its ducal castellan Theobald Pain of Gisors,[69] who had apparently held it at the time of Tinchebray but returned it to the ducal custody soon afterward at Henry's urging and probably for a price.[70] Theobald Pain relinquished the castle to Henry *tam blandiciis quam minis* ("as much by incentives as by threats"). From the time he conquered Normandy it was Henry's policy to resume control of previously ducal lands and castles granted away by Curthose,[71] and he clearly claimed the traditional right, recorded in clause 4 of the *Consuetudines et iusticie* of 1091 to limit the building of baronial castles and to place his own garrisons in them when he chose.[72] One can merely observe that it is characteristic of Louis VI's lifelong policies that his initial hostilities with Henry should result from demands involving castles and homage. And it is just as characteristic of Henry's policies on castles and homage that he should concede Louis neither. Henry could be just as adamant about refusing homage as Anselm had been.[73]

Crossing to Normandy in summer 1108, Henry resisted Louis' demands. Early in 1109, Louis endeavored to make his point by

---

[68] *AO*, ep. 461; Suger, *Louis le Gros*, pp. 102–106.
[69] OV, 5:308, 309 n. 3.
[70] Suger, *Louis le Gros*, p. 102.
[71] OV, 6:94.
[72] Haskins, *NI*, p. 282, and see above, p. 84; in general, see Green, "Henry I and the Aristocracy of Normandy," p. 167.
[73] WM, *GR*, 2:496; *MMI*, p. 38.

pillaging and burning the French properties of Henry's powerful *fidelis* Robert count of Meulan. Advancing northwest from Meulan toward Normandy, Louis encountered Henry along the eastern frontier of the duchy where, in spring 1109, the two kings parleyed from opposite sides of the River Epte at an obscure site known as the Planches-de-Neaufles (the modern Neaufles-Saint-Martin). At this point the Epte was spanned by a dilapidated bridge that threatened a ducking to anyone who strode across it too purposefully.

There the kings negotiated, surrounded by their armies, much as Rolf and Charles the Simple were said to have done at Saint-Clair-sur-Epte about 911.[74] In Louis' entourage were such notable princes as Robert II count of Flanders, Theobald count of Blois, William II count of Nevers, Hugh duke of Burgundy, and numerous archbishops and bishops. The members of Henry's following are not named (no Anglo-Norman chronicler reports on the meeting), but Henry appears to have been undaunted. The negotiations were stormy, and yet they ended with a truce. None of the issues was resolved; Henry kept both disputed castles and rendered no homage. Suger asserts, improbably, that Louis launched an unsuccessful attack against Gisors immediately thereafter. Whatever the case, the kings exchanged hostages and then, shortly afterward, each returned to his homeland.[75]

For the next two years Louis and Henry attended to their own affairs in France and England respectively. Besides concluding final arrangements for Maud's betrothal to the German monarch and raising her immense dowry, Henry I helped negotiate a temporary settlement of the bitter Canterbury–York profession dispute that Anselm had left unresolved at his death. The king also supervised the conversion of the wealthy abbey of Ely into a bishopric, appointing as its first bishop Hervey bishop of Bangor, a man of secular tastes whom Anselm had disliked. Hervey used his acquaintanceship with the king to free himself from all responsibility for the unfriendly Welsh inhabitants of his former diocese, who had driven him from Bangor into the royal court, and to settle instead into his opulent new Cambridgeshire see.[76] At a great council at Nottingham in October, Henry duly constituted the bishopric of Ely, by the authority of Pope Paschal, while at the same time granting the valuable town of Spaldwick (Hunts.) as compensation to the curial bishop Robert Bloet of Lincoln, from whose diocese the new bishopric had been carved.[77]

[74] Suger, *Louis le Gros*, pp. 104–110.
[75] Ibid., pp. 110–112; *AO*, ep. 461; Farrer, *Itin.*, p. 51; Luchaire, *Louis VI*, p. 40.
[76] *AO*, epp. 404, 441; Vaughn, *Anselm of Bec and Robert of Meulan*, pp. 320–321; Barlow, *English Church: 1066–1154*, p. 69.
[77] *Liber eliensis*, pp. 245–246, 249–250.

The years of truce (1109–1111) witnessed complex hostile diplomatic maneuverings between the kings of England and France—
although some of these intrigues prove difficult to discern or interpret.
It was probably shortly after the Neaufles meeting, for example, that a
family feud in the lordship of La Roche-Guyon ("Guy's Rock") on the
lower Seine resulted in the murder of a loyal French lord, Guy of La
Roche-Guyon, along with his wife and children, by his Norman-born
brother-in-law, William, who thereupon took possession of the lordship.[78] The castle of La Roche-Guyon is situated high on a hillside overlooking the Seine and the French Vexin. A short hike upward from the
castle brings one to the ridge of the hill which, looking southwest, commands a sweeping view of the Epte valley and eastern Normandy.

The castle was thus of great strategic importance in any struggle
between the French and the Normans. But although Suger, our one
source for this episode, hints that Henry I may have been privy to this
coup, one cannot be certain. Suger does tell us that men of the French
Vexin were so horrified by the grisly murders perpetrated by William
of La Roche-Guyon and his men that, encouraged by Louis VI, they
attacked the castle, captured William and his cohorts, and, evidently on
the French king's instruction, tortured them to death—mutilating
some, disemboweling others, and ripping William's heart from his body
and thrusting it onto a pike. William and a number of his men were
then cast into the Seine in the hope that they would float down to
Rouen and teach the Normans a grim and memorable lesson.[79]

Whether or not the unfortunate William of La Roche-Guyon had the
tacit support of the Anglo-Norman regime, Henry was suffering much
greater diplomatic reversals in the months and years just following the
Neaufles meeting. Most important, the accession of Fulk V in 1109
meant that a newly aggressive Anjou would threaten Normandy as never
before. The situation on Normandy's southern frontier became even
more menacing when Fulk V, having married Eremburga the daughter
and heir of Count Helias, inherited Maine *jure uxoris* on Helias' death
in 1110. Whereas Helias had been Henry I's friend and *fidelis*, Fulk V
rejected Henry's suzerainty over Maine and refused to do him homage
for it.[80] Robert II count of Flanders, despite having renewed his money-
fief treaty with Henry I in mid-May 1110,[81] joined the Franco-Angevin
coalition shortly afterward and took up arms against the Anglo-Norman
monarch, who now found himself threatened by three major allied
powers. The threat eased in 1111 when Robert II of Flanders died of

[78] Suger, *Louis le Gros*, pp. 112–118.
[79] Ibid., pp. 118–122.
[80] *MMI*, pp. 254, 281.
[81] *RRAN* 2, no. 941.

an injury while campaigning with Louis VI, leaving a child heir. Indeed, several of the military and diplomatic confrontations between Henry and Louis during the seventeen years between 1111 and 1128 were affected dramatically by the strange coincidence that four successive counts of Flanders—Robert II, Baldwin VII, Charles the Good, and William Clito—suffered violent and premature deaths.[82]

Despite the loss of suzerainty over Maine and the development of a dangerous new Franco-Angevin alliance, Henry was far more successful than Louis in suppressing opposition in his dominions and promoting rebellion in his neighbors'. Henry won allies beyond his frontiers by means of bribes, intrigues, and strategic marriages, and he discouraged potential rebels within his dominions with the aid of a remarkably alert intelligence system. Orderic credits Henry with being so thoroughly familiar with secret plots against him as to astonish the plotters, and he observes elsewhere, in connection with the quarrels of 1109–1113, that Henry swept away the designs of his enemies like cobwebs and crushed them without shedding the blood of his own men.[83]

Following Orderic's hints, one can reasonably suspect that the sweeping away of cobwebs was exemplified by the singular abundance of arrests and forfeitures of Anglo-Norman magnates during the troubled years between 1109 and 1113. In 1110, as the Anglo-Saxon chronicler reports without explanation, Henry disseised and exiled William Malet, William Baynard, and Philip of Braose, the last-named being restored in 1112. At about the same time, 1110 or shortly thereafter, Roger of Abitôt, sheriff of Worcestershire and constable of Worcester Castle, was deprived of his lands and offices because, as William of Malmesbury explains, with headlong madness he had ordered the assassination of a royal official.[84] In these same years (1109–ca. 1114) Robert of Lacy was deprived of his great Yorkshire honor of Pontefract.[85] In Normandy in 1112 Henry ordered the exile of William Crispin (a Tinchebray captive whom Henry had released after the battle), along with William count of Evreux and his wife Countess Helwise, all three of whom were forgiven and reseised in the peace settlement of 1113.[86]

Henry's temporary banishment of Count William and Countess Helwise can probably be explained at least in part by their kinship connections with Henry's major external enemies. The count and

---

[82] *MMI*, pp. 256, 258, 260, 281.

[83] OV, 6:176.

[84] WM, *GP*, p. 283; on the date of Roger's fall see *The Cartulary of Worcester Cathedral Priory*, pp. xxv, 26–27.

[85] *Lancashire Pipe Rolls*, p. 383; *VCH, Leicestershire*, 1:314–315; *RRAN* 2, nos 918, 1030. Robert had lost his lands by the time of the Lindsey Survey (AD 1115–1118).

[86] *ASC, s.a.* 1112; OV, 6:148 and n. 2, 180.

countess of Evreux, who were childless and growing old, intended to leave their county to their nephew Amaury (III) de Montfort, the son of William of Evreux's sister Agnes. (See genealogy of the counts of Evreux, p. 245.) Amaury's own kin ties, chiefly through his sister Bertrade de Montfort, would place him at the nexus of international opposition to Henry I. Bertrade had been countess of Anjou as the third wife of Fulk IV and she was the mother of the current count, Fulk V. She had scandalized Christendom by leaving her Angevin husband for King Philip I of France and then, astonishingly, persuading the two great princes to become friends.[87] Amaury, as Bertrade's older brother, had emerged as a major influence at both the Angevin and French courts, and Orderic places him at the center of the Franco-Angevin coalition of 1109–1113. It was Amaury, Orderic writes, who incited his nephew Fulk V to launch raids against Normandy and to appeal to Louis VI for military support. The threat of border raids by the Angevins and their allies prompted Henry to build two new frontier castles, at Nonancourt and Illiers-l'Evêque in early 1112. And it was no coincidence that Count William and Countess Helwise, Amaury's uncle and aunt, found refuge during their exile at the court of Anjou.[88] With Amaury scheduled to become the next count of the wealthy Norman county of Evreux, there was trouble ahead.

Henry's most significant arrest during these years was that of Robert of Bellême. In the crisis of 1109–1113, Robert had once again betrayed his oath of fealty to Henry I and had joined the Franco-Angevin coalition against him. Robert then committed the grave error of turning up at Henry's court at Bonneville in early November 1112, allegedly as an envoy of Louis VI.[89] But even if Robert had indeed claimed to be a French envoy, Henry regarded him not as a foreign ambassador but as a rogue *vicomte* whom the king had pardoned after Tinchebray and reappointed to the Norman *vicomtés* of Argentan, Exmes, and Falaise. These offices carried the responsibility of collecting and delivering the royal revenues from the three *vicomtés*. Having rendered no account of these revenues, Robert was in default. At Bonneville in 1112, as in England in 1102, he was required to answer to this and several other formal charges against him: Why had he acted against his lord's

---

[87] On Bertrade's skill in reconciling her first husband with her second and making close friends of both, see OV, 4:260–262, Suger, *Louis le Gros*, pp. 122–124.

[88] OV, 6:176, 180; Orderic implies that Amaury was a frequent guest at the court of Count William and Helwise: ibid., p. 204.

[89] Ibid., pp. 178, 256 and n. 7: as Chibnall states, there is no other evidence that he went as an envoy of the French king, and as a person who had betrayed Henry repeatedly, "he would have been an extremely ill-chosen one"; but it is hard to explain why Robert of Bellême would otherwise venture into Henry's court.

interests? Why had he failed to come to his court after being summoned three times? Orderic also alludes to other formal charges without specifying them and concludes by stating that "by a just judgement of the royal court" Robert of Bellême was sentenced to imprisonment for his many crimes against both God and the king. Robert was first confined in the castle of Cherbourg and then, on Henry's return to England, he was imprisoned at Wareham. The Pipe Roll of 1130 reports an annual payment of twenty pounds five shillings for his maintenance expenses, and that is the last we hear of him.[90] Not long after the arrest, Henry besieged the strategic Bellême frontier stronghold of Alençon and took it after a brief siege.[91]

Orderic, who was never a great admirer of Robert of Bellême, reports a surge of elation among the Normans as news of his arrest spread through the duchy. "The people of God, freed from the bandit's yoke, rejoiced and thanked God their liberator, and wished a long and prosperous life to King Henry."[92] It is very interesting that Orderic elsewhere includes "Robert of Bellême, with forces of Angevins and Manceaux," among the supporters of William Clito against Henry I, and still again Orderic reports that Robert of Bellême "did everything in his power to help the distinguished exile who was the duke's son."[93] Since Robert of Bellême was *hors de combat* from 4 November 1112 onward, Orderic's statements demonstrate that Clito had by that time already emerged, even though still a child of seven or eight, as his royal uncle's rival for the rule of Normandy (and perhaps England as well) and as the focus of international opposition to Henry I.

It was probably in 1110 or 1111, at a time when Henry was arresting or exiling a number of unreliable barons, that he attempted unsuccessfully to have the young William Clito arrested. He sent orders to Robert of Beauchamp, *vicomte* of Arques, to take William Clito by surprise in the castle of Saint-Saens.[94] When the *vicomte* arrived, Clito's guardian Helias happened to be absent, but friends of the child snatched him from his bed and took him eastward out of Normandy. Helias of Saint-Saens quickly joined them and became William Clito's protector and tutor, wandering in exile for a time and then settling at

---

[90] *PR 31 Henry I*, p. 12; FW, 2:66; HH, p. 238; *ASC, s.a.* 1112; WM, *GR*, 2:475. Robert of Bellême's allowances were in excess of 13d. per day, more than William of Mortain's 10.5d. per day, and far above a contemporary knight's wages of 6d. per day: Hollister, *Military Organization of Norman England*, p. 206 and n. 1; above, this chapter, n. 4. All our evidence (on Ranulf Flambard, Robert Curthose, William of Mortain, and Robert of Bellême) points to the conclusion that Henry maintained his high-status captives in considerable comfort.

[91] OV, 6:178.

[92] Ibid.

[93] OV, 6:368, 164.

[94] OV, 6:162–164.

the court of the count of Flanders. Helias sought out powerful support for Clito from all quarters and found many great men, in and out of Normandy, who were willing to turn against Henry I in behalf of his nephew. Above all, Helias and Clito were backed by Robert of Bellême, and Robert and Helias between them, soliciting the support of Louis and several of his great princes, "bombarded them with envoys and letters."[95] Robert of Bellême's arrest in 1112 thus deprived Clito of one of his chief supporters.

Conversely, Henry worked during these years to win the backing of magnates in the dominions of his enemies. "Many of the nobles of Maine," Orderic writes, "went over to Henry's side, and after doing fealty surrendered their castles to him."[96] One such noble family was that of Patrick of Sources, lord of an important castle of that name in central Maine, to whom Henry gave the English lands of Ernulf of Hesdin, who had perished on the First Crusade. Patrick became a regular member of Henry I's court and a frequent attester of his charters.[97] Another noble family of Maine may have been won over, or subsequently rewarded, by Henry's grant of the forfeited Lacy honor of Pontefract to Hugh of Laval.[98] Hugh was the uncle and guardian of Guy IV, heir to the Laval estates in Maine, and there is evidence that Guy of Laval, perhaps through Hugh's intercession, may have married an otherwise unknown bastard daughter of Henry I's named Emma.[99] Still another of the royal daughters was wed at an undiscoverable date to Roscelin *vicomte* of Maine and lord of Beaumont-le-Vicomte. Two of Roscelin's major castles, Fresnay and Beaumont-le-Vicomte, controlled the route between Alençon and Le Mans, and a third, Sainte-Suzanne, dominated central Maine. Moreover, Roscelin evidently received lands in England from Henry I: he is recorded in the Pipe Roll of 1130

---

[95] OV, 6:164.

[96] OV, 6:176.

[97] RRAN 2, nos 492, 544, 937, 960, 1005, 1517, 1553, 1567, 1675, 1826, 1939; Sanders, *Baronies*, pp. 124–125.

[98] Wightman, *Lacy Family*, pp. 66–67; Wightman inclines toward a later date (1114–1118) and associates it with the hostilities of 1116–1119. Although I think that the earlier date range of 1109–ca. 1114 is the more likely (above, this chapter, n. 80), it remains possible that the honor was in royal hands for an appreciable time between Robert's forfeiture and Hugh's arrival: ibid., pp. 243–244.

[99] Bertrand de Broussillon, *La Maison de Laval*, 1:79: ". . . on prétend même que l'abbaye de Clermont aurait conservé longtemps une tombe sur laquelle on lisait: EMMA ANGLORUM REGIS FILIA DOMINAQUE LAVALLENSIS." The author dismisses this tradition on the grounds that Robert of Torigny omits "Emma" from his list of Henry's daughters, but the list is by no means complete. Emma is absent from the list of Henry I's illegitimate daughters in *CP*, 11, app. D, pp. 112–121.

as being pardoned two marks on the forest pleas of Robert Arundel in Devon.[100] Henry also forged an alliance with Hamelin, lord of the crucially important Manceau barony of Mayenne (ca. 1112–ca. 1118), in which he exchanged lands in Devon worth some fifty pounds a year for the strategic Manceaux frontier castles of Ambrières and Gorron.[101] Thus, although Fulk V was officially count of Maine, Henry enjoyed the friendship and allegiance of several of Maine's most powerful baronies: Sourches, Laval, Beaumont-le-Vicomte, and Mayenne. The winning of friends in Maine may well have been on Henry's mind when in 1111 he raised Geoffrey Brito, dean of Le Mans Cathedral and a favorite of the late Count Helias, to the archbishopric of Rouen, recently made vacant by the death of Archbishop William Bonne-Ame in 1110.[102] And although there is no explicit evidence to show that Henry instigated the rebellion of 1112 in Anjou, he was at least convenienced by the diversion of Fulk V's military resources at the height of the international conflict. The rebellion could not have been better timed.[103]

Meanwhile, between 1111 and 1113 King Louis VI was contending, not always successfully, with the largest rebellion of his reign. Robert of Meulan, whose county in the French Vexin Louis had pillaged in 1109 and again in 1110, settled scores in 1111 by seizing and plundering Paris while the French king was some miles to the southeast in Melun.[104] In the same year the young Theobald count of Blois, perhaps on the advice of his mother Adela countess of Blois (Henry's sister), broke with Louis and allied himself with Henry.[105] By 1112 a considerable number of French magnates had joined Theobald in an uprising against Louis. The coalition included Lancelin of Bulles lord of Dammartin, Payn of Montjai, Ralph of Beaugenci, Milo of Brai *vicomte* of Troyes, Hugh of Crécy lord of Châteaufort, Guy of Rochefort, Hugh

---

[100] *CP*, 11, app. D, p. 116; *PR 31 Henry I*, p. 155; I am drawing here from an unpublished paper by Richard E. Barton, "Lordship and Pacification: The Norman Dukes in Maine, *ca.* 1060–1135," presented at the Haskins Conference, Houston, 1992.

[101] *Book of Fees*, 1:86: "Et Henricus Rex senex dedit illud manerium [Supereton'] Hamelin de Cheduana in escambium de Ambreres et de Gurreham." Henry renewed the agreement with Hamelin's successor, Juhel of Mayenne, and sealed it with the gift of a gold cup: ibid., 1:97; *Cartulaire Manceau de Marmoutier*, 2:15–17. Again, I am happy to acknowledge the help of Richard E. Barton, "Lordship and Pacification" (see n. 100, this chapter).

[102] *OV*, 5:236; 6:172. I am indebted to my former student, Professor David S. Spear, for this suggestion. Hugh the Chanter (pp. 82, 89) hints that Archbishop Geoffrey was involved in the peace negotiations of 1119–1120 between Thurstan archbishop of York, Louis VI, and the papal curia.

[103] Chartrou, *L'Anjou*, p. 27.

[104] Luchaire, *Louis VI*, nos 72, 103, 111; Anonymous of Laon, in *HF*, 12:678; the episode might possibly be dated as early as 1110; Luchaire favors ca. 12 March 1111.

[105] Luchaire, *Louis VI*, nos 117, 121.

count of Troyes, and Hugh du Puiset, supported, Suger adds, by an army of Normans.[106] An oft-repeated example of Louis' persistent struggles with what used to be called the "robber barons" of the Ile de France is his capture and destruction of the castle of Le Puiset on three separate occasions, yet each of the three sieges occurred in years of serious hostilities between Louis and Henry—1111, 1112, and 1118—and on the second of them Louis was able to take the castle only after the departure of five hundred Norman knights who had been assisting in its defense.[107] Orderic describes Louis at this time as being too much occupied to disturb the king of England by invading Normandy.[108]

Henry was winning other allies against France by marrying or betrothing royal offspring to important neighboring princes. Two such alliances can be dated firmly to the months immediately preceding the Franco-Norman peace of March 1113. The betrothal early in 1113 of Henry's nine-year-old son, William Adelin, to Matilda daughter of Fulk V of Anjou drew Anjou from the French into the Anglo-Norman orbit (as would their marriage in 1119 and the betrothal and marriage of the empress Maud to Geoffrey count of Anjou amidst the Flemish succession crisis of 1127–1128).[109] Similarly, the union between Henry's natural daughter Maud and Conan III of Brittany almost certainly occurred just before the Franco-Norman peace of 1113 and was intended, as Orderic explains, to establish a bond of peace between the Anglo-Norman monarch and the Breton ducal house.[110]

Among the numerous marriages that Henry sought to arrange between his bastard daughters and neighboring princes, one more at least was evidently associated with the peace of 1113. A letter of Ivo of Chartres to King Henry protests and forbids the betrothal of one of Henry's daughters (unnamed) to Hugh fitz Gervase of Châteauneuf-en-Thymerais, a major frontier magnate in the county of Chartres.[111] The letter can be dated loosely by Bishop Ivo's death in late 1116 and the fact that Gervase of Châteauneuf was in arms against Henry during the war of 1111–1113.[112] It looks very much as though the

---

[106] Ibid., no. 134; Suger, *Louis le Gros*, pp. 146–148.

[107] Suger, *Louis le Gros*, pp. 158–168, especially p. 162; Luchaire, *Louis VI*, nos 114, 134, 236; cf. Hallam, *Capetian France*, p. 116; Dunbabin, *France in the Making*, p. 296.

[108] OV, 6:176–178.

[109] WM, *HN*, pp. 2–3.

[110] OV, 2:352; 6:174 and n. 4, 180.

[111] *PL* 162, cols 265–266.

[112] OV, 6:176. Gervase's wife, Mabel, was a niece of Robert of Bellême; their son Hugh later (ca. 1123) married Aubree, sister of Waleran of Meulan, to seal a military alliance between Hugh and Waleran against Henry I in connection with the general hostilities of 1123–1124: OV, 6:623 and n. 3; Crouch, *Beaumont Twins*, pp. 16–17.

marriage plan that Ivo blocked was intended to draw the family of Châteauneuf into the Anglo-Norman alliance network in connection with the peace of 1113 and that it exemplified the same policy that brought about William Adelin's betrothal to Matilda of Anjou and Maud's to Conan of Brittany.

As a consequence of Henry's astute diplomacy, the peace of Normandy remained unbroken during these years. After spending Candlemas 1113 (2–3 February) at Orderic's abbey of Saint-Evroul, granting the monks generous privileges and being welcomed into the monastic fraternity,[113] Henry proceeded to a decisive meeting with Fulk V near Alençon. There, in late February, Henry arranged the afore-mentioned peace with Anjou and sealed it with the betrothal of William Adelin (now nine years old) to Fulk V's daughter Matilda. Henry agreed to pardon major adherents to the Angevin cause: Amaury de Montfort, his uncle William of Evreux, and (once again) William Crispin. The problem of Maine was settled as well (for the time being), when Fulk, as a part of the overall agreement, did homage to Henry for the long-disputed county.[114] Fulk retained direct control of Maine and its revenues, but his recognition of Henry's suzerainty restored the Anglo-Norman overlordship that had prevailed at the time of Count Helias. The overlordship was immensely important to Henry, for although intangible, it was a privilege that both his father and his brother William Rufus had enjoyed. In actuality, they had exercised more than mere overlordship; Henry I was willing to settle for suzerainty alone. It was an ancestral prerogative no more tangible than investitures but, to Henry, perhaps no less significant.[115]

Henry's peace with Anjou had precisely the effect on Louis VI that Henry had intended. Beset with rebellions and losing supporters one after another, the French king found himself almost totally isolated. Bereft of his Angevin ally, Louis came to terms within a month. At his request, Henry met him at the village of Ormeteau-Ferre near Gisors during the last week in March 1113. There both kings swore to keep the peace and bound themselves in an alliance of friendship.[116] Louis acquiesced to all that had been in contention between them and more,

---

[113] OV, 6:174–176; *RRAN* 2, no. 1019.

[114] OV, 6:180; Luchaire, *Louis VI*, no. 157; Chartrou, *L'Anjou*, pp. 6–7.

[115] Henry is styled *Dei gratia rex Anglorum et Normannorum dux atque Cenomannensium princeps* in a charter of 1113 confirming gifts to Saint-Evroul, dated *Anno quo comes Andegavensis mecum pacem fecit et Cenomannum de me, meus homo factus, recepit*: *RRAN* 2, no. 1019; cf. OV, 6:174. See, further, *Le Livre de serfs de Marmoutier*, pl. 175 (no. 50A): "In hoc rotulo continentur hi qui ab anno incarnationis dominicae (MCXIII), ipse est annus concordiae H. regis Anglorum cum F. Andegavensi comite, recognoscentes se servos beati Martini, recognita sua dederunt." (Thanks to Richard Barton for supplying this last reference.)

[116] Luchaire, *Louis VI*, no. 158.

conceding to Henry the overlordship of Maine (which Fulk had already promised him), Bellême, and Brittany. Duke Alan Fergant of Brittany had already become Henry's vassal, and their relationship had been sealed by the betrothal of Henry's natural daughter Maud to Alan's son Conan.[117]

After this general peace, there remained only one pocket of resistance to Henry, the garrison of the formidable castle of Bellême on Normandy's southern frontier. For although Henry's great adversary Robert of Bellême was now out of the picture, there remained Robert's son, William Talvas, who had inherited the county of Ponthieu (to the northeast of Normandy) from his mother Agnes, Robert of Bellême's unfortunate, abused wife.[118] Although William Talvas was then preoccupied with the defense of his mother's county, the commanders of the garrison at Bellême, trusting in its great strength, prepared to hold it against King Henry. But the victorious king, drawing on his allies old and new, assembled a huge army that included, in addition to his own Normans, the forces of Fulk count of Anjou, Theobald count of Blois, Rotrou count of Perche, "and other great magnates."[119] Through a combination of force, cunning, and luck, Henry's men succeeded in forcing their way through a half-open gate. They overwhelmed the hilltop town and when the garrison of the citadel continued to resist, they set it afire and burned it to the ground. As Orderic states, concluding the eleventh book of his history:

> Henry returned victorious to England after making peace with all his neighbours, and for five years he governed the kingdom and the duchy on opposite sides of the Channel in great tranquillity, and his friends devoutly offered praise to the Lord God of hosts who orders all things mightily and well. Amen.[120]

Orderic's passage vividly reflects the sense of triumph and accomplishment that Henry felt on the conclusion of his peace with Anjou and France in early 1113. His territorial ambitions never extended beyond the restoration of his father's dominions; his prime goals were peace with his neighbors and the curbing of violence within the Anglo-Norman world. Through astute diplomacy, a precocious intelligence

---

[117] OV, 6:174 and n. 4, 180.
[118] Ibid., p. 300; cf. *Recueil des actes des comtes de Pontieu*, no. 18: a charter of Count William Talvas, acting as lord of Bellême, which must have been issued during the interval between November 1112, when Henry I arrested his father, and April 1113, when Henry captured the fortress of Bellême (afterward ceding it to Rotrou count of Perche).
[119] OV, 6:182.
[120] Ibid.

system, and an abundance of marriageable bastard daughters, he had quelled the threats of France and Anjou while shielding Normandy and its people from the horrors of warfare with its attendant scorched-earth tactics. But France and Anjou were only momentarily placated: a new and hostile young count, Baldwin of Flanders, was approaching maturity, and William Clito remained at large.

Chapter 6

THE WHEEL OF FORTUNE

Writing of the years following Henry I's diplomatic triumphs of 1113, Suger of Saint-Denis remarks:

> The king of England had been enjoying amazing luck after a long and wonderful series of successes. But now he found himself troubled by a different and unlucky turn of events, like someone falling down from atop fortune's wheel.[1]

Suger goes on to explain that Henry now faced coordinated attacks from Louis VI (whose treaty of friendship proved short-lived), Fulk V of Anjou, and the young Baldwin VII count of Flanders (who is not reported to have settled with Henry in 1113). The three princes forged a coalition in behalf of William Clito, and their combined assaults against Normandy in 1118–1119, along with defections by some of his own Norman barons, constituted the most formidable military challenge that Henry was ever to encounter.

The trouble began not long after the peace of 1113, when Baldwin VII began launching a series of raids against northeastern Normandy. William Clito resided at Baldwin's court, and the two young men seem to have developed a bond of deep mutual affection. The raids may have commenced as early as 1114, when Baldwin VII issued an apparently genuine charter from Ypres while on the verge of leading a military campaign against Normandy, but they did not begin to pose a serious threat to Henry I for another two or three years.[2]

In July 1113 Henry had crossed to England, evidently confident that his recent settlement with Louis VI and Fulk V would hold, and at

---

[1] Suger, *Louis le Gros*, p. 188; on the ubiquitousness of the wheel of fortune metaphor in the Anglo-Norman era see Mason, "Magnates, Curiales, and the Wheel of Fortune."

[2] *Actes des comtes de Flandre*, no. 66. Clito entered Baldwin's court at about the age of ten (ca. 1112/1113) and was knighted by him at fourteen (in 1116): Hermann of Tournai, "De restauratione," *MGH, SS*, 14:284–289. The future count, Charles "the Good," was also very active at Baldwin's court as his closest adviser, and Baldwin is said to have entrusted the governance of Flanders to him while he was fighting in Normandy: ibid., p. 284.

Christmas he presided over a great court and crown-wearing ceremony at his new castle at Windsor.[3] The following year witnessed a continuation of Henry's successes. In January 1114 his daughter Maud married the emperor Henry V in an impressive wedding ceremony at Worms Cathedral (the superb Romanesque edifice that stands to this day and was then still under construction), and in midsummer Henry I led a triumphant royal foray into Wales.

The year 1114 also saw the appointment of two new archbishops. For Canterbury King Henry had proposed Faritius abbot of Abingdon, a learned Italian doctor who had served as physician to both the king and queen. The English magnates and prelates, however, much preferred a Norman to a "foreigner." Arguing speciously that a physician whose hands had been contaminated by the urine of women should never serve as archbishop, they proposed Ralph d'Escures, former abbot of Sées and bishop of Rochester, who had been a close friend of Archbishop Anselm's. The king, more concerned with cultivating the regard of his great men than in having his own way in a matter of mere secondary interest to him, yielded to their wishes. After a five-year vacancy at Canterbury following Anselm's death, the witty, easygoing Ralph d'Escures was elected to the archbishopric.[4] Shortly afterward, Henry appointed a talented royal chaplain and close friend, Thurstan of Bayeux, to the archbishopric of York on the premature death in February 1114 of the grossly fat Archbishop Thomas II, who had died of overeating.[5] As time progressed, the two new archbishops became locked in holy combat over the long-festering issue of Canterbury's claim to primacy and Archbishop Ralph's refusal to consecrate Archbishop-elect Thurstan without first receiving his written profession of obedience. The dispute would eventually become entangled with Henry's effort to achieve peace with France, but for the moment the military and ecclesiastical storm clouds still hung low on the horizon.

The success of Henry's Welsh expedition of 1114, the first in his reign, stood in sharp contrast to the previous royal offensive against Wales, by William Rufus in 1097, which was effectively resisted and accomplished little or nothing.[6] The Worcester chronicler reported that Rufus had intended to kill every last Welshman.[7] Whether Rufus had any such dark hope, and despite the Welsh fear in 1114 that Henry I

---

[3] *ASC, s.a.* 1114; on New Windsor see ibid., *s.a.* 1110, and above, pp. 114–115 and notes.

[4] WM, *GP*, pp. 125–128; Eadmer, *HN*, pp. 221–223; *Councils and Synods*, 1: part 2, pp. 707–709.

[5] Barlow, *English Church: 1066–1154*, p. 82 and n. 126 with references.

[6] Barlow, *Rufus*, pp. 370–371: Rufus seems to have launched two Welsh expeditions in 1097, the first by no means successful and the second even less so.

[7] FW, 2:40–41.

intended to exterminate them all "so that the name of the Britons should nevermore be called to mind,"[8] Henry's goal was in fact neither genocide nor conquest but simply the assurance that Welsh princes would submit to his overlordship, which was based on the claims of Anglo-Saxon kings to hegemony over all Britain but which Henry intended to exercise with far greater effectiveness than before.

Henry faced a fluid situation along the Welsh frontier. The large and compact semi-independent marcher earldoms created by the Conqueror—Herefordshire, Shropshire, and Cheshire—no longer dominated Anglo-Welsh relations after the defeat of the Montgomerys in 1102. The earldom of Hereford had fallen into royal hands on the failure of the earls' rebellion in 1075, and the death of Hugh earl of Chester in 1101 had left his earldom under royal wardship, with its child heir, Richard of Chester, being reared at Henry's court. The expulsion of the Montgomerys had brought both Shropshire (from Robert of Bellême) and the earldom of Pembroke (from Arnulf of Montgomery) into the king's fold, and Henry proceeded to integrate both regions into his kingdomwide administrative system. Extensive areas of major Norman penetration in south Wales, much of which had been conquered and colonized under the first two Williams, now passed into the control of Henry or his greater and lesser barons. Among the great curial magnates and prelates who acquired substantial Welsh lands through Henry's gift were Henry of Beaumont earl of Warwick in Gower (1106); Richard of Beaumais bishop of London, as the king's governor of Shropshire and the former Montgomery lands to the west (ca. 1102); Roger bishop of Salisbury in Kidwelly (ca. 1106); Gilbert fitz Richard of Clare in Ceredigion (1110) and later Gilbert of Clare's younger brother Walter fitz Richard in lower Gwent (1119); Brian fitz Count in Abergavenny (1119); Miles of Gloucester in Brecon (1121); the king's son Robert earl of Gloucester in Glamorgan (1121/1122 or earlier);[9] and the curial bishop Bernard of St David's, former chancellor of Queen Matilda, safeguarding the king's interests (and his own) in Dyfed in the far southwest (1115). Western Dyfed had already been tightly secured by Henry's settlement there of a large group of industrious, loyal, and pugnacious Flemings (ca. 1107–1110).[10]

These centers of Norman authority resulted not from major military campaigns under Henry I but from conquests under his royal

---

[8] *Brut*, trans. Jones, p. 37; Davies, *Age of Conquest*, p. 42.

[9] The *terminus a quo* of Robert of Gloucester's lordship of Glamorgan (and the other lands of Robert fitz Hamon) could well antedate his elevation to the status of earl: *Earldom of Gloucester Charters*, p. 152 n.

[10] WM, *GR*, 2:365–366, 477; Davies, *Age of Conquest*, pp. 41, 98–99, and "Henry I in Wales," pp. 143–147; *Brut*, trans. Jones, pp. 41–42.

1. The third abbey church of Cluny (dedicated in 1130) was the largest and most magnificent basilica of its time in western Europe (excepting Old St Peter's). Henry I contributed significantly to its construction. View from the southeast by Lallemand, ca. 1787.

2. Restoration of the nave of Cluny, third abbey church, ca. 1088–1130, Kenneth J. Conant. The nave collapsed in 1125 and it is possible that Henry financed the reconstruction.

3. Cluny, third abbey church, exterior of the extant south arm of the great transept, ca. 1095–1100.

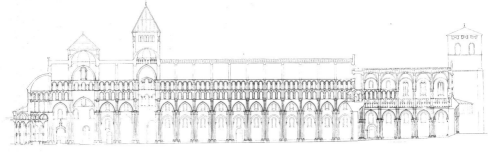

4. Cluny, third abbey church, longitudinal section, Kenneth J. Conant.

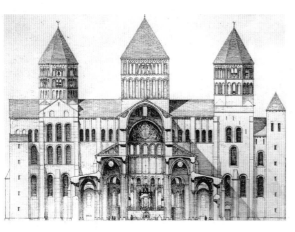

5. Cluny, third abbey church, cross-section of the nave, elevation of the large transept, Kenneth J. Conant.

ncip te consecratio regni consecrationis regn

6. Illumination of the
coronation of Henry I in
1100.

7. Illumination of the
coronation of Henry I from
Matthew Paris' *Flores
historiarum* (mid-thirteenth
century).

8. The great seal of Henry I, appended to the foundation charter of Reading Abbey, 1125.

9. The twelfth-century seal of Reading Abbey depicts the Virgin seated on a throne with the Christ Child, who lifts his right hand in benediction.

10. The fourteenth-century seal of Reading Abbey shows the Virgin and Child on one side (left) and the founder, Henry I, with crown and scepter on the other (right).

11. The foundation charter of Reading Abbey, 1125 (detail). Henry granted the abbey broad rights and immunities and endowed the monastery lavishly. The charter emphasizes the abbey's mission of providing hospitality to the poor, pilgrims, and guests.

12. The earliest known English carving of the coronation of the Virgin Mary was found on an unfinished capital at Reading Abbey. The cult of the Virgin gained strength in the early twelfth century through the support of churchmen associated with Henry I.

13–15. King Henry I's three dreams of 1131, recounted by John of Worcester ca. 1140, reflect the burdens of kingship as Henry is menaced successively by members of the three orders of society: (*counter-clockwise from upper left*) peasants, knights, and prelates.

16. A rough crossing of the Channel in June 1131 caused Henry I to forswear the danegeld tax for seven years and make a pilgrimage to Bury St Edmunds.

17. Four kings of England: William the Conqueror, William Rufus, Henry I, and Stephen, from the *Historia Anglorum* by Matthew Paris, 1250–59.

18. Portchester castle, once a Roman fort and later part of the defenses of the Saxon Shore, was strengthened by the Normans in the late eleventh century. The castle was controlled by Henry's prominent *curialis* William de Pont de l'Arche, who held the keys to the treasury at Winchester, just twenty miles north of this natural harbor. The fortified keep and bailey protected shipments of bullion to and from Normandy. The canons of Southwick were first established at Portchester with Henry's support. Exterior view of the keep.

19. A reconstruction drawing by Terry Ball showing how Portchester castle may have looked ca. 1120.

20. The impregnable abbey of Mont-Saint-Michel, which Henry controlled from 1088 as count of the Cotentin, sheltered the young prince from his two brothers in 1091.

21. Mont-Saint-Michel, interior of the basilica, ca. 1100.

predecessors, along with creeping local aggression in Henry's own time and destabilizing political rivalries and murderous feuds among Welsh princes. Indeed, Henry put an end to Norman advances in north Wales, accepting the fealty of Prince Gruffudd ap Cynan and permitting him to consolidate his power in the region over several decades. Gruffudd, as C. P. Lewis aptly writes, "fell into Henry I's greedy embrace just at the moment when royal policy was switching from direct intervention to arm's-length clientage."[11] The king took a number of central Welsh princes under his protection as well. He insisted that they respect his suzerainty and maintain at least a degree of peace with neighboring Welsh lords, but nothing more. As R. R. Davies succinctly expresses it, "Wales was not high on Henry's agenda of preoccupations and priorities."[12] Nevertheless, the intelligent planning and preparation that Henry and his counselors devoted to the exercise of his suzerainty in Wales and to his Welsh campaigns (1114 and 1121) resulted in "an era of peace which was unparalleled in the history of the region."[13] Lynn Nelson seems to deplore Henry's policy of permitting much of Welsh society to develop unmolested by Anglo-Norman armies or the savage rivalries of Welsh princes, a policy "which was to make the ultimate conquest of Wales extremely difficult."[14] But since Henry's goal was hegemony, not conquest, the idea of paving the way for Edward I did not occur to him. Nevertheless, the overlordship that he maintained with the support of Anglo-Norman settlers and Welsh princes alike won him a towering position in the history of medieval Wales unequaled until the late thirteenth century.[15] As the contemporary Welsh chronicler remarked, Henry "had subdued under his authority all the island of Britain and its mighty ones." He was "the man against whom no one could prevail except God himself."[16]

Henry launched his campaign of 1114 to restore peace between several Welsh princes and to heighten their respect for his kingly authority after a royal absence from Wales of some seventeen years. One Welsh princeling, Owain ap Cadwgan of Powys (north-central Wales), had been especially troublesome, having recently avenged himself on a rival Welsh prince by gouging out his eyes.[17] Henry's campaign of

---

[11] Lewis, "Gruffudd ap Cynan and the Normans," p. 77; see, in general, ibid.; Davies, "Henry I in Wales," pp. 138–140; and *Medieval Prince of Wales*, ed. and trans. Evans.

[12] Davies, *Age of Conquest*, p. 40; cf. Nelson, *Normans in South Wales*, pp. 123 and *passim*.

[13] Davies, "Henry I and Wales," p. 133: "Wales enjoyed an unparalleled period of peace, plenty, and prosperity." Similarly, Nelson, *Normans in South Wales*, p. 124.

[14] Nelson, *Normans in South Wales*, p. 124.

[15] Davies, *Age of Conquest*, p. 40.

[16] *Brut*, trans. Jones, p. 42.

[17] *Annales Cambriae*, p. 35; *Brut*, trans. Jones, pp. 36–37.

1114, unlike Rufus' unsuccessful efforts in 1097, was both bloodless and overwhelmingly successful. Like most of Henry's campaigns, it was meticulously prepared and organized. The king launched three military columns into Wales, one of them from the east led by Henry himself, another from Cornwall and Dyfed led by Gilbert fitz Richard of Clare lord of Ceredigion, and a third from the north led by Richard earl of Chester (now in his later teens) and Alexander king of Scots, who, as husband of one of Henry I's natural daughters and brother of Queen Matilda, was at once Henry's son-in-law and brother-in-law. Alexander's participation in the campaign exemplifies the close relationship, bound by ties of kinship, between the English and Scottish crowns under Henry I.[18] The princes of Powys and Gwynedd (northeastern Wales), evidently overawed, submitted to Henry and became his vassals and *fideles*. Owain ap Cadwgan, the last to submit, joined Henry's court for a time and accepted the honor of knighthood from him. Owain also accepted Henry's invitation to accompany the royal expedition to Normandy in the coming autumn.[19]

In September 1114 Henry crossed to Normandy with the intention of safeguarding his son's succession and held his Christmas court in Rouen. At some point in his brief Norman stay, perhaps in spring 1115, Henry assembled his Norman magnates in Rouen and had them swear fealty to William Adelin.[20] He also sent envoys to the French royal court, offering a large sum of money in return for Louis' conceding Normandy to William Adelin and receiving William's "profession" (*professio*) for the duchy.[21] Louis, who was by no means immune to the influence of silver,[22] was on the point of agreeing to the proposal but was dissuaded by William II count of Nevers.[23] Thus, instead of accepting William Adelin's submission, King Louis gave his full support

---

[18] *Brut*, trans. Jones, p. 37.

[19] Ibid., pp. 36–38; *ASC*, s.a. 1114.

[20] *ASC*, s.a. 1115; *RRAN* 2, no. 1074. Haskins (*NI*, p. 312), in a rare misreading of the *Anglo-Saxon Chronicle*, dates the oath-taking at Christmas 1114; but cf. Farrer, *Itin.*, p. 73, where spring 1115 is suggested; the *ASC* reports the fealty ceremony immediately following an account of the Christmas court, but all that one can conclude from this is that the oaths were rendered some time after Christmas during Henry's 1114–1115 sojourn in Normandy.

[21] *Liber de Hyda*, p. 309; the date is not provided, but the Hyde chronicler places the offer at some time subsequent to the Gisors peace of 1113 and before the next outbreak of hostilities, which ended with the peace of mid-1120. He also alludes to the presence at Louis' court of William II count of Nevers, who was taken captive sometime between 11 April and 8 November 1115 and remained a prisoner until the hostilities had ceased: OV, 4:337; Luchaire, *Louis VI*, no. 203.

[22] Luchaire, *Louis VI*, pp. xxxv–xxxvi.

[23] Below, pp. 244–245 (genealogy), 271.

to William Clito,[24] thereby rejecting the legitimacy of Henry's authority and instigating a war that would disrupt Normandy and France for the next several years.

The exact nature of Normandy's feudal subordination to the French monarchy was a complex, debatable, and long-standing issue. From the time of its origin (about 911) Normandy had been under the vague overlordship of the kings of France, to whom the Norman dukes had occasionally rendered homage. But ever since the Norman conquest of England, the dukes of Normandy, as kings themselves, had avoided doing homage for Normandy to the kings of France.[25] The offer that Henry made and Louis rejected constituted a new strategy, adapted to the danger posed by Clito's claim to Normandy and Henry's need of French support. It was a compromise characteristic of Henry's astute diplomacy: without humbling himself by rendering homage personally, he would place Louis under the moral obligation of a good lord to reject Clito's pretensions and accept the legitimacy of Henry's rule and the succession rights of his son and heir. This strategy was not altogether without precedent. Two centuries before, the Viking Rolf, having done homage to the king of France, subsequently associated his son William Longsword with him in the duchy and had William do homage to Charles the Simple at the frontier castle of Eu.[26] And Robert Curthose had, in his father's lifetime, done homage for Maine to the count of Anjou circa 1063 and again in 1091, thereby legitimizing William the Conqueror's own de facto power over Maine without obliging the Conqueror to humble himself before an Angevin count.[27] It is possible that Curthose did homage to King Philip I for Normandy in the Conqueror's lifetime and with his approval, conceivably just before the conquest of England when William formally proclaimed him his heir and successor in Philip's presence,[28] but no explicit evidence of any such homage exists. In any event neither Robert Curthose nor William Longsword had played the role that Henry was calling on his son to play in 1115. For Curthose's and William Longsword's fathers

[24] *Liber de Hyda*, pp. 309, 319, cf. p. 308, stating that Louis VI had granted Normandy to Clito on a prior occasion, apparently in 1111 or 1112—but the chronicler's chronology is hazy.

[25] The exception, Duke Robert Curthose, had of course never been king. On the general subject, see *MMI*, pp. 17–40; Lemarignier, *Hommage en marche*, pp. 9–72; *Brevis relatio*, p. 19. (Here as elsewhere I am grateful to Elisabeth M. C. van Houts for providing me with a copy of her as yet unpublished and unpaginated new edition of the *Brevis relatio*.)

[26] Lot, *Fidèles ou vassaux?* pp. 183–184.

[27] David, *Curthose*, pp. 9–11, 34; OV, 2:304, 310. Curthose occasionally attested as count of Maine, but Duke William actually kept the province in his own hands.

[28] David, *Curthose*, p. 12.

had themselves done homage to French kings on previous occasions, whereas Henry I had not. Henry, in urging that his son render homage in his place, was proposing an essentially novel approach to the restructuring of Normandy's feudal relationship with France. It was an arrangement that Louis VI would eventually accept, but only after more than four years of warfare.

Shortly before leaving Normandy in mid-1115, Henry spent several days with the papal legate Anselm, abbot of S. Saba (Rome) and nephew of the late Archbishop Anselm, who was on his way northward to England bearing the pallium for Archbishop Ralph (which Paschal II had granted very grudgingly). Anselm of S. Saba also brought with him a long and intemperate papal letter to the king and his bishops. Paschal accused Henry of disregarding papal customs and privileges over the Anglo-Norman Church, blocking appeals to Rome, failing to obtain papal permission to hold kingdomwide synods or to translate bishops (presumably Ralph d'Escures from Rochester to Canterbury), and withholding payments of Peter's Pence. Paschal warned of dire papal sanctions if these wrongs were not promptly corrected.[29] The pope's anger may have been kindled in part by Henry's insistence on defending Normandy's accustomed ecclesiastical autonomy by prohibiting Norman churchmen from attending legatine councils in France. This policy had prompted the zealous papal legate Cuno, cardinal-bishop of Palestrina, to suspend all the bishops and abbots of Normandy for disregarding his summons to attend a legatine council at Châlons-sur-Marne in July 1115—after they had similarly ignored his summonses to two previous councils.[30] To Henry, Cuno and Paschal were flouting the traditional rights of Anglo-Norman rulers and their metropolitans to manage their churches without undue interference from the pope and his legates. The king's position had been dear to the heart of Archbishop Anselm, who would have been appalled to know that his own nephew and namesake was now serving as papal legate in England. But Henry's policy ran counter to the growing international pretensions of the twelfth-century papacy. Indeed, Paschal's letter of 1115 seemed to condemn the process by which Archbishop Anselm had convened his own primatial councils of 1102 and 1108.[31]

Having crossed to England in July 1115, Henry addressed these and other matters at a great council at Westminster in mid-September. To

---

[29] Eadmer, *HN*, pp. 232–233; Brett, *English Church*, pp. 36–37, 73; *Councils and Synods*, 1: part 2, pp. 708–716.

[30] Eadmer, *HN*, p. 234; WM, *GP*, p. 129; Brett, *English Church*, p. 37 with references.

[31] Brett, *English Church*, p. 37; Theodor Schieffer, *Die päpstlichen Legaten in Frankreich*, pp. 198–203; FW, 2:68; WM, *GP*, p. 129.

Cardinal Cuno's suspensions and Paschal's unexpectedly furious letter, Henry responded with his accustomed policy of conciliation and delay. He sent envoys to Cardinal Cuno to seek his advice about the Canterbury–York dispute—and perhaps, more important, to negotiate on the status of the Norman clergy, about whose sentence of suspension we hear nothing further.[32] To Rome he once again sent the veteran diplomat William Warelwast bishop of Exeter, who had become blind but remained a canny and devoted royal servant. William Warelwast failed to move Pope Paschal, although he did manage to avert the threatened sanctions. Moreover, the time and distance involved in his journey, combined with Henry's skill at equivocation and delay, served to postpone the crisis while Henry attended to more urgent dangers.

In 1116 Paschal sent Anselm of S. Saba back to Henry with full legatine authority, as "apostolic vicar" over the English Church, but Henry kept the legate at bay by detaining him in Normandy— with lavish hospitality—for no less than four years.[33] In the meantime, Henry dispatched yet another mission to Rome (1116–1117), led by Archbishop Ralph, to negotiate on the matter of legates and, of course, the York profession.[34] The archbishop fell seriously ill on the journey and his mission was unsuccessful. He never did manage to see Paschal face to face because a military threat by Emperor Henry V and rebellion in Rome had driven the pope into exile in Benevento and Archbishop Ralph was too ill to venture from Rome into the Norman south on roads that were nearly impassable and alleged to be infested with robbers. Ralph did obtain a papal letter, but it was merely pro forma: it confirmed Canterbury's traditional privileges but failed to stipulate what these privileges might be. Meanwhile, the crisis in the Holy City diverted Paschal's attention from England, and papal pressure against Anglo-Norman ecclesiastical autonomy was further diminished by Paschal's death on 21 January 1118, just after his return to Rome from exile.

Henry's Westminster court of September 1115, where the king and his council discussed Paschal's complaints, also witnessed the election of Bernard the queen's chancellor to the Welsh see of St David's. The see had fallen vacant earlier in 1115 at the death of Wilfrid, the last

---

[32] Hugh the Chanter, p. 60 and n. 2; Hugh says nothing about the issue of the Norman clergy, nor would we expect him to do so since his account is always narrowly focused on York; one can hardly suppose, however, that the matter was overlooked.

[33] Eadmer, *HN*, p. 239: Hugh the Chanter, p. 90; Henry may well have promised Anselm the abbacy of the lavishly endowed Bury St Edmunds, to which Anselm was advanced in 1121.

[34] Brett, *English Church*, pp. 37–40; Hugh the Chanter, pp. 78–84; Bethell, "William of Corbeil," pp. 150–153.

Welsh bishop of St David's, and his replacement by Bernard established
for the first time a strong Anglo-Norman presence in southwestern
Wales. Bernard was devoted to the king and attended his court frequently. Having observed at close hand the contentious machinations
of the Canterbury–York dispute, Bernard after a time launched a
campaign (ultimately unsuccessful but exceedingly annoying to Canterbury) to make St David's the primatial see of Wales.[35]

Shortly after presiding over a festive Christmas court at St Albans
(1115), where the vast new abbey church was consecrated in the presence of the royal family and a great assemblage of prelates, earls,
and barons,[36] Henry turned once again to the ever-simmering Canterbury–York dispute. From the beginning, Thurstan had assured his York
canons that he would not under any circumstances profess obedience
in writing to Archbishop Ralph. His chief argument and that of
the York canons was that a metropolitan could not rightly profess
obedience to anyone but the pope. Understandably, the papal curia was
in complete agreement with this stance. The pope's previous support
of Archbishop Anselm's claim to primacy over York was an aberration,
counter to the centralizing policies of the high medieval papal
curia and occasioned only by Anselm's international celebrity and
his courageous service to the papacy. Now, with Anselm out of the
picture, the papacy was forthrightly on the side of York, as Thurstan
well understood. If the archbishop of Canterbury refused to consecrate him without the profession, Thurstan intended to turn to the
pope for advice, support, and, if necessary, consecration.[37] But King
Henry, who very much preferred to have Anglo-Norman ecclesiastical
disputes settled within his own dominions, would not permit Thurstan
to travel to Rome—and Ralph, of course, continued to withhold consecration in the absence of a profession.[38] The controversy was thus at
a standstill.

Henry does not seem to have had any strong convictions about
the quarrel. He would have found it, in Frank Barlow's words, incon-
venient and embarrassing.[39] It has been argued that the Norman kings
supported Canterbury over York because of their fear of northern

[35] Davies, *Age of Conquest,* pp. 190–191.
[36] *ASC, s.a.* 1116; *Gesta abbatum monasterii S. Albani,* 1:71. The church was largely
built under Abbot Paul of Caen (1077–1088); portions of the Norman structure
survive in the transepts and the north side of the nave, whose massive piers are
decorated with splendid thirteenth- and fourteenth-century frescoes (only recently
renovated and restored).
[37] Hugh the Chanter, p. 60; see Nicholl, *Thurstan,* pp. 49–52, and Bethell,
"William of Corbeil," pp. 151–154, for the complex maneuverings.
[38] Hugh the Chanter, p. 64; see Nicholl, *Thurstan,* pp. 49–52, and Bethell,
"William of Corbeil," pp. 151–154.
[39] Barlow, *English Church: 1066–1154,* p. 41.

separatism,[40] but in Henry's time, when the north was peaceful and relations with Scotland downright affectionate, there can have been no such fear. So for some two years after Thurstan's nomination in 1114 Henry equivocated, in the frail hope that the two archbishops might somehow settle their differences without a royal commitment to either side. But for all his skill in the art of creative delay, Henry could not forever evade his unwelcome responsibility to decide between the primacy of Canterbury and the autonomy of York. In 1116, under intense pressure from both sides, he decided for Canterbury, probably because the opposite decision would have earned him more enemies.

Shortly before departing for Normandy in early spring 1116, Henry convened a great council at Salisbury on Passion Sunday (19 March) where he had his English magnates render homage to his son William as his heir, as the Normans had done the previous year.[41] Once this important ceremony was performed, the Canterbury–York conflict came up once again. Henry, having been constrained to settle the matter decisively, had ordered Thurstan to profess to Canterbury on pain of being deposed from his archbishopric and suffering the king's hatred for himself and his relatives (including, presumably, his brother Audoin bishop of Evreux). On their way to the Salisbury court, Thurstan and his party had encountered a messenger bearing a letter from Pope Paschal to the York clergy and another addressed to Archbishop Ralph d'Escures, confirming Thurstan's election and commanding that he be consecrated without the profession, preferably by the archbishop of Canterbury, or, if he refused, by another bishop. Fearing an explosion of anger at the royal *curia*, Thurstan dared not make the letters public. But in the long run, as Denis Bethell observed, the pope's unequivocal prohibition of the York profession doomed the Canterbury struggle for primacy in Britain as "a lost cause."[42]

For the moment, however, Thurstan was on the defensive and under heavy attack. Henry first sent four of his closest magnate-counselors— Robert count of Meulan, William of Warenne earl of Surrey, William of Tancarville the master chamberlain, and the highly favored *curialis* Nigel d'Aubigny—to convey his ultimatum to Thurstan and to receive Thurstan's answer. Thurstan refused to yield. Arriving in the king's own presence, he shocked the royal court by publicly relinquishing his archbishopric, thereby withdrawing from the conflict and shielding his kinspeople from the king's *malevolentia*. Henry offered Thurstan his hand,

[40] E.g., with qualifications, by Mary Cheney in her important article, "Some Observations on a Papal Privilege of 1120 for the Archbishops of York," p. 430.

[41] Eadmer, *HN*, p. 237; the English magnates did homage to William then and there, whereas the prelates promised to do so on his succession to the throne.

[42] Bethell, "William of Corbeil," p. 151.

and Thurstan grasped it and "resigned what the king had given him."
According to Hugh the Chanter, most of the courtiers were in tears,
and Henry himself sighed and wept that an old friend should abdicate
from one of the highest ecclesiastical dignities in the realm.[43]

As it turned out, Thurstan's resignation was less significant than it
appeared to be. The York cathedral chapter continued to recognize
him as archbishop-elect, as did the pope, and King Henry did so as
well. Indeed, as time passed, Thurstan himself came to the conclusion
that he lacked the canonical authority to resign the spiritual responsibilities of his office to anyone but the pope. He accompanied the
royal party on Henry's crossing to Normandy in April 1116. Having
requested and been refused royal permission to visit the papal court,
he remained long thereafter in Henry's entourage, where he was
treated with honor and always addressed as "archbishop."[44] In time,
under pressure from Pope Paschal, the king reinstated him in the temporalities of his see.[45]

Henry's return to Normandy after a stay in England of less than nine
months was provoked by the spread of military hostilities on the fringes
of the duchy and by the breakdown of diplomatic relations with the
king of France. Baldwin of Flanders may have begun raiding Normandy
as early as 1114. And the Hyde chronicle reports that when Louis VI
in 1115 refused Henry's offer of an act of homage by William Adelin,
the French king broke his peace with Henry by throwing his support
behind William Clito.[46] The counselor who persuaded Louis to follow
this course, William II count of Nevers, was taken prisoner shortly afterward while on a French royal expedition.[47] Count William was the
brother of Helwise, the imperious countess of Evreux, who had long
been an enemy of Henry I until her death the previous year. Helwise,
in turn, was the aunt of Amaury de Montfort, an even more dedicated
enemy of Henry I and the person who stood to inherit the Norman
county of Evreux on the death of Helwise's aged and unstable husband,
William count of Evreux (see genealogical chart of the counts of
Evreux, p. 245). William of Nevers quickly fell into the hands of Henry's
nephew and Louis' adversary, Theobald count of Blois, who held him
captive for several years.[48] The Anglo-Saxon chronicler, echoed by

[43] Hugh the Chanter, pp. 70–72.

[44] Henry crossed "shortly after Easter," which fell on 2 April in 1116: *ASC, s.a.*
1116; Hugh the Chanter, p. 76. Soon after Henry's arrival in Normandy, Ralph
d'Escures departed on his aforementioned fruitless visit to Rome: above, p. 241.

[45] Ca. February 1118; see Eadmer, *HN*, p. 244; Hugh the Chanter, p. 92; Nicholl,
Thurstan, pp. 57–58.

[46] *Liber de Hyda*, p. 309.

[47] Ibid.

[48] Luchaire, *Louis VI*, pp. lxxxix–xc, 101–102 (no. 203).

THE COUNTS OF EVREUX

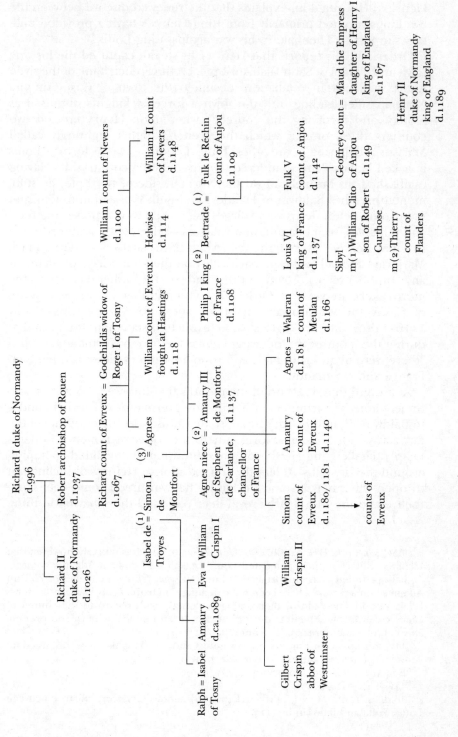

Henry of Huntingdon, explains that the renewed discord between the two kings resulted primarily from King Henry's having provided military support to Theobald in his war against King Louis.[49]

Orderic Vitalis reports that Henry I by stealth captured the historic town and citadel of Saint-Clair-sur-Epte, on the French bank of the river. Louis, evidently in retaliation, occupied the town of Gasny on the Norman side, leading into the town a force of knights disguised as monks, and fortifying the church,[50] whereupon Henry erected two counter-castles, one of which the French knights slightingly called Malassis ("Ill-placed"), the other, Trulla Leporis ("Hare's form"). Louis attacked Malassis and plundered the surrounding countryside. Having established his bridgehead on the Norman side of the Epte, he summoned his allies Baldwin of Flanders and Fulk V of Anjou to join him in burning fields, destroying villages, plows and tools, and seizing food and valuables from peasants and villagers—pillaging "a land made rich by a long peace."[51] Although these events have usually been dated 1118, Marjorie Chibnall argues persuasively that they could have occurred at any point between 1116 and 1118.[52] Indeed, the earlier date seems the more likely, in view of Orderic's comment that after the capture of Gasny the warfare continued for about four years (presumably 1116–1120) and the Anglo-Saxon chronicler's statement for 1116 that during the months just following Henry's return to Normandy in April "there were many cruel raids and robberies and castles taken between France and Normandy."[53]

At around that time and in the months that followed, hostilities continued along the frontiers of Normandy. Hermann of Tournai alludes to Baldwin VII and his knights, at some undisclosed date, riding all the way across northeastern Normandy to the tower of Rouen ("Conan's Leap"), challenging Henry to fight, and, when he declined, galloping around the city walls. At length, in frustration at Henry's disinclination to open the city gates and do battle, Baldwin freed some deer from their enclosure in a nearby royal deer park and then, having nothing

---

[49] *ASC, s.a.* 1116; HH, p. 460; cf. *Liber de Hyda*, p. 309. It is unlikely, however, that Henry's military support antedated Louis' rejection of William Adelin's homage. To have provided such support against Louis VI *before* raising the matter of William Adelin's homage would have been self-defeating. Luchaire, *Louis VI*, no. 201, shows Louis VI and Theobald of Blois acting in concert with regard to the church of Chartres, probably sometime during the first seven months of 1115 and presumably before the outbreak of hostilities between them.

[50] OV, 6:184; according to Suger, Louis and his knights were disguised as "travelers" (*viatores*): Suger, *Louis le Gros*, p. 186.

[51] Suger, *Louis le Gros*, pp. 186–188; OV, 6:186.

[52] OV, 6:184–185 n. 3.

[53] Ibid., p. 186; *ASC, s.a.* 1116; HH (p. 460) alludes to a sworn alliance between Louis, Fulk, and Baldwin in 1117.

else to do, returned home.[54] Similarly, William of Malmesbury reports that Henry I responded to a raid on northeastern Normandy by Louis VI by barricading himself and his troops in the castle of Rouen while Louis' army burned and pillaged within four miles of the city.[55] And the Anglo-Saxon chronicler reports that in summer 1117 Count Baldwin and King Louis raided northeastern Normandy together but remained only one night and returned without a fight, fearing the arrival of Henry with an army of English, Norman, and Breton mercenaries.[56] Thus, from about mid-1116 serious warfare afflicted the *pays* of Talou and Caux in the northeast (where several magnates were sympathetic to Baldwin VII and Clito) and the eastern and southern frontiers as well.[57] But it did not begin to disrupt interior districts of Normandy until after mid-1118.

The war began in earnest following the deaths of three of the most eminent persons in Henry's realm: William count of Evreux on 18 April 1118, Queen Matilda on 1 May, and Robert count of Meulan on 5 June (Robert may have retired in 1116/1117 to his family monastery of Saint-Leger, Préaux). "After these persons had died," Orderic laments, "great trials began for the Normans."[58] The effectiveness of Henry I's governance was seriously damaged by the loss of his capable wife, who had served effectively and devotedly as his English regent, and of Robert of Meulan, his sagacious adviser, who had contributed significantly, so contemporaries stated, to the political

[54] Hermann of Tournai, "De restauratione," *MGH, SS*, 14:284; see also Suger, *Louis le Gros*, p. 194, reporting that Count Baldwin had been harassing King Henry with bitter attacks and frequent invasions of Normandy.

[55] WM, *GR*, 2:481.

[56] *ASC, s.a.* 1117; HH, p. 460; cf. *Liber de Hyda*, p. 315.

[57] Contemporary writers include among Clito's adherents ca. 1117–1119 three of the foremost lords of northeastern Normandy: Henry count of Eu, Stephen count of Aumale, and Hugh of Gournay: OV, 6:188, 368; Suger, *Louis le Gros*, p. 190; *Liber de Hyda*, p. 313; other magnates of the area, including Walter Giffard III at Longueville and William of Warenne at Bellencombre and Saint-Saens, remained firmly loyal to King Henry: OV, 6:222, 236; *Liber de Hyda*, pp. 316–317. On the problem of loyalty among Norman frontier barons see the illuminating article by Judith Green, "Henry I and the Aristocracy of Normandy," pp. 161–173, especially 164–165.

[58] OV, 6:188; on Robert of Meulan's death see Crouch, *Beaumont Twins*, pp. 3–4; Vaughn, *Anselm of Bec and Robert of Meulan*, pp. 359–361. Although Robert was a habitual attester of royal charters, he cannot be shown to have attested after Henry's crossing to Normandy in April 1116; Crouch states that Robert died in England whereas Vaughn suggests that he retired to Préaux, and although there is no direct evidence for either conclusion, circumstances seem to favor Préaux. On the queen's death see *Liber de Hyda*, pp. 311–313, and Huneycutt, "'Another Esther in Our Times.'" Henry afterward commanded that the sacristan of Westminster Abbey be paid one halfpenny daily to keep a light burning before Queen Matilda's tomb forever: *RRAN* 2, no. 1377.

and diplomatic acumen of Henry's regime. William count of Evreux, however, was neither devoted nor sagacious, but his death precipitated a crisis in Normandy by permitting his county of Evreux to pass to his nephew, Henry's premier enemy, Amaury III de Montfort. Amaury, as the brother of the celebrated and notorious Bertrade de Montfort, was the uncle of Fulk V and a kinsman by marriage of Louis VI (see Evreux genealogy, p. 245 above). He enjoyed an intimate friendship with both princes and was indeed the primary connecting link between them. He had forged a coalition between them in 1111–1113 and did so once again in 1116.[59] Moreover, as heir to the county of Evreux, he threatened to establish a major hostile presence in the heart of Normandy.

Henry did all that he could to keep Amaury out of Evreux. With the endorsement of Audoin bishop of Evreux (Thurstan of York's brother), he refused Amaury's claim to the county and, for the next half-year, kept his own garrison in the castle of Evreux under the constableship of a baron of the region, William Pointel.[60] But on 7 October 1118, while Henry was attending a provincial council of the Norman Church in Rouen, William Pointel, reflecting back on his warm and long-standing association with Amaury de Montfort at the court of the late Count William, betrayed the citadel of Evreux to Amaury. William Pointel and his co-conspirators then seized the surrounding town, plundered Bishop Audoin's episcopal palace, and spread devastation far and wide across the surrounding county. Audoin, who had absented himself from Henry's Rouen council because of the military threat to Evreux, now had to flee for his life. He spent the next year in exile from his episcopal city, and Orderic reports that he displayed his mourning for his lost cathedral by refusing to shave until it was restored to him.[61]

During the months just preceding the betrayal of Evreux to Amaury, Henry's cherished peace in Normandy began to disintegrate. He found himself beset by attacks across his southern and eastern frontiers by Fulk V, Louis VI, and Baldwin VII, sometimes acting in concert, and joined by a growing number of rebellious Norman barons with castles near the borders of Anjou, France, and Flanders. As in 1110–1113, Henry responded to reports of disloyalty by arresting potential rebels. Two northeastern magnates, Henry count of Eu and Hugh of Gournay, were taken prisoner at Rouen about 1117.[62] Afterward William of Warenne, a kinsman of Hugh of Gournay, persuaded King Henry to

[59] Suger, *Louis le Gros*, p. 186.
[60] On William Pointel see OV, 6:188, 189 n. 6, 204; Le Prévost, *Notes . . . de l'Eure*, 1:138–139.
[61] OV, 6:204.
[62] Ibid., 6:190; Suger, *Louis le Gros*, p. 190; *Liber de Hyda*, p. 313.

release both men on promise of their good behavior, and in June 1118, on the king's recommendation and blessing, Hugh gave his sister, Gundreda of Gournay, in marriage to Henry's wealthy magnate-*curialis*, Nigel of Aubigny. Henry, so Orderic declares, had raised Hugh at the royal court "like his own son" and had invested him with the arms of knighthood and enriched him. Yet despite his promise of good behavior, and on the very day of Gundreda's marriage, Hugh withdrew from the wedding celebrations and took up arms against the king. He gathered a band of rebels around him, fortified his castles, and laid waste to the *pays* of Caux and Talou with fire and plunder, kidnapping peasants and their families (including infants in their cradles) and terrorizing and bringing ruin to the country people for miles around.

There can be little question that Hugh and the two other major rebels of the northeast, Henry count of Eu and Stephen of Aumale, were in close touch with Count Baldwin of Flanders and to a degree enjoyed his protection. Around the time of Hugh's rebellion Baldwin was conducting military operations in the *pays* of Talou northwest of Aumale, near the royal castle of Arques and the rebel stronghold of Eu. Henry count of Eu, Orderic states, "was one of the first sympathizers to help the rebels," and Henry I's cousin Stephen of Aumale, into whose castle Baldwin retired when he was wounded, was "one of his closest supporters."[63]

Similarly, rebellion along the southern frontier of Normandy enjoyed the support and encouragement of Fulk of Anjou. In summer 1118 Robert Giroie, whose family had cofounded Orderic's monastery of Saint-Evroul, joined the rebellion and held the Giroie castle of Saint-Céneri against King Henry. Count Fulk came to Saint-Céneri in late July at Robert's invitation with an armed force of some five hundred men. The Angevins then laid siege to the stronghold of La Motte Gautier-de-Clinchamps, a former Bellême castle in Maine that Henry had strengthened and garrisoned with knights from his own military household. At the news of the siege, Henry rushed southwest to nearby Alençon where he summoned military contingents from all Normandy—presumably the quotas of knights owed by most major Norman landholders.[64] But before Henry could reach La Motte Gautier, its garrison, beset by repeated assaults, surrendered on 1

---

[63] OV, 6:190; 280 (Count Stephen "contra dominum cognatumque suum regem rebellauit et Guillelmum Clitonem atque Balduinum Flandriam in castris suis receptos diutius adiuuit"); WM, *GR*, 2:479; *Liber de Hyda*, p. 315; HH, p. 462; after Count Baldwin's death, Henry count of Eu shifted his support back to King Henry and fought on his side at Brémule, 20 August 1119: OV, 6:236.

[64] OV, 6:194; on the knights quotas see Hollister, *Military Organization of Norman England*, pp. 77–86; Keefe, *Feudal Assessments*, pp. 141–153.

August to the Angevins, who razed the fortress and returned home joyfully. The defeated garrison made their way to Alençon where Henry awaited them—and their explanations—none too happily.[65]

Seeking assistance in the defense of southern Normandy against the Angevins, Henry granted to his nephew Theobald of Blois the strategic town of Alençon along with Sées, La Roche Mabile, and the several other former holdings and strongholds of Robert of Bellême in southern Normandy. Theobald, with Henry's permission, regranted them to Stephen, his younger brother. Stephen of Blois, who was already count of Mortain in Normandy and lord of the honor of Eye in England, was on course to becoming one of the wealthiest magnates of his generation.[66] Yet the future career of this highly born noble, the future king of England (though Henry would never have guessed it), was to be checkered at best. And Stephen's troubles, unluckily for Henry, were not long in coming.

The loyalty of Norman magnates continued to erode. It is difficult sometimes to distinguish between royalists and rebels, for as in many such rebellions a substantial number of barons were fence-sitters, trying to determine the direction of the political winds, and their loyalties oscillated. Some eighteen Norman magnates, Orderic observes, "remained passively frozen in their treachery."[67] The lords of Grandmesnil, Courcy, and Montpinçon all contemplated rebellion but finally, as Henry's fortunes revived, decided against it.[68] Richer of Laigle, resenting Henry's decision to grant his father's English lands to his younger brothers rather than to himself, threatened to join the rebellion unless the king changed his mind. With the allegiance of the Norman baronage eroding, Henry did reconsider and granted the family's English lands to Richer, but it was too late: Richer had already contracted to deliver his castle of Laigle, the fortress in which Henry had once parleyed with Anselm, to Louis VI. On hearing of Henry's new decision, Richer tried to withdraw from his agreement with Louis VI, but Louis attacked his castle, and in the ensuing battle the town of Laigle burned to the ground. On 3 September Louis occupied the citadel overlooking the ruined town and commended it to the care of William Crispin and Amaury de Montfort. With the town in ashes, members of the French garrison for whom there was no room in the castle pitched tents amidst the charred ruins surrounding it. Since the

<hr />

[65] OV, 6:194–196; on the tendency for rebellions in 1118–1119 to be concentrated on or near the frontiers of Normandy and to be supported by the hostile neighboring powers of Flanders, France, and Anjou, see Green, "Henry I and the Aristocracy of Normandy," pp. 164–165.

[66] Davis, *King Stephen*, pp. 6–9.

[67] OV, 6:194.

[68] Ibid., p. 216.

Frenchmen had no source of food, they foraged off the surrounding lands, looting and impoverishing the local peasantry. King Henry came swiftly to retake the castle, but, according to Orderic, he was informed by a trusted counselor, his chamberlain William of Tancarville, that Rouen was under attack. He hurried back to defend it, only to find that William of Tancarville's report was incorrect.[69]

From Rouen, Henry led a force northeastward to Hugh of Gournay's castle of La Ferté-en-Bray, but torrential rains forced him to abandon his siege. As he departed, he laid waste the surrounding region and then turned southwest to invest Neubourg, the seat of Robert of Neubourg, son of King Henry's old friend, Henry earl of Warwick. Robert of Neubourg had joined the rebellion because of a land dispute with Waleran, son of Robert of Meulan, who was under Henry I's protection. Henry stormed Neubourg and burned it to the ground.[70]

Shortly afterward the raids and pillaging in the northeast of Normandy ceased permanently when, in September 1118, Baldwin VII was mortally wounded while attacking the *pays* of Talou and returned to Flanders as an invalid. Henry I responded magnanimously by sending a skilled physician to attend him, but the physician was unable to save him. Baldwin died on 17 June 1119 as a newly professed monk of the Cluniac house of Saint-Bertin. Orderic suggests that his fatal illness resulted from his overindulgence on the night after receiving his wound: drinking mead, eating freshly killed meat, and sleeping with a woman.[71] Baldwin's successor, Charles "the Good," brought an end to the Flemish attacks on Normandy and from 1119 kept the peace with Henry.[72]

Although Baldwin's fatal wound removed the hostile pressure from the northeastern districts of Normandy and reduced Louis VI's

---

[69] Ibid., p. 198: this story is difficult to accept because William of Tancarville had long been one of Henry's most intimate *familiares* and remained so afterward. Orderic suggests that William was moved by pity for the Frenchmen at Laigle who were trembling with cold and terror.

[70] Ibid., p. 200.

[71] Ibid., p 190; *Liber de Hyda*, p. 315, Suger, *Louis le Gros*, p. 194, and HH, p. 462; all say that he was wounded at Eu, whereas WM, *GR*, 2:479, places his wounding at Arques, attributes his illness to a meal of goose with garlic (exacerbated by after-dinner sex), and attests to Henry's sending the physician to care for Baldwin.

[72] OV, 6:190; although he was in Louis VI's army at Chartres shortly after the battle of Brémule (Suger, *Louis le Gros*, pp. 198–200), he is not named as a participant in that battle. According to Walter of Thérouanne, Charles' succession was threatened by a civil war with Baldwin VII's mother, Countess Clemence (sister of Pope Calixtus II and aunt of Adelaide queen of France), with the secret support of Louis VI: *Vita Karoli*, p. 542; cf. *Liber de Hyda*, pp. 320–321, WM, *GR*, 2:479, and Galbert, *Histoire*, p. 176, indicating that King Henry and Count Charles renewed the traditional Anglo-Flemish money-fief agreement. Orderic places Charles at Henry's Norman court at Rouen in 1124 (6:352–354).

coalition of princes from three to two, Henry's strategic good fortune
was offset soon afterward by the aforementioned disaster at Evreux,
whose citadel was betrayed on 7 October to Amaury de Montfort. In
the following month Henry undertook a full-scale siege of Laigle,
but the French garrison continued to hold out. Theobald of Blois
was unhorsed in the course of the attack, and Henry was almost killed
when a stone struck his head but was deflected by his helmet.[73] Henry's
troubles grew even worse when the misrule of his nephew Stephen
of Blois gave rise to an urban rebellion in Alençon, which Stephen
had been commissioned to defend in Henry's behalf. Stephen's taxes
and repression of the townspeople (which included making hostages
of wives and children and permitting some of the wives to be raped)
put in jeopardy Henry's control of his most important bastion in
southern Normandy.

The first step taken against Stephen by the Alençon burghers was to
contact Fulk V of Anjou and offer him the lordship of their town. Again,
domestic rebellion was made possible by international political rivalries. Count Fulk responded to the appeal from Alençon by raising an
army of mounted knights, archers, and foot soldiers and leading them
to the rescue. In late December 1118 he entered Alençon by night, captured the city, and laid siege to the castle. Henry I, hearing the disastrous news, called for the aid of Count Theobald and his knights,
summoned Norman and English forces to his banner, and advanced
on Alençon. The first division of Henry's army, led by Theobald and
Stephen, seems to have moved ahead too swiftly and to have lost touch
with King Henry and the main body of troops; the advance was turned
back with heavy losses. With the two armies locked in combat, an
Angevin relief force attacked Henry's army and did much damage,
wounding Count Theobald with a blow to the head. Then Count Fulk
emerged from the fray and launched a cavalry charge, backed by
archers, that won the day. Henry's army withdrew, his castle garrison
subsequently surrendered, and his city of Alençon passed into the
hands of Fulk V. It was the single major military defeat of Henry's
career.[74] And as the news of Henry's defeat spread, the Norman rebellion spread with it.[75]

---

[73] OV, 6:204.

[74] The sources bearing on the battle of Alençon are in many respects confusing
and unsatisfactory: see Chartrou, L'Anjou, pp. 11–13; Morillo, Warfare, pp.
170–171; Bradbury, "Battles in England and Normandy," in Strickland, ed., Anglo-
Norman Warfare, pp. 188–189; Chroniques des comtes d'Anjou et des seigneurs d'Amboise,
ed. Halphern and Poupardin, pp. 155–161; Chroniques des comtes d'Anjou, ed.
Marchegay and Salmon, pp. 144–151; OV, 6:206–208. David Bates views the
Alençon uprising in a larger regional context: "Normandy and England after
1066," p. 858, citing Thompson, "Family and Influence."

[75] OV, 6:208, 214–216.

With the coming of the new year, Henry's troubles continued, as more and more Norman barons, sensing that his fortunes were failing, joined the rebellion—or threatened to do so unless Henry granted them more lands and castles. Louis staged still another coup when he and his troops slipped secretly into the strategic town of Les Andelys on the Seine, deep within the *Vexin normand*. Shouting an English war cry, they entered the citadel and then, changing their shouts to the French war cry, "Montjoie," they overcame the Anglo-Norman garrison.[76] The French remained in Les Andelys for many months thereafter, making it a major French outpost in the heart of eastern Normandy. Henry, in response, strengthened the defenses of Noyon-sur-Andelle, several miles to the north, and stationed one hundred knights there.[77]

In February 1119 Henry suffered what was perhaps an even greater affliction on hearing that Eustace of Breteuil and his wife Juliana, evidently at the urging of Amaury de Montfort, were on the verge of joining the rebellion. This was a grave threat to Henry's lordship of Normandy, and a sorrow as well. To begin with, Breteuil was one of the greatest and wealthiest honors in Normandy, and its loss would be crippling to Henry's cause.[78] Moreover, the defection of the lord and lady of Breteuil would have been a source of grief to Henry personally. Eustace, the natural son of William of Breteuil, had ascended to his lordship fifteen years before, against formidable competition, with the king's support; his desertion of Henry now would have seemed thankless at best. And his wife Juliana was Henry's own natural daughter.

The issue was the castle of Ivry, to which, because of Henry's embattled condition, Eustace could allege an ambiguous ancestral claim and threaten to rebel if it were not granted.[79] Henry put Eustace off with his accustomed vague assurances, and to ensure his loyalty a hostage exchange was arranged between Eustace and Juliana's two daughters (Henry I's granddaughters) and the son of Ralph Harnec, the constable of Ivry. There then occurred a series of events that are at once tragic and incomprehensible. Orderic Vitalis is our only source for these events, and his account defies belief. On the advice of the

---

[76] Ibid., p. 216 and notes. Henry's natural son Richard fell into Louis' hands, but was graciously released without ransom. Of the present twin towns of Les Andelys, only Le Grand Andelys existed at the time.

[77] Ibid., p. 218.

[78] Hollister, "Greater Domesday Tenants-in-Chief," pp. 221–226, 243–247.

[79] Possession of Ivry was disputed between the family of Breteuil and the descendants of Ascelin Goel, whose son, Robert Goel, having rebelled briefly, now supported Henry I and was in possession of Ivry: *CP*, 8:208–211; Le Prévost, *Notes . . . de l'Eure*, 2:287–288; OV, 4:114, 202, 286–288, 6:40, 228–230.

omnipresent Amaury de Montfort (who perhaps was endeavoring to effect a definitive break between Eustace and King Henry), Eustace put out the eyes of his young hostage, Ralph Harnec's son, and sent the blinded boy back to his father. Why Eustace would have mutilated an innocent young man—and thereby put his own daughters in the gravest jeopardy—is impossible to fathom. Ralph Harnec, appalled and enraged at his son's mutilation, confronted Henry and demanded vengeance. Henry, deeply moved by Eustace's seemingly gratuitous atrocity and in accordance with the custom of hostage exchanges, handed over his two granddaughters. Ralph thereupon avenged the blinding of his son by putting out their eyes and cutting off the tips of their noses. "Thus," writes Orderic, "innocent childhood, alas, suffered for the sins of the fathers."[80]

On hearing of the blinding of their daughters, Eustace and Juliana were deeply distressed. Eustace prepared his castles to resist assault and sent Juliana with a band of knights to defend the citadel at Breteuil. But the burghers of Breteuil, anxious not to offend King Henry, sent word that they were prepared to open the gates of the city to him. Henry, cautioning his knights to take no plunder in Breteuil, entered the city and laid siege to the castle, where Juliana commanded an increasingly dispirited garrison. She offered to parley with her father, and when he met her she suddenly drew a crossbow and shot a bolt at him—but missed. Henry thereupon confined Juliana to the castle, destroying the drawbridge and forbidding her to depart. She was constrained to surrender the castle to her father, but he found it impossible to forgive her attempt to murder him and he kept her confined in the tower. She was left with no choice but to leap down from the castle walls into the frozen waters of the moat. Orderic suggests that she suffered the ultimate humiliation of having her legs and bare buttocks exposed as she leapt downward, but to Juliana that was perhaps the least of her worries.

Juliana withdrew to seek the comfort of her husband at their castle of Pacy, and Henry rewarded the townspeople of Breteuil generously. He forestalled the possibility of restoring the honor of Breteuil to Eustace and Juliana at some future truce by granting it to the Breton, Ralph of Gael, a kinsman of the late William of Breteuil, who held it in strict homage to the king "and boldly attacked the enemies of the

---

[80] OV, 6:210–212; several twentieth-century historians have drastically and misleadingly oversimplified this lamentable episode, omitting Ralph Harnec and his mutilated son from the account and asserting without further explanation that the king put out the eyes of his own granddaughters, presumably on a sadistic whim.

realm everywhere." Henry thus reduced Eustace from one of the great lords of Normandy to a minor castellan.[81]

The warfare that raged through southern and eastern Normandy resulted in widespread disruption, death, and impoverishment. The normal means of overcoming a military opponent in this era was not to defeat him in battle but to ravage his estates, burn his crops and villages, and kill or kidnap his peasants, as reports of the Norman warfare of 1117–1119 repeatedly disclose. Occasionally, the war might result in the calamity of a city being burned to the ground: Laigle in 1118, Evreux (as we shall see) in 1119. And in England, which was spared the horrors of combat and pillage, one hears anguished protests against taxation of unprecedented severity, as Henry sought to employ the wealth of England to restore the peace of Normandy.

The Anglo-Saxon chronicler, always sensitive to high taxes, complained of them on several occasions during the reign, but only during the infrequent years when Henry was at war.[82] In 1118 the chronicler deplored Henry's taxes, yet he understood perfectly well the reason for them. Because of the hostilities in Normandy,

> the king was very much distressed and lost a great deal both in money and in land, and the people who troubled him most were his own men, who frequently deserted and betrayed him and went over to his enemies, and gave their castles up to them for the injury and betrayal of the king. England paid dear for all this, because of the various taxes that never ceased in the course of all this year.[83]

The betrayal by supposedly faithful magnates—Eustace of Breteuil, Hugh of Gournay, Robert of Neubourg, and others—had affected Henry deeply, suggesting to him that his most strenuous efforts to contain the rebellion were being thwarted by the defections of powerful lords whom he had trusted. Indeed, Count Fulk's capture of Alençon, along with the losses of such crucial bulwarks as Evreux, Les

---

[81] Ibid., p. 214; in the end, the king permitted Eustace and Juliana to retain Pacy and to receive rents on lands in England worth three hundred silver marks a year, which enabled the couple to continue to live in style. Juliana, in her later years, retired to the fashionable new abbey of Fontevrault: OV, 6:278; Ralph of Gael soon afterward withdrew to his lands in Brittany, marrying his daughter Amice to Richard the king's son, who then became lord of Breteuil; after Richard's death in 1120, Amice married Robert earl of Leicester, who thereupon acquired the lordship of Breteuil: ibid. and n. 2; Le Prévost, *Notes . . . de l'Eure*, 1:415–416.

[82] *ASC*, s.a. 1104, 1110 (the one exception, when Henry was raising money for Maud's dowry), 1116, 1118, 1124; HH, pp. 460–462 (1117), "because of the king's pressing needs" owing to the warfare in Normandy.

[83] *ASC*, s.a. 1118.

Andelys, Laigle, Gournay, and, very nearly, Breteuil seem for a time to have daunted the king. "He was unable to trust his own men," Orderic observes. "Some even who ate at his table favoured the cause of his nephew and his other enemies and, by prying into his secrets, greatly helped these men."[84]

Having had his life threatened, first at Laigle, then by his own daughter at Breteuil, Henry was also confronted with an assassination plot within his own household, hatched by an unnamed treasurer-chamberlain assisted by lesser royal servants. We have two independent accounts of the plot. Suger reports that the leader was a chamberlain whose name began with the letter *H*, who had been closely associated with the king and had been enriched and made famous by him. Once the plot was exposed, Henry treated the would-be assassin with great mercy, Suger says, having him blinded and castrated rather than hanged as he deserved.[85] William of Malmesbury tells us simply that the culprit was a certain chamberlain of low birth who rose to fame as custodian of the royal treasury.[86] If he was as famous as Malmesbury and Suger assert, his name should appear somewhere in the relatively abundant records of the period, yet for many years he remained unidentified. I have suggested that the culprit was Herbert the Chamberlain, who was the only man known to have been styled treasurer at the time and the only chamberlain of the entire reign to have a name beginning with *H*.[87] Herbert is such an obvious candidate that he would doubtless have been identified much sooner were it not for the deep-set tradition that he remained in office until 1129 or 1130. But in fact there is every likelihood that he surrendered his office in or before 1120. There is no charter or chronicle evidence of his being alive at any time after 1118; indeed, the charter evidence suggests that his lands had passed to his eldest son, Herbert fitz Herbert, by 1121.[88] The king was greatly unnerved by this third attempt on his life in less than a year. He took

---

[84] OV, 6:200; on Henry's near failure of nerve, cf. *Liber de Hyda*, p. 316.

[85] Suger, *Louis le Gros*, p. 190.

[86] WM, *GR*, 2:488.

[87] *MMI*, pp. 214–215. Two much later manuscripts of Suger extend the assassin's name, one of them to Hue, the other to Henry, but both are mere guesses; on King Henry's chamberlains see *RRAN* 2:xiii–xv. Herbert the Chamberlain acquired some properties in Yorkshire and Gloucestershire under Henry I (*EYC*, 1:35–38); at some point after 1086 he or his son acquired three knights fees *in capite* in Berkshire and Wiltshire and subtenancies of the bishops of Winchester and Chichester and the abbot of Abingdon: *RBE*, 1:31, 45, 199, 205, 246, 307.

[88] The latest definite date at which Herbert the Chamberlain's name occurs is 1111: *RBE. RRAN* 2, no. 1000. A charter of Herbert fitz Herbert confirming his brother William's gift of Weaverthorpe church to Nostell Priory (*EYC*, 1, no. 26) is confirmed by Thurstan archbishop of York (*EYC*, 1, no. 27) and subsequently by Henry I in a solemn diploma of 1121–1127, very probably 10 January 1122 (*EYC*,

precautions against further threats by changing beds frequently, increasing his armed guards, and sleeping with a sword and shield close at hand. His fears have been regarded by some historians as neurotic, by others as eminently sensible.[89]

Nevertheless, Henry's cause in Normandy was far from lost. Despite the defections of such great lords as Eustace of Breteuil, Hugh of Gournay, Henry count of Eu (who rejoined Henry's side after Baldwin VII's injury), Stephen of Aumale, Robert of Neubourg, and Robert Giroie and the unreliability of others, many important Norman magnates remained committed royalists. Orderic names among Henry's firm backers Richard earl of Chester, Ranulf le Meschin *vicomte* of Bayeux (future earl of Chester), William of Warenne, William of Roumare, Waleran count of Meulan, and Walter Giffard, each of them in possession of strongly fortified family castles and with significant interests on both sides of the Channel.[90] Besides these loyal magnates and their castles, Henry could rely on a large network of ducal strongholds directly subject to his own control and garrisoned by reliable soldiers of his *familia*. Castles in each of the episcopal cities—Rouen, Bayeux, Coutances, Avranches, Lisieux, and Sées—were defended by such men, as were the royal castles at Caen, Falaise, Exmes, Fécamp, Lillebonne, Arques, Nonancourt, Vernon, Illiers l'Evêque, Châteauneuf-sur-Epte (which successfully resisted a siege by Louis VI), Argentan, Neufchâtel-en-Bray, Noyon-sur-Andelle, and elsewhere throughout the duchy.[91] These fortresses were in safe hands, for although magnates might shift sides with the winds, knights of the *familia regis* did not.

3, no. 1428 and n.; *RRAN* 2, no. 1312). Henry's confirmation (original lost) is described by Farrer as "doubtful" (*Itin.*, p. 110 n. 3) but is accepted as authentic by the editors of *RRAN* 2. The signatories present no problems; Henry I's style, *dei gratia rex Anglorum et dux Normannorum*, although uncharacteristic of contemporary chancery practice, is quite acceptable in a beneficiary-drafted diploma such as is in question here. Eyton, *Antiquities of Shropshire*, 7:149, found it puzzling that Herbert the Chamberlain's heirs could be granting at such an early date while their father lived on until ca. 1129, but his objection begs the whole question. Herbert fitz Herbert married Henry I's mistress, Sibyl Corbet (ibid., 7: 149; *CP*, 11, app. D, p. 108), but did not inherit his father's treasury chamberlainship, which evidently passed to Henry I's *curialis* Geoffrey of Clinton: *MMI*, pp. 214–215. Herbert fitz Herbert's younger brother, William fitz Herbert, went on to a stormy career as archbishop of York in Stephen's reign and was subsequently canonized: ibid., p. 215 and n. 3.

[89] Suger, *Louis le Gros*, p. 190.

[90] OV, 6:222; on William of Roumare's loyalty see ibid., pp. 194, 236; he, along with Walter Giffard III, William II of Warenne, and others fought on Henry's side at the climactic battle of Brémule: ibid., p. 236; *Liber de Hyda*, p. 317; William of Tancarville (who also fought at Brémule) and Ralph III of Tosny occur on Orderic's list as well, but other passages suggest that their loyalty may have been questionable: OV, 6:198–200, 244.

[91] OV, 6:198–200, 244; Yver, "Châteaux forts," pp. 83–90, 94–99; *GND*, 2:250.

ese professional warriors, paid by the king in both wages and sus-
nce, have been the subject of valuable studies by Marjorie Chibnall
and J. O. Prestwich.[92] The military training, mobility, and skills of
the military *familia* proved an invaluable asset to Henry (and to his
royal predecessors and successors), particularly in the Norman wars of
1118–1119 and 1123–1124. In peacetime they might number a couple
of hundred, but in times of military crisis their numbers could swell
into the thousands. Many of them were trained and equipped as knights
(though some possessed little more than their arms, armor, and a
horse) whereas others were well-trained infantrymen or archers. Some
were knightly adventurers drawn from distant lands into Henry's
service by stories of his generosity and the high reputation of his court.
Most of them were relatively poor though ambitious, but in their
upper echelons and among their leaders were younger siblings of high
birth in search of good wages and wealthy heiresses, and sometimes
their upper ranks might even include a well-born son and heir waiting
for his father to die.[93] Since the livelihood of most warriors of the
familia regis depended entirely on the king's wages and maintenance
and, if they fought well, his rewards, they were devotedly loyal. As one
of their leaders warned them on the verge of battle in 1124, "[If we
shirk our duty] how shall we ever dare to enter the king's presence? We
shall deserve to forfeit both our wages and our honor, and . . . shall
never again be entitled to eat the king's bread."[94] Henry's military
familia constituted, in short, something between a royal bodyguard
(some of whom could be detached to serve the king from afar) and a
small standing army.

Yet one must be careful not to exaggerate the scope and effectiveness of Henry's military *familia*. Although it was clearly an excellent
fighting force, well trained and usually loyal, it was by no means invincible. For example, some 140 knights of the *familia*, led by the brothers Roger and John of Saint-Jean and entrusted with defending La
Motte Gautier-de-Clinchamps, surrendered to Fulk of Anjou in July
1118 after a siege of eight days. Similar garrisons may well have been
responsible for the loss of the citadels of Evreux, Alençon, and Les
Andelys, and there is evidence to suggest that another such garrison
later succumbed to an Angevin siege of the castle of Gorron in Maine.[95]

---

[92] Chibnall, "Mercenaries and the *familia regis*"; Prestwich, "The Military Household of the Norman Kings"; see also Morillo, *Warfare*, pp. 60–66.

[93] An example of a knight in the later category is Henry, heir to Joscelin of Berry
Pomeroy, Devon: Chibnall, "Mercenaries and the *familia regis*," ed. Strickland, pp.
86–87; on volunteers from afar see Map, *De nugis curialium*, pp. 438, 470.

[94] OV, 6:348–350.

[95] Ibid., pp. 194–196, 204, 208; *RRAN* 2, no. 1422 (cf. *Book of Fees*, 1:86, 97); for
an exception to the loyalty of Henry's military *familia* see OV, 6:350–352.

Further, one must distinguish between the paid knights of the *familia regis* and the common mercenaries that Henry might use in time of crisis, such as the Bretons whom he routinely hired, and the Breton and English garrison that defended the castle of Bures in Le Talou in 1118.[96] There has been a hazardous tendency, moreover, to translate the Latin term *familia regis* as "military household"—a term that does not appear in the Latin sources. In actuality members of the king's *familia* need not necessarily have been warriors at all—or at least not primarily warriors.[97] The term *familiaris* signifies a person close to the king—not simply a member of his guard but often a royal counselor or administrator or judge, or one who might serve the king in several capacities, for example Thomas of Saint-Jean, who, with two younger brothers, sometimes led mercenary contingents or commanded castle garrisons in the king's behalf but who also served for several years as sheriff of Oxfordshire.[98] And to include magnates of the highest rank as "members" of the king's military *familia* simply because they commanded knightly contingents at major battles (as great magnates ordinarily did) stretches the meaning of "military *familia*" beyond recognition. Wealthy royal *familiares* such as Robert count of Meulan, William of Warenne earl of Surrey, Ranulf earl of Chester, and David king of Scots are not likely to have appeared on any muster lists of the *familia regis*, or to have received the small daily wages that were paid to warriors in the *familia*, or to have participated regularly in routine military exercises with companies of paid knights. Waleran count of Meulan, for example, although allegedly a "member" of the military *familia regis*, is known to have expressed deep contempt for the "country bumpkins" of Henry's military household. Consequently, the question of whether these great magnates were or were not "members" of Henry's military *familia* is probably meaningless.[99] The persons who do actually seem to be commanders serving in the military

---

[96] OV, 6:190; cf. WM, *GR*, 2:478 on Henry's use of Breton mercenaries.

[97] In the twelfth century every able-bodied man of status was expected to fight when necessary; Henry I's chancellor Waldric, for example, fought in the royal army at Tinchebray and is reported to have been responsible for taking Robert Curthose prisoner: OV, 6:90.

[98] *RRAN* 2, no. 1422; Green, *English Sheriffs*, p. 69; OV, 6:84, 194; Green points out that members of the king's *familia* were both military and nonmilitary: *Government*, p. 20. On this point, see also Warren, *Henry II*, pp. 305, 309–311; Takayama, "*Familiares regis* and the Royal Inner Council."

[99] Prestwich, "Military Household of the Norman Kings," ed. Strickland, pp. 105–119; cf. OV, 6:350–351. If great landholders who (1) frequented the royal court and (2) participated in a royal military expedition were *ipso facto* members of the king's military *familia*, then one would have to include in that "standing military force" such extremely unlikely persons as Robert Bloet bishop of Lincoln, a frequent attester of royal charters who led a royal force at the siege of Tickhill in 1102, or even St Anselm, who camped with his knights at Pevensey in 1101.

familia—knights of the lesser nobility such as Ralph the Red of Pont-Echanfray and Odo Borleng, or younger sons such as Engenulf and Geoffrey of Laigle and William of Grandcourt (a son of Count Henry of Eu)[100]—were the elite members of the group, the captains, whose unnamed troops were clearly of lesser status and who therefore cannot be regarded as representative of the far humbler rank and file of the military *familia.*

The most celebrated captain in Henry's military *familia* during the war of 1118–1119 was Ralph the Red of Pont-Echanfray, whose family castle of Pont-Echanfray near Saint-Evroul brought him under the scrutiny of Orderic Vitalis and made him one of Orderic's heroes. In his youth Ralph had followed Bohemund to the Holy Land and had visited both Constantinople and Jerusalem. In 1118–1119 he was a stalwart defender of King Henry's cause, leading the defense of south-central Normandy. On one occasion he rescued Richard the courageous bastard son of Henry I and thereby suffered capture himself by the troops of Louis VI (he was quickly ransomed). On another occasion he commanded a siege castle against Amaury de Montfort's citadel at Evreux, and on still another he dashed to the rescue of Breteuil when it was under French attack and rushed furiously all over the battlefield in its defense.[101] Ralph the Red and his men, along with other devoted members of Henry's military *familia,* did much to preserve the integrity of the king's Norman dominions against the attacks of his external and internal enemies. Henry I would doubtless have elevated Ralph to high station had he not drowned in 1120 in the disaster of the White Ship.

After his defeat at Alençon, and doubtless much earlier, King Henry sought to make peace with his enemies. To Amaury de Montfort he offered lordship over the county of Evreux if Amaury would surrender the citadel to Henry and permit it to be defended by a royal garrison, but Amaury contemptuously refused. Indeed, Amaury continued to function as the heart and soul of the rebellion:

> He often galloped out at night at breakneck speed from one fortress to another, rousing everyone with ceaseless vigilance, encouraging his sworn allies and instructing them to guard their castles well, to keep sleepless watch against cunning spies, and to be bold and politic in harassing the neighbouring settlements.[102]

And his close ally, Louis VI, from his advance base at Les Andelys, continually sent out his troops to burn and pillage the Norman Vexin.[103]

---

[100] Chibnall, "Mercenaries and the *familia regis,*" ed. Strickland, pp. 86–87.
[101] OV, 6:198, 220–222, 230–232, 246, 250.
[102] Ibid., p. 220.
[103] Suger, *Louis le Gros,* pp. 194–196; OV, 6:216–218.

Gradually, however, the struggle began to turn in Henry's favor. As Suger expresses it, returning to his metaphor of the wheel of fortune, "Having harshly whipped and tormented him for some time, the divine mercy ordered that he be spared and compassionately raised from the abyss into which he had descended: the wheel now brought him up again from the depths of misfortune to the heights of success."[104] Henry, beset by enemy garrisons within the borders of Normandy— Fulk V at Alençon, Amaury at Evreux, Louis VI at Les Andelys—determined to split the alliance against him by coming to terms with Anjou. In May 1119 his emissaries worked out an agreement with Fulk that removed him from Louis VI's alliance and joined him in friendship with Henry I. In return for a large (and undisclosed) sum of money from Henry, Fulk agreed to marry his eldest daughter, Matilda, to Henry's son and heir, William Adelin, and to grant as her dowry the long-disputed overlordship of Maine (along with direct control of several strategic Manceaux castles) and the recently conquered frontier stronghold of Alençon.[105] The long-delayed marriage of William and Matilda, which had first been agreed on in 1113, took place in the cathedral of Lisieux in June 1119.[106] Fulk then departed for a visit to Jerusalem, apparently committing the lordship of Maine to Henry I, to be restored to Fulk on his return.[107]

The correlation between Norman baronial rebellions and the menaces of neighboring principalities, which has been noticed before, is further disclosed by the immediate cessation of rebellions in southern Normandy after the rapprochement between Henry and Fulk. At Fulk's request, Henry pardoned Robert Giroie of Saint-Céneri and restored his castles to him.[108] Also at Fulk's request, Henry restored the important holdings of the Bellême family to Robert of Bellême's son and heir, William Talvas count of Ponthieu, who received at that time the city of Alençon, the town and nunnery of Almenesches, and other traditional Bellême properties, except for their citadels, which

---

[104] Suger, *Louis le Gros*, p. 192.

[105] OV, 6:224; Chartrou, *L'Anjou*, p. 13; WM, *GR*, 2:495.

[106] OV, 6:224; *Chroniques des comtes d'Anjou et des seigneurs d'Amboise*, ed. Halphen and Poupardin, p. 161; SD, 2:258; *ASC, s.a.* 1119; WM, *GR*, 2:482; *RRAN* 2, no. 1204a (Rouen), which probably dates from this occasion, records a gift of two English estates by Henry I and his son William to Bishop Reginald of Angers and his cathedral. At the time of the marriage, William Adelin would have been about sixteen years old and Matilda of Anjou no more than twelve: *MMI*, p. 255 n. 33.

[107] Ibid. But Malmesbury alone reports the disposition of Maine, and he could well be confused. Cf. Norgate, *Angevin Kings*, 1:238–239.

[108] OV, 6:224: Henry regranted to Robert the castles of Montreuil and Echauffour; toward the end of May another rebel stronghold, La Ferté-Fresnel, surrendered to Henry, and its lord, Richard of Fresnel, retired to become a monk at Saint-Evroul: ibid., p. 222.

Henry assigned to his own garrisons.[109] Fulk's defection from his
alliance with Louis VI infuriated the French. Suger doubtless spoke for
many when he complained that the count of Anjou, although having
earlier pledged himself to Louis by a solemn act of homage,

> now put greed before fidelity and, crazed by treachery, gave his
> daughter in marriage to William son of the king of the English
> without consulting King Louis. He deceitfully betrayed his sworn
> word to combat King Henry and allied himself to the English king
> by ties of friendship.[110]

Having by now managed to establish friendly relations with both Flanders and Anjou, Henry, after mid-1119, had to contend with only one
major enemy rather than three.

Nevertheless, Louis VI, with his outpost deep inside the Norman
Vexin at Les Andelys, remained a formidable opponent. And Amaury
de Montfort, despite his Angevin connections, continued to nurse his
hatred of Henry I and remained at Louis' side. Henry again sent
representatives to Amaury urging him to accept comital authority in
Evreux in return for Henry's control of the citadel, but Amaury
remained defiant.

Finally, in summer 1119 Henry made what Orderic describes as a terrible progress through Normandy. He burned his enemies' strongholds
and villages, including the Breteuil castle of Pont-Saint-Pierre far to the
west of Normandy's Epte frontier.[111] King Louis, for his part, continued
to pillage and devastate crops, villages, and peasants in the Norman
Vexin from his base at Les Andelys.[112] In July Henry turned again to
Amaury's garrison at Evreux, accompanied by his intrepid natural son
Richard, his nephew Stephen of Blois, Audoin the bearded refugee-
bishop of Evreux, and a large force of Normans, probably drawn from
the king's military *familia*. Failing to penetrate the defenses of the city,
Henry turned to Bishop Audoin and said (according to Orderic): "Do
you see, my lord bishop, that we are thrown back by our foes, and that
only by fire can we force them to submit?" But if a fire is set, Henry
continued, churches will be burned and the innocent will suffer.
Requesting Bishop Audoin's advice, Henry assured him that if God

---

[109] OV, 6:222. As count of Ponthieu, William Talvas had probably cooperated with
Count Baldwin VII in his raids on Normandy until Baldwin's battle wound of
September 1118 removed him from combat.

[110] Suger, *Louis le Gros*, pp. 194–196; Suger neglected to remind his readers that
about six years earlier (in 1113) Fulk had sworn fealty to Henry I and had become
his vassal for Maine: OV, 6:180; above, p. 231.

[111] OV, 6:226.

[112] Ibid., pp. 226–228, 236; Suger, *Louis le Gros*, p. 196.

granted him victory, "then with God's help the damage to the church shall be repaired, because we will gladly donate large sums from our treasure so that the houses of God shall be built, so I believe, better than before."[113] This last offer evidently persuaded Bishop Audoin, who had been deeply troubled by the choice that Henry had asked him to make but who now advised the king to proceed with the burning. So the fire was lit, the raging flames quickly spread and, since it was the dry season, consumed the city totally. Bishop Audoin's cathedral church of St Mary's burned to the ground and the city's inhabitants scattered in all directions.

Amaury's garrison in the citadel, however, remained in place and continued to defy the king.[114] The defenders of Evreux included the royal half-brothers Philip and Florus, sons of the late King Philip I and Amaury's sister Queen Bertrade. Amaury himself was otherwise occupied, with Eustace and Juliana of Breteuil at their castle of Pacy, perhaps commiserating with them over the burning of their castle of Pont-Saint-Pierre. On hearing of the burning of his own city of Evreux, Amaury bewailed its destruction and sent for help to King Louis, who was just then besieging Henry I's frontier fortress of Châteauneuf-sur-Epte. Abandoning the siege, Louis returned briefly to his own dominions for reinforcements and then, around mid-August, moved on to Les Andelys accompanied by many of the great lords of his realm. On 20 August they proceeded through the Norman Vexin toward Henry's stronghold of Noyon-sur-Andelle, which Louis hoped to take with the help of traitors among Henry's garrison. That same morning, Henry heard Mass at Noyon-sur-Andelle and then, accompanied by his chief magnates, led an army southward through the Norman Vexin, unaware that Louis had returned from France and was on his way to Noyon.[115] Without realizing it, the two kings were advancing toward one of the decisive battles of their reigns.

Henry's scouts spotted Louis' army from their vantage point atop a hill called Verclives overlooking a flat plain known to the natives of the region as Brémule (where a modern farm complex now stands bearing the same name). The view from Verclives is today obscured by vegetation growing along the edges of the hilltop, but in the early twelfth century the outlook was largely unobstructed. Suger reports that Henry's men tried to confuse the French by lighting fires on the plain that would leap up and throw Louis' knights into disarray, but J. O. Prestwich has made the perceptive suggestion that the fires were

---

[113] OV, 6:228.

[114] Ibid.; subsequently, Henry did pay for the rebuilding of the cathedral church, whose magnificent Romanesque nave of the 1120s survives to this day; see GND, 2:256.

[115] OV, 6:234.

probably set by the French themselves, "following the normal practice of ravaging and devastation."[116] Henry, with the advance warning provided by his well-placed scouts, was able to deploy his army carefully and effectively. Our fullest sources for the battle—the Hyde chronicler, Orderic, Suger, and Henry of Huntingdon—are not in perfect accord, but they agree that Henry applied his keen intelligence and tactical knowledge to the deployment of his men into cavalry and infantry lines, the latter including large numbers of dismounted knights under his own command, whereas Louis VI and his knights galloped headlong into the fray.

Suger deplores the recklessness of his hero: "King Louis and his men thought it unworthy to plan carefully for battle and rushed against the foe in a bold but careless attack."[117] Henry's force, which Orderic estimates to have been five hundred knights, included the king's son William Adelin, his bastard sons Richard and Robert (future earl of Gloucester), William of Warenne and Walter Giffard (earls of Surrey and Buckingham), Roger fitz Richard of Clare, William of Roumare, Nigel of Aubigny, William of Tancarville (who again advised Henry not to fight), and, back on Henry's side again, Henry count of Eu.[118] Louis' force, some four hundred knights according to Orderic, included William Clito, William of Garlande seneschal of France and commander of the king's army, William Crispin (whom Henry had pardoned in 1106 and again in 1113), and a number of great French magnates. Standing aloof from the battle were two former Norman rebels of the northeast, Stephen of Aumale and Hugh of Gournay, along with (*very* surprisingly and inexplicably) Clito's tutor and protector, Helias of Saint-Saens.[119] The impetuous French charge against the Anglo-Normans broke the forward line of Henry's knights, but the French were then thrown into confusion by the next line consisting of dismounted Normans arrayed in "surprisingly well-aligned and positioned ranks."[120] The Anglo-Normans partially surrounded the French and succeeded in taking a great many prisoners, some of high status. William Crispin, chagrined to be facing defeat and capture once again, spotted King Henry on the battlefield. Galloping toward the monarch

---

[116] Suger, *Louis le Gros*, p. 196; Prestwich, "Military Intelligence," p. 12; cf. OV, 6:236, reporting that on the eve of battle the French set fire to a barn belonging to monks of Buscheron (Noyon) and that the Anglo-Normans took their bearings from the rising smoke.

[117] Suger, *Louis le Gros*, p. 196; the other sources agree: *Liber de Hyda*, p. 317; HH, pp. 462–464; OV, 6:236–240.

[118] OV, 6:236, 240; *Liber de Hyda*, p. 317.

[119] OV, 6:236; *Liber de Hyda*, p. 318; the fact that all the important former rebels from the northeast were now either neutral or in Henry's army can be explained by the withdrawal of Flanders from the war.

[120] Suger, *Louis le Gros*, p. 196.

"whom he hated above all others," he struck a blow with his sword to the head of the dismounted king, but the blow was deflected by the collar of the royal hauberk, and for the fourth time in a year Henry was saved from assassination. Roger fitz Richard of Clare struck William Crispin from his horse and on to the ground, took him prisoner, and then flung himself over William's body to save him from the vengeance of Henry's friends.[121]

The men in the French army who eluded capture, including Louis VI and William Clito, fled back to Les Andelys. Louis is said to have got lost in the forest on the way back and to have been led to Les Andelys by a peasant who did not recognize him (and later regretted deeply that he had not demanded a larger reward). Orderic reports that Henry's army took some 140 prisoners and also captured King Louis' standard and his splendidly saddled and bridled horse, along with William Clito's palfrey. Henry kept the standard as a souvenir of his victory, but he chivalrously returned Louis' warhorse to him, and William Adelin, following his father's example, returned William Clito's palfrey along with various gifts.[122] Henry returned to Rouen "amidst the sounds of battle cries and the chanting of the clergy and glorified God who is the lord of hosts."[123]

Brémule was a small battle, involving armies of only a few hundred on each side and probably lasting less than an hour. Orderic reports the estimate that only three knights were killed in the fray, the remainder having been protected by their armor, by the preference of the combatants for ransoms rather than corpses, and by their sense of brotherhood in arms and the fear of God.[124] But although the battle at Brémule was brief, it was decisive. The war produced a few more skirmishes, but they were anticlimactic. Shortly after Brémule, Louis VI, at the urging of Amaury de Montfort (who also had been absent from the battle), summoned a huge but ill-trained army, including parish levies led by their priests, to invade Normandy once again and endeavor to recover Breteuil for Eustace and Juliana. But when the French reached Breteuil (17 September), they were driven back by Ralph of Gael, the current lord of the castle, who thumbed his nose at the French by keeping his portals open while defending them with his knights. Ralph was quickly reinforced by Henry's troops led by his son Richard, Ralph the Red, and others, and, shortly afterward, by Henry himself. Again,

---

[121] OV, 6:238; cf. *Liber de Hyda*, p. 318; HH, p. 464, which adds that when William Crispin struck the king his hauberk was forced a little way into his head, causing his blood to gush out; Henry of Huntingdon adds that it was the king himself (rather than Roger fitz Richard) who struck back at William Crispin and knocked him off his horse.
[122] OV, 6:238–240. *Liber de Hyda* (p. 318) reports that Henry took 114 captives.
[123] HH, p. 464.
[124] OV, 6:238–240.

the French and their king fled homeward.[125] Suger adds that King
Louis, after his futile attempt on Breteuil, sought vengeance against
Henry's ally Theobald of Blois by advancing on his city of Chartres with
the intention of burning it down. But Louis called a halt to the project
when the cathedral clergy and townspeople overawed him by displaying their most sacred relic, the chemise of the Virgin Mary.[126] Suger,
who preferred to end his chapters with French royal victories, implies
that Louis continued to carry on his campaign against Henry, but
his account is suspiciously vague and supplies no details. Other writers
say nothing about any further fighting. It seems likely that after
Breteuil and Chartres, the discouraged French king quietly ceased all
military operations against Henry and his supporters. And the rebellion in Normandy, deprived of any major external support, continued
to lose steam.

A great papal council convened at Reims on 18 October 1119, providing Louis with the opportunity of protesting directly to the papal
curia against the wrongs that Henry had purportedly committed. The
Holy See was now ruled by its third pope in less than two years: Paschal
II had died in January 1118 and his successor, Gelasius II, shortly afterward. The new pope, Guy, former archbishop of Vienne, was a cadet
member of the comital family of Burgundy and had taken the name
Calixtus II (1119–1124). Like Gelasius before him, Calixtus was kept
from exercising power in Rome by an antipope backed by Emperor
Henry V. The pope and his court found refuge and protection in the
kingdom of Louis VI, whose wife, Queen Adelaide, granddaughter of
William Tête-Hardi count of Burgundy, was the pope's niece. At this
time the sons, daughters, and grandchildren of William Tête-Hardi
occupied positions of high distinction across Western Europe: besides
Pope Calixtus and Queen Adelaide, they included a far-flung family
network of dukes, duchesses, counts, countesses, and archbishops, in
France, ducal Burgundy, Flanders, and Castile.[127]

---

[125] Ibid., pp. 244–248; Suger, *Louis le Gros*, pp. 198–200. Suger adds that King
Louis, on his way to Breteuil, had burned down the castle of Ivry, and Orderic
asserts that a group of French knights, after the impasse at Breteuil, attempted to
seize the Norman castle of Tillières but without success: OV, 6:248.

[126] Suger, *Louis le Gros*, p. 200; the chemise is still on exhibit in the cathedral
treasury. The *Chronique de Morigny*, p. 31, states that Chartres was indeed partially
burned at the time.

[127] Bouchard, *Sword, Miter, and Cloister*, pp. 273–275: among Count William's sons
and daughters were Stephen count of Burgundy, Raynald II count of Macon,
Raymond husband of Urraca heiress of the kingdom of Castile, Hugh archbishop
of Besançon, Pope Calixtus, Sibyl duchess of Burgundy, Ermentrude countess of
Montbéliard, Gisela countess of Maurienne, and Clemence countess of Flanders
(Baldwin VII's mother).

The Council of Reims was a significant occasion in the life of the Western Church, so much so that Henry I permitted his prelates to attend it, reversing his previous policy of forbidding the participation of Anglo-Norman churchmen in synods beyond his frontiers and outside his control. But Henry prohibited his prelates from taking legal complaints against each other to the pope at Reims and thereby challenging his traditional right to adjudicate such complaints within his own dominions.[128] The council dealt with a variety of issues, of which several were of particular importance to Henry I's regime. To Pope Calixtus and his curia, of course, the crucial issue was the fierce and seemingly interminable struggle between papacy and empire, intensified by the activities of imperial troops and rebellious Romans, and the occupation of the Holy City by the antipope Maurice of Braga (Gregory VIII). These disputes induced the Council of Reims to declare a recess for several days for a parley between pope and emperor at Mouzon in the Ardennes. Their negotiations ended dismally, however, with the two parties as far from agreement as ever.[129]

The Franco-Norman war was also on the agenda at Reims where, on 21 October, Louis VI addressed the council at length. Louis raised a number of complaints: Henry's invasions in 1105–1106 of Normandy ("which is a part of my realm"), his "atrocious" imprisonment of Robert Curthose ("who is a vassal of mine"), his disinheritance of William Clito (who was just then at Louis' side), the arrest and imprisonment "in a grim dungeon" of Louis' envoy Robert of Bellême, his complicity in the rebellion of Count Theobald of Blois and in Theobald's imprisonment of William count of Nevers, and other malfeasances. When Geoffrey archbishop of Rouen rose to rebut these charges, he was shouted down by the French majority at the council. And when the bearded Audoin bishop of Evreux rose to attack Amaury de Montfort for his role in seizing the castle of Evreux, driving him from his episcopal palace, and having the city burned, he too was shouted down by one of Amaury's chaplains, backed by all the French in "a great uproar."

When the tumult had died down, Calixtus addressed the council. He urged peace between the two parties and promised to do all he could to achieve it. He further commanded the French and Anglo-Normans to observe the Truce of God "as Pope Urban of blessed memory established it at the Council of Clermont." This last command can only have helped the Anglo-Norman cause, for Henry continued to hold virtually all of Normandy and, having no designs on lands in France, had every

---

[128] OV, 6:252; above, p. 240; on the council see Robert, *Calixte II*, pp. 61 ff., and *Councils and Synods*, 1: part 2, pp. 718–721.

[129] OV, 6:264–266; Hesso Scholasticus, *Relatio de concilio Remensi*, pp. 21–28; Henry V and Calixtus would subsequently come to terms on investitures and related issues at Worms in 1122.

reason to seek peace.[130] The pope clearly had more urgent priorities than the favoring of a royal kinsman such as Louis VI whose prospects were fading, and he preferred not to make an enemy of the most powerful monarch in Western Europe, whose adversaries, one after another, were petitioning him for terms of peace.[131]

The Council of Reims ended on 30 October, about twelve days after it began. Shortly thereafter, Amaury de Montfort, whom Henry was besieging fiercely at Evreux, sued for peace. Through the mediation of Theobald of Blois, Henry accepted Amaury's surrender of the citadel of Evreux and garrisoned it with his own knights. Henry, in turn, granted Amaury the county of Evreux "to his great satisfaction" (but to Henry's later regret). It was at about this time that Eustace and Juliana, formerly "of Breteuil," made peace with Henry through the mediation of Henry's son and Juliana's brother, Richard, who would shortly afterward, very briefly, become lord of Breteuil. Robert of Neubourg surrendered as well, receiving back his burned-out castle, and Hugh of Gournay, "seeing that stronger men had abandoned him," asked for the king's pardon and received it. And when Henry assembled an army against Stephen "count" of Aumale, Stephen surrendered too.[132] It may also have been at this time that Henry arranged the marriage between his natural daughter Alice (or Aline) and Matthew of Montmorency, son of Burchard of Montmorency, constable of France, whom Henry had captured in the course of Louis VI's impetuous charge at Brémule and whom Henry released immediately after the battle.[133]

Near Aumale Henry negotiated with William Clito, whom he had perhaps not seen face to face since 1106 when Clito was not quite four years old.[134] Clito (who had recently turned seventeen) pleaded for his father's release, swearing that he and his father would go to Jerusalem and never again trouble Henry's dominions. Henry, victorious over a plethora of forsworn enemies and the target of murder attempts by several of them, refused to set Robert Curthose free. But he did promise to enrich and befriend Clito in return for his submission. Orderic, reporting on Henry's meeting with Calixtus II just afterward near Gisors, quotes the king as saying that he had offered Clito authority over three English counties and a place at his court where he might learn the art of government. Henry alleged that he would have favored his nephew as a son, or so Orderic tells us.[135] But Clito rejected the offer

---

[130] OV, 6:256–264; cf. SD, 2:254–256; *Liber de Hyda*, p. 310.
[131] Calixtus was also related to Henry I, although more distantly: Calixtus' grandmother Adeliza was a sister of Duke Robert I of Normandy, Henry I's grandfather.
[132] OV, 6:276–280.
[133] Ibid., pp. 236–242; *CP*, 11, app. D, p. 117.
[134] "Chron. de Hida," in *Liber de Hyda*, pp. 320–321.
[135] OV, 6:288.

out of respect for his captive father (whom he cannot have remembered very clearly) and resumed his life as a landless wanderer in the company of Helias of Saint-Saens. Had he chosen to become an Anglo-Norman earl and courtier, the loss of the royal son and heir a year thereafter might well have deflected the succession to him—unless, of course, he had chosen to board the White Ship himself. But even in the best of circumstances, it would have been painful for Henry to offer the succession to the person against whose claims he had struggled so long. And there was always the hazard that, in theory at least, recognizing Clito's right to succeed might have cast doubt on Henry's right to rule. If Clito were the rightful heir, why should he not be the rightful king?[136]

Still another issue raised at the Council of Reims was that of the primatial authority of Canterbury over the archbishopric of York. On the eve of the council the two archbishops were at an impasse: Thurstan insisted on being consecrated without professing obedience to Canterbury; Ralph refused to consecrate Thurstan without the profession.[137] By October 1119 both Thurstan and Ralph had been in and out of King Henry's Norman court for quite some time. Henry, engaged as he was in a desperate struggle with Louis VI, Baldwin VII, Fulk V, rebellious *fideles*, and would-be assassins within his own household, must at times have regarded his contending archbishops as a pair of horseflies buzzing around the head of a gladiator fighting for his life. In December 1118, when Hugh the Chanter reports the exchange of icy words between Archbishops Ralph and Thurstan, Henry was suffering the greatest defeat of his career at Alençon.[138]

Archbishop Thurstan, a former comrade of Henry I's and a cleric with an attractive blend of holiness and sophistication, was a veteran of the royal chapel and brother of one of Henry's most ardent supporters in the Norman war, Audoin bishop of Evreux, "the Bearded One." It was also said that Thurstan alone among the Anglo-Norman episcopate enjoyed the affection of Louis VI.[139] This fact may cast light on Thurstan's otherwise mysterious reply in spring 1119 to Henry's entreaty that he return to England: "If I stay here until you also return," Thurstan responded, "I may be able to be of some use to you."[140]

Later in the year, after the victory at Brémule had bolstered his position in Normandy, Henry let Thurstan depart for the papal council at Reims. The Canterbury sources assert that Thurstan promised Henry that he would refuse papal consecration, whereas Hugh the Chanter

---

[136] Le Patourel, "The Norman Succession, 996–1135," p. 245.
[137] Above, pp. 235, 241–244.
[138] Hugh the Chanter, p. 100; OV, 6:206–208; above, p. 252 and n. 74.
[139] Hugh the Chanter, pp. 100, 108, 160.
[140] Ibid., p. 108.

denies it.[141] Whatever the case, Calixtus consecrated Thurstan at the beginning of the council, and Henry, angered by this act of blatant interference in the affairs of his Church, thereupon prohibited Thurstan's return to England or Normandy. Thurstan stayed with the papal court as it departed Reims and traveled through France.

Despite this dangerous conflict, so Hugh the Chanter asserts, Thurstan, almost from the moment of his consecration, began working through his friend Cardinal Cuno of Palestrina to arrange a treaty with France. For Henry ardently desired to crown his achievement of 1118–1119 with a definitive peace with all his former enemies and with their guarantee that William Adelin would succeed him.

Eadmer, chagrined by Thurstan's consecration without the profession to Canterbury, reported a widespread opinion that Thurstan "could never have presumed to behave as he did in so great a matter had he not noticed that the king was a willing party to it."[142] Some evidently believed that Henry and Thurstan had an understanding from the beginning, which is possible but unlikely. It is true that Thurstan's consecration was irrelevant to Henry's interests, though disastrous to Canterbury's, and that Henry's real advantage lay in appearing to back Canterbury stalwartly while availing himself of Thurstan's diplomatic talents. But in accepting papal consecration Thurstan was defying Henry's will, and even the most prudent of monarchs can lose their tempers on such occasions. There was also the realization that Calixtus II, in consecrating Thurstan against Henry's wishes, had knocked a gaping hole in the traditional Anglo-Norman "wall around England," proclaimed by William I, defended by Henry I, and avidly endorsed by Canterbury.[143] Indeed, in opposing unprecedented papal interference in Anglo-Norman ecclesiastical affairs, Henry was again, as in the investiture controversy, defending traditional royal customs and prerogatives against a new papal monarchy on the march.[144] In consecrating Thurstan, as in sponsoring legatine councils, the papacy was blazing new trails at the expense of royal autonomy within the Anglo-Norman dominions. Henry, in the role of resolute conservative pitted once more against the political aggressiveness of the Gregorian papacy, responded by banishing Thurstan.

---

[141] Ibid., pp. 112–114; Eadmer, *HN*, p. 255, followed by John of Worcester, p. 14.

[142] Eadmer, *HN*, p. 257; cf. Nicholl, *Thurstan*, p. 64.

[143] Eadmer, *HN*, p. 10, suggests that William was asserting royal rights against both the papacy and Canterbury; but see Brett, *English Church*, pp. 34–62.

[144] Again, these royal customs were first set forth explicitly by William I only because they had not been challenged by the weak, pre-Gregorian papacy in the days of the Anglo-Saxon kings. Edward the Confessor had sent a bishop and two abbots to Pope Leo IX's council of Reims in 1049, out of curiosity (*Councils and Synods*, 1: part 1, pp. 521–523), but that was the end of it.

Calixtus, despite this seeming impasse, perhaps swayed by Thurstan's urgings, met Henry near Gisors on 23 November 1119.[145] Thurstan at this point was clearly working hand in glove with Cardinal Cuno of Palestrina toward a reconciliation between the two kings. Although Cuno had earlier been at odds with Henry over the issue of Anglo-Norman prelates' attending legatine councils beyond the Norman frontiers, the two men had evidently become reconciled, at least to a degree, and Cuno had been a guest at Henry's metropolitan synod of Rouen in October 1118 where the cardinal appealed for Anglo-Norman support for the papacy in its struggle with Henry V and the antipope Gregory VIII.[146] The meeting between Henry and Calixtus was the first occasion since Cnut's reign that an English king had met a pope face to face. King Henry made his headquarters in the castle of Gisors, Calixtus stayed at Chaumont-en-Vexin, and they conferred at a church halfway between.[147] Neither English archbishop was present. The main topic, as Calixtus had promised, was peace between the French and the Anglo-Normans. The pope repeated the complaints brought against Henry by Louis at the Council of Reims, and Henry responded effectively (according to Orderic), running through the arguments that he and his supporters had made often before: that under Curthose's incompetent rule the Normans lived in anarchy and terror and their Church was tormented by unrestrained acts of violence, that Curthose was well treated in his castle-prison, that Henry had offered to honor, empower, and enrich William Clito, that he would urge Count Theobald to release William count of Nevers, and that, above all, Henry wanted peace with France. These arguments were effective because, by all indications, they were true. Calixtus accepted them, conveyed them to the French court, and continued working for peace. William of Malmesbury adds that the pope's admiration of the Anglo-Normans was enhanced by a display of dialectical skill by the late Robert of Meulan's teenaged twins, Waleran count of Meulan and Robert earl of Leicester, who debated with great effect against the Roman cardinals. The pope's good will was further nourished by Henry's generous gifts.[148]

Henry and Calixtus also discussed the ecclesiastical issues of papal legates and the Canterbury–York controversy but without reaching any resolution. Henry requested the pope's assurance that he would send

---

[145] Hugh the Chanter, pp. 126–132; OV, 6:282–290.

[146] Above, p. 240; OV, 6:202.

[147] The editors of *Councils and Synods*, 1: part 2, p. 721 n. 2, suggest, very plausibly, Trie-Château (arr. Beauvais).

[148] WM, *GR*, 2:482; OV, 6:282–290, corroborated in general by Hugh the Chanter, pp. 126–128; *Councils and Synods*, 1: part 2, pp. 721–722.

no future legates, but Calixtus gave no definite reply.[149] On the matter of Thurstan's consecration and Henry's response of banishing Thurstan from England, there was no resolution; the York writer Hugh the Chanter was obviously irritated that Henry and Calixtus, despite their impasse, had a most cordial meeting.[150] On its completion, Thurstan of necessity remained with the papal court as it continued to travel through France. In March 1120 Calixtus, on the verge of returning to Italy, granted Thurstan a papal bull permanently exempting archbishops of York from the profession to Canterbury and another bull threatening an interdict on England and the suspension of Archbishop Ralph unless the king readmitted Thurstan to his see. The two bulls, together, were the fulfillment of York's fondest dreams.

Shortly after the pope's departure for Italy, Thurstan visited Countess Adela of Blois and her son, Count Theobald II, Henry's nephew and military ally. Adela, Henry's favorite sister, was also Thurstan's spiritual daughter and one of the most astute politicians of her era. According to Hugh the Chanter's eyewitness report, Thurstan "did not entirely conceal from them what he had done and what he carried." News of the interdict threat reached Henry, but the papal letter itself was never presented to him; it was later preserved in the church of York as a memento of the victory.[151] Thereafter Thurstan avoided the company of Louis VI "out of prudence," because there was still strife between Louis and Henry.[152] But through the mediation of Cardinal Cuno the exiled archbishop is reported to have taken great pains to procure a peace between the two kings, "being the man on the Norman side in whom Louis had the most confidence."[153]

Thurstan's itinerary during the weeks following his visit to Adela suggests shuttle diplomacy. He immediately sought out Cardinal Cuno, then returned to confer with the countess while Cuno spent Easter (18 April) with Louis VI at Senlis. Two days after Easter, Thurstan again met with Cuno at Dammartin and then returned to Adela to help arrange for her entry into religious life, while at the same time contacting Henry through messengers.[154] A meeting was then arranged between Cuno and Henry on 30 May at Henry's castle of Vernon on the Norman frontier, where Henry agreed to restore Thurstan to York provided that the archbishop would delay his return until Henry had squared matters with Canterbury.[155] Shortly thereafter the peace between Henry and

---

[149] Eadmer, *HN*, p. 258; Brett, *English Church*, p. 40.
[150] Hugh the Chanter, pp. 126–132.
[151] Ibid., pp. 152, 154–156.
[152] Ibid., p. 152.
[153] Ibid., p. 160.
[154] Ibid., p. 154.
[155] Ibid., pp. 158–160.

Louis was ratified. Symeon of Durham agreed with Hugh the Chanter that Thurstan had played the central role in the negotiations.[156] Perhaps the papal interdict, leaked but never delivered, was not intended as a serious threat (for Calixtus, battling with the emperor and his antipope, would not lightly forgo Henry's support) but as a shield with which Henry could—and did—deflect the wrath of Canterbury when he permitted Thurstan to assume his archbishopric without the profession.[157] As the Anglo-Saxon chronicler observed, "Archbishop Thurstan was reconciled to the king through the pope, and came into this country and received his bishopric, though it was very displeasing to the archbishop of Canterbury."[158] It also seems unlikely that a person as deeply involved in the politics of her age as Adela of Blois would have taken the veil until the terms of a mutually accepted peace between her son, her brother, and the king of France had been arranged.[159]

With the approach of peace, it is useful to look back on the preceding years of warfare and draw what conclusions one can. First, the fact that William Clito remained alive and at large gave Henry's enemies, both internal and external, the unique advantage of a plausible rival to support. Second, during these times of crisis, bonds of fealty proved surprisingly fragile as former oath-bound *fideles*—William Crispin, Eustace of Breteuil, Hugh of Gournay, Robert of Neubourg, Amaury de Montfort—changed loyalties in accordance with their personal advantages and impulses. Third, the geographical patterns of rebellion within Normandy leave no doubt that domestic uprisings were tightly linked to and made possible by the hostilities of external principalities; thus, the northeastern Norman rebellions ceased when Flanders withdrew, those of southern Normandy died out when Henry reached an accommodation with Anjou, and the cessation of French attacks ended hostilities among rebellious barons in the east. Finally, the months of invasion and rebellion make amply clear the ghastly consequences of medieval warfare (burned fields, villages, and cities, kidnapped or murdered peasant families) and show with even greater

---

[156] SD, 2:258; cf. WM, *GR*, 2:496: "Veruntamen tam splendidae et excogitatae pacis serenum, tam omnium spes in speculam erectas, confudit humanae sortis varietas."

[157] At Christmas 1120 Henry explained to Archbishop Ralph and his suffragan bishops the consequences of not readmitting Thurstan: "Intelligens archiepiscopus sagittam hanc prius in se infigi, episcopi uero ignominiam regi reputantes in regno suo Christianitatem interdici, ut eum reuocaret et concesserunt et consiliati sunt". Hugh the Chanter, p. 164.

[158] *ASC, s.a* 1120.

[159] WM, *GR*, 2:496: Louis shortly afterward conceded legal possession of Normandy to William Adelin and accepted his homage "enimvero socero tunc annitente, simulque Thetbaldo filio Stephani et Adalae."

clarity the reasons why the majority of Henry I's subjects appreciated so deeply the peace that he maintained throughout most of the years of his reign. The wars of 1118–1119 seriously afflicted only the outer reaches of Normandy and for only about fifteen months. For Henry's remaining years the agrarian economy in by far the greater part of the duchy flourished undisturbed and its inhabitants lived, worked, and prayed in safety.

In mid-1120 Louis agreed to a peace with Henry. The formalities took place at an unrecorded point on the Franco-Norman frontier some-time between 30 May and 29 September 1120 (probably in June). The terms were essentially those that Henry had offered Louis in 1115 before the war commenced. Persuaded by Henry's military triumphs as well as his money, Louis VI granted Normandy to William Adelin to be held of him, and William did homage to Louis, "just as Rollo, the first duke of Normandy, had promised in perpetual right."[160] One must not permit the subsequent catastrophe of the White Ship to obscure the fact that the peace of 1120 was a dazzling diplomatic triumph for Henry I. It held the promise of ensuring peace between the two monarchies for the next generation.

The most striking aspect of the peace of 1120 is that Henry had managed to win the full benefit of Louis VI's lordship while eluding the responsibility and embarrassment of personal vassalage. The solution was attractive, if not thoroughly logical, and served as the chief precedent for future acts of homage—of King Stephen's son Eustace to Louis VI in 1137 and to Louis VII in 1140, and of Henry, son of David king of Scots, to King Stephen in 1136.[161] When William Adelin "received Normandy" from Louis VI, did he thereby become "duke," or coruler with his father, or was his status in the duchy merely nominal? The question is important in understanding the full significance of the 1120 homage, but the answer is not easily found. William's name appears in no extant charter that can be dated securely within the brief period between the peace of mid-1120 and the death of the young prince on 25 November of that year in the wreck of the White Ship. The Hyde writer speaks of Henry's desire to relinquish the realm

---

[160] "Ex Anonymi Blandinensis appencicula ad Sigbertum," *HF*, 14:16: "sicut Rollo primus Normanniae dux jure perpetuo promiserat." See also Hugh the Chanter, pp. 158–160, reporting the meeting between Cardinal Cuno and Henry I at Vernon on 30 May and adding that the peace between Louis VI and Henry I was concluded *non longo post tempore*, thanks largely to Thurstan's mediation; cf. *Liber de Hyda*, p. 319, mentioning Henry's concession of an annuity to Louis VI from the English royal revenues; see further WM, *GR*, 2:496; SD, 2:258.

[161] HH, p. 706; OV, 5:81; *MMI*, p. 42 n. 140.

to his son, and the Winchester annalist goes so far as to say that at the time of the homage to Louis, William received Normandy by his father's grant.[162] But this last phrase cannot be interpreted strictly without corroborative evidence, and there is none. Much more valuable is the evidence of Hugh the Chanter, who was in Normandy in 1120 and was closely involved in the high politics of the period. Hugh calls William Adelin, in the closing days of his life, *rex et dux designatus*.[163] The possibility that this term may have been an official title is suggested by William's attestation of a royal charter of June 1119 as *Dei gratia rex designatus*, at a time when he had not yet received Normandy from Louis but had previously been named Henry's heir to the kingdom of England.[164] One might seek an analogy in Eustace, son of King Stephen, who in 1137 did homage for Normandy to Louis VI as a part of a treaty that Stephen concluded with Louis "on the same terms" as Henry I had done.[165] Eustace lived on for some years, ultimately acquiring the county of Boulogne and adopting the comital style, but he played no significant role in the governance of either Normandy or England and was never styled *dux Normannorum* or even *dux designatus*.[166] Conversely, sometime between 1098 and 1100 the future Louis VI was associated with his father on the throne and titled *rex designatus*, after which time he used the title regularly and took a vigorous part in the royal governance, whether jointly with his father or on his own initiative.[167]

But one cannot safely equate Capetian with Anglo-Norman customs, nor can one define the position of a *designatus* without taking into account the relative age, vigor, or ambition of father and son. Eustace was a child when he did homage to Louis VI, and a few years later King Stephen had lost the province of Normandy to Geoffrey count of Anjou. Louis became *rex designatus* at about seventeen or eighteen and continued in that capacity for nearly a decade while his father slipped into an early dotage. At the peace of 1120 William Adelin was probably nearing eighteen, while Henry I was a vigorous fifty-one and apparently not in the least prepared to relinquish his control of Normandy or England. At some time after the meeting with Louis Henry arranged

---

[162] *Liber de Hyda*, p. 319; *Ann. Wint.*, p. 46.

[163] Hugh the Chanter, p. 99, cf. p. 97: Hugh was in Normandy and France in the company of Archbishop Thurstan; both were at Vernon on 30 May.

[164] *RRAN* 2, no. 1204 (Rouen, 1119, ?June); *ASC*, *s.a.* 1115; Eadmer, *HN*, p. 237.

[165] HH, p. 708; OV, 5:81; Orderic mistakenly has Louis grant Normandy directly to Stephen "sicut antecessor ejus tenuerat."

[166] Eustace is normally *filius regis* or *comes* (of Boulogne); *RRAN* 3, no. 921, is attested by *Eustachio filio et herede meo*; Stephen subsequently tried without success to have Eustace crowned.

[167] Luchaire, *Louis VI*, nos 4–55 *passim* and pp. 289–293; on the use of the term *rex designatus* in Norman Sicily see Ménager, "L'Institution monarchique," p. 448.

for William to receive renewed oaths from the Norman barons,[168] but charter evidence makes it clear that on the eve of the White Ship disaster William had no real authority. In a charter of 1119–1120 Henry and his son jointly grant Norman lands to the bishop of Angers (William having just been wed to Matilda of Anjou), and in 1120 William concurs in Henry's confirmation of a benefaction to an English Tironian house.[169] But Henry I remained very much in control. On 21 November 1120, at the Norman embarkation port of Barfleur, Henry convoked a council "of my bishops and barons," at which time a charter was issued confirming the lands and privileges of the great west Norman abbey of Cérisy-la-Forêt. The confirmation was granted neither by William Adelin, nor by William and his father jointly, but by the king alone—by *Henricus rex Anglorum*.[170] What titles and authority William might subsequently have received we cannot know. But when his White Ship set off from Barfleur he was still a mere *designatus*; his father remained master of the Anglo-Norman state. And that being true, the significance of the 1120 homage becomes clear: it bound the king of France to Henry's succession plan without binding the lord of Normandy to the king of France.

On the early evening of 25 November 1120 Henry sailed with his fleet out of Barfleur for a triumphant return to England. After more than four years of arduous struggle in Normandy, he had achieved a "brilliant and carefully crafted peace."[171] It was late in the year for a major Channel crossing, but not dangerously so; the evening was clear, fair, and moonless, and a southerly breeze blew across the water.[172]

Orderic tells the plausible story that a certain Thomas son of Stephen approached Henry on the eve of his departure with the assertion that Stephen son of Alrard, his father, had piloted William the Conqueror's ship across the Channel in 1066. Thomas asked that Henry cross to England in his newly refitted vessel, the White Ship, and Henry, declining the offer but thanking the captain, agreed to entrust his

---

[168] *Ann. Wint.*, p. 46; SD, 2:258.

[169] *RRAN* 2, nos 1204a, 1223. William had previously served briefly and nominally as regent in England between Queen Matilda's death in May 1118 and his own departure for Normandy a year later to join his father; the actual work of government was performed by seasoned royal administrators: nos 1189, 1191–1192, 1201–1202.

[170] *Monasticon*, 6:1075 (*RRAN* 2, no. 1233).

[171] WM, *GR*, 2:496.

[172] Le Patourel, *Norman Empire*, pp. 175–176; William I and William II had each crossed in December, but none of Henry I's other crossings occurred later than September. On the weather, see OV, 6:296–298; Orderic wrongly reports that the moon was full: ibid., p. 299 n. 1.

sons, William Adelin and Richard, to the White Ship. Richard, a hero of the recent wars, was now lord of Breteuil, having recently married its heiress, but he traveled without his new wife aboard the White Ship, as did William Adelin, whose bride Matilda of Anjou crossed in another vessel.[173]

William Adelin and Richard were joined by a jubilant, high-spirited band of young noblemen and noblewomen: Henry's natural daughter Matilda countess of Perche (unaccompanied by her husband Count Rotrou), Richard earl of Chester and his wife Matilda of Blois, along with his tutor and half-brother Othuer son of the late Count Hugh, the now-celebrated hero Ralph the Red of Pont-Echanfray who awaited lavish rewards in England, the two sons of the long-departed Ivo of Grandmesnil who also anticipated significant benefactions on their return, and a number of important officials of the royal household along with the king's treasure. Altogether, Orderic estimates, the White Ship carried some three hundred passengers and crewmen.

There were also casks of wine aboard, which William Adelin gave to the sailors at their request and of which everyone partook amply. Indeed, passengers and crew alike were exuberantly inebriated, so much so that Count Stephen of Blois and several companions disembarked, realizing "that there was too great a crowd of wild and headstrong young men aboard." Count Stephen, moreover, was suffering from diarrhea and was not in a festive mood; his diarrhea probably determined the history of England during the nineteen years between 1135 and 1154.[174] As Thomas son of Stephen set out from the dock at Barfleur, his riotous passengers urged him and his rowers to overtake the king's fleet, which was already out in the open sea. The rowers, tipsy from their wine, made the ship leap forward and race through the harbor, and the helmsman, just as drunk as they were, paid scant attention to his steering. Consequently, the port side of the ship crashed against a large rock that lay hidden beneath the sea by the high tide and the ship capsized, sending to their deaths the heir to the English throne and his many companions among the high nobility— and bringing to ruin King Henry's peace of 1120. The peace had hinged on William Adelin's marriage to Matilda of Anjou and on his homage to Louis VI. With William Adelin gone, the alliances with both Anjou and France were severed and there was no obvious heir to Henry's throne.[175]

---

[173] OV, 6:296.

[174] Ibid.

[175] OV, 6:296, and WM, *GR*, 2:496–498, both agree that the passengers and crew were drunk. For other accounts of this celebrated and long-remembered disaster, see SD, 2:259; Eadmer, *HN*, pp. 288–289; HH, pp. 466, 594; Hugh the Chanter, p. 164.

From the top of the lighthouse that now stands on the cliff at Barfleur, the rock that the White Ship struck is clearly visible, even at high tide, as a brown shadow just beneath the surface of the water. But on the moonless night of 25 November 1120, the rock would have been invisible. And the pilot and rowers were evidently too inebriated to remember its location.

The wreck of the White Ship was the most catastrophic maritime disaster of the Middle Ages. The destruction of the new ship, carrying a plethora of the rich and famous of their time, is reminiscent of the sinking of the *Titanic*, except that some of the passengers of the *Titanic* survived whereas the only survivor of the White Ship was a butcher of Rouen named Burold, who clung to a spar throughout much of the night. Burold is thought to be the source of several stories about the last moments of the disaster, all of them probably apocryphal.[176] Moreover, the White Ship passengers constituted a much greater proportion of the ruling class of their period than did those aboard the *Titanic* and included, of course, the single plausible heir to the kingdom. As William of Malmesbury expressed it,

Many regions looked forward to the governance of this boy, for it was supposed that King Edward the Confessor's prediction would be consummated in him. It was said that now might it be expected that England's hopes, like the tree cut down, would, through this young man, again blossom and produce fruit, and thus put an end to her woes; but God saw otherwise.[177]

On the first day after his return to England, Henry was kept in ignorance of the disaster. Nobody dared tell him. As Orderic says, "The magnates wept bitterly in private and mourned inconsolably for their beloved kinfolk and friends, but in the king's presence they struggled to restrain their tears."[178] But on the next day Count Theobald, who had accompanied the king on his return to England, had a young boy throw himself weeping at the king's feet and tell him of the catastrophe. "Immediately Henry fell to the ground, overcome with anguish."[179] He would have seen all his hopes for peace falling in ruins. Most painful of all, perhaps, was the consuming grief that a father feels for the

---

[176] William Adelin is said to have perished in his brave attempt to save his sister Matilda of Perche from drowning, and Thomas son of Stephen, on hearing that William Adelin had drowned, is reported to have deliberately drowned himself in fear of the king's wrath: WM, *GR*, 2:496–497; OV, 6:298.

[177] WM, *GR*, 2:495–496.

[178] OV, 6:300.

[179] Ibid.

sudden, accidental death of a beloved and promising son about to enter his adulthood.

If Henry was, as the Welsh chronicler declared, "the man against whom no one could prevail except God himself," it could perhaps be concluded that God, in a singularly cruel and capricious mood, had prevailed indeed.[180]

[180] *Brut*, trans. Jones, p. 42.

Chapter 7

THE LAST BATTLES

In various ways the calamity of the White Ship cast its shadow into the future. Much of Henry I's political activity during the years that followed was shaped, directly or indirectly, by that single disaster. The death of William Adelin made it vital that the king remarry and produce another son. For as matters now stood, William Clito was the most plausible heir to Henry's throne, and Henry had fought long and determinedly to thwart his succession. On Epiphany (6 January) 1121, having taken counsel with a large assemblage of his prelates and barons at London, Henry announced that he would marry Adeliza, daughter of Godfrey VII "the Bearded," count of Louvain and duke of Lower Lorraine.[1] Negotiations for the marriage may have commenced before the White Ship disaster; if so, William Adelin's death would have intensified the urgency of the marriage and probably hastened it. From London Henry dispatched a delegation to Dover to meet Adeliza and escort her to Windsor, his favorite castle, where, on Friday 29 January, they were married in an imposing ceremony before a great crowd of Anglo-Norman notables.[2]

The festivities were marred by an embarrassing dispute regarding the primatial rights of Archbishop Ralph d'Escures. In earlier, happier times the archbishop of Canterbury had been described as witty and genial, but by now, having suffered a protracted illness and a long and luckless conflict with York, he had become decidedly querulous. Although prevented by a speech impediment from performing the wedding ceremony, Ralph was too proud and stubborn to relinquish his traditional right to do so. Roger of Salisbury, as diocesan bishop, claimed the privilege of acting in his place, but Ralph insisted on choosing his own deputy and appointed William Giffard bishop of Winchester to do the honors.

Having won his point, Ralph next had an altercation with Henry I. The king had placed the royal crown on his own head before

---

[1] JW, p. 15; *RRAN* 2, nos 1241–1245; Leyser, *Communications and Power*, pp. 97–98 and n. 2.

[2] JW, p. 16, for the date; Adeliza was evidently on her way to England at Henry's invitation when he took counsel with his great men. See also OV, 6:308; SD, 2:259; *RRAN* 2, nos 1247–1253.

entering the hall the following day—either absent-mindedly or
in deference to Ralph's illness. The archbishop was enraged and
demanded that the crown be removed immediately. Since Henry
had no objection (and doubtless wished to avoid a scene), he complied
with good cheer. Ralph took the crown and then grudgingly placed
it back on Henry's head himself. The archbishop then exercised his
right of personally consecrating and crowning the new queen.[3]

Several sources agree that Adeliza was a beautiful woman and
that Henry was drawn to her for that reason.[4] She had the further
advantage of being the daughter of a major prince whose dominions were strategically situated between Flanders and northwestern Germany. Moreover, she was a young woman (*puella*) in
her early child-bearing years, and as a descendant of Charlemagne
in the male line she was of sufficient nobility to be a fitting consort
for a king. She brought no land to the marriage, but neither had
Edith-Matilda—and land was not one of Henry's pressing needs at
the moment. Adeliza was nubile, intelligent, good-natured, and
fond of her royal husband. She is reported by Geoffrey Gaimar
to have commissioned a poet named David (otherwise unidentified)
to write a rhymed vernacular chronicle celebrating Henry I. Had
it survived it would have been the first known poem in the French
language.[5]

One distinguished guest at the Windsor court, Thurstan of York,
showed up a few days late for the wedding. While in Rouen, Thurstan
had received Henry's official permission to return to England. He
crossed the Channel on 31 January and went directly to Windsor where
he was warmly received by Henry and his new queen and many
others at court—although not by Archbishop Ralph.[6] A few days
later Thurstan continued on to York, where he is said to have been
greeted by an elated crowd and to have read aloud the papal privilege
restoring him to his archiepiscopal throne.[7] At a great Pentecost
court at Westminster (29 May), Henry and Adeliza were crowned for
a second time by Archbishop Ralph—without unseemly incident as far
as we know.[8]

---

[3] Eadmer, *HN*, pp. 290, 293; Brett, *English Church*, pp. 69–70.

[4] HH, pp. 464–466; *ASC, s.a.* 1121; JW, p. 15; Eadmer, *HN*, p. 296.

[5] Wertheimer, "Adeliza of Louvain"; John Horace Round's biographical sketch of
Adeliza in the *DNB*, 1:137–138, will be superseded by Lois L. Huneycutt's sketch
in the *New DNB* (forthcoming). On David's poem see Short, ed., "Gaimar's 'Epilogue'," ll. 6481–6501, p. 325, and Ian Short's valuable remarks in ibid., p. 326.

[6] Hugh the Chanter, pp. 164–166; Eadmer, *HN*, pp. 291–292. In the Anglo-Saxon
chronicler's words (*s.a.* 1120), Thurstan's reinstatement was "very displeasing" to
the archbishop of Canterbury.

[7] Hugh the Chanter, p. 166.

[8] HH, p. 469; *ASC, s.a.* 1121; *RRAN* 2, no. 1292.

Henry was soon obliged to repair another piece of damage to his realm resulting from the wreck of the White Ship. A kin-group of Welsh princes who ruled Powys in north-central Wales, having heard that Richard earl of Chester had drowned, burst into two of his castles, slaughtered many of his people, and pillaged his lands. The princes who joined in this onslaught were Maredudd ap Bleddyn and three of his nephews, the sons of Cadwgan ap Bleddyn. King Henry, who had long been endeavoring to curb such behavior throughout his dominions, led a large army into north Wales in June.[9] In the course of the campaign Henry's army was attacked by a band of Maredudd's young archers, who killed some of the Anglo-Norman warriors, wounded others, and struck Henry I himself with an arrow, which was deflected by his armor and ricocheted harmlessly away. Once again Henry had avoided death in battle, but, although frightened, he ordered his army to pitch their tents, parleyed with the archers, and arranged a peaceful meeting with Maredudd ap Bleddyn. Surprised by Henry's affable behavior and overawed by the size of his army, Maredudd and his kinsmen made peace, and they did so on terms that were, as before in 1114, heavily in Henry's favor. The Welsh gave Henry gifts, hostages, and a tribute of some ten thousand head of cattle. On their promise of good behavior Henry led his army home from Wales, once more triumphant.[10] Never again did he have occasion to return.

Henry's grief at the death of his son was also a major motive for the foundation of the great abbey of Reading. The king established the monastery in 1121 and enriched it on an immensely generous scale, comparable to that of William the Conqueror's Battle Abbey.[11] From the beginning and for generations its monks followed the Cluniac observance. The founding monks, some from Cluny, others from the Cluniac priory of Lewes in Sussex, settled at Reading on 18 June 1121. During its first twenty-two months the foundation seems to have been a Cluniac dependency and was ruled by an obscure prior named Peter, who had been sent from Cluny at Henry I's request. But on 18 April 1123 Reading became an independent abbey under Hugh of Amiens, the abbey's first abbot and

---

[9] SD, 2:263; *ASC, s.a.* 1121.

[10] SD, 2:263; *Brut,* trans. Jones, pp. 47–48; *Annales Cambriae,* p. 37. Henry's narrow escape from an arrow while marching into Wales is retold in slightly garbled form in WM, *GR,* 2:477–478.

[11] *Reading Abbey Cartularies,* 1:13–22, 33–36, 129; *RRAN* 2, nos 1238, 1418, 1423, 1427. On the foundation of Reading, see Stafford, *"Cherchez la femme."*

Henry's good friend. Hugh had entered religious life as a monk of Cluny and had served as prior of Limoges from around 1115 and prior of Lewes between 1120 and 1123. Seven years later Henry appointed Hugh to the archbishopric of Rouen.[12]

Henry was very much in charge of the process by which the new abbey was established. For its endowment, he combined the manors and churches that had once belonged to three long-defunct Anglo-Saxon religious houses—Leominster, Cholsey, and an earlier Reading—along with additional lands and churches. Most of the properties in question had been absorbed long before into the royal demesne. Some of them, however, had passed into the hands of other Anglo-Norman abbeys and Henry made careful arrangements to have them exchanged for equivalent possessions elsewhere. In one such transaction, for example, Henry named various estates and incomes in Sussex that he was granting to Battle Abbey in exchange for its properties at Reading.[13] Similarly, Henry arranged for Mont-Saint-Michel to cede to Reading Abbey the churches of Cholsey and Wargrave (a few miles northwest and northeast of Reading respectively) in exchange for lands in Devon.[14] Reading Abbey's extensive possessions, enumerated in Henry I's foundation charter of 1125, were to enjoy immunities and liberties of unsurpassed scope, including freedom from shire and hundred exactions, gelds, aids, and all customs. Henry I even granted his abbey its own mint and moneyer in London and, a few years later, a four-day fair at Reading.[15] The abbey also acquired an impressive relic collection, which continued to grow throughout the twelfth century and beyond. The most celebrated relic of all was the hand of St James the Apostle, which the empress Maud brought from Germany in 1125 and which was donated to

---

[12] Knowles et al., *Heads of Religious Houses*, p. 74; *RRAN* 2, no. 1427; *Reading Abbey Cartularies*, 1:14–15, 25–26. Reading received a confirmation charter from Pope Calixtus II dated 19 June 1123 and an official foundation charter from Henry I dated 1125: ibid., vol. 1, nos 139, 1.

[13] *Reading Abbey Cartularies*, 1:16–17 and no. 1 (*RRAN* 2, no. 1427); *RRAN* 2, no. 1238, an interpolated version, purportedly issued at Portsmouth, of what is probably a lost original relating to the exchange for Battle's holdings in Reading: the two addressees in the *Regesta* text, Ralph bishop of Chichester and William fitz Ansger, died in 1123 and *ante* 1122 respectively, and for this and other reasons the *Regesta* editors date it Nov.–Dec. 1120; but the charter also alludes to a later transaction that cannot antedate 1129; *Chron. Battle*, pp. 122–124 and 124 n. 1 (cf. *RRAN* 2, no. 1650, and *Ancient Charters*, no. 15, pp. 17–18).

[14] *RRAN* 2, no. 1418, and pp. 350–351; *Reading Abbey Cartularies*, 1:39.

[15] *Reading Abbey Cartularies*, 1:18 and nos 1, 7, and 8; *RRAN* 2:xxv and nos 1472, 1864.

Reading, almost certainly by Henry I sometime between 1126 and 1133.[16]

The king set the general direction of religious life at Reading. It was Henry who determined that his new foundation would follow the customs of Cluny. He was an admirer and benefactor of the Cluniac order, and one of his favorite nephews, Henry of Blois, was a Cluniac monk (whom Henry I would appoint abbot of Glastonbury in 1126 and bishop of Winchester in 1129). Indeed, King Henry contributed decisively to the building of the great Burgundian abbey church, Cluny III, whose vast dimensions and splendid sculpture and frescoes made it the largest and most impressive church in Christendom and whose pointed nave arches constituted a significant early step toward the development of the Gothic style.[17] Along with its majestic architecture, Cluny

[16] Leyser, "Frederick Barbarossa, Henry II and the Hand of St James," in *Medieval Germany and Its Neighbours*, pp. 225–231; by the late twelfth century the abbey's collection included 29 relics of Christ, 6 of the Virgin Mary, 19 of the Old Testament prophets, and 14 of the apostles.

[17] The two major contributors to the building of Cluny III were King Alfonso VI of Leon-Castile and Henry I: *Letters of Peter the Venerable*, 1: no. 89; see Peter the Venerable's eulogy celebrating Henry I and his unparalleled contributions to the building of Cluny III, in Dietrich Lohrmann, "Pierre le Vénérable," p. 191; cf. ibid., pp. 191–203; Conant, *Cluny*, pp. 80–82. Exactly which of the two kings was responsible for the construction of which portions of the great church remains unclear because we lack precise evidence on the time schedule of the royal contributions, the amounts contributed, and the exact timetable of construction. We know that the building of Cluny III commenced about 1084/1086 and proceeded from east to west until the early 1120s, when the great nave was largely completed. In 1125 the nave vaulting collapsed (probably bringing down all or part of the nave walls): thus, OV, 6:314; Map, *De nugis curialium*, pp. 436–438; the necessity of rebuilding after this disaster delayed the dedication of Cluny III (by Pope Innocent II) until late October 1130: see Conant, *Cluny*, pp. 82–97, for a tentative schedule of the phases of construction. The chief designer of the abbey, Hugh abbot of Cluny, and its first major donor, Alfonso VI, both died in 1109, and it has been hypothesized, not unreasonably, that Henry I was thereafter its foremost benefactor: ibid., p. 99: Conant suggests that Henry's support may have commenced ca. 1110; similarly, Brooke and Mynors, in Map, *De nugis curialium*, pp. 436–437 n. 4; see Brooke, "Princes and Kings as Patrons of Monasteries," p. 138, where Brooke remarks, "This is a remarkable fact, since it must have involved liberating resources on a massive scale for Henry to be remembered as one of the chief builders of this immensely costly church." And although there is no decisive evidence that Henry's benefactions commenced as early as 1109, it is possible, conversely, that they began even earlier (though surely not before 1106, when Henry was preoccupied elsewhere). According to the late testimony of Walter Map (ca. 1180s) Alfonso VI, having turned miserly in his later years, discontinued his patronage well before his death, at a point when he had brought the foundations of the church (nave?) barely to ground level, whereupon Henry I began underwriting the building program and continued his support until its completion, including the work of reconstruction after the collapse of the vaulting: *De nugis curialium*, p. 436; this account receives some support from indications that King Alfonso's finances were in fragile condi-

remained in the 1120s, as it had been for generations, a religious community widely admired for its moral rectitude and devotion to ecclesiastical reform.[18] It was very likely this distinctive combination of magnificence and piety that prompted Henry to choose Cluny as the model for his new foundation. At this point in his life, he was quite prepared to give his unstinted support to most of the current tenets of monastic reform. Yet he also regarded Reading as a monument to his Anglo-Norman royal predecessors, including his dead son William.[19] Indeed, Henry intended Reading to be his own mausoleum.[20] In

tion during his later years, forcing him at times to suspend his annual payments to Cluny: Reilly, *The Kingdom of Leon-Castilla*, pp. 211–212, 219, 376. The scale of the building funds supplied by the two kings cannot be compared because we have no record of Henry's contributions; we do have Henry's charter granting the community of Cluny £100 a year in perpetuity (£60 from the king's farm of London and £40 from the farm of Lincoln: *RRAN* 2, no. 1691), but this grant cannot have been intended to support major construction because the charter is dated 1131, the year after the dedication of Cluny III; Walter Map, who was aware of Henry's annual gift of £100, explains that it was intended for the upkeep of the church building: *De nugis curialium*, p. 438. As for Henry's support of the construction itself, we know only that it was very generous. Thus, Walter Map credits Henry with building and completing from its foundations "a work of marvelous greatness": ibid., pp. 436–438; according to Robert of Torigny, "He had built at great part at his own expense the church of Cluny": *GND*, 2:254; and an inscription near the sacristy of Cluny III itself coupled the names of St Hugh, the designer of the church, with the person whom the Cluniacs remembered as its chief benefactor: "Constructore Sancto Hugone, favente Henrico I Anglorum rege" (Conant, *Cluny*, p. 99, with the author's comment, "On oublie Alfonse VI ici").

Given the several variables and imponderables reviewed above, the likeliest hypothesis is the account furnished by Walter Map which, if we allow for some exaggeration and substitute "nave" for "church," provides a coherent sequence of events and accords with our other evidence. Henry would thus have been primarily responsible for underwriting the construction and subsequent rebuilding of the great nave, perhaps even *a fundamentis* as Walter Map boasts. See especially the discussion in chapter 10 below, pp. 413–33. [CWH wrote this long note before he started work on chapter 10. Had he lived, he would perhaps have shortened this note and incorporated the information into that chapter—ACF.]

[18] Cluny continued to flourish during the 1120s despite an unsavory quarrel between Abbot Pons, who resigned in 1122 but attempted unsuccessfully to recover his office in 1125, and his successor, Abbot Peter the Venerable (1122–1157). The conflict is interpreted by current scholars as, in part, a struggle between traditional Cluniac monasticism (Pons) and new ideas of monastic reform (Peter). Another conflict, relatively short-lived, pitted Peter the Venerable against St Bernard and his advocacy of Cistercian reform ideas. These reforms were in fact by no means unattractive to Peter, who introduced many of them into the customs of Cluny and who, apart from this one clash, enjoyed a cordial relationship with Bernard: see now Lawrence, *Medieval Monasticism*, pp. 108, 193–196 with references.

[19] *Reading Abbey Cartularies*, 1: no. 1.

[20] Ibid., p. 14. There is no direct or strictly contemporary evidence that Henry planned to be entombed at Reading. But it is a reasonable inference from the

accordance with the ethos of Cluny, the aura of holiness surrounding his new abbey would be accompanied by a dignity and splendor befitting the majesty of the royal family.

Henry's foundation charter for Reading, in Professor Brian Kemp's words, "reads like a programme of contemporary monastic reform in a Black Monk context."[21] Many of its provisions, probably suggested by Hugh of Amiens, echo reform ideas that were being instituted or contemplated just then at Cluny itself. Thus, the terms of Henry's charter set Reading apart from the greater English abbeys of pre-Conquest origin in a variety of ways. Reading, for example, held its properties by free alms tenure rather than by knights service and, indeed, was forbidden to create knights fees on its lands. The abbot and monks were to hold the abbey's property in common, not divide it between them. During abbatial vacancies the monastic property was to be administered by the prior and monks, not by royal agents for the king's profit. New abbots were to be chosen by the free election of the monks, not by the mandate of the king or an ecclesiastical superior. Offices of the abbey and its possessions were not to be hereditary but subject to appointment and dismissal by the abbot and monks. The abbot was not to grant monastic lands to his kinspeople. And the traditional Benedictine custom of accepting and educating child oblates was forbidden; only consenting adults were to be admitted into the community.[22]

These and similar provisions reflected the views of up-to-date Benedictine reformers throughout contemporary Western Christendom. But Henry's foundation charter also imposed a special responsibility that was singular to Reading: to feed and shelter visitors, pilgrims, and the poor. Caring for such people is an obligation of all Benedictine abbeys, but for the abbot and monks of Reading the duty was expressed with singular force and was taken very seriously.[23] It testified to King Henry's charitable side and to his practical nature as well. For with its bustling road and river traffic, Reading was the ideal site for a great monastic community that specialized in offering hospitality and compassion to weary travelers. Situated between the

events following Henry's death in December 1135, in which a large and noble entourage, surely with the intention of honoring the king's wishes, accompanied his corpse on the arduous journey through wintry weather from his deathbed at Lyons-la-Forêt in east-central Normandy to Rouen, thence to Caen (where the company waited four weeks for a good wind), and finally across the Channel to Reading for his funeral and burial on 4 January 1136: OV, 6:448–450; *RRAN* 3:xxxix and nos 386–387, 591.

[21] *Reading Abbey Cartularies*, 1:18.

[22] Ibid., 1:18 and no. 1; oblates were just then passing out of fashion at Cluny itself and were prohibited by the new Cistercian order.

[23] Ibid., 1:13.

Thames and the Kennet, and at the fork of the great west road that carried all the traffic from London to the towns of the southwest, Reading was a singularly important crossroads for merchants, pilgrims, and other travelers.[24]

Even in its initial years Reading's hospitality was legendary. As William of Malmesbury expressed it, Henry I built the monastery

> in a place designed for the reception of nearly all those who might be traveling to the more populous towns of England, a place where he placed monks of the Cluniac order who are at this day a noble model of holiness and an example of tireless and admirable hospitality. Here may be seen what is peculiar to this place, for guests, arriving constantly, consume more than the residents themselves . . . May they endeavor, by God's grace, to continue living in virtue. I do not blush at praising men of holiness and admiring in others the excellence that I lack myself.[25]

In late October 1122, while Henry was touring northern England, he received the news that Archbishop Ralph d'Escures had died.[26] The king would have been made aware shortly afterward of a papal summons to the major prelates of all Christendom to attend a general council in Rome on 18 March 1123—known later as the First Lateran Council.[27] The pope's summons may have prodded Henry to unusually swift action, perhaps to avoid papal or conciliar criticism for permitting a long vacancy at Canterbury. Whatever the case, Henry summoned a council to meet at Gloucester on 2 February 1123 to elect a new archbishop.[28] The king may well have come to dread by now the tedious power struggles that accompanied the succession to either of the two English archbishoprics. The succession of 1123 was to be no exception. Indeed, the strife over the archiepiscopal election and consecration deprived the new archbishop of any hope of reaching Rome in time for Calixtus II's ecumenical council.

The prelates at Gloucester split into two contending blocs, one of them—the monastic party—headed by the Canterbury monks and enjoying a degree of support from many of the lay magnates; the other—the episcopal party—led by the chief curialist bishop, Roger

---

[24] Ibid., 1, nos 1, 224; Leyser, "Hand of St James," in *Medieval Germany and Its Neighbours*, pp. 228–229; WM, *GR*, 2:489; WM, *GP*, p. 193. The importance of Reading's location is well explained by Knowles, *Monastic Order*, p. 281.

[25] WM, *GR*, 2:489.

[26] SD, 2:267; Eadmer, *HN*, p. 302; JW, p. 17.

[27] Hugh the Chanter, p. 182; *Regesta pontificum romanorum*, 1:809–811; Robert, *Calixte II*, pp. 162–177; *Councils and Synods*, 1: part 2, pp. 728–730.

[28] ASC, *s.a.* 1123; Hugh the Chanter, pp. 182–184.

of Salisbury, who had been supported by Robert Bloet bishop of Lincoln until his death a few weeks before the Gloucester council. The great difficulty was that the Canterbury monks claimed the right to elect the archbishop because he headed their monastic community, whereas the bishops made the same claim because the archbishop was their own superior as well, to whom they professed obedience. The Canterbury faction insisted that the new archbishop be a monk, as all previous archbishops had been. The bishops refused to continue being ruled by a monk and demanded that a secular clerk be elected. Henry sided with the bishops, doubtless because they played a far greater role than the Canterbury monks in the governance of the kingdom and because of the influence of Roger bishop of Salisbury. The monks could indeed choose their archbishop, but only from a short list provided by the bishops—which, predictably, included no monks. The Canterbury monks held firm for two days in refusing this "compromise," but at length they submitted to the royal will and elected a well-regarded regular canon, William of Corbeil, prior of the Augustinian house of St Osyth and something of a religious reformer.[29]

There next arose the question of William of Corbeil's consecration. Archbishop Thurstan agreed to consecrate him in accordance with the ancient custom that one of the two archbishops would normally consecrate the other. But William, adapting quickly to the Canterbury style, refused Thurstan's offer unless Thurstan agreed to acknowledge in the course of the ceremony that William was primate of the whole of Britain. Thurstan refused, and his followers resorted to harsh words. William responded by having himself consecrated by his own vicar and senior suffragan, Richard bishop of London, along with other Canterbury suffragans.[30]

The two archbishops then set out for Rome (mid-March 1123) in tardy but obedient response to the summons to the papal council. Even though they traveled in separate entourages, they remained on tolerable terms with one another. Arriving in Rome much too late for the council but three days ahead of William and the Canterbury group, Thurstan and his entourage were warmly and affectionately welcomed by the pope and his court. The company from Canterbury, however, received a wintry reception. Pope Calixtus, who had serious doubts about the validity of William of Corbeil's election and consecration, kept the archbishop waiting for a week or more before granting him

[29] *Councils and Synods*, 1: part 2, pp. 726–727; *ASC*, *s.a.* 1123; Bethell, "English Black Monks," pp. 674–681; Leyser, *Medieval Germany and Its Neighbours*, pp. 209–210; Hugh the Chanter, pp. 182–184.

[30] *Councils and Synods*, 1: part 2, p. 726; Hugh the Chanter, pp. 184–186.

an audience.[31] William hoped to receive a pallium, but it was far from certain whether Calixtus would grant it. The papal court questioned the legality of the election on several grounds: the Canterbury monks had been denied the decisive vote; the consecration was performed by suffragans rather than by the archbishop of York as was customary and took place at the royal court rather than in Canterbury Cathedral; and the monastic community of Canterbury was to be ruled by a canon rather than a monk. In the end, however, the pope and his court were won over by letters in Archbishop William's behalf by Henry I and his son-in-law Emperor Henry V—whose momentous reconciliation with Calixtus had occurred at Worms only a year before—and by the pleas of Thurstan who, having won his decisive battle with Canterbury, was now at pains to be as helpful as possible to Archbishop William and King Henry. The papal court was further influenced, so the Anglo-Saxon chronicler reports, by "the thing that overcomes all the world . . . that is, gold and silver," and Archbishop William thereupon received his pallium.[32] But when the Canterbury party raised once again the issue of the York profession of obedience and attempted to demonstrate their position by presenting a comprehensive portfolio of papal privileges that had been carefully manufactured at Canterbury, the bearers of the forgeries were laughed out of court, or so Thurstan's biographer Hugh the Chanter gleefully asserts. Thurstan declined to undertake a formal defense of the York case on the grounds that he had not been forewarned and had not brought the appropriate documentation to Rome. Pope Calixtus settled the matter, for then, by resolving to have the issue adjudicated and settled once and for all by a papal legate presiding at a council in England.[33] In normal circumstances this plan would have alarmed Archbishop William and King Henry alike. But for both men the circumstances were anything but normal. William of Corbeil was nearly at the end of the road in the Canterbury–York profession issue and might conceivably relinquish much in return for any possible papal support in the great cause. And if the issue were to be resolved at a legatine council in southern England, the setting would be much friendlier to Canterbury than it would be in Rome. As for Henry, the time was approaching when he would find himself in desperate need of papal support against Fulk V, even at the cost of a papal legate roaming at large through England. For while the two archbishops

---

[31] One week according to the Anglo-Saxon chronicler (s.a. 1123); a fortnight according to Hugh the Chanter (p. 190).

[32] Hugh the Chanter, p. 190; Nicholl, *Thurstan*, pp. 87–88; *ASC*, s.a. 1123; SD, 2:272.

[33] Hugh the Chanter, pp. 192–200; SD, 2:273.

maneuvered at the papal court, Henry's peace with Anjou was swiftly unraveling.

Returning from his visit to Jerusalem probably in late 1121, Fulk V had requested the return of his daughter Matilda, William Adelin's young widow, and Henry had regretfully sent her back from England to her Angevin homeland.[34] Late in the following year, envoys of the count of Anjou visited Henry I's Christmas court at Dunstable and asked that he return Matilda's dowry, but early in 1123, probably in February, they departed in anger, having failed to persuade Henry to give the dowry back. The result was a decisive fracture of the former alliance with Anjou.[35]

One must not suppose that Henry's break with Anjou was a product of the royal avarice. Indeed, Henry tried to gladden the departing messengers with gifts. As the Durham chronicler informs us, the dowry consisted not of money but of lands, towns, and castles—presumably in Maine, for which William Adelin had rendered homage to Fulk V at the time of the wedding.[36] The comital holdings in Maine available to Fulk V to grant as dowry were severely limited, for the preponderance of the province was in the possession of entrenched aristocratic families, occupying such districts as Beaumont-le-Vicomte, Mayenne, Sable, Laval, Ballon, La Ferté Bernard, Saint-Calais, Sourches, and Sainte-Suzanne. Fulk V's direct comital and demesne holdings in Maine were limited to the city and immediate surroundings of Le Mans itself along with a few strongholds far to the south that Count Helias had inherited as his patrimony or had acquired *jure uxoris*: La Flèche, Château-du-Loire, Mayet, Outille, and Le Grand-Luce.[37] It is extraordinarily unlikely that the dowry could have included the comital stronghold of Le Mans itself; the sources provide no indication whatever that an Anglo-Norman garrison was introduced into Le Mans during the brief period between the marriage of 1119 and William Adelin's death in 1120 or that Henry I ever held the city. Nor is it plausible that he acquired Helias' castles near the southern frontier of Maine, which would have been impossible for him to defend. Of what, then, did the

---

[34] SD, 2:263; ASC. s.a. 1121; Orderic (6:330) asserts that Matilda remained in England for several years as Henry's honored guest before being called home and that the king intended to arrange a distinguished marriage for her; but on this point the testimony of Symeon and the Anglo-Saxon chronicler is preferable; Fulk was back in Anjou before 29 January 1122 at the latest: Chartrou, *L'Anjou*, p. 15 n. 2.

[35] ASC, s.a. 1123; WM, GR, 2:498.

[36] SD, 2:267: ". . . terras, urbes, et castella quae in dotem fuerant data filiae ipsius comitis."

[37] Latouche, *Maine*, pp. 48–49, 59–65.

dowry actually consist? Although it is never explicitly identified, Robert of Torigny provides the names of three major castles in Mayenne in northern Maine which Henry I had garrisoned and which were in his possession in 1135: Ambrières, Gorron, and Colmont.[38] These castles and the districts they controlled, along with the old Bellême citadel of Alençon that Henry lost in December 1118 but recovered in 1119, could well have been the tangible portions of the dowry. We know of no other Manceaux castles that Henry ever possessed.

The castles in question all had Anglo-Norman associations. Fulk had returned the citadel of Alençon to Henry in the marriage settlement of mid-1119 after having held it for only half a year. Ambrières had first been fortified in 1054 by William the Conqueror,[39] and the *Book of Fees* reports that Hamelin lord of Mayenne, perhaps shortly before the marriage of William Adelin and Matilda of Anjou, granted both Ambrières and Gorron to Henry I in exchange for lands in western England.[40] Robert of Torigny speaks of Henry I strengthening the defenses of Ambrières and of building or restoring Colmont, and some years later, at Henry's death, Geoffrey of Anjou and the empress Maud seized without difficulty three of Henry's castles in Maine—Ambrières, Gorron, and Colmont—which they promptly granted to Juhel of Mayenne in return for his support, on the grounds that they were *in terra sua*.[41] The precise tenurial history of these castles cannot be reconstructed, but it seems likely that at least two of them had been given to Henry *in escambium* before the marriage arrangements of 1119 and by Hamelin of Mayenne rather than his overlord Fulk V. If so, and if Fulk was now demanding that they revert to him, Henry's refusal does not seem unreasonable.[42] If the dowry was also viewed as including the Norman frontier citadel of Alençon,[43] the king would have been particularly reluctant to accommodate the Angevin request.

---

[38] RT, *Chron.*, 1:197, 199, 335.

[39] Latouche, *Maine*, pp. 31, 61.

[40] *Book of Fees*, 1:86; cf. 1:97: Hamelin attested a royal charter of 1118 (October?) issued at Arganchy, resolving a dispute between the abbeys of Caen and Savigny; his successor Juhel of Mayenne signed a charter of Henry I's for Saint-Pierre-sur-Dives between 1123 and 1128 (*RRAN* 2, no. 1569) and is known to have held lands in Devon in 1130: *PR 31 Henry I*, pp. 152–153; Henry strengthened Ambrières ca. 1123: RT, *Chron.*, 1:164–165.

[41] RT, *Chron.*, 1:197, 199, 335; *GND*, 2:250.

[42] Gorron appears to have fallen into the hands of Fulk V in the course of the fighting ca. 1123–1124, and around this time Thomas of St John, a commander in Henry's military *familia*, was held captive there: *MMI*, p. 286; *RRAN* 2, no. 1422; Colmont (the modern Châtillon-sur-Colmont) may have been newly built between 1119 and 1135: *GND*, 2:250, cf. 252, where Robert of Torigny gently chides Henry for fortifying places beyond the Norman frontiers.

[43] OV, 6:224; it is conceivable, though highly unlikely, that other former Bellême castles in Maine and on its frontiers, such as those at Mamers, Blèves, Peray,

Like the wars of 1118–1119, the rebellion of 1123–1124 was orchestrated by Amaury de Montfort. Orderic describes Amaury (for whom he always shows sympathy and respect) as becoming intensely irritated at the activities of royal officials who were "running wild" in his county of Evreux while King Henry remained in England ignorant of all such goings on.[44] Orderic's criticism of unscrupulous officials ("worse than bandits") is of course a topos that runs back to the publicans of the Gospels and beyond—and forward to the complaints of local "militias" who long to secede from the bureaucratized commonwealth of contemporary America. Amaury, unlike other Norman counts, was not accustomed to the constraints of Anglo-Norman governance. As a wealthy and powerful magnate with extensive family holdings in the lands beyond the Norman frontier, where a lord could rule unhampered by mendacious bureaucrats, Amaury resented the bustle of royal administrators across his Norman county of Evreux, where even the comital castle was occupied by a royal garrison.

Amaury resolved to repudiate once again his homage and fealty to Henry I.[45] He made common cause with his nephew Fulk V of Anjou, who was nursing his grievance with regard to the dowry. Amaury persuaded Fulk to spit in Henry's eye by arranging a marriage between his second daughter, Sibyl of Anjou, and William Clito. Arriving at the Angevin court with his tutors and attendants, Clito was betrothed and then married to Sibyl, and Fulk granted him the county of Maine as his marriage portion until such time as Clito could recover Normandy.[46] Amaury then organized a Norman rebellion, persuading a number of magnates, several of them quite young and impressionable, to take up arms against the king.

The most eminent of the rebels under Amaury's baton was Henry I's own protégé, Waleran count of Meulan, still in his late teens. Waleran was the elder of Robert of Meulan's twin sons and lord of the Risle Valley strongholds of Beaumont (the present Beaumont-le-Roger), Brionne, and Pont-Audemer along with the castle of Vatteville to the

---

Saosnes, and Ortieuse, were at issue as well: see Louise, *Seigneurie de Bellême*, vol. 2 (= part 3), pp. 21–50; Latouche, *Maine*, p. 62; OV, 5:234. In 1119 Henry had returned to William Talvas all the Bellême lands in southern Normandy except their citadels, which he kept in his own possession (OV, 6:224; RT, *Chron.*, 1:200); William Talvas evidently controlled the bulk of his family possessions in northern Maine both before and after 1119, and there is no reason to suppose that the marriage settlement had obliged him to forfeit his Manceaux castles.

[44] OV, 6:330–332.

[45] Amaury had accepted Henry's pardon in 1113 and had clearly done homage to Henry in 1119: ibid., pp. 180, 278.

[46] Ibid., pp. 164–166, 332. Sibyl's older sister, William Adelin's widow Matilda, had already retired to Fontevrault while still in her teens: Chartrou, *L'Anjou*, p. 16 n. 3.

north in the forest of Brotonne. Joining Waleran in the conspiracy was his Risle Valley neighbor, Hugh lord of Montfort-sur-Risle (unrelated to Amaury). Other rebels included Hugh of Châteauneuf-en-Thymerais (across the Norman frontier in the county of Chartres), and William Lovel lord of Bréval on the French side of Normandy's eastern frontier.[47] Also in rebellion, but acting largely on his own, was William lord of the important honor of Roumare and the stepson of Ranulf le Meschin *vicomte* of Bayeux. Ranulf had been advanced to the earldom of Chester on the death of his cousin Richard, who had perished in the White Ship, but in accepting the earldom Ranulf was obliged to relinquish to the king some of the lands of his wife Lucy in Cumbria; William of Roumare, Lucy's son by a former marriage, felt himself cheated in the process.[48]

The rebellion gained cohesion from the fact that Waleran had given three of his sisters in marriage to three powerful lords who, then or subsequently, joined the uprising against Henry I. His sister Adelina married Hugh of Montfort, his sister Matilda married William Louvel lord of Bréval, and his sister Aubreye married Hugh of Châteauneuf-en-Thymerais, whose earlier betrothal to a natural daughter of Henry I had been blocked by Ivo of Chartres on the grounds of consanguinity.[49]

The conspiracy appears to have been contemplated as early as 1122, several months before Fulk V's envoys returned empty-handed from Henry I's court, and the marriages between the rebel leaders and the Beaumont sisters had probably occurred by the end of that year.[50] As David Crouch has observed, the rebel leaders had no significant holdings in England, whereas several of the most important of them— Amaury, Waleran, William Louvel, Hugh of Châteauneuf—held extensive lands across the Norman frontier in France; they were thus neither predominantly Norman nor Anglo-Norman, but Franco-Norman.[51]

In late April 1123 Henry, whose finely tuned intelligence network provided adequate warning of the coming storm, sent two of his most

---

[47] OV, 6:332; Crouch, *Beaumont Twins*, pp. 14–17.

[48] OV, 6:332–334; *CP*, 7:667–668, 743–746.

[49] OV, 6:332; Crouch, *Beaumont Twins*, pp. 15–17; White, "Career of Waleran," p. 24 n.; *CP*, 7:526 n. On Hugh of Châteauneuf's earlier betrothal see Hollister, "Greater Domesday Tenants-in-Chief," pp. 231–232, and above, pp. 42 n. 73, 230–231.

[50] Crouch, *Beaumont Twins*, p. 15. Orderic implies that the marriages immediately preceded the rebellion, but his language allows the possibility that one or more of them antedated the conspiracy and had little or nothing to do with its inception: OV, 6:332. Le Prévost proposes that the marriage of Adeline and Hugh of Montfort occurred about a decade before the rebellion: *Notes . . . de l'Eure*, 2:416.

[51] Crouch, *Beaumont Twins*, pp. 14–15, 19.

trusted magnates to see to the defense of Normandy. His son Robert, now raised to the earldom of Gloucester, was stationed in the Cotentin, and Henry entrusted Ranulf le Meschin earl of Chester with the royal citadel at Evreux in the heart of Amaury's county.[52]

In September 1123 Amaury de Montfort, Waleran of Meulan, and the other rebel leaders met secretly on the eve of their armed rebellion at a new Beaumont castle that Waleran had built next to the abbey of La Croix-Saint-Leufroy near Evreux. There, as Orderic puts it, they "united in a general conspiracy" to make war on Henry I.[53] At about the same time, probably in the closing months of 1123, William Clito, supported by Angevin forces, began attacking Henry from the south.[54] The sources provide no details on the warfare on the Angevin frontier, and it is uncertain whether Henry's enemies in Anjou ever penetrated into Normandy, but there is evidence that they captured the "dowry" castle of Gorron in Mayenne.[55]

Henry had crossed to Normandy the previous June. The secret plots, Orderic observes, "had not escaped the king's notice,"[56] and he undertook a series of carefully considered measures to defend the duchy. He strengthened the fortifications of the city and castle of Rouen (where the name "Conan's Leap" was still remembered), and at the castle of Caen he erected a great tower. He also reinforced his strongholds at Arques, Gisors, and Vernon on the eastern frontier, Falaise, Argentan, and Exmes in the south, Vire and Gavray in the west, and Domfront and Ambrières across the Norman frontier.[57] Having assembled a huge army at Rouen, he set out in October 1123 but kept his purpose and destination confidential. His plan was clearly to keep the rebels off balance and avoid the kind of back-to-the-wall defensive campaign that he had been forced to wage in late 1118.

Henry's initial purpose was to detach Hugh of Montfort from the coalition. Hugh was one of the duchy's wealthier landholders—lord of Montfort-sur-Risle and Coquainvilliers in central Normandy with some fifty-five knights fees. He was not only the husband of Waleran's sister, Adelina, but also the father of another Waleran.[58] Summoning

---

[52] SD, 2:267; OV, 6:334, 348.

[53] OV, 6:334 and 474 (stating that Waleran built a castle at La Croix-Saint-Leufroy).

[54] SD, 2:274; cf. ASC, s.a. 1124.

[55] RRAN 2, no. 1422; above, this chapter, n. 42; Boussard, "Thomas de Saint-Jean-le-Thomas," pp. 87–96; on the family, CP, 11:340–346. Thomas appears to have crossed to Normandy with the king in 1123: RRAN 2, nos 1400–1401, 1418.

[56] OV, 6:334; ASC, s.a. 1123.

[57] RT, Chron., 1:164–165.

[58] OV, 6:336; above, n. 50; Crouch (Beaumont Twins, p. 15 n. 61) expresses some doubt about the child's name. On the family's wealth, see Hollister, "Greater

Hugh to his court, Henry demanded that he hand over his castle of Montfort-sur-Risle.[59] Hugh had no choice but to assent, and Henry sent him off to open the castle doors to the royal knights who accompanied him. But Hugh, suddenly spurring on his swift horse, outrode the king's men and arrived at his castle ahead of them. He assigned its defense to his wife Adelina and others and then galloped on to the nearby Beaumont castle of Brionne to warn Waleran that the rebels' secret was out and that they must prepare for open battle. When Henry heard the news, he quickly launched an attack on Montfort-sur-Risle, joined by Robert of Gloucester and Nigel of Aubigny from the Cotentin with a company of Breton mercenaries. The royal force set the town afire and after a month-long siege Henry accepted the surrender of the castle's defenders and restored them to favor. He offered generous terms to Hugh's wife Adelina, out of respect for her late father, his old friend Robert of Meulan. Henry would restore all the Montfort lands to Adelina and Hugh, except for the castle, if Hugh would return to Henry in peace and obedience. But Hugh refused the terms and remained with Waleran and the rebellion—a grave mistake, as matters turned out.[60]

At around this time, perhaps during the siege of Montfort, Henry led a force a few miles up the River Risle, past the abbey of Bec, to Brionne. Waleran had meanwhile departed the castle and had established his base farther upriver at Beaumont. Henry's troops set the town of Brionne afire and attacked the garrison that Waleran had left to guard the tower. When the garrison proved impossible to dislodge, Henry returned to Montfort and then moved northward down the river with his full force against the formidable Beaumont castle of Pont-Audemer, perched high on a bluff overlooking the town.[61]

Henry's siege of Pont-Audemer began in late October 1123 and dragged on to about mid-December.[62] The king's troops burned and occupied the town and ravaged the countryside around it in a circuit of more than twenty miles to deprive the garrison in the tower of food and supplies. But although Henry attacked the castle resolutely, Waleran's defenders managed to hold out for about seven weeks. His

---

Domesday Tenants-in-Chief," pp. 239–240, 243 (where the fourth person on the Ship List should be Hugh of Montfort rather than Hugh of Avranches), 246.

[59] Recall that Norman dukes since at least William the Conqueror's time had asserted their right to garrison any of their vassals' fortresses at will: Haskins, *NI*, p. 282; above, chapter 2, p. 84 and n. 241.

[60] OV, 6:334–336.

[61] The town and castle are well described in Crouch, *Beaumont Twins*, p. 18 and n. 72 with references; see further Le Prévost, *Notes . . . de l'Eure*, 2:550.

[62] OV, 6:336, 340; SD, 2:274: the Durham writer seems to have received direct testimony of these events.

garrison, numbering some 140 men, included Louis VI's own chef along with a number of French knights, suggesting not only that Waleran and Amaury both had an abundance of friends at the French court but also, very likely, that Louis VI himself was deeply interested in the rebellion.[63]

Henry I assumed personal charge of the siege. Orderic describes the fifty-five-year-old monarch as hurrying to and fro like a young knight, energetically helping with anything that needed doing, encouraging everyone, smiling and joking, even instructing his carpenters in the construction of a wooden siege tower.[64] At length, when the tower was rolled into position it stood some twenty-four feet above the walls of the castle. The besiegers were thus able to fire their arrows down into the castle and to pelt its interior with huge stones. Having had enough of this, the rebel garrison surrendered to the king, and he permitted them to march out with honor and proceed wherever they chose. Unfortunately for the royal cause, a number of them chose to join Count Waleran and the French at Beaumont.[65]

The townspeople of Pont-Audemer suffered much from this warfare. Not only was their city burned by Henry's forces; his Breton mercenaries, who were experienced scavengers, dug up and seized a great many valuables that the townspeople had buried for safekeeping: chests of gold, silver, rich garments, and the like. As a final blow, when the inhabitants were well advanced in rebuilding their town, Count Waleran returned with a band of raiders and burned everything down again.[66]

By the time Henry's men occupied the fortress of Pont-Audemer, winter had settled on Normandy and military activity subsided. There were skirmishes and attacks on rebel castles, some successful, some not. And Amaury joined with William Crispin (Henry's old enemy) in an elaborate but unsuccessful attempt to capture the great frontier castle of Gisors by trickery. But no major warfare erupted until the following spring. During a long and unusually wet winter, Henry permitted his troops as well as the humble people of the countryside to remain in peace through the Advent season and beyond. His household troops that now garrisoned the citadels at Montfort-sur-Risle and Pont-Audemer received instructions to protect the country people against hostile raids, and the same was required of other nearby royal garrisons. Evreux remained under the command of

---

[63] OV, 6:340, 342; Waleran also commanded a large contingent of French knights at Beaumont.

[64] Ibid., pp. 340–342.

[65] SD, 2:273–274; OV, 6:342.

[66] SD, 2:274.

Ranulf earl of Chester, whose authority now replaced Amaury's throughout the entire county, and the centers of resistance were limited largely to Waleran's remaining strongholds of Beaumont, Brionne, and Vatteville. Beaumont had been reinforced by some two hundred French knights who, under Waleran's command, engaged in plundering and burning the surrounding countryside and torment-ing its peasants. Vatteville, near the Seine in the forest of Brotonne, was being closely watched by a royal garrison encamped in a nearby siege castle.[67]

It was a nasty winter in Normandy and England alike. The Anglo-Saxon chronicler laments that poor weather resulted in stunted crops during the winter growing season. There was a great shortage of wheat, and soaring food prices generated widespread hunger among the poor. The problem was exacerbated, the chronicler adds, by the miserably bad quality of the coins being produced by English mints—so bad that a pound's worth of coins would purchase only a shilling's worth of goods.[68] The resulting hardship led to increased thievery: the chronicler laments that in December 1124 the king's justice Ralph Basset, at a court in *Hundehoge*, Leicestershire, hanged forty-four thieves ("more thieves than had ever been hanged before") and mutilated six more. And as always in time of war, taxes were abnormally harsh. "The man who had any property," the Anglo-Saxon chronicler complains, "was deprived of it by severe taxes and severe courts; the man who had none died of hunger."[69]

Similar troubles afflicted Normandy, where Robert of Torigny reports that the coins reaching the duchy in 1123–1124 from English mints were largely of tin rather than silver. As a result, Henry's soldiers complained vigorously to him about the worthlessness of their wages.[70] Henry thereupon issued his famous order to Roger of Salisbury in England to punish all minters who could justly be accused of the crime by cutting off their right hands and having them castrated. These sanctions were in keeping with traditional English laws against false coining, and Henry received general praise and gratitude for enforcing them: "It was done very justly," the Anglo-Saxon

---

[67] Ibid.; OV, 6:342–346.

[68] *ASC, s.a.* 1124, dating the worst of the problem between Christmas 1123 and early February 1124.

[69] Ibid.; on this episode, and its legal background, see Hudson, *Common Law*, pp. 77–79. The Durham writer and the Anglo-Saxon chronicler both complain of the accompanying heavy taxes: SD, 2:274–275 (1123); *ASC, s.a.* 1124.

[70] *GND*, 2:238.

chronicler observed, because the minters "had ruined all the country with their great false dealing."[71]

On the night of 25 March 1124 a rebel force moved secretly northward through the forest of Brotonne to overthrow Henry's siege castle and relieve Vatteville. All the chief rebel leaders took part: Waleran, his three brothers-in-law—Hugh of Montfort, Hugh of Châteauneuf, and William Louvel—and Amaury, who was in command. On the following morning, having reprovisioned Waleran's castle, the rebels stormed the royal siege castle and captured its commander, Walter of Valiquerville, seizing him with an iron hook while he stood on the rampart and dragging him into captivity. Having occupied the siege tower, Waleran led a plundering raid on the nearby houses and churches to steal more provisions for his garrison. Then, "raging like a mad boar," he asserted his authority over the surrounding forest by capturing a number of peasants whom he found cutting wood there and proceeding to chop off their feet.[72]

Meanwhile at Evreux, scouts informed Ranulf of Chester of the rebels' covert expedition to Vatteville. Sensing a rare opportunity, Ranulf contacted his fellow castellans Henry of la Pommeraye at Pont-Authou, Odo Borleng at Bernay, and William of Harcourt, a Beaumont vassal who had declined to rebel against the king,[73] and urged them to lay an ambush for the rebels on their way from Vatteville back to Beau-

[71] *ASC, s.a.* 1124, probably reflecting the views of the humbler classes; recall Eadmer's praise of the similar legislation against false minters that Henry issued in 1108 on the advice of St Anselm and others: *HN*, pp. 192–193 (and above, p. 212): "from this, great good resulted at once to the whole kingdom." See in general Blackburn, "Coinage and Currency," pp. 64–66: of some 150 moneyers working in England ca. 1124, the Margan annalist reports that 94 were mutilated: *Annales monastici*, 1:11; Robert of Torigny praises Henry even more lavishly than Eadmer and the Anglo-Saxon chronicler, pointing out that he punished the false minters as they deserved rather than enriching himself by simply fining them: "Oh what a guardian of justice and scourge of crime!" Here was a king who "spurned money for love of justice": *GND*, 2:238; notwithstanding Robert of Torigny's praise, the Pipe Roll of 1130 reports that a certain Brand *monetarius* owed £20 in 1129 "that he might not be mutilated with the other moneyers": *PR 31 Henry I*, p. 42. The coining of false money was punishable by excommunication in the canons of church councils, most recently the First Lateran Council of 1123: SD, 2:272; cf. *Councils and Synods*, 1: part 2, pp. 728–730.

[72] OV, 6:346–348.

[73] Orderic reports that Ranulf summoned his comrades "Henry and Odo and William" without further identification: 6:348; just previously, however, he mentions, as leaders of Henry I's household troops, Ranulf (Rannulfus) "of Bayeux" (i.e., *vicomte* of Bayeux and Avranches and earl of Chester) at Evreux, Henry son of Joscelin of la Pommeraye at the castle of Pont-Anthou, and Odo Borleng at the

mont. Each of the three appears to have been an experienced leader of Henry I's military *familia*, and they were quick to comply, bringing a total of three hundred troops to the ambush point. On 26 March they deployed their forces in an open space, awaiting the rebel force "coming out of the forest of Brotonne and returning to Beaumont."[74] All sources agree that the subsequent battle occurred at a place not far from the town of Bourgthéroulde, southwest of Rouen, and a fragment of a Rouen chronicle places the battleground between Bourgthéroulde and the village of Boissy-le-Châtel a few miles farther to the southwest.[75] But Orderic, who is by far the most detailed and reliable source, reports that Henry's troops engaged the rebels when they emerged from the forest of Brotonne en route to Beaumont, and if that is true, the vicinity of Boissy-la-Châtel is impossible. Orderic, and Orderic alone, identifies the location of the battle as a field next to the village of Rougemontier, on the present N175 between Rouen and Pont-Audemer.[76] Rougemontier is near the southern edge of the forest of Brotonne and seven or eight miles to the northwest of Bourgthéroulde. Crossing the N175 at Rougemontier, a smaller road leads due north toward the forest of Brotonne in the direction of Vatteville and south toward Brionne and Beaumont. Le Prévost notes the tradition of a much earlier, well-traveled road that ran past Rougemontier from La Mailleraie (in the forest of Brotonne due east of Vatteville) to Brionne—and thence up the Risle

castle of Bernay, and adds that William son of Robert Harcourt also remained loyal and served the king but does not identify his castle (if any): 6:346. When Orderic mentions "William" a second time, he is almost certain to have had in mind, again, William Harcourt, not William of Tancarville the chamberlain as was suggested very tentatively by Chibnall: "Mercenaries and the *familia regis* I," p. 88, n. 29. Henry of Huntingdon's statement that William of Tancarville fought at Bourgthéroulde and personally captured Waleran, Hugh of Montfort, and Hugh of Châteauneuf (HH, p. 472) is impossible to reconcile with Orderic's identification of Odo Borleng as the leader of the royal force; William of Tancarville, a great Norman magnate and chamberlain of Normandy and England (below, pp. 362 n. 2, 364 n. 69, 366), is unlikely to have been serving under a mercenary captain of unknown parentage. Nor would Orderic, who provides by far the best account of the battle, be apt to overlook William of Tancarville's great feat if it had actually occurred. It seems much likelier that Henry of Huntingdon was simply wrong about William of Tancarville being at the battle.

[74] OV, 6:348.

[75] *HF*, 12:784; cf. Crouch, *Beaumont Twins*, p. 21 and n. 92. Robert of Torigny, a portion of whose account of the battle has perished, reports that it was fought "haud procul a villa, quam uocant Burgum Turoldi": *GND*, 2:236.

[76] ". . . in campo exeuntes de Brotona et Bellum-montem repetentes vii kalendas Aprilis prestolati sunt": OV, 6:348; ". . . in territorio Rubri Monasterii": ibid., p. 356. If the battle had been fought between Bourgthéroulde and Boissy-la-Châtel, the rebels would have had to skirt the forest of La Londe after they had emerged from the forest of Brotonne, which of course is not how Orderic describes it.

to Beaumont.[77] Rougemontier was thus a crossroads village, and it lay almost exactly on a straight line between Vatteville and Beaumont. If, indeed, Henry's military *familia* was encamped in its environs, they would have been ideally placed to waylay Amaury and Waleran and their troops.

When the rebel column appeared along the road out of the forest, some members of the king's *familia* were intimidated, quailing before men of such noble status. But one of their leaders, Odo Borleng, lifted their spirits with a heartening exhortation, challenging his men to stop the rebels from devastating Normandy with impunity. He then proposed a battle plan, stipulating "that one section of our men dismount for battle and fight on foot, while the rest remain mounted ready for the fray." He also proposed that a rank of archers stand in the flanks of the first line with instructions to wound the enemy's horses. He urged his men to show courage: if we fail, he said to the royal *familia*, "how shall we ever dare to enter the king's presence? We shall deserve to forfeit both our wages and our honour, and never be entitled, so I think, to eat the king's bread."[78]

Amaury, aware of the hazards of the ambush, urged the rebels to avoid battle. But the young Waleran, hotheaded and eager for glory, derided King Henry's military *familia* as "country bumpkins and mercenaries" and led a charge against them with forty knights—much as Louis VI had impetuously charged the Anglo-Norman line at Brémule back in 1119 and with a similarly disastrous outcome. Waleran's horse, wounded by the archers, fell beneath him, and he was captured before reaching the enemy line. His companions and their horses were struck down by arrows as well. Beset by archers both mounted and on foot, who took aim at their horses and their unshielded right sides, the rebel knights were unhorsed before they could deliver a blow. Waleran, Hugh of Montfort, and Hugh of Châteauneuf-en-Thymerais all fell captive to Henry's men. William Louvel escaped and fled home across the Eure to Bréval. Amaury de Montfort used his famous powers of persuasion to induce one of the royalist knights, William of Grandcourt, to set him free and thus spare him from a long captivity in one of Henry's castles. And William of Grandcourt, aware that he no longer had a future in Henry I's service, fled with Amaury into exile in France.[79]

The battle of Rougemontier, or Bourgthéroulde as it is usually called, cannot have lasted for more than half an hour, and it entailed no

---

[77] Le Prévost, *Notes . . . de l'Eure*, 3:40.

[78] OV, 6:348–350.

[79] OV, 6:248–252; *GND*, 2:234–236; William of Grandcourt was a younger son of the count of Eu. On the punishment of the captured rebels see Crouch, *Beaumont Twins*, p. 23.

clashes of arms in the traditional sense. Yet it marked a decisive end to
the rebellion of 1123–1124, and even though Henry I was not present,
it can properly be regarded as his last battle. For the final dozen years
of his reign, as Robert of Torigny observed, "the duchy of Normandy
and the kingdom of England were completely at peace."[80]

When Henry, at Caen, heard the news of Rougemontier, he was
astonished and overjoyed. But there was still some mopping up to do.
Moving on to Rouen, he conferred punishment on at least three captives of Rougemontier. Two of them, Geoffrey of Tourville and Odard
of Le Pin, had betrayed him and joined the rebels after swearing liege
homage to him. The third, Luke of La Barre, after serving in the rebel
garrison at Pont-Audemer and being pardoned when it surrendered,
had joined the rebels again at Beaumont and fought in their ranks at
Rougemontier, in violation of the laws of war. Further, he had ridiculed
the king by singing comic and obscene songs about him, thus committing what was in English law the capital offense of slander against
the king's person.[81] All three men, moreover, had been captured in
battle rather than having engaged in a formal submission—as a
besieged castle garrison or a free but subdued magnate might do—and
all were therefore legally at the mercy of the king and his court. Henry's
decision was to have them blinded (rather than to inflict the more
serious punishment of death). But Luke, choosing not to go eyeless
through life, beat his head against the stone wall of the hall "like a
madman" until he fell dead.

Although neither the punishments that Henry inflicted at Rouen in
1124 nor his burning of towns in the course of the war exceeded legal
or customary practice, this was clearly a period when Henry was sternly
unforgiving. His treatment of the handful of traitors captured at Rougemontier was overshadowed back in England by the plight of Roger of
Salisbury's minters and Ralph Basset's thieves. Henry's darker mood
during 1123–1124 may have been engendered by his profound disappointment in the treason of Waleran of Meulan and Hugh of Montfort,
both of whom had been reared and cared for at his court and whom
he seems to have regarded almost as adopted children. More generally,
the king who aspired to be a *rex pacificus* was obliged to witness the
sanguinary violation of the peace of Normandy by the perils and

---

[80] *GND*, 2:236.
[81] OV, 6:352–354; cf. Powicke, *Loss of Normandy*, p. 245; on slander of the king,
Leges Henrici Primi, p. 108: among crimes against the king that put the offender in
the royal mercy is *quicumque despectus uel maliloquium de eo*; cf. Jean le Foyer, *Exposé
du droit pénal normand au XIIIe siècle*, pp. 123, 232–233; and *MMI*, pp. 291–301.
Several historians, overlooking the severity of the law on this point, have concluded
wrongly from Henry's objections to Luke's behavior that the king had a morbid
dislike of ridicule.

pillagings of a second major rebellion, brought about by the absence of a royal son and heir. It must have seemed that the tragic consequences of the White Ship disaster would never abate.

For a time Waleran's castles continued to hold out against the king, even though their lord was Henry's prisoner. Turning to this final problem, Henry occupied Vatteville without difficulty and razed it to the ground. Toward the end of April he began his siege of Brionne, a great square stone keep whose ruins still stand on the hillside above the town.[82] The siege is mentioned by three well-placed writers: Robert of Torigny, Orderic Vitalis, and the author of the Bec treatise "De libertate beccensis monasterii."[83] Since Brionne is only three or four miles from Bec, the testimony of Robert of Torigny, later prior of Bec, and that of the Bec author of "De libertate" should be especially illuminating, although Orderic, employing his usual good sources, provides valuable testimony as well. Robert of Torigny, however, did not enter the Bec community until 1128, four years after the siege, and since his account differs drastically from those of Orderic and the author of "De libertate," it seems likely that Robert was misinformed. He reports that Henry took Brionne by assault rather than voluntary surrender and that he then blinded the castellan (whose name Robert of Torigny does not seem to know); the mutilation persuaded the garrison up the Risle at Beaumont to submit without resistance.

Orderic tells a fuller and quite different story: Henry immediately threw up two siege towers at Brionne which soon compelled the garrison to surrender peacefully. Nothing is said about an assault on the castle or about blinding the castellan (still unnamed); indeed, Orderic suggests that the defense of both remaining rebel castles, Brionne and Beaumont, was under the command of Waleran's steward and guardian, Morin of Le Pin. Beaumont then submitted peacefully, Orderic continues, because at Henry's instigation the captive Count Waleran had instructed Morin to surrender it and Morin did so, "albeit tardily." Henry afterward had Morin banished from Normandy on the grounds that he had played the role of evil counselor in inducing the young count to join the rebellion.[84]

The account in "De libertate beccensis monasterii" seems to be derived from the firsthand observations of Bec monks who were present

---

[82] Chatelain, Donjons romans des pays d'ouest, pp. 115–117.

[83] GND, 2:236; OV, 6:354; HF, 14:274–275; the siege is also mentioned, briefly and not very helpfully, in the Vita Bosonis, PL 150, cols 727–729; these last two treatises are well translated in Vaughn, Abbey of Bec, pp. 126–143.

[84] OV, 6:356; King Stephen, at Waleran's urging, pardoned Morin and readmitted him to the Anglo-Norman dominions, where he ended his days at the priory of Dunstable: Crouch, Beaumont Twins, p. 23.

at the siege of Brionne. Unfortunately for military historians, these monks were not interested in the siege. They were interested instead in having their newly elected abbot, Boso, installed in his office without doing homage to King Henry or professing canonical obedience to Archbishop Geoffrey of Rouen. Nevertheless, "De libertate" corroborates Orderic's testimony and contradicts Robert of Torigny's.[85] The siege ended, the "De libertate" writer states, in a peaceful surrender by the rebel garrison, and its commander was neither blinded nor even named. At the time of the surrender, Henry is described as in a quiet, tranquil mood, and as accompanied by three Norman bishops— Audoin of Evreux, John of Lisieux, and Geoffrey archbishop of Rouen—along with the saintly Boso abbot of Bec. None of these churchmen is apt to have looked on calmly while Henry blatantly violated the customs of war by putting out the eyes of a castellan who had come to terms peacefully. Such an act might be justified if the castellan had betrayed an oath of homage to Henry or had been taken captive in an assault, but we know of no such oath and there was evidently no assault. Henry subsequently developed an intimate friendship with Abbot Boso, whom he respected for his deep piety and keen intelligence.[86]

Orderic and the "De libertate" author both suggest that the siege was short. The latter writer has it commence well after the death of Boso's predecessor, the abbot William of Beaumont, on 16 April 1124.[87] Some days then elapsed during which the monks proceeded to elect their prior Boso as their new abbot, to overcome his reluctance to accept the office, and to inform Henry I at Rouen of their election. Then, after returning to Bec, they revisited Henry in Rouen "a few days later," after which Henry moved south and began the siege, probably toward the end of April.[88] After the subsequent surrender of Brionne, Henry visited his castle of Sainte-Vaubourg to refresh himself, returned to Rouen a few days later, and then, after several days in Rouen, sent for Boso and conferred with him at the Bec priory of Notre-Dame du Pré (La Bonne-Nouvelle) on 18 May.[89] If this chronology can be accepted,

---

[85] The account in the treatise on the liberties of Bec is concerned almost exclusively with the election of Abbot Boso (1124–1136), but because some of the negotiations with the king occurred at the siege of Brionne the Bec writer could not avoid the campaign altogether.

[86] *HF*, 14:275; *GND*, 2:254; *PL* 150, cols 728–729. Many years earlier, ca. 1094, Archbishop Anselm had summoned Boso from Bec to England to help him with the writing of *Cur Deus homo*, in which Anselm named Boso as the interlocutor: Southern, *Anselm: A Portrait*, pp. 202–203; of all Anselm's pupils, Southern observes, Boso showed the most aptitude for philosophy.

[87] *HF*, 14:274–275; Porée, *Bec*, p. 279; see ibid., pp. 280–288.

[88] According to Orderic (6:354) the siege began in April.

[89] *HF*, 14:274–275; cf. *Vita Bosonis*, *PL* 150, cols 727–729.

the siege of Brionne lasted about two weeks and the surrender of Beaumont occurred around the middle of May.

Without the ambush at Rougemontier, the rebellion would have stretched on and perhaps expanded. Orderic asserts that the castellans of seven castles were on the verge of revolt—including the Clare castles of Bienfaite and Orbec and the stronghold of the late royalist hero Ralph the Red at Pont-Echanfray. But as news of the rebels' catastrophe quickly spread, their erstwhile confederates lay low and hoped to be ignored by the king's justices. With the total collapse of the insurrection, rebels remaining at large such as William Louvel and the irrepressible Amaury de Montfort humbled themselves before King Henry and received his pardon and their Norman lands—abandoning once again the cause of William Clito. The captives of Rougemontier were less fortunate: Waleran of Meulan and Hugh of Châteauneuf spent the next five years in captivity, and Hugh of Montfort, who had scorned Henry's offer of peace and pardon in 1123, was still a prisoner well into Stephen's reign.[90]

In the meantime, Henry had launched major diplomatic offensives against both France and Anjou in order to minimize their support of the Norman rebels and prevent the sort of direct military intervention in Normandy that had caused him such grave difficulties in 1118–1119. With respect to Anjou, Henry began working with the papacy to obtain an annulment of the marriage between Sibyl of Anjou and William Clito. It cannot be determined exactly when these efforts commenced, but Henry's extraordinarily complex and expensive negotiations with the papal court culminated in a bull formally annulling the marriage, issued by Calixtus II on 26 August 1124.[91] The canonical hindrance was that the marriage was within the seven prohibited degrees. This objection was perfectly correct, but a challenge on precisely the same grounds could have been raised against the marriage in 1119 of William Adelin and Matilda of Anjou.[92] Indeed, the Church usually tolerated such marriages unless someone objected strongly to them. Henry did indeed object and accompanied his objection with a flood

[90] OV, 6:356; GND, 2:236; Waleran received custody of Hugh's honor of Montfort under King Stephen and consequently seemed more than content that Hugh remain a captive, despite their being in-laws; Waleran was released and reinstated in his lands (except the castles) on the death of William Clito, because rebellion against Henry was thereafter out of the question. Crouch's suggestion that Waleran's sister Isabel may have persuaded Henry to release Waleran in return for her sexual favors is a wild though fascinating guess.

[91] HF, 15:251; Chartrou, L'Anjou, p. 17 and n. 4; OV, 6:164–166.

[92] MMI, p. 287 and n. 104; the subsequent marriage of the empress Maud and Geoffrey of Anjou presented exactly the same difficulties.

of money into the papal treasury; he might also have pointed out that clause 8 of the canons of the First Lateran Council, issued just the year before, pronounced as "accursed" the contractors of consanguineous marriages and the offspring of them and branded all such marriages "infamous and abominable."[93] By whatever means, Henry won over the papal legate Gérard bishop of Angoulême, who issued an official condemnation of the marriage. Pope Calixtus, under pressure from his brother-in-law Louis VI not to act hastily, sent two more legates—the cardinals Peter Pierleoni and Gregory of S. Angelo—to examine the case at a council at Chartres in 1124. Since the results of the council were inconclusive, Calixtus sent yet another legate, John of Crema, who annulled the marriage anew and pronounced an interdict on all territories that William Clito might visit unless he was separated from his wife within a fixed time. It was this sentence that Calixtus ordained in his bull of 26 August. Fulk was enraged; he threw the papal envoys into prison (briefly), singed their whiskers, and burned their letters, and the pope responded by excommunicating Fulk and placing an interdict on all his lands. Overawed by the pope's heavy spiritual artillery— and perhaps aspiring to ascend someday, with papal blessing, to the throne of Jerusalem—Fulk submitted.[94] Thus, as Orderic ruefully observes, William Clito "was driven out by the Angevins and forced to beg the help of foreigners."[95]

While unknitting the Angevin marriage, Henry was also engaged in keeping the French king too occupied to interfere seriously in Normandy. Well before the battle of Rougemontier, rumors must have been reaching Louis VI of a projected invasion of France by the German emperor Henry V. The military expedition was not actually launched until summer 1124, but the mere threat of it would have kept Louis at home, preparing to defend his dominions. In August (or possibly July) Henry V, by the counsel of his father-in-law Henry I, led his forces against Reims.[96] From Henry I's perspective, the expedition accomplished its purpose admirably by pinning Louis down during the crucial months, but from Henry V's it was a failure. Once his army encountered the French, the imperial forces turned back without a fight, overawed by the unprecedented kingdomwide coalition that Louis VI had organized, perhaps intimidated by the great red *oriflamme* banner of Saint-Denis around

---

[93] SD, 2:271.
[94] Chartrou, *L'Anjou*, pp. 17–18 and n. 1; seven years later Fulk did in fact ascend the throne of Jerusalem: Mayer, *The Crusades*, pp. 82–83.
[95] OV, 6:166.
[96] Suger, *Louis le Gros*, pp. 218–230; Luchaire, *Louis VI*, no. 349 and references; *MMI*, pp. 286–287 and nn. 102, 103.

which the French rallied, and, just possibly, terrified by an eclipse of the sun.[97]

In return for annulling Clito's marriage to Sibyl of Anjou, Henry had poured money into the papal coffers, but there was a further price to pay. For the first time in his reign, Henry was prepared to permit a papal legate to exercise full legatine jurisdiction in Britain, including the convening of a major council in Westminster and the authority to visit churches throughout the realm.[98] The legate, appropriately, was the cardinal-priest John of Crema who had arranged the decisive papal annulment of Clito's marriage to Sibyl in summer 1124. Almost immediately after having annulled the marriage, John proceeded to Normandy where Henry, as was his wont with legates, detained him for a number of months. Pope Calixtus died on 13 December and was succeeded by Honorius II, who confirmed John of Crema's legatine authority. But even before receiving the papal confirmation, John traveled to England in Lent 1125, arriving in time to say Mass in Canterbury Cathedral at Easter (29 March). He subsequently set out on a series of visitations that included, according to the Anglo-Saxon chronicler, every bishopric and abbey in England.[99]

Honorius, in the meantime, dispatched a series of bulls empowering John of Crema to exercise his legatine authority not only in England but in Scotland as well, where King Alexander, Henry I's son-in-law, had just been succeeded by his younger brother David, earl of Huntingdon and Northampton and a close friend and longtime courtier of Henry I's. As William of Malmesbury put it, artlessly and with more than a touch of Anglo-Norman chauvinism, David was "a youth more courtly than [his brothers] who, polished since

---

[97] *MMI*, p. 287 and n. 103; Bur, *Suger*, pp. 115–120. Louis VI's army included such friends of Henry I as Theobald count of Blois and Charles count of Flanders: Luchaire, *Louis VI*, no. 349. The expedition cannot be dated precisely: Luchaire, in reviewing the evidence, concludes that it occurred some time after 25 July and before the end of August, pointing out that Henry V was at Worms on 25 July and that several contemporary writers place the invasion in August. Luchaire further points out that Lambert of Waterlos, writing a generation later, places the expedition "intrante mense augusto" but gets the year wrong; and that, according to the *Auctorium laudunense*, Henry V withdrew on 14 August. The solar eclipse of 11 August 1124 would have been visible from Reims at about noon (though the path of totality lay to the north of France): Von Oppolzer, *Canon of Eclipses* [*Canon der Finsternisse*], pp. 222–223 and chart 111; Galbert of Bruges reports that the eclipse, even though only partial, was an awesome sight signifying an oncoming calamity: *Histoire*, p. 5.

[98] For John of Crema's legateship in England see *Councils and Synods*, 1: part 2, pp. 730–741; Schieffer, *Die päpstlichen Legaten in Frankreich*, pp. 225–226; Tillmann, *Die papstlegaten in England*, pp. 27–30; Brett, *English Church*, pp. 42–47; Chartrou, *L'Anjou*, p. 17 and n. 4; Hicks, "The Anglo-Papal Bargain of 1125."

[99] *ASC*, *s.a.* 1125.

boyhood by intercourse and familiarity with us, had rubbed off all the rust of his Scottish barbarism."[100] John of Crema met with King David at Roxburgh and then proceeded south to Westminster to convene his legatine council.[101]

The Westminster council of 8 September 1125 was the only council in Henry I's reign to be presided over by a legate from Rome. It covered the general papal reform agenda of the early twelfth century including a number of the canons of the Lateran Council of 1123. Its severe strictures against clerical marriage had the predictable effect of alienating married clergy. Henry of Huntingdon, who had inherited his office from his father and had no intention of abandoning his wife and child, understandably disliked John of Crema's prohibition of clerical marriage. He rejoiced in being able to report the rumor (whether false or true) that just following the council of Westminster John had been discovered with a prostitute and had to retire home in shame.[102]

A similar story with different details and a different setting—but clearly another version of the same rumor—is told by the Winchester annalist: John of Crema repeatedly summoned Ranulf Flambard bishop of Durham to answer for various wrongdoings, including incontinence, but the bishop responded with a series of excuses. At length John of Crema visited Ranulf at Durham and was entertained lavishly. Having consumed an abundance of wine, the legate found himself attracted to a young woman, a niece of Bishop Ranulf himself. Cardinal John arranged to have her meet him later in his bedroom, and, with Bishop Ranulf's connivance, she did so. As they were making love in the legate's bed, Bishop Ranulf, with a company of attendants, burst into the room with torches and goblets and, standing around John of Crema's bed, they shouted, "Benedicte! Benedicte!" Ranulf Flambard then explained, "My lord, it is the custom in our land that whenever a nobleman is about to be married his friends shall show him this respect and courtesy. So rise, sir, and drink from my cup. If you don't, you shall at once drink from another cup after which you shall thirst no more." The legate rose naked from the bed and drank half the goblet and the bishop withdrew from the room, no longer concerned about the legate's charges against him. John of Crema is reported to have departed before dawn with the bishop's niece and hastened back to Rome.[103]

Neither story is at all likely, and they can hardly both be true. Indeed, John of Crema returned to Rome in the company of both English

[100] WM, GR, 2:476–477.
[101] Councils and Synods, 1: part 2, p. 732.
[102] HH, pp. 472–474.
[103] Ann. Wint., pp. 47–48.

archbishops. But as the editors of *Councils and Synods* have observed, John of Crema's career may not have been altogether free of sexual transgressions, and either Henry of Huntingdon's story or that of the Winchester annalist may conceivably have been based on some substratum of fact.[104]

That Cardinal John did not flee England in disgrace is suggested by the compromise scheme that he negotiated between the two archbishops before his departure: Canterbury would cede three bishoprics to York (Chester, Bangor, and St Asaph's—the first two very poor, the third unoccupied) in return for a spoken—but not written— profession of obedience. When the archbishops arrived at Rome they rejected the arrangement. Instead, with the assistance of Thurstan of York, William of Canterbury received the *ex officio* papal legateship for England. It had been a goal dear to the heart of St Anselm, and Henry I had been seeking it as a basis for compromise between Canterbury and York since at least 1120.[105] For William of Corbeil it was the best compromise that could be imagined under the circumstances, and for Archbishop Thurstan, wise prelate that he was, it was a welcome, altogether acceptable settlement. On his return, William of Corbeil held his own legatine council at Westminster on 13–16 May 1127 at which he covered the standard reform agenda and produced no surprises.[106]

By the mid-1120s Henry I's failure to conceive a child by Adeliza of Louvain was becoming an urgent problem. "In grief that the woman did not conceive, and in fear that she would always be barren," he was obliged to look elsewhere for an heir.[107] To turn to a nephew would

---

[104] *Councils and Synods*, 1: part 2, p. 732.

[105] Hugh the Chanter, p. 87; Nicholl, *Thurstan*, pp. 96–97; *Councils and Synods*, 1: part 2, pp. 741–743 with references; *AO*, ep. 214.

[106] *Councils and Synods*, 1: part 2, pp. 743–749; Archbishop Thurstan, who was quarreling again with Archbishop William over a relatively minor matter, declined to attend.

[107] WM, *HN*, p. 3; similarly Hildebert of Lavardin's replies to Adeliza's letters to him, now lost, requesting advice and solace on her childlessness: *PL* 171, cols 179–181, 189–191. Adeliza failed to conceive during her fifteen-year marriage to Henry I, for reasons that remain obscure. Unlike Edith-Matilda, Adeliza accompanied Henry on almost all his travels. Robert of Torigny, writing probably in the late 1130s, reports that Henry's illegitimate children included at that time three young men who were *adhuc iuuenes* and an unmarried daughter, which suggests (but does not prove) that the king was still fit at the time of his marriage to Adeliza in January 1121: *GND*, 2:248–250. After Henry I's death, Adeliza married the king's master butler, William II d'Aubigny, and bore him several sons: Wertheimer, "Adeliza of Louvain," p. 110; RT, *Chron.*, 1:215, 2:19.

have been to reverse a quarter-century of diplomacy. But the empress Maud, Henry's one remaining legitimate child, came into the succession picture in May 1125 at the death of her husband, the emperor Henry V.[108] In 1126 she joined her father in Normandy at his command and, it is said, with regret. Now in her mid-twenties, she had lived in Germany since she was eight and had evidently enjoyed being an empress. Maud shared with her father the attribute of porphyrogeniture he had once claimed in his own behalf. Just as Henry had been the only one among the Conqueror's sons to be born in the purple, so too had Maud been born of a reigning king and of a royal mother whose ancestors had been kings of the Anglo-Saxons. Despite the White Ship, Edward the Confessor's green tree might yet be grafted. Henry himself took the idea of the joined royal lines very seriously, in part because it provided further justification for the succession of his own children. He would later commend the empress to his barons as the one rightful heir, with Norman kings as her grandfather, uncle, and father and Old English kings in her mother's lineage.[109]

Maud's great impediment was her gender. It would have been widely doubted that a woman could rule Normandy or England without a husband to uphold her interests, and the great hope would have been that she give Henry I a royal grandson. Accordingly, it was essential that Maud's succession right be affirmed by the Anglo-Norman magnates and prelates through solemn oaths. Before the disaster of the White Ship, Henry I's English and Norman courts had sworn oaths to William Adelin in separate ceremonies.[110] In the case of Maud, however, a single great court sufficed: it met at Windsor at Christmas 1126 and adjourned to Westminster a few days later, where the oaths were taken. The courtiers swore to uphold the succession not only of Maud but also of her legitimate son, if she should have one. In short, Henry's great men committed themselves to the rule of the future Henry II some six years before his birth.[111]

But since the future of the Anglo-Norman monarchy was at issue, the decision in favor of Maud was not made rashly. John of Worcester states that before making his choice Henry had taken counsel with his great men, and William of Malmesbury adds that he arrived at his decision

---

[108] See Leyser, "Anglo-Norman Succession," in Leyser, *Communications and Power*, pp. 97–114. Leyser's suggestion that Henry V and the empress Maud may have coveted the Anglo-Norman succession is interesting but beyond any possibility of proof.

[109] WM, *HN*, pp. 3–4; see *MMI*, pp. 145–169.

[110] Above, pp. 238, 243.

[111] Some, including perhaps Henry I himself, may have worried that Maud would prove as infertile as Adeliza; the childlessness of the empress' previous marriage cannot have been entirely the fault of Henry V, who is known to have had bastards.

"after deliberating long and deeply."[112] On the nature of these deliberations contemporary writers are silent; they disclose neither what
alternatives if any to Maud's succession were considered, nor what
advice the king received, nor from whom. But buried in the sources are
certain clues that point to a clash of opinion at the court of 1126—a
dispute between Maud's friends and opponents which divided Henry's
curiales and dimly foreshadowed the savage political factions of the next
reign.

Besides the empress, Henry and his advisers may have considered
the claims of two or three royal nephews: Theobald count of Blois or
his younger brother Stephen (both sons of Henry's sister Adela), and,
indeed, William Clito himself. At Henry I's death in December 1135,
Count Theobald, a longtime friend and ally of the late king, entered
Normandy and rallied baronial support for his cause, but he then withdrew, reluctantly, on hearing of Stephen's accession to the throne of
England. As for Stephen, he had been vastly enriched by Henry, who
granted him the county of Mortain in western Normandy and huge
tracts of land in England.[113] He had the further advantage of being well
acquainted with the Anglo-Norman magnates. Contemporary writers
speak not a word about his candidacy until after Henry I's death, but
it may perhaps be significant that in 1125, by Henry's arrangement, he
was wed to Matilda of Boulogne, daughter and heiress of Count Eustace
III.[114] Matilda of Boulogne's mother, Mary of Scotland, was the sister of
the late Queen Matilda, Henry's first wife, and like her a descendant
of Alfred the Great and Edmund Ironside. Stephen's children would
thus graft the Norman and Anglo-Saxon royal branches no less truly
than the children of Henry I and Queen Matilda. Henry cannot have
been unaware of this fact. At the time that he was arranging the marriage (probably 1124 or 1125) the empress Maud was still reigning in
Germany and unavailable. Until she was widowed in late May 1125,
Henry may have taken Stephen's candidacy seriously.

But Henry's chief motive in marrying Stephen to Matilda of
Boulogne could have been the establishment of a trusted nephew
in the county of Boulogne rather than a second grafting of the green
tree. Boulogne, with its thriving port of Wissant, was strategically
situated directly across the Channel from Romney and Dover. It lay
southwest of Flanders and just to the north of Ponthieu, which was
ruled in the mid-1120s by William Talvas, Robert of Bellême's son

---

[112] JW, p. 27; WM, *HN*, p. 3.
[113] On Theobald and the Norman magnates see OV, 6:454; RT, *Chron.*, 1:198,
305–306; on Stephen, Davis, *King Stephen*, pp. 7–10. Stephen's danegeld exemptions for 1129–1130 mark him as one of the three wealthiest magnates in England.
[114] *CDF*, no. 1385.

and no friend of Henry's. The county of Ponthieu was thus caught between Henry's prongs, with Normandy to the south and Boulogne to the north.[115]

In Henry's view the countship of Boulogne probably seemed more suitable to Stephen's capacities than the throne of England. For although he was loyal, rich, affable, and well connected, it was becoming clear that statecraft was not one of Stephen's strengths. His best known political and military disasters lay in the future, but it is suggestive that when friends were urging his cause in December 1135 they stressed that the assistance of his wise brothers, Count Theobald and Henry bishop of Winchester, would "bring to greater perfection whatever is thought to be lacking in him."[116] In reflecting on Stephen's suitability for the throne, Henry can hardly have forgotten the one major military debacle of the reign, at Alençon in December 1118. The king had assigned the governance of Alençon to Stephen, whose misrule prompted its citizens to invite Fulk V through their gates. It is, moreover, indicative of Stephen's own modest ambitions in the period after his marriage that he named his first son "Eustace," the favored name of the comital family of Boulogne. The empress at least had the good sense to name her first son "Henry" rather than "Fulk"; if Stephen had dreamed of royal status for himself and his heirs, he might have named his own first son "Henry" too, harking back through his mother and maternal grandmother to Henry I of France and thereby avoiding any taint of unseemly ambition. The naming of Eustace, along with the crossed signals between Theobald and Stephen in December 1135, convey the impression that Stephen's bid for the throne was hasty and improvised. There is nothing to indicate that he was a serious candidate in the deliberations of 1126.

It has been suggested that Henry might have settled the succession on his eldest bastard son, Robert earl of Gloucester. Robert was able, well educated, immensely wealthy, and a *curialis*-administrator of the king's inner circle.[117] But his illegitimacy drastically weakened his candidacy. His bastard grandfather, William the Conqueror, had been the product

---

[115] William Talvas granted Ponthieu to his son Guy about 1129 (when Guy cannot have been more than fifteen years old): Thompson, "William Talvas, Count of Ponthieu," pp. 172–173 and 172 n. 18.

[116] *Gesta Stephani*, p. 8.

[117] Ibid.; Davis, *King Stephen*, pp. 13–15. Through his marriage to the heiress of Robert fitz Hamon and through royal gifts, Robert of Gloucester acquired lands in 23 shires as well as in Wales (Glamorgan) and western Normandy (Creully and Torigny); his English holdings enjoyed extremely high danegeld exemptions in 1128–1130 (of more than £125) and were later assessed at over 200 knights fees. He was created earl of Gloucester between 1121 and 1122 and attested 96 royal charters between 1113 and 1135, making him the most frequently attesting layman of his era: *RRAN* 2, nos 1015a–1973 *passim*.

of an earlier, far different age and had won the throne over the dead
bodies of Anglo-Saxons. In 1119 the bastard William of Ypres had failed
in his attempt on the Flemish succession and would fail again in 1127,
when Flemish townspeople pledged to reject him as their count "because
he is illegitimate."[118] In England the tradition against bastard kings runs
all the way back to the council of Chelsea of AD 787, and in the early
twelfth century, with ecclesiastical reform nearing high tide, the selection of Robert of Gloucester would have been, at best, inauspicious.[119]

There remains William Clito. As the Conqueror's one surviving legitimate grandson in the male line and the only son of the Conqueror's
eldest son, Clito had the best hereditary claim of all—better, according
to the theory of primogeniture, than Henry I's own. In late 1126 Clito
was twenty-four years old. He was by many accounts a young man of considerable charm and military prowess.[120] A few years before, Henry had
offered to accept Clito into his kingdom and court and to enrich him and
treat him as a son, if Clito would come to terms. And although Clito
declined the offer, the two men parted without rancor.[121] Yet even in the
best of circumstances it would have been painful for Henry to offer the
succession to the person against whose claims he had struggled so long.
And there was always the hazard that, in theory at least, recognizing
Clito's right to succeed might have cast doubt on Henry's own right to
rule. If Clito were the rightful heir, why should he not be the rightful
king?[122]

Nevertheless, Clito's case remained strong, and he continued to draw
ardent supporters from among the Anglo-Normans. Some, like the
rebels of 1123–1124, would have put him on Henry's throne immediately. But there were others, in no sense rebels, who looked ahead to
his peaceful succession on Henry's death. John of Worcester reports
that the news of Clito's own death from a battle wound in 1128 provoked universal grief, while Henry of Huntingdon adds that Clito was
the king's sole rightful heir to the crown and was judged worthy of it
in the expectation of all.[123] These are strong words, coming as they do
from English writers by no means hostile to King Henry. They reflect
a widespread opinion, following the death of William Adelin, that

[118] Galbert, *Histoire*, p. 76.
[119] *Councils*, ed. Haddan and Stubbs, 3:453; John, *Orbis Britanniae*, p. 33; *Gesetze*,
ed. Liebermann, 1:662, 3:341; see more generally, Chibnall, *Empress Matilda*, p. 53.
[120] In addition to the references previously cited, see the "Chronicle of Rouen"
(*s.a.* 1128) where Clito is described as "miles nulli comparabilis probitate": *HF*,
12:785.
[121] Above, pp. 268–269.
[122] Le Patourel, "The Norman Succession, 996–1135," p. 245.
[123] JW, p. 29; HH, p. 594.

although Henry merited allegiance as long as he lived, Clito should succeed him. By all accounts, this view was sufficiently prevalent to make William Clito Maud's chief rival in the deliberations of 1126. He is the only claimant apart from the empress herself who is known to have enjoyed substantial support.

On 11 September 1126, after "agreements with the princes of France had been confirmed in a manner that satisfied the victorious king," Henry crossed from Normandy to England.[124] He was accompanied by Queen Adeliza and the empress Maud, along with a company of high-ranking magnates and prelates. The king's fleet also carried two rebel leaders whom his forces had captured in 1124: Waleran of Meulan and Hugh fitz Gervase of Châteauneuf. On their arrival in England, Waleran was incarcerated at Bridgnorth and Hugh fitz Gervase at the royal castle at Windsor.

The succession issue had probably already been under discussion at the king's court in Normandy,[125] but now, in England, the debate began in earnest. Henry's close friend and brother-in-law, King David of Scots, joined his court that autumn along with two other neighboring princes—Conan duke of Brittany and Rotrou count of Perche—*fideles* and sons-in-law of the king. And from Normandy came such major dignitaries as Geoffrey archbishop of Rouen and John bishop of Lisieux, the head of Henry's Norman administration.[126]

The debate over the succession may well be reflected in the Anglo-Saxon chronicler's reports of changes in the custody of two important royal prisoners. At some point in late 1126 the king had Waleran of Meulan transferred from Bridgnorth, where he had been guarded by Payn fitz John, sheriff of Shropshire, to Brian fitz Count's castle at Wallingford. Similarly, Henry had Robert Curthose removed from Bishop Roger of Salisbury's custody at Devizes Castle and placed in Robert of Gloucester's custody at Bristol. This was done, the chronicler adds, on the advice of the empress, seconded by her uncle, King David.

---

[124] HH, p. 476; SD, 2:281.

[125] Attending Henry's court at Rouen in 1125, besides Queen Adeliza and the empress (who would have been roughly the same age), were such dignitaries as his three archbishops, the legate John of Crema, and a plethora of bishops, abbots, and *comites* of both England and Normandy: *RRAN* 2, nos 1425–1427; cf. *Chron. Battle*, pp. 132–134, reporting a royal edict of 1125 summoning all vacant English churches to send delegates to the king in Normandy to receive new prelates.

[126] *ASC, s.a.* 1126; Hugh the Chanter, p. 216; *RRAN* 2, no. 1466. Also present at Henry's autumn courts were Audoin bishop of Evreux, William of Tancarville the chamberlain, William archbishop of Canterbury, Thurstan archbishop of York, and many other magnates and prelates: ibid., nos 1459–1461, 1463, 1466–1467, 1475.

It looks as though Maud was maneuvering for the succession by ensuring that the kingdom's most valuable political prisoners would be in the hands of dependable friends. These friends evidently included Robert earl of Gloucester, Brian fitz Count, and King David, but not Roger of Salisbury or Payn fitz John.[127]

Brian fitz Count, lord of Wallingford, was a bastard son of Alan Fergant duke of Brittany and half-brother of Alan's successor, Duke Conan. Reared in the royal household, Brian was a close friend and associate of his fellow bastard Robert earl of Gloucester. Both young men had prospered enormously in Henry's service. Brian, through the royal favor, had married Maud heiress of Wallingford and had received other lands as well, including the important lordship of Abergavenny in south Wales. By 1126 he was a trusted royal counselor and administrator and would soon rise to the important household office of constable.[128] Brian and Robert of Gloucester were subsequently chosen to escort Maud to Normandy in 1127 for her betrothal to Geoffrey of Anjou, and Roger bishop of Salisbury later complained that King Henry had consulted no one about the marriage except Robert of Gloucester, Brian fitz Count, and John bishop of Lisieux.[129] In short, among the men on whom Henry and his daughter would depend during the delicate marriage negotiations of 1127 were the very persons who had favored Maud's succession in the debate of the previous autumn. Their dual role as Maud's adherents and as Henry's counselors on the Angevin marriage casts doubt on the chronicle evidence that Maud entered the marriage unwillingly. Roger of Salisbury

[127] *ASC, s.a.* 1126. Hugh of Montfort had already been imprisoned at Earl Robert's castle at Gloucester: ibid., 1124. That the safekeeping of high-status prisoners was of crucial political importance is made clear by the nearly catastrophic consequences of Ranulf Flambard's escape from the Tower of London in 1101 (above, pp. 133 ff.); in 1129–1130 the *curialis* Aubrey de Vere received a heavy fine for permitting a prisoner to escape: *PR 31 Henry I*, p. 53.

[128] On Brian's career see Southern, *Medieval Humanism*, p. 220; Stenton, *English Feudalism*, p. 236 n.; Round, *Studies in Peerage and Family History*, pp. 210–212; *RRAN* 3:xx; *PR 31 Henry I*, pp. 129–131, shows Robert of Gloucester and Brian fitz Count functioning as co-auditors of the Winchester treasury ca. 1128–1129; the pipe roll also shows Brian enjoying a very substantial danegeld exemption of £72 9s. 4d. (the fifth highest exemption of any person in England) for lands in 11 shires. He attested more than 40 royal charters between 1125 and 1135, and his tenants owed him more than 100 knights: *RBE*, pp. 308–310; Sanders, *Baronies*, p. 93.

[129] *ASC, s.a.* 1127; WM, *HN*, p. 5. John bishop of Lisieux, the head of Henry's Norman administration, was with the king in England in autumn 1126 (*RRAN* 2, no. 1466). He had reason to favor Maud over Clito, having been at Henry's side in the war of 1123–1124 against Clito's supporters (OV, 6:340). Years before, as archdeacon of Sées, he had fled Normandy during the closing years of Robert Curthose's anarchic rule and had found refuge with Henry in England: OV, 6:142–144.

was not consulted on the marriage, evidently because he supported the losing side in 1126. Maud did not trust him.

Clito's supporters at Henry's court in autumn 1126 may well have gathered around Roger bishop of Salisbury, regent of England and master of the exchequer. That Roger was disinclined toward Maud has already been suggested. He would later insist that he had sworn to support the empress only on condition that she not marry outside the realm without the explicit agreement of the king's chief men.[130] William of Malmesbury, who reports these words, obviously doubts the veracity of one "who knew how to adapt himself to any occasion." It can be assumed that Roger, who owed everything to Henry's favor, would do precisely as the king commanded and render the required oath without conditions. Moreover, Roger and his fellow lords had sworn subsequent oaths to Maud in 1131 and (probably) 1133, after her marriage to Geoffrey of Anjou.[131] Nevertheless, Roger's protestations convey the strong implication that he was hostile toward Maud's succession in the discussions of 1126, and the implication is reinforced by the transfer of Robert Curthose from Devizes to Bristol.

Roger's doubts about Maud need not in themselves imply that he favored naming Clito as heir in her place. Roger does not seem to have known Clito personally and is nowhere quoted as expressing an opinion on his candidacy. Nevertheless, Clito was the most likely alternative to Maud. Roger's attitude toward him can perhaps be inferred from the glowing accounts of Clito's career in the writings of Henry of Huntingdon. As archdeacon of Huntingdon, Henry was the direct ecclesiastical subordinate of Alexander bishop of Lincoln. Henry's *Historia Anglorum* was written at Bishop Alexander's request and was dedicated to him.[132] Bishop Alexander, in turn, was Roger of Salisbury's nephew, former ward, and closest political ally.[133] Roger and his kinsmen formed a tightly knit ecclesiastical family that had risen from obscurity in King Henry's service. On all matters of state they thought as one.[134] While it

[130] WM, *HN*, pp. 15–16.
[131] Ibid., p. 10; Roger of Hoveden, *Chronica*, 1:187; Ralph of Diceto, *Opera historica*, 1:246.
[132] HH, pp. lvii, 4–8, 474, 496.
[133] Reared in his uncle's household, Alexander began his ecclesiastical career in 1121 as archdeacon of Salisbury and obtained the very wealthy see of Lincoln in 1123 through Roger's influence: *ASC, s.a.* 1123.
[134] Besides Roger and Alexander, the group included Roger's nephew Nigel, royal treasurer and subsequently bishop of Ely (1133–1169); Roger's nephew (or son) Adelelm, who was to become King Stephen's treasurer; Roger's son Roger "le Poer," King Stephen's chancellor; and several archdeacons. Later generations of the family would produce distinguished royal officials such as Richard fitz Nigel—author of the *Dialogus de scaccario*—and William of Ely: Kealey, *Roger of Salisbury* (*passim*).

would be an exaggeration to regard Henry of Huntingdon simply as a spokesman for Roger's family, it is nevertheless suggestive that in the preface to his *Historia Anglorum* Henry entreats Bishop Alexander to praise what is written well and correct what is not.[135]

Of all contemporary writers, Henry of Huntingdon is William Clito's warmest advocate. Most chroniclers are ambivalent, viewing Clito as brave and likable but impulsive and tragically ill-starred—William *Miser* ("the Pitiable"), as John of Worcester calls him.[136] But Henry of Huntingdon, although he cannot have actually met Clito, describes him as the hero of the age, a warrior of irresistible courage, a youth of immortal fame.[137] Henry of Huntingdon's primary channel into high politics was the court of Bishop Alexander, which he attended faithfully and knew intimately. Roger of Salisbury's hostility toward Maud could well be mirrored in Henry of Huntingdon's suggestion that her machinations in 1135 propelled King Henry into his fatal illness and in his later allusion to her "insufferable arrogance."[138] It seems probable that Henry of Huntingdon's attitude toward Clito likewise reflects the viewpoint of Bishops Roger and Alexander.

Both sides of the succession debate were well represented at Henry's court in late 1126. A royal charter probably issued at Portsmouth on Henry's return from Normandy in September is attested by the empress Maud, Brian fitz Count, and six others; shortly afterward the king was in Rockingham with (among others) Robert of Gloucester, Brian fitz Count, Alexander bishop of Lincoln, and probably also Roger of Salisbury, Nigel his nephew, and Payn fitz John.[139] At Woodstock that same autumn the king's attendants included King David, Robert of Gloucester, John of Lisieux, Roger of Salisbury, Payn fitz John, and Brian fitz Count.[140] The two groups consisted of similar sorts of men—those raised to high position by Henry and frequenters of his court. Their differences were neither ideological nor economic but seem to have depended largely on their estimate of their candidate's ability to rule effectively and uphold their interests. John of Lisieux, Robert of Gloucester, and Brian fitz Count had all been involved in warfare against Clito's supporters in Normandy and may have found Clito hard to swallow. They would surely have met Maud in Normandy before the September crossing, and all three may have formed attachments to her.

---

[135] HH, p. 6.
[136] JW, p. 29.
[137] HH, pp. 482, 594, 836–837 (Clito's epitaph, by the poet Walo, quoted by Henry of Huntingdon).
[138] Ibid., pp. 490, 738.
[139] *RRAN* 2, nos 1448 (a possible forgery), 1459, 1461, and 1463.
[140] Ibid., no. 1466; cf. no. 1467. Queen Adeliza, Rotrou count of Perche, and a number of others were also with Henry at Woodstock, his favorite hunting place.

King David and Robert of Gloucester may have been swayed by their kinship to Maud,[141] but their chief motive was probably nothing more or less than personal affection.

What was in Henry's own mind in 1126? His inclination toward Maud is evident from the very fact that he summoned her home. But he had not seen her since her departure as a child more than sixteen years before, and he would probably have withheld his final decision until he could judge at first hand her capacity to succeed him.[142] By 1126 it must have been clear to him that fixing the succession on Clito would not only please many of his subjects but would also ensure peace with Louis VI. Indeed, in 1126 Louis appears to have been entertaining some hope that Henry would choose Clito as his successor, and as long as the decision remained unresolved Louis made not a move against Henry' dominions. All through the year Clito wandered and waited, and Louis did nothing to help him—or to alarm Henry. In the summer Henry, for the first and last time in his reign, sent troops to serve on a French royal campaign, dispatching a contingent of Norman knights to Louis' expedition against the Auvergne.[143] It was a promising sign. As northern Christendom awaited the decision of Henry's court, relations between the two monarchs became more amicable than they had been in years.

The oath-taking ceremony for Maud on 1 January 1127 was attended by a glittering assemblage of Anglo-Norman magnates and prelates. Perhaps as a deliberate irony, Roger of Salisbury was given the honor

---

[141] But Robert of Gloucester, Maud's half-brother, was also the first cousin of both William Clito and Stephen. King David, Maud's uncle, was unrelated to Clito but was the uncle of Stephen's wife. Brian fitz Count was distantly related to Maud, Clito, and Stephen: Duke Richard I of Normandy (942–996) was the great-great-great-grandfather of all four. (See the Anglo-Norman genealogy above, p. xxii.)

[142] The Waverley annalist asserts that Henry summoned the empress to England early in 1122 but that she was prevented from completing her journey ("so it was said") by Charles count of Flanders, who refused to let her cross his lands: *Annales monastici*, 2:218; although the Waverley annals are a late authority, the story may be true: Henry of Huntingdon (p. 468) places Henry in Kent after Pentecost (14 May), at about the time the Waverley annalist has him at Canterbury awaiting Maud's arrival. Count Charles was on generally good terms with Henry at the time (*Liber de Hyda*, p. 320: OV, 6:352–354), but the trouble may have arisen from hostilities between Count Charles and Emperor Henry V; the emperor led an army to Liège in 1122 and was strongly supported by Godfrey of Louvain, Queen Adeliza's father, who had earlier tried to prevent Charles' succession: A. Wauters, "Godefroid Ier, comte de Louvain," pp. 846–847; *Actes des comtes de Flandre*, no. 108 (p. 249); Walter of Thérouanne, *Vita Karoli*, MGH, SS, 12:542; Chibnall, *Empress Matilda*, pp. 38–39; Von Knonau, *Jahrbücher des deutschen Reichs*, pp. 273–277.

[143] Suger, *Louis le Gros*, pp. 234–236, also reporting the participation of Charles count of Flanders.

of supervising the proceedings. William archbishop of Canterbury took the first oath, followed by the bishops, abbots, and magnates.[144] King David, possibly by accident, took the oath ahead of the abbots, who objected vehemently to being upstaged by a layman. There was also what has been described as a friendly dispute between Stephen and Robert of Gloucester as to who should swear first. But the ceremony accomplished its purpose: the great men of the realm were oath-bound to support Maud and her heirs if Henry should die without a legitimate son.[145]

The oaths to Maud set off a diplomatic explosion. The news that Henry was to deflect the succession from Clito prompted Louis VI to urge the barons at his own Christmas court to consider ways of helping the young prince. Before the end of January Louis had married his wife's half-sister, Jeanne of Montferrat, to Clito and endowed him with the lordship of the French Vexin. Shortly thereafter, Clito led an armed band to Henry's frontier castle of Gisors and issued a formal claim on Normandy, whereupon some Normans are said to have rendered him the respect due their natural lord.[146]

On 2 March the situation changed dramatically. Charles of Flanders was murdered at Mass in the church of St Donatian in Bruges by conspirators associated with a powerful Flemish administrative family of humble origins known as the Erembalds. Count Charles died without a son and heir and without having had the opportunity to designate a successor. The result was widespread insurrection and looting and the beginnings of civil warfare between several aspirants to the comital office. By 13 March Louis VI, as overlord of the murdered count, had journeyed to the city of Arras in southern Flanders to quell the anarchy, punish the murderers, and arrange for the selection of the new

---

[144] The best account, albeit misdated, is in JW, pp. 27–28; on the date see Round, *Geoffrey de Mandeville*, pp. 31–32. It is possible that Henry's gift of Rochester Castle to Archbishop William at just this time bolstered the archbishop's enthusiasm in supporting the succession arrangement and taking the first oath: *MMI*, pp. 158–160. Notice, too, that on the occasion of a second round of oaths to support the empress Maud's succession, at Northampton on 8 September 1131, Henry granted Malmesbury Abbey to Roger "ut dominium suum et sedem propriam": *RRAN* 2, no. 1715; WM, *HN*, p. 10.

[145] For the friendly dispute between Stephen and Robert of Gloucester (which Stephen won), see WM, *HN*, p. 4. The Durham writer adds that the assemblage also swore to honor any gifts that Henry granted to Queen Adeliza (SD, 2:281–282), doubtless in reference to the great honor centering on Arundel that Henry granted to Adeliza in dower; she did in fact retain the honor after Henry's death, and it became, through Adeliza's second husband William of Aubigny and their heirs, the earldom of Arundel (or Chichester, or Sussex): *Gesta Stephani*, pp. 86–89; WM, *HN*, pp. 34–35; JW, p. 55; OV, 6:534; *CP*, 1:233–237.

[146] Luchaire, *Louis VI*, nos 4, 5; OV, 6:368–370.

count.[147] On Louis' advice and command, the Flemings chose William Clito over several other candidates with various claims of kinship to the comital house.[148] Clito was successfully installed as count and, by promising good government and granting privileges, he won the support of the leading towns of this highly industrialized province: Arras, Saint-Omer, Bruges, Ypres, Ghent, Lille, and others. Meanwhile Clito and Louis VI proceeded to hunt down participants in the murder conspiracy and to inflict severe punishments, some of them quite appalling, on them and their followers.[149] By early May 1127 the new regime seemed sufficiently well established for Louis VI to depart Flanders and leave its governance to Clito.[150] As he established himself more firmly, Clito became an increasingly ominous threat to the stability of Henry I's realm. The new count of Flanders was by no means ready to abandon his designs on Normandy.[151] On the contrary, he was in a position to advance them more forcefully than ever before. Henry could now anticipate a renewal of the Franco-Flemish-Angevin coalition that had nearly wrested his duchy from him nine years earlier.

When Henry heard the news at his Easter court at Woodstock, he was "much distressed,"[152] and in the months that followed he devoted

---

[147] Walter of Thérouanne, *Vita Karoli*, *MGH*, *SS*, 12:557; Galbert, *Histoire*, pp. 75–77, 81–84; Ganshof, "Trois mandements perdus," pp. 117–130; on Louis' activities in Flanders see Ganshof, "Le Roi de France en Flandre," pp. 204–228; on the Flemish crisis in general, Nicholas, *Medieval Flanders*, pp. 62–66.

[148] Walter of Thérouanne, *Vita Karoli*, *MGH*, *SS*, 12:557–558; Hermann of Tournai, "De restauratione," *MGH*, *SS*, 14:288; Clito's claim was through his grandmother, Matilda of Flanders, wife of William the Conqueror.

[149] Galbert, *Histoire*, pp. 92, 125–126, 128–129 and *passim*; William Clito and Louis VI subjected large numbers of their captives to grisly tortures and agonizing executions, the vengeance extending beyond the murderers and their fellow conspirators to their followers, many of whom were presumably innocent. Suger (*Louis le Gros*, pp. 246–248) writes approvingly of Louis VI's brutal punishments; see in general *MMI*, pp. 297–298.

[150] On 6 May: Galbert, *Histoire*, p. 126.

[151] Robert of Torigny states that Henry's Anglo-Norman dominions enjoyed undisturbed peace from 1124 to 1135 despite Clito's doing his best to disturb them during his brief tenure as count of Flanders: *GND*, 2:236. Clito's various hopes are suggested by the language of his charter to Saint-Omer of 14 April 1127: "Si contigerit mihi aliquo tempore preter terram Flandriae aliam conquirere, aut si concordia pacis inter me et avunculum meum eos liberos ab omni teloneo et ab omni consuetudine in concordia illa recipi faciam": *Actes des comtes de Flandre*, no. 127, cl. 7. In his comital charters Clito styles himself *Guilielmus* (or *Willelmus*) "Dei gratia comes Flandrie, filius Roberti comitis Normannie" (ibid., no. 125; cf. no. 128). He avoided claiming the Norman duchy as his own because his father still lived.

[152] HH, p. 476; cf. p. 606, where Henry of Huntingdon states (with the tendentious exaggeration characteristic of his *De contemptu mundi*), "What care struck him down when his nephew William obtained Flanders and Henry thought that he would himself certainly lose the crown of the kingdom" (trans. Greenway).

money, energy, and all his diplomatic ingenuity to the goal of fore-
stalling the impending alliance and shaking Clito's hold on Flanders.
Had he merely watched and waited, he could have faced a Norman
rebellion, supported by outside intervention, such as had accompanied
his hostilities with France and Anjou in 1118–1119 and 1123–1124. To
preserve the peace of his cross-Channel dominions, it was essential that
Henry move swiftly and keep his enemies off balance. This policy of
what might be termed "aggressive defense" had worked well for him
in past crises, with the exception of the wars of 1118–1119. Now in
1127–1128, as in 1111–1113,[153] Henry's diplomacy was so effective as
to safeguard Normandy against all external threats. The duchy enjoyed
absolute peace throughout the crisis.

  Thus, Henry kept Clito occupied by secretly sending money to
various disappointed claimants to the comital title, placing himself
nominally at their head and encouraging them all until he could
discern which of them might prevail.[154] He prohibited the shipment of
English wool to Flanders, damaging its textile industries and enkindling
opposition to the new count within the Flemish cloth towns.[155] In
August 1127 he arranged for his nephew Stephen to make war on Flanders from Boulogne, but Clito's retaliatory attacks forced Stephen to
conclude a three-year truce.[156] Henry also, as we shall see, entered into
negotiations with Fulk V to ensure that Anjou would not lend support
to Clito.

  As a result of Henry's machinations and Clito's increasingly inept
handling of Flemish burghers, opposition was beginning to develop in
the towns. It began in Bruges in mid-September 1127 and then spread
to Lille, Saint-Omer, Ghent, and Ypres, until by spring 1128 the county
was in a state of general rebellion.[157] The feeling was swiftly growing

---

[153] Above, pp. 225–233.
[154] Galbert, *Histoire*, pp. 78, 141, 144–147; *HF*, 15:341; Walter of Thérouanne,
Vita Karoli, MGH, SS, 12:557–558. Clito's leading rivals were William of Ypres,
Baldwin of Hainault, Arnold nephew of Charles the Good, and Charles' cousin
Thierry of Alsace, all of whom had hereditary claims to the county. Henry I's claim
was through his mother (Clito's grandmother) Matilda of Flanders; although he
did make his claim public (ibid., p. 558; SD, 2:282), he undertook no serious effort
to acquire the province for himself. His claim served as a symbol to which other
claimants, otherwise mutually hostile, could rally. He put it forward, in Ganshof's
words, "moins dans l'espoir de pouvoir s'en rendre maître que dans le but d'en
chasser son neveu": "Le Roi de France en Flandre," p. 210.
[155] Galbert, *Histoire*, pp. 140–141, 152.
[156] OV, 6:370–372; Walter of Thérouanne, *Vita Karoli, MGH, SS*, 12:557.
[157] Galbert, *Histoire*, pp. 132–134, 137–158; Clito offended the Flemish townspeople by imposing "unjust" exactions and heavy fines, by appointing castellans
whom the burghers regarded as oppressive, and by reneging on his earlier pledges
to remit tolls—some of which had been granted in fief by previous counts to barons
of the various regions, who objected vigorously to losing them.

that William Clito should be replaced by Thierry of Alsace, Charles the Good's first cousin and grandson of Robert I of Flanders, whose hereditary claim was better than Clito's and who promised Flemish townspeople more generous terms than Clito had offered. Late in March 1128 Clito sent a letter to Louis VI pleading for aid against the intrigues of his uncle, Henry I, and Louis responded by returning to Flanders in April.[158] On 6 May he convoked a council in Arras at which the archbishop of Reims excommunicated Thierry and his sympathizers and laid an interdict on Lille, a center of Thierry's support.[159] Later in the month, in the midst of besieging Lille, Louis suddenly withdrew and hastened back to France, leaving Clito once again on his own.[160]

The reason for Louis VI's abrupt withdrawal is almost surely a military feint undertaken by Henry I against the Ile de France. As Henry of Huntingdon describes it, Henry I marched in arms into France because the French king was supporting his nephew and enemy. For eight days Henry sat with his army at the castle of Epernon between Paris and Chartres "as safely as if he were in his own kingdom," forcing Louis VI to give no further aid to the count of Flanders. When Louis returned to protect Paris, Henry pulled his army back into Normandy.[161]

Epernon was one of the major castles of Amaury de Montfort, Henry's chief opponent for the past fifteen years. Henry's feat in entering Amaury's castle unopposed was made possible by a recent, revolutionary upheaval in Louis VI's household and administration. Sometime in the later 1120s, Amaury had taken in marriage Agnes, niece of the chief administrator of France, Stephen of Garlande, chancellor and seneschal of Louis VI and his chief adviser.[162] There is

---

[158] Galbert, *Histoire*, pp. 158–159; Hermann de Tournai, "De restauratione," *MGH, SS*, 14:288–289.

[159] *HF*, 15:341; Luchaire, *Louis VI*, nos 405, 407, 410, 412; Galbert, *Histoire*, pp. 151–152, 158–159; Hermann de Tournai, "De restauratione," *MGH, SS*, p. 289.

[160] Galbert, *Histoire*, pp. 158–159; Luchaire, *Louis VI*, no. 412, suggesting the date of 21 May.

[161] HH, pp. 478–480; Henry of Huntingdon, the only source that reports this event, provides the year, 1128, but not the month. Louis' sudden retreat into France suggests strongly that Henry's advance on Epernon occurred in May. Charter evidence indicates that Louis was back in Paris by summer: Luchaire, *Louis VI*, no. 417.

[162] Amaury received as Agnes' dowry the Garlande castle of Rochefort. Although the Garlandes were a nonnoble family, four Garlande brothers, Anseau, William, Gilbert, and Stephen, played central roles in Louis VI's administration: Gilbert had been royal butler since 1112; Anseau (father of Amaury de Montfort's wife, Agnes) was seneschal until his death in 1118, at which time the seneschalship passed to his brother William and, on William's death in 1120, to Stephen of Garlande, who combined the office with the chancellorship, which he had held since 1108. On

evidence that Stephen planned to bequeath his seneschalship to Amaury, thereby compromising the integrity of the French royal administration by reinforcing the hereditary nature of one of its key household offices. As a result of this plan (among other reasons) Stephen aroused the opposition of various figures in Louis' regime, in particular his queen, Adelaide of Murienne. Having married Louis in 1115, Adelaide found herself at odds with Stephen of Garlande and his family who, until the marriage, had been virtually all-powerful at the royal court. A rivalry developed between Stephen and the queen, whose influence increased in 1119 with the election of her brother to the papacy as Calixtus II and in 1127 with the marriage of her half-sister, Jeanne de Montferrat, to William Clito. It was evidently Adelaide who, despite Stephen of Garlande's misgivings, persuaded Louis VI to intervene in Flanders in Clito's and Jeanne's behalf. In late 1127, through Adelaide's influence, Louis VI stripped Stephen of his offices of chancellor and seneschal and at the same time deprived Stephen's brother, Gilbert, of the master butlership of the royal household. Stephen and Gilbert were both exiled from the royal court, and Queen Adelaide had the pleasure of ordering Stephen's several elegant houses in Paris leveled to the ground.[163]

Amaury de Montfort, whose ambitions had unexpectedly linked him to a family that had suffered the royal *malevolentia*, now found himself rejected and reviled by Louis and his queen. He and Stephen of Garlande responded by making common cause with Henry I and Theobald of Blois. Louis retaliated by attacking, seizing, and razing Stephen's castle of Livry near Paris—in the course of which Louis was seriously wounded and his cousin Ralph count of Vermandois lost an eye.[164] Ralph went on to become royal seneschal in Stephen of Garlande's place, and Amaury, count of Evreux and mastermind of the Norman rebellions of 1118–1119 and 1123–1124, caused no further trouble in the duchy. William Clito, now married to Queen Adelaide's half-sister, no longer commanded his support.[165]

Shortly after the news of Clito's advancement to the countship of Flanders reached England, Henry once again sought a rapprochement with

Stephen's overriding influence as royal counselor see *Chronique de Morigny*, p. 27; see, more generally, Luchaire, *Louis VI*, pp. xliii–liii.

[163] Luchaire, *Louis VI*, nos 399, 426; Bur, *Suger*, pp. 133–134.

[164] The modern Livry-Gargan seven miles northeast of Paris. See Luchaire, *Louis VI*, no. 420; Suger, *Louis le Gros*, p. 117; on Louis' war with Amaury de Montfort see *HF*, 15:374.

[165] Henry I and Amaury de Montfort never seem to have become good friends, but Amaury does attest a Norman charter of Henry's ca. 1131: *RRAN* 2, no. 1701.

Fulk of Anjou.[166] As before, the accord was to be sealed by a m̵
this time between Fulk's son and heir Geoffrey and the empress Mau..
There seem to have been objections from members of Henry's court,
although they were probably not raised at the time, and the empress
herself, as a widow in her mid-twenties, may have been hesitant to marry
a fourteen-year-old boy, the heir to a mere county.[167] But the plan proceeded, and Maud and her supporters doubtless appreciated its necessity. At Pentecost (22 May) 1127 Henry sent the empress to Normandy,
accompanied by Robert of Gloucester and Brian fitz Count. Henry
himself crossed on 26 August, and not long afterward he betrothed his
daughter to Geoffrey.[168] The following year, on Whitsunday, 10 June
1128, Henry knighted Geoffrey in Rouen, in a ceremony that John of
Marmoutier, writing sixty years later, described in chivalric terms that
seem somewhat anachronistic. The ceremony is said to have begun by
Geoffrey taking what would in later years become the traditional ceremonial bath. He was then attired in a cloth-of-gold tunic and a purple
cloak and escorted into the king's presence. He received a pair of
golden spurs and a shield emblazoned with lions, and King Henry
girded him with a splendid sword. Thirty young companions of

---

[166] WM, *HN*, p. 2.

[167] Robert of Torigny (*GND*, 2:240) states that Henry I gave Maud in marriage to
Geoffrey "despite her reluctance" and then provides a long passage explaining
(rather apologetically) that "although the rank of count of Anjou is lower than that
of Roman emperor," the Angevin counts were nevertheless of an extremely distinguished lineage and were descendants of Charlemagne (pp. 242–244). See further,
WM, *HN*, p. 5. The oft-repeated assertion that opposition to the marriage resulted
from the Normans' hatred of Angevins seems much exaggerated; during the rebellions of 1118–1119 and 1123–1124, some Norman barons did not hesitate to make
common cause with the count of Anjou: *MMI*, p. 163. See in general Chibnall,
Empress Matilda, p. 55.

[168] HH, p. 476; SD, 2:282. Chartrou (*L'Anjou*, pp. 21–22), who has sometimes
been misread on this point, dates the betrothal to the period between 22 May and
the end of August 1127. *MMI*, p. 261 and n. 63: a charter of John bishop of Sées,
dated at Sées in the year 1127, sixth indiction (September 1127–September 1128),
bears the words *Signum Henrici regis Anglorum. Quando dedit filiam suam Gaufredo
comiti Andegavensi juniori: RRAN* 2, pp. 360–361: appendix, no. CCVI (no. 1548);
original in the Archives départementales de l'Orne, H. 2159: the king's *signum* is
on the right of the lower margin of the original charter and is enclosed in a circle;
the names of the other signatories are on the left. Round (*CDF*, no. 1192 n. 5) suggests that the king's *signum* may have been added later, although the charter itself
states that the transaction of autumn/winter 1127 was concluded on the king's
advice; in the unlikely event that the charter date of 1127 does not pertain to the
king's attestation, the phrase *quando dedit filiam suam Gaufredo* could conceivably
refer to the wedding on 17 June 1128 (at which John bishop of Sées assisted) rather
than to the betrothal. Henry was probably in Rouen in the later months of 1127
(*RRAN* 2: nos 1545, 1547), and a later chronicle tradition makes Rouen the site
of the betrothal: *Ann. Wint.*, 2:48 (in a passage based on Matthew Paris).

Geoffrey were knighted at the same time, and Henry bestowed horses
and arms on them. There followed a week of feasts and tournaments,
culminating in a great wedding ceremony.[169]

On 17 June Geoffrey and Maud were married in the cathedral of Le
Mans by the bishop of Le Mans, Guy of Ploermel, assisted by John
bishop of Sées, in the presence of Count Fulk and King Henry.[170] Fulk
at once associated his fourteen-year-old son in the governance of Anjou,
and in the following year Geoffrey became sole count when Fulk
departed once again for the Holy Land to marry the heiress of the
kingdom of Jerusalem.[171]

In the absence of any written agreement, one is left uncertain as
to exactly what Maud's marriage implied with respect to the succession.
According to the customs of the times Geoffrey le Bel would have
become heir to England and Normandy *jure uxoris*, just as his father
was about to become coruler of Jerusalem. But Henry had been known
to bend the customs of inheritance among his own barons,[172] and there
are good reasons to doubt that he intended Geoffrey as his successor.
Rather, Geoffrey was, in Orderic's words, to act as a "stipendiary
commander in his wife's behalf,"[173] seeing to it that the empress and
her hoped-for heirs received their proper inheritance. He was to
provide her with sons, uphold her interests, and, for his own part,
be content with Anjou. The Durham chronicle asserts that in the
absence of heirs Geoffrey was to inherit the English crown, but
this seems dubious. In the years following the marriage Henry
did nothing whatever to prepare Geoffrey for the throne. Geoffrey
acquired no lands in England or Normandy and so far as is known was
never at Henry's court or in his presence after 1128. He received
no oaths from the Anglo-Norman barons and was virtually unknown

---

[169] John of Marmoutier, "Vita Gaufredi," p. 178: Keen, *Chivalry*, pp. 64–65; cf.
Flori, *L'Essor de la chevalerie*, pp. 266–267.

[170] Chartrou, *L'Anjou*, pp. 22–23; Chibnall, *Empress Matilda*, p. 56; *MMI*, p. 261.
The dating of the marriage presents formidable problems that Kate Norgate has
satisfactorily solved: *Angevin Kings*, 1:258–260. The site of the marriage was the
splendid Romanesque cathedral of Le Mans of the eleventh and twelfth centuries,
much of the nave of which survives.

[171] Chartrou, *L'Anjou*, pp. 23–24; Chibnall, *Empress Matilda*, p. 56. Fulk had been
negotiating concurrently with Henry I and with envoys from the kingdom of
Jerusalem who offered him the hand of Melisende, daughter and heiress of Baldwin
II, king of Jerusalem. Fulk had been a widower since the death of his first wife,
Eremburga of Maine, in 1126. As a result of his marriage to Melisende, his son
Geoffrey became, like the empress, the offspring of a king (although not born in
the purple).

[172] Note the cases of the earldom of Huntingdon and the honor of Eudo *Dapifer*.
CP, 6:638–642; *MMI*, pp. 117–128.

[173] OV, 6:482.

to them.[174] Henry was probably being deliberately vague, as was his wont, and keeping his options open. In any event, the success of the marriage as a workable solution to the succession issue depended on the birth of a son and heir, and in this sense the whole plan was a gamble. Maud, a widow of twenty-five, had as yet borne no children.[175]

In the meantime, Clito continued to fight for his survival against recalcitrant Flemish townspeople and nobles. Thierry of Alsace had by now emerged, with Henry's aid, as Clito's chief rival for the countship. Clito again proved his prowess as a warrior and commander, fighting against Thierry and his other enemies with considerable success. But in late July 1128 he was mortally wounded while leading an assault on Thierry's castle of Aalst.[176] Clito was twenty-five years old when he died, probably on 28 July, having been wounded in the hand and bedridden several days before. His death, as sudden and unexpected as William Adelin's had been, occurred less than six weeks after the marriage that his rule in Flanders had precipitated.

For a brief period, Orderic says, Clito's followers, including the ever faithful Helias of Saint-Saens, kept his death a secret and carried on the fight. Then, at length, they parleyed with Thierry's castellan, led him into Clito's tent, and showed him the dead body of their young lord: "Look," they said, "and see what you have done. You have killed your lord and thus have plunged countless knights into mourning." The castellan, weeping, had Clito's body escorted to the abbey of Saint-Bertin in the town of Saint-Omer, where Clito was posthumously enrolled as a monk and was buried. The messenger who brought the news to King Henry carried letters that Clito had written on his deathbed, asking his uncle's forgiveness for all the wrongs he had done and asking Henry to pardon and receive back into favor all those who had supported him if they returned to their loyalty. Henry abided by Clito's last wishes and received many who returned to him. Others among Clito's followers, distraught at his death, set out on crusade.[177]

---

[174] Symeon's remarks on continental events in 1127–1128 are subject to caution: *MMI*, p. 262, n. 68; on Geoffrey's role in Henry I's succession plans see Chibnall, *Empress Matilda*, pp. 56–57, 65.

[175] Hermann of Tournai ("De restauratione," *MGH, SS*, 14:282) says that Maud bore a son who lived only a short while.

[176] Galbert, *Histoire*, p. 171; OV, 6:376–378; on Thierry's support from Henry I, see HH, pp. 280–282. Henry of Huntingdon, who is an unashamed admirer of William Clito, assures his readers that had Clito not been wounded, Aalst would have surrendered the following day; "Mars has died on earth," grieves Henry of Huntingdon, paraphrasing the poet Walo, "the gods lament an equal god" (HH, p. 182).

[177] OV, 6:376–378.

With Clito's death, Henry's diplomatic troubles were virtually at an end. Clito had always been the one viable alternative to Henry's rule and his succession plans, and now the peace of his cross-Channel dominions was assured. Henry was free to release Waleran of Meulan from imprisonment at Wallingford and Hugh of Châteauneuf from Windsor. Hugh left for home, and Henry began taking steps to restore Waleran's property and status.[178] For the rest of his reign the king remained at peace with Amaury de Montfort. Thierry of Alsace became count of Flanders without further opposition and made close alliances with both Louis VI and Henry I.[179] A few years later, "on the advice of the king of England," Thierry wed William Clito's former wife, Sibyl of Anjou, now the sister-in-law of the empress Maud.[180] And in 1129 Henry concluded a peace with King Louis VI that would endure until the end of the reign. Thus, as the Durham chronicler states, Henry's enemies on every side were either conquered or reconciled, and prosperity everywhere smiled on him.[181] Owing to Clito's death, the political and diplomatic tranquillity that the king had sought and nearly attained on the eve of the White Ship disaster was achieved at last; the survival of his regime would never again be threatened. In mid-July 1129, with peace established "in France, Flanders, Normandy, Brittany, Maine, and Anjou, Henry returned joyfully to England."[182]

---

[178] *MMI*, pp. 185–186; Crouch, *Beaumont Twins*, p. 25; *ASC, s.a.* 1129; SD, 2:283.
[179] OV, 6:378; Thierry renewed the traditional money-fief treaty with England: Galbert, *Histoire*, p. 176.
[180] OV, 2:378.
[181] SD, 2:283.
[182] HH, p. 482 and n. 257.

Chapter 8

KING AND MAGNATES

At the beginning of his reign Henry had promised to establish "a firm peace in all my kingdom" and ordered "that this peace shall henceforth be kept."[1] From that time on, he proceeded to construct a regime more rigorous in its maintenance of peace and good order than any that England or the Continent had known since Roman times. Even the peace of the empire of Charlemagne had been disturbed by private feuds and local military clashes, sometimes even between bishops and abbots, and in the centuries that followed, the problem of local and regional violence became much worse.[2] The same was true in Anglo-Saxon England, even in Edward the Confessor's reign, the happy memories of which conveniently overlooked various rebellions, exiles, and political murders.[3] In the post-Conquest generation, most of the new magnates whom William the Conqueror enriched remained devoted to him and frequented his court (see table 8.1), but the reign was nevertheless "a period of jarring and violent tenurial discontinuity" marked by rebellions, invasions, and the systematic pillaging by Normans and other French-men of the properties of the Anglo-Saxon laity and the Church.[4] After the Conqueror's death, Normandy suffered a deluge of lawless-ness and violence under Robert Curthose,[5] while social disruption

---

[1] Coronation Charter, cl. 12: *Select Charters*, ed. Stubbs and Davis, p. 119; above, pp. 108–112. On Henry and his magnates see Southern, *Medieval Humanism*, pp. 206–233; Green, *Government*, pp. 1–24, 226–286 *passim*; *MMI*, pp. 97–189. Charlotte Newman, in her valuable study *The Anglo-Norman Nobility in the Reign of Henry I*, employs a different methodology from mine, calculating baronial attestations year by year (pp. 92–100, 182–196), but our general conclusions are similar (see especially p. 140: "The magnates received conspicuous favor—they were granted large estates, married great heiresses, and attended court on state occasions"). On the post-Conquest aristocracy in general, see J. C. Holt's brilliant paper "Politics and Property in Early Medieval England."

[2] Fichtenau, *The Carolingian Empire*, pp. 122–123, 137–138, and, by the same author, *Living in the Tenth Century*, pp. 382–383, 385–386, 391.

[3] Fleming, *Kings and Lords*, p. 55.

[4] Ibid., pp. 184–214. "There are numerous accounts from each reign of aristocratic disaffection and revolt" (p. 215).

[5] David, *Curthose* (*passim*).

Table 8.1. Relationship between Landed Wealth and Frequency of Attestation among English Magnates Alive in 1087

Ten greatest English lay landholders	Land income (£ per year)	William I attestations	Rank of lay attesters
Odo of Bayeux (deprived 1082)	3,000	34	2
Robert of Mortain	2,100	30.5	4
Roger of Montgomery	2,100	40	1
William I of Warenne	1,165	8	
Alan lord of Richmond	1,100 + waste	21	7
Hugh earl of Chester	800	15.5	9
Richard of Clare	780	11	11
Geoffrey of Coutances	780	34	3
Geoffrey of Mandeville	780	0*	
Eustace II count of Boulogne	770	0**	

Total of attesters in top 15: 7 of 10.
* Sheriff: five charters of William I addressed to him.
** Spends much of the reign in Boulogne.

in Rufus' England, although less ubiquitous, remained a serious affliction.

William Rufus' reign witnessed two major revolts, a systematic corruption of royal law through the abuses and swindlings of Ranulf Flambard, who managed the royal courts, and the pillaging of church properties by the same Ranulf, acting in the king's behalf.[6] In the first of the two revolts (1088), the heads of at least six of England's ten wealthiest Domesday families (see table 8.1) supported the succession of Robert Curthose to the English throne: Odo of Bayeux, Robert of Mortain, Roger of Montgomery, Gilbert of Clare, Geoffrey of Coutances, and Eustace of Boulogne—along with barons of only slightly lesser wealth such as Roger Bigod, William of Eu, Roger of Lacy, and Hugh of Grandmesnil. Rufus was confronted, in short, with the hostility of the very families that the Conqueror had so lavishly favored. Only two of England's ten wealthiest magnates, Hugh earl of Chester and William I of Warenne, are known to have supported Rufus. He survived the uprising thanks in part to Curthose's inability to launch an invasion, just as Henry I would later prevail against a similar magnate coalition in 1101, again as a consequence of Curthose's ineptitude. But by 1105–1106, as we have seen, Henry had won most of the Anglo-Norman baronage over to his cause, whereas Rufus, seven years after the initial rebellion, confronted once again in 1095 a coalition

[6] Barlow, *Rufus*, p. 200; Hollister, "William II, Henry I, and the Anglo-Norman Church," *Culture of Christendom*, pp. 189–200.

of England's wealthiest families—Montgomery, Clare, Lacy, Eu, Mowbray (the rebel Robert of Mowbray was Geoffrey of Coutances' nephew and heir)—and he narrowly escaped being murdered in an ambush. At that time no major magnates are known to have supported Rufus.[7] Had he lived beyond August 1100, his determination to keep Curthose from recovering Normandy could have precipitated another, larger rebellion.[8] Sir Richard Southern makes the perceptive observation that when Rufus died "the country was ready for a revolution, which might well have swept away much of the structure of royal government."[9]

The split between Rufus and his magnates that the rebellions suggest is confirmed by an analysis of the witness lists on his charters (see table 8.2). Only one representative of the ten wealthiest Domesday families, Hugh earl of Chester, attests with any frequency. Rufus' other major attesters tended to be landholders of middling wealth, several of them household officials: Eudo *Dapifer*, Hamo *Dapifer*, Roger Bigod (also a *dapifer*), and Urse of Abitôt (constable and sheriff). On Henry I's accession, the allegiance of the great magnate families remained dubious for a time, but through a blend of firmness and astute royal patronage, Henry managed to develop a loyal aristocracy and establish a firm peace throughout his realm.[10]

Henry's peace was made possible by the tradition and reality of strong kingship in England, buttressed by an abundance of royal demesne revenues resulting from the territorial rearrangements of 1066,[11] and by the long-standing (if sometimes ineffectual) Anglo-Saxon and Anglo-Norman opposition to private warfare. But these advantages could be translated into a stable, enduring peace only through intelligent and tenacious royal leadership over a period of time. During his first tumultuous year Henry dared not risk offending any magnates. But once his throne was reasonably secure, after the treaty of July 1101, he began taking measures not only to win the allegiance of the barons through patronage (marriages, high offices, grants of land) but also to curb regional violence and private war.

---

[7] *MMI*, pp. 101–102.
[8] OV, 5:280; *MMI*, pp. 66–67.
[9] Southern, *Medieval Humanism*, p. 231.
[10] Above, pp. 153–163, 171–184; see, in particular, the tables on pp. 172 and 175.
[11] *MMI*, p. 97; *CMH*, 5:505; Green, "William Rufus, Henry I, and the Royal Demesne"; Clarke, *English Nobility*, pp. 162–163. On the sophistication of Anglo-Saxon royal government see Campbell, "Observations on English Government," pp. 155–170. William I acquired not only the *terra regis* of Edward the Confessor but also the vast lands confiscated from the Godwines and some of their followers: see Fleming, *Kings and Lords*, pp. 66–69.

Table 8.2. Relationship between Frequency at Court and Landed Wealth: 1101 (The 9 leading lay *curiales* of William II alive in 1100)

	Wm. II attestations	Addressee	Office	Land income (£ per year)	Norman lands
Eudo *Dapifer*	37	0	Steward	415	Middle
Roger Bigod *Dapifer*	28	2	Steward, sheriff	450	Small
Robert fitz Hamon*	21	0		300+ Wales	Large
Robert count of Meulan	16	1		? 100	Large
Urse of Abitôt	12	5	Constable, sheriff	90	Very small
Hamo II *Dapifer*	9	11.5	Steward, sheriff	128	None
William Peverel of Nottingham	9	2.5	? Local justiciar	250	Middle
Hugh earl of Chester	8.5	0	[Earl]	800	Large
Henry earl of Warwick*	8	1	[Earl]	325	Middle
Total				2,858	

*Much enriched under William II.

Let us review briefly some of these activities.[12] Henry disseised William II of Warenne earl of Surrey (son and heir of the great Domesday lord), probably on the grounds that Earl William's men had, without legal warrant, seized the lands and men of Herbert bishop of Norwich in Thornham (Norfolk). Similarly, Henry brought Ivo of Grandmesnil to trial and levied a heavy fine against him for waging private war and engaging in the accustomed military tactic of burning his neighbors' crops. Ivo was forced into exile and mortgaged his lands to Robert count of Meulan.[13] The king's successful military campaign against Robert of Bellême in 1102 was prompted in part by Robert's flouting of custom in building the stronghold of Bridgnorth without royal permission.[14] After the forfeiture of Robert of Bellême's earldom of Shrewsbury and his forced departure from England, Henry instituted legal action against Bellême's nephew, the demanding and troublesome William count of Mortain and earl of Cornwall, charging

[12] See also chapter 3, above.
[13] OV, 6:18; above, pp. 154, 172–173.
[14] *Brut*, trans. Jones, p. 23.

him with seizing neighboring lands illegally. William responded by leaving for Normandy in a rage and declaring for Robert Curthose, whereupon Henry confiscated the earldom of Cornwall.[15] William of Mortain was taken prisoner two years later at Tinchebray and incarcerated in the Tower of London for the remainder of the reign. The forfeitures of Robert of Bellême and William of Mortain marked the end, in Henry's England, of private military feuds and the unsanctioned building of castles or the purloining or ravaging of neighbors' lands. In the place of such private enterprise, Henry gradually expanded and reformed the system of shire courts and regularized the use of royal justices in eyre.[16] Law came to supersede violence as the means of settling property disputes.

Henry's reform of the itinerant royal court was another step in the direction of imposing law and discipline on his baronage. At the beginning of the reign barons tended to be unruly. Some were exchanging tasteless jokes about Henry and Queen Matilda; the Clares and Giffards and their retainers were bullying Henry's court. Much worse, royal courtiers continued during Henry's opening years, as in the time of Rufus and Curthose, to pillage and torment inhabitants of the villages through which the court passed.[17] Henry brought these practices to an end around 1108 by imposing severe sanctions against misbehavior while granting uniform stipends for court attendance.

Henry's strict rules against curial looting and sexual harassment, along with his policy of discouraging his courtiers from wearing extravagant clothing, curly-toed shoes, and the flowing locks so deplored by reform churchmen, may have resulted in some of his courtiers feeling shackled. One modern scholar has cautiously implied that such restrictions were "uncourtly."[18] But life at Henry's court remained lively and exuberant, marked by feasts, rich gifts, sports, gallantry, hilarity and "decent mirth."[19] It was also, compared to other royal courts elsewhere and later, notably stable in its membership after the reforms of 1108 and firm in its loyalty.[20] The one exception

---

[15] Above, pp. 182–183.
[16] WM, *GR*, 2:473; *ASC, s.a.* 1104; above, pp. 212–213.
[17] Above, pp. 213–215; WM, *GR*, 2:487.
[18] Jaeger, *Origins of Courtliness*, pp. 179–181, 193–195, 231; Hollister, "Courtly Culture and Courtly Style," pp. 10–11. Constraints against long hair were not notably successful in Henry's reign: see WM, *HN*, pp. 5–6.
[19] Above, pp. 215–216; Gaimar, *L'Estoire des Engleis*, ed. Bell, p. 206; Map, *De nugis curialium*, pp. 438, 470–472; cf. WM, *GR*, 2:488 (in reference to Henry I): "Facetiarum pro tempore plenus; nec pro mole negotiorum, cum se communioni dedisset, minus jocundus."
[20] Green, *Government*, pp. 169–170; the stability of the court was of course diminished by losses from the White Ship disaster.

in the course of the entire reign, Malmesbury states, was the assassination conspiracy of 1118 led by "a certain chamberlain" of modest estate, whose resulting fall from grace was hardly comparable in impact to the fall of the Erembalds in Flanders or the Garlandes in France.[21]

The alleged downfall of two other, much more important members of Henry's court has been misinterpreted, creating the false impression that court life was as hazardous and slippery under Henry I as it later became in Tudor times. First, the arrest of the justiciar–sheriff–treasury chamberlain Geoffrey of Clinton in 1130 has been wrongly seen as marking the end of his curial career. In fact Geoffrey, having been charged with some unspecified act of treason, was arrested only briefly. He was promptly acquitted in King Henry's court, at a hearing presided over by David king of Scots. Afterward Geoffrey resumed his curial role and continued to attest royal charters until his death (ca. 1132/1133).[22]

Second, there is the supposed fall of the great *curialis* Robert Bloet bishop of Lincoln, recorded so memorably by Henry of Huntingdon and echoed in the writings of several modern scholars.[23] The tale originates in the treatise *De contemptu mundi*, the morose and moralizing letter to "Walter," written by Henry of Huntingdon many years after Bishop Robert's death.[24] To add to his collection of examples of great men suffering painful reverses (the unifying theme of his essay), Henry of Huntingdon reports that late in life Bishop Robert complained of having recently lost two cases in the royal courts and thus of having fallen afoul of the cold, inscrutable Henry I after having served him faithfully over many years. It happens that records survive of two pleas that Bishop Robert lost during his final years, very likely the two that he complained of losing. In one, a royal inquest jury decided against him in his dispute with St Augustine's, Canterbury, over the lordship of Royton, Kent, but Robert was nevertheless permitted to hold the property from the abbot indefinitely, free of the castle guard and host service that normally pertained to it.[25] The other plea resulted in a royal mandate concerning the manor of Lessness, Kent, which Robert held of Westminster Abbey: Robert was to render to the abbey, in return

[21] WM, *GR*, 2:488; Suger, *Louis le Gros*, p. 190; above, pp. 318, 321–322.

[22] Southern, *Medieval Humanism*, p. 217; Green, *Government*, pp. 33, 170, 216; OV, 4:276; HH, p. 486; *RRAN* 2, nos 420 (Chartres, 23 January 1131), 1688 (Rouen, 1131), 1715–1716 (both Northampton, 8 September 1131), 1798 (1131–1133),

[23] E.g., Southern, *Medieval Humanism*, pp. 224–225; Green, *Government*, p. 188; Newman, *Anglo-Norman Nobility*, pp. 93–94.

[24] HH, pp. 586–588.

[25] *RRAN* 2, no. 1283 (AD 1121?).

for the manor, the services that he himself had earlier agreed to provide.[26] In short, Robert's losses in both cases were trivial.

That Henry's court might find in favor of St Augustine's or Westminster Abbey, presumably on the basis of sound evidence, cannot be taken to indicate a Luciferian fall from heaven on Bishop Robert's part. Losing a plea or two would doubtless be irritating, and Robert probably grumbled about it in the hearing of his young archdeacon, Henry of Huntingdon, perhaps over a goblet or two of good wine. Many years later, when Henry of Huntingdon was casting about for examples of the transitory nature of worldly success, he recalled Robert Bloet's two lost pleas and used them for all they were worth. But charter evidence discloses Robert attesting royal acts without interruption until on 10 January 1123 he suffered a fatal stroke while riding at King Henry's side in the royal deer park at Woodstock, discussing affairs of state with him and Roger of Salisbury. "Lord king, I am dying," the bishop said as he sank down on his horse. Henry, quickly dismounting, caught Bishop Robert as he fell, escorted him into the royal dwelling, and remained at his bedside until he died.[27] Robert's influence lingered on when, in early February at Gloucester, King Henry was persuaded to permit the election of the regular canon William of Corbeil to the archbishopric of Canterbury, despite the bitter complaints of the Canterbury monks, through the influence of the bishop of Salisbury "and the bishop of Lincoln before his death."[28] Robert Bloet's plunge from royal favor is clearly one of Henry of Huntingdon's moralizing pipe dreams. In actuality, no major *curialis* of Henry I's fell from the king's good graces for any appreciable interval of time during the final quarter-century of his rule.[29] In comparison to other, later regimes in English history, Henry's was stable beyond all measure.

The same is true of the stability and heritability of aristocratic tenures after the anxious opening years of the reign. Throughout its final twenty years, from approximately 1115 to 1135, tenures and inheritances in England were secure. No important family forfeited its lands during that period. Having endured a sequence of tenurial upheavals following the Norman Conquest, members of the aristocracy in England could now depend on retaining possession of their family

[26] Ibid., no. 1383 (AD 1121–Jan. 1123). Conversely, *RRAN* 2, no. 1254 (AD 1120–1122), reports the restoration to Bishop Robert of two Lincolnshire estates belonging to the royal domain.

[27] HH, pp. 470, 586–588, where Henry of Huntingdon seems to chide the king for being unable to cure the fallen bishop; see further *ASC, s.a.* 1123; SD, 2:268.

[28] *ASC, s.a.* 1123.

[29] One possible exception: the would-be assassin Herbert the Chamberlain was a relatively small fish, and his downfall cannot be ascribed to an inscrutable royal whim.

estates.[30] During Henry's last two decades, the integrity of baronial landholdings was threatened neither by the aggression of hostile neighbors nor by royal confiscation, but only by a failure of heirs.

In Normandy, because of the crises of 1111–1113, 1118–1119, and 1123–1124, forfeitures were more common than in England: in 1112 Robert of Bellême lost his freedom and his continental possessions (most of which passed to his son, William Talvas), and the leading Franco-Norman rebels captured at Rougemontier in 1124—Waleran of Meulan, Hugh of Montfort, and Hugh of Châteauneuf—were imprisoned for a time.[31] More significant, however, is the considerable number of Norman rebels whom Henry disseised and then restored: William and Helwise of Evreux, William Crispin, Amaury de Montfort, Robert of Neubourg, and others. Even Waleran of Meulan recovered his lands and the king's favor after five years' imprisonment. Eustace and Juliana lost Breteuil permanently but were compensated with revenues from England.[32] To describe Henry's regime as a "reign of terror" is to misunderstand it profoundly. His goal was not to destroy his nobles or take vengeance on them but to mold them into trustworthy participants in his regime.

In the course of time, Henry achieved this goal. A substantial number of his magnates supported Henry's peace and profited from his lordship. He succeeded in shaping a royalist baronage in England and to a lesser but significant extent in Normandy, a baronage bound to him not by fear so much as by gratitude for past and present favors and the hope of future ones. Because he was disinclined toward military aggression and therefore had no supply of newly conquered lands such as William I had utilized to enrich his own men, Henry was obliged to reach elsewhere for the means of rewarding his supporters. The *terra regis* had been moderately enhanced by the forfeitures of such families as the earls of Hereford (1075), Shrewsbury (1102), and Cornwall (1104), but about 1113/1114 such forfeitures ceased. And because the engine of foreign conquest no longer rolled, lands, offices, and privileges had to be distributed with caution and finesse. In this connection,

---

[30] DeAragon, "Growth of Secure Inheritance"; cf. Newman, *Anglo-Norman Nobility*, p. 117. Notice, too, the instances of magnates' being disseised and then restored: William of Warenne and Philip of Braose in England and, in Normandy, William of Evreux, Amaury de Montfort, William Crispin, Waleran of Meulan, and William Talvas.

[31] Above, p. 304; Waleran and Hugh of Châteauneuf were rehabilitated in 1129; Hugh of Montfort, who had earlier rejected Henry's offer of pardon and the restoration of his lands, remained in custody after Henry's death, perhaps at the instigation of Waleran, who acquired custody of the Montfort honor: Crouch, *Beaumont Twins*, pp. 29–30.

[32] Above, pp. 254–255, 268.

Henry's notable administrative reforms[33]—the exchequer with its pipe rolls, the system of judicial eyres, the reorganized treasury and expanded chancery—must be viewed not only as revenue-raising devices but also as means of systematizing the allotment of royal patronage to great and small alike. It was important to modernize the instruments of revenue collection in order to supplement the income from a gradually diminishing royal demesne[34] with new sources of income or old sources more rigorously audited. But it was likewise important to have exact records of exemptions from danegeld, *auxilium burgi*, and *murdrum*, of the marriages of heiresses to royal favorites, of debts that might be collected swiftly, or permitted to run on year after year, or pardoned altogether because of the king's love of the earl of Leicester or the lord of Pontefract. The pipe rolls are records not only of debts and payments but also of debts pardoned or left uncollected, taxes forgiven, income relinquished, all for the sake of patronage. The Pipe Roll of 1130 records payments into the treasury of about £24,200, but it also reports some £40,000 still owing, along with exemptions and pardons of well over £5,000.[35] To describe such a political system as "predatory" is altogether implausible.

It is possible to examine Henry I's baronial policies, at least in very general terms, by estimating the relative wealth of his great landholders, the frequency of their attendance at the royal court, and the patronage that the king bestowed on them, their close kinspeople, and sometimes their clients. The names of magnates, prelates, and officials on the witness lists of royal charters (of which more than 1,500 survive) provide a rough but indispensable gauge of their attendance at court and proximity to the king.[36] Evidence of Henry's patronage of various magnates and their families is to be found in both narrative and record sources of the reign, most abundantly in the Pipe Roll of 1130. Their relative wealth is much more difficult to measure. Domesday Book becomes an increasingly poor index of baronial estate values as Henry's reign progresses. Some impression of baronial wealth can be derived from the old enfeoffment totals (the number of knights enfeoffed by the death of Henry I) in Henry II's *Cartae baronum*: any magnate who

---

[33] To be discussed in chapter 9, below.

[34] Green, "William Rufus, Henry I and the Royal Demesne."

[35] Green, *Government*, pp. 220–225; *MMI*, p. 177; my figures include rough estimates of counties and revenues that had been recorded on lost or illegible membranes of the Pipe Roll of 1130 and therefore differ slightly from Green's totals.

[36] Below, p. 361 ff. It has been objected that witnesses might attest for various reasons, or that their names might be added later, or that witness lists do not include everyone present at court; such objections have no merit when one contrasts an occasional visitor who attests three charters over ten years with a *curialis* who attests thirty over the same period. See also appendix, p. 499 ff. below.

had enfeoffed one hundred or one hundred and fifty knights on his estates by 1135 must have been, to say the least, comfortably well off. Again, the danegeld exemptions on baronial demesnes recorded in the Pipe Roll of 1130 reflect baronial wealth in some instances, but unfortunately not in most. The difficulty is that danegeld exemptions measure not only demesne values (at the rate of two shillings on the hide) but royal favor as well: magnates who were seldom at court received minuscule exemptions, if any.[37] Despite these difficulties, I have formulated a list of Henry's magnates about 1125–1135 divided according to their probable landed wealth. The division is based on old enfeoffment totals, supplemented by Domesday data when the honors in question appear to have remained stable and by 1130 danegeld exemptions when they are high enough to suggest that the entire demesne is exempt. As far as possible I have tried to follow the classification system developed by William Corbett in the *Cambridge Medieval History* to measure the wealth of Domesday magnates, although, to repeat, my data are distinctly less reliable than his.[38] I begin with class AA: three "supermagnates"—Robert of Gloucester and Stephen of Blois with about 300 fees each, and Roger bishop of Salisbury, whose danegeld exemption total in 1130 suggests comparable wealth.[39] Next, class A: eight lay magnates with 100 to 200 fees. Then, class B: a dozen or so laymen with about 60 to 90 fees. And finally, class C: about thirty laymen with 30 to 60 fees. The methodology, although admittedly precarious, does provide a valuable general picture—blurred but not seriously misleading. And one can hardly arrive at any meaningful conclusions about Henry I's policies toward his wealthiest barons without having some reasonably clear notion as to who they were. The prosopographical approach that I have proposed (see appendix below) can provide a useful corrective to the often repeated charges that Henry I's regime repressed its magnates, dominated them by terror and savage reprisals, and transformed them into a powder keg that exploded on Henry's death. Instead of the traditional picture of

---

[37] For example, Walter Giffard earl of Buckingham, Robert of Ferrers, and Henry count of Eu rarely attest royal charters; Walter Giffard has no danegeld exemptions, and the exemptions for Robert of Ferrers and Henry of Eu are trivial: *PR 31 Henry I* (*passim*).

[38] *CMH*, 5:508–511.

[39] The Pipe Roll of 1130 records danegeld exemptions on Roger's lands in excess of £150, indicating at least 1,500 demesne hides or, very roughly, £1,500 a year from his demesne alone. I have classified Roger as a magnate rather than a prelate because the bulk of his landed wealth was clearly nonepiscopal: the total value of the bishop of Salisbury's Domesday manors, demesne and enfeoffed, was £580 a year. Cf. WM, *HN*, p. 31: Stephen arrested Roger in 1139 not as a bishop but as a royal servant and castellan, much as William I had arrested Odo not as bishop of Bayeux but as earl of Kent.

undifferentiated barons steaming with resentment, it may be illuminating to examine these barons individually.

Some historians have restricted the term *magnate* in Henry I's reign to the heirs of what they call "the old Conquest baronage." I prefer the more straightforward definition: a magnate is, quite simply, a very wealthy landholder. The timeworn distinction between old and new families raises the question: What do we mean by "old"? Were there indeed any "old" magnate families in England at Henry I's accession? Henry's so-called old Conquest magnates in 1100 were William I's "new men" or their sons—the beneficiaries of a prodigious land redistribution that had occurred in stages over the previous thirty-odd years. Moreover, it seems probable that the Conqueror's companions themselves represented a Norman aristocracy "of comparatively recent growth."[40] Most of the Conquest families had been dominant in Normandy for only a generation or two. William I's half-brothers, Robert of Mortain and Odo of Bayeux, recipients of tremendously lucrative earldoms in England, were sons of a relatively obscure Norman *vicomte*, Herluin of Conteville, and his wife Herlève, whose liaison with Duke Robert I had had such momentous consequences but who was herself a mere burgher's daughter. Odo became bishop of Bayeux only about 1050; Robert became count of Mortain in 1055. Accordingly, the forfeitures suffered by Odo in 1088 and by Robert of Mortain's son William in 1104 can hardly be viewed as a ruthless uprooting of ancient families.

Henry's wealthiest magnates in the period 1125–1135 came from a variety of backgrounds. Some were heirs of the richest (class A) Conquest families: Clare, Chester, Richmond, Warenne. Others represented families with lesser but growing English wealth: Beaumont, Bigod. Still others were younger, noninheriting sons or recognized bastards of royal or comital fathers: Robert earl of Gloucester, Stephen of Blois, Brian fitz Count. Only one among the eleven class AA and class

---

[40] Douglas, *William the Conqueror*, p. 89 and, more generally, pp. 83–104; Le Patourel, "Norman Barons," *passim*; Musset, "L'Aristocratie normande au XIe siècle," pp. 88–94. More recently David Bates has contended that the Conquest aristocracy of Normandy was old after all, arguing not from prosopographical evidence (of which there is virtually none) but from the theories of medieval aristocratic development on the Continent proposed by such scholars as Gerd Tellenbach, Karl Schmid, and Georges Duby: Bates, *Normandy before 1066*, pp. 34–36, 133–134; echoed in Chibnall, *Anglo-Norman England*, p. 162; cf. Tellenbach, "Zur Erforschung des hochmittelalterlichen Adels," 1:318–336; Schmid, "The Structure of the Nobility in the Earlier Middle Ages," pp. 37–59; Duby, *Chivalrous Society*, pp. 59–80, 94–111, 134–157. Hollister ("Greater Domesday Tenants-in-Chief," pp. 230–235) employs prosopographical evidence to argue, against Bates' thesis, that the Conqueror's companions did indeed constitute a recently risen aristocracy.

A magnates, Roger of Salisbury, had truly risen from the dust.[41] (I venture to suggest that a regime so conservative as to prohibit the rise of new men would be neither very successful nor very attractive.)

Four of Henry's eleven wealthiest magnates—Roger of Salisbury, Robert of Gloucester, Brian fitz Count, and Hugh Bigod—figure among the ten most frequent baronial attesters of his charters, and three others were bound to the king by ties of kinship, gratitude, or both. Stephen of Blois owed everything to Henry; Ranulf le Meschin had been advanced by royal favor to the earldom of Chester; and Robert earl of Leicester owed his substantial Norman honor of Breteuil to Henry and his English earldom to Henry's generosity toward his father, Robert of Meulan. Seven of the eleven represented families of either the greater or lesser baronage under William the Conqueror.[42] Eight were receiving substantial danegeld exemptions ranging from £20 to more than £150 in 1129–1130.[43] One of the eleven, Stephen of Richmond, was absent for most of the reign attending to his considerable estates in Brittany. He caused no trouble, did no personal service to Henry, and received no immunity from danegeld, but his other pardons, exemptions, and assorted benefits from the king place him among the ten most favored men in England in 1129–1130.[44] Nine of the eleven magnates of classes AA and A were men, or the sons of men, who had profited substantially from Henry's favor. From the truce of 1101 until Henry's death in 1135, none of the eleven, or their fathers, had opposed the king either in England or in Normandy.

My division of the magnates into classes is obviously fuzzy at the boundaries separating class A from class B and class B from class C. But the trend toward royalist magnates pierces these boundaries. At the top of class B one encounters two *curiales* and royal servants, Geoffrey of Clinton and Nigel of Aubigny, along with David king of Scots who owed everything to Henry. Farther down in the Bs are William of Aubigny

---

[41] In order to avoid suggesting a precise rank order that my methodology cannot support, I have chosen not to list in tabular form the magnates who appear to make up these several classes. The three class AA magnates in 1125–1135 are Robert of Gloucester, Stephen of Blois, and Roger of Salisbury. The eight magnates in class A are Stephen of Richmond, Ranulf I and II earls of Chester, Robert earl of Leicester, William of Warenne earl of Surrey, Richard fitz Gilbert of Clare, Roger earl of Warwick, Hugh Bigod, and Brian fitz Count. Geoffrey of Clinton, with a demesne exemption of £59 in 1130, may well have enjoyed comparable wealth; although Southern regarded him as a middle-ranking landholder, the exemption suggests that his demesne alone may have been worth some £600 a year; Corbett's class A begins at £750, but the figure includes both demesne and enfeoffed manors.

[42] Stephen of Richmond, Ranulf of Chester, Robert of Leicester, William of Warenne, Richard of Clare, Roger of Warwick, and Hugh Bigod.

[43] All but Stephen of Richmond, Richard of Clare, and Roger of Warwick.

[44] Mooers, "Patronage and the Pipe Roll of 1130," pp. 293–294.

Pincerna (butler), a frequently attesting member of the royal household, Walter fitz Richard who received his barony of Netherwent from the king some time before 1119, Robert fitz Richard to whom Henry gave the Baynard honor of Little Dunmow, and William Maltravers whom Henry had planted in the forfeited Lacy honor of Pontefract.[45] These last two elevations exemplify a policy, to which the late R. H. C. Davis called our attention, of creating royalist magnates by placing them on the forfeited lands of the king's enemies. Robert of Lacy and William Baynard had both been disseised for treason around 1110–1113, presumably for conspiring to support William Clito. Should Clito ever prevail over Henry I, the Lacy and Baynard honors would doubtless be restored to the families that had held them previously and had supported the good cause. The new holders thus had a compelling reason to back their king.

Notice, too, that Walter fitz Richard of Netherwent and Robert fitz Richard of Little Dunmow were younger brothers of the class A magnate Gilbert of Clare and of Roger lord of Bienfaite and Orbec in Normandy. Gilbert of Clare was the magnate who, with his kinsmen and entourage, had caused such a rumpus at Henry's court during his initial year. Henry, who seldom held a grudge when it was against his interest, had favored Gilbert in 1110 with the lordship of Ceredigion in Wales.[46] All Gilbert's lands passed on his death in 1117 to Richard, his eldest son. Henry's generosity to Gilbert and the two Clare cadets had the effect of putting the entire cross-Channel Clare family in his debt. If any of the Clares had been tempted to betray Henry for Clito, the temptation would have been dampened by the realization that a victory for Clito would probably cost their kinsman Robert his barony of Little Dunmow. In 1119, at the climactic battle of Brémule, Roger fitz Richard, the Norman Clare, was in the first rank of Henry's army.[47] When the Vexin baron William Crispin struck at Henry's head with his sword, it was Roger fitz Richard who knocked William Crispin to earth, thereby perhaps saving Henry's life.[48]

The conversion of the Clares was an impressive achievement. The family had participated in the rebellion against Rufus in 1088; they had conspired against him in 1095, as well as bullying Henry in the early months of his reign. When Curthose invaded in 1101 Gilbert of Clare apparently sat on the fence while his uncle, Walter II Giffard, joined

---

[45] Sanders, *Baronies*, pp. 110, 129, 138. Of the twelve class B barons, at least seven were either *curiales* of Henry I or deeply beholden to him.
[46] Above, p. 236.
[47] OV, 6:234–236; "Chron. de Hida," in *Liber de Hyda*, pp. 316–317; "De libertate beccensis monasterii," 5:604, placing Roger fitz Richard at Henry's side at the siege of Brionne in 1124.
[48] OV, 6:238; above, pp. 264–265.

the duke's army.[49] But Henry's gift of Ceredigion to Gilbert and his handsome provisions for Gilbert's younger brothers evidently had their effect. The Clares and Giffards remained royalists for the rest of the reign.

Henry's baronial policy shows to even greater effect in his handling of William II of Warenne earl of Surrey, whose father's Domesday estates were exceeded in wealth only by those of Odo of Bayeux, Roger of Montgomery, and William of Mortain.[50] William I of Warenne had fought for the Conqueror at Hastings, helped crush the earls' rebellion in 1075, and died in mid-1088 of a wound received while fighting for Rufus during the rebellion of that year. Either to ensure William of Warenne's loyalty in 1088 or to reward it, Rufus advanced him to the earldom of Surrey. His son and heir, William II of Warenne, succeeded to his father's new title and his lands in England, and he also seems to have inherited the Norman patrimony centering on the castles of Mortemer and Bellencombre in upper Normandy. Like other young magnates of his generation, he was not the dependable royalist that his father had been. He played a part in the sporadic baronial warfare of Curthose's earlier years in Normandy. Sometime in the 1090s he is reported to have unsuccessfully sought the hand of the Scottish princess Edith-Matilda, and, as previously remarked, her subsequent marriage to Henry I may have been the cause of William's alleged habit of taunting the new king with a derisive nickname.[51] Henry ignored the insult and made an effort to win William of Warenne's allegiance by offering him a royal bastard daughter in marriage. Archbishop Anselm, however, quashed the project on the grounds of consanguinity, and we find William of Warenne among the rebels who welcomed Robert Curthose's invasion of mid-1101. Having exiled William to Normandy and seized his earldom, Henry reinstated him two years later at the request of Curthose, who in exchange relinquished the annuity of three thousand marks that Henry had granted him. During the years that followed, in Orderic's words, William "throve as one of Henry's closest friends and councillors."[52]

Orderic's observation is borne out by other evidence. As we have seen, William of Warenne served as one of Henry's chief military commanders at the battle of Tinchebray. And in 1110 or shortly thereafter Henry secured William's loyalty for all time by granting him the castle and lordship of Saint-Saens in upper Normandy. Henry had seized the

---

[49] Above, pp. 132–133.
[50] *MMI*, pp. 137–144, 181–182.
[51] Ibid., pp. 140–142, 181, 315; above, p. 132; Wace, *Roman de Rou*, 2:275–276.
[52] OV, 6:14.

honor when its previous lord, Helias of Saint-Saens, accompanied William Clito in his flight from Normandy just ahead of the royal officials whom Henry had sent to apprehend him. It happens that the castle of Saint-Saens lies about three miles up the River Varenne from the Warenne castle of Bellencombre. Henry's grant to William was thus another instance of the royal policy of granting forfeited enemy holdings to his supporters in order to guarantee their continued loyalty. In Orderic's words, Henry gave Saint-Saens to William of Warenne "to secure his loyal support and resolute defence against enemy attacks."[53] The new lordship constituted a valuable and strategic addition to the Warenne holdings in upper Normandy, and William would have realized that should Clito ever return in triumph, Saint-Saens would be restored to Helias, Clito's guardian, brother-in-law, and companion in exile.

Accordingly, William of Warenne now became a *familiaris* of the king and an ardent royalist. Having attested only once (or possibly twice) for Rufus, he witnessed a total of sixty-nine of Henry I's surviving charters. In 1111 he was sitting as a judge in Henry's court in Normandy, and in 1119, at the climactic battle of Brémule, William of Warenne fought alongside Roger fitz Richard, the Norman Clare, in the front rank of Henry's victorious army. William is quoted as telling the king on the eve of battle:

> There is no one who can persuade me to treason. . . . I and my kinsmen here and now place ourselves in mortal opposition to the king of France and are totally faithful to you. . . . I will support this undertaking, with my men, in the first rank of your army and will myself sustain the full weight of battle.[54]

William's danegeld exemptions in 1129–1130 came to the tidy sum of £104—the third-highest figure among the English baronage—testifying not only to the value of his lands but to the warm affection of his monarch. When Henry lay dying at Lyons-la-Forêt in 1135 Earl William was at his bedside, and he was one of the five *comites* who escorted the royal corpse to Rouen for embalming.[55]

Henry I did not squander lands and privileges on his magnates, for his resources, unlike King William I's, were limited, and he intended neither to impoverish himself nor to raise magnates to such heights as to rival their monarch. This William of Mortain discovered to his sorrow

---

[53] Ibid., p. 164; by 1150, however, Saint-Saens was back in the hands of Helias' descendants.

[54] "Chron. de Hida," in *Liber de Hyda*, pp. 316–317.

[55] *MMI*, pp. 143–144.

when Henry denied his request to add his uncle's earldom of Kent to his own earldom of Cornwall.[56] When the king's old friend Hugh earl of Chester died in 1101, Henry reared Richard, Hugh's seven-year-old son and heir, at the royal court, and in time arranged a distinguished marriage for him. Richard's bride, Matilda of Blois, was the sister of Stephen and Count Theobald and the king's own niece. Richard of Chester, like Roger fitz Richard and William of Warenne, was absolutely loyal to Henry in the crisis of 1118–1119.[57] Henry had meanwhile raised Othuer, Earl Hugh's bastard and Richard's half-brother, to a position of considerable wealth, entrusting him with the custody of the Tower of London.[58] Tragically, Richard of Chester perished in the White Ship disaster of 1120 along with his wife Matilda of Blois and his half-brother Othuer. Since Richard and Matilda had no offspring, the flexible inheritance customs of the time would have permitted Chester to revert to the king.[59] Nevertheless, Henry granted the earldom to Ranulf le Meschin, Richard's first cousin, a devoted royalist of long standing who may well have participated in the successful effort to convince Robert Curthose to free Henry from captivity in 1089. Ranulf had fought heroically for Henry in the battle of Tinchebray and had given him staunch support in the crisis of 1118–1119.[60] Ranulf was already a wealthy Anglo-Norman baron—*vicomte* of the Bessin, lord of extensive lands in Cumberland, and, through his thrice-married wife Lucy, a major landholder in Lincolnshire. In exchange for his advancement to the earldom of Chester—England's seventh or eighth wealthiest Domesday honor—and to Earl Richard's Norman *vicomté* of Avranches, Ranulf gave to the king most of Lucy's estates, apparently with her permission, and his own lands in Cumberland.[61] The exchange aroused conflicts in later years between the monarchy and Lucy's heir, William of Roumare,[62] but Ranulf le Meschin seems to have accepted the arrangement with good cheer: he had gained a comital title and a fortune, and Henry had prevented the formation of a baronial agglomeration of dangerous proportions.[63] Although not a major figure at

---

[56] Above, pp. 182–183.

[57] OV, 6:222, 304; above, p. 257.

[58] *MMI*, pp. 120–123.

[59] The honor of Eudo *Dapifer* escheated to the crown at about this time under similar circumstances.

[60] OV, 6:84, 88, 222–224.

[61] *CP*, 3:155; 7:668, 745.

[62] Above, p. 293.

[63] On the vast estates the earls of Chester might have controlled had they made good all their claims see Jolliffe, *Constitutional History*, p. 172. Ranulf seems to have held for a time the lands between Ribble and Mersey that Henry had seized in 1102 from Robert of Bellême's brother, Roger the Poitevin; White, "King Stephen, Duke Henry and Ranulf de Gerons, Earl of Chester," p. 558.

court, Ranulf attested Henry's charters with some frequency, particularly after his advancement to the earldom.[64] His loyalty was such that Henry sent him to Normandy in 1123 to take a major role in its defense against Angevin aggression and baronial rebellion.[65] At Ranulf's death in 1129, the earldom passed quietly to his son, Ranulf II, who is reported in the Pipe Roll of 1130 as owing a thousand marks of his father's debt for the land of Earl Hugh.[66]

This pipe roll entry is of exceptional importance in that it suggests a form of royal patronage—the deliberate noncollection of a debt—that occurs repeatedly in the pipe rolls of Henry II. The run of annual pipe rolls from 1156 onward discloses a pattern in which royal favorites often pay little or nothing on a debt over a long period of years and, in the end, are sometimes pardoned altogether.[67] This kind of policy is virtually impossible to perceive in Henry I's reign, where only the single pipe roll survives. Sir Frank Stenton and others built their theory of Henry I's repression on evidence from the roll of 1130 for baronial debts rather than baronial payments. To quote Stenton, "The £102 16s. 8d. laid on Simon de Beauchamp because he had been the pledge of a man whom he did not produce in court seems grotesquely severe."[68] But Simon in fact paid less than a third of the fine (£33 6s. 8d.) and, for all we know, may never have paid the rest. The Chester relief seems to disclose precisely such a policy of noncollection. The round figure of one thousand marks suggests that it may have been the full original assessment. Earl Ranulf II paid nothing on it in 1130. It is described as his father's debt, which probably indicates that it was the full relief assessed on the earldom when Ranulf le Meschin received it back in 1121. Further, the designation of the honor as the land of Earl Hugh may well imply that Earl Richard, who acceded to the earldom as a child on Hugh's death in 1101 and grew up in the royal court, had paid no relief by the time of his own death in 1120 in the White Ship—probably because the king had custody of the honor during Richard's long minority. Whatever the case, Earl Ranulf le Meschin was evidently permitted to leave unpaid throughout his eight-year tenure what was probably the full relief on his earldom. Such was Henry's policy toward a faithful earl, an old friend, and a singularly wealthy noble. It demonstrates how king and magnates could prosper together in the new era of exchequer accounting

---

[64] Eleven attestations in the eight years between his advancement in 1121 and his death in 1129: *RRAN* 2, nos 1243–1602 *passim*.

[65] SD, 2:267–268.

[66] *PR 31 Henry I*, p. 110. Young Ranulf received danegeld exemptions on 210 demesne hides in addition to his Chester lands, which owed no geld.

[67] Keefe, *Feudal Assessments*, pp. 116–140.

[68] Stenton, *English Feudalism*, pp. 221–222, from *PR 31 Henry I*, p. 103.

just as in the land-grabbing, swashbuckling years of William the Conqueror.

Thus far we have been concentrating on the great Domesday honors that remained intact or expanded only modestly under Henry I. Other families, of middling wealth under the Conqueror and Rufus, were raised to the heights of class A only under Henry I. Orderic states that immediately on his accession Henry, apparently in contrast to Rufus, eschewed the advice of rash young men and followed the counsel of wise, older men, among whom Robert of Meulan, Hugh of Chester, Richard of Redvers, and Roger Bigod are singled out by name.[69] The notion of the good king being surrounded by wise and seasoned advisers is of course a medieval political cliché, and, despite Orderic's implication, three of the four men he names had attested regularly for William Rufus. Only Richard of Redvers was new to the *curia*. A baron of western Normandy, he had been a loyal friend during Henry's turbulent youth and now became a frequent witness of royal charters. Henry granted him a very substantial barony, chiefly in Devon and the Isle of Wight, carved out of *terra regis* and the vast honor forfeited by Roger earl of Hereford in 1075. Although Roger Bigod and Robert of Meulan had been major attesters for Rufus, it was Henry who catapulted them into the top echelon of the English landholding aristocracy. Roger Bigod's Domesday lands, worth £450 a year, kept him in the lower circles of Corbett's class B barons. But the family prospered, chiefly as a result of Henry I's gifts to Roger, and to such a degree that the Bigod *carta* of 1166 reports the very impressive total of 125 knights having been enfeoffed by 1135. Roger and later his son Hugh served as royal stewards and figured among the most frequent lay attesters of Henry's charters.[70]

Robert, count of Meulan and lord of Beaumont, was a lord of immense wealth on the Continent but held a Domesday estate of only about £250, placing him toward the bottom of Corbett's class C. Henry permitted him to acquire, from the disgraced Ivo of Grandmesnil, the considerable Grandmesnil family estates centering on Leicester, plus chunks of the forfeited earldom of William of Mortain in the rape of Pevensey and elsewhere, along with portions of *terra regis*.[71] He became the first earl of Leicester, a notable achievement in a regime that did not create new earldoms with careless abandon, and his successor

---

[69] OV, 5:298; cf. FW, 2:57.
[70] Sanders, *Baronies*, pp. 46–47; *CP*, 9:575–579.
[71] Fox, "Honour and Earldom of Leicester," pp. 385–388; Mason, *William the First and the Sussex Rapes*, p. 20.

in early Angevin times answered for 157 knights fees, a figure that suggests prodigious wealth.[72] Robert earned his fortune by serving as Henry's chief adviser, his most frequent lay attester, his alter ego.[73] Robert's twin sons, Waleran and Robert, were raised in the royal court and, as we have seen, became *comites* of Meulan and Leicester respectively on their father's death in 1118. Robert earl of Leicester always remained loyal to Henry I, whereas Waleran, whose lands were chiefly in Normandy and France, rebelled in 1123–1124 and paid for it with five years of imprisonment.[74] The Pipe Roll of 1130, which dates from shortly after Waleran's release, discloses the fiscal dimensions of both the royal anger and the royal love. Waleran is charged one hundred marks for the recovery of his modest estates in Dorset (but pays none of it), while at the same time the flow of royal patronage is resumed: he receives danegeld exemptions on forty-six demesne hides in 1129, fifty-two in 1130, and is among those royal favorites exempted from the *murdrum* fine.[75] Waleran learned Henry's lesson well: he attested the king's charters regularly thereafter and did not rebel again.[76]

An important minority of Henry I's class A and AA magnates inherited nothing in England or Normandy and owed their entire fortunes to Henry. Brian fitz Count, a bastard son of the count of Brittany, rose through royal gifts and a marriage to Maud heiress of Wallingford to become one of Henry's wealthiest magnates and most active *curiales*—with danegeld exemptions on 720 demesne hides.[77] Robert earl of Gloucester and Stephen of Blois rose still higher, again through royal gifts and strategic marriages.[78] Stephen of Blois' English fortune derived primarily from the forfeited honors of Henry's enemies, William Malet and Roger the Poitevin (Robert of Bellême's brother), and from Stephen's marriage to the heiress Matilda of Boulogne.[79]

Henry's three wealthiest English landholders—Robert of Gloucester, Stephen of Blois, and Roger bishop of Salisbury—were in a class apart. Nobody else approached them in landed wealth. And all three were

---

[72] In 1172, 157 knights fees; no earlier enfeoffment data exists for the Beaumont earldom of Leicester: Keefe, *Feudal Assessments*, p. 162.

[73] See Walker, "King Henry I's 'Old Men,' " pp. 3–5; Le Patourel, *Feudal Empires*, pp. vi, 12–15.

[74] Above, pp. 292–304. Robert earl of Leicester supported Stephen almost to the end, and served as one of Henry II's chief justiciars: *CP*, 7:527–530.

[75] *PR 31 Henry I*, pp. 13–16 and *passim*.

[76] See in general Crouch, *Beaumont Twins* (*passim*). On Waleran's attestations for Henry I after his release: *RRAN* 2, nos 1607, 1688–1690, 1693, 1699, 1702, 1711. Waleran was at Henry's deathbed in 1135 and was one of five *comites* who bore the royal corpse from Lyons-la-Forêt to Rouen.

[77] Southern, *Medieval Humanism*, p. 220.

[78] *Earldom of Gloucester Charters*, p. 3; *CP*, 5:683–684.

[79] Davis, *King Stephen*, pp. 4–10.

Henry's creations and unswerving *fideles*. Stephen's ascent has been described as Henry's single act of folly—forced on him by his need of an alliance with Stephen's brother, Theobald count of Blois.[80] But it should be clear from our foregoing discussions of war and diplomacy on the Continent that Theobald needed Henry's support at least as much as Henry needed Theobald's. Indeed, Henry's elevation of Stephen and Robert of Gloucester is better seen as an expression of deliberate royal policy, uninfluenced by diplomatic factors. A comparison of Corbett's classification of the foremost landholders under William the Conqueror with my parallel classification of those under Henry I discloses a striking similarity in the overall distribution of baronial wealth between 1086 and 1125–1135. William I's "super-honors"—those of Odo, Robert of Mortain, and Roger of Montgomery—had all perished by 1104, but by the mid-1120s others had been constructed in their places. Henry I's "super-honors" appear to have been of approximately the magnitude of William I's. And, significantly, Henry's two greatest hereditary honors were both granted to close kinsmen—a nephew and a natural son—just as two of William's three had been created for his half-brothers.[81] Both kings were, in effect, creating appanages—placing trusted kinsmen at the top of the baronial hierarchy. The policy had been followed by the Conqueror's ducal ancestors, who entrusted their kinsmen with the great frontier counties of Eu, Evreux, and Mortain.[82] It was of course a Capetian policy as well; in one form or another it influenced most of the rulers of medieval Christendom. It often led to difficulties: William I cast his brother Odo into prison; Odo and Robert of Mortain both rebelled against Rufus; Stephen seized the English throne after Henry I's death and against his wishes. But as long as Henry lived, Stephen and Robert of Gloucester remained the most ardent of royalists. It is beyond the capacity of most leaders, even the ablest of them, to control events after their deaths.

During the last decade of the reign, Henry's reconstructed baronage was firmly in place. The forfeiture of honors that marked the half-century following the Norman Conquest had diminished after Tinchebray and ceased altogether after about 1113.[83] By 1125 the honors of Robert of Gloucester, Stephen of Blois, and Brian fitz Count were squarely in place. The magnate class in England was

---

[80] Southern, *Medieval Humanism*, p. 213.

[81] William I's third "super-magnate," Roger of Montgomery, was also connected, though more distantly, to the royal family: Hollister, "Greater Domesday Tenants-in-Chief," pp. 231–233.

[82] Douglas, "The Earliest Norman Counts."

[83] Again, DeAragon, "Growth of Secure Inheritance."

unwaveringly royalist and even, to a degree, curialist. There was no pressure cooker.

The extent of the transformation is evident when one contrasts the struggle between magnates and *curiales* in the rebellion-invasion of 1101 with the backstairs maneuverings twenty-five years later at Henry's court between the supporters and opponents of the empress Maud. The courtiers on both sides of the issue were similar kinds of men. All had been enriched by Henry I; all had frequented his court and attested his charters; all were royalists. Their support or dislike of Maud seems to have depended largely on personal factors. The issue was resolved, for the time being, entirely within the confines of the court and with such adroitness that Roger of Salisbury, who was clearly no friend of Maud's, was himself put in charge of the oath-taking ceremony.[84] The empress must have enjoyed that.

Nevertheless, warfare between the two factions did break out some years later, after Henry I's death. Several historians have attributed the strife to the explosion of baronial discontent, exacerbated by the impracticality of Henry's succession plan in the face of alleged Anglo-Norman baronial hostility toward Angevin counts and female rulers. But no historian has endeavored to identify the magnates whose alleged discontent set off the explosion. In actuality, the civil war was the product of a political stalemate in which, as a result of political difficulties beyond Henry's control, his designated successor to whom the baronage was oath-bound found herself pitted against a crowned and anointed king. "Stephen's reign is so confused and so messy," writes Edmund King, "not because the aristocracy was reacting against strong government but because they had accepted it. . . . Having learned to live with a strong king, to accept his peace and adapt their strategy to his power, they found it difficult to manage without one."[85]

Henry I's regime was firmly based on the support of great landholders. From beginning to end Henry worked to create a royalist baronage and, especially in England, he succeeded in doing so. He understood the truth that most barons, even Anglo-Norman barons, were as a group neither turbulent nor particularistic but anxious to safeguard their family wealth or, better yet, augment it. Henry's magnates discovered that rebellion involved high risks but that loyalty to the king and association with his court brought security and enrichment. This was the key to Henry's peace.

---

[84] Above, pp. 317–318.
[85] King, "King Stephen and the Anglo-Norman Aristocracy," p. 192; in general, see below, pp. 475 ff., and *MMI*, p. 262.

The conclusion that the baronage flourished under Henry I has been challenged by some modern historians, but it was understood clearly by his own contemporaries. As William of Malmesbury expressed it, "Firm in the administration of justice, he ruled the common people gently, the nobles graciously. . . . Thus, in consequence of the righteousness of his conduct, he was venerated by the nobility and loved by the commoners."[86] Malmesbury's testimony receives forceful independent corroboration from Orderic Vitalis, who praises King Henry for safeguarding his people by giving them just laws and protecting them from unjust extortions and robbers. Orderic's summary of Henry's policy toward his subjects provides an appropriate conclusion to this chapter:

From the beginning of his reign he wisely recommended himself to all, inviting them into his favour with royal gifts. He treated the magnates with honour and generosity, adding to their wealth and estates, and by placating them in this way he won their loyalty.[87]

[86] WM, *GR*, 2:487.
[87] OV, 5:296.

Chapter 9

LAW AND GOVERNANCE

The reign of Henry I stands as the most creative in the Anglo-Norman era.[1] With its long peace and stability, Henry's regime contributed much to the development of English medieval institutions: the centralizing, ever tightening control of the *curia regis* over the administration of kingdom and duchy, the emergence of the exchequer with its sophisticated accounting procedures, the proliferation of royal justices, and the concentration of authority over exchequer, judicature, and English and Norman viceregencies in the hands of an elite group of skillful and loyal servants.[2] Subsequent kings, despite the machine's steady growth, had less success with the system than Henry I. He was solvent, they were not—perhaps because he kept the peace, as they could not. And he achieved that goal not simply by developing the new administrative machinery but by placing it firmly under the control of some twenty or thirty loyal *curiales*. In their hands the machine kept the treasury full for the defense of the Anglo-Norman state. Just as

---

[1] The writing of this chapter has been enormously eased by Judith Green's work on Henry I's governance and John Hudson's on Anglo-Norman law. See Green, *The Government of England under Henry I*. Hudson's contributions to our understanding of Anglo-Norman law include "Life-Grants of Land and the Development of Inheritance in Anglo-Norman England," "Anglo-Norman Land Law and the Origins of Property," and *The Formation of the English Common Law: Law and Society in England from the Norman Conquest to Magna Carta*. These indispensable studies, along with other recent and valuable scholarship, have influenced my own conclusions and have provided an abundance of detailed evidence (statistical and otherwise) that need not be repeated here. Among the most important are Mark Blackburn, "Coinage and Currency under Henry I: A Review" (building on the work of such numismatists as M. Dolley, D. M. Metcalf, and E. J. Harris); Paul Dalton, *Conquest, Anarchy, and Lordship: Yorkshire, 1066–1154*; Stephanie L. Mooers, "A Reevaluation of Royal Justice under Henry I of England"; W. L. Warren, *The Governance of Norman and Angevin England, 1086–1272*; David Bates, "The Earliest Norman Writs" and "Normandy and England after 1066"; David Crouch, "Normans and Anglo-Normans: A Divided Aristocracy," pp. 51–67; John Le Patourel, *The Norman Empire*; and, underlying these works, a long, noble tradition of scholarship on English and Norman constitutional, legal, and administrative history.

[2] I have touched on Anglo-Norman governance in my discussion of record sources in chapter 1 of this book and in earlier essays, several of which will be

important, it enabled Henry I to tighten his hold on his dominions and to enforce royal justice as never before.

Two of the most significant aspects of Henry I's rule, the growth of royal justice and the elimination of private warfare, are closely related. More and more, over the thirty-five years of the reign, royal adjudication came to replace violent self-help in the settlement of disputes, especially those involving property. The reformed and reorganized royal court, making its rounds in England and Normandy, became the chief source of royal justice, governance, and patronage. Henry's itinerant justices by the late 1120s were attending to royal judicial business in almost all the shires of England. This remarkable centralization and systematization allowed Henry to keep the peace in England and Normandy alike—thirty-three unbroken years in England (1102–1135) and a period of twenty-nine years in Normandy interrupted only twice (ca. 1118–1119 and 1123–1124) by disturbances on the frontiers, largely provoked by neighboring powers. The *Anglo-Saxon Chronicle* in 1135 praised Henry for having given England "peace for man and beast." Orderic Vitalis summed up Henry's policies in familiar terms: "He always devoted himself, until the end of his life, to preserving peace . . ." William of Malmesbury credited Henry with giving Normandy "a peace such as no age remembers, such as his father himself . . . was never able to effect." Even Suger of Saint-Denis remarked that when Louis VI invaded Normandy about 1118 he entered a land long accustomed to peace.[3]

In the generations following Henry I's death (after the aberration of Stephen's reign), royal justice and administration continued to grow despite occasional episodes of regional violence.[4] The correlation between domestic peace and administrative growth is thus far from

reviewed and summarized here; see, in particular, the introduction and essays in *Monarachy, Magnates, and Institutions* (*MMI*), especially, "The Origins of the English Treasury," "The Rise of Administrative Kingship: Henry I," "The Making of the Angevin Empire," and "Henry I and the Invisible Transformation of Medieval England"; as well as "Anglo-Norman Political Culture and the Twelfth-Century Renaissance."

[3] *ASC, s.a.* 1135; OV, 6:99; WM, *GR*, 2:476; Suger, *Louis le Gros*, pp. 184–186.

[4] John Hudson in *Land, Law, and Lordship in Anglo-Norman England* attempts to give Anglo-Norman administration and justice their fair place in the evolution of English law. Hudson's reassessment of legal development in land law in the years before 1135 undermines the traditional idea of an Angevin great leap forward. Hudson concludes: "If [my] various arguments concerning customs and thought, courts, royal involvement, and the consequent limitation of seignorial discretion are correct, Henry I's reign was probably one of major change. . . . The developments of land law from *c.* 1166 are of course striking, but they were most notably an acceleration of administrative change, not an unprecedented leap forward" (pp. 279–281).

exact, but under Henry I the two went hand in hand. A total absence of private war in England and a startling growth in government and records are the outward signs of Henry's fundamental shift in the style of governance. No novel political philosophy animated his rule. Rather, Henry saw himself as the good steward of his inherited dominions and privileges. The novelty of his reign is to be found neither in his goals nor in his political assumptions but in the development of a new, highly effective means to achieve conventional ends.

An unprecedented expansion of the royal administration marked the reign of the Conqueror's youngest son. James Campbell has aptly described this growth as a step in the transformation of the English state from a Carolingian type into a twelfth-century type. W. L. Warren viewed the process as a major shift in balance, in which the monarchy became much more actively interventionist than its Anglo-Saxon predecessor had been. Whereas pre-Conquest kings "had organized their realm into self-managing parts and concerned themselves largely with matters which transcended the parts or involved the kingdom as a whole," the authority of the Norman monarchy reached out increasingly into the activities of individual subjects.[5]

But although Henry I's regime was in some sense a New Monarchy, in other, fundamental respects it was firmly rooted in traditional Anglo-Saxon political institutions.[6] Henry's intention to uphold the laws of Edward the Confessor is embodied not only in his coronation charter but also in the *Quadripartitus*, the *Leges Henrici Primi*, and a body of related legal works.[7] As Patrick Wormald observed, the unfolding of legal thought and practice under Henry I ensured "that it would be on the foundations of a long-established and specifically English system that future development would build."[8]

Henry's regime, like those of his Anglo-Norman predecessors, preserved the Old English system of shires, sheriffs, and shire courts, hundreds and hundred courts, hides and carucates, boroughs and markets, and much else—including the institution of monarchy itself. An Anglo-Saxon *ordo* was almost certainly used at Henry's coronation, and early in his reign he commanded that shire and hundred courts be held at the same places and on the same terms as in the days of King Edward.[9] Two

---

[5] Campbell, "Anglo-Norman State," p. 171; Warren, *Governance*, quote on p. 65. See also Hudson, *Land, Law, and Lordship*, on increasing royal involvement in justice and the affairs of the landed.

[6] Among the great abundance of studies on the precociousness of Anglo-Saxon government, see especially Campbell, "Observations," pp. 155–170.

[7] See above, chapter 1, pp. 28–29.

[8] Wormald, "*Laga Eadwardi*," p. 266.

[9] On the *Third English Ordo* see above, pp. 107–108; on the ordinance on shire and hundred courts, *RRAN* 2, no. 892, and above, pp. 212–213.

of the most notable monuments to the sophistication of Old English royal government, the danegeld and the managed coinage system, continued into the Anglo-Norman era, and both became important components of Henry I's fiscal administration.

The danegeld was a land tax of considerable flexibility, levied since Ethelred the Unready's reign at rates of one or more shillings per hide or carucate. The sums of money in tribute to the Danes raised during the crisis years of Ethelred and Cnut could be spectacularly high—exceeding Henry I's danegeld income in 1129–1130 by tenfold or more.[10] By the Confessor's reign the danegeld had ceased to be a tribute payment and had become a lucrative source of revenue for the royal treasury. Edward is said to have abolished the tax in 1051, but it was reinstituted either later in his reign or in the Conqueror's.[11] In 1084 William I levied a danegeld of six shillings per hide, which was extraordinarily high by Anglo-Norman standards, and another danegeld appears to have been recorded for 1086.[12] There is some evidence, indeed, that danegeld was levied annually by the Conqueror and by Rufus, who is reported to have imposed a geld at the unusually high rate of four shillings per hide in 1096 in connection with his agreement to take Normandy in pawn from Curthose for ten thousand marks.[13] William of Malmesbury complains that whenever William Rufus levied a geld, Ranulf Flambard would double the rate.[14] Henry I's highest reported geld was three shillings per hide in 1110, on the occasion of his daughter Maud's

[10] In contrast to the approximately £2,375 in danegeld payments recorded in the Pipe Roll of 1130 (Green, *Government*, table 1, p. 223), the *Anglo-Saxon Chronicle* reports payments to the Danes, in geld or tribute, of £16,000 in 994, £24,000 in 1002, £36,000 in 1007, £48,000 in 1012, and £82,500 in 1018 for Cnut and his forces. This last sum, if one assumes that it was raised by a tax on land, would amount to a rate of 20 shillings on the hide without any pardons or arrears, as compared with 2 shillings on the hide in 1129–1130—along with a great many pardons and some arrears: Lawson, *Cnut: The Danes in England in the Early Eleventh Century*, pp. 189–196. The reliability of the *ASC* figures has been challenged by John Gillingham and defended by Lawson, Pauline Stafford, and others: Gillingham, "'The Most Precious Jewel in the English Crown'"; Lawson, "'Those Stories Look True'"; Gillingham, "Chronicles and Coins as Evidence"; Lawson, "Danegeld and Heregeld Once More"; Stafford, *Unification and Conquest*, pp. 142–143; Blackburn, "Aethelred's Coinage and the Payment of Tribute," pp. 156–169.

[11] FW, 1:204; a number of Domesday passages mention the existence of danegeld *TRE*, e.g., *DB*, 1:336b; see Hollister, *Anglo-Saxon Military Institutions*, p. 20.

[12] *ASC*, s.a. 1083 ("after Christmas"); Green, "Danegeld," pp. 241–242.

[13] *Gesetze*, ed. Liebermann, 1:636 (from the *Leges Edwardi Confessoris*); Green, *Aristocracy of Norman England*, p. 234.

[14] WM, *GR*, 2:369.

marriage to Henry V,[15] but later in the reign, as is clear from the Pipe Roll of 1130, the usual rate was two shillings per hide.[16]

Perhaps as significant as Henry's recorded danegeld income of £2,375 in 1129–1130 are his danegeld pardons *per breve regis* of some £1,811—more than three-quarters of his danegeld revenue. According to the *Dialogus de scaccario* of late Henry II, exchequer officials and sheriffs were exempt from the danegeld, and this rule may be reflected in the generous exemptions of Roger of Salisbury and various sheriffs. But the recipients of many of the highest geld pardons in 1129–1130— Robert of Gloucester, William of Warenne, Brian fitz Count, William archbishop of Canterbury, Henry bishop of Winchester, Stephen of Blois, and others—cannot be so explained. The danegeld pardons on these and similar individuals are clearly acts of royal favor directed toward the king's frequently attesting *familiares* and his closest kinsmen. They demonstrate the importance of danegeld not only in the raising of royal revenues but also in the distribution of royal favors.[17]

The sources show that Henry I's regime might occasionally levy land taxes other than danegeld, although on exactly what grounds or occasions is unclear. One might reasonably associate such additional gelds with the war years in which the Anglo-Saxon chronicler complained of unusually high taxes. A charter of 1103–1107, for example, pardons an estate of Westminster Abbey from all gelds and especially *de novo geldo propter hidagium*, which could well refer to taxation associated with Henry's Norman campaigns against Robert Curthose in 1105 and 1106.[18]

John of Worcester states that King Henry, threatened by a tempest while crossing the Channel in August 1131, promised to suspend the danegeld for seven years if God granted him a safe crossing.[19] It was a costly promise, but not ruinously so during the placid, final years of his reign when Henry enjoyed peace with all his neighbors, in Britain and on the Continent, and had doubtless completed his long line of strongholds along the Norman frontier. Henry of Huntingdon reports that King Stephen promised not to levy danegeld but that he failed to keep his promise, and we know that the tax was collected during the early

---

[15] HH, pp. 456, 457 n. 159; as Diana Greenway points out, the marriage of a lord's eldest daughter was one of the three customary occasions for a feudal aid.

[16] *PR 31 Henry I (passim)*; HH, p. 704. Earlier in the reign, danegeld may have been charged at 1 shilling per hide, the per annum rate recorded in the *Leges Henrici Primi*, p. 120, and repeated in the *Leges Edwardi Confessoris: Gesetze*, ed. Liebermann, 1:634.

[17] Mooers, "Patronage in the Pipe Roll of 1130"; Green, "Danegeld," pp. 246–251.

[18] *RRAN* 2, no. 851; Green, "Danegeld," pp. 253–254, and *Government*, p. 78.

[19] JW, pp. 33–34.

years of Henry II. Eventually it gave way to other methods of taxation,
but throughout much or all of Henry I's reign it was a valuable source
of both royal revenue and royal patronage.[20]
     Another element of the Anglo-Saxon heritage, the highly complex
system of coinage that dates from the reign of Edgar the Peaceable
(perhaps from about 973), also served Henry well. In its fully developed form, some sixty or more mints, each in a separate borough, were
producing standardized silver pennies of high quality, with the name
of the mint and minter on each of them. Coin types were changed at
periodic intervals—every six years under Ethelred and Cnut, every two
or three years thereafter—and only coins of the current type were
acceptable for the payment of royal farms or fines. These frequent
changes required that coins of the superseded type be brought in for
exchange, and the moneyers charged a fee for reminting, a portion of
which they paid to the king.[21] There was opportunity for further profit
if the new type contained less silver than the old one, and it has been
suggested that William the Conqueror's *monetagium* was a tax levied in
lieu of such manipulations.
     The constant reissuing of coins in new types was both lucrative and
cumbersome. The process was particularly difficult in the early twelfth
century, when the supply of European silver was dwindling[22] and, as we
have seen, when debasement and forgery caused Henry to take severe
retribution against his minters. Since all coins of the era are undated,
there has been much debate as to the sequence of the fifteen coin types
attributed to the reign.[23] The most plausible sequence has been
advanced by Mark Blackburn, whose hypothesis is both radical and persuasive. Blackburn suggests that Henry I's coinage reforms took place
in three stages: first, the introduction of round halfpennies, about 1107;
second, about 1108, the order to snick (or cut) each coin before it left
the mint—to prevent the production of plated forgeries; and third and
most important, in about 1125, the abandonment of the Anglo-Saxon
system of periodic recoinages. Blackburn associates the 1124 mutilation
of the moneyers with the final shift, from the type 14 coin to the type
15, a shift that witnessed the dismissal of more than half the moneyers
in England and the elimination of twenty-eight mints.[24] In these various
reforms, especially those of the 1120s, Blackburn sees the glimmerings

----

[20] HH, p. 704; Green, "Danegeld," pp. 254–258.
[21] Stewart, "Coinage and Recoinage after Edgar's Reforms," pp. 455–485.
[22] Blackburn, "Coinage and Currency," pp. 52–53, 73–74.
[23] Andrew, "A Numismatic History"; Brooke, *Catalogue: Norman Kings*; Dolley, *The
Norman Conquest and the English Coinage*; Seaby, "Henry I Coin Types"; Conte and
Archibald, "Five Round Halfpennies"; Blackburn, "Coinage and Currency," pp.
49–81.
[24] Blackburn, "Coinage and Currency," pp. 65–73.

of a deliberate economic policy, noting that the rationalization of the minting system took place in a period of "intense administrative reform." After careful consideration of the potential impact on revenues, Henry and his advisers, Roger of Salisbury in particular, apparently undertook such a fundamental change in monetary policy to maintain quality but also to avoid the major loss of silver coins that occurred with each recoinage when people retained some coin of the older type for use in private transactions.[25]

Both Sally Harvey and James Campbell have shown how the Anglo-Norman conqueror kings profited from the precocious Anglo-Saxon governmental system. In her analyses of Domesday Book, Harvey emphasizes the pre-Domesday documentation at Winchester as well as the sophisticated Anglo-Saxon treasury practices that underlay the administrative enterprises of the Anglo-Normans. She cites in particular "the exchequer, its accounting of royal revenues from shires, from geld, and from feudal incidents, and its court on tenurial rights as prominent features of the reign of Henry I."[26] Campbell identifies the great feats of organization achieved by Anglo-Saxon government—danegeld levies, regular minting and reminting processes, an elaborate fort system—and deems these part of the indispensable Anglo-Saxon legacy that gave the Anglo-Normans powers that other states lacked.[27] We cannot fail to add to that list the basic organization of the realm and its assessment system to provide for military defense.[28]

Pondering the origins of the systems of administration of the Old English state and those of its successors, Campbell zeroes in on the problem of evidence. He argues that research and experience have taught us to be wary of drawing negative conclusions about origins or ancestry from the silence of traditional kinds of written sources. The absence of such sources—that is, their failure to survive—cannot be considered proof of the absence of ancestry of any particular system.[29] For what would we know of the connection of Anglo-Saxon and Anglo-Norman institutions without that incomparable monolith, Domesday Book, or the isolated Pipe Roll of 1130? Neither enterprise can seriously be considered the initial effort of an infant administration, yet the silence of the Anglo-Saxon sources on such topics as accounting

---

[25] Ibid., pp. 72, 75.

[26] Harvey, "Domesday Book and Anglo-Norman Governance," p. 193, and "Domesday Book and Its Predecessors."

[27] Campbell, "Anglo-Norman State," pp. 167, 172. See also Campbell's comment on the relationship between Carolingian and Anglo-Saxon administrative achievements and his suggestive words on the survival of administrative skills in Normandy: "Observations," p. 167, and "Anglo-Norman State," pp. 185–186.

[28] Hollister, "1066," MMI, pp. 1–16.

[29] Campbell, "Anglo-Norman State," pp. 179, 187, 188, and passim.

and minting procedures contrasts with the evidence in the Domesday survey for a tradition of inquests or in the pipe roll for the development of sophisticated accounting methods. The physical remains themselves—the surveys, the financial systems, even the coins, these products of successful Anglo-Norman efforts—allow us to infer the existence of predecessors. Nonetheless, as Campbell acknowledges, the transformation of Anglo-Saxon systems, in their uniformity and complexity, into elements of the twelfth-century medieval state, some of them simpler and more immediate, can involve a distinct change in attitudes and powers of government.[30] This is a valuable perspective from which to view the Anglo-Norman kings' ability to adapt as well as to invent in their organization of the realm.

While the kingdom that Henry I inherited had grown more efficient over the decades after 1066, the pace of adaptation and invention accelerated in the years when Henry's machine worked to centralize and stabilize government. The exchequer, perhaps the best known cogwheel of Henry's evolving administrative system, emerges from the mist around 1110 under the direction of Roger of Salisbury.[31] Despite extensive investigations, its origins remain obscure. The *Dialogus de scaccario* from the end of the century implies that Roger did not invent the exchequer but did much to improve and modernize it.[32] Doubtless it evolved out of the ancient practice of sheriffs' bringing their revenues annually to the central English treasury, located at Winchester since Anglo-Saxon times. Chroniclers alluded to a general administrative and legal reorganization undertaken by Henry on both sides of the Channel in the years immediately following his conquest of Normandy in 1106. This activity, combined with the raising of a huge aid for his daughter's betrothal in 1110, may have stimulated the accounting reforms that produced what we know as the English exchequer—the abacus accounting procedure, a court of audit, and pipe rolls recording receipts from the sheriffs and their shires.[33]

From about 1110 onward we encounter mounting evidence of the complex accounting process that appears in detail in the Pipe Roll of 1130 (the one surviving example of the series of fiscal records

---

[30] Campbell, "Observations," p. 169, and "Anglo-Norman State," p. 172.

[31] Henry I to *baronibus de scaccario*, attested by Roger of Salisbury and Ranulf the Chancellor; *RRAN* 2, no. 963. This, the earliest known reference to the exchequer by name, deals with the aid of 1110.

[32] *Dialogus de scaccario*, 42.

[33] OV, 6:92–94; FW, 2:57; Eadmer, *HN*, 192–193. And see Poole, *Exchequer*.

produced annually throughout most of Henry's reign).[34] A passage in the Abingdon chronicle preserves a full list of the officials who sat at the Winchester treasury during the Michaelmas exchequer session of AD 1111. The exchequer was so new at this point that the justices were not yet termed *barones de scaccario* and the session itself was described as being *in thesauro* rather than *ad scaccarium*. But there can be no doubt that the account in question is the earliest recorded description of the exchequer court in action.[35] Later in the Abingdon chronicle we read of a panel of *justitiae regis* who in 1119 heard a plea for the exemption of the abbey from danegeld, a hearing that almost certainly represents some of the exchequer barons sitting at another Michaelmas session at Winchester.[36]

Up to a point, there is general agreement on how the exchequer process worked. Twice each year, at Easter and at Michaelmas, separate groups of royal administrators went to the Winchester treasury and to the Norman treasury to audit the accounts of the sheriffs and *vicomtes* over the famous checkered cloth. The title "barons of the exchequer," as contemporary records referred to the members of these courts of audit, has given rise to some confusion because it suggests a body of full-time exchequer officials. Certainly the exchequer eventually became "a permanent financial bureau" and a "central organ of government,"[37] but at its inception under Henry I the exchequer was merely a semiannual auditing procedure, nothing more or less than a highly effective device for increasing curial supervision of the sheriffs and *vicomtes* and a means of applying the latest systematic procedures to the collection of royal revenues and the dispensing of royal patronage. The exchequer was not yet a department, not yet an institution—it was simply an occasion.

The collection of revenues was one of the strengths of the administration of Henry I. The king and Roger of Salisbury were able to raise large sums on special occasions (the betrothal of Maud, the two campaigns in Normandy), without serious complaint, and apparently to take in on a regular basis substantially more funds than Henry's predecessors or successors. Moreover, Henry emerged solvent at the end of the periods of warfare on the Norman frontiers and left a full treasury at the end of his reign. Judith Green has analyzed the sources

---

[34] *PR 31 Henry I.* Annual pipe rolls survive from AD 1156 onward and can be used (with caution) to illuminate the roll of 1130. Further illumination (along with some phantom images) is provided by Richard fitz Nigel's *Dialogus de scaccario* from late in Henry II's reign.

[35] *RRAN* 2, no. 1000; *Chron. Ab.*, p. 116.

[36] *RRAN* 2, no. 1211.

[37] Stenton, *English Justice*, p. 59; West, *Justiciarships*, pp. 19–20.

of the king's revenues as revealed in the Pipe Roll of 1130.[38] In that year, perhaps one of Henry's more successful years (which Green suggests may account for the preservation of this unique roll), the royal treasury took in almost £23,000, a sum not to be matched by his successors for a half-century. Roughly half of that sum came from revenues from royal lands, of which the sons of the Conqueror held less and less over time as lands were alienated to buy loyalty. Yet by 1130 Henry I was taking in more money, as Green notes, by raising rents and improving land management, than his predecessors had with more land in the royal demesne. Payment in coin rather than in kind resulted in more accurate returns (and may have been involved in the ultimate decision to reform the coinage system, dated by Blackburn to just a few years before 1130) and certainly marked an improvement over in-kind payments by simplifying the process and making funds quickly available.

The high yield from royal justice revealed by the pipe roll shows the heightened activity of Henry's administration in developing new sources of revenue unique to the Anglo-Norman kings.[39] The selling of offices, the exploitation of the feudal "incidents" of relief, wardship, and marriage, as well as the income from pleas and the issue of writs significantly increased the potential royal income but also recorded the impetus toward centralization and systematization so characteristic of Henry's administration. One is struck by the great proliferation of justices of all kinds under Henry I: justices of groups of shires, individual shires, hundreds, boroughs, and royal demesne lands.[40] To differentiate among these various sorts of judges can be treacherous, for contemporaries had not yet developed a technical vocabulary to distinguish shire justices from itinerant justices, a term which itself does not appear until the 1170s. The semantic problem at least is resolved for us midway through the reign, when the activities of the men considered justiciars of individual shires began to blend into those of the "itinerant justices." Ralph Basset, whose judicial activities left their mark in at least eleven shires in the roll of 1130, had earlier been on eyre in two others, Huntingdonshire in 1116 and Leicestershire in 1124.[41] We know of his activities in these years only through isolated chronicle

---

[38] Green, *Government*, chap. 4.

[39] Ibid., p. 92. See *EHD*, 2:434, no. 44, for an order protecting the jurisdiction of the bishop of Lincoln in order to ensure the flow of royal revenues.

[40] *Leges Henrici Primi*, pp. 98, 132, 183, 195, 212; *PR 31 Henry I*, p. 91; Stenton, *English Justice*, p. 57; OV, 3:348, 6:330–332; *Gesta Stephani*, p. 24; Hurnard, "Local Justice," pp. 522–524; and Cronne, "Local Justiciar," p. 22.

[41] Van Caenegem, "Public Prosecution of Crime in Twelfth-Century England," pp. 51–61; Richardson and Sayles, *Governance*, pp. 185–187; *RRAN* 2:xviii; and Cronne, "Local Justiciar," p. 33. For one of many references to *judices* of the county and

references, but for the period roughly from 1125 to 1130 the pipe roll provides a relatively full picture. From the pipe roll and charter evidence we can see that by the late 1120s the shire justiciars had evolved into justices with larger responsibilities—men who would have been described by a later generation as "justices in eyre"—all dispensing the king's profitable justice.[42]

John Hudson, in his work on land and law in Anglo-Norman England, stresses the considerable royal involvement of the Anglo-Norman kings, Henry I in particular, in the administration of justice, but Hudson cautions against the view that royal intervention in the affairs of lords and their men represented aggression against the seigneurial system. Hudson considers this understanding too confrontational; he prefers, as do I, to emphasize the community of shared interests served by the exercise of royal power such as Henry I's.[43] The justice of the king's vassals helped to maintain the peace of the realm; should that justice be contested or fail, the king's justice could fill the breach: a royal writ ordering settlement in the shire court,[44] a summons before a royal justice or court, or the visitation of a royal sheriff.[45] Such assertive royal action by Henry I produced no known outcry, much less a revolt, and testifies to the harmony that existed between Henry and his barons, who participated in and benefited from the king's strong judicial arm. In the history of the development of the English common law, these innovations from the first third of the twelfth century reveal an advancement toward coherent, centralized government, which challenges the long-standing assumption of a fundamental disjunction between the legal history of the reigns of Henry I and Henry II.

In addition to using his judges as a means of maintaining peace and

---

hundreds, see *PR 31 Henry I*, p. 97. It has been my good fortune to have access to a much fuller and more rigorous list of local justiciars: Frederick Hok-ming Cheung, unpublished paper, "Local Justiciars under Henry I." For Ralph Basset, see *ASC*, s.a. 1124, and OV, 3:351. Since the reference to Ralph at Huntingdon in 1116 occurs in Orderic's account of the case of Bricstan of Chatteris, William T. Reedy has concluded that Ralph "did not hear 'pleas' " but only one plea: "Origins of the General Eyre," p. 705. But Bricstan's indictment for usury and concealment of treasure was a matter of only routine interest to the *curia regis* and would surely not alone have drawn together the great court that Orderic described.

[42] The single known exception to this trend was Henry I's charter to the citizens of London (ca. 1133) that granted them the privilege of electing a justice to supervise crown pleas and pleadings in London and Middlesex: *RRAN* 2, no. 1645. Although the authenticity of this charter has recently been questioned, I continue to regard it as a genuine act of Henry I (see my *MMI*, pp. 191–208).

[43] Hudson, *Land, Law, and Lordship*, p. 5.

[44] *RRAN* 2, no. 892; *Gesetze*, ed. Liebermann, 1:524 (in Hudson, *Land, Law, and Lordship*, p. 279 n. 102).

[45] Hudson, *Land, Law and Lordship*, p. 279 and notes.

order, Henry also used his sheriffs. Shrievalties, like the justiciarships, underwent transformation as the king and his *curia* tightened control. Generally speaking, Henry appointed fewer magnates as sheriffs, choosing instead less exalted, more pliable men.[46] While some of these appointments were no doubt influenced by wealthy curial magnates who secured the selection of a friend or client as sheriff of a county,[47] the king constantly shuffled sheriffs in and out of shires and as the reign progressed Henry moved increasingly to appoint *curiales* to the office. The Pipe Roll of 1130 discloses an extraordinary experiment in centralization: two of Henry's most trusted curial administrators, Richard Basset and Aubrey de Vere, were by then joint sheriffs of no fewer than eleven shires, while many of the remaining shires were in the hands of *curiales* such as the constable Miles of Gloucester and the treasury chamberlains Geoffrey of Clinton and William of Pont de l'Arche. All but the last of these men were active concurrently as itinerant justices and were sometimes to be found on judicial eyres in the very shires that they held as sheriffs. Indeed, the joint sheriffs Basset and de Vere were to all intents and purposes "sheriffs in eyre." They did not farm their shires in the traditional manner but seem to have functioned instead as *custodes*, responsible to the king for the whole of the royal revenues.[48] This intense degree of curialization may have been relaxed slightly during the closing years of the reign, but the sheriffs remained to the end under the strictest royal control.

The engine behind the system was of course the king and the *curia regis*. Henry's reign saw the strengthening of the centripetal forces inherent in feudal society. The king's court, moving incessantly across southern England and Normandy, controlled all aspects of governance. Its membership fluctuated constantly. Some individuals were almost always in attendance, others frequently so, and still others occasionally or rarely. Besides officials and servants of the royal household, the court included royal advisers and *familiares* without household titles— what used to be called, in reference to the American presidency, the "kitchen cabinet." Henry I's court might also include visiting foreign princes, royal and comital heirs-apparent and bastards with their tutors and servants, merchants who supplied the royal entourage, camp followers, and plaintiffs and favor-seekers—often local prelates—from

[46] Here I correct my previous conclusion: William A. Morris (*Medieval English Sheriff*, pp. 41–75) was mistaken in believing that the Conqueror routinely appointed magnates as sheriffs. See Green, "Sheriffs."

[47] Green, "Sheriffs," pp. 136–138, 145; Crouch, "Geoffrey de Clinton and Roger, Earl of Warwick," pp. 113–124.

[48] Round, *Geoffrey de Mandeville*, pp. 297–298; *PR 31 Henry I*, p. 63.

the districts through which the court was traveling or sometimes from afar.

At the heart of the *curia* was the royal household staff, whose organization and fixed allowances were recorded in detail in the *Constitutio domus regis* of about 1136. The chief household officers, echoing continental custom, were the chancellor, stewards, master butler, master chamberlain, and constables. To these traditional officials Henry added a new one, the household treasurer. Scholars used to dispute whether the *Constitutio domus regis* described the English household or the Norman, but they now generally agree that the *domus regis* accompanied the king wherever he might be.[49] The frequency with which Henry's household officials attested royal or administrative *acta* emanating from Normandy and from England supports the conclusion.[50] When due weight is given to the survival of Henry's English charters in far greater numbers than his Norman charters, it becomes clear that most members of Henry's household crossed regularly with the *curia* and attested with some frequency on both sides of the Channel (see table 9.1). But certain household officials concentrated their activities on one side of the Channel or the other. The steward Robert de la Haye attested a great many royal acts in Normandy but few in England, and the same is true of the chamberlains William fitz Odo and William of Glastonbury and, to a lesser extent, the steward Robert of Courcy. Conversely, certain household officers attested charters primarily in England: the steward Adam of Port and the constables Walter of Beauchamp, Walter and Miles of Gloucester, and Nigel and Robert of Oilli.[51]

Analysis of attestation can help to illuminate the administrative activities of Henry I's chancellors: Ranulf (1107–1122) and Geoffrey Rufus (1123–1133) both attest enormous numbers of surviving royal charters, some from Normandy but far more from England.[52] When Henry was in Normandy, his chancellor was often away from the

---

[49] For the *Constitutio domus regis* see *Dialogus de scaccario*, pp. 128–135; above, pp. 213–216; White, "Household of the Norman Kings," pp. 127–159; *RRAN* 2:ix–xvii; Le Patourel, *Norman Empire*, pp. 135–137.

[50] On the validity of attestation analysis, see my appendix, pp. 499 ff. below.

[51] The responsibilities of Walter and Miles of Gloucester (father and son) included the custody of Gloucester Castle. Walter of Beauchamp's constableship seems to have been associated with Worcester Castle, and Nigel and Robert of Oilli (father and son) were responsible for Oxford Castle: *RRAN* 2:xv–xvi; Robert of Oilli, although he attested heavily in England, was rather more active in Normandy than his father had been.

[52] Ranulf attested 163 charters, of which 134 are certainly or probably from England and 22 certainly or probably from Normandy; of Geoffrey Rufus' 115 attestations, about 95 are English and about 15 are Norman (a few are of undetermined origin). Even allowing for the much greater survival rate of

Table 9.1. Officers of the Royal Household, 1130

Office	Officers of the Household
Chancellor	Geoffrey Rufus* (XE)
Keeper of the Seal	Robert *de Sigillo** (X)
Stewards	Hugh Bigod* (X)
	Humphrey of Bohun* (X)
	Robert of Courcy (XN)[1]
	Robert de la Haye* (N)
	(?) William Martel (X)
	(?) Robert fitz Richard (Clare) (X)
Master Butler	William of Aubigny *Pincerna** (X)
Treasurer	Nigel *nepos episcopi** (bp. Ely, 1133+) (X)
Chamberlains of the Winchester Treasury	William de Pont de l'Arche* (X)
	Geoffrey of Clinton* (X)
Chamberlains of the Camera Curiae	William de Pont de l'Arche* (X)
	Osbert of Pont de l'Arche (X)
	William Maudit (X)
Chamberlain of England and Normandy	(?) Rabel of Tancarville (N)[2]
Norman Chamberlains (?)	William fitz Odo (N)[3]
	William of Glastonbury (N)
Constables	Robert de Vere* (X)
	Miles of Gloucester* (E)
	Robert of Oilli (XE)
	Walter of Beauchamp (E)
	Brian fitz Count* (attested as constable in 1131) (XN)
Assistant Constables (?)	Roger of Oilli (E)
	Henry of la Pommeraye (X)
Marshals	John fitz Gilbert (X)
	Wigan the Marshal (N[?])

Source: Hollister, *MMI*, p. 226.
Note: An asterisk (*) designates a *curialis*, that is, a man whose attestations demonstrate frequent participation in the king's court (see my *MMI*, p. 242 and table 4, for further refinement). In their roles as attesters of royal acts, E = 91–100% English attestations; XE = 81–90% English; X = 51–80% English; XN = 50–64% Norman; and N = 65–100% Norman. (Some adjustment has been made for the greater survival expectancy of charters from England; pre-1106 charters have been excluded from all computations regarding English versus Norman attestations.)
[1] Robert of Courcy attested thirty-seven acts between 1113 and 1135 (1.7/year), but thirty-five of those attestations occurred between 1126 and 1135 (4.1/year).
[2] Rabel "inherited" the Anglo-Norman chamberlainship from his father, William of Tancarville* (X), who died in 1129. But there is no concrete evidence that Rabel performed any functions of the chamberlainship under Henry I. In 1133 the *curialis* Aubrey de Vere received the master chamberlainship "of all England," but he was at times with Henry in Normandy between 1133 and 1135; see *RRAN* 2, nos 1777, 1913–1915, 1960.
[3] William fitz Odo averaged 1.9 attestations per year, which places him about thirty-second among attesters active in 1130. But the disproportionate loss of Norman acts causes a systematic underestimation of the curial activity of primarily Norman attesters.

itinerant court, engaged in administrative work in England. And since the Anglo-Norman chancery was inseparable from the royal court, the household scriptorium must often have functioned without the chancellor's direct supervision. During the latter half of Henry's reign, the chancery staff included about four scribes, under the direction of a subchancellor known as the "master of the scriptorium" or keeper of the king's seal.[53] Robert *de Sigillo* occupied this office from 1121 to 1135, and his nearly one hundred attestations, nicely balanced between England and Normandy, suggest that he was regularly with the king's court. The frequency and ease with which the chancery functioned without the chancellor's presence doubtless influenced Henry's decision to leave the chancellorship vacant after Geoffrey Rufus' promotion to the see of Durham in 1133 and may also explain why Henry was willing to double Robert *de Sigillo*'s wages.[54]

That an important minority of royal household officials concentrated their activities on only one side of the Channel is not surprising. Once Henry had rejoined the duchy to the kingdom, he had to depend on some sort of regional governing body to supervise Normandy when he was in England and England when he was in Normandy. His predecessors, William I and William II, faced with the same problem of dual governance, had handled it with a variety of ad hoc arrangements. William I left the kingdom in charge of various great men at different times—men like William fitz Osbern, Odo bishop of Bayeux, and Archbishop Lanfranc.[55] The Conqueror likewise entrusted Normandy to such notables as Queen Matilda, Roger of Montgomery, and Roger of Beaumont. Under William Rufus, whose joint rule of Normandy and England extended only from 1096 to 1100, the first hint of a more specialized English viceregency appeared. Initially, William II's omnicompetent minister Ranulf Flambard served as coregent with Walchelin bishop of Winchester, but in 1099 Rufus committed England to Flambard alone, to be assisted

English charters, it remains clear that both men were often in England while the king was in Normandy.

[53] Bishop, *Scriptores regis*, p. 30. From an analysis of scribal hands, Bishop has identified two royal scribes active at Henry's accession in 1100; their number had risen to at least four by mid-reign and seems to have remained at about that level until Henry's death.

[54] For Robert, see *RRAN* 2:x, and *Dialogus de scaccario*, p. 129; of Robert's attestations, 56 percent are from England, 44 percent from Normandy; his contemporary, the chancellor Geoffrey Rufus, attested 86 percent from England and 14 percent from Normandy. On the probable vacancy of the chancellorship after 1133, see Johnson, "The Last Chancellor of Henry I."

[55] Bates, "Origins of the Justiciarship," pp. 1–12, stresses the importance of Bishop Odo.

by Hamo *Dapifer* sheriff of Kent and Urse of Abitôt sheriff of Worcestershire.[56] These administrative beginnnings, aborted by Rufus' death in August 1100, foreshadowed the development of more stable and elaborate viceregal arrangements in the years following Henry's conquest of Normandy in 1106. From about 1107 onward the Norman viceregal court was headed by John bishop of Lisieux, whose numerous attestations of royal charters disclose that he was almost constantly at Henry's side in Normandy but seldom crossed with the king to England. His name occurs at the head of lists of Norman justices, usually followed by that of the seneschal or steward Robert de la Haye, whose overwhelmingly Norman attestations suggest that his administrative duties were limited primarily to the duchy. He was evidently the chief layman in the Norman viceregal court and its second in command. Others active in the Norman viceregency include the household officials William of Glastonbury and Robert of Courcy, whose names occur chiefly in the Norman records of the reign.[57]

Charles Homer Haskins rigorously examined the personnel of Henry I's courts some eighty years ago, and relatively little has since been added to his fundamental work.[58] But it is now possible, through comprehensive attestation analysis, to sift out the predominantly Norman figures from the cross-Channel *curiales* whose names sometimes appear in Norman documents as judges and administrative officials. A panel of judges hearing a Norman plea of AD 1111 included Geoffrey archbishop of Rouen (who attested chiefly in Normandy) and the Norman "viceroy" John bishop of Lisieux, along with five lay magnates, at least four of whom held lands and attested substantially on both sides of the Channel.[59] Similar analyses of the other documents that Haskins assembled disclose a Norman viceregal core group that sometimes functioned on its own, sometimes expanded into a larger court of bishops and magnates, and usually merged into the king's traveling entourage when Henry was in Normandy. Even when on its own, the viceregal

---

[56] Douglas, *William the Conqueror*, pp. 185–186, 207; Barlow, *Rufus*, pp. 376, 399; *Ann. Wint.*, 2:39. Bishop Walchelin died in January 1098, and Flambard was advanced to the bishopric of Durham in June 1099, before becoming sole regent. The sources are silent on Rufus' viceregal administration in Normandy.

[57] Haskins, *NI*, pp. 88–89, 120, 307; *RRAN* 2, nos 1184, 1352, 1422, 1579, 1584, 1593.

[58] See, however, Yver, "Le Développement du pouvoir ducal en Normandie," pp. 183–204; Le Patourel, *Norman Empire*, pp. 121–354 *passim*; Bates, "Earliest Norman Writs," pp. 266–284.

[59] The magnate-judges were Robert count of Meulan, William of Warenne, Gilbert of Laigle lord of Pevensey, and William the Chamberlain of Tancarville. A fifth judge, William of Ferrars, was doubtless a Norman figure, but he did not attest sufficiently to be placed with certainty: Haskins, *NI*, pp. 91–92.

court was itinerant, meeting sometimes at Rouen, sometimes at Caen, and less often elsewhere in the duchy. Its members spent most of their time in Normandy, but on rare occasions one or another of them turned up in the royal entourage in England, leaving their Norman viceregal duties to subordinates or other household officers.[60]

In England Queen Matilda usually served as regent during King Henry's absences. Archbishop Anselm, however, may have occupied the position sometime between his return from exile in 1106 and his death in spring 1109, and after Matilda's death on 1 May 1118, the teenaged William Adelin headed the English regency for a year.[61] But these altogether traditional arrangements were supplemented by a clearly identifiable body of viceregal administrators: the witness lists of charters issued by Matilda and William Adelin as regents disclose that in England as in Normandy a viceregal court of relatively stable and expert membership was developing. At its head was Henry's foremost administrator, Roger bishop of Salisbury, who attested no fewer than nine of Matilda's and William Adelin's surviving *acta* and whose name, when it occurs with others, almost always heads the list. Other figures in the English viceregency included Robert Bloet bishop of Lincoln, Richard of Beaumais bishop of London, Ranulf the Chancellor, the stewards Adam of Port and William of Courcy, the constables Walter of Gloucester and Nigel of Oilli, and the royal justice Ralph Basset.[62] The stewards and constables on this list are among the household officials who attest primarily in England. Indeed, the attestations of almost all those in the English viceregal core group are very largely limited to

---

[60] John of Lisieux traveled to England, for example, in late 1126 to join the deliberations on the royal succession that culminated in the empress Maud's designation at the Christmas court: *RRAN* 2, no. 1466; John of Lisieux and Robert de la Haye were both apparently with the king at York in late 1122: ibid., no. 1338; both John and Robert were absent because of illness from a Norman court of ca. 1129 where Robert, chaplain to the bishop of Lisieux, and the steward Robert of Courcy seem to have acted in their places: ibid., no. 1584.

[61] Bates rightly stresses the custom of assigning viceregal responsibilities to royal spouses and close kinsmen: "Origins of the Justiciarship"; Rufus, of course, was both sonless and spouseless. On Matilda's viceregencies see *RRAN* 2, nos 971, 1000–1001, 1190, 1198; and *Cartulary of Worcester Cathedral Priory*, nos 40, 262; on Anselm, *AO*, ep. 407; Eadmer, *HN*, p. 197. Matilda II was probably in Normandy in 1107, but she was in England with Anselm in 1108 or early 1109 when she issued the charter, on Anselm's advice, that established the Augustinian house of Holy Trinity, Aldgate: *RRAN* 2, nos 808–809, 906; on William Adelin see ibid., nos 1189, 1191–1192, 1201–1202.

[62] For Roger see *RRAN* 2, nos 906, 909, 1090, 1189–1190, 1192, 1201; *Cartulary of Worcester Cathedral Priory*, nos 40, 262. Roger is the first or sole witness to all of these acts except no. 906, for which he was the second of three episcopal attesters. For the English viceregal group see also *RRAN* 2, nos 971, 1001, 1129, 1180, 1191, 1198.

royal acts issued in England. Ranulf the Chancellor was the only official who crossed the Channel at various times in the king's service, but
even he attested many more charters in England than in Normandy.
Clearly, then, the chancellor was in part a cross-Channel *curialis* and in
part a member of the English viceregency.

One particularly illuminating document provides a view of the
English viceregal court meeting at Brampton, Huntingdonshire, in
1116. The "judges" (*judices*) included several men who were active
in Matilda's and William Adelin's regency administrations: Roger
bishop of Salisbury, Robert Bloet bishop of Lincoln, Walter of
Gloucester, and Ralph Basset.[63] Similarly, a plea recorded in the
Abingdon chronicle (circa 1101) was heard in the presence of Roger
bishop of Salisbury, Robert bishop of Lincoln, *et multis regis baronibus*;
another Abingdon plea (circa 1111) was heard by Roger of Salisbury,
Robert of Lincoln, Richard of London, "and many royal barons," and
still another (1119) by Roger of Salisbury, Robert of Lincoln, Ranulf
the Chancellor, and Ralph Basset.[64] The membership of these courts,
corroborated by the witness lists of viceregal charters, thus discloses
a select and stable body of viceregal administrators based in England
and led by Roger bishop of Salisbury, with functions and membership
that closely parallel those of the Norman viceregal body headed by
John bishop of Lisieux.

Until 1119 the queen or prince headed the English viceregency.
But the members of the viceregal court, and Roger of Salisbury in
particular, exercised strong influence on Matilda and William Adelin.
Herbert bishop of Norwich, in begging a favor of Bishop Roger during
one of Henry I's absences, was confident that "you will not find our
lady the queen difficult, for . . . she takes advantage of your advice
in all matters."[65] Chroniclers described Roger as *secundus a rege*, but the
phrase reflects an insular rather than an Anglo-Norman perspective.
When Henry was negotiating with Louis VI on the River Epte, or fighting for survival in the Norman Vexin or the Risle Valley, he was
accompanied by his great cross-Channel attesters and intimate counselors—magnates such as Robert count of Meulan, Robert earl of
Gloucester, Brian fitz Count, William the Chamberlain of Tancarville,
and Hugh Bigod—who as a whole differed from the two viceregal
groups in that they were all laymen of immense wealth. One must
bear in mind a distinction between administrators and counselors.

---

[63] *English Lawsuits*, 1:176 (no. 205); the two remaining judges at Brampton are
Gilbert sheriff of Huntingdonshire and Hugh of Leicester sheriff of Leicestershire.
[64] Ibid., 1:128 (no. 162), 157–158 (no. 189), 182 (no. 215).
[65] *Epistolae Herberti de Losinga . . . Osberti de Clara, et Elmeri prioris cantuariensis*, no.
26.

While Henry's closest magnate-*familiares* accompanied him back and forth across the Channel, Roger of Salisbury remained in England attending to the king's interests.

Having made the distinction between administrators and counselors, I must immediately qualify it. Norman-English attestation patterns do not indicate three groups—Normans, English, and crossers. The groups blend across whatever lines of demarcation one might impose on them. Moreover, Henry's top administrators—his viceregal people—could and did counsel him on matters of high import, even if not on a continuous basis. By the 1120s Roger bishop of Salisbury exercised a powerful influence on English episcopal and abbatial appointments, much to the chagrin of the Anglo-Saxon chronicler.[66] And Roger's counterpart in Normandy, John bishop of Lisieux, was one of the very few people whom Henry consulted on the issue of the empress Maud's marriage to Geoffrey of Anjou—or so Roger of Salisbury later grumbled.[67] Conversely, great cross-Channel magnate-counselors could involve themselves in administration, as judges, of course, and also, in the persons of Robert of Gloucester and Brian fitz Count, as treasury auditors.[68] Robert count of Meulan had created his own baronial exchequer within a very few years of the earliest reliable evidence for the existence of a royal *scaccarium*, and both he and Robert of Gloucester developed administrative machinery for their own honors patterned after the royal model.[69] But although Henry's chief administrators might give him advice and although his greatest cross-Channel counselors had the wits to adapt the latest royal administrative innovations to their own honorial uses, the distinction between them remains useful. Robert of Meulan and Roger of Salisbury served the king in drastically different capacities.

Such are the contours of Henry I's administrative machine. At its center was the itinerant royal *curia* of household officials and *familiares*. Ranging outward were the English and Norman viceregencies with their semiannual exchequer sessions and the fixed treasuries with their chamberlains, coins, and records. At the grassroots level were the sheriffs, *vicomtes*, and local justices whose responsibilities, at least in

---

[66] *ASC*, s.a. 1123, 1131.

[67] William of Malmesbury reports, with a touch of skepticism, Roger of Salisbury's complaint that the king had conferred about the marriage only with Robert of Gloucester, Brian fitz Count, and John bishop of Lisieux (*HN*, p. 5).

[68] *PR 31 Henry I*, p. 130.

[69] Stenton, *English Feudalism*, pp. 69–70; Crouch, *Beaumont Twins*, pp. 140, 145, 163–166; Vaughn, *Anselm of Bec and Robert of Meulan*, pp. 354–356.

England,[70] passed more and more under the expert supervision of
curiales exercising authority over large regions. Overall, the reign was
marked by an ever-increasing concentration of authority in the
hands of an elite group of administrators who gave the system its
cohesion.

I have argued above that Henry's government represented a quali-
tative difference in style from that of his predecessors, that his administrative mechanisms constituted novel means to traditional ends.
Perhaps in conclusion it would be wise to review some of the half-
hidden factors that elucidate this decisive shift in orientation. Henry's
regime marked a drift toward systematization and explicitness, not only
in the major administrative innovations just discussed but also in such
matters as the standardization of measures and coins, the establishment
of regulations governing the conduct, wages, and perquisites of the
royal household, the granting of fixed stipends for barons attending
court, and the common use of royal writs purged of superfluous ver-
biage and cast in the most starkly economical style.[71] Royal patronage,
while an age-old practice, was now systematized as never before. Writs
granting lands and privileges were copied and preserved in the treasury at Winchester. Under Henry I the expansion of the Anglo-Norman
regnum ceased, halting with it the expansion of royal estates and the
winning of new lands to bestow on *fideles*. The Anglo-Norman monarchy survived this lowering of expectations by tightening its judicial and
fiscal procedures.[72]

The trend toward systematization was accompanied, appropriately,
by growing literacy and mastery of Latin among Henry's magnates and
administrators and by a substantial increase in written records.[73] The
outpouring of governmental documents that Henry's regime amply
produced—including about fifteen hundred charters, compared to
fewer than five hundred for the reigns of William I and William II—
exemplifies what Michael Clanchy describes as the great historical
transition "from memory to written record."[74] Henry's government produced the first records of the newly constituted exchequer, the Pipe

---

[70] The disappearance of all Henry I's Norman exchequer rolls leaves the situation in Normandy unclear. A passage from the Troarn cartulary shows the "king's
justice" William Tanetin first sitting at Caen with John of Lisieux and later settling
the case on his own: Haskins, *NI*, p. 98.
[71] See, for example, *Royal Writs in England from the Conquest to Glanvill*, pp.
252–253; Kealey, "Anglo-Norman Policy," p. 343; *Constitutio domus regis*, in *Dialogus
de scaccario*, pp. 128–135; Hollister, "Rise of Administrative Kingship," in *MMI*, pp.
224–245.
[72] See Green, "William Rufus, Henry I, and the Royal Demesne."
[73] Richardson and Sayles, *Governance*, pp. 269–284; Turner, "The *Miles literatus*."
[74] Clanchy, *From Memory to Written Record*.

Roll of 1130, by far the earliest surviving kingdomwide financial survey in the history of humankind. The same administration produced an elaborate record, again the first of its kind, of the organization, rank, and emoluments of the royal household: the *Constitutio domus regis*. The anonymous administrator who wrote the first treatise on English law, the *Leges Henrici Primi*, is probably also the author of a significant companion treatise, the so-called *Quadripartitus*. The two treatises are best seen as products of a concerted effort to make explicit the idealized pre-Conquest "law of Edward the Confessor," which Henry I had undertaken to restore. It is characteristic of the twelfth-century renaissance that these two documents rest on deep foundations yet build on them with a self-awareness and coherence that is altogether new.

This novel perception of the world—as rational order open to human intellectual exploration—gave rise to a great upsurge in systematic thinking, in theology and law, architecture, sculpture, literature, music and the other arts, and in the writing of history and political organization as well. Henry I surrounded himself with systematizers, but no one was more systematic than Henry himself. "He inquired into everything," Orderic remarks, "and retained all he heard in his tenacious memory. He wished to know all the business of officials and dignitaries; and since he was an assiduous ruler, he kept an eye on all the happenings in England and Normandy."[75]

---

[75] OV, 6:100.

Chapter 10

KING AND CHURCH

Vir prudentissimus Henricus . . .
—Suger, *Vie de Louis le Gros*, chap. 1.

The church of God has enjoyed riches and honours, and every religious order flourished greatly to the glory of the Creator. Monks and clerks bear witness to this, for they increased in number and distinction during his reign. Hermits can add their testimony, for they cut down dense woods and now give praise in high-roofed monasteries and spiritual palaces built there, chanting glory to God with peace of mind in the places where formerly robber outlaws used to hide to perform their evil deeds.
—Orderic Vitalis 5:294–296.

Frank Barlow concluded his important work on the Anglo-Norman Church by noting Henry II's nostalgia for the orderly relationship of *regnum* and *sacerdotium* in the era of his grandfather. Whether or not Henry II recognized what he owed to Henry I's administrative talent, he clearly viewed his grandfather's religious policy as an ecclesiastical standard. The grandson's backward glance over a period of imbalance also reminds us of Henry I's effort, after the excesses of William Rufus' reign, to restore the relationship of Church and state achieved by the Conqueror. Barlow reasons that the skill of all three Norman kings produced a solid working system, "a polity out of tamed feudalism and the skill of the church."[1] He emphasizes that the English Church, while absorbing numerous foreign currents over the centuries, retained its acknowledged national character. Barlow details this character sensibly and thoughtfully, sketching personalities in honest, graphic strokes. Since the appearance of his volume over twenty years ago, it has formed the basis of our understanding of the Anglo-Norman Church, the kings and their bishops. Recent scholars have continued to work on the basis

---

[1] Barlow, *English Church: 1066–1154*, p. 8.

of his suggestive ideas toward a deeper understanding of the development of the Church and state under individual Anglo-Norman kings, an effort that has sometimes cast the central characters in a different light as warranted by new interpretations of the evidence.

Martin Brett, like his mentor R. W. Southern, pointed out how much evidence exists for the history of the English Church in the early twelfth century yet how much still remained to be done. *The English Church under Henry I*, Brett's foundational work on the organization of the Church in the reign of Henry I, established the context for the activities of the king he labeled a most "elusive character" and shows how the Church grew into a virtual department of state.[2] The harmony achieved resembled that maintained by the Conqueror and Lanfranc. But without the long presence of a single-minded archbishop and partner, Henry's "policy," as it developed during his long reign, was more reactive, more nuanced. His consistent goal was to maintain firm control of the Church, but the varying challenges he faced over the years required more patience, more flexibility, more finesse than his father or brother displayed. Brett observed that the harmony of Church and state under Henry I resulted from careful ecclesiastical patronage, creating a coherent group of bishops whose interests paralleled those of the king.[3] Brett describes Henry's power and influence, so revered by his grandson Henry II, as "more pervasive but less malign than [that exercised] in the Holy Roman Empire."[4] The king's practical approach to royal control of the Church can be read as an extension of his policy toward the lay aristocracy. Henry consistently rewarded talented and loyal supporters with lands and status, he worked them hard (as Southern noted so long ago), and he linked their success to that of the administration. Research has probed the nature of Henry's appointments to the episcopacy, detailed the background of ecclesiastical appointees raised to magnate status, and evaluated these prelates for qualities that contributed to the stability of the regime: experience in the royal bureaucracy, administrative or diplomatic skill, family connections, or prestige in the religious world.

Brett's work richly documents the rise of papal influence over the English monarchy. Neither the distance from Rome nor the insistence of both the king and his archbishops on their prerogatives long stayed Rome's march. Even if the Gregorian reform movement failed to achieve its most sweeping goals, the popes in the twelfth century played an international role, intervening in the national churches, particularly as arbiters of legal disputes over conflicting jurisdictions: metropolitans

[2] Brett, *English Church*, p. 3
[3] Ibid., p. 111.
[4] Ibid., p. 66.

versus archbishops, abbots versus bishops and archbishops, kings versus archbishops. In this atmosphere the impetus for precision in documentation placed a premium on papal pronouncements, privileges, confirmations, and reconfirmations. In the process bishops and abbots became more and more part of an administrative structure sensitive to the demands of both popes and kings.

Bishops were becoming important players in government. Everett Crosby compared the role of the bishops in the coronation of Henry I in 1100 and in that of Stephen of Blois in 1135.[5] In opposition to the old argument that Henry I abused the Church and Stephen offered redress, Crosby contends that between 1100 and 1135 the basis for ecclesiastical power was laid and that Stephen's promises constituted recognition of that power. To what then do we attribute this remarkable development in the Church? To William the Conqueror and Lanfranc, who grafted Norman authority onto the Anglo-Saxon tradition of royal and archiepiscopal cooperation, giving the Anglo-Norman Church the basis for power in the political world. To the temper and folly of William Rufus, whose predations made the Church an aggrieved party eager to protect itself—or at least to receive fair treatment in the courts, royal and papal. To the reform of the Church universal and the growing influence of the papacy. To the search for precision and the new litigiousness arising from the revival of learning. And ultimately to the youngest son of the Conqueror, whose style of personal government and whose pragmatic and tempered policies guaranteed the loyalty of his ecclesiastical servants in his lifetime but ultimately gave them the power and organization to improve their position against a lesser man, Stephen, and to challenge and nominally win against a greater one, Henry II.

A man of praiseworthy devotion to God . . .
                                    —William of Malmesbury, *GR*, 5:413

Henry I was a much better friend to the Anglo-Norman Church than current opinion is inclined to grant. Many modern historians in the field have rejected as monkish exaggeration the almost universal praise of Henry by contemporaries in favor of a one-sided portrait of the king as calculating, avaricious, and brutal, dismissing the comments of Robert of Torigny, Eadmer, Orderic Vitalis, William of Malmesbury, and the chroniclers at Battle and Abingdon. It is time for a more modulated understanding of the king's motivations and actions. I certainly

[5] Crosby, "Organization of the English Episcopate," pp. 4–6.

do not intend to argue the case for Henry's canonization. For as a ruler he was shrewd and calculating, and he knew the value of loyalty, lands, and possessions. But he could also be unaccountably forgiving in victory, humble in the face of his sins (or dreams of them), humorous in the face of immovable objects, and loyal and generous to his family and friends in the religious and secular worlds.

Henry I was not only an Anglo-Norman king following in the footsteps of his predecessors but also an innovator whose policies evolved in a unique way in reaction to new currents and new challenges. Both the Anglo-Saxon kings and the Norman dukes expected to control the Church, almost as part of the ducal or royal demesne. Certainly by the late eleventh century the Norman rulers considered their bishops and abbots as ecclesiastical barons, powerful elements in the maintenance of order. Influenced by these traditions, Henry I saw himself as the good steward of his inherited domains and privileges, responsible for preserving them all and passing them intact to his heirs. Thus he wrote to Pope Paschal II.[6] On approving the election of Boso as abbot of Bec in 1124, Henry made a statement that reveals his conception of his role in ecclesiastical affairs: "You must be abbot within your order, and I shall be abbot in external affairs."[7] The king adamantly defended his right to appoint bishops and abbots, to assume control of church property during a vacancy, to resolve church problems in the royal council, usually in the presence of the bishops, abbots, and magnates of the realm, to approve appeals to Rome, and to authorize or deny attempts by the pope or his legates to exercise authority in the realm.

Such goals were also those of William the Conqueror and William Rufus. Yet Henry I's policies were not merely those of his father or his brother "disguised under a veneer of bureaucracy and custom,"[8] a conclusion that derives from recent efforts to redeem William Rufus from the vilifications of monk-historians and eminent Victorian scholars. Frank Barlow, in his erudite biography of Rufus, credits him with confirming the royal power in England and restoring ducal rights in Normandy. But Barlow acknowledges no substantial differences in the ecclesiastical policies of William I, William II, and Henry I, apart from variations in style: "Rufus was a slightly more polished version of his father, although by no means as smooth as his younger brother, Henry."[9] Unfortunately, efforts to rehabilitate William Rufus have reinforced stereotypes of Henry I as the cruel, exploitative manipulator of

[6] AO, ep. 215; cf. Vita Beati Lanfranci, PL 150:32.
[7] "On the Liberty of the Abbey of Bec," in Vaughn, Abbey of Bec, p. 143.
[8] Mason, "William Rufus," p. 15.
[9] See Barlow, English Church: 1066–1154, pp. 67, 70, 91, 297–298, and Barlow, Rufus, pp. 181–182, 434–435.

his servants. This hypothesis—that Henry pursued essentially the same policies toward the Church that Rufus did but disguised them with soothing words and slick public relations—is simply not true.[10]

The stylistic difference between the two regimes, a matter on which all would agree, emerges vividly in the contemporary sources. Eadmer's *Historia novorum* provides numerous striking vignettes: Ranulf Flambard, "full of insolence and self-importance," creating a furore at Anselm's archiepiscopal enthronement ceremony by launching a lawsuit against Canterbury,[11] or Rufus responding to Anselm's refusal to contribute to the Norman expedition of 1094:

> Yesterday I hated him with great hatred; today I hate him with still greater hatred, and he can be certain that tomorrow and thereafter I shall hate him continually with ever fiercer and more bitter hatred. I absolutely refuse any longer to regard him as father or archbishop. As for his blessings and prayers, I utterly abominate them and spew them from me.[12]

With Henry I we enter a world of gentle words and circumlocutions. In early 1106 Henry replied by letter to Anselm's complaint that he was levying improper fines against churchmen by promising "an explanation that will be so satisfactory to you that, when you and I come to talk it over, I am certain that you will not blame me for what I have done."[13] Earlier, during Anselm's exile resulting from the impasse over investiture, Henry wrote in honeyed words, grieving that Anselm declined to follow his predecessor Lanfranc in permitting the king to invest prelates for "I would wish to have no mortal man with me more willingly than you."[14] Anselm replied with a firm refusal framed in similarly affectionate words: if Henry would only relinquish investitures, "with no other king or prince on earth would I so willingly live, no other so willingly serve."[15]

Similarities in substance between the two kings' attitude to the Church exist, but they are shared by virtually all competent medieval princes: a need for revenues, which can become an urgent need in time of war,[16] and a determination to uphold inherited royal customs. Rufus

---

[10] The material that follows here (pp. 374–391) is extracted from Hollister, "William II, Henry I, and the Anglo-Norman Church," in *Culture of Christendom*, pp. 183–205.

[11] Eadmer, *HN*, p. 41.

[12] Ibid., p. 52.

[13] *AO*, ep. 392. Cf. Brett, *English Church*, p. 7, who states that Henry I is "an elusive character with a marked capacity for concealing his motives and emotions."

[14] *AO*, ep. 318 (*an.* 1104).

[15] Ibid., ep. 319.

[16] See Southern, *Medieval Humanism*, p. 188: "Flambard initiated the tireless

repeatedly accused Anselm of trying to rob him of the crown and jewel of his sovereignty,[17] and Henry, in an otherwise friendly letter to Paschal II, assured him that, "so long as I live, the dignities and usages of the English realm shall not be diminished."[18]

Apart from such predictable similarities, the two kings had different policies toward the Church both in style and in substance.[19] Rufus has been credited with defending England against the newly aggressive Gregorian papacy,[20] but in fact no such defense occurred in Rufus' reign because none was needed. As Sally Vaughn demonstrated in her book on Anselm and Robert of Meulan,[21] the issues dividing Anselm and Rufus had nothing directly to do with Gregorian reform. They had to do with what Anselm regarded as Rufus' assault on the dignities of Canterbury as embodied in the customs of Lanfranc. Anselm was no less determined than William Rufus and Henry I to uphold the customs and honors of his stewardship. As he said in a letter of 1108 to Thomas II, archbishop-elect of York, "You can be very certain that I shall strive in every possible way to see that the Church [of Canterbury] does not lose one scrap of her prestige in my time."[22] Anselm assumed precisely this position with respect to Rufus. They quarreled over the enfeoffment of royal knights on Canterbury estates (which Lanfanc had struggled so long to recover);[23] they squabbled over Rufus' refusal to fill vacant abbacies or to permit Anselm to summon a primatial reform council (in the tradition of Lanfranc, not Hildebrand);[24] and they argued over the canonical requirement that Anselm receive his archiepiscopal pallium from Pope Urban II—whom Anselm had recognized while abbot of Bec but whom Rufus had declined to recognize until 1095 because of the rival claim of the antipope Clement III.[25] With Anselm needing a pallium and Rufus refusing to recognize either pope, trouble was inevitable—but it had nothing to do with lay investiture or clerical homage.[26]

---

search for money for foreign conquest which is the hall-mark of English government in the Middle Ages."

[17] Eadmer, *HN*, pp. 53, 54, 58.

[18] *AO*, ep. 215.

[19] Emma Mason's "William Rufus and the Benedictine Order," *Anglo-Norman Studies* 21 (1998, 1999): 113–141, appeared after Warren Hollister's death [ACF].

[20] Callahan, Jr., "The Making of a Monster"; for a dissenting opinion see Chandler, "Historical Revision and the English Monarchy."

[21] I am indebted to Sally N. Vaughn, *Anselm of Bec and Robert of Meulan*, esp. chapters 5–7, for much of this argument.

[22] *AO*, ep. 455.

[23] Eadmer, *HN*, pp. 48–50.

[24] Ibid.

[25] Ibid., pp. 52–53.

[26] See, in general, Vaughn, *Anselm of Bec and Robert of Meulan*, pp. 149–203.

Anselm's disputes with both Rufus and Henry I, and the exile he suffered in both their reigns, suggest a similarity in the policies of the two regimes that on closer scrutiny proves to be an illusion. The issues dividing Anselm and Rufus were utterly unlike those dividing Anselm and Henry I, who, when he recalled the archbishop from exile immediately after being crowned, did so with the full intention of respecting the dignities of Canterbury as Anselm interpreted them.[27] But while in exile Anselm had attended the Roman synod of 1099 where he had witnessed and affirmed the solemn papal and synodal condemnation of lay investiture and clerical homage.[28] The English investiture controversy thus commenced abruptly on Anselm's return from exile in September 1100. It constituted a fundamental reorientation of Anselm's relationship with the English monarchy; rather than Anselm striving to defend the lands and customs of Canterbury, Henry I was obliged to defend basic prerogatives of the crown. Whereas Rufus had denied Anselm the customs of Lanfranc, the papacy, through Anselm's agency, was endeavoring to deny Henry the customs of William the Conqueror. The filling of episcopal and abbatial vacancies that had accumulated under Rufus was now delayed not by royal policy as before but by Henry's insistence on continuing to invest prelates-elect and Anselm's refusal to consecrate such individuals on the grounds of the papal ban.[29] Anselm's former mantle as defender of his stewardship now passed to Henry. Pope Paschal II dropped the issue of clerical homage fairly early in the controversy,[30] but the conflict over investiture persisted, eventually propelling Anselm into a second exile, which continued until Henry I, under the pressure of a Norman war, agreed in 1105 to abandon the custom.[31]

The investiture controversy was thus, in essence, a struggle between Henry I, defending royal custom, and the papacy, which placed truth above custom. Anselm, who never expressed any personal concern about lay investiture, was caught in the middle, unable to cooperate with the king without betraying the pope. The agreement of 1105, ratified

---

[27] *AO*, ep. 212; see ep. 210, wherein Anselm states to Paschal II the conditions on which he might return to England.

[28] Eadmer, *HN*, p. 114; Pope Paschal II recalled the condemnation as having occurred at the council of Bari in 1098, which Anselm also attended, *AO*, ep. 282 (Paschal II to Anselm), "Reverendae in Christo memoriae praedecessoris nostri domni Urbani tempore, apud Barim collecto venerabilium episcoporum et abbatum ex diversis partibus concilio, in quo tua religio et nos ipsi interfuimus, sicut fratres qui nobiscum aderant reminiscuntur, in eandem pestem excommunicationis est prolata sententia" (in reference to the investiture of churches).

[29] See, in general, Vaughn, *Anselm of Bec and Robert of Meulan*, pp. 214–216.

[30] Southern, *Anselm and His Biographer*, pp. 171–193.

[31] Vaughn, *Anselm of Bec and Robert of Meulan*, pp. 283–295.

at Bec in 1106 and at Westminster in 1107,[32] was less a compromise (although Paschal formally conceded clerical homage) than a surrender by Henry, mediated by Anselm, of a highly valued but ultimately dispensable customary ritual. With the settlement, relations between Anselm and the monarchy became, for the first time, untroubled.

Henry, then, claimed that the relationship between Lanfranc and William the Conqueror was the paradigm of his own relationship with the archbishop of Canterbury. His ecclesiastical councils bear out the claim. "Canterbury's superior governmental powers," in Barlow's words, "consisted almost entirely in the right to hold what were usually called by contemporary writers general councils of the English Church."[33] It is not always possible to determine whether such councils were primatial, provincial or legatine, or to distinguish them absolutely from royal councils: the archbishops and bishops participated routinely in royal councils, and the king and lay magnates usually attended ecclesiastical councils. The same was true in Normandy where, for example, the business of the council of Lillebonne in 1080 included both ecclesiastical discipline and ducal jurisdiction.[34] Lillebonne was the last of a series of synods of the province of Rouen under William the Conqueror. Raymonde Foreville has identified no fewer than sixteen and possibly seventeen such Norman synods during William's rule, ranging from the 1040s to 1080, most of them presided over by the archbishop of Rouen or by the duke and archbishop jointly, and dealing with ecclesiastical reform and discipline.[35] In England, Lanfranc presided over reform councils, usually jointly with the king, in 1072, 1075, 1076, 1077–1078, 1080, and 1085. These councils reformed and reshaped the English Church, enacting legislation against simony and clerical marriage, licensing the relocations of several episcopal sees, delineating and reinforcing episcopal jurisdictional authority, and prohibiting irregular sacramental and liturgical practices.[36]

With the accession of Rufus, ecclesiastical councils ceased. Two were held in Normandy under Duke Robert Curthose but none whatever in England, even during King William II's initial two years when Lanfranc was still living. Archbishop Anselm pressed Rufus repeatedly for permission to summon a reform council, but Rufus would not be budged: "I will deal with these things when I think fit," he told Anselm in 1094, "not at your pleasure but at mine . . . Enough . . . say no more about

---

[32] *Councils and Synods*, 1: part 2, pp. 689–694.
[33] Barlow, *English Church: 1066–1154*, p. 120.
[34] Foreville, "The Synod of the Province of Rouen," p. 26.
[35] Ibid., pp. 21–27.
[36] Barlow, *English Church: 1066–1154*, pp. 119–128; *Councils and Synods*, 1: part 2, pp. 591–634.

it."[37] Florence of Worcester reports that Anselm had his final quarrel with Rufus in 1097 "because from the time of his having been made archbishop he had not been allowed to hold a synod and correct the evil practices which had grown up in all parts of England, so he crossed the sea."[38] In Normandy, after two synods of the province of Rouen under Robert Curthose's rule (1091 and February 1096), such assemblies ceased after Curthose pawned the duchy to Rufus and departed for the crusade.[39]

Henry I differed dramatically from Rufus in his attitude toward ecclesiastical councils. Anselm presided over two great primatial councils during his six years in England under Henry I, the first of which, at Westminster at Michaelmas 1102, produced ecclesiastical legislation that Martin Brett describes as being "on a scale which not even the most impressive of Lanfranc's councils had achieved."[40] After Anselm's second reform council in 1108,[41] there is a hiatus corresponding approximately to the Canterbury vacancy (1109–1114) following Anselm's death and the pontificate of his successor, Archbishop Ralph d'Escures (1114–1122). Ralph's unsuccessful struggle to obtain a profession of obedience from Thurstan, archbishop of York, and the crippling paralytic stroke from which he never fully recovered doubtless limited his ability to preside at any church council in England.[42]

Raymonde Foreville has isolated four general synods in Normandy under Henry I's rule—in 1106 at Lisieux, in 1118 at Rouen, in 1119 at Lisieux, and in 1128 at Rouen[43]—to which should be added a fifth synod presided over by Archbishop William Bonne-Ame at Rouen in 1108. In England, after Ralph d'Escures' death in 1122 and the elevation in 1123 of William of Corbeil to the archbishopric, the councils resume. William of Corbeil returned from Rome with his empowering pallium in mid-1123, and although the first general council of his pontificate was presided over by the papal legate John of

---

[37] Eadmer, *HN*, pp. 48–49.

[38] FW, 2:41.

[39] Foreville, "The Synod of the Province of Rouen," p. 22.

[40] Brett, *English Church*, p. 76; see also *Councils and Synods*, 1: part 2, pp. 668–688.

[41] *Councils and Synods*, 1: part 2, pp. 694–704; I omit the council at Westminster in August 1107 which ratified the investiture settlement.

[42] OV, 6:318 and notes; Eadmer, *HN*, pp. 239, 243, 248–249, 259; WM, *GP*, pp. 128–132. There is no evidence that Archbishop Ralph asked Henry for permission to hold a primatial council, and his itinerary and troubles make it unlikely that he did so.

[43] Foreville, "The Synod of the Province of Rouen," p. 22; OV, 4:264. I am not, however, entirely convinced that the council of 1106 can correctly be termed a synod; the synod at Rouen in 1119 may possibly have been diocesan rather than provincial, OV, 6:290. See, in general, Spear, "Norman Episcopate," pp. 145–160.

Crema at Westminster in September 1125,[44] much to Canterbury's chagrin, Archbishop William himself, with Henry I's backing, obtained from the pope an *ex officio* legateship over Britain in 1126.[45] He proceeded to convene general councils at Westminster in 1127 and at London in 1129.[46] A final council, at London in April 1132, was convened by papal order for the purpose of resolving the long-standing dispute between the Welsh bishoprics of Llandaff and St David's before a tribunal headed by all three Anglo-Norman archbishops: Canterbury, York, and Rouen.[47]

Henry I, in short, reverted to his father's policy of collaborating with his archbishops in convening a series of general councils of both the English and Norman Churches, and the English councils during his reign might have been even more numerous had it not been for Archbishop Ralph's long absence and paralytic stroke. Rufus, then, is the aberration.[48]

Whether Henry I's ecclesiastical policy was Rufus' writ large turns on the issue of regalian right during episcopal and abbatial vacancies. Anselm, Eadmer, the Anglo-Saxon chronicler, the Winchester annalist, and other contemporaries castigated Rufus for permitting churches to lie vacant for excessive periods of time and despoiling them of their wealth,[49] whereas under Henry I such criticism ceased. It is nevertheless clear that royal appropriation of the revenues of vacant bishoprics and abbeys also occurred under William the Conqueror, Henry I, and their successors. Margaret Howell, in her comprehensive study of regalian right, concluded that "the difference between the practice of William I and that of William II in respect to vacant sees and abbeys was the difference of use and abuse."[50] She points out, however, that despite the chorus of contemporary complaints about Rufus' despoliation of churches, he can be shown to have treated two of them gently. In a writ of 1095 or 1096 he commanded that the prior and monks of

---

[44] *Councils and Synods*, 1: part 2, pp. 725–727, 730–741. Archbishop William was probably deterred from summoning a council in 1123–1125 by Henry's absence in Normandy and by Pope Calixtus II's promise in 1123 to send a legate to England to settle the primacy issue.

[45] Ibid., pp. 742–743 with references. See, in general, Bethell, "William of Corbeil."

[46] *Councils and Synods*, 1: part 2, pp. 743–754.

[47] Ibid., pp. 757–761; other ecclesiastical business appears to have been transacted at this council as well. See Brett, *English Church*, p. 80, for a possible additional English ecclesiastical council in 1102–1103 or 1107–1108.

[48] See Barlow, *Rufus*, p. 373.

[49] Eadmer, *HN*, pp. 49–50; *AO*, ep. 206; *ASC, s. a.* 1100; *Ann. Wint.*, 2:39; and OV, 5:202.

[50] Howell, *Regalian Right*, p. 12.

the vacant bishopric of Worcester should have unchallenged possession of the property appropriated for their maintenance.[51] And a Durham chronicler reports that during the vacancy of 1096–1099, although Rufus appropriated three hundred pounds annually from the see, he took nothing from the monks but, on the contrary, was generous and beneficent toward them.[52] From an analysis of the Pipe Roll of 1130, Howell finds that Henry I's regime was making a much tidier profit from the two initial years of the subsequent Durham vacancy of 1128–1133: "The profligate Rufus," she concludes ironically, "had taken £300 a year from the bishopric of Durham during the previous vacancy; the Lion of Justice reaped a clear profit of over £1,200 from the regular issues of this vacancy in two years."[53]

This Worcester and Durham evidence must, however, be interpreted with great caution. The Worcester writ is probably concurrent with a brief truce in the otherwise stormy relations between Rufus and Anselm—lasting from May 1095 into the early months of 1097—during the course of which Rufus entrusted Anselm with the defense of southeastern England during the Mowbray rebellion. Anselm also at this time contributed personally to Rufus' great fund-raising effort for the pawning of Normandy that enabled Duke Robert Curthose to join the First Crusade.[54] It was a period during which Rufus was on his best behavior.[55] The gentle treatment of Durham, however, is probably to be explained by the likelihood that Ranulf Flambard, who administered the vacant see along with many other bishoprics and abbeys, knew that Rufus intended him to be its next bishop. If so, he had good reason to desist from plundering the see he was himself to assume in 1099.

Apart from these two instances, the evidence against Rufus and Flambard is damning.[56] On the death of Paul abbot of St Albans in 1093, a St Albans writer reports that Rufus "held the monastery in his hands and mercilessly impoverished it by leveling the groves and by extorting

---

[51] Ibid., p. 16; *Cartulary of Worcester Cathedral Priory*, no. 5.

[52] Howell, *Regalian Right*, p. 16; SD, 1:135.

[53] Howell, *Regalian Right*, p. 29; from *PR 31 Henry I*, pp. 130–133; see p. 140 for traces of royal revenues from the bishoprics of Hereford and Coventry and the abbey of Chertsey.

[54] Barlow, *Rufus*, pp. 343–373; Vaughn, *Anselm of Bec and Robert of Meulan*, pp. 191–195. The Worcester vacancy, by which the writ can be dated, ran from 19/20 January 1095 to 8 June 1096.

[55] Rufus appointed the Bec monk Henry to the abbey of Battle in June 1096 and a monk of Lessay, Richard d'Aubigny, to St Albans in 1097. Anselm's close ties to Bec, Lessay, and St Albans suggest that he was consulted. The truce period also witnessed the filling of vacancies, without evidence of simony, at Hereford, Worcester (as above), and probably Winchcombe.

[56] Jared, "English Ecclesiastical Vacancies."

money from the men of St Albans."[57] At Abingdon, vacant from February 1097 to the end of the reign, the house chronicler reports that Rufus put the abbey into the hands of a certain Modbert, who managed affairs "not for the advancement of the church but for the wealth of the royal purse"; he lavished church property on his kinsmen and friends to such a degree that of eighty ploughs only eighteen remained, and of eighty monks only thirty-two survived.[58] Not before Henry I filled the vacancy in 1100 with the learned monk Faritius did the abbey begin growing again.[59] Orderic, in describing Rufus' policy of allowing the monks of vacant houses barely enough for food and clothing, diverting the rest into the royal coffers, singles out Bury St Edmunds (vacant after December 1097) and Ely (vacant after 1093) as victims of these policies.[60] Similarly, Anselm, writing to Paschal II in 1099 or 1100, states that when he left England in 1097 the king seized his entire archbishopric and converted it to his own use, "allowing only for the bare food and clothing of our monks."[61] Speaking more generally, the Winchester annalist reports that by 1097 Ranulf Flambard held sixteen bishoprics and abbeys "in extreme poverty."[62]

Eadmer describes the earlier Canterbury vacancy (1089–1093) in terrifying detail, asserting that Rufus auctioned the custody of the archbishopric to the highest bidder year after year, putting the monks on the slenderest of rations, permitting tax collectors to barge into the precincts of the monastery and intimidate the monks, driving many of them away, and granting out lands as fees for the king's knights.[63] Eadmer adds that the king inflicted similar suffering on vacant churches throughout England,[64] and although recent historians have been skeptical of this testimony, it is corroborated, as we have seen, not only by the general complaints of other observers but also by independent accounts relating specifically to Abingdon, St Albans, Ely, Bury St Edmunds, and Canterbury during its subsequent vacancy. The

---

[57] *Gesta abbatum monasterii S. Albani*, 1:65; cf. *AO*, ep. 203, where Anselm alludes to the tribulations of the St Albans monks.

[58] *Chron. Ab.*, 2:42, 285; Knowles, *Monastic Order*, p. 180.

[59] *Chron. Ab.*, 2:285.

[60] *OV*, 5:202; *Liber eliensis*, pp. 218–219, 223, 234; Howell, *Regalian Right*, pp. 14–15, qualifies Orderic by pointing out that the separation of conventual property may not yet have occurred at Ely or Bury St Edmunds. Cf. Southern, *Medieval Humanism*, p. 190.

[61] *AO*, ep. 210; cf. WM, *GP*, pp. 92, 97.

[62] *Ann. Wint.*, 2:39. Southern, *Medieval Humanism*, pp. 191–192, regards this statement as quite plausible. He adds that although Flambard's practices were not unprecedented, "it was the stripping away of all pretence, and the naked search for profit, that shocked contemporaries."

[63] Eadmer, *HN*, pp. 26, 39–40.

[64] Ibid., pp. 26–27.

monastic writers who bear witness to these practices are not conspiring to slander the reputation of a high-spirited king; they are not inventing abuses; they are in a state of shock. Even at Durham, where Rufus' hand lay gently, it was observed that "his conduct toward other monasteries was ferocious."[65]

Although Henry I continued the Anglo-Norman royal policy of appropriating episcopal and abbatial lands during vacancies, the chorus of complaints about abusive practices suddenly hushed at the new king's accession and are rarely heard thereafter. Indeed, there is much to suggest that Henry made a conscious effort to protect vacant churches. At Battle, during the vacancy of 1102–1107 (doubtless lengthened by the investiture impasse), the king's administrator, a monk of Saint-Calais named Geoffrey, won the hearts of the community. As the Battle chronicler reports, "Under his care, the storerooms were soon restocked with supplies, the rights of the church and the honor of the brothers revived, and the prosperity of the estates renewed."[66] At Geoffrey's death, the king entrusted the abbey to Gunter abbot of Thorney, who deputized his nephew Ralph to care for the Battle monks; when they complained about him he was removed, the monks being permitted to manage their own affairs until a new abbot was appointed at the Westminster council of 1107.[67] At Bury a charter of 1108 specified that during any vacancy the king's officials were to claim no power over manors belonging to the house.[68]

Lest this evidence seem tainted on the grounds that Battle was a royal *Eigenkloster* that even Rufus had handled with care, let us return to Abingdon. There, during the vacancy following the death of Abbot Faritius in 1117, the royal custodian Warenger, in striking contrast to Rufus' Modbert, is portrayed in the Abingdon Chronicle "as a most bounteous mother, he always nurtured us sincerely."[69] Eadmer attests to similar royal circumspection in his account of the Canterbury

---

[65] SD, 1:128: "in alia monasteria et ecclesias ferocius ageret . . . ," in reference to the vacancy created by William of Saint-Calais' exile in 1088–1091, during which Rufus' administration was also mild—except for the unfortunate necessity of sending a royal army against Bishop William in 1088 which "laid waste the land of the bishopric with fire and pillage." See also ibid., 1:176, and the entry for 1092 in the Winchester annals (*Ann. Wint.*, in *Annales monastici*, 2:37), following a notice of Ranulf Flambard's taking custody of the bishopric of Lincoln and Chertsey Abbey: "Praedictus vero Radulphus vir quo in malo nemo subtilior, ecclesias sibi commissas expoliavit bonis omnibus, et divites simul et pauperes ad tantam deduxit inopiam, ut mallent mori quam sub ejus vivere dominatu."

[66] *Chron. Battle*, p. 108. For the chronicler's less enthusiastic notice of a vacancy under Rufus, ibid., pp. 100–102.

[67] Ibid., p. 116.

[68] *RRAN* 2, no. 1079.

[69] *Chron. Ab.*, 2:159.

vacancy resulting from Anselm's exile of 1103–1106: Henry confiscated the archiepiscopal revenues but entrusted their collection to two of Archbishop Anselm's own men, "with the pious intention, as may reasonably be believed, that they would take greater pains than others would to see that their lord's men and possessions were not vexed, oppressed, or laid waste, for everyone knew that they had been bound to him by a special tie of fealty and by solemn oath."[70] Since Eadmer expresses no complaint regarding the landed revenues reserved for the Christ Church monks, Henry is unlikely to have touched them. Again, during the five-year Canterbury vacancy following Anselm's death in 1109, Henry appropriated the archiepiscopal revenues but permitted the monks to retain their own revenues, which they used in part for the beautification of their church. Resisting the urging of evil counselors, Henry is quoted by Eadmer as insisting that these monastic revenues be devoted to "the increase and glory of God's house . . . so that in my time, my mother church should grow rather than suffer detriment."[71] Whether these are Henry's words or Eadmer's invention, they testify to royal policy toward monastic lands as perceived by a well-placed contemporary monk who had ascribed, from firsthand observation, a drastically harsher policy to William Rufus.

Comparison of the two Durham vacancies—under Rufus in 1096–1099 and under Henry I in 1128–1133—has been taken as proof that despite all narrative evidence to the contrary, Henry squeezed harder than Rufus.[72] Although some questions regarding revenue sources remain unanswered and doubtless unanswerable, an analysis of the pipe roll evidence for the first two years of the 1128–1133 vacancy makes it clear that the bishopric was worth some £750 or £800 a year to Henry I, as against Rufus' £300. But these figures must be viewed in the context of the intervening twenty-nine-year pontificate of one of the great fund-raising masters of the age, Ranulf Flambard himself. It seems probable that the revenues accounted for by Henry I's collector at Durham, including an episcopal farm divided into two parts and totaling about £650 a year, resulted not from their own initiative but

---

[70] Eadmer, *HN*, p. 159. Eadmer hints that the two custodians did not altogether fulfill this hope, but he provides no details. *AO*, ep. 293, from Anselm in exile to Gundulf, bishop of Rochester, implies that the Canterbury monks retained their lands but that Henry I was attempting to tax them. Ibid., ep. 331 (1104), Anselm to Ernulf, prior of Canterbury, further indicates that the monks continued to hold their lands and revenue, and ep. 349 (early 1105) refers again to the money that the Canterbury monks were forced to pay to the king—presumably to support his approaching campaign to conquer Normandy.

[71] Eadmer, *HN*, p. 221.

[72] Howell, *Regalian Right*, p. 29; Mason, "William Rufus: Myth and Reality," pp. 1–20, esp. p. 15.

nbard's—that they were simply taking over a preexisting machine constructed in the course of his long pontificate.[73] ability is corroborated by a passage in the *Historia dunel-* porting that Bishop Ranulf, who had supported Robert Curthose's invasion of England in 1101 and had subsequently been restored to his see, thereafter sought persistently but vainly to win King Henry's full favor through lavish gifts. Consequently, the Durham writer continues, Ranulf's hand "lay heavily on the see, demanding from it many immoderate sums of money with which to buy the good will of the king and his *familiares*."[74] At Flambard's death in 1128, the Durham writer reports simply that the bishopric was entrusted to two local barons "that they might collect the taxes due to the king."[75] The monks left no recorded complaints of their treatment during the vacancy. Indeed, at that very moment they were making architectural history, building the majestic vaulting of the Durham cathedral nave, with its great transverse pointed arches and vault ribs that evoke our awe and point the way toward Gothic. By the end of the vacancy, the Durham writer proudly informs us, the vaulting was completed.[76] The monks can hardly have been impoverished by Henry's agents.

Margaret Howell made the valuable suggestion that Henry I's promise in his coronation charter, repeated at the investiture settlement at Bec in 1106, to neither lease nor sell nor take anything from the demesnes or benefices of vacant churches, did not constitute a repudiation of regalian right but merely of its abuse.[77] William the

---

[73] On the revenues, see Howell, *Regalian Right*, pp. 25–29, and Barlow, *Rufus*, p. 237. Note in particular the opening sections of the Durham account in *PR 31 Henry I*, pp. 128 (canceled) and 130, where the chief collector, Geoffrey Escolland, renders account of £82 18s. 6d. of the remainder of the farm from Bishop Ranulf's time. Ranulf died on 5 September 1128, and the figure, which is slightly over 20 percent of Geoffrey's portions of the farms of Michaelmas 1128–1129 and 1129–1130 (£429), must have included revenues owed to the bishop during the closing months of his life. What extent of the 1127–1128 Michaelmas year the £82 18s. 6d. "remainder" covered is not disclosed, but there is nothing to indicate that the farm was raised at Michaelmas 1128. See further Richardson and Sayles, *Governance*, pp. 225–226.

[74] SD, 2:138–139.

[75] Ibid., 1:141.

[76] Ibid., pp. 139, 141. Ranulf carried the walls of the nave up to the roof; the monks devoted themselves during the vacancy to the further building of the nave and finished it: "Eo tempore navis ecclesiae Dunelmensis monachis operi instantibus peracta est." It is on the basis of this passage that architectural historians are able to provide a tight date range for the building of the Durham nave vaults: e.g., Bony, *French Gothic Architecture*, p. 10: "The central space of the nave . . . is known to have been vaulted between 1128 and 1133."

[77] Howell, *Regalian Right*, pp. 20–24, concluding with the statement: "It is certain that Henry I continued to exercise a claim to the issues of vacant sees and abbeys; it seems a likely hypothesis that he never renounced it."

Conqueror seems to have taken the revenues of vacant churches in both Normandy and England, and the custom appears to extend even farther back into pre-Conquest Normandy and Carolingian Francia.[78] Henry's promise to Anselm at Bec is described explicitly as the renunciation of Rufus' policy of letting churches out at rent, "which had never been done before."[79] The evidence suggests that Henry did not, in fact, pursue a policy of letting churches out at rent, or of making them the objects of bidding wars, or of alienating their property through sale or forced enfeoffment, or of intimidating or impoverishing their monks. The examples reviewed here suggest a policy whereby Henry's custodians appropriated abbatial revenues of vacant churches and rendered strict account of these revenues at the exchequer. The custodians do not appear to have been notoriously ruthless, and some of them were well loved by the monks, who themselves were left in charge of their own allotted lands.

The average length of vacancies under Rufus and Henry I is a problem because the two reigns differ so sharply in duration and circumstances. Barlow has pointed out that the episcopal vacancies over which Henry I had control averaged eighteen months, whereas Rufus' episcopal vacancies averaged just over two years, dropping to just over one year "if we subtract the three longest vacancies."[80] These figures, however, can be altogether misleading, as Barlow himself warns us. They apply only to bishoprics, whereas Rufus' policies weighed more heavily on abbeys.[81] The Anglo-Saxon chronicler grieved that Rufus, at the time of his death, was keeping vacant three bishoprics and eleven abbeys;[82] since these remarkably numerous vacancies were filled as a consequence not of Rufus' volition but of his death, the statistic for

---

[78] Ibid., pp. 7–11.

[79] Eadmer, *HN*, p. 183.

[80] Barlow, *English Church: 1066–1154*, pp. 67–68, 77. I make it fifteen months for episcopal vacancies between 1107 and 1135, dropping to seven and a half months if we subtract the longest vacancy (Canterbury, 1109–1114).

[81] Barlow, *Rufus*, pp. 182–185: "He gradually allowed the monasteries to become acephalous . . . ," at p. 184.

[82] *ASC, s.a.* 1100; Malmesbury makes it three bishoprics and twelve abbeys, WM, *GR*, ed. Mynors (book) 4: (chap.) 333.8–9 [all *GR* references hereafter are to book and chapter in the Mynors edition]. The bishoprics were Canterbury, Winchester, and Salisbury; the figures on vacant abbeys cannot be confirmed because of the patchiness of the surviving evidence on abbatial successions at all but the wealthiest houses. Among those definitely or probably vacant in 1100 are Glastonbury, Ely, Bury St Edmunds, St Augustine's, Canterbury, Abingdon, New Minster, Winchester, Peterborough, and Chertsey. The editors of *Councils and Synods*, 2: part 2, p. 653 and n. 2, suggest rounding out the list with Milton, Mulchelney, and Cerne, in each of which the evidence on abbatial tenures is ambiguous. That the scandal of Rufus' exploitation of churches was not limited

average lengths of vacancies during his reign is meaningless as a gauge of royal policy. Perhaps when Rufus died he had been on the point of filling the vacant sees of Salisbury and Winchester and of recalling Anselm to Canterbury, but there is no hint of any such intention in the surviving evidence.[83]

The condition of the English Church at Rufus' death is particularly striking when one considers the vacant sees and abbeys in the order of their wealth and then applies to them the classification scheme developed by W. J. Corbett for categorizing the annual incomes of Domesday magnates.[84] The two class A bishoprics, Canterbury and Winchester, with revenues in excess of £750 a year, were both in the king's hands. Moving down, and excluding bishoprics in which no vacancy occurred during the reign, one of the two class B sees (over £400), Salisbury, was also vacant; the other, Lincoln, was occupied by the former chancellor, Bishop Robert Bloet. The record improves as one descends to class C (£200–£400) and class D (£100–£200), with Worcester, Norwich, Bath, Hereford, Durham, and Chichester all occupied by appointees of Rufus. His apparent preference for wealthy churches extended to abbeys as well. Of the six abbeys of class A and B—Glastonbury, Ely, Bury St Edmunds, St Augustine's, Westminster, and Abingdon—all were in the king's hands in 1100, save Westminster, where Abbot Gilbert Crispin had been ruling since the Conqueror's reign,

---

to English observers is made clear by Hugh of Flavigny's description of the legatine commission that Urban II sent in 1096 to warn Rufus "about the many illicit things that were done by him: i.e., about the bishoprics and abbeys that he held in his hands, for which he had provided no pastor and in which he had assumed to himself the rents and revenues; about simony; and about the fornication of clerics": *MGH, SS*, 8:474.

[83] Barlow, *English Church: 1066–1154*, p. 71, suggests that Anselm's absence prevented Rufus from filling Canterbury suffragan sees and obliged him to appoint Flambard to Durham, in the province of York, rather than to Winchester. There is no evidence, however, that Rufus ever intended Winchester for Ranulf or that deference to the exiled Anselm prevented Rufus from filling sees in the province of Canterbury. Henry I's effort in 1102, when at loggerheads with Anselm, to have Gerard, archbishop of York, consecrate bishops-elect of Hereford, Winchester, and Salisbury seems narrowly to have missed success when the bishops-elect declined consecration; it is most unlikely that, with Anselm abroad and Rufus in firm control, Flambard would have renounced the golden opportunity of enthronement at Winchester had he been offered it (Eadmer, *HN*, pp. 145–146). In 1091, during the Canterbury vacancy following Lanfranc's death, Rufus appointed Ralph Luffa to Chichester and Herbert Losinga to Norwich, and both were consecrated by Thomas, archbishop of York.

[84] *CMH* 5:508–511. My figures for the wealth of Domesday bishoprics are drawn primarily from Brett, *English Church*, p. 103 n. 1, with Hereford calculated at £280, Durham at £300 (as above), and York at £235 but almost certainly underreported, ibid., p. 72 n. 1.

thereby denying Rufus his opportunity.[85] Indeed, of the eight English abbeys with Domesday values exceeding £300 a year, all but two were in the king's hands in 1100, the aforementioned Westminster and Ramsey, to which Rufus had appointed Aldwin in 1091. The king's motive in making this one exception is made clear by Aldwin's subsequent deposition for simony at Anselm's council of 1102, along with Guy abbot of Pershore and Wimund abbot of Tavistock, both of whom also appear to have bought their prelacies from Rufus.[86] This interesting configuration of vacancies and simoniacal abbots at the close of Rufus' reign is almost equally evident in the English episcopate. Two of Rufus' nominations, Anselm to Canterbury and Robert Bloet to Lincoln, were made concurrently in March 1093 when Rufus lay at death's door and was desperate to make amends with his Almighty Lord.[87] On recovering, Rufus repudiated his various deathbed benefactions, but he was stuck with having received nothing in return for these episcopal appointments. Henry of Huntingdon states that Rufus "ached that he had not sold the bishopric of Lincoln" and adds that in the following year he made good his loss by charging Robert Bloet £5,000 for a favorable royal decision against claims on the diocese of Lincoln by the archbishop of York—a payoff that Henry of Huntingdon describes explicitly as simony.[88] If the sum was indeed £5,000, it was the equivalent of the bishop of Lincoln's entire annual Domesday revenues over a period of approximately eight years. Rufus had rather less luck with Anselm, from whom he tried unsuccessfully to wring £2,000, allegedly toward the expenses of a Norman expedition, a few weeks after Anselm's archiepiscopal enthronement.[89] There is unequivocal evidence of simony in

[85] Figures are from Knowles, *Monastic Order*, pp. 702–703. That St Augustine's, Canterbury (£635), which fell vacant in 1093, remained so until after Rufus' death is strongly suggested by Eadmer, *HN*, pp. 188–191, where the abbot-elect, Hugh, is described in 1107 as a monk of Bec. If, as seems most likely, Anselm recommended Hugh for the office, he is unlikely to have done so before Rufus' death. See Knowles et al., *Heads of Religious Houses*, p. 36.

[86] Eadmer, *HN*, p. 142: Wimund of Tavistock clearly took office under Rufus, for which see Knowles et al., *Heads of Religious Houses*, p. 72, and it is unlikely that Guy of Pershore, who is described as a consecrated abbot in 1102, could have arranged to be consecrated after Anselm's return in September 1100, when he prohibited the consecration of invested abbots.

[87] Eadmer, *HN*, pp. 30–37; *ASC*, s.a. 1093.

[88] HH, pp. 416–418, where Henry, a loyal archdeacon of the diocese of Lincoln, ascribes the sin of simony to Rufus, not Robert Bloet. The Winchester annalist (*Ann. Wint.*, 2:37) tells the same story but reduces the charge to three thousand marks.

[89] Eadmer, *HN*, pp. 143–145. Anselm, rather surprisingly, offered £500, which Rufus rejected as insufficient. Anselm correctly saw the transaction as being tainted with simony (*AO*, ep. 176). In the later twelfth century Canterbury scutages were running £80 or less: *RBE*, 1:22, 49.

Rufus' appointments of Ranulf Flambard to Durham, Herbert Losinga to Norwich, and Herbert's father Robert to New Minster, Winchester.[90] In a breathtaking act of alienation the king sold the vacant and previously independent abbey of Bath, with its buildings, estates, and monks, to John de Villula, bishop of Wells, who made it his new episcopal headquarters; in 1092, in consequence of the king's harassments, Odo abbot of Chertsey resigned and his abbey passed into Flambard's hands, where it remained until Rufus' death.[91] The king permitted Thurstan abbot of Glastonbury, who had been banished to Normandy by the Conqueror for perpetrating a scandalous riot, to return to England on the payment of £500, although the hostility of the Glastonbury monks prevented him from actually resuming his abbatial office.[92]

In virtually all of Rufus' transactions with his wealthier bishoprics and abbeys, the determining factor was money—whether the predictable annual issues of vacated prelacies or the larger, one-time payoff of simoniacal purchase. William of Malmesbury observes that this royal exploitation began in earnest only after Lanfranc's death in 1089 and that it then grew progressively more severe during the remaining years of the reign.[93] The Anglo-Saxon chronicler draws a clear parallel between Rufus' policies of simony and the exploitation of ecclesiastical vacancies, viewing them as two sides of a single coin: "He kept down God's church, and all the bishoprics and abbacies whose incumbents died in his days he sold for money or kept in his own hands and let out for rent."[94] We know from independent evidence that of the eight bishoprics of Corbett's classes A–C vacated since Lanfranc's death, six were either vacant or held by known simoniacs in 1100—including all four in classes A and B[95]—and of the eleven class A–C abbeys in which vacancies occurred, eight were vacant in 1100 and a ninth is known to have

---

[90] *AO*, ep. 214; WM, *GP*, p. 274; see ibid., p. 151, which reports that Herbert Losinga paid Rufus one thousand marks for the bishopric of Norwich and the abbey of New Minster.

[91] WM, *GR*, 4:340.1; *GP*, p. 194; *Ann. Wint.*, 2:37; Abbot Odo resumed his office in 1100 after Rufus' death, ibid., 2:40.

[92] WM, *GP*, p. 197; *De antiquitate Glastonie ecclesie*, pp. 156–158. Barlow, *Rufus*, p. 180, observes, more generally, that simony was probably blatant in Rufus' reign.

[93] WM, *GR*, 4:312–314.2.

[94] *ASC*, *s.a.* 1100; similarly, WM, *GR*, 4:314.2–3: "sacri aecclesiarum honores mortuis pastoribus venum locati; namque audita morte cuiuslibet episcopi vel abbatis, confestim clericus regis eo mittebatur, qui omnia inuenta scripto exciperet, omnesque in posterum redditus fisco regio inferret. Interea querebatur quis idoneus in loco defuncti idoneus substitueretur, non pro morum sed pro nummorum experimento, dabaturque tandem honor, ut ita dicam, nudus, magno tamen emptus."

[95] Canterbury (£1,860 including the lands reserved for the monks but appropriated by Rufus in 1097, for which see above, this chapter, n. 61), vacant;

been purchased; these nine abbeys included the eight wealthiest.[96] There is also evidence of three and perhaps four additional abbots having bought their offices from Rufus.[97] We can by no means be confident that all such transactions have left traces in our surviving sources.

Otherwise expressed, taking the total Domesday values of all class A–C bishoprics and abbeys, including those that did not fall vacant under Rufus, 60 percent of the wealth of all English churches worth £200 per year or more was in the royal hands in 1100; this figure breaks down to 48 percent of the episcopal lands (or £3,360) and 75 percent of the monastic lands (or £4,245).[98] If one adds the class A–C bishoprics and abbeys whose prelates are known to have paid Rufus large sums of money in connection with their elevation, the figures rise to 67 percent of episcopal lands, 81 percent of monastic lands, and 73 percent of all such lands. And because our evidence on instances of simony may well be incomplete, these figures must be regarded as minimal. Finally, if one excludes churches in which no vacancies had occurred since Lanfranc's death—that is, if one considers only those

[96] Winchester (£920), vacant; Lincoln (£660), simony (although Henry of Huntingdon blames the simony on Rufus, not Robert Bloet, for which see above, this chapter, n. 88); Salisbury (£580), vacant; Exeter (£460), Osborn: 1072–1103; London (£440 plus London), Maurice: 1085–1107; Worcester (£390), Samson: 1096–1112, no evidence of simony, for which see above, this chapter, n. 55; Norwich (£360), Herbert: 1091–1119, simony; Wells (£285), John: 1088–1122, appointed under Lanfranc, relocates see at Bath; Hereford (£280?), Gerard: 1096–Dec. 1100, no evidence of simony, for which see above, this chapter, n. 55; York (£235 plus), Thomas 1: 1070–Nov. 11—?; Rochester (£220), Gundulf: 1077–1108; Durham (£205 in Domesday Book, £300 in 1096–1099), Ranulf: 1099–1128, simony. Of the two bishoprics below class C, Chichester (£142), with Ralph Luffa, 1091–1123, appears unexceptionable, and Chester (£95) had no vacancy during Rufus' reign. I have omitted from consideration the lands reserved by the bishop of Winchester for his monks (£600) because, despite Orderic's implication that Flambard seized them in 1098 (OV, 5:202), there is no direct evidence to this effect.

[96] Glastonbury (£827), vacant; Ely (£769), vacant; Bury St Edmunds (£640), vacant; St Augustine's, Canterbury (£635), probably vacant, for which see above, this chapter, n. 85; Westminster (£584), Gilbert Crispin: 1085(?)–1117; Abingdon (£462), vacant; New Minster, Winchester (£390), vacant; Ramsey (£358), Aldwin: 1091–1102, 1107–1112, simony; Peterborough (£323), probably vacant; St Albans (£270), Richard d'Aubigny: 1097–1119, no simony, for which see above, this chapter, n. 55; Battle (£212), Henry: 1096–1102, no simony, for which see above, this chapter, n. 55; Chertsey (£199), vacant.

[97] Robert of Losinga, New Minster, Winchester: post-1088–1098; Wimund, Tavistock: 1096–1102; Guy, Pershore: deposed 1102, reinstated, for which see above, this chapter, n. 86; and perhaps Hamo of Cerne, for whom see Knowles et al., *Heads of Religious Houses*, p. 37.

[98] If one adds the two remaining bishoprics (of class D and E), the percentage of episcopal lands in royal custody descends from 48 percent to 46.5 percent.

that Rufus had an opportunity to confiscate—73 percent of their lands were in royal custody at the time of his final hunt and another 16 percent were in the hands of known simoniacs, making an overall total of 89 percent of the landed wealth of England's more substantial churches falling into Rufus' possession. In the Anglo-Saxon chronicler's words, this land Rufus "sold for money or kept in his own hands." These statistics make clear that statements such as this cannot be dismissed as monkish malice or savage caricatures. They are directly on target.

There is an evident connection between Rufus' systematic policy of leasing or selling churches and his adamant refusal to permit a general church council. Such a council would not only have brought to a head, as Barlow points out, the diametrically opposed views of Anselm and Rufus' circle on the practice of sodomy,[99] but also, and more to the point, it would have provided a legislative body and high tribunal to condemn simony and the royal exploitation of vacant churches.[100] Given the nature of Rufus' ecclesiastical policy, a council was out of the question. The series of church councils during the following reign bears witness to an overall redirection of royal policy. With the accession of Henry I, the systematic exploitation of churches ceased. Henry promised at his coronation, "because the kingdom has been oppressed by unjust exactions," neither to lease, despoil nor sell churches,[101] and he immediately set about to fill the vacancies. He restored Canterbury to Anselm and Chertsey to Odo, and he nominated prelates to Winchester, Abingdon, Ely, Bury St Edmunds, and New Minster, Winchester, all by the end of 1100. Glastonbury and Peterborough acquired prelates in 1101, Salisbury in 1102. The effects of this policy of restoration were fully realized only after mid-1107, when the resolution of his impasse with Anselm over investiture and consecration resulted in a torrent of episcopal and abbatial consecrations—"so many," the Anglo-Saxon chronicler marvels, "that nobody could remember that so many had ever been given together before."[102]

Henry was not a saintly king. He could squeeze the Church, especially at times when he was involved in war on the Continent. In 1105–1106 Anselm accused him of twisting the clerical celibacy rulings of the council of 1102 to his own fiscal advantage by collecting fines from offending clergy to fill the war chest for his campaign to conquer

---

[99] Barlow, *Rufus*, p. 373.
[100] The leasing of churches was evidently no longer a problem at the time of Anselm's primatial council of 1102, but simony and sodomy were both condemned and, as we have seen, several simoniacs were deposed, *Councils and Synods*, 1: part 2, pp. 668–688.
[101] *EHD*, 2:433; Howell, *Regalian Right*, pp. 20–24.
[102] *ASC, s.a.* 1107.

Normandy.[103] A similar accusation was made with respect to Archbishop William's council of 1129 by Henry of Huntingdon, a married, hereditary archdeacon whose comments on canonical censures of married clergy are always testy and not altogether reliable.[104] The Anglo-Saxon chronicler complains of severe taxes in the years when Henry was engaged in warfare on the Continent: 1103–1105, 1116–1119, 1124, and also in 1110, when Henry took an aid of three shillings from every hide for his daughter's marriage to the emperor.[105]

Allegations of simony are rare: Martin Brett was able to find only two concrete instances of it throughout the thirty-five-year reign, and he regards neither reference as entirely credible.[106] There remains the tirade against Henry's ecclesiastical policies attributed by the *Gesta Stephani* to "the chief leaders of the church" at King Stephen's council of spring 1136, including the charge that "he had shut or opened the door of the church more commonly with the key of Simon than with that of Peter."[107] The absence of earlier complaints, as Brett suggests, "may possibly have been dictated by prudence."[108] But the churchmen's accusation, which seems curiously self-incriminating, bears the mark of rhetorical exaggeration intended to elicit from Stephen his charter of liberties for the Church: "The king listened patiently, freely granted them their requests, and gave orders that the freedom of the church should be firm and inviolable . . . and he would have kept his word had it not been that perverse counsellors . . . and actual imperious need . . . urged him to break these promises."[109] Among Stephen's promises was his renunciation of regalian right: the administration and revenues of vacant churches were henceforth to remain with the churches themselves.[110] This concession, as Margaret Howell observes, constituted a significant break from royal practice stretching back to the Norman Conquest and forward through the Middle Ages.[111]

---

[103] *AO*, epp. 391–394; Eadmer, *HN*, pp. 171–177; and above, p. 374. Eadmer alludes to further severe taxation of churches in the interval between the Norman campaigns of 1105 and 1106.

[104] HH, p. 484; cf. Partner, *Serious Entertainments*, pp. 41–47.

[105] *ASC*, in the indicated years, and HH, p. 456. The normal danegeld rate was two shillings on the hide.

[106] Brett, *English Church*, p. 105.

[107] *Gesta Stephani*, pp. 24–26. The probable author, Robert, bishop of Bath, a protégé of Henry, bishop of Winchester, was consecrated at exactly this time.

[108] Brett, *English Church*, p. 105.

[109] *Gesta Stephani*, pp. 26–28.

[110] *RRAN* 3, no. 271.

[111] Howell, *Regalian Right*, pp. 21, 29–30; Stephen did in fact administer vacant churches, at least occasionally, and the practice was fully reinstated by Henry II and his successors.

*shops] were the pillars of the kingdom and the sunbeams
s at this time.*

—Henry of Huntingdon, 7:40

Against these various, scattered charges must be balanced Henry's consistent and beneficent attention to the Church. During his reign two new bishoprics were established,[112] the last to be created before the Reformation, and the Anglo-Norman Church made significant progress toward integrating the Welsh bishops into the English circle. Royal support of the new movement of Augustinian canons and the king's approval of the first Cistercian foundations gave the regular canons and the white monks their entrance into England. In fact, J. C. Dickinson cites the age of Henry I as the golden era of the expansion of the Augustinian order in England.[113] Henry also engaged in considerable patronage of traditional Benedictine foundations in England, Normandy, and even outside the realm. C. N. L. Brooke argues that the differences between the various religious orders were barely apparent to contemporaries,[114] and Henry's I's eclectic patronage shows that he did not distinguish between approaches to spirituality. The sheer number of gifts and confirmations and the breadth of the king's interest argue against a mere cynical attempt—by a supposedly parsimonious king—to buy salvation or to secure royal servants.

The establishment of the see of Ely took place in 1109 and that of Carlisle in 1133.[115] Ely, founded in the first flush of vigor as Henry undertook court and church reform, was carved out of the overlarge diocese of Lincoln. The plan was apparently first proposed early in the reign by the abbot of Ely and then revived in 1108 by the king or possibly by the eventual appointee. The decision to establish the see was made at a royal council attended by barons and bishops.[116] Eadmer makes the initiative come from the king, but he emphasizes the

---

[112] In addition, the see of Whithorn was established in the mid-1120s under the patronage of Henry's son-in-law Fergus of Galloway and assigned to the province of York: see Nicholl, *Thurstan*, pp. 137–139, and Brett, *English Church*, pp. 24–25 with notes.

[113] Dickinson, *Origins of the Austin Canons*, p. 139.

[114] Brooke, "Monk and Canon," pp. 115, 129. See also Franklin, "The Bishops of Winchester and the Monastic Revolution," esp. p. 47.

[115] In addition, in 1101 the various plans for the see of Thetford finally resulted in its placement at Norwich by Herbert Losinga. Henry and Anselm both sanctioned the move as well as the replacement of secular canons by monks; Henry then gave Herbert and the cathedral the manor of Thorpe: see *RRAN* 2, nos 547, 548, 549.

[116] *RRAN* 2, no. 919: the witness list shows this council as a family affair—the king, queen, the eight-year-old Maud *sponsa regis Romanorum*, plus Stephen of Aumale.

cooperation of king and archbishop and includes Anselm's letter to Pope Paschal II to underline the archbishop's consent to the decision.[117] The first bishop appointed to Ely was the royal clerk Hervey, who had been expelled by the Welsh from his first see at Bangor in northern Wales and had subsequently been an unsuccessful candidate for the see of Lisieux.[118] Hervey attended Anselm's council of 1102 at London and was probably also present with the unspecified bishops at the court and council in 1108, so he must have been known to the archbishop. Eadmer noticeably does not mention Hervey as among the bishops who supported Anselm against Thomas of York in 1109 (after Anselm's death); perhaps this is why he rather snidely remarks that Hervey received the see of Ely by "much asking, much promising, and many services" only after the archbishop had died.[119] Certainly Hervey was a faithful curial bishop, attesting many charters and receiving a good number of gifts from the king.[120] The establishment of this diocese and the appointment of the first bishop is an early example of royal involvement in the affairs of the Church, for the pattern of decision making throughout the reign varies little. The king consulted, then decided—he would have argued that this process fulfilled the agreement at Laigle. The king was seldom crossed.

Martin Brett's thorough survey of church councils shows that most discussion of church business took place on the occasion of royal councils. Except for specific reforming councils, many of the "church" councils of the reign can more readily be viewed as "committees" of the royal council held in the presence of the relevant parties.[121] The importance of the royal initiative in matters of ecclesiastical elections and appointments illustrates Henry's "close and continuous" management of the Church.[122] But despite the king's direct involvement in church matters, he was never so rash or tactless as to claim, like William Rufus, that he would do with his churches and abbeys as he pleased.[123] Henry's style was more subtle. He preferred to use his considerable diplomatic skills in careful preparation and in persuasion. We need only recall

---

[117] Eadmer, *HN*, pp. 194 ff. Later in the history Eadmer describes the decision as having been made "by the king and princes" (p. 211).

[118] Barlow, *English Church: 1066–1154*, p. 69.

[119] Eadmer, *HN*, p. 212.

[120] *RRAN* 2, nos (attestations) 1038, 1039, 1301, 1317, 1411, 1428; (gifts) 945, 771, 1029, 1421, 1499, 1501, 1542, 1576, 1620, 1656. The bishop of Ely and the abbot of Thorney contended for jurisdiction on a number of occasions, and despite Hervey's favor, the king issued some rather harsh admonitions against the bishop in favor of the abbot: *RRAN* 2, nos 1168, 1731; see Brett, *English Church*, pp. 85–88, on Ely, its rights, and the abbey of Thorney.

[121] Brett, *English Church*, e.g., pp. 5, 80; see also Knowles, *Monastic Order*, p. 397.

[122] Brett, *English Church*, p. 98.

[123] Eadmer, *HN*, pp. 49–50.

Robert of Meulan's advice to the young king that he should attempt to gain his ends peacefully, through soft words and promises.[124] Occasionally it was the king who was persuaded (recall the 1114 election to the see of Canterbury). But always it was the king who consented.

The creation of the see of Carlisle in 1133, in the later years of the reign, seems also to have been preceded by long discussions. J. C. Dickinson recognized that the establishment of the see resolved a number of vexing problems, including the relationship between the aggrieved archbishop of York and the Scottish bishops, which could have affected the good relations between David king of the Scots and Henry, his kinsman by marriage. Brett suggests that when the two kings met at Christmas 1126 they reached a compromise (probably to avoid an appeal to Rome) that allowed Thurstan to consecrate Scottish bishops but denied him the profession of obedience he so desperately wanted. This settlement, if such it was, resembles those proposed by Henry in the Canterbury–York dispute and follows the pattern of Henry's efforts to resolve crises through compromise. Henry visited Carlisle around this time—he ordered the construction of a castle and walls (and paid for them)—an example of the king's concern for stability in his border regions, in this case Cumbria, which Dickinson calls a sort of no-man's-land without a frontier. The formal establishment of the diocese in 1133, the year that Innocent II granted Archbishop Thurstan the right to divide dioceses and create new bishoprics, partially fulfilled the latter's desire for suffragans and made the political and ecclesiastical boundaries of England coincide.[125]

Although Norman political control over Wales was imperfect in the early twelfth century, the Welsh sees were nonetheless considered subordinate to Canterbury and, when bishops were in place, acted as a link between the independent Welsh and the advancing Anglo-Normans.[126] Early in the reign Archbishop Anselm threatened the two southern Welsh bishops, at Llandaff and St David's, perhaps for contraventions of Anselm's program of reform. Wilfrid of St David's apparently made amends and received the approval of Canterbury; at his death the king then appointed the queen's chancellor, the Norman Bernard, to that see. In 1107 the Welshman Urban received the see of Llandaff. He was said to have been a priest of Worcester as well as archdeacon of Llandaff, but the sources are disputed. In the north, at Bangor, where Rufus' appointee the Breton Hervey had been expelled, the local

---

[124] See OV, 5:316, and Vaughn, *Anselm of Bec and Robert of Meulan*, p. 165.
[125] Brett, *English Church*, p. 26; see the foundation of Nostell priory and the bishopric of Carlisle, below p. 398.
[126] I (ACF) acknowledge a great debt to Martin Brett, *English Church*, on this subject.

prince took the initiative in 1120 by writing (somewhat threateningly) to Ralph at Canterbury to request that a certain Scot named David (possibly a royal clerk) be consecrated to the long-vacant see.[127] This appointment brought the northern Church closer to Canterbury and must have helped to improve relations between the Welsh and the Anglo-Normans. Archbishop Ralph also seems to have taken an interest in Wales, for according to the Book of Llandaff he advised building a new cathedral in that diocese and granted a special indulgence to those who contributed.[128]

Brett notes that as the reign progressed the bishops of Wales began to appear regularly at councils and consecrations "as loyal, and sometimes diligent, suffragans."[129] They also began to appear at court to a greater or lesser degree, depending on their relations with the king. Wilfrid of St David's consented to only one charter, by Roger of Salisbury, in 1114,[130] and Hervey of Bangor attested two, in 1103 and 1107.[131] But Hervey undertook a royal mission to Rome for the king in 1108, and after he received the see of Ely he appeared at court on at least ten occasions. His successor at Bangor, however, David, whose appointment came at the instigation of the Welsh, was only at the royal court twice, just after his appointment.[132] In contrast, the numerous attestations of the Norman Bernard of St David's over his twenty years in office rank him as one of the most faithful members of the king's entourage, in both England and Normandy. In addition to at least forty-five attestations of royal charters, Bernard also acted as the king's emissary to the pope, at Reims in 1119 and 1131 and at Rome in 1120.

Urban of Llandaff witnessed more than five of the king's charters.[133] He was well enough acquainted with the system to challenge the king's son Robert of Gloucester in court in 1126 and to clarify his own court's jurisdictional rights.[134] The following year Urban sought first royal, then papal assistance in a jurisdictional dispute with his episcopal neighbors, Hereford and St David's. Not satisfied with the response from Archbishop William, he appealed to Rome. Ultimately, in 1132, in a con-

---

[127] Barlow, *English Church: 1066–1154*, p. 84.
[128] Brett, *English Church*, p. 85. Ralph of Canterbury was formerly abbot of Saint-Martin of Sées, which sent the first monks to the independent house at Shrewsbury and which had dependent priories at Pembroke (in Wales) and at Lancaster (in England).
[129] Ibid., p. 30.
[130] *RRAN* 2, no. 1042 (21 July 1114).
[131] Ibid., nos 675, 828.
[132] Ibid., nos 1243, 1245.
[133] Ibid., nos 847, 1091, 1202, 1243, 1245, 1485.
[134] Ibid., no. 1466.

cession to the independence of the Anglo-Norman Church, the
pope ordered Urban to appear before the three Anglo-Norman
archbishops—York, Canterbury, and Rouen—for resolution of the
conflict. They ruled against Llandaff, whereupon the resolute Urban
set off for Rome for yet another appeal. In all he visited the pope
four times (without royal complaint), in 1128, 1129, 1131 (in France),
and 1134; he died in Rome on his last trip.

By the end of Rufus' reign, the episcopal sees had all been established in recognized centers. By the end of the reign of Henry I the
number of sees in England and Wales had been increased to twenty.
Martin Brett sums up: "Under Henry it was as easy to speak of his
church as his kingdom," for the kingdom was now coterminous with
the provinces of York and Canterbury.[135]

> *The illustrious king [Henry], whose deeds we are describing,
> was very generous not only to the most powerful of this world, but
> also, a more remarkable and profitable quality, to the religious.
> Bishops, abbots, poor monks and flocks of nuns not only of
> France and Aquitaine but of Burgundy and Italy testify to
> his generosity, for they annually receive much from him in
> benefactions.*
>   —Robert of Torigny (*GND*, 2:252–253)

> *The wise king surpassed almost all other princes of his time in
> both clemency and wealth. By his clemency he endowed churches,
> monasteries and the poor people of his land. By his infinite abun-
> dance of wealth he maintained . . . soldiers in various places near
> his enemies . . . by force of arms prevent[ing] these people from
> robbing churches and the poor.*
>   —Robert of Torigny (*GND*, 2:236–237)

The flood of new religious foundations in Normandy and England after
the Norman Conquest testifies to the wealth and health of the Anglo-
Norman monarchy and aristocracy. The new power of the feudal class
as well as the growing importance of the honorial barons and the
curiales, the heightened interest in new forms of monastic life, the more
traditional search for intercession and confraternity, the opening of

---

[135] Brett, *English Church*, p. 12.

undeveloped, uncolonized land, all contributed to this explosion in religious foundations. Christopher Brooke remarks on the proliferation of patrons lavishing resources on an "unparalleled variety of religious houses."[136] Marjorie Chibnall concludes her brief survey of monastic foundations in England and Normandy 1066–1189 by directing attention to "the interplay of religious and social change" and to the relationship between piety and politics.[137]

Henry clearly recognized the advantages. Dickinson calls the era of Henry I a golden age and describes the "potent bond" between Henry I and the Augustinian canons.[138] Dickinson attributes the success of the regular canons in England in general to the support of the monarchy and to the enthusiasm of clerics for a return to the apostolic communal life. Queen Matilda's foundation of Holy Trinity, Aldgate, in 1107/1108, undertaken with the counsel of Archbishop Anselm and the support of the king, was colonized from the first house of Augustinian canons in England, St Botolph's at Colchester. The first prior, Norman, a former student of Anselm's, became the queen's confessor.[139] The success of Holy Trinity, which subsequently founded a whole series of daughter houses, and its distinguished pedigree established the order in England. By the end of the reign there were at least forty-three houses of regular canons, fully three-quarters of which were founded by individuals close to the king:[140] the royal favorite Gilbert sheriff of Surrey, Cambridge, and Huntingdon; Richard Bassett, at one time sheriff of eleven counties; the royal treasurer and chamberlain Geoffrey de Clinton; the sheriff of Oxford Robert d'Oilli II; William de Pont de l'Arche, sheriff of Wiltshire and Hampshire; Geoffrey fitz Pain; Pain Peverel; and, surprisingly, even the king's former minstrel and "clerk," Rahere. The king's bishops—Archbishop Anselm, William Giffard, William Warelwast, Richard de Beaumais, and the powerful Roger of Salisbury—were equally supportive.

The king himself either founded or aided in the foundation of many of the new houses of Augustinian canons. Henry confirmed and reconfirmed the privileges of Holy Trinity, Aldgate, the only religious foundation within the city walls, and throughout his reign gave the priory numerous additional liberties as well as freedom from subjection to

---

[136] Brooke, "Monk and Canon," p. 110.
[137] Chibnall, "Monastic Foundations," pp. 38, 48. See also Cownie, *Religious Patronage in Anglo-Norman England*, esp. pp. 7, 8, 9, and chap. 11.
[138] Dickinson, *Origins of the Austin Canons*, pp. 139, 129. See also Dickinson, "Saint Anselm and the First Regular Canons in England," pp. 541–546.
[139] Later in the reign, we will see the king's confessor establish an Augustinian priory in the north at Nostell, with Henry's aid.
[140] Dickinson, *Origins of the Austin Canons*, pp. 125, 130.

neighboring jurisdictions.[141] He provided the site for St Bartholomew's hospital for the poor, founded by Rahere just outside the city walls in Smithfield, and he granted the priory the important right of choosing Rahere's successor.[142] Both the queen and Henry seem to have been interested in the monastery founded by the queen's chaplain at Llanthony (Monmouthshire) and then colonized by canons regular.[143] In 1131 Robert de Béthune, the prior of Llanthony, received the bishopric of Hereford (the next canon to receive an episcopal see after William of Corbeil). The priory of St Frideswide in Oxford, colonized from Aldgate, seems to owe its foundation to the early efforts of Roger of Salisbury, but Henry, who endowed the canons substantially in 1122, is claimed as the legal founder.[144] The first prior was said to be a royal chaplain and all the early priors were esteemed as learned men.

At the urging of his Augustinian confessor Adelulf (or Athelulf/ Athelwold), Henry assisted a struggling group of clerks at Nostell in the north to find a new site and to adopt the regular life.[145] Adelulf became the first prior of Nostell around 1122 and a decade later, in 1133, he was appointed the first bishop of Carlisle, where he installed a chapter of Augustinian canons, the only cathedral in England with such a chapter.[146] Southwick priory records also celebrate the king's donation of the church of Portchester, the first site of the priory, and his confirmation of the land in Southwick given by William of Pont de l'Arche, sheriff of Hampshire.[147] The story of Southwick is an interesting one

---

[141] *RRAN* 2, nos 897, 898, 908, 909, 915, 1315, 1316, 1493, 1514, 1529; Christelow, "A Moveable Feast," p. 188, no. 5, citing *Royal Writs*, ed. Van Caenegem, no. 17.

[142] *RRAN* 2, nos 1794, 1795, 1943, 1761. Dickinson, *Origins of the Austin Canons*, p. 140 n. 1, says St Bartholomew's was never well funded, the canons living "on alms, not revenues."

[143] *RRAN* 2, nos 1681, 1738, 1748, all confirmations; apparently the king and queen were discouraged from favoring and enlarging the community: see Brooke, "Monk and Canon," p. 126, citing *Monasticon*, 6:129–131.

[144] *RRAN* 2, nos 1342, 1343, 1957.

[145] Ibid., nos 1207, 1217, 1225, 1287, 1461, 1628, 1775, 1856.

[146] The diocese of Sées received Augustinian canons in 1131 (*GC* 11:160–161, *Instrumenta*, no. 7). Adelulf seems to have continued to attend the king as confessor, for he attested in England: *RRAN* 2, nos 1764 (for a gift at the establishment of a hospital of canons regular [1134/1135] at Falaise) and 1767 (gift to Whitby Abbey); at Rouen: *RRAN* 2, nos 1900, 1902, 1911, 1913 (all 1134–1135); and at Falaise: *RRAN* 2, nos 1915, 1919; Adelulf was also probably at Rouen in 1130 with the pope: *RRAN* 2, no. 1691 n. See also Wightman, "Henry I and the Foundation of Nostell Priory," pp. 57–60.

[147] *RRAN* 2, no. 1787. See Mason, "The King, the Chamberlain, and Southwick Priory," pp. 1–10, and Franklin, "The Bishops of Winchester and the Monastic Revolution," p. 50.

and illustrates the importance of royal participation and confirmation to the health and security of a religious foundation, not to mention the prestige that accrued to founders, noble and royal.[148]

Henry's greatest foundation of Augustinian canons was that at Cirencester in Gloucestershire. First mentioned by John of Worcester when building commenced in 1117, the foundation was an abbey from the very beginning. Established on the considerable lands of secular canons, Cirencester was munificently endowed by the king.[149] The first abbot, the Norman Serlo, was appointed in 1131. For his own salvation and for the souls of his son William and his wife Matilda, Henry also founded a priory at Dunstable in 1131/1132 as a daughter house of Holy Trinity, Aldgate, and he installed as prior Bernard, the brother of Norman, first prior of Aldgate.[150] The king gave the canons his own lands, that is, the manor and borough of Dunstable, only reserving for himself certain houses and gardens, where he often lodged over the years. Henry also established the priories at Bridlington, Wellow-by-Grimsby, and St Denis by Southampton as well as the Augustinian chapters at Carlisle in northern England and at Sées in Normandy.[151] All these benefactions (and the appointment of several canons to episcopal sees and of William of Corbeil, prior of Saint Osyth's, to the archiepiscopal see of Canterbury) validate Robert of Torigny's assertion of Henry's reputation for piety and Dickinson's proposed link between court and convent.[152]

The king of England . . . as is known throughout all the lands of the world, exceeds all Christian princes of his time in prudence, in [good] works, and in generosity.
—Peter the Venerable, *De miraculis* 2:10 (*PL* 189:921)

Traditional Benedictine monasteries prospered in the Anglo-Norman world of the twelfth century. Both Domesday Book and the Pipe Roll of 1130 show the cathedral monasteries and the major Benedictine monasteries as among the greatest landholders in the realm, with

---

[148] See Herbert, "The Transformation of Hermitages," pp. 131–145, esp. p. 144.
[149] Brett, *English Church*, p. 139 n. 1, says that Cirencester was the largest foundation of the reign, with an endowment of sixteen churches once held by Reginbald the chancellor. See *Cartulary of Cirencester Abbey*, esp. pp. xix, xxi.
[150] *RRAN* 2, no. 1827.
[151] Ibid., nos 1334 (Bridlington, under royal protection), 1508 (St Denis, gift of land); *GC* 11, *Instrumenta*, pp. 160–161 (*an.* 1131). Henry was generous to the new canons at Sées: see Haskins, *NI*, pp. 300–303, 307, nos 11, 12, 22.
[152] *GND*, 2:216–217, 2:252–257.

myriad royal privileges and exemptions from financial and service obligations. John Van Engen has argued that Benedictine monasteries held their own in the early twelfth century, despite growing competition from new orders, and that the number of monks recruited reached its peak under Henry I.[153] Van Engen disputes Dom David Knowles' conclusion that this last flowering of Benedictine culture was a kind of time lag resulting from the importation of Norman enthusiasm. In fact, Van Engen deems unjustified the very idea of a crisis in traditional monasticism, first articulated (without the word *crisis*) by contemporaries as criticism of the "soft" Benedictine life and then echoed by many later historians.[154] Contemporary criticism came from *rivals*, he stresses, advocates of a radically different approach to spirituality. In a sense, this shift in mentality represents one of the perennial paradoxes in the monastic movement itself, what Jeffrey Burton Russell called the impetus toward withdrawal versus the impetus toward conversion. The cyclical "reform" of the institution of monasticism involved focus on one or the other pole. What was really at issue in the twelfth century, claims Van Engen, was the *prosperity* of the Benedictine order, not its spiritual decadence. Traditional Benedictine goals, when analyzed, reveal a set of attitudes based on an open relationship with secular society. Monks were "*in* the world but not *of* it";[155] they were intercessors at the Divine Court. Hence, over time, prayer and the liturgy grew more and more elaborate as the sites of celebration grew larger and more opulent, the very signs of spiritual success. Benedictine monks had to be literate and moral, and these two qualities attracted a high class of recruits and students. Success generated more success, including gifts of lands, precious objects, and relics.

The right of the Anglo-Norman kings to appoint their abbots formed part of their Norman inheritance. It had long been understood that royal or ducal investiture conferred only the temporalities of a church, or, as Ivo of Chartres expressed it, the "manors, farms, and rents conferred on the church by the generosity of kings and princes"; spiritual authority was conferred by episcopal consecration alone.[156] While the Norman monasteries were strictly subordinate to the feudal sovereign, the community of abbots in England had a more personal, cooperative relationship with the English king.[157] Between 1066 and 1135 the English kings appointed over sixty new heads of monastic houses,

---

[153] Van Engen, "The 'Crisis of Cenobitism' Reconsidered."
[154] See Leclercq, "The Monastic Crisis of the Eleventh and Twelfth Centuries," pp. 217–237, and Brooke, "Monk and Canon," p. 118.
[155] Van Engen, "The 'Crisis of Cenobitism' Reconsidered," p. 303 (italics added).
[156] See n. 305 below, this chapter, and Hollister, "Saint Anselm on Lay Investiture," pp. 257 and 157 n. 68.
[157] Knowles, *Monastic Order*, pp. 92–93.

founded new monasteries following the Benedictine rule, and favored many of the older, wealthy English houses, which by the time of Henry I were almost completely under Norman leadership. Henry I's benefactions fall into a number of categories: major and minor grants in England; Norman patronage; benefactions to nunneries, to hospitals, and to hermits; and patronage of Cluniac houses.[158]

The Benedictine houses in England that the *Regesta regum anglonormannorum* records as having the greatest number of grants of lands, privileges, and exemptions during the reign of Henry I were, in order, Abingdon (with more than 23 significant grants), Ramsey (21), Battle (14), Gloucester (11), Reading (10), and St Augustine's, Canterbury (9).[159] All but Gloucester ranked among the wealthiest in the land.[160] Faritius, the royal physician and monk of Malmesbury whom Henry appointed abbot of Abingdon, was a favorite, having the ear of the king. In addition to receiving such grants as a wood, a mill, a chapel, and several hides of land as well as freedom from tolls and customs, Faritius (and his successor Vincent) also regularly sought and secured the king's enforcement of rights and freedoms challenged by neighbors and overzealous royal and local officials.[161] In all, Henry appointed three abbots to the Wessex house over his long reign: Faritius, the Italian so favored that the king once tried to make him archbishop of Canterbury; Vincent, a monk of Jumièges; and Ingulf prior of Winchester.

Ramsey, in the fenlands of East Anglia, second in the number of grants from the king, also received three abbots from Henry I: a monk of St Albans, a monk of Caen, and a certain Walter, who was elected in 1133. The abbots of Ramsey in the early twelfth century seem not to have been intimates of the royal court but nonetheless merited the notice and assistance of the king, who ordered on a number of occasions that the monks receive their rights and dues.[162] The Conqueror's foundation at Battle continued to be distinguished by his son. The Battle chronicle, lauding itself as well as Henry I,

---

[158] Most of the benefactions cited here come from *RRAN* 2, Farrer (*Itin.*). and *CDF*. Christelow, "A Moveable Feast," p. 188–189 n. 5, provides a list of royal grants and notices *not* in these sources.

[159] These figures are approximate and for comparative purposes; they emphasize substantive royal grants and exclude most general confirmations.

[160] Frank Barlow says that Henry I "hankered after aristocratic monasticism": *English Church: 1066–1154*, p. 90.

[161] *RRAN* 2, nos 521, 815, 856, 974, 1133; Fulk, an illegitimate son of Henry I, seems to have been a monk at Abingdon: *EHD*, vol. 2, table 4. Cownie, *Religious Patronage in Anglo-Norman England*, p. 47, counts 81 writs and charters in *Chron. Ab.* illustrating royal favor for Faritius.

[162] *RRAN* 2, nos 1262, 1632.

says that Henry defended the church "as the ensign of the Crown . . . fortified it with the powers of his charters, [and] with care exalted its position," especially noting Henry's compensatory gifts to the abbey of Marmoutier (which had sent the initial contingent of monks to Battle) in return for recognition of the English abbey's independence. Henry's gifts were mostly of the monetary kind (he freed the well-endowed Battle monks and the abbey's men from all customs, tolls, gelds, scots, and services), but the chronicle also records the gift of two churches and some land in Carmarthen. The king ordered that no one molest the monks, including any sheriff or minister, "on pain of the King's forfeiture." In addition, Henry assured the abbot's court of "royal privilege": all pleas were to come to the abbot's court; should resolution fail there, the suit would be held in the king's court in the presence of the abbot and the justiciar.[163] During Henry's reign two abbots of Battle were elected, one a monk of Bec, Caen, and Rochester, verifying the continuance of Norman influence, particularly that of Bec. The second, appointed by the king and subsequently elected by the Battle monks, was from Canterbury.

Gloucester, with its one hundred monks, participated in the royal largesse, perhaps because of its location near the Welsh frontier and because of the occasional presence of the royal court (the hunting in the nearby Forest of Dean was excellent). Henry's brother Robert Curthose was buried here and Henry made a special gift of land to pay for the candles to burn for the soul of the former duke. Henry approved three abbots for Gloucester during his long reign, all from within the monastery. Peter, the prior, was elected abbot in 1107; William Godeman was appointed in 1113; and a member of the de Lacy family became abbot in 1130. The latter two bishops attracted more royal attention than their predecessor.[164]

Henry's generosity to St Augustine's, Canterbury, is typical of his religious grants elsewhere: here a fair or market, there a church, a manor, or hunting rights. These documents reveal the king's appellate role. Quite a few charters rectify damages done to St Augustine's by local landholders, burgesses, or even other religious houses.[165] The injunction "to do right" is often invoked.

---

[163] *Chron. Battle,* pp. 108 ("the ensign . . ."), 114–116 (gifts to Marmoutier), 124 (gifts in Carmarthen); *RRAN* 2, no. 1806 (exemption from tolls and admonition against molesters).

[164] *ASC, s.a.* 1113 (William Godeman). Christelow, "A Moveable Feast," table B, p. 199, and p. 188, n. 5, for a grant of a royal manor (citing *Historia et cartularium monasterii Sancti Petri Gloucestriae,* 1:110–111). See also Cownie, *Religious Patronage in Anglo-Norman England,* chap. 3, "St Peter's, Gloucester" (p. 61 for the grant mentioned here), and "Gloucester Abbey, 1066–1135: An Illustration of Religious Patronage in Anglo-Norman England," pp. 143–157.

[165] *RRAN* 2, nos 678–679, 944, 1078, 1141–1142, 1189–1192, 1283, 1314. These

It is tempting here to draw some conclusions about Henry's appointments to these and other Benedictine monasteries.[166] In the first two decades of Henry's reign 37 abbots took office. Of those, the sources specify that 6 were elected (at Battle, Chertsey, Gloucester, Peterborough, Winchester, and Hyde); only 6 abbots came from across the Channel or beyond. Mid-reign, Henry filled 47 abbacies, of which 5 abbots were elected (Battle, Bury, St Albans, Tewkesbury, Westminister); 11 came from beyond the Channel. Late in Henry's reign 17 abbacies fell vacant and were filled; only 2 abbots (Chertsey and Ramsey) are reported to have been elected and none of the new abbots was a foreigner.[167] Such sketchy evidence may suggest that Henry did not insist on appointing all his abbots and that some of the major monasteries played a role in the selection of their abbots. The "elected" candidate may have been presented to the monastery (as happened at Battle at least once), but since 6 of the 13 elected came from within their own houses (Battle, Gloucester, Hyde) at least half the selections do not appear to be appointments in disguise. A number of the documents in the *Regesta* 2 permit institutions to elect a head, suggesting that in Henry's realm this was a privilege, not a right.[168]

Royal benefactions in Normandy do not equal those to the prominent English houses, but they reveal the king's same broad interests. The abbey of Bec, the first monastic home of Robert of Torigny, the primary contemporary source for Henry's piety, received the king's greatest notice in Normandy. Henry visited Bec at least four times during his reign (in 1106, 1113, 1124, and 1130)[169] and showed real affection for Abbot Boso (1124–1136),[170] refusing to order the abbot to make a written profession to the archbishop of Rouen. In a rare glimpse of the king's insight into character and even perhaps of his

examples plus those mentioned above for Abingdon and Ramsey amplify the picture of the administrative and legal activity of the royal court sketched above in chapter 9.

[166] I (ACF) have used Knowles et al., *Heads of Religious Houses*, as my principal source here. I have excluded abbots of dependent monasteries who recruited from the mother house in Normandy: e.g., Sées monks to Arundel.

[167] The Cistercian abbey of Fountains elected its first abbot in 1132.

[168] See St Bartholomew's, *RRAN* 2, nos 1794–1795; Bury, no. 1079; Tynemouth, no. 1331; St Mary's York, no. 1276; Montébourg, no. 825; Conches (*GC* 11, *Instrumenta*, no. 5; *RRAN* 2, no. 1701, on right to elect abbot freely); Saint-Pierre sur Dives (see n. 191 below, this chapter); Glastonbury, no. 1226; at Sherborne the king stipulated that the *confirmation* of election by the monks remained with the crown: no. 1325.

[169] Christelow, "A Moveable Feast," table B.

[170] *GND*, 2:254–255; RT, *Chron.*, s.a. 1124. Boso was well known to Anselm, and thus no doubt well acquainted with Henry I; Boso was with Anselm almost constantly from 1093 until 1109 (Vaughn, *Abbey of Bec*, pp. 56, 127 ["Life of Boso"]).

sense of humor, Henry told the archbishop he might *try* to force Boso to profess but Henry doubted the outcome would please him.[171] In addition to the usual exemptions from tolls and grants of liberties and customs, Henry gave the abbot of Bec the right to plead exclusively in the royal court.[172] He also took firm action against the abbot's townsmen, who had taken advantage of the abbot's gentle rule to menace the monks—thereafter the townsmen were forbidden to bear arms in town under pain of a serious penalty.[173] Henry dutifully confirmed a wealth of private donations to the famous abbey and also showed interest in the abbey's daughter houses, at Envermeu and especially at St Neot's in Huntingdonshire.[174] The king was often at Rouen when in Normandy, and he indulged his love of building by completing his mother's plans for a daughter house of Bec just outside the city. Robert of Torigny, albeit prejudiced, celebrates all the work undertaken by the king at Notre-Dame du Pré (La Bonne-Nouvelle) and hails the promises made for future benevolences.[175] (In 1130 the king did give the Bec monks at Rouen four houses in the city.[176]) Henry also built himself a residence adjoining the monastery, which suggests that he frequented the Bec monks there.[177] When the king died, although his body was transferred for burial at Reading, some of his internal organs were interred at Le Pré as the obvious site of preference. Henry's daughter Maud also favored the monks at Bec, and she even demanded that her father grant her the right to be buried there.

The king's role in the foundation of the abbey of Mortemer (diocese of Rouen) provides an especially good example of Henry's eclectic patronage.[178] In the early 1130s a group of monks who had lost the support of their patrons began to seek a new site—and presumably a new patron—and were even considering a move outside the realm, to Limoges. In a strong statement Henry prohibited the monks from leaving the region—the sensitive Norman Vexin—and urged them to

---

[171] "On the Liberties of the Abbey of Bec," in Vaughn, *Abbey of Bec*, p. 141. Orderic reports that Henry argued the abbots' case against the bishops at the synod of Rouen in 1128 (6:390–391).

[172] *RRAN* 2, no. 1213.

[173] The fine was 18s. or 60s., depending on intent: *RRAN* 2, nos 1434, 1900, 1901.

[174] Envermeu: *RRAN* 2, nos 794, 1086, 1577; St Neot's: 1766, 1969, 1970.

[175] The promises were unfulfilled because of the king's death. *GND*, 2:252–253; see *RRAN* 2, nos 792 (royal assent to gift of Notre-Dame du Pré to Bec), 1290 (royal gifts).

[176] *CDF*, no. 262; WM, *HN*, chap. 457: "distinguished by no small endowments."

[177] See Chibnall, "The Empress Matilda and Bec-Hellouin," esp. pp. 37–38.

[178] On Mortemer, see *GC* 11:307–309; Bouvet, "Le Récit de la fondation de Mortemer"; "Chronicon monasterii Mortui-maris," p. 1438; Chibnall, "Monastic Foundations," p. 44. Charters by Stephen and Henry II confirm earlier grants and mention Henry I as founder: *CDF*, nos 1404, 1408.

seek a new site that he could give them and thus act as their founder. The monks were attracted to a *secretissima vallis* in the forest of Lyons, where three hermits were already living. When Henry heard that the hermits, "whom he loved very much," were willing to receive the homeless monks, he readily agreed to sponsor the new foundation and promised *multa bona*. Indeed, he handed over the place to the abbot and pledged himself solemnly as founder. Henry visited the monks and gave them land in the forest for a grange, granting them liberties and immunities throughout his realm and the right to use the whole forest freely. In the two years before the king died, he financed the construction of the abbey buildings, later described as impressive. In this one instance Henry first patronized hermits, then supported a more permanent regular foundation;[179] the king did not live to see the abbot offer himself and his monastery to the new Cistercian order, which had just begun to establish itself in England with royal approval. Mortemer thus became the first of the new order in Normandy, to be joined by Savigny, another of Henry's interests, a decade later.

The young abbey of Saint-Georges de Boscherville (founded in 1112/1113), on the Seine downstream from Rouen, attracted a surprising number of grants for a new foundation, perhaps because of the sponsorship of Henry's chamberlain William de Tancarville.[180] Henry himself gave the new abbey his port of Bénouville near Fécamp.[181] The abbey seems to have rapidly acquired cross-Channel possessions that the king confirmed along with liberties, customs, and exemptions.[182] Not far away the monastery of Beaubec, at the head of the Andelle, received the right not to be impleaded except before the king or the chief justiciar; in return the king asked for nothing "but the prayers of the monks."[183]

Other grants and confirmations in Normandy are spread rather evenly over the better-known Benedictine monasteries, many of them ducal foundations (identified by an asterisk). At *Fécamp the king made three settlements to restore jurisdiction to the abbot: once against the Braose family, once over the port of Winchelsea against the count of Eu, and once over the incursion of royal huntsmen,[184] demonstrating the constant attention required to rein in landholders and

---

[179] Recall similar scenarios at Llanthony and Nostell, among others, in England.
[180] *RRAN* 2, no. 1012. Grant, "Architectural Relations between England and Normandy," p. 129, notes that the architectural style of Boscherville in the 1120s reflects the influence of Reading and Caen.
[181] *RRAN* 2, no. 1596.
[182] Ibid., nos 1099–1100.
[183] Ibid., no. 1270.
[184] Ibid., nos 626, 1690, 1689.

royal officials. Henry carefully explained that his persistence in the case of Fécamp was what was required for a "royal foundation" whose property was to be held "as freely as if in the royal demesne," a frequent phrase in the king's charters.[185]

While Fécamp was one of the largest holders of land in England (£200 in Domesday Book), Henry also paid attention to the less well known houses. In a precept from the latter half of his reign Henry announces that the abbot and church of Notre-Dame de *Montébourg (diocese of Coutances) in Henry's first Norman possession, the Cotentin, hold their lands as peacefully as the abbey of Fécamp, for the king has released to them in free alms all his rights. A particularly stern admonition warns against doing any wrong to the abbey that the king considers "his own chapel."[186]

Saint-Martin of Troarn, on the Dives river not far from the Channel, received grants in England (at Horsley in 1129) and in Normandy (at Notre-Dame du Désert in Vassy, Calvados) for the creation of daughter houses.[187] The king also settled a lawsuit in the abbot's favor between Saint-Martin and Roger de Gratapancia and ordered the monks of La Couture not to implead Saint-Martin regarding the church Henry had given them at Vire.[188] The distinguished abbey of *Jumièges received two important grants in Henry's early years. The monks also success-fully brought a suit before the royal court at Rouen to recover an alien-ated possession there; at another point the king promised to restore to the abbey what royal officials had apparently extracted after a great fish was caught at Quilleboeuf.[189]

The monastery that the Conqueror had founded at Caen, Saint-Etienne, sought assistance from the royal court many times and bene-fited from a number of royal confirmations as well as grants made in the presence of the king. Henry himself gave the monastery the manor of Burton Bradstock in Dorset as part of an exchange for the coveted crown and royal regalia that his father had left to the abbey.[190]

Elsewhere in Normandy, evidence survives for the king's notice of the monasteries of *Saint-Wandrille, *Saint-Ouen (Rouen), Saint-

[185] Ibid., no. 1689.

[186] Ibid., nos 1953 (free alms), 825, 826, 1018, 1155, 1708, 1682–1684, 1950 (admonition); Christelow, "A Moveable Feast," pp. 188–189 n. 5, citing BN MS lat. 10087.

[187] RRAN 2, nos 719 (Horsley), 1023 (Vassy).

[188] Ibid., no. 1570 (an. 1129; William Talvas, count of Ponthieu, witnesses); ibid., no. 1088a (Vire).

[189] Ibid., nos 638, 912, 1002 (Rouen suit), and CDF, no. 154; RRAN 2, no. 842 and CDF, no. 155 (Quilleboeuf).

[190] RRAN 2, nos 1184, 1188, 1215, 1341, 1352, 1593, 1672; (Burton Bradstock) 601; (regalia) 1575.

Pierre sur Dives,[191] Notre-Dame of Bayeux, Préaux, Saint-Valéry, Saint-Evroul, Beaumont-le-Roger, Holy Trinity at Aunay, and Saint-Pierre de Châtillon at Conches (Evreux).[192] Even outside the boundaries of the duchy, in the sphere of Norman influence, Henry was generous. He contributed to the abbey church of Saints Sergius and Bacchus[193] and to the abbey of Saint-Nicholas[194] at Angers as well as to the cathedral of Saint-Maurice there.[195] Both Henry and Matilda were on excellent terms with Hildebert of Lavardin, bishop of Le Mans and later archbishop of Tours, who wrote many letters to members of the English royal family. In particular, he thanked Queen Matilda for the gift of two candelabra. In later years Henry himself made a gift of an annual rent to the bishop and canons of Le Mans Cathedral, at the baptism of Maud's son Henry (1133).[196] The celebrated canonist-bishop of Chartres, Ivo, also corresponded with Henry I and Matilda; he thanked Matilda for a chasuble she had sent, plus a gift of bells (apparently an Anglo-Norman specialty),[197] and he successfully beseeched the royal family to contribute to the repair of the cathedral roof, which required re-leading.[198] The monks of Saint-Père at Chartres received royal protection, a clarification of their rights in an inquiry, plus a gift of tithes from the king.[199]

---

[191] The abbey of Saint-Pierre sur Dives received an especially long confirmation charter in 1108 (and again in 1124) in which the king took the abbey "in manu mea et protectione mea est liberrima ab omnium subjectione sicut proprium dominium meum," apparently out of guilt for the burning of the abbey and its *villae* (in the struggles against Curthose), which the king admits was his fault. The monks were also given the right to free election. *GC* 11:156–160, *Instrumenta*, nos 4, 5, and 6.

[192] See note 168 above, this chapter, for the right to free election at Conches as part of a long confirmation of 1130.

[193] *RRAN* 2, no. 735a.

[194] Ibid., no. 1602.

[195] Ibid., nos 1204a, 1920a. Henry also settled a dispute between the bishop of Angers and the count of Anjou, ibid., no. 1920a; see below, this chapter, p. 451.

[196] Hildebert of Lavardin, Letters, *PL* 171: book 1: epp. 12, 7, 9, 13, 14, 18; book 3: epp. 11, 12, 13, 14; these letters show the relationship to have been a family affair. See also Dieudonné, *Hildebert de Lavardin*, esp. discussion of Hildebert's English letters. Henry himself was in Le Mans for Maud's wedding in June 1128: see Christelow, "A Moveable Feast." On Henry's gift to the cathedral, see Chibnall, *Empress Matilda*, p. 61, citing *Actus pontificum cenomannis*, p. 432.

[197] See below, this chapter, p. 428.

[198] *Lettres de Saint Ives*, nos 108, 109, 121, 145, 176 (a letter of sympathy on the death of Matilda's brother, king of Scotland), 263. Lead was one of the products mined in England. See also Musset, "Le Mécenat des princes normands au XIe siècle," p. 130 (citing "Nécrologe de Notre-Dame de Chartres," in *Cartulaire de Notre-Dame de Chartres*, 3:204).

[199] *RRAN* 2, nos 1229, 1931–1932; *CDF*, no. 1258; Haskins, *NI*, pp. 304–305 (app. F, no. 16), 223, both citing BN MS lat. 9221, nos 6 and 7; *Cartulaire de l'abbaye de Saint-Père de Chartres*, 2:640 (no. 25, Bon Molino tithes), 659 (no. 55, confirmation

Henry also supported the English possessions of a number of foreign
monasteries, for example, Saint-Pierre de la Couture at Le Mans,[200] the
pre-Conquest abbey of St Peter's of Ghent,[201] Saint-Rémi of Reims in
Shropshire,[202] and Notre-Dame, La Sauve Majeure (Gironde) near
Bordeaux.[203] The monks of the Loire abbey of Marmoutier, a favorite
of the Norman dukes and kings, received the church of Corsham in
Wiltshire, a confirmation of their Norman and English lands, rights in
the Cotentin at Héauville, and rights for their colony at Holy Trinity,
York, founded by Ralph Paynel early in the reign.[204] In 1126 Henry
settled a suit between Marmoutier and the bishop of Sées in favor of
the abbey.[205] And finally, sometime between 1126 and 1129, the
Cluniac nunnery of Marcigny (Saône-et-Loire), where Henry's sister
Adela of Blois had retired around 1122, received a grant of liberties
and freedom from customs as well as the stipulation that the nuns could
not be impleaded except in the presence of the king.[206]

*He cultivated religious reverently and supported the poor and
helpless with sumptuous alms.*
                        —Richard of Hexham, "The Acts of King Stephen,"
                              in *The Priory of Hexham*, p. 67.

On and across the southern frontier Henry paid considerable attention
to two hermits who eventually founded small reform congregations,
Vital of Savigny and Bernard of Tiron. Vital, a complex individual of
many talents, seems to have begun his religious career as a canon at
the court of Robert of Mortain.[207] He spent considerable time thereafter on the road as an itinerant preacher condemning vice and disorder. His renown was such that he was invited to Anselm's primatial
council of London in 1102, where Vital preached in French and was
said to have been understood by English listeners. The hermit was
asked to mediate between Henry I and Robert Curthose, perhaps

by Henry II of another gift by Henry I). Louis VI was also a great benefactor of
Saint-Père: ibid., 2:270, 445–446, 455, 456, 460, 638.
[200] *RRAN* 2, no. 960.
[201] Ibid., nos 730, 934, 1148.
[202] Ibid., no. 618 (1102).
[203] Ibid., no. 1652.
[204] Ibid., nos 593, 679, 1948, 1638; *CDF*, no. 1180. See n. 163 above, this chapter,
for royal grants to Marmoutier which confirm the independence of Battle Abbey.
[205] *RRAN* 2, nos 1439, 1548.
[206] Ibid., no. 1599a.
[207] Dom Claude Auvrey, *Histoire de la congrégation de Savigny.*

because of Vital's former connection with Robert of Mortain, who was supporting Curthose at that point. Not until 1112, after much wandering, did Vital settle down with his followers in the forest of Savigny, not far from Mortain, on the southern frontier, where he received lands from Raoul I seigneur of Forgères, a supporter of Henry I in 1106. The king immediately exempted the monks from all transportation dues in Normandy and England.[208] Henry I then confirmed all the donations to the small community, under a reformed Benedictine rule, and added customs, liberties, and exemptions for the Savigny monks and the daughter houses that sprouted rapidly in England.[209] Henry also granted the monks a number of churches (for example, Dompierre [or Dampierre] in Normandy) as well as vineyards from his own and the queen's demesne.[210]

Bernard of Tiron followed a similarly circuitous road to the reformed communal life, having shown some difficulty fitting into the traditional monastic establishment of the late eleventh century. When he finally founded Tiron, just south of the Norman frontier in the diocese of Chartres, his house was quick to attract gifts in Normandy and elsewhere in the northwest. Henry I confirmed gifts in his regions, exempted the monks from tolls, and took the personal step of granting the monks fifteen silver marks annually for proper shoes.[211] Robert of Torigny also says that the king, who contributed to abbey and cathedral construction in many regions, made great contributions toward the construction of the abbey's domestic buildings and was solely responsible for the dormitory, which he ordered to be built from scratch at his expense and in his memory.[212] In 1120 the king and his son William also granted the Tironian abbey of St Mary's, Cameis, in Wales complete independence of all secular power and the right of free election of the abbot.[213]

Other isolated individuals with even less political or economic importance merited the king's attention from time to time. Perhaps their names were presented as worthy causes by individuals close to the king. In 1103, for instance, "for the soul of Queen Matilda," Henry granted

---

[208] Poulle, "Savigny and England," p. 162, citing the cartulary of Savigny, no. 4.

[209] *CDF*, nos 792, 793, 795; Poulle speaks of "constant royal protection": "Savigny and England," pp. 166, 162, noting at least forty-one twelfth-century royal charters; see *RRAN* 2, nos 1003, 1015, 1183, 1433, 1588a, 1573, 1909, 1941. By 1132 there were twelve Savignac daughter houses; in 1147 the Savignac houses merged with the Cistercians.

[210] *CDF*, no. 793 (Dompierre); *RRAN* 2, nos 1016, 1212.

[211] *RRAN* 2, nos 1074, 1169, 1187, 1223, 1236, 1294, 1874–1875; *CDF*, nos 994–998, 1004, 1005.

[212] *GND*, 2:254–255.

[213] *CDF*, no. 997.

Osmund the priest and his brethren at Goathland (diocese of York) "that place [Goathland]" in order to support the poor. Later Henry added ploughland and pasturage.[214] The mention of Matilda, already known for her religious benefactions and her close relationship with Archbishop Anselm, suggests that it was the queen who prompted this particular royal notice.[215] Ultimately, the Goathland brethren gave up the eremitic life (perhaps their numbers had increased or the poor had become too numerous) and they joined the monks at the monastery of Whitby, an action for which Henry I's approval was sought.[216] In the king's second decade of rule, Matilda overtly intervened on behalf of a hermit and persuaded the king to allow the monk Malger "and his servants" to be conveyed to the forest at Luffield, where Henry ordered that he was to be protected.[217] On another occasion, from Rouen, Henry granted to Peter, a clerk of St Martin, the site of *Mara* in Wilton near the church of Holy Trinity "for the making of houses or cells."[218]

If Henry's notice could fall on isolated individuals, it could also extend to the weak, the poor, and the outcasts of society. A sizable number of hospitals benefited from the royal purse.[219] Early in the reign Queen Matilda established the hospital of St Giles in Holborn in London for forty lepers.[220] About mid-reign Henry granted ten perches of land to the hospital of Harbledown in Kent "to assart and cultivate."[221] The king also granted and confirmed lands given to the hospital of St Peter's, York, threatening any who made wrongful claims against the brethren with a ten-pound fine.[222] By mid-century this hospital, renamed St Leonard's, had become one of the greatest in England.

---

[214] *RRAN* 2, nos 891, 926.
[215] Brooke, "Monk and Canon," p. 122, and Brooke, "Princes and Kings," pp. 125–152, p. 147, emphasizes the role of the queen.
[216] *RRAN* 2, no. 927 (ca. 1109?).
[217] *RRAN* 2, no. 1198; this individual is evidently Mauger, the first prior of the Benedictine house of St Mary's, Luffield, founded by the earl of Leicester 1116 × 1118 or 1124; see Knowles et al., *Heads of Religious Houses*, p. 53, and *Monasticon*, 4:345 and nos 1–3.
[218] *RRAN* 2, no. 1709.
[219] Nicholas Orme and Margaret Webster (*The English Hospital*) note the proliferation of hospitals in the twelfth century: 68 new hospitals appeared between 1080 and 1150, roughly half for lepers and 25 linked to monasteries (pp. 11, 23, 35). Edward Kealey ("Anglo-Norman Policy," p. 350) cited the foundation of 43 hospitals in Henry's time and praised the king and his administrators for their "authentic interest" in public health (p. 351)
[220] Knowles and Hadcock, *Medieval Religious Houses*, "Hospitals."
[221] *RRAN* 2, no. 1260.
[222] Ibid., no. 1327.

St Bartholomew's, the London priory of canons established in 1123 by Henry's former clerk Rahere at Smithfield for the sick, the poor, and wayfarers, received protection from the king as well as gifts of a number of churches and chapels. The king also specified that the canons were to have the right to elect Rahere's successor when the time came.[223] Henry gave St Paul's hospital of the poor at Norwich his "firm peace" and granted it churches, sheep, and tithes in Norfolk.[224]

Henry himself founded the leper hospital of St Bartholomew's at Oxford sometime before 1129.[225] He is also credited with founding the leper hospital of St Giles in Shrewsbury and possibly the Lincoln leper hospital of Holy Innocents.[226] After the foundation of the abbey of Cirencester for Augustinian canons, Henry also established there the hospital of St John the Evangelist for the poor, stipulating that the hospital was to be provisioned by the abbey.[227] In the years 1130–1135, at the royal abbey at Reading, the second abbot, Ansger, built the leper hospital of St Mary Magdalen, an undertaking that certainly had the moral and probably the financial support of the king. Also late in the reign the king made a per diem grant to the Norwich hospital of St Paul for the poor.[228] About 1135 Queen Adeliza, in one of the few surviving notices of her actions, followed the royal lead and founded the hospital of St Giles at Wilton for lepers and the poor.[229]

Across the Channel, the king founded the leprosary-chapel of St James at Rauville-la-Place (Manche). He supported the canons at the hospital at Falaise as well as the hospital of St Giles at Pont-Audemer, the lepers of Rouen, and the infirm at St Mary Magdalen's at Boulogne.[230] In 1135 he provided for an annual gift of ten pounds

---

[223] Ibid., nos 1761, 1794–1795, 1943.

[224] Ibid., no. 1954.

[225] Knowles and Hadcock, *Medieval Religious Houses*, p. 383.

[226] Ibid., p. 391 (Shrewsbury: probably founded late in the reign); ibid., p. 371 (Lincoln).

[227] Ibid., p. 352.

[228] Farrer, *Itin.*, no. 673.

[229] Ibid., p. 403.

[230] Christelow, "A Moveable Feast," p. 188–189 n. 5, citing Renault, "Nouvelles recherches sur les léprosaries et maladeries en Normandie," p. 142 (Rauville-la-Place); *RRAN* 2, nos 1742, 1764 (Falaise); *CDF*, no. 238 (Pont-Audemer); Christelow, "A Moveable Feast," p. 188–189, no. 5, citing Archives nationales (Paris), MS K. 23B, no. 15, item 22 (a monthly stipend to the lepers of Rouen); *RRAN* 2, no. 1924 (confirmation to Boulogne hospital). A charter of Henry II says that Henry I "caused to be founded and built" the leper hospital at Pont-Audemer in 1135: *Recueil des actes de Henri II*, 1: no. 250; see also for Pont-Audemer White, "Career of Waleran" (see p. 26); *RRAN* 2, no. 1918; *CDF*, no. 240.

rouennais to the leper hospital of Le Grand Beaulieu at Chartres.[231] The *Anglo-Saxon Chronicle* and Henry of Huntingdon both report that in 1128 Hugh of the Knights Templar visited Rouen and England and took away much wealth, in gold and silver. The London Temple seems to have been founded at this time, but there is no record of Henry's involvement. In Normandy, however, Robert of Torigny mentions that Henry made annual contributions in arms and "necessaries" and that he also gave land near Avranches so that the knights could build the Hospital of Jerusalem at Villedieu.[232] Taken together, these benefactions document a broad sense of social responsibility in the royal family and a concern for the poor and the sick.

Although nuns and anchoresses did not hold high status in the twelfth century, especially in England, neither the king nor his wealthy clerics and nobles ignored female religious. Archbishop Ralph and Thurstan of York acted to help the anchorite Christina of Markyate find a suitable place of retirement. During Henry's reign at least twenty-five new nunneries were founded, almost tripling the number of houses for women religious.[233] The king himself patronized the few important foundations for women in England: Shaftesbury;[234] Romsey, where Edith-Matilda spent part of her youth;[235] Malling, where the monastery was taken under the king's protection;[236] and St Mary's, Elstow.[237] By confirming possessions in England, Henry also lent his support to Marcigny (Saône-et-Loire), the foundation of St Hugh of Cluny where the king's sister Adela had taken the veil around 1122.[238] In 1129 Henry favored the house of Fontevrault, near Saumur in Anjou, where his widowed daughter-in-law Matilda had retired some years after the wreck of the White Ship (Matilda eventually became abbess).[239] In that

---

[231] *GND*, 2:254–255; *RRAN* 2, no. 1917. Henry also exempted the hospital from customs (Christelow, "A Moveable Feast," p. 188–189, n. 5, citing BN MS nouv. acq. lat. 1408, fol. 351v). The hospital was founded by Theobald II of Chartres around 1054, and around 1115 Ivo of Chartres is believed to have given the rule of St Augustine to the priests and brothers there: *Cartulaire de Notre-Dame de Chartres*, 1:17 n. 3.

[232] *GND*, 2:256–257.

[233] Knowles, *Monastic Order*, p. 711.

[234] *RRAN* 2, nos 1165, 1347.

[235] Ibid., nos 802, 883, 957, 1160. Eadmer, *HN*, p. 123, says Wilton rather than Romsey; William of Malmesbury mentions both Romsey and Wilton (WM, *GR*, 5:418).

[236] *RRAN* 2, nos 634, 943, 1398 (royal protection).

[237] Ibid., nos 1828–1829.

[238] Ibid., no. 1599a.

[239] Henry I's natural daughter Juliana, wife of Eustace of Breteuil, also retired to Fontevrault (OV, 6:278). The future Henry II patronized Fontevrault substantially; as duke of Normandy and count of Anjou he twice mentioned his aunt Matilda as abbess of Fontevrault in the early 1150s: *CDF*, nos 1059, 1060.

year the nuns received an extraordinarily generous sum as an annual gift: one hundred pounds in money of Rouen and fifty marks of silver from England.[240] The empress Maud also attested this charter, whose date suggests that the gift followed her marriage to Geoffrey of Anjou.[241] Shortly thereafter, in 1131, in Chartres, Henry seems to have doubled the English grant, specifying one hundred pounds from the farms of London and Winchester in England. The king also stipulated that the grant was "inviolable for ever" and that it had been confirmed at his entreaty by Pope Innocent II as well as by the bishops, barons, and people of his kingdom and of Normandy.[242]

The king made grants to his mother's foundation of *La Trinité at Caen, where a sister was abbess until 1127, giving the nuns a number of valuable manors in England.[243] Smaller communities also benefited from royal attention, including the house of Sainte-Marie Villers-Canivet (Calvados),[244] the nuns at Saint-Amand,[245] and those at Saint-Paul in Rouen, where the king's precept threatened violators of the Saint-Paul nuns' peace with a startling hundred-ounce fine in gold.[246]

Among all the kings of the Latin West, who for the last three hundred years have testified their affection for the church of Cluny . . . Henry, king of the English and duke of Normandy, has surpassed all others in his gifts and has shown more than an ordinary share of love and attachment to [Cluny]. It was he who perfected that grand basilica, commenced under the auspices and donations of Alfonso, king of Spain, exceeding all other known churches in the Christian world in its construction and beauty.

—Peter the Venerable, Mandatory epistle, 1155–1156
(*Recueil des chartes de l'abbaye de Cluny*, vol. 5, no. 4183)

---

[240] *RRAN* 2, nos 1580–1581.
[241] In 1141 Maud as "Lady of the English" gave the nuns fifty silver marks annually (downsizing?) "for the safety of my realm": *CDF*, no. 1056.
[242] *RRAN* 2, no. 1687.
[243] Ibid., nos 1692, 1928. Southern, "The Place of Henry I," p. 163 n. 3, notes the great value of the gift to Holy Trinity. Molinier, *Les Obituaires français au moyen âge*, p. 77, says another daughter of the Conqueror, Matilda, was abbess of Caen until 1113; see also Douglas, *William the Conqueror*, app. C. A granddaughter of Henry I's, Maud, by an illegitimate daughter, Elizabeth, seems to have become abbess of the ducal foundation of Montivilliers (Seine-Maritime), but we find no mention of the abbey among Henry's benefactions: see *EHD*, table 4, and *GC*, 11:282D.
[244] *RRAN* 2, no. 1919.
[245] Ibid., nos 829, 1271, 1962; *CDF*, no. 96.
[246] *RRAN* 2, no. 1965.

Of all Henry's religious interests, his attentions to the distant abbey of Cluny in Burgundy are among the most provocative and the most elusive. Robert of Torigny, writing in the 1140s at Bec specifically about Henry's reign, praised the king for his important foundations and his many pious works, adding an impressive catalog of gifts that highlights benefactions to the celebrated Burgundian abbey and to the Cluniac monks in England. Robert is the first to specify that Henry was responsible for "the major part" of the building of the new basilica at Cluny (called Cluny III), a declaration that piques the imagination and immediately raises a host of questions.[247] Later in the century Walter Map, whose interest in "trifles" before his time might otherwise warrant suspicion, appears to echo (but exaggerate) Robert of Torigny.[248] Map claims that Henry "completed from the foundations the monastery [sic] of Cluny." He then explains that the church financed by Alfonso VI of Spain had fallen to the ground, with the result that Henry had to rebuild the basilica completely, a provocative statement that at least accords with the documented 1125 collapse of the vaulting of the cathedral nave. Between these two reports we are fortunate to have the highly reliable "mandatory letter" of Peter the Venerable, probably dated 1156, in which the abbot of Cluny ordered regular prayers said in all Cluniac houses for Henry's daughter, the empress Maud, and in which he specified that among the benefactors of the abbey of Cluny "Henry, King of the English, Duke of Normandy, has surpassed all others."[249]

The letter of Peter the Venerable succeeds in reconciling history and hagiography. We know that Alfonso of Spain contributed massively to the construction of the new basilica on and off until his death in 1109.[250] This is the same year in which Abbot Hugh, the initiator of plans and work on the monastery and basilica, died, as did Anselm of Canterbury, who had spent quite some time in exile in Burgundy and visited his friend Abbot Hugh a number of times during the years of construction. The archbishop thus was an early link between England and Cluny. After 1109 the credit for Cluny III seems to belong to Henry I. Little has been made of this serious and expensive enterprise by the English king, for beyond these statements, which reveal a strong contemporary tradition, the evidence for dispersement of major funds

---

[247] *GND*, 2:254–255.

[248] Map, *De nugis curialium*, pp. 436–438.

[249] *Charters and Records among the Archives of the Ancient Abbey of Cluni from 1077–1534*, 2:104–105, and *Record-Evidences among the Archives of the Ancient Abbey of Cluni*, pp. 42–44; *Recueil des chartes de l'abbaye de Cluny*, 5: no. 4183.

[250] See Reilly, *The Kingdom of Léon-Castilla*; Conant, *Cluny*, p. 81 n. 22, says Alfonso VI paid for roughly half the church, of an estimated 1968 sum of fifty million dollars.

is sparse and the king's motivation unclear. He no doubt knew that he was contributing to the most renowned monastery in Western Europe, an establishment of noble lineage that attracted holy men of aristocratic background, an abbey under the protection of the Holy See and wholly independent of secular authority, and an institution that in the eleventh century provided much of the impetus for monastic reform throughout the Christian West. But Henry could only have guessed that the new basilica he was helping to complete would become the largest and most magnificent church in the West (except for Old St Peter's). The high Romanesque baroque style embodied in Cluny III, with its innovative two-towered façade (mid-twelfth century) and sculptured grand portal, set the standard for cathedral architecture for the century. Even the mistakes at Cluny were fruitful, for the rebuilding of the nave, which Henry is said to have financed, introduced the flying buttresses that would distinguish the new architecture of the Gothic.[251]

Most of the surviving charters verifying Henry's interest in Cluny appear in the *Regesta*, Round's *Calendar of Documents Preserved in France*, and collections of Cluny charters.[252] The problem is that these documents do not provide nearly enough in grants of land and funds to build or rebuild a basilica. But, as Christopher Brooke observes, exactly what kings gave to religious foundations is difficult to determine, for the documents that have survived hide as much as they reveal.[253] In the case of Cluny, the extant charters begin early in Henry's reign, are reinforced by a host of other benefactions in 1121–1122 , and climax in 1130/1131, the year of the dedication of the basilica by Pope Innocent II.

In 1102/1103 Henry confirmed William Giffard's major grant of nine *mansiones* on the great street of London to St Peter of Cluny and its renowned daughter house, Saint-Martin des Champs in Paris.[254] (Around this time Henry's cousin Stephen of Aumale made a grant of a church in Normandy to Saint-Martin des Champs.[255]) The alien

---

[251] See Conant, *Cluny*, and Conant, "Cluniac Building during the Abbacy of Peter the Venerable," pp. 121–127.

[252] *Recueil des chartes de l'abbaye de Cluny*, nos 1091–1210. *Bibliotheca cluniacensis*, ed. Marrier.

[253] Brooke, "Princes and Kings," p. 127. See also Lucien Musset's discussion of sources of revenue for monastic construction ("Le Mécenat des princes normands au XIe siècle," pp. 130–134), in which he notes the absence of documents to verify the accumulation of capital (as gold, jewels, etc.) which inevitably preceded construction.

[254] *RRAN* 2, no. 646; *CDF*, no. 1266. The *mansiones* were said to be in Cheap. William Giffard received this large grant from Odo of Bayeux.

[255] The church at Arènes: *CDF*, no. 1264; *Recueil des chartes et documents de Saint-Martin des Champs*, 1: no. 147.

priories of Thetford and Lenton were founded between 1104 and 1106 and it is reasonable to assume that Henry's three undated confirmations followed fairly soon after each foundation.[256] Also early in the reign Henry made gifts to the priory of St Saviour's Bermondsey, daughter house to Cluny's first and most important daughter, La Charité-sur-Loire.[257] St Andrew's Northampton, another daughter of La Charité, received confirmations of earlier gifts, to which the king added his own gift of a mill.[258] Sometime between 1106 and 1109 Henry confirmed the English possessions of the Cluniac priory of Longueville in the diocese of Rouen and added freedom from tolls, dues, and customs as well as the right to carry on industry (in this case, lead casting).[259] Probably before mid-reign Henry then offered the Northampton monks the church of the Holy Sepulchre at Northampton.[260] Mid-reign, Henry seems to have supported the Bohun family foundation of Monkton Farleigh (Wiltshire).[261] The king even linked his son with patronage of the Cluniacs. The cartulary of the abbey of Saint-Martin des Champs records a confirmation by William Adelin, probably during the last years of his short life when Henry was associating him with his rule.[262]

From mid-reign Henry's gifts to Cluny grew more substantial. In the 1120s the king made an important collection of grants: the manor of Tixover, the half-manor of Manton in Rutland, and the manor of Opford-Cluny in Huntingdonshire.[263] Then in May 1131, in an assembly at Rouen attended by some of the most distinguished religious in Western Europe, Henry offered one of the largest gifts of his life: an annual grant of one hundred marks of silver, sixty marks from the farm of London and forty marks from that of Lincoln, payable at the exchequer at Michaelmas.[264] English confirmations of this grant followed in the same year, at Northampton

---

[256] *Charters and Records . . . Cluni*, 1: nos 179, 180, 182; Henry's confirmation of Lenton was witnessed by Stephen of Aumale: *CDF*, no. 1383 (1107–1115).

[257] *RRAN* 2, nos 664–665, 962, 1021, 1350. See above, p. 97.

[258] Ibid., no. 833.

[259] *CDF*, no. 219.

[260] *RRAN* 2, no. 1318; C. N. L. Brooke calls this gift a gesture of penance: "Princes and Kings," p. 139, citing *Monasticon*, 5:191–192, as evidence that the gift took place early in the reign.

[261] *Monasticon*, 5:24–27, and no. 3 (for reference to Henry I), and *Papsturkunden*, ed. Holtzmann, 1: no. 15 (for reference to Henry I).

[262] *Recueil . . . Saint-Martin des Champs*, 2:77, no. 230.

[263] *RRAN* 2, no. 1618; the confirmation, no. 1721, which may be later, mentions that the original gift of Opford was by Ernulf de Hesding; *Charters and Records . . . Cluni*, 1:67, no. 213.

[264] *RRAN* 2, no. 1691; this grant is only surpassed by Henry's grant of a similar sum to Fontevrault: see pp. 412–413 above.

and Woodstock.[265] The conditions of payment were clearly detailed: the sum was to be paid in perpetuity, and the king specified that after his decease "his officers shall annually bring the 100 marks with the rest of the rents to his exchequer and they shall there be delivered to the agent of the abbey."[266] The confirmation by Pope Innocent II states that the gift was made in his presence at Rouen and notes the illustrious witnesses: the archbishops of Tarragona, Rouen, and Chartres, the bishops of Lisieux and Sées, the abbots Bernard of Clairvaux, Suger of Saint-Denis, and Boso of Bec, the prior of Saint Oswald's at Nostell (Henry's Augustinian confessor), as well as the count of Warenne, Robert of Gloucester, and Robert de Sigillo, among others.[267] It is even possible that Abbot Peter the Venerable of Cluny was in attendance.[268] An undated charter of King Henry sums up his attitude succinctly: "Let it be known that I have received into my hand and custody and protection the abbey of Cluny . . ."[269]

The final hard evidence comes in the form of a petition presented in 1457 to the court of Henry VI by three monks of Cluny sent by the aristocratic abbot John of Bourbon.[270] Seeking to recover possessions and rents alienated or appropriated over the years, the Cluniacs detailed their possessions in England, justifying their rights and describing their acquisitions and donors. John of Bourbon says that Abbot Hugh, in desperation about the growing number of monks and the inadequate facilities, sought assistance to accommodate the brethren[271] and to finance the building of the new basilica. He therefore went to King Henry, who, he states, was ruling in 1101 (a curious date to note; perhaps this was the date of the visit), and begged for help. Henry responded "by contributing abundantly from his treasury" (one hundred silver marks are specified durante dicto opere, annis singulis) so that building could be continued and "by sending jewels"[272] from the royal chapel so that the new church would be decorated as befitted such a magnificent structure. A few years later the king contributed another (alius) one hundred marks, in a donation inter vivos,[273] to be paid

---

[265] RRAN 2, nos 1713, 1721; CDF, no. 1386 (Woodstock), where Hugh archbishop of Rouen attested.

[266] CDF, nos 1387, 1389.

[267] RRAN 2, no. 1691; CDF, no. 1388.

[268] Letters of Peter the Venerable, 2: appendix D.

[269] Charters and Records . . . Cluni, 2:199, no. 229, citing Cluny cartulary D.

[270] Ibid., 2:76–83, no. 521; see also commentary on pp. 71–73.

[271] Hugh's building program on the monastery buildings had been under way for most of his rule. Building on the basilica commenced in the late 1080s.

[272] The jewels were also sent "etiam peregrina hinc inde querendo," a difficult passage to translate: to attract (assuming quaerendo) pilgrims/foreigners/others there?

[273] Inter vivos can mean "orally."

in perpetuity from the exchequer. The interesting aspect of this account is the precedent for sending jewels and silver (portable wealth and precious metals) and the possibility that Henry made an *oral* grant for cathedral construction some years before he made the acknowledged perpetual grant (Rouen, 1131).

Henry's benefactions to monasteries have been variously interpreted: as a sign of piety, as a mark of penance or contrition, as an effort to distinguish royal relations, and as the grand gesture intended to impress. All of these motivations probably stirred the king's complex character. Christopher Brooke suggests—more vividly—that under Henry's skin lurked two or three different men.[274] Henry's interest in Cluny and the Cluniacs does in fact seem to be partially a family affair and partially an affair of "princes and kings." Domesday Book tells us that in 1086 the English holdings of the abbey of Cluny amounted to an insignificant eighteen pounds, placing it low on the list of important landholders. Moreover, the earliest priories, excepting Lewes, were mostly dependent on La Charité-sur-Loire, illustrating the reluctance of Abbot Hugh of Cluny to send his monks into unstable lands far from home.[275]

There is, however, some Anglo-Norman precedent for Henry's attentions. When the Conqueror founded Battle Abbey, he sought monks from Marmoutier, which although not dependent on Cluny had been reformed by Cluny under Abbot Mayeul. The Conqueror and Queen Matilda apparently admired the Cluniacs, for they asked for confraternity with the Burgundian abbey. In thanks to Abbot Hugh for having sent the monk Warmond to Normandy with an affirmative response, the king and queen sent to Cluny a richly ornamented cope of heavy gold brocade. Interwoven with gold and silver, bordered with pearls and precious stones, the chasuble was said to be so heavy and stiff that it could not be folded.[276] William also asked for a group of Cluniac monks to help him with church reform, but Hugh refused, having recently supplied the Warenne foundation at Lewes (and somewhat miffed at William's suggestion of payment). There is even record of one visit of Abbot Hugh to the Conqueror in Normandy around 1078, a visit that seems associated with the foundation or royal confirmation of Lewes.[277] The Conqueror's son William Rufus is hardly known for his kindness to monasteries, but he did continue to favor his father's foundation at Battle and he specifically joined in the foundation of the

---

[274] Brooke, "Princes and Kings," p. 127.
[275] The priories of Bermondsey, Daventry, Northampton, Much Wenlock, and Pontefract were all founded in the last two decades of the century.
[276] *Charters and Records . . . Cluni,* 1:30–31.
[277] *Recueil des chartes de l'abbaye de Cluny,* 4: nos 3559–3561.

Cluniac priory of Bermondsey in London in 1089, giving the land on the south bank of the Thames for the priory.

At the beginning of Henry's reign, a surge of activity produced a number of new Cluniac foundations plus two refoundations, all with the assistance or approval of the king. Roger Bigod, the king's powerful steward, lord of Norwich Castle and holder of many possessions in Suffolk and Essex, founded St Mary's priory in Thetford (Norfolk) about 1103/1104.[278] Three royal confirmations that date to the first half of the reign followed; in 1107 the king himself visited Thetford, for the confirmation is dated "when the king stayed a while here" and has the king's cross and seal.[279] The priory was at first dependent on Lewes and then later on Cluny itself, probably after 1114 when the priory moved across the Little Ouse river. William Peverel, Henry's half-brother, a natural son of the Conqueror, founded the priory of Holy Trinity at Lenton (Nottinghamshire) sometime between 1102 and 1108. He was fortunate enough to receive a colony of twelve Cluniac monks and a prior from Lewes. The king's early confirmation (1109) mentions his own soul, that of his wife and those of his ancestors, and in particular the safety of William his son and Maud his daughter.[280] A mid-reign confirmation adds gifts of a fair, a quantity of wood, and certain royal liberties.[281] One of the witnesses to the 1109 charter was Henry's cousin Stephen of Aumale, who himself favored Cluniac foundations.[282]

About 1107 Joel de Totnes, an ancestor of the Braose family, established the small Cluniac community of St Mary Magdalen at Barnstaple in Devon, and Henry duly and repeatedly confirmed its many possessions.[283] Around the same time Daventry priory was founded by the "sheriff" of Northamptonshire with the assistance of the earl of Northampton, Simon of Senlis.[284] Montacute, founded by the powerful Robert of Mortain, lost its endowment early in Henry's reign with the defection of the young William of Mortain to Robert Curthose. One tradition maintains that the monks pleaded with King Henry for restoration but insisted on returning to their isolated Somerset site, refusing the king's offer of a larger site with the prospect of royal favor

---

[278] A "Roger count in Anglia" is also said to have been responsible for the grand refectory at Cluny; L'Huillier, *Vie de Saint Hugues*, pp. 366–367, identifies this individual as Roger Bigod. L'Huillier also suggests that Anselm proposed that Bigod ask for Cluniac monks for Thetford (p. 345).

[279] *RRAN* 2, nos 682, 834, 1084.

[280] Ibid., no. 920.

[281] Ibid., no. 1282.

[282] *CDF*, no. 1265.

[283] Ibid., no. 1267; *RRAN* 2, nos 1269, 1270; *Monasticon*, 5:198, no. 3.

[284] See *Cartulary of Daventry Priory*, pp. xvii ff.

and growth.[285] Both Ranulf the Chancellor and Ranulf the king's physician are associated with this priory, a sign of royal interest spreading.[286] Henry's nephew and namesake Henry of Blois, a monk of Cluny from about 1110 until the mid-twenties, may even have been prior at Montacute before receiving from the king the abbey of Glastonbury.[287] The Bohun family founded the priory of Monkton Farleigh at mid-reign; Hugh prior of Lewes confirmed the foundation, as did Innocent II at Rouen in 1131, mentioning the role of Henry I.[288] It seems that many of those close to the king favored the foundations that he favored (as Dickinson noted long ago in his study of the Augustinian canons).

Other connections through family and important friends link the king with Cluny. Henry seems to have followed his parents' lead. He favored Bec and its daughters, as they did, and he distinguished Cluny and sought Cluniac monks for a royal foundation. Henry, however, was successful in importing a colony of Cluniacs when in mid-reign he founded the royal abbey at Reading. Although Henry repudiated the ecclesiastical practices of his brother William Rufus, he nonetheless showed consistent interest in the Cluniac house of Bermondsey, which Rufus had helped to found.[289] Henry might also have been well disposed toward Cluny because his favorite sister Adela and her husband Stephen count of Blois admired the abbey: about 1096 they gave the monastery of Saint-German at Auxerre to Cluny.[290] Sometime in the first decade of the century they sent their young son Henry as a child to the celebrated abbey then under the guidance of the distinguished Hugh of Semur. And between 1095 and 1120 the family also gave the Cluniac nunnery of Marcigny-sur-Loire near Autun three manors in England.[291]

---

[285] Knowles et al., *Heads of Religious Houses*, citing *Itinerary of J. Leland*, 1: part 2, p. 158.

[286] *RRAN* 2, nos 1399, 1307, and p. 344, no. 14, with a royal attestation.

[287] The name Henry runs in the Blois comital family as well as in the family of Anglo-Norman kings. Knowles et al., *Heads of Religious Houses*, p. 121 and n. 3, and Knowles, *Monastic Order*, p. 282 n. 3. Lena Voss, *Heinrich von Blois*, p. 4, thinks that Henry of Blois probably came directly from Cluny to Glastonbury.

[288] See note 261 above, this chapter.

[289] *RRAN* 2, nos 664–665, 962, 1021, 1350, 1743, 1990, plus various confirmations; see above, p. 97. Barlow, *The English Church: 1066–1154*, p. 91, citing "Ann. Berm.," *Annales monastici* 3:432, recounts a dream of Henry I's in which the prior of Bermondsey saved the king from a lion.

[290] *RRAN* 2, nos 3717, 3859 (confirmation of Paschal II); *Recueil des chartes de l'abbaye de Cluny*, 5: no. 3717 (1096); Pignot, *L'Ordre de Cluny*, 2:163, says the count or countess of Blois restored the abbey sometime between the first two crusades.

[291] *Cartulaire de Marcigny-sur-Loire*, no. 172; *Monasticon*, 5:28, no. 7, for Farleigh Priory.

After the death of Stephen, Adela, a woman of great political influence with important friends,[292] made a gift and a confirmation to Saint-Martin des Champs.[293] Ultimately Adela retired to the Cluniac monastery of Marcigny.[294] That elite monastery, founded by the same Hugh of Cluny who had years earlier received Adela's young son, sheltered many noble widows and female relatives of important figures in the secular and ecclesiastical worlds.[295] Alfonso VI of Spain, Cluny's greatest donor, sent one of his daughters, Tarasia, to Marcigny to join Hugh's select group of ninety-nine women leading a life said to be more strict than that at Cluny.[296] Count William of Burgundy gave land to the nunnery around 1095 and sent his mother there sometime before 1115. Abbot Hugh's relatives—his mother, two sisters, sister-in-law, and three nieces—entered the community. Anselm of Canterbury tried to move his sister to Marcigny to provide for her widowhood.[297] Hecelina, the mother of the future abbot of Reading and archbishop of Rouen, Hugh of Amiens, also joined the distinguished nuns at Marcigny, as did the mother of Peter the Venerable in addition to two of his nieces.[298] Even the sister of Henry I's longtime seal-bearer and chancellor Robert *de Sigillo* was welcomed at the Burgundian nunnery. Robert himself was invited to enter the monastery at Cluny but instead settled at Reading.[299] While cloistered, the nuns at Marcigny maintained a certain contact with the world. Abbot Hugh visited often, as abbot of both

[292] Adela may have arranged the 1105 English investiture settlement: see below, p. 423.

[293] *Recueil . . . Saint-Martin des Champs*, 1: nos 98, 96.

[294] Stephen died early, in 1102, but Adela remained active as countess for many years, perhaps because her sons were minors and then because of the incapacity of her oldest son; see *GND*, 2:276–277, and *PL* 171:144–145 (letters of Hildebert of Lavardin, bishop of Le Mans, book 1, no. 3). Various authorities propose various dates for Adela's entrance: 1120 (Hugh the Chanter, pp. 154/155) and 1122 (*RRAN* 2, no. 1599a); there seems no reason to doubt Hugh's date, since he also reports that Thurstan accompanied Adela from Blois to Marcigny when she took the veil just after Easter 1120 (18 April).

[295] For the following information on family members at Marcigny I have relied on Wollasch, "A Cluniac Necrology from the Time of St Hugh," pp. 143–190, esp. pp. 163–164, 168, 188 n. 1, and Pignot, *L'Ordre de Cluny*, esp. 2:38.

[296] It may be worth noting here that a sister of Henry I, Agatha, was said to have been affianced to this same Spanish king, before he married Hugh of Cluny's niece; see Reilly, *The Kingdom of Leon-Castilla*, p. 47 n. 49, citing WM, *GR*, 3:276, OV, 3:114 and n. 1, and *Charters and Records . . . Cluni*, 2:105. Douglas, *William the Conqueror*, pp. 393–395, explicates the problem.

[297] Apparently the bishop of Chiusa refused permission for the move; see Southern, *Anselm and His Biographer*, pp. 9–10, citing ep. 328.

[298] Hugh of Amiens, on entering Cluny sometime around 1099, made a gift of churches for his mother at Marcigny: *Cartulaire de Marcigny-sur-Loire*, nos 171, 171b.

[299] *Letters of Peter the Venerable*, 1: no. 77, 2:150; the choice of Reading opened the door for an episcopal appointment at London later.

Marcigny and Cluny and, one suspects, as a dutiful son. Anselm of Canterbury accepted hospitality at Marcigny while in exile during Rufus' reign, and the itinerary of Peter the Venerable shows that he frequently called at Marcigny in the course of his many travels.

The presence of Anselm of Canterbury at Marcigny and at Cluny and his friendship with St Hugh constitute an important link between England, Henry I, and the abbey of St Peter. Eadmer reports visits to Cluny in 1097 and 1098. Although Anselm lodged principally with his old friend Hugh of Lyons during his two exiles, he was always welcomed joyfully at Cluny, and he once gave a well-received lecture there on eternal life.[300] In the third year of Anselm's exile he was invited by Abbot Hugh to visit Marcigny,[301] which turned out to be a momentous occasion, for Hugh related a dream in which he saw William Rufus judged and condemned at the Divine Court: the accident in the New Forest took place just a few days later.[302]

The unfortunate situation in which Anselm found himself with Henry I was not the result of doctrinaire sentiments on Anselm's part but rather a question of compliance with recent papal declarations on investiture.[303] Both the king and archbishop behaved circumspectly throughout the crisis,[304] and their relationship, so cooperative and friendly at the start of the reign, seems to have withstood the trials of the investiture standoff, with its repeated delays and appeals to Rome to reconsider the English case and the king's customary rights. We know that Anselm himself insisted on careful selection of important churchmen, so while Anselm waited in Burgundy for Henry to realize that the loss of the outward signs of investiture would not compromise his authority,[305] he partook of the hospitality of his good friends. It is hard to

---

[300] See Cousin, "Les Relations de Saint Anselme avec Cluny," pp. 439–453, esp. pp. 441–442.

[301] Eadmer, *Life of Saint Anselm*, ed. and trans. Southern, p. 123 and note.

[302] In Gilo's *Life of Saint Hugh*, printed in L'Huillier, *Vie de Saint Hugues*, p. 588.

[303] Hollister, "St Anselm on Lay Investiture," pp. 145–158; see also above, pp. 119 ff.

[304] For example, although Henry collected the Canterbury revenues during Anselm's exile, he entrusted collection to two men of the archbishop, not royal officials: Mason, "Saint Anselm's Relations with Laymen," p. 549. Henry no doubt felt grateful to Anselm for his role in gaining approval for Henry's marriage to Edith-Matilda. After Anselm's return to England, Henry was solicitous about the archbishop's health and left Anselm as regent and guardian of the queen and his children when he was in Normandy.

[305] See Ivo of Chartres' famous distinction between temporalities and spiritualities: letter to Hugh of Lyons (1097), in Yves de Chartres, *Correspondance*, pp. 238–254, and in *Lettres de Saint Ives*, ep. 61, esp. pp. 118–120. Hugh the Chanter, pp. 22–25, commented on Ivo's argument. Ivo obtained the liberty of his see from secular control as early as 1101 (*Cartulaire de Notre-Dame de Chartres*, 1:104–105, 3:225); Ivo once proposed that only concord between "la royauté et le sacerdoce peut assurer la

imagine Anselm, renowned for his gentleness in reprimand and his sweetness of temper, hardening his heart against the king to whom he extended such patience and to whom he wrote so temperately. Various authors, contemporary and modern, have singled out Anselm's famed gentleness, tact, and charity; one commentator even argues that Anselm's *politique* was to succeed through "une douceur persuasive" and not "par la contrainte," an explanation reminiscent of the *politique* of Henry himself.[306] Nor can we imagine the abbot of Cluny, a kind of monarch in his own realm, friend of the greatest men of the age, lord of an abbey that represented the old school of Church–state relations, failing to understand the importance of managing appointments to high office.

When Anselm's patience finally wore out in 1105 and he took leave of Hugh to return north, he stopped at La Charité en route to a probable showdown in Normandy. A timely illness of Adela of Blois, with whom Anselm had corresponded warmly,[307] diverted him from a direct route to Normandy. Learning of Anselm's intentions, Adela probably acted to warn Henry about the archbishop's exasperation. In fits and starts a resolution was finally reached, a compromise that seems to have satisfied all parties. Henry I was already favoring Cluniac monasteries at this time, and the queen and Anselm worked closely in the first decade of Henry's rule, promoting many religious projects together. Anselm's ties to Cluny and his admiration for the Cluniac system[308] may have prompted or encouraged the king's interest, preparing the way for English assistance in the building of the basilica. In 1107 the founder of the Cluniac priory of St Andrew's Northampton took the opportunity to confirm at court in the king's presence his foundation for the monks of La Charité, thus acquiring the royal seal of approval. Anselm and a large group of bishops witnessed this charter as well as one by the king himself giving the Northampton monks a mill and certain exemptions from tolls and customs and confirming in detail Earl Simon's gifts of the 1090s.[309]

---

securité aux choses humaines" (*Lettres de Saint Ives*, p. 119 [ep. 61]). See also the arguments put forward by Pons, abbot of Cluny, and the bishop of Châlons to Henry V much later: Pignot, *L'Ordre de Cluny*, 3:23.

[306] See Mason, "Saint Anselm's Relations with Laymen," p. 559; Cousin, "Les Relations de Saint Anselme avec Cluny," p. 449 n. 25. Hugh of Cluny called Anselm *quasi angelus dei* (noticed by Dickinson, "Saint Anselm and the First Regular Canons in England," p. 546, citing *AO*, 4:80, no. 412).

[307] Anselm visited Chartres in 1103 and his chaplain William also visited Chartres on unknown business sometime between 1102 and 1104 when he witnessed one of Adela's charters: *Recueil . . . Saint-Martin des Champs*, 1:96 (for William), and Dickinson, "Saint Anselm and the First Regular Canons in England," pp. 541–546, citing M. Rule, *The Life and Times of Saint Anselm* (London, 1883), 2:314.

[308] Barlow, *English Church: 1066–1154*, p. 185.

[309] *RRAN* 2, nos 832, 833.

Anselm's Cluny connections persisted during his last years. Hugh of Cluny wrote a number of times, asking for news and cheerfully recalling Anselm's smile and sweetness, which he said had conquered the hearts of all the Cluny monks.[310] When Hugh archbishop of Lyons died in Italy in 1106, Abbot Hugh wrote immediately to tell Anselm about the loss of his friend.[311] To contemporaries the ties extended even beyond the grave. When Abbot Hugh of Cluny died in late April 1109, just a week after Anselm, Baldwin of Tournai, Anselm's steward and companion in exile, received the news in a dream and hastened to tell the Canterbury community of the sad event.[312] According to an early historian of Cluny, it was commonly believed in the Cluniac world that Hugh and Anselm ascended to heaven together; the abbot of Afflighem (diocese of Cambrai), among others, reported seeing the event in a vision.[313]

After the death of Anselm, Henry's links to Cluny were buttressed by two important appointments. When the king decided to make a major royal foundation at Reading in the early 1120s, he had enough influence or was already respected enough at Cluny to secure a temporary prior and seven monks from Cluny itself, plus a larger contingent from St Pancras at Lewes. In 1125 Henry chose from Lewes as first abbot the scholar and theologian Hugh de Boves,[314] a descendant of the count of Amiens and a former student of Anselm at the famous school of Laon, meeting point of many upwardly mobile young clerics. Early in the century Hugh had become a monk at Cluny, where he probably knew Adela's son and Henry's nephew, Henry of Blois, before Hugh left about 1113 to become prior at Saint-Martial of Limoges.[315] When he became prior at Lewes in 1120—a post guaranteed to the most distinguished monk in the Cluniac community, excepting the priors of the mother house and her first daughter, La Charité—he must have been known to the Laon alumni in England and thus come to the attention of Henry I. Hugh remained abbot at Reading until 1129/1130, when Henry raised him to the important archiepiscopal see of Rouen. William of Malmesbury says that Hugh was devoted to Henry I, and

---

[310] AO, 4:17 (ep. 259) and 5:356 (ep. 411); see also Cousin, "Les Relations de Saint Anselme avec Cluny," pp. 449–450.

[311] Pignot, L'Ordre de Cluny, 2:175, citing PL 159:241.

[312] L'Huillier, Vie de Saint Hugues, p. 543.

[313] Pignot, L'Ordre de Cluny, 2:371–372, citing Vita by Raynaldo of Vezelay in PL 159:905–906; see also Cowdrey, Two Studies in Cluniac History, p. 106 n. 4, on the visions, and Hildebert of Lavardin's Life of St Hugh, PL 159, cols 857–894, chap. 51.

[314] See Hébert, "Hugues III d'Amiens," pp. 323–371.

[315] A "Hugone de Bovo" witnessed an undated charter of Adela of Blois to Saint-Père de Chartres: Cartulaire de l'Abbaye de Saint-Père de Chartres, 2:309 (no. 57).

with good reason, for he owed his advancement to the king.[316] Hugh could easily have played the role of intercessor for Cluny in the 1120s and 1130s, for he was a friend of the vigorous young abbot of Cluny, Peter the Venerable (1122–1156/1157).

In 1122 Pierre-Maurice de Montboisier undertook the restoration of the venerable Burgundian abbey, which had been experiencing some years of difficulty, financial and spiritual. Working to complete the abbey basilica, reorganize the abbey finances—so that it could provide for itself and its many dependents[317]—and revitalize its spiritual reputation, Peter launched a vigorous public-relations and fund-raising campaign among the kings and princes of Europe. He traveled incessantly in this effort and in order to assess the strengths and weaknesses of the whole community. In 1130 Peter visited England, with the express permission of the king,[318] and made a kind of tour of inspection, spending time with Henry of Blois, former prior of Cluny and by this date bishop of Winchester, and visiting the Cluniac abbot of Peterborough. Returning to Cluny, in October 1130 Peter saw the completion of St Hugh's grand design (after the shocking collapse of the nave vaulting in 1125) in the dedication of the new basilica by Pope Innocent II, the event calculated to fall on the anniversary of the consecration of the apse and main altar in October 1095 by Pope Urban II.[319] King Henry's sole documented donation of annual funds followed in May 1131. The following year, Peter convoked the first grand synod of priors at Cluny to begin efforts toward spiritual reform, aimed at restoring the prestige of the abbey.[320]

The affection Abbot Peter felt for the English royal family is expressed in a number of letters. In 1135, before the death of Henry I, Peter wrote to his friend Henry of Blois at Winchester of his admiration for the English king;[321] this is the oldest personal testimony of relations between

---

[316] WM, *HN*, chap. 457.

[317] There were between 300 and 400 monks at Cluny and multitudinous poor who were accustomed to seeking relief there, not to mention the spiritual and secular lords who also accepted the abbey's hospitality. *Bibliotheca cluniacensis*, pp. 1640, 1651, says there were 300 monks at Peter the Venerable's election and 460 in his later years. See also Duby, "Le Budget de l'abbaye de Cluny entre 1080 et 1155," for analysis of the Cluniac lifestyle and its financial requirements.

[318] *ASC*, s.a. 1130.

[319] Conant (*Cluny*, p. 111) gives Henry credit for supporting some of the other constructions that Peter the Venerable undertook during these years, notably the great infirmary and the great dormitory.

[320] See OV, 6:424–427 for details: 200 priors and 1,200 monks attended. Further reform decrees were promulgated in the early 1140s: Knowles, "The Reforming Decrees of Peter the Venerable," pp. 1–20. On the aims of Peter the Venerable, see Bredero, "Pierre le Vénérable," pp. 99–118, and Constable, "The Monastic Policy of Peter the Venerable," pp. 119–142.

[321] *Letters of Peter the Venerable*, 1: no. 56.

Henry I and Cluny.[322] In early 1136 Peter wrote movingly to Henry's sister Adela at Marcigny, telling her what he had learned about the death of the king and the disposition of his remains.[323] Peter explained that he was unsure of the civil situation in England but had sent messengers to Hugh of Rouen and Henry of Winchester, who would report to him and whose information he would forward as soon as possible. He assured Adela that the memorials to be held at Cluny and all Cluniac monasteries would be greater than for any other benefactor, such a calamity was the loss of Henry I for Cluny. In 1140 Peter wrote in a letter to the king of Sicily that a prince he had loved (presumably Henry) was now dead.[324] The efficacy of Cluniac prayers for Henry I passed quickly into legend. Peter the Venerable's disciple Ralph, in his life of the abbot, says that Henry appeared to one of his knights to say that he would surely be in hell without the prayers of the Cluniacs. The king then asked the knight to hurry to Lewes to urge the monks to redouble their efforts. On learning of the plea, Peter did exactly that and soon received the good news through the same knight that the king had been saved.[325]

The second appointment Henry made in the 1120s was even more significant in augmenting ties with Cluny. Peter the Venerable's friend Henry of Winchester was the youngest living son of Adela, Henry I's sister. He had become a monk at Cluny in the first decade of the century and had made important friends among members of that aristocratic community.[326] His presence at Cluny may have influenced the king in the years after the death of Anselm. Henry of Blois was among the king's favorites after the death of the king's son. The path of ecclesiastical preferment opened to him under the king's sponsorship led to the pinnacle of ecclesiastical power in England. Appointed by Henry I in 1126 to rule the abbey of Glastonbury,[327] once the wealthiest religious foundation in England, Henry of Blois worked over the

---

[322] Lohrmann, "Pierre le Vénérable et Henri Ier," p. 195.

[323] *Letters of Peter the Venerable*, 1:22, no. 15 (Constable's commentary in 2: 103–105). Pignot, *L'Ordre de Cluny*, 3:279, for French translation and Pignot's commentary.

[324] *Letters of Peter the Venerable*, 1: no. 131. Lohrmann, "Pierre le Vénérable et Henri Ier," p. 199; Lohrmann adds here that Peter the Venerable's references to Henry I throughout his works are so numerous as to indicate conviction and a basis of truth.

[325] *PL* 189:25 (chap. 13), "Vita Petri Venerabilis, auctore Rodulpho monacho ejus discipulo." This Ralph may be the Blois relative, Rodolfus of Sully, abbot from 1173 to 1176, suggests the editor.

[326] Kenneth J. Conant notes that a biographer of St Hugh marveled at the celebrated recruits (*viri celebres converterentur*) who were drawn to Cluny because of the distinction of Abbot Hugh: "Observations on the Practical Talents and Technology of the Medieval Benedictines," p. 77.

[327] Knowles, *Monastic Order*, p. 282 n. 3 (citing *RBE*, 2:752), says that Henry was perhaps also prior of Montacute.

years to restore the monastery to its former status. A man of talent and ambition,[328] he succeeded, to his own benefit and that of the monks, who never complained of his appointment or its duration.[329] When Henry received the bishopric of Winchester in 1129, he retained Glastonbury (with papal permission) and added to these possessions a deanery in London and one in Waltham.[330] By the 1140s Henry may have been the richest prelate in England, for Glastonbury was again the richest abbey (at least it was by 1166) and Winchester was second only to Canterbury in wealth. When Henry became papal legate, a post that he held from 1139 to 1143, he rivaled the archbishop of Canterbury as the most powerful churchman in the realm.

Henry of Winchester's extraordinary loyalty to Cluny, evident throughout his long career, cannot have failed to influence Henry I in his last decade. The bishop was in constant communication with Peter the Venerable, who frequently consulted him on financial matters.[331] Henry of Winchester loaned or gave the Burgundian abbey large sums of money (as well as valuable gifts) on many occasions, even demanding an inquest of the abbey's revenues as part of this assistance. For a time he himself administered the abbey and supported the monks.[332] It is no wonder that one Cluny chronicle described Henry of Winchester as *benefactor singularissimus et maximus*.[333]

---

[328] See Franklin, "The Bishops of Winchester and the Monastic Revolution," for a careful study of Henry's talents (as politician, art connoisseur, administrator, and benefactor).

[329] Knowles, *Monastic Order*, pp. 290–291 (n. 6), citing Voss, *Heinrich von Blois*, pp. 70–90. See Adam of Domerham, *Historia de rebus gestis glastoniensibus*, 2:305 ff.; the Cluniac observance was probably followed there, for a monk of Lewes was Henry's representative until 1136 and a Cluniac consuetudinary is said to have existed: Knowles, *Monastic Order*, pp. 282–283; Knowles (ibid., p. 287) describes Henry of Winchester as an administrative genius of the first order.

[330] *Papsturkunden*, ed. Holtzmann, 1, nos 30, 27 (both 1144).

[331] See *Letters of Peter the Venerable*. Letter 49 was probably written after the 1130 visit, when the abbot of Cluny no doubt consulted Henry about Cluny's financial difficulties: see Van den Eynde, "Voyages."

[332] For Henry's loans: *CDF*, no. 1395, and *Charters and Records . . . Cluni*, 2:88, no. 244; *Recueil des chartes de l'abbaye de Cluny*, 5: no. 4142. His funds may have been secretly spirited out of England by Peter the Venerable: *Letters of Peter the Venerable*, 2: app. D, *anno* 1155; Lohrmann, "Pierre le Vénérable et Henri Ier," p. 203 n. 51, citing RT, *Chron., s.a.* 1155; Van den Eynde, "Voyages," pp. 90 ff. For his gifts: Henry of Winchester seems in fact to have given to Cluny the gold and silver on the great crucifix; he "rescued" such precious metal from the Canute Cross at Hyde after the sack of Winchester in 1141: *DNB*, 26:114–116; see WM, *HN*, chap. 499, for a description of the cross; see FW, 2:133–135, for the riches Henry of Blois "rescued" at various sites in Winchester.

[333] *Bibliotheca cluniacensis*, col. 1624. Conant, "Observations on the Practical Talents and Technology of the Medieval Benedictines," p. 78. *Charters and Records . . . Cluni*, 1:81, no. 521 (letter from Abbot John of Bourbon, 1457). Van den

Other members of Henry I's family show dynastic solidarity in sharing his interest in Cluny. His daughter, the empress Maud, while in Germany, witnessed and approved a privilege for the Cluniac monks of Rüggisberg.[334] More important, she later donated a magnificent candelabrum that stood before the high altar of the new basilica at Cluny. Modeled on the candelabrum commanded of Moses by the Lord (Exod. 37:17), Maud's seven-branched exemplar stood on a pedestal seven feet high and glowed with gold, silver, jewels, and precious stones. Other gifts attributed to the empress include gold crucifixes, a fragment of the True Cross, gold-brocaded vestments embroidered with precious stones, and an unusual set of church bells, called the "Anglican" bells, which could be recognized when they tolled by their remarkable timbre, the product of a novel alloy.[335] Peter the Venerable himself visited Maud in Normandy in her later years (probably around 1155) to discuss commemorative services after her death.[336]

After Henry's death, his widow Adeliza and her husband William d'Aubigny, the king's steward and a descendant of the powerful Bigod family, continued faithfully to support Henry's foundation at Reading, which followed the Cluniac observance.[337] And Henry's favored nephew Stephen of Blois, who seized the throne in 1135 at Henry's death, confirmed all of Henry's donations to Cluny, only replacing the one-hundred-mark annual payment with the manor of Ledcombe Regis, considered equal in value.[338] Stephen too founded a royal abbey, at Faversham in Kent, which followed the Cluniac system. A number of new Cluniac foundations date from Stephen's reign, bringing the total number of foundations made between 1100 (when there were about ten) and 1160 to thirty-six.[339] Henry II, whose charters regularly refer to his grandfather's era, responded magnanimously to Cluny's pleas for assistance in the later years of his reign, at one time sending one thousand marks with the stipulation that the money was to be repaid only if he

Eynde, "Voyages," p. 91. On the number of monks at Cluny in the mid-twelfth century: Pignot, *L'Ordre de Cluny*, 2:497. The Cluny chronicle: *Bibliotheca cluniacensis*, col. 1624.

[334] Chibnall, *Empress Matilda*, p. 29.

[335] *Charters and Records . . . Cluni*, 1:18 and n. 33.

[336] Pignot, *L'Ordre de Cluny*, 3:496: a double *tricenaire* was specified, i.e., twice the usual thirty masses in thirty days.

[337] See below, this chapter, p. 440; *Reading Abbey Cartularies*, nos 268, 370, 371, 459, 534–536, 550–553, 658.

[338] *CDF*, no. 1390; the Spanish kings took similar actions throughout the twelfth century, substituting land grants for money grants. The witness list for 1390 makes the charter a family affair, including Stephen, Henry of Winchester, and Henry of Sully, plus Roger of Salisbury and his two nephews.

[339] Knowles, *Monastic Order*, p. 153.

asked for it.[340] Apparently the old saw about Cluny's ability to raise funds was valid throughout the twelfth century:

> Par tout où le vent vente
> l'abbaye de Cluny a rente.

As Kenneth Conant, the historian of the architecture of the abbey, sagely comments, "Cluny a bien su trouver des bienfaiteurs quand il était nécessaire."[341]

There remain a few other individuals of this international elite who contributed to the Cluny–England connection. Henry of Poitou, monk and prior of Cluny and then abbot of Saint-Jean d'Angély, is described by both Orderic and the *Anglo-Saxon Chronicle* as a kinsman of Henry I.[342] This ambitious churchman of uncertain spirituality, labeled by contemporaries "an ecclesiastical adventurer,"[343] received the abbey of Peterborough from Henry I in 1127. The gift could have been an expression of family ties, but reward for prior services seems more likely. Henry is said by the *Anglo-Saxon Chronicle* to have served as legate in England in 1123, but as he came with bad news about nonpayment of Peter's Pence and the faulty election of the archbishop of Canterbury, his visit cannot have been a happy experience.[344] Still, in 1124 Henry of Poitou did help annul the threatening marriage between William Clito and Sibyl of Anjou,[345] which could only have raised him in the king's favor. Once installed at Peterborough, according to the *Chronicle*, Henry of Poitou exploited the monastery and its monks and, worse, attempted to force the monastery into dependence on Cluny. Because of the king's good will, the new abbot almost succeeded, but, says the chronicler, Roger of Salisbury and his nephew Alexander of Lincoln convinced the king that a scheme was afoot. In the end the king made an about-face, asking the abbot to leave the kingdom instead.

Dietrich Lohrmann sees in this episode an attempt by Peter the Venerable (who visited England during these years and stayed at

---

[340] *CDF*, no. 1399.
[341] Conant, *Cluny*, p. 111 n. 19. Cowdrey, "Unions and Confraternity with Cluny," esp. p. 162, also comments on the ability of Cluny to augment its income through confraternity and unions.
[342] OV, 6:316/317; *ASC*, s.a. 1127.
[343] See Clark, "'This Ecclesiastical Adventurer,'" *passim*, esp. for genealogical analysis.
[344] Henry d'Angély had been a legate of the pope earlier, says Hugh the Chanter (pp. 104/105), when Henry was sent to fetch Archbishop Ralph in 1119.
[345] *ASC*, s.a. 1127. Neither OV, 6:165 nor WM, *HN*, chap. 450, mentions Henry d'Angély's role in obtaining the annulment.

Peterborough) to gain not only Peterborough but also Reading and Glastonbury for the Cluniac community.[346] But an effort to attach to Cluny one of the most English of monasteries would have been both foolhardy and doomed to failure. Moreover, the royal abbey of Reading was already following the Cluniac observance (without formal ties to Cluny and *with* the assent of Peter the Venerable) and Glastonbury was being administered for Henry of Winchester by a Lewes monk of Cluny.[347] If Peter's efforts at centralization looked like aggrandizing to Henry I, they would have been fruitless. For Peter faced a king whose skill in disarming challengers to his authority, through diplomacy or subterfuge, was seldom equaled in his times. One can scarcely believe that such a talented diplomat and fundraiser, known for his *sage politique*, would risk alienating a king he considered a valuable source of support.[348]

Peter the Venerable may have used his visit to Peterborough to remonstrate with Henry of Poitou about his irregular ambitions. The offer of Peterborough to Cluny may then have been made in order to reclaim Peter's good graces.[349] It is also possible that the king's exasperation with Henry of Angély had to do with recognition of Pope Innocent II. Through the good offices of Peter the Venerable of Cluny and Bernard of Clairvaux, most of the powers in Western Europe had accepted Innocent II as the legitimate pope over the antipope Anacletus. Only Rome, Aquitaine-Poitou, and Sicily held out. William X count of Aquitaine and the bishop of Poitiers both supported Anacletus, despite the best efforts of Peter the Venerable and St Bernard. Henry's abbey of Angély seems to have been a center of opposition, and Peter the Venerable's secretary, Peter of Poitiers, once a monk there, crowed in relief at his escape from the abbey, describing the place as "a horrible pit [of] miry clay," adding in a poem, "You draw your swords in vain / Oh men of Angély . . ."[350] If Henry d'Angély had associated himself with this dissent, then he would have incurred the wrath of both the king of England and the abbot of Cluny.[351]

---

[346] Lohrmann, "Pierre le Vénérable et Henri Ier," p. 197.

[347] Knowles, *Monastic Order*, pp. 282–283. See below, this chapter, pp. 436–437, on Reading's status.

[348] Pignot, *L'Ordre de Cluny*, 3:299; see Peter the Venerable's letter to Adela on Henry I's death, n. 323 above, this chapter, on his esteem for Henry I.

[349] Van den Eynde, "Voyages," pp. 88–89; the abbots of Saint-Jean d'Angély were often in trouble with the abbot of Cluny throughout the late eleventh and first half of the twelfth centuries, usually about subjection to Cluny; but Henry d'Angély's episcopal escapades make other pluralists look like amateurs—see Clark, " 'This Ecclesiastical Adventurer,' " *passim*; Clark notes that there had been complaints to the abbot of Cluny against Henry of Poitou before 1107 (p. 551).

[350] *Letters of Peter the Venerable*, 2: app. Q, pp. 336–337; Pignot, *L'Ordre de Cluny*, 3:156 ff.

[351] The abbot of Cluny supported Innocent II over Anacletus, a former Cluniac.

Matthew of Albano, prior of Saint-Martin des Champs, cardinal-bishop of Albano, and nephew of Hugh abbot of Reading, plays a much more important role in the Cluny connection.[352] Whether Henry I personally knew the prior of Saint-Martin des Champs when he confirmed certain gifts to the priory of Barnstaple and gave land in memory of Queen Matilda is impossible to know.[353] But these grants form part of the background for Robert of Torigny's claim that Henry did for Saint-Martin des Champs what he did for Cluny, namely, contributed significantly to its building program.[354] Although we lack solid evidence for the dispensing of major funds—as Lohrmann suggests, the lone Pipe Roll of 1130 looks lonelier still when we begin to search for major undocumented expenditures—all these personal connections, clearly important to Henry I, make Robert of Torigny's claims more believable.

In any case, by 1128 Matthew had become one of the many talented Cluniacs recruited by the papacy. In that year the king welcomed Matthew, now cardinal-bishop of Albano and papal legate, to Normandy, and, perhaps because of the recommendation of Hugh of Reading, permitted Matthew to hold a reforming synod in Rouen in that year. Dom Ursmer Berlière suggested that at this time Matthew may have influenced Hugh of Reading's appointment to the see of Rouen, for the incumbent, the archbishop Geoffrey le Breton was gravely ill in 1128 when the legate was in Normandy and the subject of a vacancy must have arisen.[355] Matthew certainly admired his relative Hugh: when Matthew was still prior at Paris he asked Hugh for instruction on certain theological points. Hugh dedicated the resulting *Dialogues* to Matthew, providing vital biographical information on their past.[356] Matthew was also esteemed by Peter the Venerable, who called on him when he was still prior of Saint-Martin des Champs to come to Cluny to help address the abbey's problems. If Matthew's successful fund raising at Paris was known to the abbot of Cluny, this could have been a reason for the

---

Henry of Poitou lived only a short time longer. Expelled from Saint-Jean d'Angély, he is said to have retired to Cluny and made a pious end. See Clark, "'This Ecclesiastical Adventurer,'" p. 560.

[352] First suggested by Lohrmann, "Pierre le Vénérable et Henri Ier."

[353] *Recueil . . . Saint-Martin des Champs*, 2:72–81, 81–83; *RRAN* 2, no. 1292, and *CDF*, no. 1269–1270.

[354] *GND*, 2:254–255; Pignot, *L'Ordre de Cluny*, 3:65, says there were 300 monks at Saint-Martin des Champs in the era of Peter the Venerable. Wollasch, *Synopse der Cluniacensischen Necrologien*, 2:673, for 2 December, notes that Henry gave one hundred shillings annually to Saint-Martin des Champs for offices to be said after his death.

[355] Berlière, "Le Cardinal Matthieu d'Albano," pp. 113–140, 280–303; see esp. p. 129.

[356] *Recueil . . . Saint-Martin des Champs*, 1:178.

invitation. In addition, Matthew's reputation as a stern disciplinarian seems to have recommended him to Peter, for internal dissent was a factor at Cluny in these years of reform. Whatever the cause for his stay, Matthew remained for two years. Peter the Venerable later asked Matthew to accompany him to Rome, in 1126, to face ex-abbot Pons before the papal court. The collapse of the nave of the basilica had just occurred, and Matthew's intimacy with Peter put him in a position to know that Cluny desperately needed funds at this particular moment.

This appearance with the abbot of Cluny at the papal court recommended Matthew to the pope, and within a year he had been elevated to cardinal-bishop. A whole series of legatine activities followed, including the visit to Normandy in 1128. When Innocent II was elected in 1130 and then forced to leave Italy, Matthew traveled with him throughout France. Matthew attended the dedication of the new basilica at Cluny in October 1130, where he must have heard praises of the king of England from Abbot Peter.[357] He followed the pope to visit Louis VI of France and stopped in Chartres, where he encountered Henry I again.[358] When the pope held a great council at Reims in 1130, Henry sent Matthew's friend Hugh of Rouen to reiterate his support for Innocent II against the antipope.

This relationship between Hugh and Matthew illuminates another part of the puzzle of international connections between Western European intellectuals, who by definition were all churchmen. Both Hugh and Matthew were from noble families of the *pays* of Laon. Both had studied at the famous school there under the direction of Anselm of Laon, schoolmaster to a group of important Anglo-Norman prelates that included William of Corbeil, Robert de Béthune bishop of Hereford, Robert of Chichester bishop of Exeter, Geoffrey le Breton archbishop of Rouen, the bishops of Le Mans and Coutances, as well as the nephews of Roger of Salisbury, Alexander (later bishop of Lincoln) and Nigel (later bishop of Ely). Early on, in 1106, the king somehow arranged the appointment of his chancellor Gaudry to the archbishopric of Laon.[359] Gaudry's successor as chancellor sent both his sons to Laon for their education.[360] And the current ran both ways. Roger of Salisbury eventually employed another Laon student, Guy of

---

[357] Peter's writings are full of praise of the king of England, among other benefactors, so it is reasonable to assume that he would have praised the principal benefactors at the dedication.

[358] Pignot, *L'Ordre de Cluny,* 3:152.

[359] Guibert of Nogent, *Self and Society,* trans. Benton, pp. 167–177. Guibert says Gaudry had an abundance of gold and silver to facilitate his acquisition of the bishopric; Gaudry was murdered in 1112.

[360] Poole, *Exchequer,* pp. 53–56; Richardson and Sayles, *Governance,* pp. 270–271.

Etampes, as master of his school at Salisbury, and he warmly welcomed a group of Laon canons in 1113 when they made a fund-raising tour to England.[361]

Some minor characters add bits of circumstantial evidence to this international web of ties to Cluny. Peter the Venerable revealed in one of his letters the existence of a "dear English notary," one Thomas of St Andrew's Northampton, whom Peter describes as the "most dear and most pleasing" of all the gifts he had received from Northampton.[362] Eustace III, count of Boulogne, Henry's brother-in-law and a distant relative (through Ethelred and Emma of Normandy) as well as Stephen of Blois' father-in-law, withdrew from the world around 1125 and entered the Cluniac monastery of Rumilly, which he had founded and favored.[363] At mid-century Peter the Venerable was traveling between England and the Continent in the company of Hugh l'Anglais, an individual about whom we know nothing but his nationality.[364]

After the death of Henry I, English relations with Cluny remained close. Henry of Winchester continued to promote Cluniacs in England whenever he could.[365] Cluniacs from Bermondsey moved on to the abbeys of Abingdon and Evesham, and as the best example of the English connection with the abbey Henry I had so admired two English abbots, William of Ramsey and Hugh of Reading, were elected to lead the celebrated Burgundian house.[366]

[Reading] was founded by him . . . in a place well suited to provide a lodging for almost all travellers to the more populous cities of England. In it he established monks of Cluny, who are at this time a distinguished exemplar of holy life and a model of inexhaustible and delightful hospitality.

—William of Malmesbury, *GR*, 5:413

---

[361] See Kealey, *Roger of Salisbury*, pp. 48–49 and notes.

[362] *Letters of Peter the Venerable*, 1: no. 45, and 2: app. R, p. 348.

[363] *CDF*, no. 1385.

[364] *PL* 189:662a.

[365] Robert of Lewes, Henry of Winchester's administrator at Glastonbury, received the see of Bath in 1136. The Frenchman Peter Moraunt, former prior of La Charité, was appointed to Malmesbury.

[366] Roger of Bermondsey moved first to Saint-Ouen in Rouen and then to Abingdon; Adam of Bermondsey received Evesham. William of Ramsey, former prior of Saint-Martin des Champs, elected abbot of Cluny in 1177, is acknowledged as the greatest benefactor of Cluny after Henry of Winchester: *Bibliotheca cluniacensis*, col. 1662; Hugh V of Cluny, former prior of Lewes and abbot of Reading, elected in 1199, was the last Englishman to rule Cluny.

The monastery of Reading [is] distinguished without by vast estates and within by an order of holy monks.
—William of Malmesbury, *HN*, chap. 462

The foundation of the abbey of Reading was Henry's first grand gesture.[367] Coming as it did after a period of war in Normandy, when Henry dramatically defeated the coalition led by the king of France,[368] the laying of the first stone in June 1121 could be described as celebratory. But because of the harrowing personal disaster that Henry suffered in the loss of the White Ship, most historians have painted the foundation in somber tones, arguing that the king was seeking pardon for his faults through pious acts, Reading being the most conspicuous of such deeds.[369] Although William of Malmesbury mentions a penance in association with the foundation and the chronicle of Battle Abbey repeats the medieval formula that Henry was disposed to build an abbey for the absolution of his sins and for the souls of his family members,[370] it is not necessary to posit grave royal faults and expiation of guilt to justify the foundation. Henry had reached the age of fifty-two. The loss of his wife and heir constitute reason enough for him to seek a fitting memorial for their souls and to add another colony of monks to those already praying for his own salvation and that of his heirs.

Most of Henry contemporaries spoke of his many "kingly enterprises" and his "praiseworthy devotion to God" expressed in his building of monasteries in England and Normandy.[371] Orderic Vitalis' impression of the king is so favorable that scholars might have taken more seriously the Saint-Evroul monk's good-hearted revelations of the human element in Henry's nature. Orderic has Henry telling the owner of the White Ship that he loved his boys (William Adelin and his natural son Richard) "as my own life." He also reports on the king's anguish and his "bitter laments," which Hugh the Chanter seconds.[372] Henry's

---

[367] See chapter 7, above, pp. 282–287.

[368] HH, p. 464: Henry describes the battle of Brémule in detail and says that the king was struck twice on the hauberk by William Crispin—a close brush with death; see also OV, 6:238, and *Liber de Hyda*, p. 318.

[369] E.g., Pignot, *L'Ordre de Cluny*, 3:34; Southern, "The Place of Henry I," p. 155. Only the *Chronicle of Battle Abbey*, pp. 122–123, repeats the medieval formula so often found in charters: "the excellent King Henry was disposed to build an abbey for the absolution of his sins and for the souls of his father, mother, and wife, and the salvation of all his heirs." See also Brooke, "Princes and Kings," p. 147, discussion comment by A. H. Bredero on the foundation of monasteries as a known penance.

[370] WM, *GP*, p. 193; *Chron. Battle*, pp. 122–123.

[371] WM, *GR*, 5, prologue, 1, 5:413.1; *GND*, 2:252–253.

[372] OV, 6:300; Hugh the Chanter, pp. 164/165.

nephew Theobald of Blois hurried to England after the disaster in 1120 to spend Christmas with the king at Brampton and offer such consolation as a family member could.[373] Hildebert of Lavardin, bishop of Le Mans and a longtime family friend, wrote to offer condolences and praised Henry for mastering himself in his misery.[374]

Pauline Stafford speaks of the foundation of Reading as a new beginning for King Henry.[375] Certainly his extraordinary activity in the years 1121–1122 shows that he had lost none of his vigor. By February 1121 he had taken a new wife.[376] There followed a host of royal grants and mandates, issued as if many men and tasks had been awaiting the king's attention. And the plans for the royal abbey at Reading became concrete.

Henry I may have been contemplating a major foundation for some time. Knowles, Brooke, and London suggest that the king once considered transforming Montacute into a royal foundation, for a late report says that Henry had offered the monks a better site (which they refused) and he may even have installed his nephew Henry of Blois as prior.[377] In 1118 Henry sent off an embassy to the Eastern Empire in search of relics, the fruit of which effort became the basis of the collection that ultimately attracted throngs of visitors to Reading.[378]

The abbey site shows careful consideration.[379] At the confluence of the Kennet and the Thames rivers, one leading west and the other north, and at the intersection of the Great West Road and routes

[373] WM, *GR*, 5:419.2.

[374] Hildebert of Lavardin, Letters, *PL* 171:290–291 (book 3, ep. 13). See A. E. Dieudonné's critical comments on this letter in *Hildebert de Lavardin*, p. 283 (his ep. 86).

[375] See Pauline Stafford's recent article (which Warren Hollister could not have seen when he wrote chapter 7 above), "*Cherchez la femme*," for a new analysis of the foundation of Reading. Stafford describes the foundation as a simultaneous act of penance and piety as well as an expression of dynastic continuity in celebration of the king's second marriage.

[376] Negotiations must have been in progress for some time. The new queen, Adeliza of Louvain, was the daughter of that Godfrey of Louvain for whom the young Maud had interceded as one of her first acts after her arrival in Germany: Chibnall, *Empress Matilda*, p. 23 n. 16. Another Godfrey of Louvain, who came to England with Adeliza, received the see of Bath in 1123 (*ASC, s.a.*), perhaps a sign of the importance of the imperial connection; see below, this chapter, pp. 456–457.

[377] Knowles et al., *Heads of Religious Houses*, pp. 121 and n. 3. See also Brooke, "Princes and Kings," p. 137 and esp. n. 40.

[378] Apparently Henry had shown an interest in relics from early in his reign; see Bethell, "The Making of a Twelfth-Century Relic Collection," pp. 66 and 69, citing (for the embassy) Aldgate Chronicle, London Guildhall MS 122, IV. f. 16; on the number of monks and visitors: Pignot, *L'Ordre de Cluny*, 3:34.

[379] As noted by WM, *GR*, 5:413. See also Stafford, "*Cherchez la femme*" (*passim*), for the basis of the endowment.

linking north and south, the house was admirably suited to its expressed purpose of providing alms and food for the poor and hospitality for the voyager and pilgrim. A West Country monastery could never have served as such a focus. Moreover Reading, on pleasant rising ground, lay a reasonable distance from the south coast and the Channel. Also within reach were Windsor, Westminster, Winchester, and Salisbury as well as Abingdon, Cirencester, and Gloucester—even Wales. The royal endowment, described by most contemporaries as lavish,[380] made it possible from the very beginning for the abbey to fulfill the mission anticipated for it by the king. A nineteenth-century historian of the abbey of Cluny estimated that by the mid-twelfth century Reading had as many as two hundred monks and, as *la grande hôtellerie de l'Angleterre*, served an equal number of "guests" daily.[381]

Unsurprisingly, Henry chose to affiliate Reading with the celebrated abbey of St Peter at Cluny, leader of the most esteemed aristocratic fraternity in Europe, renowned as a way station on the pilgrimage route to Rome and as a source of relief for legions of poor.[382] Abbot Pons willingly sent an initial complement of seven monks from Cluny along with Prior Peter to direct the work.[383] It was but two years before the royal abbey was ready to receive an abbot. The king then imported a larger colony and chose an abbot, both from Lewes, Cluny's first and foremost daughter house in England. The new abbot, who had been prior at Cluny, Saint-Martial of Limoges, and then Lewes, was the distinguished Hugh of Amiens. His aristocratic and intellectual connections in Amiens and at Laon, a region known and esteemed by Englishmen and the English monarch, placed him among the European elite.[384] Hugh's kinship with the prior of Saint-Martin des Champs, a Cluniac monastery already patronized by Henry I and his relatives, and his probable acquaintance with Henry's nephew Henry of Blois, then a monk at Cluny, help to explain his selection for the royal abbey. His

---

[380] The numerous confirmations of the abbey's possessions show a stable base of possessions from its inception: see, e.g., Richard I's confirmation in *Reading Abbey Cartularies*, 1: no. 34.

[381] Pignot, *L'Ordre de Cluny*, 3:34–35, compared Reading with La Charité, another celebrated site of hospitality; other commentators suggest between 50 and 200 monks in residence at Reading.

[382] David Knowles says the reputation of Cluny was never higher than in the days of Henry I: *Monastic Order*, p. 174.

[383] The "Annales radingenses," in *Ungedruckte Anglo-Normannische Geschichtsquellen*, pp. 9–12, suggest that monks from Lewes joined the settlement in 1121, but this may be a late addition and it seems reasonable to assume that the full complement would only be reached as building progressed.

[384] See above, p. 432.

subsequent career at Rouen shows that Henry valued him as a strong (if testy) and reliable churchman.[385]

Peter the Venerable, who succeeded Pons at Cluny in 1122, praised the English king as "our outstanding benefactor" and quickly granted the new community *societas* with Cluny, giving the abbey important rights of confraternity. The monks of Reading were to have the usual right of all Cluniacs to sit in chapter at Cluny, successive abbots were to be elected from among the monks of Reading or from Cluny itself (excluding, as usual, the grand prior), and a special trental (*tricenarium*) of memorial masses was to be granted all abbots of Reading, an honor reserved for the most important priors and abbots as well as major benefactors.[386] As Brian Kemp, editor of the Reading cartularies, notes, the charter of *societas* reveals no juridical dependency on Cluny, once the first abbot had been chosen. The last lines of the charter reinforce this conclusion: Peter the Venerable announces that every abbot-elect will be consecrated *sine contradictione* and that the rights and liberties detailed in the charter have been instituted by the will and consent of both Henry I and the abbot of Cluny.[387]

If the importance of Reading to Henry I can be gauged by the timing of the foundation, its endowment and extraordinary liberties, and its association with the splendor of Cluny, the dedication also suggests that the king was making great efforts to touch both the past and the future. Having early in his reign sought a link with the Old English royal line through marriage to Matilda, Henry now, at mid-reign, undertook "to revive the piety and glory of three ancient Anglo-Saxon monasteries"[388] destroyed by the Danes: Reading, Leominster, and Cholsey. The restoration of the churches and manors of these institutions, whose extensive lands had been incorporated into the royal demesne, set Reading on a solid territorial and financial foundation. In addition, the effort no doubt also earned Henry the approval of reform elements in the Church.

Linking his dynasty to the foundation, Henry dedicated the abbey

---

[385] See Hébert, "Hugues III d'Amiens," for an unusual assessment of Hugh's career in Rouen; see also below, pp. 446–449.

[386] *Reading Abbey Cartularies*, 1: no. 218; for confirmations by successive popes, starting in 1123, see ibid., p. 129 ff. (Papal Acts), esp. no. 146, by Adrian IV.

[387] Kemp notes that the foundation charter of Faversham granted that abbey complete freedom from all obedience and subjection to Cluny and La Charité, from which it was colonized, stipulating that Faversham was to enjoy the same freedom as Reading Abbey: *Reading Abbey Cartularies*, 1:15 n. 5, and *Monasticon*, 4:575, no. 9.

[388] Brooke, "Princes and Kings," p. 141. See Pauline Stafford's "*Cherchez la femme*" in which she "links the lands used to endow Reading with those of late Saxon queens and of female communities themselves linked to queens" (p. 4).

specifically to the memory of his parents, his brother King William, his son William and his wife Matilda, and all his predecessors and successors in honor of the Blessed Virgin Mary and St John the Evangelist. The first seal of the abbey showed the Virgin and Child with a model of the abbey.[389] As two of the incorporated monasteries had been nunneries and as the cult of the Blessed Virgin was spreading among English prelates at this time, it is no coincidence that Henry tapped this movement of popular piety for his foundation. Anselm of Bec had come to England with a number of hairs of the Virgin Mary which had been brought to him from Jerusalem,[390] and Anselm's nephew, now abbot at Bury, promoted the cult of the Immaculate Conception.[391] Lanzo of Lewes "revered God's blessed mother," said William of Malmesbury,[392] and Hugh of Amiens followed suit.[393] Even the distinguished abbot of Cluny celebrated the Virgin in poetry as part of the liturgy.[394]

Henry's impressive collection of relics ensured the abbey's significance as a place of pilgrimage. The seal of the abbey with its three scallops boldly confirms this intention with the universal medieval symbol of the pilgrim.[395] According to Denis Bethell, Henry probably acquired the former relics of Leominster, for among the Reading relics were numerous pieces from a strong pre-Conquest collection such as had existed there. Other English monasteries also donated to the new foundation, including Canterbury, Winchester, Bury, St Albans, and Westminster. Even Cluny contributed two pieces. In addition to the Old English relics, those of international importance were a fragment of the True Cross and the hand of St James, brought by Maud from the empire on her return to England in 1126.

Such foresight on the part of the king for this sole Benedictine foundation of the reign suggests that Emma Mason is right to see the abbey as an element in ensuring the stability of the realm,[396] a particular concern between 1120 and 1126. Whether the king at this point envisaged his own burial at Reading is difficult to know, but its association with his son, who had no resting place but the sea, would have placed the abbey close to Henry's heart. The magnificence of the foundation and its endowment certainly made it a site worthy of a royal

---

[389] See Hurry, *Rise and Fall of Reading Abbey*, fig. 9, p. 33.

[390] Eadmer, *HN*, pp. 181–182.

[391] Celebration of the feast of the Immaculate Conception was approved at William of Corbeil's council of 1129.

[392] WM, *GR*, 5:443.8.

[393] Hébert, "Hugues III d'Amiens," p. 329 and n. 4.

[394] Folz, "Pierre le Vénérable et la liturgie," pp. 150 n. 30, 158, has an example.

[395] See fig. 1 in Hurry, *Rise and Fall of Reading Abbey*, frontispiece.

[396] See Mason, "Royal Monastic Patronage," pp. 99–117.

mausoleum.[397] Even the presence of so many of Henry's notables and stalwarts as signatories to the formal foundation charter of 1125 illustrates the importance the king attached to his new abbey.[398]

The foundation of Reading also reveals another aspect of Henry's personality, his love of building. Robert of Torigny gives a long list of the constructions to which Henry I contributed during his lifetime. He mentions first Reading, then Cirencester, Notre-Dame du Pré, and Mortemer, followed by *habitacula* and constructions in more remote lands, including those at Tours (Marmoutier), Chartres (the cathedral),[399] Evreux (the cathedral),[400] Paris (Saint-Martin des Champs), Avranches (the hospital of Jerusalem), and of course Cluny.[401] To this list can be added the rebuilding of Bayeux cathedral.[402] William of Malmesbury points out that the Normans were all generous in their building in England, where post-Conquest structures exceeded in grandeur any of the pre-Conquest Norman basilicas.[403] Between 1066 and 1135 new churches or cathedrals were undertaken at Durham, St Albans, Norwich, Exeter, Salisbury, Gloucester, Canterbury, Rochester, York, Llandaff, Tewkesbury, Peterborough, Ramsey, and Worcester, and many were dedicated during Henry's reign. Another contemporary, Richard prior of Hexham, said of Reading: *in lumine basilicam pulcherrimi*

---

[397] After Henry I, the king's natural son Reginald, his queen Adeliza, and the eldest son of Henry II were buried at Reading.

[398] The charter (*Reading Abbey Cartularies*, no. 1), which was probably written and witnessed in Normandy, included the attestation of John of Crema, the papal legate, the archbishops of Canterbury, York, and Rouen, the bishops of Winchester, St David's, Lisieux, and Avranches, the abbots of Battle, Bury, Bec, Sées, and Mont-Saint-Michel, plus Robert of Gloucester, Brian fitz Count, William of Warenne earl of Surrey, Roger of Warwick, Humphrey of Bohun, Hugh Bigod, William Tancarville, and Stephen of Aumale, among others. Henry was rewarded with praise from his monks. Alan Coates (*Reading Abbey Collections*) notes verses written in honor of the founder by the Reading monk Robert Partes (pp. 56, 152 [no. 46]) and a (now lost) history of the deeds of Henry I by Isidorus de Summobono (pp. 28, 42).

[399] *Lettres de Saint Yves*, nos 108, 121, 263.

[400] Henry was very generous to the cathedral at Evreux (*CDF*, nos 282–290), where the bishop was a former royal chaplain. The king had been forced to burn the cathedral and town (with the bishop's permission) to defeat a baronial revolt in 1119 (see OV, 6:228–230, or *GC*, 11:573–575, for this story). At that time Henry promised the bishop that after he had retaken the town he would gratefully rebuild the cathedral better than before. Robert of Torigny says the new cathedral (dedicated in 1132) outshone all others in Neustria (*GND*, 2:256–257).

[401] *GND*, 2:254–255.

[402] WM, *GR*, 5:398.4. Bayeux was rebuilt magnificently by Henry after he was forced to burn the town and church to rescue Robert fitz Hamon before the Tinchebray victory.

[403] See a modern commentary by Fernie, "Architecture and the Effects of the Norman Conquest."

operis erexit.[404] Archaeology suggests that the Reading basilica was almost the size of St Paul's in London.[405] Building at Reading continued until the mid-twelfth century. In the early 1130s the second abbot, Ansger of Lewes, added a hospital dedicated to St Mary Magdalen, the kind of institution Henry was known to favor. After forty years of construction— although part of that time was a period of civil war—the completed basilica was finally consecrated by Thomas Becket, archbishop of Canterbury, in 1164.

After Henry's death, his family fostered his cult at Reading. On the first anniversary of the king's death, Queen Adeliza hosted a gathering of bishops and abbots at the abbey. She pledged 100 shillings' worth of land that Henry had given her, to make provision for the convent and religious persons attending the anniversary. At the ceremony itself Adeliza granted the manor of Aston to Reading plus 110 shillings annually from a hithe in London. Sometime later she arranged for lights to burn continually before Henry's tomb and the Holy Sacrament, much as Henry had done for Matilda at Westminster. William d'Aubigny, whom Adeliza married in 1138, confirmed her gifts and added his own. At Adeliza's death in 1151, she too was interred at Reading; thereafter her brother Jocelin, her son William, and Jocelin's son kept up the family's attentions to the abbey.[406]

Members of Henry's royal entourage also became benefactors. David king of Scots, who had grown up at Henry's court along with the king's sons William Adelin and Robert of Gloucester as well as Brian fitz Count, made a whole series of gifts in Perthshire and on the Isle of May which permitted Reading to establish a daughter house in Scotland.[407] The empress Maud, in the troubled times after her father's death, did her best for Reading, with the assistance of her *fideles* Robert of Gloucester, Brian fitz Count, and Milo of Hereford. Her actions, however, like Stephen's, varied with the extent of power she was able to exercise. The grant of the church "for the safety of the kingdom" seems to show the empress's assumption of control at the same time as it suggests the difficulties she faced. She made another grant when she held the title "Lady of the English." A confirmation in the mid-1140s is particularly telling, for Maud makes the grant for the souls of her father, mother, and husband, and "for the

---

[404] *Priory of Hexham*, ed. Raine, "The Acts of Stephen and the Battle of the Standard," 1:66.

[405] Hurry, *Rise and Fall of Reading Abbey*, p. 10; medieval St Paul's was still under construction during Henry's reign and was not completed until the 1240s.

[406] See *Reading Abbey Cartularies*, nos 534, 370, 451, 535, 268 and note, 269, 371, 658, 550–555, 482.

[407] Ibid., nos 1276–1285.

peace and stability of the realm."[408] Henry's grandson Henry, as duke of Normandy, made a number of confirmations in the late 1140s, no doubt in order to announce his right to do so.[409]

Stephen, the new king, who had spent most of his life at court in the company of Henry I, apparently saw nothing inconsistent in his seizure of the throne, for he manfully carried the body of his uncle on his shoulders at the royal funeral at Reading. Thereafter Stephen tried to take Reading Abbey into his care, confirming land and liberties as well as grants by his nobles.[410] The new king probably did not need the urging of his brother Henry of Winchester to identify himself with the royal abbey. Ultimately, however, Stephen gave up this effort and established his own foundation at Faversham in 1148, choosing nonetheless to maintain the family affiliation with Cluny.[411]

A superficial study of the cartularies shows that every king thereafter until the early fifteenth century carefully confirmed the lands and liberties of Reading. Royal patronage is unequivocally familial in its consistent and explicit emphasis on predecessors' confirmations, all of which maintain the extraordinary independence that Henry I had granted the monastery. Henry II, who was present at the dedication of the abbey in 1164, made a point of taking Reading under his protection, as did his sons and successors.[412] Even as late as 1398 Richard II showed his interest by refusing to confirm the abbey's possessions and immunities until the restoration of the tomb and effigy of his ancestor Henry I had been completed and the royal honor restored.[413]

I propose to behave as a good king . . .
—William of Malmesbury, *GR*, 5:405.4

Frank Barlow accurately described the Church under Henry I as an institution under new management. But Barlow's statement that the Church preferred tyrants—that is, rulers like Henry I—to bunglers

---

[408] Ibid., nos 1108, 325 and note (Brimfield manor), 267 (confirmation), 667 (Blewbury).

[409] Ibid., nos 273–275, 668, 1109.

[410] Ibid., nos 272, 451–452, 605–607, 669.

[411] The monks of Faversham came, however, from Bermondsey, a daughter house of La Charité. Faversham, like Reading, followed the Cluniac observance but remained independent. Stephen and his wife and son were buried there.

[412] *Reading Abbey Cartularies*, nos 32 (Henry II); 35, 39 (Richard I); 71 (Henry III). Richard also ordered the abbot to recall into demesne any lands that had been given in fee since the death of Henry I (no. 37); such enfeoffment was strictly forbidden by the charter of foundation.

[413] Ibid., no. 116.

ignores the favorable contemporary estimates of Henry's rule, which contrast so sharply with critiques of the reigns of Rufus or Stephen.[414] Henry I was no tyrant. Despite the difficult years at the beginning of the reign, when Henry I discovered that the rules of Church–state relations had changed, the remainder of Henry's years passed with the Church enjoying a long period of calm during which it "flourished greatly," as Orderic exulted.[415] Henry learned early that he could not win by making an enemy of the Church—in fact, he could lose everything. Both Henry of Winchester and Hugh of Rouen later vainly begged King Stephen to avoid this mistake.[416] Perhaps the chroniclers' comments on the disasters of Stephen's reign are the best evidence we have for the successes of Henry's. Orderic's eulogy for Henry I is lengthy, but his verses on the present topic are worth noting:

> In days when evil rages all through the world
> He was, I dare assert, the best of men,
> As all his noble acts clearly proclaim.
> Peace-lover, Church's *guardian* . . .[417]

The Hexham chronicler lamented that after Henry "another prince did not rise up who could forbid unjust exactions, maintain his subjects in peace and modesty, cultivate religious persons reverently, and support paupers and the weak with generous alms."[418] Even the dyspeptic Henry of Huntingdon, in one of his moralistic treatises, was forced to admit that in "the dreadful time that followed . . . what Henry had done— whether in the manner of a tyrant or of a king—seemed, in comparison with worse, to be the summit of excellence."[419]

What Henry I offered the Church is what he offered his secular elite: patronage, wealth, justice, and peace. By coming to an agreement (albeit haltingly) with Anselm—and perhaps thereby saving his realm and kingship—Henry demonstrated to the Anglo-Norman Church and the papacy that a man of different character was at the helm—not a tyrant like Rufus, not a bungler like Curthose, but a man clever enough, *politic* enough, to concede when necessary, to seek the practical middle road, to treat the Church as the vital element of the realm that it was. Throughout his long reign Henry admittedly "managed" the Church, but he did so according to accepted rules. Although he controlled

---

[414] Barlow, *English Church: 1066–1154*, pp. 13, 66.
[415] OV, 5:294.
[416] WM, *HN*, chap. 477.
[417] OV, 6:453 (italics added).
[418] Richard prior of Hexham, in his "The Acts of King Stephen," in *Priory of Hexham*, ed. Raine, 1:66–67.
[419] HH, "The Present Time," pp. 700–701.

appointments when he wished, he never again asked for homage after the 1106 settlement;[420] in many instances he allowed free elections and occasionally bowed to the will of influential bishops whose aims differed from his own. And while he maintained his regalian rights in cases of vacancies, he never exploited or plundered monasteries or sees, instead displaying the management skills characteristic of his government. He was extremely generous, facilitating the civilizing and spiritual mission of the Church and promoting its security.

No doubt there was method in the king's management and in his wide distribution of largesse. Elizabeth Hallam admitted the same for Louis VII when she noted the "watchful eye" he kept on the Church, adding: "His was a piety with valuable political consequences."[421] Henry's bishops during the course of his reign gradually came to resemble the secular nobility in their origins and talents (as did churchmen in the Church universal). A few displayed real sanctity, but most were the king's men, and they brought to their sees both their managerial skills and the king's favor. One result was the culmination of the building boom in cathedrals; another, perhaps, a sense of episcopal solidarity, which became useful in the following reigns. If the number of monastic bishops decreased as the reign progressed and monasteries no longer played a powerful role in political culture, Henry I cannot be accused of neglecting them. One can argue, as Barlow did, that the king favored traditional Benedictine aristocratic monasticism. But the king's patronage of the Augustinian canons, whose worldly needs were not great,[422] and his attentions to hermits and hospitals show the king wooing all elements of the Church. As R. W. Southern so aptly put it, Henry could give his churchmen security and "they could give him their prayers and their good opinion."[423] Henry's genius was to realize that he needed both.

Either Henry absorbed Robert of Meulan's political advice well or he was a born diplomat. It is possible that he learned in youth how to

---

[420] Only the settlement achieved by Ivo of Chartres preceded the English accommodation to the reform papacy. See n. 305 above, this chapter.

[421] Hallam, *Capetian France*, p. 196.

[422] See Herbert, "The Transformation of Hermitages into Augustinian Priories in Twelfth-Century England," who points out that founding priories was a less expensive enterprise for nobles who wanted to imitate royalty and that certain royal foundations showed obvious "political manoeuvre" (p. 142). Cirencester, as a favored royal foundation, seems not to have been embarrassed by its substantial endowment.

[423] Southern, *Medieval Humanism*, pp. 231–232. Henry also patronized the Cistercians: *RRAN* 2, no. 1820, is a blanket grant of freedom from tolls, etc., to all Cistercian abbeys and daughters of Clairvaux; he singled out the abbey of Pontigny for exemption from certain customs (Christelow, "A Moveable Feast," p. 188 n. 5, citing *Thesaurus novus anecdotorum* 3:1227–1228).

negotiate between conflicting powers in order to survive. His manner was seldom combative; nor was he hasty. He preferred to persuade, to delay, to wait for events to provide a solution. The long journey to Rome, with its well-known perils, could provide intervals of calm to keep a simmering church problem from reaching the boil. The political difficulties of the papacy with the empire and its internal problems—a series of antipopes, even the succession of five legitimate popes with very different aims—worked to reward Henry's strategy. He successfully kept any legates from exercising authority in England until the mid-1120s, and he may have permitted John of Crema to hold a council in England only because the legate and Calixtus II had supported the annulment of the marriage of William Clito and Sibyl of Anjou. In fact, no legate seems to have infringed on Henry's rights; we are almost embarrassed to see Peter Pierleone retreating with such haste in 1121 when Henry brought up the subject of those rights.[424] The popes in the second half of Henry's reign—Calixtus II, a distant relative through the Burgundian connection, and Innocent II, in particular—both had serious political problems and needed the support of the kings and their churches in the West. They therefore treated Henry with some delicacy.[425] Calixtus may have denied the primacy to Canterbury,[426] but he rewarded the archbishop (and thereby Henry I) with the legation for England. As Martin Brett says, the popes "laboured long and hard to little purpose" to extend papal control over the Church in the reign of Henry I.[427] Perhaps the popes were satisfied that English clerks and monks were increasingly appealing and traveling to Rome, without royal interference, to air their conflicts and seek redress. Diplomacy and patience, delay and division, were tactics both sides were learning to appreciate.

Only one mysterious late incident shows the king of England

---

[424] Brett, *English Church*, p. 41.

[425] Hildebert bishop of Le Mans and then archbishop of Tours in fact complained of the popes' deference to the king of France because of the threat from the Empire: Dieudonné, *Hildebert de Lavardin*, p. 105. See pp. 447–449 below, where Innocent II (*HF*, 15:378, no. 21) defers to Henry I when the king complains that Hugh archbishop of Rouen is treading on the king/duke's customs and prerogatives in his zeal for ecclesiastical reform.

[426] One has the impression that Henry was never very adamant about the Canterbury primacy, although he loyally supported the ailing Archbishop Ralph. The king accepted the defeat of Canterbury with good grace and all indications are that Thurstan of York was extremely useful to the king (before and after his long-delayed consecration). It is interesting to note that Canterbury lost its metropolitan status but that the next pope, Innocent II, granted Rouen that distinction just a few years later (1131), another example of the inconsistency (or opportunism) in papal policy so evident in the long struggle over the primacy in England.

[427] Brett, *English Church*, p. 50.

reacting forcefully against the papacy.[428] In 1128 a letter arrived from Pope Honorius II praising Abbot Hugh of Reading and peremptorily summoning him to Rome; the reasons were unspecified, but the summons, when protested, was curtly repeated that year. According to Hugh's nineteenth-century biographer, the pope was exercising his pre-eminent jurisdiction over all Cluniacs, which included the right to approve appointments and demand services.[429] In response to the papal summons, the Reading monks wrote immediately to the Holy See, begging the pope not to leave them bereft of their leader. Henry I also wrote, more authoritatively, desiring the pope *not* to insist that Hugh present himself by the specified date. Then followed a threat: if Hugh is removed, the king announces, he will take back into the royal demesne all the gifts he has made to Reading at Hugh's request and he will not appoint a successor to Hugh.[430] Hugh himself wrote to both the pope and the papal chancellor (evidently an old friend) to say that he was much distressed by the king's resistance to his departure. These rather frantic letters suggest that Hugh's first loyalty was to the papacy, and it may be that Henry for once misjudged his man.

There can be no question that Henry perceived real danger in the papal summons. One explanation is that the king simply wanted to keep Hugh from going to Rome out of fear of the well-known papal poaching of talented Cluniacs. Matthew of Albano, Hugh's kinsman, was a recent example. As prior of Saint-Martin des Champs he had gone to Rome in 1126 with Peter the Venerable to dispute charges brought by ex-abbot Pons of Cluny; Matthew never returned to Paris as prior. Instead, he was appointed cardinal-bishop of Albano and spent his remaining years traveling as a legate for Honorius and Innocent.[431] Henry's strong reaction to the summons may also have had something to do with the impending vacancy of the archiepiscopal see of Rouen.

---

[428] See Hébert, "Hugues III d'Amiens," pp. 325–371, for this story and appropriate references; see also Martin Brett's appendix of Anglo-papal contacts for 1128–1130 (*English Church*, pp. 243–244), and *Papsturkunden*, ed. Holtzmann, 3: nos 15–27.

[429] Hébert, "Hugues III d'Amiens," pp. 330–331. In 1125 Honorius confirmed the foundation of Reading, specifically mentioning Abbot Hugh, indicating that he approved of Hugh's appointment (*Reading Abbey Cartularies*, no. 140).

[430] *RRAN* 2, no. 1549; *Papsturkunden*, ed. Holtzmann, 3: no. 16.

[431] The popes sometimes used their legates harshly. Matthew of Albano traveled incessantly for the papacy, to the detriment of his health. At one point Peter the Venerable wrote to the pope to ask him to delay his order for Matthew's return to Rome from Cluny as the legate was too ill to travel. The request was not granted (although the time required for the exchange of letters perhaps gave Matthew a longer rest); Matthew died worn out, of the same malady, a few years thereafter (7 November 1135) (see Berlière, "Le Cardinal Matthieu d'Albano," pp. 291–293, 296 ff.).

When Matthew of Albano held a legatine council at Rouen in
1128, the incumbent, Geoffrey le Breton, was gravely ill (he died
within a month). The question of the vacancy was probably discussed
at the council as the king and the five suffragans of Rouen were all
present. It is not improbable that Matthew proposed his cousin Hugh
for the see of Rouen; Henry himself may have had Hugh in mind
for Rouen or he may have balked at the prospect of losing the abbot
of his royal foundation. The common feature of these suggestions
is the king's reluctance to lose Abbot Hugh—or to have the abbot's
loyalty coopted.

The king's fears proved justified. In mid-1129 Abbot Hugh finally
answered the papal summons and traveled to Rome, possibly in the
company of the legate Matthew.[432] There Honorius retained him for
some time; the pope even wrote to the monks at Reading urging them
to be prudent and disciplined in the absence of their abbot, whom he
intended to keep with him for a while. This minor contest so late in
Henry's reign reveals the delicacy of the balance of power between king
and pope. Henry realized immediately that the summons was a serious
matter. The subsequent retention of Abbot Hugh in Rome justified
his suspicions. When Hugh returned from Rome—in a surprisingly
timely manner—the reason for the summons became clear: the abbot
was charged as *specialis filius beati Petri* with collecting Peter's Pence,
the annual tithes from the English Church which were long in arrears.
This was a task usually entrusted to legates, whom Henry had often
excluded from England over the years. Hugh's subsequent report to
Honorius reveals once again the diplomatic skills of the English king—
as well as those of the abbot of Reading, who seems to have persuaded
the king to comply. Henry acceded to the request for payment (in fact,
the king guaranteed it), but he sought (and presumably received)
a reduction in the amount as well as a delay in the commencement
of payments. Henry had negotiated favorable terms, but Honorius
had found a new way to breach the defenses of the English Church.
Then the pope died.

The new pope, Innocent II, wasted no time after his election in contacting his *specialis filius* about the schism and about Peter's Pence,
seeking support for his election and funds for his struggle. When late
in 1129 or early in 1130 Hugh of Reading was elected by the clergy
of Rouen to that important see, Innocent quickly approved and

---

[432] Matthew of Albano was well known and favored by Henry I. He had been prior
of Saint-Martin des Champs, which received Henry's attentions; he had been
allowed to hold a council in Normandy in 1128; and he may in fact have been
allowed to enter England in 1129 to persuade the king to let Hugh respond to the
papal summons (see *Papsturkunden*, ed. Holtzmann, 3: nos 18, 19, 20).

confirmed his selection.[433] The letter from the clergy of Rouen requesting papal approval specified the assent of the king and the bishop of
Salisbury (in whose diocese Reading lay), pointedly noting Hugh's
release from his former jurisdictions and his subjection to the
authority of the pope alone.[434] In the autumn of 1130 Hugh crossed
with the king to Normandy and was consecrated archbishop in
September. By this time Henry had decided to support Innocent II over
the antipope Anacletus.[435] Hugh, a friend of St Bernard, who was
canvassing Western European powers for support of Innocent, and
Matthew of Albano may have helped persuade Henry. All parties met
happily in Chartres and Rouen in 1131, and Hugh was Henry's representative to the council of Reims in that year, carrying letters of support
for Innocent II, and to later councils at Montpellier and Pisa in 1134
and 1135. Relations seemed amicable.

But Hugh proved stern in his enforcement of discipline among the
secular clergy of Rouen, provoking widespread opposition,[436] and he
soon became involved in a number of disputes with Norman abbots
about profession of obedience to the metropolitan.[437] Recalling
Henry's handling of the same problem with Boso of Bec, we suppose
that Henry now made his characteristic efforts to prevent discord and
arrive at compromise.[438] In 1124 he had ordered the archbishop of
Rouen to accept Boso's verbal profession without requiring a binding
legal document. Henry wanted no open quarrels, much less excom-
munications. Hugh, however, was inflexible. Now the king began to

---

[433] Honorius II was still pope at Hugh's election, for he confirmed to Reading and
to the new abbot, Ansger, the abbey's possessions and liberties (*Reading Abbey Cartularies*, nos 141–142), but Innocent II confirmed Hugh's election to the see of
Rouen (*Papsturkunden*, ed. Holtzmann, 3: no. 26).

[434] *Spicilegium*, ed. Luc d'Achery, 3:484. In this letter the clergy of Rouen note that
the pope had at one time specified to Henry that he was keeping Hugh under "our
own law and dominion as a special cleric of St Peter and the Holy Roman Church,"
the fullest description of the authority of the pope over Cluniacs. Hugh himself
told the clergy at Rouen that he could not be elected without papal consent.

[435] Peter Pierleone, a former Cluniac and an unsuccessful legate to England.

[436] See OV, 6:292/293, where Geoffrey le Breton's enforcement of the prohibition against clerical marriage and concubinage had proved dangerous.

[437] *PL* 150:733A, "Vitae Venerabilis Theobaldi," on Hugh's demands for a profession from the abbot of Bec and the intervention of Audoin of Evreux and Peter
the Venerable of Cluny. Hugh was successful in forcing the abbots of Jumièges and
Saint-Ouen, whose documents were proved false at the Council of Reims, to profess,
at command of the pope (*HF*, 15: 961–962); he also had a long dispute with the
abbot of Saint-Wandrille (see Hébert, "Hugues III d'Amiens," pp. 343–349, and
HF, 15:377–378). Orderic (6:391) says that Henry I supported the abbots against
the bishops at the synod of Rouen in 1128.

[438] See p. 403 above, this chapter, plus Gibson, "History at Bec in the Twelfth
Century," p. 174.

weary of his archbishop's intransigence, and he appealed to the pope—an unusual resort for this English king. Either Henry was sure he could not force Hugh to change his behavior or, as is more probable, he was sure he could persuade the vulnerable pope to accede to his wishes. Apparently the problem became known in the ecclesiastical world, for Peter the Venerable and even St Bernard wrote to Hugh, and they both urged moderation.[439] Innocent II, in his response, also temporized, making a clear effort not to offend the English monarch and risk a breach: he praised Hugh's noble aims, assured him of papal support, but counseled patience.[440]

During these last years of Henry's life, Hugh performed many duties for both king and pope, traveling to the council of Montpellier in 1134 as a royal representative, resolving a conflict in the diocese of Romans for the curia, and spending time in Italy with the pope after the council of Pisa (1135), which he also attended as Henry's representative.[441] The problems of profession to the archbishop resolved themselves over time,[442] but another, more serious dispute reared its head. When the bishop of Bayeux died in 1133, Henry ordered a thorough feudal inquest for the diocese and then appointed as the new bishop a royal chaplain, his grandson Richard, illegitimate son of Robert of Gloucester. Archbishop Hugh refused to violate canon law by consecrating a bastard. For two years Richard remained unconsecrated until the pope, who had evidently been implored, finally authorized Hugh to

[439] Hébert, "Hugues III d'Amiens," p. 335, citing St Bernard's letter 25. Peter the Venerable mentioned the dispute to the pope in the hope of finding a solution that would not merit divine censure and would not offend royal majesty (*Letters of Peter the Venerable*, 1: no. 17). Hugh seems to have mellowed over time; he conceded and confirmed to Fécamp its liberties (*GC*, 11:23–24, *Instrumenta*, no. 21 [ca. 1150]); the abbot at that time was Henry of Sully, a Blois descendant and nephew of King Stephen and Henry bishop of Winchester.

[440] *HF*, 15:377–378. This half-hearted support of Hugh is reminiscent of papal politicking during Anselm's dispute with Henry I years earlier.

[441] Hébert, "Hugues III d'Amiens," p. 334.

[442] Two abbots were ordered at the Council of Reims to profess obedience to Rouen, their documents of exemption having been proved false (see Hébert, "Hugues III d'Amiens," pp. 341–342). The recalcitrant (and underage) abbot of Saint-Wandrille, Alan, who had been elected in 1125 or 1126 (see ibid., pp. 342–344), continued to protest, especially to the king (a charter of Henry I to Alan and Saint-Wandrille, dated 1128–1135, takes the abbey into the king's protection: *Recueil des chartes de l'abbaye de Saint-Wandrille*, nos 64, 65, pp. 118–119). Alan was finally deposed by his own monks, probably in 1134 (when Hugh was not in Normandy), thus ending that controversy. Hugh himself does not refer to this last problem; in his later letter of solidarity with Thomas Becket in which he recounts his early troubles with Henry I, Hugh mentions only the two abbots who were forced by the pope at Reims to accept submission to Rouen (*HF*, 15:961–962).

perform the ceremony.[443] It seems likely that Hugh's duties for the pope conveniently kept him out of the duchy at a time when his refusal to bow to the king's wishes would have precipitated conflict.

Hugh's absences eventually annoyed the king, for in 1135 Henry again wrote to the pope, this time to complain about the long delay of his archbishop outside the realm and to lament the resulting detriment to the Church of Rouen.[444] Henry may by this time have heard that Innocent had ordered the consecration of Richard to the see of Bayeux and the king may have wanted speedy action. Chroniclers also note that Henry had been hoping to return to England, in which case he would have required the archbishop of Rouen in place as one of his mainstays of government in Normandy. As it happened, Henry did not return to England. The archbishop duly consecrated Richard III bishop of Bayeux, then attended to another, more somber duty when the king urgently called him to his side at Lyons-la-Forêt.

Henry's actions in the ecclesiastical sphere were undoubtedly influenced by political as well as religious considerations. The very symbiosis of ecclesiastical and secular political authorities shows the elite of Anglo-Norman society as participants in one inchoate civil service. The juxtaposition of ecclesiastical culture, which debated and largely determined the ethics and aesthetics of the age, and high secular politics linked the sacred and the profane, the commentators and the actors, in a long-term relationship with inevitable tension. It is perhaps unhelpful to speak unilaterally of "a prevailing climate of secular control" or a policy of "political manoeuvre."[445] It is more useful to take note of the importance of monasteries "dans la politique comme dans la piété."[446] The king was willing to patronize border foundations, for example, as islands of security in ill-defined borderlands. The free spirits of the spiritual world readily accepted what aid they felt to be consistent with their vocation. The church hierarchy shared both attitudes as the civilizing mission of the Church extended the areas under the control of the local bishop and the national Church.

If the measure of a good king is the support of the powerful, the maintenance of peace and order, and the dispensing of justice, then Henry's kingship meets the criteria. The reigns of William Rufus and Stephen of Blois show by contrast how remarkable and how fragile such

---

[443] OV, 6:428, 442. Richard appears in a charter of Henry I in 1135 (*RRAN* 2, no. 1909: for Savigny, at Caen) as "Richard son of the earl of Gloucester"; he obviously had not yet been consecrated.

[444] OV, 6:443.

[445] Herbert, "The Transformation of Hermitages," pp. 144, 142.

[446] Brooke, "Princes and Kings," p. 148, discussion following article, comment by Raymonde Foreville on the Anglo-Saxon kings.

an achievement could be. Henry I seems to have been particularly proud of his success in providing justice for his churchmen. As Ivo of Chartres once explained, concord between *le royaume et le sacerdoce* was essential to the security of human society.[447]

The *Regesta* and Round's *Calendar of Documents Preserved in France* contain numerous charters in which Henry I took it upon himself or was called on to resolve problems between monasteries,[448] between bishops and monasteries,[449] between monasteries and nobles,[450] and between bishops or monasteries and secular authorities.[451] This last category is particularly interesting, for we see the king controlling his high officials (even justiciars) as well as his lesser ones (huntsmen, for example). The phrases "to do full right by" and "to be resolved immediately" are as frequent as those guaranteeing the king's peace or royal protection. Many charters establish the jurisdiction of the courts of the abbots and bishops, ordering that the churchmen are not to be impleaded except in the royal court or that they are to be "free of all pleas." The repetition of such grants of jurisdiction and the restitution of rights or sums extracted by overzealous royal officials show the constancy of royal protection.[452]

The king whose judgment warranted recourse by other authorities was a king highly regarded in the Middle Ages. Few secular authorities in the early twelfth century merited this distinction. At least one incident, probably in 1130 or 1131, when Henry was at the peak of his power and repute, reveals the English monarch arranging a concord between the king of France, his longtime rival, and the archbishop of Tours, his longtime friend. The archbishopric of Tours lay as an island of French power surrounded by the county of Anjou. Moreover, the king of France also controlled (as abbot) the abbey of the canons of Saint-Martin at Tours. Thus Hildebert of Lavardin, bishop of Le Mans, acquired a difficult charge when he was elevated to Tours. A dispute between the archbishop and the king over the right to appoint canons

---

[447] *Lettres de Saint Ives*, p. 119, no. 61 (to Hugh archbishop of Lyons).

[448] E.g., Saint-Wandrille and Saint-Vigor, Cérisy, *RRAN* 2, no. 1210; Savigny and Saint-Etienne, Caen, ibid., nos 1183, 1215, and *GC*, 11:110, *Instrumenta*, no. 10; Fécamp and Saumur, *CDF*, nos 118, 119, and Fécamp and Saint-Taurin: *GC*, 11:127, *Instrumenta*, no. 4 (*an.* 1106).

[449] Saint-Evroul and Evreux, *RRAN* 2, no. 1700; St Augustine's and Lincoln, ibid., no. 1283; Peterborough and Lincoln, ibid., no. 1911.

[450] Gloucester, ibid., no. 1485; Troarn, ibid., nos 1200, 1570; Fécamp, *CDF*, nos 118, 119, 123; Mont-Saint-Michel, *RRAN* 2, no. 1422; Ramsey, ibid., nos 967, 1262 and 1293; Sées and Marmoutier, ibid., nos 1191–1192 (where Henry is called "the father and the brother of the church of Marmoutier"), 1429, 1548; Shaftesbury, ibid., no. 1347.

[451] Ibid., no. 1920a.

[452] See, e.g., *CDF*, no. 119, or *RRAN* 2, no. 1191.

at the cathedral, complicated by internal factions among the canons, resulted in an impasse lasting four years, during which the king appropriated a large portion of the archbishop's revenues. The affair is known only through a letter Hildebert wrote thanking Henry for his assistance in resolving the conflict and restoring the cathedral's revenues.[453]

Later in the reign Henry also mediated between Ulger bishop of Angers and Geoffrey count of Anjou (Henry's son-in-law), with the assistance of the papal legate Geoffrey and Hugh, the new archbishop of Tours. Apparently the bishop had suffered serious losses as a result of the count's castle-building, and the settlement stipulated that the count was to secure reparations for the bishop and, most remarkable, that the king of England would reimburse the bishop for losses "due to the count's aggressions."[454]

England at that time abounded with great riches.
—Report of canons of Laon, 1113 (*PL*, 156:973)

We will gratefully give large sums from our treasury.
—Henry I to Audoin, bishop of Evreux
(*Gallia Christiana* 11:574)

Opulentia thesaurorum infinita . . .
—Robert of Torigny (*GND*, 2:236–237)

The mention of Henry's use of funds from his famous treasury raises the question of the sources the king tapped for his benefactions. Of the simple grants of manors, churches, tithes, and woods as well as fairs, markets, or fishing and hunting rights, only the grants of manors diminished the royal demesne. But the king also granted an exceptional number of freedoms and liberties to his monastic houses, in particular freedom from tolls, customs, gelds, and work duties in addition to jurisdictional rights and freedoms. This sort of gift subtracted from the royal income and necessitated raising resources elsewhere to replace them. But what is most difficult to assess are the gifts that do not turn up in the charter evidence although they are mentioned, even

---

[453] *PL* 171:272 (Letters, book 2, ep. 46). It is possible that Suger, through whom Henry had been known to work, facilitated this resolution.
[454] *RRAN* 2, no. 1921a.

praised, by contemporaries. Most of Henry's contributions outside the Anglo-Norman realm fall into this category, as do his gifts to building funds for specific cathedrals and monasteries. Lucien Musset has commented on the tendency of royal families to assert themselves and to vaunt their powers by highly visible patronage of religious institutions. Within the realm, it was the nobles who were impressed and were often inspired to imitate royalty. Outside the realm, major contributions no doubt demonstrated to rival powers the resources available to the English king.[455] This reasoning perhaps explains the scope of Henry's benefactions as well as his seeming preference for "les sanctuaires de grande réputation."[456] Like Emma Mason, Musset stresses the element of prestige in royal patronage; moreover, he raises the question of royal rivalry in benefactions.

The rivalry between Henry I and Louis VI of France influenced the diplomatic history of the reign and colored Henry's relations with the other mighty vassals of the king of France: the counts of Blois and Anjou. Militarily, despite the cost, Henry I triumphed against all coalitions, maintaining his frontiers and his equality (only his son offered homage to the French king). Yet without hungering for territory, Henry seems to have thirsted for renown. His religious benefactions beyond the realm could thus be viewed as demonstrations of influence and wealth or, to use a modern conceit, as conspicuous piety. Because of the absence of dates for some important benefactions by Henry I and Louis VI, it is difficult to prove a competition in endowments between the two monarchs.[457] Yet Henry sometimes almost aggressively patronized institutions also noticed by the French king. Henry had many reasons for helping Cluny, but his donations and his protection must also have rewarded him with a certain international prestige, especially after Alfonso VI of Spain (d. 1109) ceased to send funds. Henry's charter of protection is undated, but it may well have been issued in the 1120s, when the triumphant king was back from Normandy and attending to the business of the realm—and when the abbey of Cluny was in particular need of support.

At that time local religious authorities had been challenging Abbot Pons, who was also facing serious internal problems. He asked for and received help from the pope, who restated Cluny's independence of local jurisdictions, and he solicited support from Louis VI, who in 1119

---

[455] Musset, "Le Mécenat des princes normands au XIe siècle," 2:121–134, esp. pp. 121–122, speaks of "une politique consciente du mécenat, envisagé comme un moyen d'étaler leur réussite à l'intérieur de leur état et d'affirmer leur prestige à l'extérieure." See also Mason, "Royal Monastic Patronage."

[456] Musset, "Le Mécenat des princes normands au XIe siècle," 2:131.

[457] This is a topic that requires much more research; Louis' benefactions were also praised by his biographers.

(just after his defeat by Henry I) issued his charter of protection. Louis confirmed the possessions of the abbey, stressing the right of the abbot to control all his priors. The king's only qualification had to do with royal fortresses on Cluny lands, which *castra* were undoubtedly crucial in Louis VI's attempts to control his mighty vassals. (At this point Louis was about to lose the fortress of Gisors to Henry I.) The strongholds were to remain the property of the French crown but never to pass into other lay hands.[458] Shortly after his defeat in Normandy and after the granting of the charter of protection to Cluny, the French king appealed to the pope at Reims to help him against Henry I. Ultimately, Henry triumphed here too, personally persuading Calixtus that he was neither the aggressor nor the malefactor.

Henry I was on good terms with Abbot Pons, who recognized the foundation of the abbey of Reading by sending the first prior and monks desired by the king. When for some reason Pons decided to resign his abbacy and make an unauthorized pilgrimage to Jerusalem, the new abbot, Peter the Venerable, quickly recognized the independent status of Henry's abbey. In 1125, however, Pons returned and tried to seize the abbey from Peter; at the same time, say contemporaries who believed in divine judgment, the vaulting over the nave of the new basilica collapsed. The abbey was thus in distress in many ways. Rushing to the rescue of Cluny in these difficult years would have earned Henry just the kind of gratitude that Peter the Venerable went out of his way to display from that time forward; in one pertinent instance the abbot singled out the kings of England and Spain as prominent donors but then rushed on to proclaim the English king as the special benefactor of Cluny.[459] The rapid rebuilding of the nave, by 1130, when the new basilica was dedicated, demonstrates that the abbey had an angel who could provide major funds without delay. The best that Louis VI could do in his later years was to exempt Cluny from a certain *péage* and make an exchange of churches with Saint-Martin des Champs.[460]

A similar comparison can be made in relation to Henry's patronage of a less exalted institution. In the 1120s Henry issued a charter granting an annual sum to the leper hospital of Le Grand Beaulieu in Chartres.[461] In 1135 he reissued the grant, replacing the original

---

[458] *Recueil des chartes de l'abbaye de Cluny*, 5: no. 3943; Luchaire, *Louis VI*, no. 276; Pignot, *L'Ordre de Cluny*, 3:28–29; *Bibliotheca cluniacensis*, col. 575.
[459] See n. 249, this chapter.
[460] Luchaire, *Louis VI*, nos 456 (1130; the *péage* at Montereau) and 523 (1133). The exchange with Saint-Martin des Champs led to the foundation of the Benedictine nunnery of Montmartre.
[461] See n. 231, above, this chapter. To be fair, the count of Blois was Henry's nephew and Anglo-Norman patronage at Chartres had precedents.

lost in a fire.[462] In contrast, Louis VI, technically the overlord of the count of Blois but in fact at a distinct disadvantage against the Blois–Champagne union, made but one (undated) minor grant to the same leper hospital.[463] And finally, if Henry I really was the master of the grand gesture, then one of the best examples of his spirit of rivalry is his patronage of the Cluniac abbey of Saint-Martin des Champs in Paris. Although the abbey had been founded (and refounded) by Louis' predecessors and although Peter the Venerable mentions Louis as a royal donor, Louis VI's series of confirmations is overshadowed by Peter's praise of the English king and Robert of Torigny's report of Henry's important contributions to the celebrated Parisian site of hospitality.[464]

This exhibition of political, religious, and financial influence also vaunted the fabled resources of England. The country's wealth in metals had been known from prehistoric times. The acquisition of England by William the Conqueror linked the best-organized province in France with a country already producing a solid and well-respected currency.[465] Anglo-Saxon England had been able to assess its landholders and peasants in the late tenth and eleventh centuries in order to raise large sums of money for tribute. The number of mints in England and the number of coins in circulation in the late eleventh and early twelfth centuries as well as coin hoards on the Continent are further evidence of the resources on which the Anglo-Normans could draw. It is probable that Henry's undocumented benefactions were gifts of gold or silver or even (as in the case of Henry of Winchester) gifts of objects of precious metal, embellished with precious stones.

Henry I himself learned the value of liquid assets even before he

---

[462] *RRAN* 2, no. 1917.

[463] Luchaire, *Louis VI*, p. 278, no. 630 (grant of two *muids* of flour from the oven at Dourdan).

[464] *GND*, 2:254–255, says, in a section on Henry's contributions to building programs, that the king did for Saint-Martin des Champs the same as he did for Cluny, especially noting the substantial possessions granted in England. Peter the Venerable, "De Miraculis," book 2, chap. 10, *PL* 189:921, in his biography of Matthew of Albano, former prior of Saint-Martin des Champs, says that Matthew visited the English king (as he did the French king), in search of funds, seldom returning empty-handed: "Hoc maxime jam nominatus magnus ille rex Henricus faciebat . . . ab eo obsequiis honoratus, ac donis regiis oneratus." The *nécrologie* of Saint-Martin des Champs has a marginal note for the date of commemoration of Henry I's death (2 December) indicating that Henry gave the monks one hundred shillings annually for offices to be said after his death (Wollasch, *Synopse der Cluniacensischen Necrologien*, 2:673n.).

[465] Sawyer, "The Wealth of England in the Eleventh Century," elaborates on this topic and suggests that France was cash poor (as was Cluny) at a time when England had a significant money element to its economy (pp. 156, 157).

came to the throne. He had inherited a fixed (and, in his eyes, inadequate) sum from the Conqueror with which to establish himself in Normandy. He received large sums from Rufus to help in the subjugation of Normandy. Perhaps the fragility of his hold on the lands he bought or received in reward for services taught him the value of a full treasury (the only characteristic regularly vilified—and exaggerated—by Henry's contemporaries). During Henry's reign the use of gold and silver is constantly reported. The number of times Henry is said to have bought decisions at the papal curia, or secured a position for a favorite (Gaudry at Laon, for example), or paved the way for an administrative change (such as buying the support of the bishop of Lincoln for the creation of the see of Ely) probably cannot be easily counted. William of Malmesbury reports that the French king, Louis VI, was "beguiled by the prospect of spoils" from Henry's abundant gold; the Malmesbury monk continues in the same chapter to note that with "money as the go-between on one side and family ties on the other" Henry also pacified Anjou.[466] Henry regularly carried funds from his treasury back and forth from England to Normandy.[467] The vast sum collected for Maud's dowry is a good example of his ability to raise money; despite protests, Henry's functioning exchequer was able to extract this and similar emergency funds on a number of occasions. The complaints of the Anglo-Saxon chronicler serve here to emphasize the king's success. Had we more pipe rolls for the reign of Henry I, we might be able to provide evidence for the dispensing of funds not generally reflected in documents. Recall the words of the *Anglo-Saxon Chronicle* for 1128 when the grand master of the Templars came to the king in Rouen to raise funds and is reported to have left laden with gold and silver; the reception in England was equally lucrative, the report again specifying gifts of gold and silver. The gifts Henry made to Innocent II in 1131 at Rouen mention monies from the Jews of Normandy. The vast sums sent to Burgundy by the king of Spain to finance St Hugh's magnificent dream are yet another example of transfers involving hard cash.

The existence of treasuries in cathedrals and monasteries emphasizes the prevalence of portable wealth;[468] reports of objects in gold and silver being liquidated on occasion to meet financial obligations suggest that

---

[466] WM, *GR*, 5:405.1 and 405.4.

[467] Haskins, *NI*, p. 113, citing for the year 1120 OV, 4:412, 419 (ed. Le Prévost) and for 1135 OV 5:50 and RT *Chron.*, 1:201. See also Symeon of Durham (*s.a.*) reporting on the gold and silver that Henry brought to Normandy in 1105/1106.

[468] Apparently some major towns also had treasuries, for Orderic (6:50) mentions that in 1103 Henry confiscated the treasure of King Magnus of Norway (£20,000 of silver) which the citizens of Lincoln had been holding (Magnus was killed attacking Ireland).

gifts in precious metals functioned as a kind of savings account. For example, when Henry of Winchester loaned the abbey of Cluny enough money to pay off its debts, he specifically demanded that the missing gold from the great cross he had given them be restored before the debt could be absolved. When Bishop Henry left England at the accession of Henry II he either had his own treasury smuggled out of the country or he took it himself. The numerous pirates of the Mediterranean (about which Hildebert of Lavardin, bishop of Le Mans, reported to the abbot of Cluny) and the notorious brigands on the roads of Europe testify to the riches carried to and fro.[469]

But had the English government been wealthy enough to finance itself without "taxes," says P. H. Sawyer, it would have done so. The monetary wealth of the country was not limitless.[470] Sawyer proposes Germany as a source of precious metal. The discovery of silver in the Harz Mountains of Saxony in the late tenth century intensified trade between England, the Low Countries, and the Holy Roman Empire. The prevalence of English mints on the east coasts of the country is a hint, Sawyer says, of this orientation. Economic regulations dating to the reign of Ethelred II and concerning the "men of Lorraine [that is, the empire]" confirm the suggestion that the fingers of English trade reached beyond the Low Countries to the Meuse, Rhine, and Elbe rivers. Maud's expensive marriage to the emperor makes good sense if such a connection furthered the acquisition of gold and silver. And Henry's own marriage to Adeliza of Louvain, in preference to a closer alliance with France, Anjou, or even Flanders, suggests that the route east of Flanders toward Germany was on the king's mind. That the emperor launched a diversionary attack on Louis VI in 1123 (to keep the French king from aiding Norman rebels) was probably a result of these connections.

In exchange for gold, silver, and precious stones as well as for other vital imports, such as wine, mail, furs, and cloth, the English exported the commodity that would soon make England famous:

[469] Dieudonné, *Hildebert de Lavardin*, pp. 186 ff., ep. 53. SD reports the 1123 council of Rome decrees against brigands who preyed on travelers and pilgrims to Rome. Emma Cownie, in her *Religious Patronage in Anglo-Norman England*, notes numerous instances of cash gifts to monasteries; see, e.g., pp. 51, 52, 75, 77. Eadmer says that Herbert of Losinga was "robbed" on his way to Rome with money to be used at the papal curia (*HN*, p. 133).

[470] Sawyer ("The Wealth of England in the Eleventh Century," p. 159) discusses the sources of English silver in Derbyshire, the Mendips, and Wales (from tribute and from mines) but notes the low silver content of English lead ore (although this lead was useful for other purposes, as, for example, the reroofing of the Chartres cathedral that Ivo of Chartres requested of Queen Matilda).

wool.[471] Economic records for the early twelfth century are scarce, but most economic historians agree that the boom in wool production in the late twelfth century must have had a history.[472] An example often cited is the ransom of Richard I with a sum said to have been worth the wool of six million sheep. Grain may also have been exchanged for imports, and evidence for tin, coal, and iron production suggests surpluses available for exchange. Around 1130 regulations were laid down for the men of Lorraine to trade in London.[473] The thirty years of peace and order that Henry brought to England and his administrative efficiency constitute ideal conditions for economic development, just as similar conditions promoted development in Flanders. Even the king's benefactions to religious institutions have an economic component: the income, the liberties and exemptions, the markets and fairs can only have contributed to the expansion of arable land and pasturage, the production of surplus, and the flow of goods.[474]

As Henry I once said to Boso of Bec, he intended to look after outside affairs for his Church as well as for his kingdom. In the eyes of Henry's contemporaries, he was an effective guardian of the Church. In his own eyes, perhaps, as he entered his sixty-third year, content to dawdle with his grandsons in Normandy, he might have reflected with pleasure on his achievement: the Church in capable hands, his religious flourishing, the royal abbey at Reading rivaling the celebrated hospitality centers of Europe, his relations with the papacy personal and amicable (on the king's terms), and his association with Cluny crowned by the dedication of the most magnificent basilica in Christendom. Perhaps Denis Bethell summed up Henry I's ecclesiastical policy best: "Henry knew exactly how to handle the Church; he always did the right thing."[475]

---

[471] When the canons of Laon paid a visit to England in 1113, they were accompanied by Flemish merchants who brought 300 marks of silver with them to purchase wool: see Sawyer, "The Wealth of England in the Eleventh Century," pp. 162–163, citing Hermann of Tournai, *De miraculis S. Mariae laudunensis, PL* 156:975–977.
[472] Vast flocks of sheep are reported in Domesday Book.
[473] Bautier, *Economic Development of Medieval Europe*, p. 96. In 1127 Henry had forbidden trade in wool with Flanders when he was at war with William Clito (Galbert, *Histoire*, pp. 140–141, 152).
[474] See Kealey, "Anglo-Norman Policy," *passim*, for Henry's "innovative steps to direct the national economy" (p. 343). Perhaps the king's grant of the right to cast lead to the Norman monastery of Longueville (see n. 259 above, this chapter) represents a very early grant of a monopoly.
[475] Personal communication: see Hollister, "William II, Henry I, and the Anglo-Norman Church," p. 119.

Chapter 11

FINAL YEARS AND CONCLUSION

Then King Henry, when everything was at peace in France, Flanders, Normandy, Brittany, Maine, and Anjou, returned joyfully to England.

—Henry of Huntingdon, p. 482.

A.D. 1129. King Henry . . . concluded a peace between himself and the king of the Franks; he received the earldom of Flanders; he also married his daughter, the ex-empress, to the earl of Anjou; his enemies on every side were either conquered or reconciled; prosperity everywhere smiled on him . . .

—Symeon of Durham, *s.a.*

By the beginning of his fourth decade of rule, in his early sixties, King Henry I had reason to feel content. At the peak of his royal power, the king had triumphed over adversity by sheer force of will, a combination of that "invincible spirit" lauded by William of Malmesbury and the "tremendous energy" noted by Orderic Vitalis.[1] The tragedy of the White Ship had demonstrated Henry's strength of character. Despite his initial collapse at the horrific news, despite the dashing of all his hopes for an undisputed succession by a legitimate male heir, the king stoically roused himself from his grief and pragmatically turned to work.[2] The 1120s and early 1130s were arguably the king's most serious and productive years. He remarried, prudently seeking another heir. He attended to his own soul and to those of family members, giving copiously to new and to favored monastic foundations where legions of

---

[1] WM, *GR*, ed. Mynors, book 3, preface [all *GR* references hereafter are to book and chapter in the Mynors edition]; OV, 6:100.

[2] Symeon of Durham (*s.a.* 1120) speaks of Henry's stoicism, which perhaps helps to explain Hildebert of Lavardin's letter to the king after the tragedy in which Hildebert urges the king not to bury his feelings lest he take them out on his followers (Dieudonné, *Hildebert de Lavardin*, pp. 210, 283; *PL* 171, Letters, book 1, no. 12).

monks and canons would pray for the king and the royal family.[3] It is probably in the 1120s that Henry and Roger of Salisbury oiled the machine that would produce the celebrated Pipe Roll of 1130. Where flagrant corruption or treason menaced the well-being of the realm, Henry took unaccustomed strong measures.[4] He vigorously fought off what proved to be the final challenges to his rule in Normandy, out-maneuvering rebellious nobles and using his considerable diplomatic talents to subvert the involvement of his continental neighbors. And after much soul-searching the king made the fateful decision to confer the Anglo-Norman succession on his daughter, the empress Maud. The ensuing discussion in the royal court, to which important individuals were summoned from England, Scotland, and Normandy, appears to have been a real debate. Despite differing opinions, the king's wishes prevailed, and all the prelates and barons took an oath administered by Roger of Salisbury ensuring England and Normandy to Maud and thereafter to any legitimate son she might bear.[5]

His throne secure after the death of William Clito in 1128, at peace with Louis VI of France, his candidate ruling Flanders,[6] and his headstrong daughter married to the vigorous young heir of the count of Anjou, Henry could finally look forward to resting on his laurels. He pardoned and released most of his political prisoners, except of course Robert Curthose, William of Mortain, and Robert of Bellême.[7]

---

[3] According to R. W. Southern ("King Henry I," in *Medieval Humanism*, pp. 232–233, citing Cambridge MS Ff. I 27), a Bec monk reported a vision in which he saw King Henry released from hell every evening as a result of the continuous prayers of monks. Peter the Venerable's biographer Ralph reports that Henry appeared to one of his knights to ask him to urge the monks to continue their efficacious prayers (see chapter 10 above, n. 325). Henry seems to have given the monks of Saint-Martin des Champs 100 *solidi* annually to be remembered in their prayers: Wollasch, *Synopse der Cluniacensischen Necrologien*, 2, for 2 December (Saint-Martin des Champs).

[4] *Gesta Stephani*, p. 11. See Hollister, "Royal Acts of Mutilation: The Case against Henry I," *MMI*, pp. 291–301.

[5] The inclusion of Normandy in the succession buttresses the argument for Henry's rule over a true Anglo-Norman realm. See "The Anglo-Norman Succession Debate of 1126," *MMI*, pp. 145–169. The oaths to Maud were repeated at two later dates, once in 1131 at Northampton (WM, *HN*, chap. 455) and (perhaps) once in 1133 after the birth of Maud and Geoffrey's son Henry (see Roger of Hoveden, *Chronica*, 1:186–187).

[6] On Flanders see SD, *s.a.* 1128 (who makes Henry the heir of Clito, with the favor of the French king, and says that Henry then gave the county to Thierry of Alsace); HH, pp. 481–482 (who says only that Thierry of Alsace received Henry I's support); and above, chapter 7, nn. 154, 179, 180.

[7] Robert I de Stuteville was also imprisoned for life; see above, p. 205 and n. 4. Curthose died in 1134 and Robert of Bellême disappears from records around 1130. Unfortunately for Henry, Robert of Bellême's son, William Talvas, count of Ponthieu, survived and for a time carried on his father's tradition of rebellion against the English king. Hugh de Montfort was also kept in prison into Stephen's reign.

The wheel of fortune, which had raised the king to its apex in 1119 only to cast him down a short year later, now ground slowly but surely upward again in reward for the king's labors. The landless young prince, once assured by his father that he too would be a king, easily exceeded his brothers in riches and power.[8]

In September 1130, after a flurry of episcopal and abbatial appointments in England,[9] Henry took ship at Portsmouth for Normandy in the company of Hugh abbot of Reading, recently elected to the archiepiscopal see of Rouen. The voyage must have felt unusual, for the king was crossing the sea without a sense of urgency or menace. John of Worcester associates the crossing with the appearance of a shining comet in the night sky.[10] Unpressed, the royal party made a detour down the Risle Valley to the abbey of Bec,[11] perhaps to visit the ailing Boso, whom Bec writers describe as a firm favorite of the king.[12] Then Henry moved on to Rouen, where the consecration of Hugh took place—we can only guess that as an interested party the king was present, but no chronicler expressly mentions him. Some time thereafter Henry "entertained" his nephew Theobald of Blois at Vernon-sur-Seine, in the Norman Vexin.[13]

The high point of this sojourn in Normandy—perhaps the high point of the reign—took place in early January 1131, when the king traveled to Chartres to meet and recognize the exiled Innocent II as the true pope of the Western Church. According to Orderic, Henry knelt humbly at the pontiff's feet and paid him the reverence due the vicar of Christ, then bestowed many gifts on the papal entourage.[14] The pope had recently stopped at Cluny, where he was hailed and welcomed by Peter the Venerable and where he received assurance of the support of the Cluniacs in Western Europe. While at Cluny, the pope had participated in the dedication of the new basilica that Henry of England had helped to finance. Abbot Peter himself had just returned from a visit to England, where with royal permission he had made an extended

---

[8] RT, *Chron.*, *s.a.* 1106 and 1087; WM, *GR*, 5:390.
[9] Hugh of Reading to Rouen, Henry of Blois to Winchester, Roger (nephew of Geoffrey Clinton) to Chester, and Robert to Hereford; Ansger to Reading, Ingulf to Abingdon, Walter to Gloucester, and Serlo to Cirencester.
[10] JW, p. 31 n. 4.
[11] Farrer, *Itin.*, p. 133; annals of Waverley, *Annales monastici*, 2:222.
[12] "Life of Boso," in Vaughn, *Abbey of Bec*, p. 130.
[13] Farrer, *Itin.*, p. 133.
[14] OV, 6:420; also WM, *HN*, chap. 454.

tour of inspection preparatory to the grand synod of priors and abbots he had called for 1132.[15]

The visit to Chartres, capital of the county of Blois, where Henry's nephew Theobald ruled, was a luxury Henry had previously been unable to afford. Orderic says he stayed in the episcopal city a number of days, "to the delight of the French and the Romans."[16] We know of this meeting of distinguished rulers because while in Chartres Henry made a grant to the celebrated Angevin abbey of Fontevrault. Founded by Robert d'Arbrissel some thirty years earlier as part of a growing monastic reform movement, the monastery was established primarily for nuns but included a community of priests and monks to support the women.[17] Henry had already made a grant to the community in 1129,[18] probably just after Maud's marriage to Geoffrey of Anjou. William Adelin's widow, Geoffrey's sister and daughter of the count of Anjou, had chosen to become a nun at Fontevrault after her father had demanded her return from Henry's court in England. The king's 1131 grant appears to have doubled the annual sum delegated to Fontevrault from the English farms of London and Winchester, making the total one hundred marks of silver, sixty from London and forty from Winchester. The grant was confirmed at Henry's entreaty by Pope Innocent.[19]

A few months later, in May 1131, the pope honored Henry with a visit to Rouen. The papal entourage included the archbishop of Tarragona, Bernard abbot of Clairvaux,[20] Suger abbot of Saint-Denis, Geoffrey bishop of Chartres, and Boso abbot of SS. Sergius and Bacchus of Angers. The king, surrounded by his *fideles*—in particular Hugh archbishop of Rouen, his son Robert of Gloucester, the bishops John of Lisieux and John of Sées, William of Warenne, Ralph *de Sigillo*,

---

[15] Peter probably visited the king's nephew, the new bishop of Winchester, Henry of Blois, former monk of Cluny, to discuss plans for the reform of finances. See Van den Eynde, "Voyages," pp. 87 n. 166, 88, and *Letters of Peter the Venerable*, 1: no. 49.

[16] OV, 6:420.

[17] Robert of Arbrissel was a former colleague of Bernard of Tiron and Vital of Savigny, both of whom Henry I patronized, before the three hermits went their separate ways toward reforming monastic life. Many noble women were attracted to the community of Fontevrault (Henry's natural daughter Juliana [OV, 6:278] and his daughter-in-law Matilda, for instance), as they were to Marcigny, where Henry's sister Adela of Blois had retired.

[18] *RRAN* 2, nos 1580, 1581, at Rouen.

[19] Ibid., 2, no. 1687.

[20] Bernard had earlier written to Henry to encourage his support of Innocent II: Dieudonné, *Hildebert de Lavardin*, pp. 107–108; see also *HF*, 15:558, no. 19 (perhaps the letter Dieudonné cites; a letter from St Bernard to Henry I, written after Henry had given his support to Innocent II, requesting further assistance).

the chamberlain Rabel de Tancarville, the treasurer Nigel, and the king's confessor Adelulf of Nostell—used the occasion of this glittering international assembly to make his final grant to the abbey of Cluny, allocating one hundred pounds annually and in perpetuity to demonstrate his continuing interest in the new basilica. The empress Maud also signed this grant, possibly as part of Henry's effort to associate his daughter with his rule.[21] We cannot firmly date the concord that Henry arranged between the archbishop of Tours and the king of France, but the peace between France and England and the prestige Henry had earned in 1131 make this period ideal for such mediation.[22]

Henry seems to have remained in or near Rouen until June 1131, when he traveled north to Arques and Dieppe to take ship for England. A number of charters can definitely be attributed to this spring, in particular a confirmation to the oft-favored abbey of Bec as well as a formal charter approving the establishment of canons regular at the bishopric of Sées and the gift of a fee to the bishop.[23] The king then crossed to England, apparently in the company of the queen and his daughter Maud.[24] The party encountered such rough weather at sea that the king vowed, should they all survive, to collect no danegeld for seven years and to make a pilgrimage to the East Anglian abbey of Bury St Edmunds where reposed the relics of the martyred Anglo-Saxon king.[25] The presence of the royal family, in particular the king's heir Maud and possibly his favorite son Robert of Gloucester, no doubt accounts for the king's desperate plea to God. John of Worcester says the king duly fulfilled his vow.[26]

---

[21] *RRAN* 2, no. 1691; confirmed at Northampton a few months later, ibid., no. 1713. Maud also confirmed the Fontevrault grant, twice, once after 1129 (ibid., no. 1581) and later when she was Lady of the English: *RRAN* 3, no. 328. See Chibnall, *Empress Matilda*, pp. 58–59.

[22] See above, chapter 10, pp. 450–451 and nn. 453 and 475; Dieudonné, *Hildebert de Lavardin*, dates the concord between 1129 and 1131 (pp. 104–105).

[23] In 1131 the king made a grant to the bishop of Sées at Rouen (*RRAN* 2, no. 1688) and another to the bishop of Evreux at Vaudreuil (ibid., no. 1700); he also appointed Bernard as abbot of Mont-Saint-Michel (Farrer, *Itin.*, p. 136). He issued a general confirmation for Bec and Beaumont-le-Roger (*RRAN* 2, no. 1693), confirmed the installation of the canons at Sées (ibid., no. 1698), and granted a fee to the same church (Farrer, *Itin.*, no. 639). Sées would later be joined by the see of Carlisle, created in 1133, as the only two bishoprics served by a house of canons.

[24] Queen Adeliza signs or witnesses a number of charters during Henry's many visits abroad (e.g., Farrer, *Itin.*, no. 644 [1129–1135]). Maud may have arrived in Normandy as early as 1129 (SD, *s.a.* 1129); no chronicler places her specifically on the boat with Henry, although Henry of Huntingdon (p. 487) says that she returned with the king. JW, p. 33, says the king returned "cum regali curia."

[25] JW, pp. 33–34.

[26] The king was definitely at Bury in these years: *RRAN* 2, no. 1733, and Farrer, *Itin.*, no. 668.

Anselm abbot of Bury, nephew of the late archbishop Anselm, was well known to Henry. A legate to England in 1115 and 1116, he had spent three years in Normandy with the king when the threat of a coalition of powerful neighbors kept Henry preoccupied. The king was obviously unwilling to allow the legate into England unsupervised (if at all). From the time of Anselm's election as abbot of Bury in 1121, however, he enjoyed exceptional favor from the king, even though he once publicly protested the low status accorded abbots at royal councils.[27] Between 1121 and 1135 at least thirteen charters guarantee the rights, customs, and liberties of the abbot and the monks of St Edmunds. In addition, Henry wrote a personal letter to Abbot Anselm in the early 1120s (perhaps 1122) begging him not to go abroad, as his monks and the abbey's knights could not spare him.[28] Instead, in 1123, Anselm was sent to Rome with the new archbishop of Canterbury, William of Corbeil, and Bernard of St David's, Seffrid of Glastonbury, John the archdeacon of Canterbury, and a royal chaplain to secure the pallium for William of Corbeil and perhaps to defend his "election."[29] Anselm was one of the earliest to promote the cult of the Blessed Virgin, which Henry himself favored at Reading.[30] During Anselm's rule at Bury he found the means to develop the library into a first-rate collection, and, as David Knowles noted, under royal protection the already rich abbey was guaranteed steady growth.[31]

The principal royal action that attracted the notice of the chroniclers in 1131 was Henry's royal council at Northampton in September. There Henry and his notables discussed the question of the separation of Maud and her husband Geoffrey. Maud seems to have left Anjou and arrived in Rouen as early as 1129, but not until 1131 did Geoffrey ask for her return and offer suitable escort.[32] The king and council sent the empress back to her husband that fall, but not before Henry secured a second oath in support of Maud as his successor.[33] At this

---

[27] See JW, p. 27, and Chibnall, *Empress Matilda*, p. 52, for Anselm's protest at the Westminster council when oaths were sworn to support the succession of the empress Maud.

[28] E.g., *RRAN* 2, no. 1812. Anselm may have proposed a pilgrimage to St James of Compostela (ibid., no. 1340).

[29] *ASC*, s.a. 1123. The group is clearly a Canterbury-royal coalition of emissaries: Bernard of St David's often represented Henry; Seffrid of Glastonbury was the half-brother of Archbishop Ralph d'Escures and future bishop of Chichester; John the archdeacon was the nephew of Archbishop Ralph and future bishop of Rochester, appointed by William of Corbeil.

[30] See above, p. 438.

[31] Knowles, *Monastic Order*, p. 186. *RRAN*, no. 1933.

[32] *HH*, p. 486. See Chibnall, *Empress Matilda*, pp. 57–58.

[33] *WM*, *HN*, chap. 455.

council the king also granted Roger of Salisbury the abbey of Malmesbury and William of Corbeil and Canterbury the church of St Martin
at Dover.[34] The king then spent Christmas at Dunstable.

The year 1132 is little reported in the sources, where royal actions
are few and far between. The king spent Easter at Woodstock, then
moved on to Westminster, where he held a great court and considered
the dispute between the bishops of St David's and Llandaff,[35] and
finished the year at Windsor, his favorite residence. The Anglo-Saxon
chronicler reports joyously that in that year King Henry finally
recognized the error in his appointment of his kinsman Henry
d'Angély to the abbey of Peterborough and sent the scheming abbot
away.[36] The only firmly datable charters for the year are a grant of
warren to the priory of Bermondsey,[37] a per diem grant (made
at Marden) to the hospital at Falaise,[38] and the grant of a manor to
Alexander of Lincoln.[39]

In 1133, before Henry's departure for Normandy, he was at pains
to settle a great deal of important unfinished business. Within a period
of about two months, the king ended a five-year vacancy in the see of
Durham by appointing as bishop his own chancellor, Geoffrey Rufus;
he appointed his treasurer, Nigel, to the see of Ely, vacant since 1131;
he created a new bishopric at Carlisle and appointed as the first bishop
his Augustinian confessor, Adelulf prior of Nostell.[40] At the same time
he reestablished the office of master chamberlain of England after
a lapse of twenty-seven years.[41] He also granted lands and privileges
to Reading, Ramsey, Whitby, Chertsey, St Augustine's, Canterbury,
and Cirencester, to the bishoprics of York, Bath, Chichester, and
Lincoln, to the canons of Nostell, Ipswich, Holy Trinity, Aldgate, and
St Mary's, Portchester, and to the hospital of St John at Falaise.[42] He
assented to the founding of Missenden Abbey, protected the burial
rights of London churches against the claims of St Paul's Cathedral,

---

[34] Farrer, *Itin.*, nos 655, 660; *RRAN* 2, nos 1715, 1736. These grants could also
be rewards for supporting the succession of Maud.

[35] Farrer, *Itin.*, p. 143; HH, p. 488.

[36] See *ASC, s.a.* 1127, 1130, 1131, 1132.

[37] Farrer, *Itin.*, no. 676; *RRAN* 2, no. 1743.

[38] Farrer, *Itin.*, no. 677; *RRAN* 2, no. 1742.

[39] Farrer, *Itin.*, no. 678; *RRAN* 2, no. 1746.

[40] HH, p. 488; RT, *Chron., s.a.* 1133.

[41] *RRAN* 2, no. 1777; Farrer, *Itin.*, no. 698.

[42] *RRAN* 2, nos 1757 and 1789 (Reading); 1766 and 1788 (Ramsey); 1767
(Whitby); 1768 and 1781 (Chertsey); 1779 (St Augustine's); 1782 (Cirencester);
1759 (York Minster); 1762–1763 (Bath); 1769 (Chichester); 1770–1773, 1773,
1784, 1791–1792 (Lincoln); 1775 (Nostell); 1783 (Ipswich); 1785–1786 and 1792
(Aldgate); 1787 (Portchester); 1764 and Farrer, *Itin.*, no. 697 (Falaise); see also
n. 38 above, this chapter.

and confirmed the lands of his new master chamberlain, Aubrey de Vere, as well as those of Gilbert Chaylot of Chichester.[43] The evidence strongly suggests that this whirlwind of appointments, benefactions, and confirmations, some of them relating to matters of major importance, occurred during June and July 1133, just before Henry's Channel crossing in early August.

The departure of the king for Normandy was accompanied by a frightening eclipse of the sun and an earthquake, which caused great commotion in the seaports. With hindsight, the chroniclers were quick to seize on the significance of the king's departure when it turned out that this was Henry's final crossing and when it was discovered to have taken place on the very same day as his consecration in the year 1100.[44] In the autumn the king spent time at Rouen, where he issued a confirmation for Bec,[45] and Bayeux, where he probably ordered Robert of Gloucester to conduct an inquest into the fees belonging to the vacant cathedral of Bayeux. Haskins calls this feudal inquest of the bishop of Bayeux's rights and possessions from the time of Bishop Odo "the earliest detailed account . . . of the tenants and obligations of a great Norman fief."[46]

Orderic Vitalis describes the year 1134 in frightening detail as one of continuous natural disasters, including much loss of life from heat, wind, snow, floods, lightning, and fires (at Le Mans, Chartres, Alençon, Nogent, and Verneuil).[47] According to Henry of Huntingdon, however, the king spent much time at Rouen rejoicing in his grandsons, Henry, who had been born in March 1133 in Le Mans, and Geoffrey, who was born in May 1134, apparently at Rouen. Despite the joy of two strapping grandsons, however, Henry almost lost his daughter. Maud sickened immediately after childbirth, and for a while all despaired of her life. Robert of Torigny reports that she nonetheless had the energy to debate with her father about the place of her burial. She preferred Bec, while Henry argued for Rouen.[48] In the event, Maud recovered, saving Henry the anguish of finding himself with only infants to succeed him, and the king and his daughter agreed that she

---

[43] *RRAN* 2, nos 1765, 1774, 1778, 1780.
[44] JW, p. 37.
[45] Farrer, *Itin.*, no. 715.
[46] *RRAN* 2, nos 1893–1894, and Farrer, *Itin.*, no. 716 (dated 1134); Haskins, *NI*, pp. 15 ff. See *HF*, 23:699–702, and *Mémoires de la Société des Antiquaires de Normandie* (Caen, 1824–), 8:425–431, for printed versions of the inquest. See also Gleason, *Ecclesiastical Barony*, pp. 23–27, 41, which discusses the state of the bishopric and the role of Robert of Gloucester in despoiling it; Gleason argues that Henry I was concerned to establish his own rights at Bayeux through the inquest (pp. 42–44).
[47] OV, 6:434–436.
[48] RT, *Chron.*, *s.a.* (p. 193).

would eventually be buried at Bec. Perhaps this decision, if the debate actually took place, freed the king to plan his own burial at Reading.

A series of charters dated 1134 at Rouen confirm Henry's long stay there.[49] The king's movements during the rest of the year include a visit in April to Mortemer, in the forest near Lyons-la-Forêt, where he installed a colony of monks,[50] and perhaps a visit to Aumale, not too far to the northeast.[51] Visits to Verneuil in the southeast and to Falaise, Argentan, and Sées on the southwestern frontier all probably belong to 1135, when Henry spent the fall *in expeditione* because of the hostile activities of Geoffrey of Anjou and William Talvas.

Henry's plan for 1135 was to return to England. Three times he made preparations for his departure,[52] but events intervened. Angry that Archbishop Hugh of Rouen had not returned to the duchy after attending a papal council at Pisa, the king wrote a strong letter insisting that Hugh return to his cathedral and his duties.[53] (Henry may not have felt free to leave the duchy without the archbishop in place to act with the curial bishops John of Lisieux, Audoin of Evreux, and John of Sées as his regents.) Recent popes had coopted many a talented churchman, especially Cluniacs, for papal service,[54] and Innocent too had a sharp eye for a good administrator. Hugh himself may have been loath to return because he was opposed to the appointment of the proposed bishop of Bayeux, Richard, Henry's grandson, the bastard son of Robert of Gloucester. Eventually the pope sent orders for Hugh to consecrate Richard, "out of fear of the king," says Orderic.[55]

Until the fall, Henry seems to have remained in the north. A charter to the Savignac abbey of Vignats (Saint-André-en-Gouffern) is dated at

---

[49] Charters in favor of the church of Coutances (*RRAN* 2, no. 1902; Farrer, *Itin.*, no. 720; the empress Maud attests as well as other important members of the *curia*), Bec (Farrer, *Itin.*, no. 723), the bishop of Evreux (ibid., no. 722), the bishop of Lincoln (ibid., no. 717), who had come to Rouen during the year regarding a dispute with the abbey of Peterborough (ibid., no. 721 and note on p. 151).

[50] See above, chapter 10, pp. 404–405.

[51] *RRAN* 2, nos 1903 and 1904 n.

[52] OV, 6:444.

[53] Hébert, "Hugues III d'Amiens," p. 334. OV, 6:442. See above, chapter 10, pp. 448–449.

[54] See chapter 10, pp. 444–446, for a discussion of Hugh's earlier summons by Honorius II.

[55] OV, 6:442. Earlier when Innocent II ordered Hugh to temper his reform efforts, he argued for a certain deference to the power and justice of secular authority, which protected all Christians (*HF*, 15:378). Peter the Venerable wrote to the same pope in Hugh's behalf to ask for such assistance as would render to Caesar the things that belong to Caesar and to God the things that belong to God, in order to offend neither God nor the royal majesty (*Letters of Peter the Venerable*, 1: no. 17).

Caen.[56] A confirmation of the gift of Barnstaple to the Cluniac abbey of Saint-Martin des Champs in Paris is dated at Perriers-sur-Andelle,[57] near the forest of Lyons, although this document could also have been issued in November when the king arrived to hunt in the forest, just prior to his death. The most significant Norman ordinance of the reign dates from Henry's final year, 1135, and was issued at Rouen, probably before mid-year.[58] This great ordinance on the Peace and Truce of God in Normandy, issued formally by the *rex Anglorum* in council, continued Henry's centralizing process by augmenting the role of the royal court in the enforcement of the Truce of God.[59]

According to the chroniclers, the principal reason for Henry's delay in Normandy in 1135 was his growing estrangement from Maud and Geoffrey of Anjou. Although Henry's contemporaries are eager to blame Maud,[60] whose temper often irritated people, it is more likely that the friction arose from Geoffrey's demand that Henry hand over the frontier castles promised in Maud's dowry. Henry's refusal and Geoffrey's belligerence made it impossible for the king to leave the duchy. In addition, the king, whose intelligence systems always functioned well, grew suspicious of some of his marcher lords, in particular William Talvas count of Ponthieu, the heir of Robert of Bellême to whom Henry had generously restored most of his patrimony, and Roger of Tosny. Henry acted quickly, preemptively: he garrisoned Roger of Tosny's castle at Conches, and when Talvas refused royal summonses to court to respond to the king's suspicions he was disseised of all his possessions. Talvas responded by going over to Geoffrey of Anjou in September.[61] For almost four months, from August to November, reports Orderic, Henry "prowled" the southern frontier. He took Alençon and Almenesches and he enlarged the castle at Argentan. Then, as winter approached, his defenses strengthened, Henry retired to Lyons-la-Forêt in late November to hunt. As the most graphic story goes, the king regaled himself with a serving of lampreys, disobeying his

---

[56] Farrer, *Itin.*, no. 733; *RRAN* 2, no. 1909.

[57] Farrer, *Itin.*, no. 735; *RRAN* 2, no. 1912.

[58] *RRAN* 2, no 1908.

[59] According to Haskins (*NI*, p. 104), from the time of the council of Lillebonne (1080) the role of the ducal courts in the enforcement of the Truce of God had been growing. In the great ordinance Henry I fixed the fines for bishops; whatever else was appropriated from violators of the truce went to the king, in whose court the duel was to be held and whose justices collected the fine. Fittingly, the Truce of God thus became part of Henry's peace.

[60] HH, pp. 490–491, 738.

[61] OV, 6:446.

physician's orders, suffered an attack of some sort, and died within the week.[62]

Henry's unexpected death on 1 December was a great shock.[63] A man of great vigor and energy, he had scarcely ever been sick. Henry of Huntingdon is the only writer to remark casually that at Christmas 1132 the king was ill at Windsor.[64] The nature of the illness is not mentioned, and the king's hectic activity in England in early 1133 gives no indication that he might have been suffering from a serious ailment. Nor can we suspect mental distress. The king's bad dreams in 1131, reported by John of Worcester as told by the royal physician to the abbot of Winchcombe,[65] are certainly dramatic—in fact, too dramatic—but, like other chroniclers' magnification of events into portents after the fact, they bear the mark of hindsight. John, for instance, placed the tale of the three dreams just before his account of the king's difficult crossing to England: "It so happened after this [the dreams] that the king took ship for England. And lo . . ." After the dreams and the dangerous crossing comes a fantastical tale of a German nobleman and his daughter, undermining the credibility of the preceding incidents.

John of Worcester's original chronicle ended about 1128–1130, but in the late 1130s, after the death of Henry I, he revised and continued the work. The dreams were inserted at this later date (probably about 1139), along with other "marvelous" events, reflecting the Worcester chronicler's aim of edifying, perhaps even amusing his readers.[66] The description of King Henry's three dreams, one by one, is vivid. Representatives of the three orders of society—those who worked, those who fought, and those who prayed—appear, armed with appropriate weapons, sequentially in three separate royal nightmares. The king bolts out of bed—frightening away his guards and servants—to seize his ready sword or to call for help. This makes a wonderful story, which John enhances theatrically with editorial comments ("O qualis regia dignitas"), asides to the reader ("Had you been there . . . you might guess . . ."), direct address to the king ("Cease, king, cease . . ."), and the royal cries for help (no one comes!). Clearly the story was meant to be recounted aloud and to be visualized ("The king woke from his sleep terrified, leapt from

---

[62] HH, p. 490. Henry of Huntingdon is the first to mention the famous "surfeit of lampreys."

[63] Certainly neither Geoffrey nor Maud expected the king's demise, or they would not have risked war.

[64] HH, p. 489, echoed in the annals of Waverley (*Annales monastici*, 2:223).

[65] JW, pp. 32–33.

[66] Gransden, *Historical Writing*, p. 147.

his bed, his feet probably bare, to seize his arms . . ."). We can only imagine how the tale improved with repetition.

The intended audience was obviously churchmen, for the bishops, abbots, and priors are the only spirits who give a reason for their nocturnal visit: *ceu perquirentes res aecclesiae spoliatas.* Historians have always assumed that Henry was the despoiler of churches, but all the evidence is to the contrary. Many of Henry's charters show the king *restoring* possessions and funds expropriated or extorted from bishops and abbots.[67] Despite the best efforts of the best organized king of his age, local magnates and royal officials required constant supervision.

This is not to say that Henry did not suffer a nightmare.[68] But to search for deep subconscious causes is to stray from history into psychology. Henry was a practical man, a thoroughly modern monarch of his times; nothing in his comportment in the years after 1131 suggests that he was in fear for his soul or his life. His actions and their quality, his benefactions, his campaigns, even his hunting are all activities typical of other periods in his reign. Even the disregarding of his doctor's advice and the overindulgence in lampreys was probably not unprecedented.

Stephanie Mooers Christelow has charted the activities of King Henry year by year, showing that royal productivity diminished in the last years of the king's life.[69] Certainly the king was most active in his middle years and particularly after frontier challenges in Normandy had been met; in the year 1121, for example, he issued the greatest number of charters (90) of any year in the reign. The last two years of Henry's rule do in fact produce the fewest number of royal acts, but the years 1130–1135 overall compare favorably in both quantity and quality with other five-year clusters during Henry's reign. Some 228 charters were issued in this six-year period, a total representing 15.3 percent of the king's acts (only the years 1100–1104 exceed this, at 17 percent). Even if we deduct the 11 charters for the king's last year to reduce the period to five years, the percentage still remains

---

[67] For example, Farrer, *Itin.*, no. 666; chap. 10, above, nn. 184–185; *RRAN* 2, nos 522, 566, 576, 600, 694, 736, 807, 842, 997, 1038, 1142, 1186, 1239, 1409, 1411, 1416, 1422, 1510, 1637, 1662, 1682, 1689, 1775, 1803, 1853, 1902, 1962, among *many* others.

[68] Apparently Henry suffered at least two reported nightmares in thirty-five years. In an earlier dream the king was attacked by a lion and rescued by the prior of Bermondsey; see Barlow, *English Church, 1066–1154*, p. 91 n. 164 (citing Bermondsey annals, *Annales monastici*, 3:432).

[69] Christelow, "A Moveable Feast," pp. 187–228; see in particular table A, pp. 194–195.

roughly equal to that for other five-year periods (surpassing the low count for 1115–1119 and falling below the high count for 1100–1104).

Those royal charters that can be accurately dated I have mentioned in the above narrative of the king's final years. But many others can be placed only generally in these last years of the king's life. Since the king and his council or court often made decisions about Normandy while sitting in England (and the reverse), it is easier and just as informative to lump together Henry's charters for these final years in order to get a glimpse of the king's concerns throughout the realm. The king's attention generally fell first on vacant abbeys and sees. In the 1130s Henry made appointments or approved election to the abbeys of Gloucester (1130), Reading (1130), Abingdon (1130), his completed foundation at Cirencester (1130), Mont-Saint-Michel (1131), and Bardney (1134). He filled the archbishopric of Rouen in 1130 and installed canons at the bishopric of Sées in the same year.[70] He appointed bishops to Chester (1129/1130), Hereford (1130/1131), Ely (1133), Durham (1133), and Bath (1133 or 1134, via Henry of Winchester). In 1133 Henry established the new see of Carlisle and appointed his Augustinian confessor Adelulf of Nostell as the new bishop. In 1133 or 1134 Henry ordered an inquest into the holdings of the canons of the see of Bayeux,[71] preparatory to giving the see to his grandson Richard, the son of Robert of Gloucester.[72] At the same time he gave the see of Avranches to another royal chaplain, Robert of Beaufour.[73] A lover of new buildings, in 1130 the king attended the dedication of the new cathedrals at Canterbury and Rochester, and in 1133 he no doubt rejoiced in the completion of the abbey of Cirencester.[74]

Royal gifts and confirmations in England and Normandy during these years show once more the breadth of the king's largesse. Henry recognized the canons at the royal foundations of Holy Trinity, Aldgate, St Bartholomew's in London, Cirencester, Dunstable, and St Mary, Portchester, and noticed as well Augustinian houses at Braemore, Bruton, Colchester, Ipswich, and Guisborough (Yorks.).[75] He also

---

[70] For Sées see this chapter, n. 23 above.

[71] *RRAN* 2, no. 1893, and Farrer, *Itin.*, no. 716.

[72] OV, 6:429

[73] Ibid.

[74] HH, p. 487; FW, *s.a.* 1130; *RRAN* 2, no. 1728; *ASC, s.a.* 1130; Dickinson, *Origins of the Austin Canons*, p. 119.

[75] Farrer, *Itin.*, nos 1784 and 1768 (Holy Trinity), 682 and 683 (St Bartholomew's), 704 (Cirencester), 707 (Portchester; later Southwick), 689 (Braemore), 646 (Bruton), 667 (Colchester), 709 (Ipswich), 642 (Guisborough); *RRAN* 2, nos 1826–1827 (Dunstable; prob. 1131–1133).

confirmed the foundation of a new house of canons at Missenden (Bucks.), the new Cistercian foundation of Rievaulx, and a daughter house of Rievaulx at Garendon.[76] A gift to the hospital at Falaise has been noted above, in addition to which the king also made a grant to the leper hospital of Le Grand Beaulieu at Chartres and renewed the annual rent late in his life after the charter disappeared in a fire.[77] The traditional monastic establishments were not neglected. Henry remembered the nuns at Sainte-Marie Villers-Canivet, St Mary, Wikes (or Wix), Elstow, and Holy Trinity, Caen.[78] He confirmed grants to Cluny, to his Cluniac monks at Reading, and to those of Saint-Martin des Champs at Barnstaple.[79] Grants, confirmations, and settlements also exist for the important foundations at Bec and Envermeu, Fécamp, Montébourg, Conches, Saint-Georges de Boscherville, Troarn, Sées, Saint-Wandrille, Savigny, and Tiron in Normandy, Saint-Père de Chartres in Blois, and Westminster, Battle, St Augustine's, Canterbury, Chertsey, Hyde, St Peter's, Bath, Thorney, and Ramsey in England.[80] In the last decade of his life the king, as mentioned, singled out for patronage Bury St Edmunds and Abbot Anselm, almost as he had earlier favored Faritius of Abingdon.[81]

Henry's aristocratic prelates continued to play an important role in his administration. Roger of Salisbury and his nephews at Lincoln and (after 1133) at Ely maintained a powerful influence, as for example in the case of the intrusion of Henry of Poitou abbot of Saint-Jean d'Angély into the abbey of Peterborough in 1130/1131. A most extraordinary case of mistaken judgment by the king,[82] the appointment was finally reversed at the insistence of the Salisbury clan. Henry of Blois, the king's nephew at Winchester, seems to have been deputized (or deputized himself) to handle appointments during

---

[76] Farrer, *Itin.*, nos 688 (Missenden), 679 and 681 (Rievaulx; also *RRAN* 2, nos 1740–1741), 706 (Garendon).

[77] Farrer, *Itin.*, no. 627; *RRAN* 2, no. 1917.

[78] Farrer, *Itin.*, nos 728 (Villers-Canivet), 685 (Wikes, or Wix; 1123–1133; also *RRAN* 2, no. 1739), Farrer, *Itin.*, no. 693 (Elstow; 1120–1133), and *RRAN* 2, no. 1692 (Caen; 1131).

[79] Farrer, *Itin.*, no. 664 (Cluny); ibid., no. 713, and *RRAN* 2, no. 1714 (Reading); Farrer, *Itin.*, nos 604 and 735, and *RRAN* 2, no. 1912 (Saint-Martin des Champs).

[80] For Normandy: Farrer, *Itin.*, nos 647 (Bec); 651 (Envermeu); 622, 623, 625 (Fécamp); 618, 629, 643, 724 (1123–1135) (Montébourg); 644 (Conches); 649 (Boscherville); 636, 731 (1107–1135) (Troarn); 624 (Sées); 638, 652 (Saint-Wandrille); 630 (Savigny); 664a (Tiron).
For Blois: 641 (1107–1135) and 719 (1130–1135) (Saint-Père de Chartres).
For England: *RRAN* 2, no. 1988, and Farrer, *Itin.*, no. 666 (Westminster); *RRAN* 2, no. 1896 (Battle); Farrer, *Itin.*, nos 711 (St Augustine's), 699 (Chertsey), 680 (Hyde), 691 (St Peter's, Bath), 659 (Thorney), 692 and 727 (Ramsey).

[81] Farrer, *Itin.*, no. 729, and *RRAN* 2, nos 1913 and 1914.

[82] See above, p. 429.

the king's absence, as both Florence of Worcester and John of
Worcester report that Henry of Blois appointed Robert to the vacant
see of Bath in 1133/1134.[83]

The prelates also benefited from their service and proximity to the
king. Roger of Salisbury's rewards, which included the abbey of
Malmesbury and the preferment of his nephews, were many and his
power almost unlimited; after the king he was the most important
administrator in the realm.[84] Alexander of Lincoln, Roger's nephew, is
the recipient of the greatest number of charters in the last years of the
reign;[85] he is followed distantly by Godfrey of Bath,[86] Robert of Hereford,[87] Everard of Norwich,[88] and Seffrid of Chichester.[89] Audoin of
Evreux, the brother of Thurstan of York, has been mentioned above,[90]
as has the bishop of Sées, who was often at the king's side, like Audoin,
and often favored.[91] The canons of Bayeux (probably during the
vacancy in 1134) and the church of St Mary, Rouen, also record a grant
from the king.[92]

While charters to religious institutions survive in great numbers,
those to individuals and to corporate bodies are far fewer. For these
later years of Henry's life, we have a goodly number of documents
revealing the king attending to feudal arrangements: for example,
authorization for a noble to give his daughter in marriage,[93] the grant
to a royal chamberlain of a fee that had escheated to the crown, along
with the right to marry the previous holder's daughter,[94] grant of soc
and other liberties to an individual who holds of the fee of three
nobles,[95] and a number of restorations of land to sons whose fathers
had held of the king.[96]

---

[83] FW and JW, *s.a.* 1134. See Crosby, "Organization of English Episcopate," p. 4.

[84] Roger's influence may have declined somewhat as a result of his resistance to
Maud's succession and then to her marriage outside the kingdom. Nonetheless, he
had been with Henry as a prince and he was known to be loyal to the man who
had made him. Moreover, Roger was on the spot in England as regent. His danegeld
exemptions in 1128–1130 were £153 (the highest of any person in England) for
lands in fifteen shires (Kealey, *Roger of Salisbury*, p. 277 and *passim*).

[85] Farrer, *Itin.*, nos 621a, 657, 696 (1123–1133), 696a (1123–1133), 701, 702
(1123–1133), 708, 717 (1123–1133).

[86] *RRAN* 2, nos 1762–1763. Godfrey came to England with Adeliza of Louvain.

[87] Farrer, *Itin.*, no. 690.

[88] Ibid., no. 684.

[89] Ibid., no. 702 (1125–1133); *RRAN* 2, no. 1769.

[90] Farrer, *Itin.*, nos 620 (Evreux vs. Saint-Evroul) and 662.

[91] Ibid., nos 639, 653, 718.

[92] Ibid., nos 632, 725.

[93] Ibid., no. 669.

[94] Ibid., no. 661; *RRAN* 2, no. 1719.

[95] Farrer, *Itin.*, no. 687.

[96] Ibid., nos 694, 705, 712, 730.

Record also exists of Henry's confirmation of the guild of cord-wainers and shoemakers at Rouen.[97] The other corporate entity addressed by the king in his late years is perhaps the most important in the realm: the corporation of London. The much-disputed charter of liberties for the city, commonly dated to 1130–1133,[98] marks the very beginning of the city's history as an autonomous unit.[99] It grants the city the right to elect its own sheriffs and justiciars and it reduces the annual assessment of taxes to three hundred pounds.[100] Henry probably saw a fiscal advantage in both these provisions. The city was greatly in arrears in its payment of the farm, a problem that can only have been exacerbated by the fire of 1133. The reduction of the farm then makes sense if the aim was to stimulate payment. Moreover, the corporation no doubt paid handsomely for the right to elect its officials.[101]

King Henry was clearly of sound mind and body when he arrived at the forest of Lyons in autumn 1135. William of Malmesbury says that Henry became ill while hunting; Orderic reports that he sickened in the night before he was to hunt; Henry of Huntingdon gives us the more theatrical description that gripped the imaginations of later historians: the king violated his doctor's orders and dined on for-bidden fish.[102] The Huntingdon archdeacon also gets in a stab at Maud, whose betrayal, he suggests, provoked angry and bitter feelings that contributed to the king's demise. There is no consensus on the exact cause of Henry I's death, but Orderic's description is the fullest: the king, then in his sixty-eighth year, no doubt wearied from his exertions on the southern frontier, arrived at his castle in the forest on a Monday, planned to hunt the next day, but fell ill in the night; from Tuesday to Sunday his condition steadily worsened. When the seriousness of the illness became apparent, the king confessed his sins to his chap-lains and then sent for Hugh archbishop of Rouen for spiritual counsel. Robert of Gloucester also hurried to his father's bedside, as did others of his court. Henry commanded Robert to take sixty thousand pounds from the treasury at Falaise (which Robert controlled) to pay

<hr/>

[97] Ibid., no. 650; *RRAN* 2, no. 1695.
[98] Hollister favors the date posited by J. C. Russell, 1133, in *Twelfth Century Studies*, which places the charter among Henry's many acts and activities before his depar-ture for Normandy: "The Date of Henry I's Charter to London," pp. 94–102.
[99] See Hollister, "London's First Charter of Liberties: Is It Genuine?" *MMI*, pp. 192–208.
[100] Farrer, *Itin.*, no. 671; *RRAN* 2, no. 1645.
[101] Hollister, "London's First Charter of Liberties," pp. 202–207.
[102] WM, *HN*, chap. 457; OV, 6:448; HH, p. 490.

wages to Henry's household and to his stipendiary soldiers. The king then gave instructions that he was to be buried at Reading. William of Malmesbury adds that when queried about his successor Henry "assigned all lands on both sides of the sea to his daughter in lawful and lasting succession" but ignored the count of Anjou because of his "threats and insults."[103] Both monk-historians show the king making a pious end. Orderic reports that the king implored all to devote themselves to the preservation of peace and the protection of the poor. Malmesbury quotes Hugh of Rouen's letter to Pope Innocent in which the archbishop assured the pope of Henry's contrition for his sins and his arrangements for almsgiving.[104]

Henry died at night on Sunday, 1 December.[105] Archbishop Hugh and Audoin of Evreux made the assembled nobles—the celebrated five counts: Robert earl of Gloucester, William of Warenne earl of Surrey, Robert earl of Leicester, Rotrou of Mortain count of Perche, and Waleran count of Meulan—swear to accompany the body honorably to the sea. The next day a huge procession made its way to Rouen, where the body was prepared by a skillful embalmer in the archbishop's chamber.[106] The entrails were extracted and the urn with these perishables was taken for burial at Notre-Dame du Pré, one of Henry's favorite monastic churches.[107] Then the king's bier was escorted by knights, retainers, and officials to Caen by way of Pont-Audemer and Bonneville. There followed a wait of about a month "until winter should grow a little milder and bring gentler breezes."[108] During that time, says Orderic, the king's body rested at the monastery of Saint-Etienne, his father's distinguished foundation and burial place.[109] After Christmas, monks of Saint-Etienne accompanied the body across the Channel. The king was buried at Reading on 4 January 1136 "by his successor in the realm and by the bishops and magnates of the land."[110]

---

[103] OV, 6:448 (for burial at Reading); WM, *HN*, chap. 457 (for succession).

[104] WM, *HN*, chap. 458; *HF*, 15:694–695, n. 3.

[105] The date is often noted as 2 December 1135 because of the medieval practice of closing a given date at nightfall. WM, *HN*, chap. 457, says the king died "in the dead of night." Henry's obituaries in the Cluny necrologies date the commemoration of his death to 2 December. See Wollasch, *Synopse der Cluniacensischen Necrologien*, and Schnürer, *Necrologium des Cluniacenser-Priorates Münchenwiler*.

[106] OV, 6:450.

[107] Compare the sober accounts of Orderic Vitalis and William of Malmesbury with the lurid moralistic version by Henry of Huntingdon ("The Present Time," pp. 702–705).

[108] WM, *HN*, chap. 459.

[109] Henry had only in recent years negotiated with the abbey of Saint-Etienne to acquire the royal regalia left by the Conqueror to the monks: *RRAN* 2, no. 1575 (*an.* 1129).

[110] OV, 6:450.

When King Henry died . . . the peace and harmony of the kingdom were buried with him.

—*Gesta Stephani*, p. 14

Orderic's account of the disorders that broke out after King Henry's death suggests that the problems were concentrated in Normandy, as one might have expected. "By the prudent advice of wise counsellors" the various regions of Normandy were put under the authority of the king's lieutenants. William of Warenne protected Rouen and the Pays de Caux. William of Roumare, Hugh of Gournay, and other marcher lords were dispatched to the frontiers. Nonetheless, laments Orderic, "stubborn Normandy, an unhappy mother country, suffered wretchedly from her viper's brood. For on the very same day that the Normans heard that their firm ruler had died . . . they rushed out hungrily like ravening wolves to plunder and ravage mercilessly."[111] The lament then becomes part of the king's eulogy:

> Heavy sorrow oppresses every part of [Henry's] country;
> Every man now seeks to plunder the goods of others
> And abandons himself to unbridled lawlessness . . .
> The Normans abandon themselves to robbery and pillage,
> They slay and capture each other, and bind with fetters;
> They burn buildings and everything that is inside them,
> And neither spare monks nor show respect for women. . . .
> O Christ, give us a leader who will love peace and justice
> And preserve them, and lead back thy people to thee.[112]

The rest of book 13 is a litany of the strife in Normandy and the misfortunes of the duchy. Orderic punctuates his account of disunity and lack of leadership with comments on the violence committed on churches, cemeteries, peasants, and towns, the Saint-Evroul monk harshly censuring the Normans for their warlike and bold nature.[113] Even Henry of Huntingdon reports on the dreadful times that followed the king's death, with Normandy "set on fire by the treacheries of the Normans."[114]

When we consult chroniclers on the other side of the Channel, the story is little different. It was not long, John of Worcester notes, before the compact of peace was torn up. "Everyone raised his head against the other . . . devastating all, both nobles and base-born," the powerful

---

[111] Ibid.
[112] Ibid., p. 452.
[113] Ibid., pp. 454–456.
[114] HH, p. 701.

oppressing the weak.[115] The Hexham chronicler Richard announces cryptically that King Henry's justice and peace were buried with him. Prior Richard complains of the calamities and cruelties that prevailed, regretting that "no prince rose up to forbid unjust exactions, to keep his subjects in peace, or to cultivate the religious and take care of the poor and needy."[116] The *Gesta Stephani*, despite its sympathy for King Stephen, echoes Richard of Hexham: "The peace and harmony of the kingdom were buried with [King Henry]." The writer does not hesitate to describe the "grievous calamity" afflicting England:

> On his decease [there] grew up abundance of iniquity and a seed-plot of all manner of wickedness; so much that England, formerly the seat of justice, the habitation of peace, the height of piety, the mirror of religion, became thereafter a home of perversity, a haunt of strife, a training-ground of disorder, and a teacher of every kind of rebellion. . . . For every man, seized by a strange passion for violence, raged cruelly against his neighbour and reckoned himself the more glorious the more guiltily he attacked the innocent. Likewise, utterly disregarding, or rather bringing to naught, the enactments of law, whereby an undisciplined people is restrained, and abandoned to all things unlawful, they were executing most readily any crime that occurred to their minds.[117]

Even William of Malmesbury, in his reasoned and careful description of the aftermath of 1135, allows his dismay to show, describing England as "a country that was like a forest full of raging wild beasts":

> So a dreadful thing could be seen, that England, once the noblest nurse of peace, the peculiar habitation of tranquillity, had sunk to such wretchedness that even bishops or monks could not safely pass from village to village.[118]

Abbot Peter the Venerable, far away in Burgundy, verifies these portraits. Writing from Cluny to console Henry's sister Adela at Marcigny, he gently explains that he has heard that Normandy is in a state of war; he adds that he has yet to have news of England but has sent couriers to Rouen and Winchester and will inform Adela as soon as possible. Peter assures Adela that the fullest remembrances for Henry will be celebrated

---

[115] JW, pp. 40–41.
[116] Richard, prior of Hexham, "The Acts of King Stephen and the Battle of the Standard," in *Priory of Hexham*, ed. Raine, 1:64, 66–67.
[117] *Gesta Stephani*, p. 14 and pp. 2–4.
[118] WM, *HN*, chaps 483, 506.

by all Cluniacs.[119] The commemorations of Henry's death which appear in the necrologies of Saint-Martin des Champs, Marcigny, and other Cluniac foundations as well as in the cartulary of the cathedral of Notre-Dame at Chartres reveal the impact of Henry's death on those who admired the Anglo-Norman king for his piety and for his peace.[120]

The chaos that engulfed the Anglo-Norman world in 1136 resulted in civil war and the division of the realm. This instability was exactly what Henry had struggled to prevent. But because the king was at odds with Geoffrey and Maud in 1135, Maud did not rush to her father's bedside to assume her rightful inheritance and her supporters were unable to promote her cause in the crucial period when Stephen seized the throne. Had the countess managed her temper better, had Geoffrey not decided to fight for the disputed border castles, and had the count and countess of Anjou not made an ill-advised invasion of Normandy just after Henry's death,[121] Henry's plan of 1126/1127 would probably have worked, especially given the birth of the couple's two sons. It would have been impossible as well as unthinkable for Stephen to step into the breach but for the absence, indeed the hostility, of the designated heir.[122]

As all the chroniclers admit, Stephen was Henry's favorite nephew, immensely enriched and distinguished by his uncle. In 1127 he and Robert of Gloucester had disputed who was to be the first among the magnates to please the king and swear to the empress (Stephen, the older, swore first). He was considered by all his contemporaries the most honorable, the most knightly of the magnates. And, failing Maud, Stephen was also seen as the most logical candidate for the throne. Moreover, like Henry I in 1100, he was quickly on the spot. He sailed

---

[119] *Letters of Peter the Venerable*, 1: no. 15.

[120] *Cartulaire de Notre-Dame de Chartres*, 3:59, 204.

[121] RT, *Chron., s.a.* 1135; OV, 6:454 ff.

[122] See Hollister, "The Anglo-Norman Succession Debate of 1126," pp. 162–169, "Henry I and the Anglo-Norman Magnates," p. 188, and Hollister and Keefe, "The Making of the Anglo-Norman Empire," pp. 262–263, all in Hollister, *MMI*. Edmund King, in the introduction to his new edition of William of Malmesbury's *Historia novella* (pp. xli-xlii), which appeared in 1998, the year after Warren Hollister's death, argues that *Henry* was at fault for the succession crisis because of his refusal to acquiesce to Geoffrey and Maud's demand that he do fealty to them for all the fortresses of Normandy and England; they made this request (demand?) in behalf of Henry's grandsons, his lawful heirs. King argues that Robert of Torigny pinpointed this crucial aspect of a complex settlement. Thus, Henry's refusal to hand over the border fortresses, the outward signs of a complex succession settlement, can be read as a refusal to live up to the terms of that agreement. I (ACF) do not know if Hollister knew of this interpretation or whether he would have agreed. I suspect that he would not have been surprised to see Henry refusing to do homage to any other lord.

hurriedly from Wissant to England (arriving to an ominous sound of thunder, says the Malmesbury monk)[123] and soon gained the support of Roger of Salisbury, William de Pont de l'Arche, Henry of Blois bishop of Winchester, and William archbishop of Canterbury. His principal supporters turned out to be the very people who had resisted Maud's succession in 1126 and who resented the alliance with Anjou which followed.[124]

Contemporary chroniclers were obviously confounded by the unanticipated turn of events after Henry's death and found it difficult to deal with the ethical and political implications. Orderic Vitalis, as always on the side of peace and order, ignores the question of the legitimacy of Stephen's rule. When he mentions Maud, she is always "the countess" or the wife of the count of Anjou. The Saint-Evroul monk does not mention the oath until 1138, and then only as an explanation for David of Scots' invasion of England.[125] Otherwise, Orderic speaks hopefully of "King Stephen"—anointed authority—and critically of the "pernicious disturbers of the realm." His focus is the cruel suffering of the Church and the poor at the hands of barbarous nobles. He readily laments the lack of leadership, both in Normandy and in England. One gets the impression that Orderic would have supported any strong candidate who could have quelled the strife. Recall his conclusion to Henry's eulogy:

> O Christ, give us a leader who will love peace and justice and pre-
> serve them . . . [who will] smite the turbulent with the rod of justice
> that thy people may render thee service in safety.[126]

John of Worcester, a supporter of the "magnificent" King Stephen, man of piety and peace, candidly admits that all who took the oath to Maud in 1127 would become perjurers in the next reign.[127] At that point the Worcester chronicler drops the subject, never again speculating on right and wrong or the problems of political leadership.[128]

---

[123] WM, *HN*, chap. 460.

[124] See Hollister, "Anglo-Norman Succession Debate of 1126," *MMI*, pp. 145–169, for a full discussion.

[125] OV, 6:519.

[126] Ibid., p. 453.

[127] JW, p. 28. (JW gets the date wrong and makes this point for the year 1128.) The annals of Winchester (*Annales monastici*, 2:50) report that Stephen usurped the throne, "breaking the pact and oath he had made to the daughter of the lion of justice."

[128] A difficult passage in John of Worcester (p. 58) seems to refer to the problem of oaths: [King Stephen is encamped at Leominster in 1139] "Ubi quidam ex consulto regi fidelitatem iuraverunt. Quidam renuentes, hoc regi intulerunt: 'Si non iuramento, credat rex, si velit, saltim fidelibus verbis nostris.'"

The *Gesta Stephani*, in contrast, shows us how contemporaries justified or explained away Stephen's seizure of the throne.[129] Without denying the oath to Maud, the anonymous writer reports that Londoners fell back on their ancient right to choose the king, citing the need to choose quickly because of the dangers threatening the realm.[130] Stephen then traveled to Winchester, where the archbishop of Canterbury, acting as the conscience of the realm and cautioning (rhetorically?) against haste without reflection, brought up the problem of the oath all prelates and magnates had taken to Maud. There follow the various justifications for the fait accompli: the oath was invalid because it had been imposed by the king and was thus not freely given; the king knew his wishes would not be followed but felt that he had at least achieved peace in his lifetime (and possibly thereafter) through the alliance with Anjou; the king had repented of his imposition of the oath; the king on his deathbed had released his nobles and bishops from the pledge.[131] "Wherefore," says the writer,

> because it is acknowledged that any forcible exaction of an oath from anyone has made it impossible for the breaking of that oath to constitute a perjury, it is sound and eminently advisable to accept gladly as king the man whom London, the capital of the whole kingdom, has received without objection, and who moreover was a suitable candidate owing to his just claim of close relationship.[132]

Following such reasoning, the *Gesta* writer is able to mention without embarrassment the oath to Maud (which he says Stephen's opponents claimed as their justification for sowing discord) while censuring those who betrayed their oath to King Stephen in the course of the civil war.

Thus, the "nearest and dearest of all Henry's nephews," with the support of his powerful brother at Winchester and the king's regent at Salisbury, received the archbishop's approval, was given the keys to the treasury, and was consecrated king on 22 December 1135. Just ten days later King Stephen unembarrassedly carried the coffin of his uncle on his shoulders at the royal funeral at Reading. The *Gesta* writer then quickly brings the kingdom, through Stephen's efforts, back to its

---

[129] *Gesta Stephani*, pp. 8–12.

[130] Ibid., pp. 4–6. The Londoners are among the few who criticized King Henry after his death, noting his "grievous" laws (remembering his taxes?) (FW, *s.a.* 1140).

[131] *Gesta Stephani*, pp. 8–12. According to Gervase of Canterbury (RS, 1:94), Hugh Bigod said that before the king died he released his men from their oath. Ulger bishop of Angers testified at the papal court in 1139 that Hugh Bigod was not present at Henry's deathbed: John of Salisbury, *Historia pontificalis*, pp. 84–85.

[132] *Gesta Stephani*, p. 12.

"wonted tranquillity," except for some "special and very intimate friends of King Henry." These are described (in another justification) as people of low birth who had been enriched by the late king to ensure their loyalty.[133] Although offered similar enrichment by King Stephen, these men firmly refused, "both on account of the loyalty and the oath that they owed to their foster sister, King Henry's daughter, and because the noblest men of the kingdom grudged their distinction and their splendor." King Henry's men are also said to have feared losing ill-gotten gains extracted from the poor and weak. But eventually, says the *Gesta*, even these men bound themselves by fealty and an oath to King Stephen.[134]

The question of the 1127 oath arose again when Maud sought the help of her uncle, King David of Scots. David had been "vexed that Stephen had taken the tiller," but because the barons had rallied to Stephen, David had decided to wait to see what would happen.[135] Energized by Maud's appeal, however, David determined to create disorder for Stephen, and he had the help of others, says the *Gesta*, who acted for their own profit or to defend "what they regarded as justice." These seem like fair words, but in fact the *Gesta* writer, believing the rationalizations he presented at the time of Stephen's consecration, probably means that King Henry's loyalists were deluded.

The degeneration of honor brought on by the war,[136] as well as the interminable see-saw of conflict, ultimately tested the *Gesta* author's support for Stephen. By the later years of the civil war, the author is reduced to pitting Maud against Stephen at the truce table, each claiming sovereignty "by right";[137] neither elaborates, nor does the author. Thereafter, in an abrupt change of tone, after lamenting that "a kingdom of joy and quiet, tranquillity and peace" had become a place "of sadness and strife, slaughter and devastation,"[138] the *Gesta*

[133] Contrary to the traditional view that Stephen was raised to the throne by "the great Conquest baronage" and opposed by Henry I's "new men" (Jolliffe, *Constitutional History*, p. 201; Southern, *Medieval Humanism*, p. 220), it seems rather that the succession issue divided the court down the middle, with "new men" on both sides in 1126 and again in the aftermath of Henry's death. See Hollister, "Anglo-Norman Succession Debate of 1126," p. 166 and references.

[134] *Gesta Stephani*, p. 22. The man considered the chief opponent of King Stephen and the number of King Henry's loyalists vary throughout the *Gesta*.

[135] Ibid., p. 53. David and Stephen were no doubt well known to each other from their youthful days at Henry's court.

[136] See ibid., p. 152ff. These comments remind us of Thucydides' discussion of the deterioration of character in the Greek world at the time of the revolution in Corcyra during the Peloponnesian War (book 3, chaps 82–85). WM, *HN*, chap. 483, also describes the "brutalities of war."

[137] *Gesta Stephani*, p. 186.

[138] Ibid., p. 170.

author despairs of Stephen, just as Stephen himself wonders what has happened to the faith and honor of the men who should have been loyal to him.[139] From this point, as Stephen's fortunes decline, the author begins to speak of the "lawful heir and claimant to the kingdom of England,"[140] Maud's son Henry. Fickle fortune, often invoked in the *Gesta*, has abandoned Stephen.

None of these sources recognizes Maud as the heir to the throne. Yet the evolution of the *Gesta* author's sentiments suggests that had Maud behaved in a way that contemporaries could have admired, that is, more like what they thought a woman should be,[141] she might have succeeded in ruling for her eldest son, especially if she had avoided behaving so much like a queen.[142] The *Gesta* writer shows how fickle the nation in fact was: the barons and prelates "inclined" to Stephen when he was the best authority available; when Stephen was defeated by the loyalists in 1141, the same grandees rallied to Maud, until she disgraced herself.[143]

William of Malmesbury gives us the loyalist perspective on this story. An eyewitness to many of the events reported, he addresses as dispassionately as possible the ethical issues of the oath to Maud and Stephen's seizure of the throne (in the preface to book 1 of the *Historia novella* he says he will try to tell "the truth of things without any concession to dislike or favour"), and he gives us some understanding of the motivations of the principal players. Malmesbury says that from the time of Maud's marriage "all men were asserting, as though by some prophetic sign, that after [Henry's] death they would fail to keep their oath."[144] Roger of Salisbury apparently said many times in the hearing of the Malmesbury monk that he was released from his oath because he had sworn only on condition that the king should not give his daughter in marriage outside the realm without his consent and that of the great barons. Thus when Stephen arrived in England in mid-December, Roger was to his own mind free (and willing) to support the king's nephew.

Malmesbury also explains the position of Robert of Gloucester:

> He had wearied his mind with much reflection while in Normandy, on what he thought he should decide to do in this

---

[139] Ibid., p. 202.

[140] Ibid., pp. 204, 214, 222, 224.

[141] Ibid., pp. 118, 121, 135, 138. William of Malmesbury calls Maud a woman of masculine spirit (*HN*, chap. 467) and delicately but honestly notes her inability to show restraint in the enjoyment of what she had gained (chap. 498).

[142] *Gesta Stephani*, p. 118.

[143] Ibid., pp. 116, 118.

[144] WM, *HN*, chap. 452.

matter, for he saw that if he submitted to King Stephen it
would be contrary to the oath he had taken to his sister, but
[he] understood that if he resisted it would bring no advantage to
his sister or nephews and would certainly do enormous harm
to himself.[145]

The oaths that most took to Stephen turned out to be conditional.
Robert of Gloucester finally consented in 1136 to swear fealty
and homage to Stephen, but only should the king comport himself
toward the earl in a faithful way. Apparently, on reflection back
in Normandy, Robert decided that his oath to Stephen was unlawful,
citing Stephen's unlawful seizure of the throne, his own preexisting
oath to Maud, and Stephen's faithless treatment of him. "He was
indeed encouraged by the answer of many ecclesiastics whom he
had consulted on the matter [apparently not Hugh of Rouen, who
supported Stephen], to the effect that in no wise could he pass
this present life without disgrace or win blessedness in the life to
come if he neglected to keep the oath to his father's daughter."[146]
The prelates in England, says Malmesbury, also swore to support
Stephen only "for as long as he should maintain the freedom of
the Church and the strict observance of its discipline."[147] The
regularity with which Stephen's supporters changed sides during
the wars suggests that self-interest and moral confusion in general
about the binding nature of oaths and in particular about the
legality of Stephen's kingship would plague the king throughout
his reign. Stephen himself bemoaned the fickleness of his men:
"When they have chosen me king, why do they abandon me?"[148]

After the victory of Maud's supporters in 1141, the *Historia novella*
includes a long speech by Henry bishop of Winchester, the king's
brother, in which he repeats the history of the oath, explains why it was
disregarded, and proposes that because Stephen has failed as king the
empress should assume her rightful position, now that she has been
sanctioned by the clergy.[149] At this point William of Malmesbury fails
us, for when he explains how Stephen was chosen, he makes no
mention of the hostilities between Henry I and the count and countess of Anjou, merely stating that it was "tedious" waiting for Maud, "who
made delays in coming to England since her residence was in

[145] Ibid., chap. 463.
[146] Ibid., chap. 467. WM adds that Robert even produced a bull from the pope
bidding him keep his oath to Maud.
[147] Ibid., chap. 464.
[148] Ibid., chap. 466.
[149] Ibid., chap. 493.

Normandy."[150] The same error of omission occurs earlier in the *Historia novella* when Malmesbury says that after the death of King Henry, "for certain reasons, the empress and likewise her brother Robert of Gloucester, together with almost all the nobles, delayed their return to the kingdom."[151] Later, in 1139, when Malmesbury announces the arrival of Maud and Robert, he explains that the earl, "escaping at last after hampering delays," landed in England with his sister, relying on the mercy of God and "his fidelity to a lawful oath."[152] The event that Malmesbury does not mention—either out of lack of firsthand information or out of delicacy—was of course the border warfare that was going on between the king and the count and countess of Anjou at the time of Henry's death. When, after the king's death, the Angevins compounded their mistakes and invaded Normandy, having made common cause with William Talvas and Roger of Tosny, Henry's *fideles* were constrained to take up arms against Geoffrey and Maud and the rebels. Not until 1138 was the border situation resolved. Thus when Robert of Gloucester traveled to England in early 1136 and decided to submit to Stephen's rule, he was in the awkward position of supporting Stephen because he could not support Maud. This bewildering mix of allegiances, in which the players were "dragged this way and that,"[153] contributed to a climate of moral confusion that is illustrated clearly in the accounts of this difficult period in English history, all of which lament the "changeableness of fortune and the mutability of the human lot."[154]

> *His greatness showed itself in every quarter,*
> *In wealth and justice, wisdom and integrity.*
> *No better prince than he ruled on this earth . . .*
> *He was, I dare assert, the best of men,*
> *As all his noble acts clearly proclaim.*
>
> —Orderic Vitalis, 6:453

[150] Ibid. It is possible that William of Malmesbury was ignorant of the situation on the southern frontier. He does say (book 3, preface) that he is "undertaking to unravel the trackless maze of events and occurrences." Thus he may have conflated the Angevin hostilites with Maud's reaction to her exclusion. Malmesbury does point out in chap. 491 that by the 1127 oath Maud was to receive all England *and* Normandy.

[151] Ibid., chap. 460. More than once William of Malmesbury passes over events that he does not wish to recount from hearsay, in particular events across the Channel (see, e.g., *HN*, chap. 501, p. 62; chap. 514, p. 70; chap. 457, p. 12).

[152] Ibid., chap. 478. WM adds in chap. 491 that all England and Normandy had taken the oath to Maud.

[153] *Gesta Stephani*, p. 118.

[154] WM, *HN*, book 3, preface.

The continuous disturbances during King Stephen's reign contrast sharply with the long and well-documented peace of Henry's rule and offer eloquent testimony to Henry's success as king. In his first two years of power Henry quickly and effectively defended his claim to the throne, whereas Stephen ultimately failed, despite his personal and financial resources—he was after all William the Conqueror's grandson, Henry's favorite nephew, and he had Henry I's Winchester treasury. In Henry's England, after the first struggles, an unbroken peace endured for thirty-three years. In Normandy, a most difficult region to govern,[155] as Orderic sadly admits, the peace was broken during Henry's rule only twice in twenty-nine years, and then only with the stimulus of foreign support. In comparison with France, in particular, with its incessant warfare, urban riots, and mass suffering, the history of Normandy under Henry I is relatively pacific.[156]

The assessments of King Henry by chroniclers and historians of both reigns unanimously emphasize Henry's peace,[157] made possible by his strong governance. The almost universal approval Henry earned from his contemporaries[158] tells us as much about Anglo-Norman attitudes toward kingship and power as about Henry himself. But modern historians have not always read these estimates with an eye to twelfth-century attitudes. For example, contemporary reports of Henry's few harsh reprisals for treason (including false coinage)[159] persuaded many modern writers that Henry was brutal and ruthless,[160] when in fact most

---

[155] David Bates ("The Rise and Fall of Normandy," p. 23) notes that the southern Norman frontier was always a problem for the Anglo-Norman kings, with significant defections in every reign. The defection of the count of Alençon in 1203 signaled the coming loss of the entire duchy.

[156] John Le Patourel (Norman Empire, pp. 288–289) and Judith Green ("Henry I and the Aristocracy of Normandy," p. 173) agree with this comparison.

[157] See ASC, s.a. 1135; OV, 6:472; Suger, Louis le Gros, p. 186; WM, HN, chap. 458; WM, GR, 5:399. Recall the words of Henry's coronation charter: "I establish a firm peace in all my kingdom and I order that this peace shall henceforth be kept" (EHD, pp. 433–434). Edward Kealey ("Anglo-Norman Policy," p. 341) notes Henry's good repute, citing a Saxon priest and recluse, Wulfric of Haselbury, who on the day of the king's death praised his peace and justice; Kealey explains that the Norman kings served public welfare by maintaining peace and justice, "mighty accomplishments in any age."

[158] R. W. Southern made this observation thirty-nine years ago: "The Place of Henry I," p. 128.

[159] ASC, s.a. 1124; HH, p. 474. In Germanic law treason against one's lord was the supreme offense; see Hollister, "Royal Acts of Mutilation: The Case against Henry I," esp. p. 333 (in MMI, see p. 294), and Lear, Treason in Roman and Germanic Law.

[160] On Henry's supposed cruelty, see Southern, Medieval Humanism, pp. 218, 231; Brooke, London 800–1216, p. 317; and Mason, "William Rufus and the Historians," p. 15. Robert Bartlett, in his recent work on the Norman and Angevin kings, repeatedly notes Henry I's autocratic rule and ruthlessness (England under the Norman and Angevin Kings, 1075–1225 [Oxford, 2000], pp. 4, 21, 145).

reports of such firm action were in *praise* of the king for using his strong arm to prevent corruption and strife and make life "safe for man and beast."[161] Death and mutilation were standard punishments in medieval Europe, but Henry I generally avoided the former, showing more moderation than many contemporaries, and his use of mutilation was rare.[162] When contemporaries reported that Henry caused men to fear him, a theme also taken up by many modern historians, what the monastic writers meant was that the king "made brutal officials quake with fear,"[163] that he called to justice royal officials who exceeded their authority and extorted from churches and monasteries,[164] that he kept nobles from breaking the peace (even in the absence of the king) as they maneuvered to improve their own positions vis-à-vis their neighbors or the king.[165] Even a comment by the saintly Anselm reinforces the contemporary attitude that only a strong hand could protect the unarmed. Writing to Alexander king of Scots, Anselm urged him to "behave in such a way that the bad will fear you and the good will love you"[166]—an illustration of the medieval understanding of the king as God's regent, charged to protect the defenseless and smite evildoers. Robert of Torigny emphasizes the military aspect of medieval kingship when he notes with admiration that Henry kept his enemies from plundering churches and the poor "by force of arms."[167]

The maintenance of peace was not an easy task. Henry's many years in Normandy are witness to the constant attention required in a vulnerable region with fractious nobles and aggressive neighbors. But in the king's absences from England—equal to more than half the reign—no revolt ever broke out. Had Henry forced his barons into obedience by extortion and repression, as we have been told,[168] a time bomb might have exploded[169]—and long before the death of the king. Instead,

---

[161] *ASC*, s.a. 1135.

[162] See Hollister, "Royal Acts of Mutilation," *passim*. The blinding of select rebels in 1124 and mutilation of the false moneyers in 1125 are the principal examples. See also Green, *The Aristocracy of Norman England*, p. 264, on increasing leniency in punishment of treasonous aristocrats.

[163] OV, 6:248–249.

[164] See chapter 10, n. 184, and n. 67 above, this chapter.

[165] WM, *GR*, 5:410.1, says "the most remarkable thing about Henry was his ability to keep rebellions in check by fear of his name." In the *HN* (chap. 463) Malmesbury says that under Henry I "bad knights had but scant livelihood."

[166] *AO*, 5: ep. 413.

[167] *GND*, 2:236–237. Suger (*Louis le Gros*, p. 100) noted Henry's success in imposing peace on the ferocious inhabitants of Normandy by force.

[168] Stenton, *English Feudalism*, p. 257. Stenton used evidence from the Pipe Roll of 1130 to argue that Henry I controlled his magnates by extortion and repression; see above, chap. 8, for arguments to the contrary.

[169] R. H. C. Davis wrote (*King Stephen*, p. 12) that waiting for Henry to die was like waiting for a bomb to explode.

Henry's contemporaries praised his honorable and generous treatment of the magnates. "Adding to their wealth and estates," wrote Orderic, and "placating them in this way, [Henry] won their loyalty."[170] The royal example was contagious. Orderic also recounts the story of Ralph of Gael, a staunch royalist, who suspected the loyalty of Ralph of Tosny. But, taking the king's advice, says Orderic, Ralph of Gael gave the lord of Conches and Tosny an important territory at the junction of the Andelle and Seine rivers "to secure his loyalty to himself and to ensure that he [Tosny] would defend the state against public enemies with all his might."[171] To see Henry's rule as a reign of terror is thus to miss its central point: a substantial number of magnates supported Henry's peace and profited from his lordship. Henry based his success on the shaping of a royalist baronage, bound to him not by fear so much as by gratitude for past and present favors and hope of future ones.

Henry started his wooing of the important men of the realm early in his reign. His first supporters were mostly men from Rufus' court, mid-level landholders and household officials. The coronation charter was an attempt to generate wider baronial support from the magnates and the prelates. The crisis of 1101 had revealed the gulf between the wealthiest magnates, who in general supported Robert Curthose, and the middling men and royal servants, who were royalists. Once Henry had succeeded, in his practical way, in negotiating a compromise solution to the challenge of Curthose, he immediately undertook to bridge the gulf by transforming magnates into friends and *curiales*—the alternative for those who refused was dispossession and banishment. By 1102 the vast estates of the Montgomery–Bellême family were in royal hands. Robert of Bellême seems to have been the only baron to whom Henry did not offer a choice; his involvement in revolts in 1088, 1095, and 1101 and his refusal to respond to charges had apparently convinced the king of his untrustworthiness. As Southern recognized, personal loyalty was "the one virtue that Henry absolutely required from others"—and one that he himself consistently displayed.[172]

Henry made overtures to William count of Mortain and was rebuffed, after which the king confiscated the great earldom of Cornwall (1104). William of Warenne was disseised in 1101 but then reinstated and lured into the royal *curia*.[173] The *Liber de Hyda* quotes the earl as saying in

[170] OV, 5:296.

[171] OV, 6:250.

[172] Southern, "The Place of Henry I," p. 163.

[173] OV, 6:14 and n. 5. See "Magnates and Curiales in Early Norman England," *MMI*, p. 114, and "The Taming of a Turbulent Earl: Henry I and William of Warenne," ibid., pp. 137–144.

1119, on the eve of the battle of Brémule, "There is no one who can persuade me to treason."[174] Such generosity on the part of the king was to become policy as the reign progressed; other examples of men pardoned and welcomed into the royal court are Robert Malet, Walter Giffard, and Eustace of Boulogne. Eustace became the king's good friend and Robert Malet became his master chamberlain.

The confiscations of the early years were useful to a king whose financial resources at the time were not great. But to defend the realm and to patronize the magnates, Henry needed to make the system he had inherited work. The reforms that Henry and his administrators initiated, probably before 1110, continued throughout the reign;[175] they funded the castles, wars, weddings, and patronage of the king who ultimately became celebrated for his full treasury. Having eliminated his overmighty and faithless English barons, Henry worked over the years to build a loyal aristocracy of old and new men. By 1135 five of the twelve richest men in the realm—Robert of Gloucester, Roger of Salisbury, Brian fitz Count, Stephen of Mortain, and Geoffrey Clinton—owed their exalted positions to the king. They were all either bastards, younger sons, or of nonnoble lineage. Often at court, they held vast lands, fulfilled key administrative functions, and benefited in addition from a kind of backhanded patronage in which the king absolved them from payments they owed to the treasury, one of the most important being the danegeld. As Henry and his officials had learned how to make justice more profitable in their effort to centralize royal authority and as the royal courts expanded their scope and grew more significant in the resolution of disputes, the funds flowing into the exchequer increased. With better record-keeping the king was in a position to collect (or not collect) debts, fines, or other exactions. He could thus excuse his *fideles* from payments as a form of patronage. The five nobles just mentioned appear in the Pipe Roll of 1130 as holders of the greatest exemptions from the danegeld.[176] Understandably, these men, who owed everything to King Henry, were absolutely loyal to him. Others, from old families and among the richest in the realm, benefited from royal attention of an equally satisfying nature. Sons of fathers whom Henry had enriched succeeded more and more regularly to their patrimony in an example of the growing security of inheritance that stabilized the baronage

[174] *Liber de Hyda*, pp. 316–317.
[175] Recall the great ordinance on the Truce of God in Normandy of 1135 and the charter of liberties to London of ca. 1133.
[176] See Mooers (Christelow), "Patronage in the Pipe Roll of 1130."

as well as the kingdom.[177] Henry's magnates were thus a working, integral part of the system. Their conversion, as William of Malmesbury noted, had involved no loss of dignity. [178] One would be quite surprised to find such men discontented with their affluence and power, especially as the value of their lands and rents rose steadily during the tranquil and prosperous decades of Henry's long reign.

There were nonetheless occasional rebels and malcontents. With his vast treasury, his clever diplomacy (even intrigue), and his military skill (as well as that of his lieutenants), the king undermined or overwhelmed these eruptions. The most unrepentant or dangerous enemies, as mentioned above, were consigned to prison, some for life.[179] Others the king kept in custody for a time. And, to the surprise of many, a good number Henry pardoned. Orderic Vitalis comments favorably on the king's leniency: "He, being a God-fearing man and a lover of peace and justice, spared the barons *who asked forgiveness* for their misdoing and, pardoning their offences, readily welcomed them back into his favour." Later in his history Orderic labels Henry's forgiveness "shrewd graciousness."[180]

Early in the reign, Henry pardoned the notorious Ranulf Flambard as part of his truce with Robert Curthose.[181] The bishop never reformed, but neither did he ever again plot against the king.[182] The king forgave Robert Malet, Robert of Lacy, Walter Giffard, and Eustace of Boulogne for their support of Curthose. (The sons of Roger of Montgomery were not forgiven, nor was their relative William of Mortain.) Robert Curthose could not be left free to provide a focus for rebellion and was therefore imprisoned for the rest of his life— but comfortably and honorably, as Henry explained to the pope at Gisors.[183] At this point Henry engaged in an act of mercy that was to haunt him—but whether he could have done otherwise is doubtful. Arriving at Falaise, where Robert Curthose's son William was being raised, the king had the boy brought before him:

---

[177] Stenton deplored the "fundamental insecurity of a government that rested on enforced obedience": *English Feudalism*, p. 257. Poole echoed these words: *Domesday Book to Magna Carta*, p. 130, where he criticizes "premature and overrigid centralisation."

[178] WM, *GR*, 5:411.

[179] OV, 6:90: "others were kept in fetters to the day of their death, as their crimes deserved."

[180] OV, 6:278 (italics added); ibid., pp. 378–380.

[181] See *MMI*, p. 95

[182] The bishop died in 1128.

[183] OV, 6:286; Henry gave the monks of St Peter at Gloucester (where Curthose was buried) a parcel of land to fund the perpetual burning of a light for the salvation of his brother's soul (Cownie, *Religious Patronage in Anglo-Norman England*, p. 61 and n. 55).

The king looked at the child, who was trembling with fright, and comforted him with kind promises, for he had suffered too many disasters at a tender age. Then, for fear that it might be held against him if the boy came to any harm while in his hands, he decided not to keep him under his own tutelage, but instead entrusted his upbringing to Helias of Saint-Saens [Curthose's son-in-law].[184]

William Crispin, who was captured at this time with others, was pardoned, unfortunately to challenge the king again with his kinsman Amaury de Montfort, a powerful and turbulent man, according to Orderic, who would trouble the king repeatedly. Then, when "the French and the Normans and the people on their frontiers laid down their arms for a little while [1113]," Henry again pardoned William Crispin, as well as Amaury.[185] He also pardoned William count of Evreux, whom he had exiled about a year before because of suspect loyalties. The Anglo-Saxon chronicler also mentions the deprivation (1110) and then reinstatement (1112) of Philip of Braose.

After the protracted struggles of 1117–1119 between the king and his treasonous barons[186] in coalition with the counts of Anjou and Flanders and the king of France, Henry could easily have taken severe measures against the rebels. Instead, flushed with victory, having secured the support of the pope against the king of France, he once again pardoned Amaury de Montfort (who had been advising Louis VI) and even gave him the county of Evreux, which he had earlier refused to do. Henry's natural daughter Juliana and her husband, Eustace of Breteuil, along with Hugh of Gournay[187] (who had been raised at the royal court) and Robert of Neubourg, all sought and received the royal mercy. And finally Henry pardoned his cousin Stephen of Aumale, who had held out the longest against the king.[188] At the request of the count of Anjou, William Talvas, son of the infamous Robert

---

[184] OV, 6:93. See Hollister, "Anglo-Norman War and Diplomacy," *MMI*, p. 280.

[185] OV, 6:236, 240, 344. Crispin would return to menace Henry: at Brémule in 1119 he tried to kill the king; he was captured but Orderic does not specify his fate. Crispin appears again with Amaury in the 1123/1124 revolt, suggesting that he somehow escaped punishment, perhaps as an additional favor to Amaury when he received the county of Evreux.

[186] Orderic (6:194) says there were eighteen treasonous castellans who far exceeded the loyal magnates in wealth and power.

[187] Hugh acted as one of Henry's lieutenants in an effort to keep the peace in Normandy after the death of the king.

[188] See *Liber de Hyda*, pp. 320–321. Stephen had been part of the 1095 revolt against Rufus (as a replacement candidate for the throne). But in 1104 he had remained loyal to Henry (OV, 4:183), until later, under the influence of his wife, says Orderic (6:280), when he chose the losing side.

of Bellême, was granted his patrimony, although the "far-seeing" king prudently kept his own garrisons in the citadels.[189]

The defection that seems to have pained the king the most yet necessitated serious punishment was that of Waleran of Meulan in 1123–1124. The son of Henry's late friend and longtime counselor Roger of Meulan, Waleran (and his twin Robert of Leicester) had been raised at the royal court; both boys had remained loyal in the 1117–1119 troubles. But perhaps the lure of power (Orderic says Waleran was "burning to give an example of his knightly prowess" and was "boyishly" eager for a fight)[190] and the seduction of the powerful (and ungrateful) Amaury de Montfort, who resented the inroads that royal centralization was making in his county of Evreux, tempted Waleran. After the victory of Henry's troops, the king's mood was less than merciful. Some rebels were blinded (for treason), provoking a protest from the count of Flanders for what he saw as mutilation. To this Henry replied:

> My lord count, what I do is just, as I will prove conclusively. . . . [M]y liege men . . . broke faith with me when they deliberately committed treason; therefore they deserve punishment by death or mutilation. They ought rather to have sacrificed all they possessed to preserve the fealty they had sworn to me than to have given their support in any way to any man opposing the law and to have broken the covenant with their liege lord by foully betraying their trust.[191]

The count of Flanders could not argue with Henry's logic, and the sentences were carried out. Amaury had escaped, but young Waleran and his brother-in-law Hugh de Montfort were imprisoned. One would not be surprised if the story ended here, but in fact five years later Henry's heart softened toward Robert of Meulan's son and the young man was released, restored to his possessions, and kept often at court.[192] Hugh de Montfort, however, remained in prison into Stephen's reign "because he was guilty of the most serious crimes with no justification."[193] Amaury de Montfort, worn down with defeats over the years, reports Orderic, soon sought peace with Henry, reluctantly abandoned Clito, placated the king, and was "restored to the king's favor with a pardon for past crimes"; he even regained his former honors.[194]

---

[189] OV, 6:228 ("far-seeing"), ibid., p. 224 and n. 2 (on royal garrisons).
[190] OV, 6:332 and 350.
[191] Ibid., p. 352.
[192] *RRAN* 2, no. 1607 (1129); *ASC, s.a.* 1129. See p. 474 above.
[193] OV, 6:356.
[194] Ibid., p. 358.

All these examples of Henry's patronage, punishment, and pardons are quite useful in the overall assessment of the king's reign. For in these tactical responses to the problem of building and maintaining loyalty, we can readily discern the hand of the political realist. Flexible and pragmatic, Henry made his decisions case by case. The disseisin of Ranulf Flambard early in the reign signaled to the Church Henry's intention to implement reform. But by late 1101 the process of restoring the bishop was under way. Flambard never became a favorite, but both his dispossession and his restoration had served a political purpose.[195] The restoration of William of Warenne in 1102 took place when Henry held the upper hand against his brother. After chastening the duke for his uninvited landing in England and his failings in Normandy—which Orderic says prompted Curthose to renounce the pension he had received the preceding year—Henry then seems to have made a (self-interested?) gesture of good will by pardoning William of Warenne.[196] "Assured of the duke's friendship," the "politic king" restored the earl. And the earl, "duly chastened," remained faithful for the remainder of his days "as one of Henry's closest friends and counselors."[197] The restoration of the Bellême inheritance to William Talvas in 1119 was another considered act, a favor to the count of Anjou, whose daughter had just been married to Henry's son William Adelin. As William of Malmesbury pointed out, Henry always regarded Anjou with suspicion,[198] so he made efforts to please the count and ensure his support in order to prevent future coalitions of neighbors against Normandy.

The long history of Henry's pardons of Amaury de Montfort is nothing short of astonishing. But a glance at a map of northwestern France and a look into Amaury's connections indicates the potential importance of this foreign magnate.[199] That Henry handled Amaury

[195] See Hollister, "The Anglo-Norman Civil War: 1101," *MMI*, p. 95. R. W. Southern, in "Ranulf Flambard" (*Medieval Humanism*, p. 197), called the restoration of Flambard "an uncharacteristic act of clemency." I hope here to have made exactly the opposite case: Henry's treatment of the bishop of Durham was decidedly a *characteristic* act of clemency.

[196] According to Orderic (6:12), William of Warenne had complained to the duke that he had lost the valuable earldom of Surrey because of him and he asked Curthose to intercede for him with the king.

[197] OV, 6:12–14.

[198] WM, *HN*, chap. 450.

[199] Amaury (see Evreux genealogy, p. 245, above), lord of Montfort l'Amaury (Montfort en Iveline), was uncle to Fulk V count of Anjou (heir to the county of Maine); Amaury's sister Bertrade had been married to Philip I of France, thus Amaury had royal nephews; another nephew was Ralph of Conches/Tosny; the baron William Crispin was his kinsman. Orderic says Amaury's "kinsfolk abounded in wealth and resources so that he was one of the greatest among the great nobles of France" (6:188). It might be fair to say that Amaury de Montfort's one loyalty was to himself.

almost as carefully as he did his other troublesome neighbors shows the king's concern. Henry was certainly aware of the danger of creating another cross-frontier magnate if he permitted Amaury to succeed to his uncle's county of Evreux. For this reason, on the advice of the bishop of Evreux—and perhaps because Amaury had demanded the county—Henry refused the first request.[200] But later, when Henry had experienced the havoc that such a disgruntled neighbor with influential friends could create, he reversed his position, partly as a result of the intercession of his nephew Theobald of Blois, granting Evreux to the lord of Montfort l'Amaury but wisely keeping a royal garrison in the citadel.[201] When this patronage did not prevent Amaury from creating discontent among Henry's Norman barons, the king accepted the challenge, and Amaury and his compatriots were crushed at Bourgthéroulde (1124). Amaury escaped capture, but later, having lost his influence at the French royal court,[202] he sued for peace with Henry and recovered his honors.[203] In this case Henry initially acted to prevent the succession of a powerful lord whose loyalties would always be divided; but as the situation evolved, Henry revised his tactics to patronize or to punish as behavior merited and opportunity warranted.

The punishment and subsequent pardoning of Waleran of Meulan reveal both reason and sentiment in the king's reactions. In 1124 Henry seems to have chosen to make an example of Waleran's treason. William Clito was still at large and elicited the support of France and perhaps also that of the dangerous Amaury de Montfort, whose marriage to Agnes niece of the seneschal of France had given him great influence at the French court.[204] Fulk V, Amaury's nephew, had yet to be drawn into the English orbit. By 1129, however, Henry had had William Clito's marriage with Sibyl of Anjou annulled,[205] he had

---

[200] Henry was known to resent high-handed demands from his vassals. Robert count of Flanders made a similar demand (to receive the accustomed money-fief from the king of England) and Henry at first refused because of the "imperious insolence" of the request: WM, *GR*, 5:403.2.

[201] One wonders if Amaury's failure to support his allies (OV, 6:230, 250), in particular the king of France, whom he had counseled to make the disastrous concerted invasion at Breteuil, could have been a "politic" decision on his part to remove himself from the war, thus influencing the later concession of Evreux. On Amaury's problems at the French court, see Bur, *Suger*, p. 133.

[202] See above, chapter 7, pp. 321–322.

[203] OV, 6:358. Just as the count of Blois needed the support of the king of England as much as the king of England needed his good will, so Amaury seems to have wanted the county of Evreux enough to humble himself and seek pardon from Henry. Thereafter, Amaury caused Henry no trouble, as far as we know.

[204] See n. 202 above, this chapter.

[205] Henry later arranged for the marriage of Sibyl to the new count of Flanders, Thierry of Alsace.

married Maud to the heir to the county of Anjou, he had undermined the French king's support of Clito as duke of Flanders, and he had seduced Amaury de Montfort into supporting him; then Clito died. The ties of friendship, always strong in Henry I, and the prospect of a durable peace may have been crucial factors in the restoration of the headstrong young count.

Henry's greatest praise comes from the monk of Saint-Evroul and the monk of Malmesbury, both men of dual nationality who lived long enough to see Henry's peace fall to pieces. From this perspective they and others looked back on Henry's years as the good times. As did Brian fitz Count, who was reminded by the abbot of Gloucester of the golden age of his youth in the court of the king.[206] As did the Battle chronicler, who said of Henry II that he had brought back the good times of his grandfather.[207] How was the Conqueror's third son able to generate such peace and maintain it for so long? According to Orderic, Henry's "deep wisdom, military prowess, and abundance of wealth and friends" were the ingredients of success.[208] Malmesbury observes that the king was "in political wisdom second to none among kings of our day and first among all his predecessors." He also makes the crucial point that Henry I preferred to battle in the council chamber rather than on the battlefield.[209] Even Henry of Huntingdon, whose assessment of the king varied by his mood and his patron, echoed other writers in his praise of Henry's intelligence: "great in wisdom, profound in counsel, famous for his farsightedness, outstanding in arms, distinguished for his deeds, remarkable for his wealth . . ."[210]

The common denominator here is respect for the king's intelligence. A man of some education, Henry surrounded himself with capable and well-educated individuals whom he trusted and to whom he delegated great authority. The king's first counselor and adviser, Robert of Meulan, is always described as a man of great intelligence endowed with sound judgment and capable of subtle, pragmatic counsel.[211] His twin sons were educated by Faritius, the learned Italian physician and abbot of Abingdon, and the twins once successfully held a theological disputation before the pope

---

[206] Southern, *Medieval Humanism*, p. 220.

[207] *Chron. Battle*, p. 213.

[208] OV, 6:368.

[209] WM, *GR*, 5:412.

[210] HH, "De contemptu mundi," pp. 607–609. This estimate clearly sounds a little formulaic—a man in love with his own words does not radiate sincerity—but the importance of this passage is its accord with other assessments.

[211] See WM, *GR*, 5:407.

to show off Henry's sophisticated court.[212] Roger of Salisbury
who virtually ran the kingdom in the absence of the king, was the
creator and manager of an increasingly sophisticated adminis
trative and judicial machinery; he showed himself prudent, honest, and
energetic in his service to the king.[213] The bishop of Salisbury's links
to the influential school of Laon,[214] where he sent his nephews, both
of whom Henry promoted in his household and at Lincoln and Ely
indicate the high caliber of these royal servants. Robert of Béthune,
who was first appointed prior of Llanthony and then bishop of Here
ford, had also studied at Laon. Orderic praises those members
of the Norman clergy whose skills made them attractive to Henry
and useful in his administration. Bishop John of Lisieux, a former
archdeacon of Sées and royal chaplain, functioned as a prime member
of the viceregency in Normandy, where he was known for his intelli
gent handling of ecclesiastical and secular matters.[215] Audoin of Evreux,
brother of the clever Thurstan archbishop of York, often traveled
with the king in Normandy and ranked, adds Orderic, among the
most learned of his day.[216] Neither Hugh of Amiens, a distinguished
theologian who became abbot of Reading and archbishop of
Rouen, nor the Breton philosopher Gilbert de la Porrée "the Uni
versal," who became bishop of London, hesitated to accept an appoint
ment in England. The Benedictine monastic community basked
in the support of this king, who admired such leaders and intellec
tuals as Anselm and Boso of Bec and counted them among his
friends and advisers. Hildebert of Lavardin, the poet-bishop of Le
Mans and archbishop of Tours, enjoyed a long friendship with Henry
and with many members of his family, as evidenced by an extensive
correspondence. Ivo the canonist-bishop of Chartres also maintained
close ties with the Anglo-Norman kings. Peter the Venerable abbot
of Cluny was of course indebted to Henry for his great generosity,
but as one of the supporters of the celebrated abbey of Cluny
Henry joined a confraternity of powerful European luminaries
which included various popes, the invincible St Bernard of Clairvaux,

[212] Ibid.; White, "Career of Waleran," esp. p. 23. On the same occasion as the dis
putation, Calixtus also deferred to the intelligence of Henry himself, who defended
himself so plausibly, cogently, and eloquently that the pope could not censure him,
as he had planned to do (WM, *GR*, 5:406).

[213] WM, *GR*, 5:408. Henry was so confident of the bishop of Salisbury's loyalty that
the disagreement over the succession made no difference to the bishop's admin
istrative role.

[214] Roger successfully enticed Guy of Etampes, also a former Laon student, to
become master of his school in Salisbury.

[215] OV, 6:142–144.

[216] Ibid., p. 520.

and the kings of Spain and Sicily, all linked by their friendship with the abbot.

The royal family and Henry's intimates also charted a new course for England and Normandy in the twelfth-century world of literacy and letters. Both of Henry's queens patronized writers, Matilda favoring William of Malmesbury as well as a number of foreigners (complained William), Adeliza commissioning a scholar named David to write a history/biography of Henry I, which is unfortunately lost.[217] Robert of Gloucester, the king's natural son, profited from the schooling his father ordained for him and grew up, as Malmesbury said, to balance knighthood and letters.[218] He patronized William of Malmesbury and Geoffrey of Monmouth. Geoffrey Gaimar included Robert of Gloucester in the epilogue of his *Estoire des Engleis* of ca. 1136/1137 as a member of a kind of aristocratic literary circle.[219] Brian fitz Count, a constant companion of Robert of Gloucester and Henry I, must have belonged to this circle, for he showed himself well enough educated to write letters of support for Maud during Stephen's early years.[220] Maud herself followed her family's lead in literary patronage.[221] She even convinced the philosopher William of Conches to abandon the French schools for the Norman ducal court in order to tutor her son, the future Henry II.[222]

A literate ruler, a literate government: these aspects of the English monarchy in the first third of the twelfth century place Henry's court within the intellectual-literary-artistic movement that Haskins termed the "Renaissance of the Twelfth Century." Henry's government was moving throughout the reign toward greater centralization, systematization, and specialization as order replaced disorder, as responsibility and accountability displaced self-interest and localism. That the exploitation of power by royal officials was difficult to control goes without saying,[223] but in addition to this rather common failing of bureaucratic government, another aspect piqued contemporaries. Frank Barlow noticed an unhealthy atmosphere of "greed and ambition" in the Benedictine monastic world of the early twelfth century,[224]

---

[217] Short, "Gaimar's 'Epilogue,'" pp. 323, 327, 340.

[218] WM, *HN*, chaps 446, 449.

[219] Ibid.

[220] H. W. C. Davis, "Henry of Blois and Brian fitz Count"; Chibnall, *Empress Matilda*, pp. 84–85; *Letters and Charters of Gilbert Foliot*, pp. 60–66.

[221] WM, *GR*, ep. 2, pp. 6–8

[222] Haskins, "Adelard of Bath and Henry Plantagenet," p. 516; Warren, *Henry II*, p. 39.

[223] See OV's long diatribe, 6:331. I have noted elsewhere in this work the many instances in which the king *rectified* such illegal activities (see chapter 10, note 184, and above, this chapter, nn. 67 and 164).

[224] Barlow, *The English Church: 1066–1154*, p. 198.

but his terms seem also to echo the language and opinions of many contemporaries on royal government. For the only ill repute Henry suffered in his own time arose from his government's success in collecting and amassing revenues. The development of systematic financial institutions with standardized procedures no doubt shocked Henry's subjects, who were unaccustomed to the fingers of government reaching so effectively into their pockets as royal officials spread out into the shires. What we are seeing is not greed, but need: an ambitious government, as it grows bigger and better, requires more officials and more taxes. Lacking the spoils of conquest, the Henrician administration managed its resources more and more carefully, funding the system (and the peace) from established sources based on the regular "contributions" of the governed—a novelty in the early twelfth century which would, in each incarnation in later generations, produce similar cries of outrage.

Such government was still personal government and required a strong hand at the top. But the implicit contract between the ruler and the ruled, the mutual responsibility that such a relationship entailed, did not permit oppression and extortion. Henry's tactics for securing the loyalty of his magnates have an eminent reasonableness, for the king offered tangible rewards, such as lands and titles, and less tangible benefits, such as power, access to the king's ear, and a blind eye to debts. The king described by some as cold and inscrutable in fact worked hard to entice his supporters into his company; he repeated his overtures; he forgave the repentant. Those who joined him willingly enjoyed the king's favor and the respect of their colleagues. Surprisingly, no chroniclers or historians complain of royal favoritism, although it is clear that there were favorites. Apparently the respect accorded the king extended to his *fideles*. Perhaps the social mobility evident in Henry's recruitment made jealousy impossible. Even Stephen's chroniclers can say little critical of Robert of Gloucester or Brian fitz Count, both noted for their knightly qualities of honor and fidelity. Perhaps this lack of criticism was also a result of the king's strong sense of justice. Suger was the first to call Henry "the lion of justice."[225] Although he used the metaphor to emphasize the king's power to make men tremble, this justice also demonstrated the evenhandedness of a centralized system in which the unprotected—a monastery, even a royal scribe, for example—could seek redress for the actions of the inevitable unscrupulous baron or royal official.

The art of compromise also goes hand in hand with the rationality of Henry's system. The king's treatment of the magnates—his domestic policy, so to speak—from beginning to end exhibits constant

---

[225] Suger, *Louis le Gros*, pp. 102–103 (chap. 16), citing Geoffrey of Monmouth.

attempts to reach accommodation. Everett Crosby notes the same quality in the king's selection of his bishops.[226] Similar efforts can be seen in Henry's dealings with his neighbors—his foreign policy. He sought good relations and stable frontiers above all else as part of a consistent effort to avoid war and bloodshed. Henry is unique among his Anglo-Norman predecessors and his European contemporaries in seeking no further conquests once he had secured the Anglo-Norman realm of his father. He eschewed the heroic model of Arthur popularized by Geoffrey of Monmouth in which the English king eventually marched into Rome. Henry equally disdained the path trod by Charlemagne, or the Crusaders, or indeed his own father. Raised in the hard school of poverty, with few expectations, Henry seems to have recognized the difficulty of financing and controlling unlimited expansion. His brother Rufus had planned to occupy Poitiers and perhaps even to rule France; his grandson Henry II had seemingly limitless ambitions. But Henry, the peacemaker, sought the possible. A glance at his policies regarding Wales, Scotland, or Maine, even Flanders,[227] shows that he was content with nominal suzerainty over his traditional vassals— nothing more. As king, he had no intention of humbling himself to swear homage and fealty to Louis VI for Normandy, although he allowed his son to do so. He never requested such submission by David king of Scots, presumably because David had given homage and fealty when he received the earldom of Huntingdon. Henry was realist enough to demand no greater precision.[228]

Overall, one might say that King Henry I was a master builder: of men, of personal relationships, of institutions, of a myriad religious establishments from great cathedrals and monasteries to the *habitacula* of hermits, of a ring of castles on the Welsh and Norman[229] frontiers to protect his renowned peace, safeguard the countryside, and keep the barns full.[230] The king even interested himself in a canal to facilitate water transport to Lincoln from the River Trent, and he contributed to

---

[226] Crosby, "The Organization of the English Episcopate," p. 27.

[227] Thierry of Flanders apparently did homage to Henry I, as a charter of Henry II shows (OV, 6:378/379 n. 4).

[228] This understanding of the king explains why Henry was so mystified by the Canterbury–York struggle over the primacy and the unwillingness of archbishops to accept general professions of obedience from important abbots. Henry, the pragmatist, always seemed to be trying to reach a compromise that the principal parties, often ideologues, found odious.

[229] RT, *Chron.*, s.a. 1135 (pp. 196–197), lists the important constructions on the Norman frontier: Neufchâtel-en-Bray, Châteauneuf-sur-Epte, Verneuil, Nonancourt, Bonsmoulins, Lyons-la-Forêt, le Vaudreuil, Evreux, Alençon, and Coutances. We should not fail to mention New Windsor, which the king built for himself. See also above, pp. 90–93, 115, 185, 188, 189, 199, 263, 404, 405, 409, 431, 439.

[230] Suger, *Louis le Gros*, p. 103.

the construction of a road for pilgrims over the Alps leading to Rome.[231] During his reign Henry, his bishops, abbots, and barons presided over the reconstruction or rebuilding of almost every major abbey church and cathedral in England. The energetic Normans had begun this work in the 1070s and 1080s, but, as any reader of the *Anglo-Saxon Chronicle* will notice immediately, frequent fires meant frequent reconstruction. This challenge created new opportunities for architects and artisans to introduce improvements in craftsmanship and structure and to display greater originality in decorative elements, all of which distinguished English high Romanesque architecture and contributed to the new continental style, the Gothic.[232]

The wealth and stability of the Anglo-Norman realm under Henry I as well as the generosity of the king and his magnates permitted the "visionary program" that these "grandiose concepts" embodied.[233] The evidence lies in such monasteries as St Albans, Bury St Edmunds, St Swithin's in Winchester, Peterborough, Ely, Ramsey, Gloucester, St Werburgh's at Chester, Tewkesbury, Crowland, and later Fountains, Rievaulx, Furness, and Melrose, and in the new or enlarged cathedrals of Canterbury, St Paul's, Rochester, Evreux, and Bayeux.

Like an architect, Henry conceived and designed a great governmental edifice: he laid solid foundations, cut his stones to true shapes, improved the structure to bear greater weight, and buttressed where necessary to maintain the integrity of the whole. The stones that Henry piled up, to quote William of Malmesbury quoting Wulfstan of Worcester,[234] would prove durable. The green tree that Henry had reunited when he joined the Norman and Old English lines bore fruit in his own reign and would blossom again, even luxuriantly, in the reign of his grandson.[235]

---

[231] SD, *s.a.* 1121; *GND*, 2:254–255.
[232] See Harvey, *The Master Builders*, and Rowley, *The Norman Heritage: 1066–1200*, esp. pp. 139–143.
[233] Harvey, *The Master Builders*, pp. 19–20.
[234] WM, *GP*, p. 283.
[235] WM, *GR*, 2:226.

APPENDIX

CHARTER ATTESTATIONS AND THE ROYAL ENTOURAGE

A number of times throughout this book I have listed the most frequent attesters of surviving royal charters across various time periods, on the plausible assumption that such persons attended the king's court more regularly than other high-status individuals and were therefore, presumably, his closest associates. The results of this methodology, as I have pointed out in earlier works, can only be approximate:

> For obvious reasons, the correlation between charter attestations and attendance at court is imperfect: one could be at court and not attest, and it is possible that a person's name might occasionally appear on a witness list without his having been present at the time the charter was issued. Nevertheless, attestations remain our surest means of determining which people were habitually in the royal entourage.[1]

David Bates, in a recent paper, used his expertise as editor of the new *Regesta* of William the Conqueror to elaborate substantially on my caveats and to challenge the soundness of my witness-counting methodology.[2] His reservations deserve serious consideration. It is of course essential, as he points out, to consider in one's analysis all the genuine charters at hand, to exclude forgeries, and to approach "improved" charters warily. To this end, Bates' comprehensive new *Regesta* of William I will be invaluable, adding as it does some seventy-two *acta* overlooked in the original *Regesta* 1 (1913) and in the *errata and addenda* section of *Regesta* 2 (1956) and significantly refining evaluations of the validity and nature of the *acta*.[3]

Bates' remarks are also valuable in that they remind us of the distinction between writs of various sorts (common in England but not in

---

[1] *MMI*, p. 98; cf. p. xiii.
[2] David Bates, "The Prosopographical Study of Anglo-Norman Royal Charters." I am grateful to Professor Bates for his kindness in sending me an offprint. For a cogent counter-argument, supporting the correlation between attestations and appearances at court, see Keefe, "Counting Those Who Count."
[3] David Bates' new *Regesta regum anglo-normannorum* appeared in 1998 (ACF).

Normandy before Tinchebray), solemn diplomas attested by *signa*, short diplomas with relatively few *signa*, memoranda recording pleas, and *pancartes,* which embody multiple witness lists and record a number of benefactions and transactions across time. Bates rightly stresses the complexities of charter production and witness selection, including the tendency for some attesters to have been chosen because of their association with the charter's beneficiary. He suggests that the loss of a single monastic archive might distort the overall distribution of attesters.

As against these several cautions, it must be stressed that the approximately two thousand royal charters issued between 1066 and 1135 (of which about fifteen hundred are from Henry I's reign) constitute a database of far more than adequate size to factor out anomalies in the nature and production of individual charters. The several thousand witnesses of Anglo-Norman charters comprise an immense variety of individuals.[4]

This point emerges strikingly from Bates' own effort at a much more sophisticated analysis of the charter attesters of William the Conqueror than my own. Bates endeavors to refine my methodology by adding his seventy-two new *acta* to those in the 1913 and 1956 *Regestae* (on which I was obliged to depend), by eliminating all *acta* that the original *Regesta* editors accepted as genuine but were subsequently rejected by Bates and others as forgeries, and then by filtering out all remaining *acta* except those with multiple high-status *signa* and with attesters who have no apparent connection with the contents of a diploma. The outcome of this elaborate methodological enhancement is a list of names that are disappointingly familiar: Roger of Montgomery, Robert count of Mortain, Roger of Beaumont, Robert count of Meulan, Alan lord of Richmond, and Hugh earl of Chester. Bates concludes, "These six—probably unsurprisingly—are as good as identical with the six leading lay magnates identified by very different methods by Hollister."[5] I am happy to agree, having myself earlier identified William I's six most frequently attesting laymen as Roger of Montgomery, Robert count of Mortain, Robert count of Meulan, Roger of Beaumont, Alan lord of Richmond, and Hugh earl of Chester. Indeed, since Bates' list echoes my own earlier list so unerringly, the import of his criticism is not easy to grasp.[6]

---

[4] Contemporary French royal charters, by comparison, are much less useful in identifying members of the king's entourage beyond the five great household officers who ordinarily attest: the dapifer, constable, butler, treasurer, and chancellor (*per manum*): *Recueil des actes de Louis VI, roi de France (1108–1137).*

[5] Bates, "Prosopographical Study," p. 96.

[6] *MMI,* p. 109: the six magnates on my list attest, respectively, 40 charters, 30.5, 23, 21, 21, and 15.5.

Let us look next at the *acta* of William Rufus and their bearing on what I have perceived to be an important change in the nature of Rufus' entourage. Of the nine most frequent lay attesters of his *acta* (predominantly writs), five are magnates and four are household officials with only moderate landed endowments.[7] Three of the magnates hold comital titles but only one (Hugh earl of Chester) belongs to a Domesday class A landholding family. Bates regards my attestation statistics for Rufus' reign as "almost totally irrelevant to the topic being discussed" because of the preponderance of English writs over Anglo-Norman diplomas. Diplomas, Bates supposes, are more likely than writs to bear the attestations of magnates; yet as we have just seen, magnates constitute the majority of high attesters of Rufus' writs. Perhaps Bates means that diplomas are more apt to be signed only by the very wealthiest magnates rather than by lesser ones, but why this should be so I am not sure.[8]

The likelihood that Rufus' most frequent attesters were indeed often at his court is suggested by the fact that all of them are prominently mentioned in contemporary narrative sources. Their appearance in royal charters should therefore not be surprising. Of the magnates, for example, Robert count of Meulan is portrayed by Eadmer as Rufus' constant companion and chief adviser in the king's conflict with Anselm. Robert of Meulan's brother, Henry earl of Warwick, is known to have been Rufus' good friend as well, and so too are Robert fitz Hamon and Hugh earl of Chester,[9] along with Robert fitz Hamon's brother Hamo II *Dapifer*, Eudo *Dapifer*, and Urse sheriff of Worcester. In short, Rufus' leading attesters are precisely the men whom we would have otherwise expected them to be. Our various historical sources are mutually consistent to a reassuring degree.

The "topic being discussed," to which my statistics are alleged to be irrelevant, is the drastic reduction of attestations by Domesday class A landholding families from all but the earliest of Rufus' charters and the degree to which this development indicates, as I have suggested elsewhere, a growing divergence between Rufus' *familiares* and his

---

[7] Ibid., p. 110: Rufus' most frequent attesters of genuine *acta* calendared in *RRAN* 1 are Eudo *Dapifer* (37 attestations), Roger Bigod *Dapifer* (28), Robert fitz Hamon (21), Robert count of Meulan (16), Urse of Abitôt constable and sheriff of Worcestershire (12), Hamo II *Dapifer* (9), William Peverel of Nottingham (9), Hugh earl of Chester (8.5), and Henry earl of Warwick (8).

[8] Since the lists of *signa* on solemn diplomas, often issued at great courts, tend to be substantially longer than the lists of witnesses on writs, diplomas are more likely than writs to include the attestations of great magnates. But the *signa* on diplomas also include, in greater abundance, the same lesser magnates and *curiales* whose names appear on writs. As a result, analyses of the *most frequent* attesters of diplomas and writs produce much the same results.

[9] See above, pp. 58–59, 79 and n. 221, 95–96, 99, 116, 132–133.

wealthiest magnates. Once again, the attestation statistics are corroborated by other evidence. Rufus was confronted with two general baronial rebellions during his thirteen-year reign, the first of which, in 1088, involved most of the Domesday class A families. In the second of them (1095), many of the greatest landholders again joined forces against the king, this time in a sworn conspiracy to have Rufus murdered (a fate that he barely eluded by being warned of an ambush in the nick of time). "Earls and men of similar rank," Orderic declares, "had knowingly been parties to the treacherous confederacy."[10] It seems unlikely that Rufus and his erstwhile murderers could afterward have consorted cheerfully together at the royal court.

Henry I, on the contrary, faced only one rebellion in England during his thirty-five-year reign (and it occurred in his initial year). Again, Henry I's coronation charter promising his nobility relief from Rufus' oppressions contrasts sharply with Stephen's coronation charter promising his nobles all the liberties and good laws that Henry I had given them.[11] The chroniclers confirm these impressions. Orderic asserts that Rufus' government bore heavily on rich and poor alike: the king bound some to him by generosity but held everyone else in check by force or fear, whereas Henry I placated all groups. William of Malmesbury declares that Rufus was mourned chiefly by his mercenary knights and unlamented by others because he permitted their property to be plundered; and Malmesbury describes Rufus' financial alter ego, Ranulf Flambard, not only as an exterminator of the poor but also, significantly, as a "despoiler of the rich." Eadmer depicts Rufus at the council of Rockingham as being backed by his hand-picked bench of bishops but opposed by the magnates. According to the Worcester chronicler, Rufus "pillaged the richer men of England by depriving them of their wealth and lands."[12]

The conclusion that a person's absence from Rufus' witness lists indicates that he was rarely at court receives striking confirmation in the case of Robert Malet, Domesday lord of Eye, with estates in Suffolk, Yorkshire, and several other counties. Robert served for a time as sheriff of Suffolk under William the Conqueror and resumed the office under Henry I, who advanced him to the master chamberlainship. Robert Malet attested at least five of the Conqueror's surviving charters and

---

[10] OV, 4:281–285; *MMI*, p. 103.

[11] Above, pp. 110–111; *Select Charters*, ed. Stubbs and Davis, p. 142.

[12] OV, 4:178, 5:296; WM, *GR* (RS) 2:369, 379; Eadmer, *HN*, pp. 53–67; FW, 2:46; cf. "The Prefaces of *Quadripartitus*," ed. and trans. Richard Sharpe, p. 165: [After bewailing the miseries suffered under William Rufus]: ". . . when we were worn out and almost done for, the peaceful times of the king and duke of Normandy . . . Henry son of William the great, brought back the longed-for joys of peace and our former happiness."

nineteen of Henry I's between about 1100 and 1105. The fact that he neither attested nor was addressed in any of Rufus' surviving charters led me to the cautious conclusion (in 1977) that he did not serve "in an important office in Rufus's administration."[13] That my conclusion was not unreasonable is demonstrated by C. P. Lewis in an article published in 1989, cleverly entitled "The King and Eye."[14] In it, on the basis of new evidence unknown to me or to any of his predecessors, Lewis demonstrated that Rufus, toward the beginning of his reign, disseised Robert Malet of his honor of Eye and granted it to Roger the Poitevin (brother of Robert of Bellême). Later "Henry I deprived Roger to restore it to Robert."[15] Thus, Robert Malet's attestation statistics accurately reflect the ups and downs of his career under the first three Norman kings.

Let me turn finally to the much better documented reign of Henry I. Here once again the relationship between attestation frequency and other evidence is overwhelming. At the opening of the reign, for example, the men named by Orderic as Henry's chief counselors (Robert of Meulan, Hugh of Chester, Richard of Redvers, and Roger Bigod) are among the most frequent attesters of the king's early charters.[16] Later in the reign, men named in narrative sources as members of Henry's inner circle—Roger of Salisbury, Robert Bloet, Ranulf the Chancellor, Robert of Gloucester, Brian fitz Count, Henry bishop of Winchester—are also among the preeminent attesters, and those of them who were alive in 1129–1130 are named in the Pipe Roll of 1130 as foremost recipients of danegeld exemptions.[17]

The number of Henry's charters that has survived, whether published or not, obviously constitutes only a fraction of the total originally issued by the royal chancery. What that fraction might be one can only estimate very roughly and with considerable uncertainty. Michael Clanchy has offered the educated guess that the total number of Henry I's surviving charters should be multiplied by about one hundred.[18] Using Clanchy's multiplier, we arrive at a total output for the reign of more than 150,000 charters, or some 4,400 per year, which is compatible with T. A. M. Bishop's estimate that in 1130 Henry's chancery

[13] *MMI*, pp. 130–131.

[14] Lewis, "The King and Eye," pp. 569–589.

[15] Ibid., p. 576.

[16] OV, 5:298; similarly, the magnates named by William of Malmesbury as loyal to Henry in the crisis of 1101: Robert of Meulan, Richard of Redvers, Robert fitz Hamon, Roger Bigod, and Henry earl of Warwick: WM, *GR* (RS), 2:471.

[17] ASC, s.a. 1123–1135, *passim*; WM, *GR*, and WM, *HN*, *passim*; HH, pp. 416–418, 460, 468–470; *PR 31 Henry I*, *passim*. My point is so obvious that further references seem unnecessary.

[18] Clanchy, *From Memory to Written Record*, pp. 57–60.

was employing about four scribes—requiring the not unreasonable output per scribe of three charters a day.[19] Whatever the correct multiplier might be, it is clear that the output of royal charters per year was increasing dramatically through the reigns of the Norman and Angevin kings (Stephen's reign excepted).[20]

Since only a small percentage of Henry I's charters has survived, the question arises: how typical are the surviving charters relative to the much larger original body? Here again, certainty is impossible, but it should be borne in mind that considerably more of Henry I's charters have survived from England than from Normandy, even though Henry spent more time south of the Channel than north of it. Between his conquest of the duchy in 1106 and his death in 1135, Henry spent 210 months in Normandy and only 140 in England, yet of the 980 royal charters from these years whose origins are certain or probable, 765 emanated from England and a mere 215 from the Continent.[21] Because of this markedly disproportionate survival rate of English to Norman charters, I will continue, as in the past, to weigh charters issued from Normandy more heavily than those from England.[22]

One must also recognize that certain kinds of charter are more apt to have survived than others. Whereas charters granting or confirming property, especially to churches, would normally have been preserved for posterity in archives or recorded in cartularies, charters conveying royal orders of temporary duration are unlikely to have been preserved once the orders took effect. We know from chronicle evidence, for example, that Henry regularly summoned his chief magnates and prelates to great councils by sending individual writs to each of them.[23] Again, the *Pipe Roll of 31 Henry I* mentions nearly three hundred otherwise unknown royal writs granting annual exemptions from gelds

---

[19] Bishop, *Scriptores regis*, p. 32.

[20] See Clanchy, *From Memory to Written Record*, p. 60, fig. 1. Charters surviving from the combined reigns of William I and II (1066–1100: a time span only slightly shorter than the reign of Henry I) come to little more than a third of Henry I's total: 351 for William I (I am grateful to David Bates for supplying me with this figure from his *Regesta* of William the Conqueror [published 1998—ACF]) and roughly 180 for William II (from *RRAN* 1)—a total of about 530 for both reigns as against about 1,550 for Henry I. Clanchy suggests that the constant rise in annual charter production between the reigns of Edward the Confessor and Henry II can be explained not only by the growing trend toward literate governance but also by the surge in population over these years and the dramatic increase (at least tenfold) in the number of religious houses.

[21] *MMI*, p. 227 n. 10; Le Patourel, *Norman Empire*, pp. 124, 175–176.

[22] *MMI*, pp. 226, 227 n. 18.

[23] E.g. *ASC, s.a.* 1123: "The king sent his writs over all England and ordered all his bishops and abbots and nobles to come to him for his council meeting on Candlemas Day at Gloucester, and they did so."

and fines to favored individuals, and one can reasonably conclude that Henry's chancery issued a comparable number of similar writs each year, none of which has survived.[24] Such writs would necessarily have been very brief and would have been witnessed by no more than one or two royal intimates, in contrast to more formal grants authenticated by a number of witnesses or solemn diplomas, often issued during great royal councils, which might be signed by as many as several dozen people. The attesters of these diplomas customarily included a number of courtiers of the king's inner circle (who formed the core of all great councils), but they also included many others who were rarely at court and seldom witnessed charters—abbots, for example, who normally remained in their monasteries unless summoned to major councils, or lay magnates of sedentary, apolitical disposition who attended court only when necessary, or humbler men who had come in their lords' retinues. A comprehensive analysis of the witnesses of Henry I's surviving charters would thus include, along with *curiales* more or less regularly in the king's company, a great number of relatively infrequent attesters who attended court only on special occasions. If, however, one excludes these large assemblages from the analysis and considers only the witness lists of charters emanating from the smaller itinerating court, the result should be to filter out many of the people who attended court only occasionally and to bring the king's regular companions into even greater prominence.

This assumption is confirmed by an analysis of actual charters and their attesters. In a previous study of all Henry's genuine charters calendared in the *Regesta* 2, I listed the most frequent witnesses in the years around AD 1111 and again around 1131, limiting my lists to *curiales* who attested surviving charters at the rate of at least 1.5 per year.[25] I identified 24 such attesters in 1111 and 38 in 1131, for a total of 56 (counting as only 1 an attester who occurred on both lists). To these *curiales* I added 5 others who died before 1111 (Roger Bigod, Robert fitz Hamon, Robert Malet, Hugh earl of Chester, and Richard of Redvers), along with Ralph d'Escures, archbishop of Canterbury, whose archiepiscopal career fell between 1111 and 1131. The attestations of these 62 *curiales* (attesting at a rate of between 1.5 and 11.5 a year) constitute roughly half of all attestations throughout the thirty-five-year reign, the others being scattered among many hundreds of less frequent attesters.

Let us therefore reverse Bates' focus on longer attestation lists and *omit* charters with multiple attesters (normally issued at large councils), in order better to identify persons in the king's day-by-day entourage.

---

[24] Bishop, *Scriptores regis*, p. 32; Clanchy, *From Memory to Written Record*, p. 58.
[25] *MMI*, p. 241.

If we use charters with 5 attesters as our cut-off point, the percentage of attestations by the 62 aforementioned *curiales* rises from one-half to about two-thirds of the total. And if one limits the sample to the 716 charters bearing no more than two attestations, it rises to 83 percent, the remainder being primarily lesser members of the royal household and regional officials. Finally, if one considers only charters with a single attestation, the attestations of the 62 *curiales* constitute no less than 86 percent of the total. And as we perform these successive analyses, the most frequent attesters within the curial group pull farther ahead of the others at each step. In short, there is every reason to conclude that the group of administrators and advisers who frequented the king's itinerant court and attested surviving royal charters most often would have been all the more conspicuous in the witness lists of charters that have perished.

BIBLIOGRAPHY

PRIMARY SOURCES

Abelard, Peter. *Peter Abelard's "Ethics."* Ed. D. E. Luscombe. Oxford, 1971.

Actes de Guillaume le Conquérant et de la reine Mathilde pour les abbayes caennaises. Ed. Lucien Musset. Caen, 1967.

Actes des comtes de Flandre, 1071–1128. Ed. Fernand Vercauteren. Brussels, 1938.

Actus pontificum cenomannis in urbe degentium. Ed. G. Busson and A. Ledru. Le Mans, 1902.

Adam of Domerham. *Historia de rebus gestis glastoniensibus.* Ed. T. Hearne. 2 vols. London, 1727.

Aelred of Rievaulx. *Vita S. Edwardi regis et confessoris. PL,* vol. 195. Paris, 1855.

Ancient Charters, Royal and Private, Prior to AD 1200. Ed. J. H. Round. London, 1959.

Anderson, Alan Orr. *Early Sources of Scottish History.* Corrected edn. 2 vols. Stamford, Lincs., 1990.

Anglo-Latin Satirical Poets and Epigrammists of the Twelfth Century. Ed. Thomas Wright. Rolls Series, vol. 59 (in 2 vols.). London, 1872.

Anglo-Saxon Chronicle. Ed. Dorothy Whitelock. New Jersey, 1961.

Anglo-Saxon Chronicle: A Collaborative Edition. Ed. David M. Dumville and Simon Keynes. Cambridge, 1983–.

Annales Cambriae. Ed. John Williams ab Ithel. Rolls Series, vol. 20. London, 1860.

"Annales de Saint-Aubin." In *Recueil d'annales angevines et vendômoises.* Ed. Louis Halphen. Paris, 1903.

"Annales de Waverleia." In *Annales monastici,* vol. 36, part 2.

"Annales du Mont-Saint-Michel." In RT, *Chronique,* vol. 2. Ed. Léopold Delisle. Rouen, 1873.

"Annales Monasterii de Wintonia." In *Annales monastici,* vol. 36, part 2.

Annales monastici. Ed. Henry Richards Luard. Rolls Series, vol. 36 (in 5 vols.). London, 1864–1869.

"Annales radingenses." In *Ungedruckte Anglo-Normannische Geschichtsquellen.* Ed. F. Liebermann. Strasbourg, 1879.

"Annals de Margan." In *Annales monastici,* vol. 36, part 1.

Bayeux. *Antiquus cartularius ecclesiae baiocensis (Livre noir).* Ed. V. Bourienne. 2 vols. Rouen, 1902–1903.

Beati Lanfranci Archiepiscopi Cantuariensis opera omnia. Ed. J. A. Giles. Oxford, 1844.

Bibliotheca cluniacensis. Ed. Martin Marrier. Paris, 1614. Macon, 1915.

Book of Fees/Liber feodorum. 3 vols. London, 1920–1931. Repr. 1971.

Brenhinedd y Saesson, in *Myvrian Archaeology of Wales.* Ed. Owen Jones, Edward Williams, and W. O. Pughe. 2nd edn. Denbigh, 1870.

Brevis relatio de Willelmo nobilissimo comite Normannorum. In *Scriptores rerum gestarum Willelmi Conquestoris.* Ed. J. A. Giles. London, 1845.

Brut y Tywysogyon or the Chronicle of the Princes, Peniarth, MS. 20 Version. Trans. Thomas Jones. Cardiff, 1952.

Calendar of Documents Preserved in France, Illustrative of the History of Great Britain and Ireland. Ed. J. H. Round. Vol. 1, AD 918–1206. London, 1889.

Canterbury Professions. Ed. Michael Richter. Torquay, 1973.

Cartulaire de l'abbaye de Saint-Père de Chartres. Ed. M. Guérard. 2 vols. Paris, 1840.

Cartulaire de l'église de Notre-Dame de Chartres. Ed. E. de Lépinois and Lucien Merlet. 3 vols in 2. Chartres, 1862–1865.

Cartulaire de Marcigny-sur-Loire, 1045–1144. Ed. Jean Richard. Dijon, 1957.

Cartulaire Manceau de Marmoutier. Ed. E. Laurain. Laval, 1911–1945.

Cartularium monasterii de Rameseia. Ed. William Hart and Revd. Ponsonby A. Lyons. Rolls Series, vol. 79. London, 1884–1893.

Cartulary of Cirencester Abbey. Ed. Charles D. Ross. 2 vols. London, 1964.

Cartulary of Daventry Priory. Ed. M. J. Franklin. Northampton, 1988.

Cartulary of Worcester Cathedral Priory, Register I. Ed. R. R. Darlington. London, 1968.

Charters and Documents Illustrating the History of the Cathedral, City and Diocese of Salisbury in the Twelfth and Thirteenth Centuries. Ed. W. D. Macray. Rolls Series, vol. 97. London, 1891.

Charters and Records among the Archives of the Ancient Abbey of Cluni from 1077 to 1534. Ed. G. F. Duckett. 2 vols. Lewes, 1888.

Charters of Norwich Cathedral Priory, Part One. Ed. Barbara Dodwell. London, 1974.

Charters of the Honor of Mowbray, 1107–1191. Ed. D. E. Greenway. London, 1972.

Charters of the Redvers Family and the Earldom of Devon, 1090–1217. Ed. Robert Bearman. Exeter, 1994.

"Chronica monasterii de Hida juxta Wintoniam." In *Liber monasterii de Hyda.*

Chronicle of Battle Abbey. Ed. Eleanor Searle. Oxford, 1980.

"Chronicle of Rouen." In *HF,* 12: 784–786.

Chronicles of the Reigns of Stephen, Henry II, and Richard I. Ed. Richard Howlett. Rolls Series, vol. 82 (in 4 vols.). London, 1884–1889. Reprint 1964.

Chronicon abbatiae rameseiensis. Ed. W. D. Macray. Rolls Series, vol. 83. London, 1886.

Chronicon beccense abbatiae. PL, vol. 150, cols. 639–696. Paris, 1854.

Chronicon monasterii de Abingdon. Ed. Joseph Stevenson. Rolls Series, vol. 2 (in 2 vols.). London, 1858.

"Chronicon monasterii Mortui-maris." In *Thesaurus novus anecdotorum,* vol. 3.

Chronique de Morigny (1095–1152). Ed. Léon Mirot. 2nd edn. Paris, 1912.

Chronique du Bec. Ed. A. Porée. Rouen, 1883.

Chroniques des comtes d'Anjou et des seigneurs d'Amboise. Ed. Louis Halphen and René Poupardin. Paris, 1913.

Chroniques des comtes d'Anjou. Ed. P. Marchegay and A. Salmon. 2nd edn. in 2 parts. Paris, 1871.

Clarius of Sens. "Chronicon S. Petri Vivi Senonensis." In *HF*, vol. 12.

Concilia rotomagensis provinciae. Ed. Guillaume Bessin. Rouen, 1717.

Constitutio domus regis. See Fitz Nigel, Richard.

Corpus juris canonici. Ed. Emil Friedberg. 2nd edn. Leipzig, 1879. Repr. Graz, 1959.

Coucher Book of Selby. Ed. J. T. Fowler. 2 vols. Yorkshire, 1891–1893.

Councils and Ecclesiastical Documents Relating to Great Britain and Ireland. Ed. A. W. Haddan and William Stubbs. 3 vols. in 4. Oxford, 1869–1878.

Councils and Synods with Other Documents Relating to the English Church. Ed. Dorothy Whitelock, Martin Brett, and C. N. L. Brooke. Vol. 1, AD 871–1204, Part 1, 871–1066, Part 2, 1066–1204. Oxford, 1981.

De antiquitate Glastonie ecclesie. Ed. John Scott. Woodbridge, Suffolk, 1981.

"De libertate beccensis monasterii," *Annales ordinis sancti Benedicti,* vol. 5, pp. 601–605. Ed. Jean Mabillon. Paris, 1703–1739.

Dialogus de scaccario. See Fitz Nigel, Richard.

Diplomatic Documents Preserved in the Public Record Office. Vol. 1. Ed. Pierre Chaplais. London, 1964.

Domesday Monachorum of Christ Church. Ed. David C. Douglas. London, 1944.

Durham Episcopal Charters, 1071–1152. Ed. H. S. Offler. Gateshead, 1968.

Eadmer. *Historia novorum in Anglia.* Ed. Martin Rule. Rolls Series, vol. 81. London, 1884.

——. *Life of St Anselm.* Ed. and trans. R. W. Southern. Oxford, 1962.

——. *Vita Sancti Anselmi.* Ed. Martin Rule. Rolls Series, vol. 81. London, 1884.

Earldom of Gloucester Charters. Ed. Robert B. Patterson. Oxford, 1973.

Early Sources of Scottish History. Ed. Alan Orr Anderson. 2 vols. Corrected edn. Stamford, Lincs., 1990.

Early Yorkshire Charters. Ed. William Farrer and C. T. Clay. 12 vols. Edinburgh, 1914–1965.

Early Yorkshire Families. Ed. Charles Travis Clay. Leeds, 1973.

English Historical Documents. Ed. and trans. David C. Douglas and George Greenway. Vol. 2: 1066–1189. 2nd edn. New York, 1981.

English Lawsuits from William I to Richard I. Ed. R. C. Van Caenegem. 2 vols. London, 1990–1991.

Epistolae Herberti de Losinga, primi episcopi norwicensis, Osberti de Clara et Elmeri prioris cantuariensis. Ed. Robert Anstruther. Brussels, 1846.

Facsimiles of English Royal Writs to AD 1100. Ed. T. A. M. Bishop and P. Chaplais. Oxford, 1957.

Fitz Nigel, Richard. *Dialogus de scaccario and Constitutio domus regis.* Ed. and trans. Charles Johnson; corrections by F. E. L. Carter and D. E. Greenway. Oxford, 1983.

Florence of Worcester. *Chronicon ex chronicis.* Ed. B. Thorpe. 2 vols. London, 1848–1849.

Gaimar, Geoffrey. *L'Estoire des Engleis*. Ed. Alexander Bell. Oxford, 1960. Repr. New York, 1971.

Galbert of Bruges. *Histoire du meurtre de Charles le Bon*. Ed. Henri Pirenne. Paris, 1891.

———. *The Murder of Charles the Good, Count of Flanders*. Trans. James Bruce Ross. Rev. edn. New York, 1967.

Gallia Christiana in provincias ecclesiasticas distributa qua series et historia archiepiscorum, episcoporum et abbatum Franciae vicinarumque ditionum ab origine ecclesiarum ad nostra tempora deducitur et probatur ex authenticis documentis ad calcem appositis. 16 vols. Paris, 1715–1865.

Geoffrey of Monmouth. *The "Historia regum Britanniae" of Geoffrey of Monmouth*. Ed. Acton Griscom. London, 1929.

Gervase of Canterbury. *The Historical Work of Gervase of Canterbury*. Ed. William Stubbs. Rolls Series, vol. 73 (in 2 vols.). London, 1879–1880. Repr. 1965.

Die Gesetze der Angelsachsen. Ed. Felix Liebermann. 3 vols. Halle, 1903–1916.

Gesta abbatum monasterii S. Albani a Thoma Walsingham. Ed. Henry T. Riley. Rolls Series, vol. 28 (in 3 vols.). Part 4. London, 1867–1869.

Gesta normannorum ducum. Ed. Jean Marx. Rouen and Paris, 1914.

Gesta normannorum ducum of William of Jumièges, Orderic Vitalis, and Robert of Torigni. Ed. and trans. Elisabeth M. C. van Houts. 2 vols. Oxford, 1992–1995.

Gesta regis Henrici Secundi Benedicti abbatis. Ed. William Stubbs. Rolls Series, vol. 49. London, 1867.

Gesta Stephani. Ed. K. R. Potter and R. H. C. Davis. Rev. edn. London, 1976.

Gesta Stephani regis Anglorum, in *Chronicles of the Reigns of Stephen, Henry II, and Richard*. Ed. R. Howlett. Rolls Series, vol. 82. London, 1884–1889.

Gilbert of Limerick. *Liber de statu ecclesiae. PL*, vol. 159. Paris, 1854.

Great Rolls of the Pipe for the Second, Third, and Fourth Years of the Reign of King Henry the Second, AD 1155–1156, 1156–1157, 1157–1158. Ed. Joseph Hunter. London, 1844.

Gregorii VII regestum. MGH, Epistolae selectae. Berlin, 1920.

Guibert of Nogent. *Histoire de sa vie (1053–1124)* [De vita sua]. Ed. Georges Bourgin. Paris, 1907.

———. *Self and Society in Medieval France: The Memoirs of Abbot Guibert of Nogent (1064–c. 1125)*. Trans. John F. Benton. New York, 1970.

Guide historique et monumental de Domfront. Association pour la restauration du château de Domfront, 1990.

Handbook of British Chronology. Ed. E. B. Fryde, D. E. Greenway, S. Porter, and I. Roy. 3rd edn. London, 1986.

Henry of Huntingdon. *Historia Anglorum*. Ed. Diana Greenway. Oxford, 1996.

Herbert of Losinga. *The Life, Letters, and Sermons of Bishop Herbert de Losinga*. Ed. Edward Gouldburn and Henry Symonds. 2 vols. London, 1878.

———. *Epistolae Herberti de Losinga primi episcopi Norwicensis, Osberti de Clara, et Elmeri prioris Cantuariensis*. Ed. Robert Anstruther. Brussels and London, 1846.

Herefordshire Domesday. Ed. V. H. Galbraith and James Tait. Pipe Roll Society, n.s. 25. 1927–1928.

Hermann of Tournai. *De miraculis S. Mariae laudunensis. PL*, vol. 156. Paris, 1881.

——. "Liber de restauratione monasterii S. Martini tornacensis." Ed. G. Waitz. *MGH, SS*, vol. 14. Berlin, 1956.

Hermannus Laudunensis monachus. *De miraculis B. Mariae Laudunensis libris tribus*. In *HF*, 12:266–272.

Hesso Scholasticus. *Relatio de concilio remensi*. Ed. Wilhelm Wattenbach. *MGH, Libelli de Lite*, vol. 3. Hanover, 1956.

Hildebert of Lavardin. *Hildeberti cenomannensis episcopi carmina minora*. Ed. A. Brian Scott. Leipzig, 1969.

Historia et cartularium monasterii Sancti Petri Gloucestriae. Ed. W. H. Hart. 3 vols. Rolls Series, vol. 33. London, 1863.

Hugh of Flavigny. *Chronicon*. Ed. G. H. Pertz et al. *MGH, SS*, vol. 8. Hanover, 1826.

Hugh the Chanter. *The History of the Church of York, 1066–1127*. Ed. Charles Johnson, M. Brett, C. N. L. Brooke, and M. Winterbottom. Oxford, 1990.

Itinerary of John Leland. Ed. L. Toulmin Smith. 5 vols. Oxford, 1907–1910.

Ivo of Chartres. See Yves of Chartres.

John of Hexham, in *Symeonis monachi opera omnia*. Ed. T. Arnold. Rolls Series, vol. 75, part 2. London, 1885.

John of Marmoutier. "Vita Gaufredi." In *Chroniques des comtes d'Anjou et des seigneurs d'Amboise*. Ed. Louis Halphen and René Poupardin. Paris, 1913.

John of Salisbury. *Historia pontificalis*. Ed. Marjorie Chibnall. Oxford, 1986.

John of Worcester. *Chronicle*. Ed. J. R. H. Weaver. Oxford, 1908.

Lancashire Pipe Rolls of 31 Henry I, AD 1130, and of the Reigns of Henry II, AD 1155–1189; Richard I, AD 1189–1199; and King John, AD 1199–1216. Ed. William Farrer. Liverpool, 1902.

Leges Henrici Primi. Ed. L. J. Downer. Oxford, 1972.

Leicestershire Survey, c. AD 1130. Ed. C. F. Slade. Leicester, 1956.

Letters and Charters of Gilbert Foliot. Ed. Z. N. Brooke, Adrian Morey, and C. N. L. Brooke. London, 1967.

Letters of Lanfranc, Archbishop of Canterbury. Ed. Helen Clover and Margaret Gibson. Oxford, 1979.

Letters of Peter the Venerable. Ed. Giles Constable. 2 vols. Cambridge, Mass., 1967.

Letters of Saint Anselm of Canterbury. Ed. Walter Fröhlich. 3 vols. Kalamazoo, 1990–1994.

Lettres de Saint Ives. Ed. and trans. Lucien Merlet. Chartres, 1885.

Liber eliensis. Ed. E. O. Blake. London, 1962.

Liber feodorum. See *Book of Fees*.

Liber monasterii de Hyda. Ed. Edward Edwards. Rolls Series, vol. 45. London, 1866.

Liber S. Marie de Dryburgh. Ed. John Spottiswoode. Edinburgh, 1847.

Life, Letters, and Sermons of Bishop Herbert de Losinga. Ed. Edward Meyrick Gouldburn and Henry Symonds. 2 vols. Oxford, 1878.

Life of King Edward Who Rests at Westminster. Ed. Frank Barlow. 2nd edn. Oxford, 1992.

Lincolnshire Domesday and the Lindsey Survey. Ed. C. W. Foster and Thomas Longley. Lincoln, 1924. Repr. Gainsborough, 1976.

Le Livre de serfs de Marmoutier. Ed. André Salmon. Tours, 1864.

Louis le Gros: Annales de sa vie et de son règne. Ed. Achille Luchaire. Paris, 1890.

Magni rotuli scaccarii Normanniae sub regibus Angliae. Ed. Thomas Stapleton. 2 vols. London, 1840–1844.

Map, Walter. *De nugis curialium/Courtiers' Trifles.* Ed. and trans. M. R. James. Rev. by C. N. L. Brooke and R. A. B. Mynors. Oxford, 1983.

Matthew Paris. *Chronica majora.* Ed. Henry Richards Luard. Rolls Series, vol. 57 (in 7 vols.). London, 1872–1883.

Medieval Prince of Wales, A: The Life of Gruffudd ap Cynan. Ed. and trans. D. Simon Evans. Felinfach, 1990.

Monasticon anglicanum. Ed. Thomas Dugdale. 6 vols. in 8. London, 1817–1830.

"Monumenta bambergensis." Ed. P. Jaffé. In *Bibliotheca rerum germanicarum,* vol. 5. Berlin, 1869.

Monumenta Germaniae historica. Munich, 1819–1969.

Neustria pia. Ed. Artur Dumonstier. Rouen, 1663.

Norman Anonymous. *Die Texte des Normannischen Anonymus.* Ed. Karl Pellens. Wiesbaden, 1966.

"On the liberty of the abbey of Bec" [De libertate beccensis monasterii]. Trans. Sally N. Vaughn. In Vaughn, *The Abbey of Bec and the Anglo-Norman State.*

Orderic Vitalis. *Historia ecclesiastica/The Ecclesiastical History.* Ed. and trans. Marjorie Chibnall. 6 vols. Oxford, 1969–1980.

———. *Historia ecclesiastica libri tredecim.* Ed. Auguste Le Prevost. 5 vols. Paris, 1838–1855.

Otto of Freising. *The Two Cities.* Trans. C. C. Mierow. New York, 1928.

Outline Itinerary of King Henry the First. Ed. William Farrer. Oxford, 1920.

Papsturkunden in England. Ed. Walther Holtzmann. 3 vols. Abhandlungen der Gesellschaft der Wissenschaften in Göttingen, Phil.-Hist. Klasse, neue Folge, 25 (1930–1931), 3 Folge, 14/15 (1935–1936), 33. 1952.

Patrologia cursus completus. Series latina. Ed. J.-P. Migne. 221 vols. Paris, 1844–1864. Repr. 1958–.

Peterborough Chronicle. Ed. Cecily Clark. 2nd edn. Oxford, 1970.

Pipe Roll of 31 Henry I, Michaelmas, 1130. Ed. Joseph Hunter. Rev. edn. London, 1929.

The Pontifical of Magdalen College. Ed. H. A. Wilson. London, 1910.

"Preface to the *Quadripartitus.*" Trans. Richard Sharpe. In George Garnett and John Hudson, eds, *Law and Government in Medieval England and Normandy.*

The Priory of Hexham. Ed. James Raine. 2 vols. Surtees Society 44. Durham, 1864–1865.

Quadripartitus, ein englisches Rechtsbuch von 1114. Ed. Felix Liebermann. Halle, 1892.

Ralph of Diceto. *Abbreviationes chronichorum*, in *Opera historica*. Ed. William Stubbs. Rolls Series, vol. 68 (in 2 vols.). London, 1876.

Reading Abbey Cartularies: British Library Manuscripts Egerton 3031, Harley 1708 and Cotton Vespasian E XXV. Ed. B. R. Kemp. 2 vols. London, 1986–1987.

Record-Evidences among the Archives of the Ancient Abbey of Cluni. Ed. Sir G. F. Duckett. Lewes, 1886.

Recueil d'annales angevines et vendômoises. Ed. Louis Halphen. Paris, 1903.

Recueil des actes de Henri II. Ed. Léopold Delisle. 3 vols. Paris, 1909–1916.

Recueil des actes de Louis VI, roi de France (1108–1137). Ed. Jean Dufour. 3 vols. Paris, 1992–1993.

Recueil des actes de Philippe Ier, roi de France (1059–1108). Ed. M. Prou. Paris, 1908.

Recueil des actes des comtes de Pontieu, 1026–1279. Ed. Clovis Brunel. Paris, 1930.

Recueil des actes des ducs de Normandie de 911 à 1066. Ed. Marie Fauroux. Caen, 1961.

Recueil des chartes de l'abbaye de Cluny. Ed. Auguste Bernard and Alexandre Bruel. 6 vols. Vol. 5: 1091–1210. Paris, 1894.

"Recueil des chartes de l'abbaye de Saint-Wandrille." In Ferdinand Lot, *Etudes sur l'abbaye de Saint-Wandrille*. Paris, 1913.

Recueil des chartes et documents de Saint-Martin des Champs. Ed. Joseph Depoin. 2 vols. Paris, 1912.

Recueil des historiens des Gaules et de la France. Ed. Martin Bouquet. 24 vols in 25. Vol. 12: *Opera omnia B Lanfranci*. Vol. 15: *Reigns of Philip I, Louis VI, Louis VII*. Repr. Farnborough, 1967–1968.

Red Book of the Exchequer. Ed. Hubert Hall. Rolls Series, vol. 99 (in 3 vols.). London, 1896.

Regesta pontificum romanorum. 2nd edn. Ed. P. Jaffé; rev. W. Wattenbach, S. Lowenfeld, F. Kaltenbrunner, and P. Ewald. 2 vols. Leipzig, 1885–1888.

Regesta regum anglo-normannorum. Vol. 1: *Regesta Willelmi Rufi*, ed. H. W. C. Davis. Vol. 2: *Regesta Henrici Primi*, ed. C. Johnson and H. A. Cronne. Vol. 3: *Regesta Regis Stephani ac Mathildis imperatricis ac Gaufridi et Henrici ducum normannorum, 1135–1154*, ed. H. A. Cronne and R. H. C. Davis. Oxford, 1913–1969.

Regesta regum anglo-normannorum: The Acta of William I (1066–1087). Ed. David Bates. Oxford, 1998.

Registrum antiquissimum of the Cathedral Church of Lincoln. Ed. C. W. Foster. Hereford, 1931.

Richard Fitz Nigel. *Dialogus de scaccario and Constitutio domus regis*. Ed. and trans. Charles Johnson; corrections by F. E. L. Carter and D. E. Greenway. Oxford and New York, 1983.

Richard of Hexham. "Historia de gestis Regis Stephani et de Bello de Standardii." In *Chronicles of the Reigns of Stephen, Henry II, and Richard*, vol. 82, part 3. Ed. R. Howlett. Rolls Series, vol. 82 (in 4 vols.). London, 1884–1889. See also *The Priory of Hexham*.

Robert of Torigny. See *Gesta normannorum ducum* for his interpolations of William of Jumièges' *GND*.

———. *Chronicle of Robert of Torigni*. In Richard Howlett, ed., *Chronicles of the*

Reigns of Stephen, Henry II, and Richard I, vol. 82, part 4. Rolls Series, vol. 82. London, 1884–1889. Repr. 1964.

———. *Chronique*. Ed. Léopold Delisle. 2 vols. Rouen, 1872–1873.

Roger of Hoveden. *Chronica magistra*. Ed. William Stubbs. Rolls Series, vol. 51. London, 1868–1871.

Royal Writs in England from the Conquest to Glanvill. Ed. R. C. Van Caenegem. London, 1959.

S. *Anselmi cantuariensis archiepiscopi opera omnia*. Ed. Francis S. Schmitt. 6 vols. Stuttgart, 1946–1961. Repr. 1968.

Scriptores rerum gestarum Willelmi Conquestoris. Ed. J. A. Giles. London, 1845. Repr. New York, 1967.

Select Charters and Other Illustrations of English Constitutional History from the Earliest Times to the Reign of Edward the First. Ed. William Stubbs and H. W. C. Davis. 9th edn. Oxford, 1921.

Serlo of Bayeux. "De capta Bajocensium civitate." In *Anglo-Latin Satirical Poets and Epigrammists of the Twelfth Century*. Ed. Thomas Wright. Rolls Series, vol. 59 (in 2 vols.). London, 1872.

Spicilegium, sive Collectio veterum aliquot scriptorum ubi in Galliae bibliothecis delituerant. Ed. Luc d'Achery. 3 vols. Paris, 1723.

Suger. *The Deeds of Louis the Fat*. Trans. Richard C. Cusimano and John Moorhead. Washington, DC, 1992.

———. *Vie de Louis VI le Gros*. Ed. Henri Waquet. Paris, 1964.

Symeon of Durham. *Historia ecclesiae dunelmensis*, in *Symeonis monachi opera omnia*. Ed. Thomas Arnold. Rolls Series, vol. 75 (2 vols.). London, 1882–1885.

———. *Symeonis Dunelmensis opera et collectanea*. Ed. John Hodgson Hinde. Durham, 1868.

Textus roffensis. Ed. Thomas Hearne. Oxford, 1720. Facsimile edn, ed. Peter Sawyer. 2 vols. Copenhagen, 1957–1962.

Thesaurus novus anecdotorum. Ed. Edward Martène. 5 vols. Paris, 1717. Repr. 1968.

Two of the Saxon Chronicles Parallel. Ed. John Earle and Charles Plummer. 2 vols. Oxford, 1892–1889.

Ungedruckte Anglo-Normannische Geschichtsquellen. Ed. F. Liebermann. Strasbourg, 1879.

Vetus registrum sarisbereiense, alias Dictum Registrum S. Osmundi episcopi. Ed. W. Rich-Jones. Rolls Series, vol. 78. London, 1883–1884.

Victoria County History of Northampton. London, 1902–1937. Repr. Folkestone, 1970.

Victoria County History of Worcester. London, 1901–1924. Repr. Folkestone, 1971.

Vita Beati Lanfranci. PL, vol. 150, cols. 29–58.

Vita Bosonis. In *PL*, vol. 150, cols. 723–734. Paris, 1854.

Vita Gundulfi. Ed. Rodney Thomson. Toronto, 1977.

Vita Wulfstani of William of Malmesbury. Ed. Reginald R. Darlington. London, 1928.

Wace. *Le Roman de Rou de Wace*. Ed. A. J. Holden. 3 vols. Paris, 1970.

Walter of Thérouanne. *Vita Karoli comitis Flandriae. MGH, SS*, vol. 12. Hanover, 1963.

William of Jumièges. See *Gesta normannorum ducum*.

William of Malmesbury. *Gesta regum Anglorum.* Ed. and trans. R. A. B. Mynors; completed by R. M. Thomson and M. Winterbottom. 2 vols. Oxford and New York, 1998.

——. *Gesta regum Anglorum.* Ed. W. Stubbs. Rolls Series, vol. 90 (in 2 vols.). London, 1887–1889.

——. *Gestis pontificum Anglorum.* Ed. N. E. S. A. Hamilton. Rolls Series, vol. 52. London, 1870.

——. *Historia novella.* Ed. and trans. K. R. Potter. London, 1955.

——. *Historia novella: The Contemporary History.* Ed. Edmund King. Trans. K. R. Potter. Oxford, 1998.

William of Poitiers. *Histoire de Guillaume le Conquérant/Gesta Guillelmi ducis Normannorum et regis Anglorum.* Ed. and trans. Raymonde Foreville. Paris, 1952.

Winchester in the Early Middle Ages: An Edition and Discussion of the Winton Domesday. Ed. F. Barlow, Martin Biddle, Olaf von Ferlitzen, and D. J. Keene. Winchester Studies 1. Oxford, 1976.

Yves de Chartres. *Correspondance 1090–1098.* Ed. Jean Leclercq. Paris, 1949.

SECONDARY SOURCES

Abels, Richard. *Lordship and Military Obligation in Anglo-Saxon England.* Berkeley, 1988.

Alexander, James W. "Herbert of Norwich, 1091–1119: Studies in the History of Norman England." *Studies in Medieval and Renaissance History* 6 (1969): 115–232.

Andrew, W. J. "A Numismatic History of the Reign of Henry I, 1100–1135." *Numismatic Chronicle* 1 (1901): 1–515.

Auvrey, Dom Claude. *Histoire de la congrégation de Savigny.* 2 vols. Paris, 1896–1897.

Bachrach, Bernard S. *The Anatomy of a Little War: A Diplomatic and Military History of the Gundovald Affair, 567–585.* Boulder, Colorado, 1995.

——. *Fulk Nerra, the Neo-Roman Consul, 987–1040.* Berkeley, 1993.

——. "The Idea of the Angevin Empire." *Albion* 10 (1978): 293–299.

Barlow, Frank. *Edward the Confessor.* London, 1970.

——. *The English Church: 1066–1154.* London, 1979.

——, ed. *The Life of King Edward Who Rests at Westminster.* 2nd edn. Oxford, 1992.

——. *Thomas Becket.* Berkeley, 1986.

——. *William Rufus.* Berkeley, 1983.

Barrow, G. W. S. *The Anglo-Norman Era of Scottish History.* Oxford, 1980.

——. *The Kingdom of the Scots: Government, Church and Society from the Eleventh to the Fourteenth Century.* London, 1973.

——. *Robert Bruce.* Berkeley, 1965.

Barton, Richard E. "Helias of Maine, Henry I, and the Importance of Friendship." Unpublished paper given at Kalamazoo, 1996.

Bates, David. *A Bibliography of Domesday Book.* Woodbridge, Suffolk, 1986.

——. "The Character and Career of Odo, Bishop of Bayeux." *Speculum* 50 (1975): 1–20.

——. "The Earliest Norman Writs." *English Historical Review* 100 (1985): 266–284.

——. "Normandy and England after 1066." *English Historical Review* 104 (1989): 851–880.

——. *Normandy before 1066.* New York, 1982.

——. "The Origins of the Justiciarship." *Anglo-Norman Studies* 4 (1981): 1–12.

——. "The Prosopographical Study of Anglo-Norman Royal Charters." In *Family Trees and the Roots of Politics*, pp. 89–102. Ed. K. S. B. Keats-Rohan. Woodbridge, Suffolk, 1997.

——. "The Rise and Fall of Normandy." In David Bates and Anne Curry, eds, *England and Normandy in the Middle Ages.*

——. *William the Conqueror.* London, 1989.

Bates, David, and Anne Curry, eds. *England and Normandy in the Middle Ages.* London, 1994.

Bautier, Robert-Henri. *The Economic Development of Medieval Europe.* London, 1971.

Bayle, Maylis. "La Priorale Saint-Symphorien (Domfront), décors et date de construction." *Le Domfront médiéval* 3 (1985): 9–15.

Beckerman, John S. "Succession in Normandy, 1087, and in England, 1066: The Role of Testamentary Custom." *Speculum* 47 (1972): 258–260.

Berlière, D. Ursmer. "Le Cardinal Matthieu d'Albano." *Revue bénédictine* 18 (1901): 113–140, 280–303.

Bertrand de Broussillon, Arthur. *La Maison de Laval, 1020–1605.* 5 vols. Paris, 1895–1903.

Besse, J.-M. *Abbayes et prieurés de l'ancienne France.* Vol. 7: *Province ecclésiastique de Rouen.* Ligugé, 1914.

Bethell, Denis. "English Black Monks and Episcopal Elections in the 1120s." *English Historical Review* 84 (1969): 673–698.

——. "The Making of a Twelfth-Century Relic Collection." In *Popular Belief and Practice.* Studies in Church History 8. Ed. G. J. Cuming and D. Baker. Cambridge, 1972.

——. "William of Corbeil and the Canterbury–York Dispute." *Journal of Ecclesiastical History* 19 (2) (1968): 145–159.

Biddle, Martin. "Seasonal Festivals and Residence: Winchester, Westminster, and Gloucester in the Tenth to Twelfth Centuries." *Anglo-Norman Studies* 8 (1985): 51–72.

Biddle Martin, ed. *Winchester in the Early Middle Ages.* Oxford, 1976.

Bishop, T. A. M. *Scriptores regis.* Oxford, 1961.

Bisson, Thomas N. "The 'Feudal Revolution.'" *Past and Present* 142 (1994): 6–42.

Blackburn, Mark. "Aethelred's Coinage and the Payment of Tribute." In *The Battle of Maldon, AD 991.* Ed. Donald Scragg. Oxford, 1991.

——. "Coinage and Currency under Henry I: A Review." *Anglo-Norman Studies* 13 (1990/1991): 49–81.

Bliese, John. "The Battle Rhetoric of Aelred of Rievaulx." *Haskins Society Journal* 1 (1989): 99–107.

Bloch, Marc. "La Vie de S. Edouard le Confesseur par Osbert de Clare." *Analecta bollandiana* 41 (1923): 5–131.

Blumenthal, Uta-Renate. *The Early Councils of Pope Paschal II, 1100–1110.* Toronto, 1978.

Böhmer, Heinrich. "Der sogenannte Serlo von Bayeux und die ihm zugeschriebenen Gedichte." *Neues Archiv der Gesellschaft fur ältere deutsche Geschichtskunde* 22 (1897): 701–738.

———. *The Investiture Controversy: Church and Monarchy from the Ninth to the Twelfth Century.* Philadelphia, 1988.

Bony, Jean. *French Gothic Architecture of the Twelfth and Thirteenth Centuries.* Berkeley, 1983.

Boswell, John. *Christianity, Social Tolerance, and Homosexuality: Gay People in Western Europe from the Beginning of the Christian Era to the Fourteenth Century.* Chicago, 1980.

Bouchard, Constance. *Sword, Miter, and Cloister: Nobility and the Church in Burgundy, 980–1198.* Ithaca, New York, 1987.

Boussard, Jacques. "Le Comté de Mortain au XIe siècle." *Le Moyen âge* 58 (1952): 253–279.

———. "La Seigneurie de Bellême aux Xe et XIe siècles." In *Mélanges d'histoire du moyen âge dédiés à la mémoire de Louis Halphen,* vol. 1. Paris, 1951.

———. "Thomas de Saint-Jean-le-Thomas et l'abbaye du Mont-Saint-Michel." In *Droit privé et institutions régionales: Etudes historiques offertes à Jean Yver.* Paris, 1976.

Bouvet, J. "Le Récit de la Fondation de Mortemer." *Collectanea Ordinis Cisterciensium Reformatorum* 22 (1960): 149–168.

Bradbury, Jim. "Battles in England and Normandy, 1066–1154." *Anglo-Norman Studies* 6 (1983/1984): 1–12. Repr. in Matthew Strickland, ed., *Anglo-Norman Warfare.*

Bredero, Adriaan. "Pierre le Vénérable: Les Commencements de son abbatiat." In *Pierre Abélard/Pierre le Vénérable.*

Brett, Martin. *The English Church under Henry I.* London, 1975.

———. "John of Worcester and His Contemporaries." In *The Writing of History in the Middle Ages: Essays Presented to Richard William Southern.* Ed. R. H. C. Davis and J. M. Wallace-Hadrill. Oxford, 1981.

Brooke, C. N. L. *London, 800–1216: The Shaping of a City.* London, 1975.

———. "Monk and Canon: Some Patterns of Monastic Patronage in the Religious Life of the Twelfth Century." In *Monks, Hermits, and the Ascetic Tradition.* Studies in Church History 22. Ed. W. J. Sheils. Oxford, 1985.

———. "Princes and Kings as Patrons of Monasteries: Normandy and England." In *Il Monachesimo e la riforma ecclesiastica, 1049–1122.* Milan, 1971.

———. *The Saxon and Norman Kings.* 2nd edn. London, 1978.

Brooke, George C. *A Catalogue of English Coins in the British Museum: The Norman Kings.* 2 vols. London, 1916.

Brown, R. Allen, H. M. Colvin, and A. J. Taylor, eds. *The History of the King's Works: The Middle Ages.* 2 vols. London, 1963.

Bruckmann, J. "The *Ordines* of the Third Recension of the Medieval English Coronation Order." In *Essays in Medieval History Presented to Bertie Wilkinson.* Ed. T. A. Sandquist and M. R. Powicke. Toronto, 1969.

Bur, Michel. *Suger, abbé de Saint-Denis, régent de France.* Paris, 1991.

Callahan, Thomas, Jr. "The Making of a Monster: The Historical Image of William Rufus." *Journal of Medieval History* 7 (1981): 175–185.

Cambridge Medieval History. Vol. 5: *Contest of Empire and Papacy.* Ed. J. R. Tanner, W. W. Previté-Orton, and Z. N. Brooke. Cambridge, 1957.

Campbell, James. "Observations on English Government from the Tenth to the Twelfth Century." In Campbell, *Essays in Anglo-Saxon History.* London, 1986.

———. "The Significance of the Anglo-Norman State in the Administrative History of Western Europe." In Campbell, *Essays in Anglo-Saxon History.* London, 1986.

Chandler, Victoria. "Historical Revision and the English Monarchy: The Case of William II and His Barons." *Indiana Social Studies Quarterly* 33 (1980): 41–48.

Chanteux, Henri. "Recueil des actes de Henri Ier Beauclerc duc de Normandie." Thesis, Ecole de Chartes, 1932.

Chaplais, Pierre. "William of Saint-Calais and the Domesday Survey." In *Domesday Studies: Papers Read at the Novocentenary Conference of the Royal Historical Society and the Institute of British Geographers.* Ed. J. C. Holt. Woodbridge, Suffolk, 1987.

Chartrou, Josèphe. *L'Anjou de 1109 à 1151: Foulque de Jérsualem et Geoffroi Plantagenet.* Paris, 1928.

Chatelan, André. *Donjons romans des pays d'ouest.* Paris, 1973.

Cheney, Mary. "Some Observations on a Papal Privilege of 1120 for the Archbishops of York." *Journal of Ecclesiastical History* 31 (4) (1980): 429–439.

Chenu, M.-D. *Nature, Man, and Society in the Twelfth Century.* Ed. Jerome Taylor and Lester K. Little. Chicago, 1968.

Chesnel, P. *Le Cotentin et l'Avranchin sous les ducs de Normandie, 911–1204.* Caen, 1912.

Chibnall, Marjorie [also see Morgan, Marjorie]. *Anglo-Norman England, 1066–1166.* New York, 1987.

———. "The Empress Matilda and Bec-Hellouin." *Anglo-Norman Studies* 10 (1987): 35–48.

———. *The Empress Matilda: Queen Consort, Queen Mother and Lady of the English.* Oxford, 1991.

———. "Mercenaries and the *familia regis* under Henry I." *History* 62 (1977): 15–23; also in Matthew Strickland, ed. *Anglo-Norman Warfare.*

———. "Monastic Foundations in England and Normandy, 1066–1189." In David Bates and Anne Curry, eds. *England and Normandy in the Middle Ages.*

———. "The Relations of St Anselm with the English Dependencies of the Abbey of Bec, 1079–1093." In *Spicilegium beccense,* vol. 1. Paris, 1959.

———. "Robert of Bellême and the Castle of Tickhill." In *Droit privé et institutions régionales: Etudes historiques offertes à Jean Yver.* Paris, 1976.

———. "Women in Orderic Vitalis." *Haskins Society Journal* 2 (1990): 105–121.

———. *The World of Orderic Vitalis.* Oxford, 1984.

Christelow, Stephanie Mooers [also see Mooers, Stephanie]. "A Moveable

Feast? Itineration and the Centralization of Government under Henry I." *Albion* 28 (1996): 187–228.

Clanchy, Michael T. *From Memory to Written Record: England, 1066–1307.* 2nd edn. Oxford, 1993.

Clark, Cecily. "'This Ecclesiastical Adventurer': Henry of Saint-Jean d'Angély." *English Historical Review* 84 (1969): 548–560.

Clark, Kenneth. *Civilisation: A Personal View.* New York, 1969.

Clark, Mary Amanda. "Ralph d'Escures: Anglo-Norman Abbot and Archbishop." Ph.D. dissertation, University of California, Santa Barbara, 1975.

Clarke, Peter A. *The English Nobility under Edward the Confessor.* Oxford, 1994.

Classen, Peter. "*Res gestae*, Universal History, Apocalypse: Visions of Past and Future." In *Renaissance and Renewal in the Twelfth Century.* Ed. Robert L. Benson and Giles Constable. Cambridge, Mass., 1982.

Coates, Alan. *The Reading Abbey Collections from Foundation to Dispersal.* Oxford, 1999.

Complete Peerage of England, Scotland, Ireland, Great Britain and the United Kingdom. New edn, rev. and enl. Ed. Vicary Gibbs. 13 vols in 14. London, 1910–1959.

Conant, Kenneth J. "Cluniac Building during the Abbacy of Peter the Venerable." In *Petrus Venerabilis, 1156–1956.* Ed. Giles Constable and James Kritzeck. Rome, 1956.

——. *Cluny: Les Eglises et la maison du chef d'ordre.* Cambridge, Mass., and Macon, 1968.

——. "Observations on the Practical Talents and Technology of the Medieval Benedictines." In Noreen Hunt, ed. *Cluniac Monasticism in the Central Middle Ages.*

Constable, Giles. "The Monastic Policy of Peter the Venerable." In *Pierre Abélard/Pierre le Vénérable.*

Conte, W. J. and M. M. Archibald. "Five Round Halfpennies of Henry I: A Further Case for Reappraisal of the Chronology of Types." *Numismatic Circular* (1990): 232–236.

Corbett, William John. "The Development of the Duchy of Normandy and the Norman Conquest of England" and "England, 1087–1154." In *CMH*, vol. 5, chaps 15 and 16.

Cousin, Patrice. "Les Relations de Saint Anselme avec Cluny." In *Spicilegium beccense*, vol. 1. Paris, 1959.

Cowdrey, H. E. J. "The Anglo-Norman *Laudes regiae.*" *Viator* 12 (1981): 37–78.

——. *Two Studies in Cluniac History, 1049–1126.* Rome, 1978.

——. "Unions and Confraternity with Cluny." *Journal of Ecclesiastical History* 16 (1965): 152–162.

Cownie, Emma. "Gloucester Abbey, 1066–1135: An Illustration of Religious Patronage in Anglo-Norman England." In David Bates and Anne Curry, eds. *England and Normandy in the Middle Ages.*

——. *Religious Patronage in Anglo-Norman England, 1066–1135.* New York, 1998.

Craster, H. H. E. "A Contemporary Record of the Pontificate of Ranulf Flambard." *Archaeologia Aeliana*, 4th ser., 7 (1930): 33–56.

——. "The Red Book of Durham." *English Historical Review* 40 (1925): 504–532.

Cronne, Henry A. "The [Office of] Local Justiciar in England under the Norman Kings." *Birmingham Historical Journal* 6 (1957): 18–38.

Crosby, Everett U. "The Organization of the English Episcopate under Henry I." In *Studies in Medieval and Renaissance History*, vol. 4. Ed. William M. Bowsky. Lincoln, Nebraska, 1967.

Crouch, David. *The Beaumont Twins: The Roots and Branches of Power in the Twelfth Century.* Cambridge, 1986.

——. "Geoffrey de Clinton and Roger Earl of Warwick: New Men and Magnates in the Reign of Henry I." *Bulletin of the Institute of Historical Research* 55 (1982): 113–124.

——. "Normans and Anglo-Normans: A Divided Aristocracy." In David Bates and Anne Curry, eds. *England and Normandy in the Middle Ages.*

Dagron, Gilbert. "Nés dans le pourpre." *Travaux et mémoires*, Collège de France, Centre de recherche d'histoire et civilisation de Byzance 12 (1994): 105–142.

Dalton, Paul. *Conquest, Anarchy and Lordship: Yorkshire, 1066–1154.* Cambridge, 1994.

Darby, H. C. *Domesday Book: Studies.* London, 1987.

——. *Domesday England.* Cambridge, 1977.

Darlington, R. R. *Anglo-Norman Historians.* London, 1947.

Darlington, R. R. and P. McGurk. "The *Chronicon ex chronicis* of 'Florence' of Worcester and Its Use of Sources for English History before 1066." *Anglo-Norman Studies* 5 (1982/1983): 185–196.

David, C. W. "The Claim of King Henry I to Be Called Learned." In *Anniversary Essays in Mediaeval History by Students of Charles Homer Haskins.* Boston and New York, 1929.

——. *Robert Curthose, Duke of Normandy.* Cambridge, Mass., 1920.

Davies, R. R. *The Age of Conquest: Wales, 1063–1415.* Oxford, 1987.

——. "Henry I in Wales." *Studies in Medieval History Presented to R. H. C. Davis.* Ed. Henry Mayr-Harting and R. I. Moore. London, 1985.

Davis, H. W. C. "A Contemporary Account of the Battle of Tinchebrai." *English Historical Review* 24 (1909): 728–732. Correction: *English Historical Review* 25 (1910): 295–296.

——. *England under the Normans and Angevins.* London, 1905; 13th edn. 1949.

——. "Henry of Blois and Brian fitz Count." *English Historical Review* 25 (1910): 297–303.

Davis, R. H. C. *King Stephen, 1135–1154.* 3rd edn. London, 1990.

——. *The Normans and Their Myth.* London, 1976.

——. "William of Jumièges, Robert Curthose, and the Norman Succession." *English Historical Review* 95 (1980): 597–606.

DeAragon, RaGena. "The Growth of Secure Inheritance in Anglo-Norman England." *Journal of Medieval History* 8 (1982): 381–393.

Delisle, Léopold. *Histoire du château et des sires de Saint-Sauveur-le-Vicomte, suivie de pièces justificatives [Preuves].* Paris, 1867.

Dickinson, John C. *The Origins of the Austin Canons and Their Introduction into England.* London, 1950.

——. "Saint Anselm and the First Regular Canons in England." In *Spicilegium beccense*, vol. 1, pp. 541–546. Paris, 1959.

Dictionary of National Biography. Oxford, 1921–1922. Repr. 1937–1938.

Dieudonné, A. *Hildebert de Lavardin.* Paris, 1898.

Dolley, Michael. *The Norman Conquest and the English Coinage.* London, 1966.

Douglas, David C. "The Earliest Norman Counts." *English Historical Review* 61 (1946): 129–156.

——. *William the Conqueror: The Norman Impact upon England.* Berkeley, 1964.

du Monstier, Arthur. *Neustria Pia seu de omnibus et singulis abbatiis et prioratibus totius Normaniae.* Rouen, 1663.

du Motey, Vicomte. *Robert II de Bellême et son temps.* Paris, 1923.

Dubois, Dom J. "Les Dépendances de l'abbaye du Mont Saint-Michel et la vie monastique dans les prieurés." In *Millénaire monastique du Mont Saint-Michel.* Ed. P. Lethielleux. Paris, 1966.

Duby, Georges. "Le Budget de l'Abbaye de Cluny entre 1080 et 1155." *Annales: Economies, sociétés, civilisations* 7 (2) (1952): 155–171.

——. *The Chivalrous Society.* Berkeley, 1977.

Dunbabin, Jean. *France in the Making, 843–1180.* Oxford, 1985.

Duncan, Archibald A. M. *Scotland: The Making of the Kingdom.* New York, 1975.

Dupont, Pierre. "Nouvelles recherches sur la famille de Bellême (I)." *Le Domfront médiéval* 6 (1988): 33–49.

Engles, L. J. "*De obitu Willelmi ducis Normannorum regisque Anglorum:* Texte, modèles, valeur et origine." In *Mélanges Christine Mohrmann: Nouveau recueil offert par ses anciens élèves.* Utrecht, 1973.

English, Barbara. *A Study in Feudal Society: The Lords of Holderness, 1086–1260.* Oxford, 1979.

——. "William the Conqueror and the Anglo-Norman Succession." *Historical Research* 64 (1991): 221–236.

Eyton, R. W. *Antiquities of Shropshire.* 12 vols. London, 1854–1860.

Farmer, Hugh. "William of Malmesbury's Life and Works." *Journal of Ecclesiastical History* 13 (1962): 39–54.

Fernie, E. C. "Architecture and the Effects of the Norman Conquest." In David Bates and Anne Curry, eds. *England and Normandy in the Middle Ages.*

Fichtenau, Heinrich. *The Carolingian Empire.* Trans. Peter Munz. Oxford, 1957. Repr. Toronto, 1978.

——. *Living in the Tenth Century: Mentalities and Social Orders.* Trans. Patrick Geary. Chicago, 1991.

Fleming, Robin. *Kings and Lords in Conquest England.* Cambridge, 1991.

Fliche, Augustin. *Le Règne de Philippe Ier, roi de France (1060–1108).* Paris, 1912.

Flint, Valerie I. J. "The Date of the Chronicle of 'Florence' of Worcester." *Revue bénédictine* 86 (1976): 115–119.

——. "The 'School of Laon': A Reconsideration." *Recherches de théologie ancienne et médiévale* 43 (1976): 89–110.

Flori, Jean. *L'Essor de la chevalerie, XIe–XIIe siècles.* Geneva, 1986.

Folz, Robert. "Pierre le Vénérable et la liturgie." In *Pierre Abélard/Pierre le Vénérable*.

Foreville, Raymonde. "Le Sacre des rois anglo-normands et angevins et le serment du sacre (XIe–XIIe siècles)." *Anglo-Norman Studies* 1 (1978): 49–62.

——. "The Synod of the Province of Rouen in the Eleventh and Twelfth Centuries." In *Church and Government in the Middle Ages: Essays Presented to C. R. Cheney*. Ed. C. N. L. Brooke et al. Cambridge, 1976.

Fox, Levi. "The Honour and Earldom of Leicester: Origin and Descent, 1066–1399." *English Historical Review* 54 (1939): 385–402.

Franklin, M. J. "The Bishops of Winchester and the Monastic Revolution." *Anglo-Norman Studies* 12 (1989/1990): 47–65.

Freeman, Edward A. *The History of the Norman Conquest of England*. 6 vols. Oxford, 1867–1879. 2nd edn. Chicago, 1974.

——. *The Reign of William Rufus and the Accession of Henry the First*. 2 vols. Oxford, 1882. Repr. New York, 1970.

Fröhlich, Walter. *Die bischoflichen Kollegen Erzbischof Anselms von Canterbury*. Munich, 1971.

——. "The Genesis of the Collections of Anselm's Letters." *American Benedictine Review* 35 (1984): 249–266.

——. "The Letters Omitted from Anselm's Collection of Letters." *Anglo-Norman Studies* 6 (1983/1984): 58–71.

Galbraith, V. H. "Girard the Chancellor." *English Historical Review* 46 (1931): 77–79.

——. "The Literacy of the Medieval English Kings." In *Kings and Chronicles: Essays in English Medieval History*. London, 1982.

Ganshof, F. L. "Le Roi de France en Flandre en 1127 et 1128." *Revue historique de droit français et étranger* 27 (1949): 204–228.

——. "Trois mandements perdus du roi de France Louis VI intéressant la Flandre." *Annales de la Société d'émulation de Bruges* 87 (1950): 117–130.

Garnett, George and John Hudson, eds. *Law and Government in Medieval England and Normandy: Essays in Honor of Sir James Holt*. Cambridge, 1994.

Gem, R. D. H. "The Romanesque Rebuilding of Westminster Abbey (with a Reconstruction by W. T. Ball)." *Anglo-Norman Studies* 3 (1980/1981): 33–60, 203–207.

Gibson, Margaret. "History at Bec in the Twelfth Century." In *The Writing of History in the Middle Ages: Essays Presented to Richard William Southern*. Ed. R. H. C. Davis and J. M. Wallace-Hadrill. Oxford, 1981.

Gillingham, John. "Chronicles and Coins as Evidence for Levels of Tribute and Taxation in Late Tenth- and Early Eleventh-Century England." *English Historical Review* 105 (1990): 939–950.

——. "Henry of Huntingdon and the Twelfth-Century Revival of the English Nation." In *Concepts of National Identity in the Middle Ages*. Ed. Simon Forde, Lesley Johnson, and Alan V. Murray. Leeds, 1995.

——. "Kingship, Chivalry, and Love: Political and Cultural Values in the Earliest History Written in French: Geoffrey Gaimar's *Estoire des Engleis*." In *Anglo-Norman Political Culture and the Twelfth-Century Renaissance*. Ed. C. Warren Hollister. Woodbridge, Suffolk, 1997.

——. "'The Most Precious Jewel in the English Crown': Levels of Danegeld and Heregeld in the Early Eleventh Century." *English Historical Review* 104 (1989): 373–384.

———. *Richard the Lionheart.* 2nd edn. London, 1989.

———. "1066 and the Introduction of Chivalry into England." In George Garnett and John Hudson, eds. *Law and Government in Medieval England and Normandy: Essays in Honour of Sir James Holt.*

Gleason, Sarell E. *An Ecclesiastical Barony of the Middle Ages: The Bishopric of Bayeux, 1066–1204.* Cambridge, Mass., 1936.

Golding, Brian. "Robert of Mortain." *Anglo-Norman Studies* 13 (1990/1991): 119–144.

Gransden, Antonia. *Historical Writing in England c. 550 to c. 1307.* London, 1974.

Grant, Lindy. *Abbot Suger of Saint-Denis.* London and New York, 1998.

———. "Architectural Relations between England and Normandy, 1100–1204." In David Bates and Anne Curry, eds. *England and Normandy in the Middle Ages.*

Green, Judith A. *The Aristocracy of Norman England.* Cambridge, 1997.

———. *English Sheriffs to 1154.* London, 1990.

———. *The Government of England under Henry I.* Cambridge, 1986.

———. "King Henry I and the Aristocracy of Normandy." In *La "France anglaise" au moyen âge: Colloque des historiens médiévistes français et britanniques,* Actes du congrès national des sociétés savantes, section d'histoire médiévale et de philologie 111.1. Paris, 1988.

———. "The Last Century of Danegeld." *English Historical Review* 96 (1981): 241–258.

———. "Lords of the Norman Vexin." In *War and Government in the Middle Ages: Essays in Honour of J. O. Prestwich.* Ed. John Gillingham and J. C. Holt. Cambridge, 1984.

———. "The Sheriffs of William the Conqueror." *Anglo-Norman Studies* 5 (1982/1983): 129–145.

———. "William Rufus, Henry I and the Royal Demesne." *History* 64 (1979): 337–352.

Greenway, Diana. "Henry of Huntingdon and the Manuscripts of His *Historia Anglorum.*" *Anglo-Norman Studies* 9 (1986/1987): 103–126.

Grierson, Philip. "Domesday Book, the Geld *de moneta* and *monetagium*: A Forgotten Minting Reform." *British Numismatic Journal* 55 (1985): 84–94.

Grinnell-Milne, Duncan. *The Killing of William Rufus.* Newton Abbot, 1968.

Guillot, Olivier. *Le Comte d'Anjou et son entourage au XIe siècle.* 2 vols. Paris, 1972.

Guillot, Olivier and Yves Sassier. *Pouvoirs et institutions dans la France médiévale.* 2 vols. Paris, 1994.

Hallam, Elizabeth M. *Capetian France, 980–1328.* London, 1980.

Harvey, John. *The Master Builders: Architecture in the Middle Ages.* New York, 1971.

Harvey, Sally. "Domesday Book and Anglo-Norman Governance." *Transactions of the Royal Historical Society,* 5th ser., 25 (1975): 175–193.

———. "Domesday Book and Its Predecessors." *English Historical Review* 86 (1971): 753–773.

Haskins, Charles Homer. "Adelard of Bath and Henry Plantagenet." *English Historical Review* 28 (1913): 515–516.
——. *Norman Institutions*. Cambridge, Mass., 1918.
——. *Studies in the History of Medieval Science*. Oxford, 1927.
Hébert, P. "Un Archevêque de Rouen au XIIe siècle: Hugues III d'Amiens, 1130–1164." *Revue des questions historiques*, n.s. 20 (1898): 325–371.
Herbert, Jane. "The Transformation of Hermitages into Augustinian Priories in Twelfth-Century England." In *Monks, Hermits, and the Ascetic Tradition*, Studies in Church History 22. Ed. W. J. Sheils. Oxford, 1985.
Hicks, Sandy Burton. "The Anglo-Papal Bargain of 1125: The Legatine Mission of John of Crema." *Albion* 8 (1976): 301–310.
Hollister, C. Warren. *Anglo-Saxon Military Institutions on the Eve of the Norman Conquest*. Oxford, 1962.
——. "The Aristocracy." In Edmund King, ed. *The Anarchy of Stephen's Reign*. Oxford, 1994.
——. "The Campaign of 1102 against Robert of Bellême." In *Studies in Medieval History Presented to R. Allen Brown*. Ed. Christopher Harper-Bill, Christopher Holdsworth, and Janet L. Nelson. Woodbridge, Suffolk, 1989.
——. "Courtly Culture and Courtly Style in the Anglo-Norman World." *Albion* 20 (1988): 1–18.
——. "The Greater Domesday Tenants-in-Chief." In *Domesday Studies: Papers Read at the Novocentenary Conference of the Royal Historical Society and the Institute of British Geographers*. Ed. J. C. Holt. Woodbridge, Suffolk, 1987.
——. "The Magnates of Stephen's Reign: Reluctant Anarchists." *Haskins Society Journal* 5 (1993): 77–87.
——. *The Military Organization of Norman England*. Oxford, 1965.
——. *Monarchy, Magnates, and Institutions in the Anglo-Norman World*. London, 1986.
——. "Royal Acts of Mutilation: The Case against Henry I." *Albion* 10 (4) (1978): 330–340. Reprinted in *MMI*, pp. 291–301.
——. "St Anselm on Lay Investiture." *Anglo-Norman Studies* 10 (1988): 145–158.
——. "The Strange Death of William Rufus." *Speculum* 48 (1973): 637–653. Reprinted in *MMI*, pp. 59–75.
——. "The Viceregal Court of Henry I." In *Law, Custom, and the Social Fabric in Medieval Europe. Essays in Honor of Bryce Lyon*. Ed. Bernard S. Bachrach and David Nicholas. Kalamazoo, 1990.
——. "William II, Henry I, and the Anglo-Norman Church: Difference in Style or Change in Substance?" *Peritia* 6–7 (1987–1988): 119–140. Repr. with revisions in *The Culture of Christendom: Essays in Medieval History in Memory of Denis L. T. Bethell*. Ed. Marc A. Meyer. London, 1993.
Holt, J. C. *Domesday Studies: Papers Read at the Novocentenary Conference of the Royal Historical Society and the Institute of British Geographers, Winchester, 1986*. Woodbridge, Suffolk, 1987.
——. "Politics and Property in Early Medieval England." *Past and Present* 57 (1972): 3–52.
Howell, Margaret. *Regalian Right in Medieval England*. London, 1962.
Hudson, John. "Administration, Family, and Perceptions of the Past in Late

Twelfth-Century England: Richard Fitz Nigel and the Dialogue of the Exchequer." In *The Perception of the Past in Twelfth-Century Europe*. Ed. Paul Magdalino. London, 1992.

———. "Anglo-Norman Land Law and the Origins of Property." In George Garnett and John Hudson, eds. *Law and Government in Medieval England and Normandy*.

———. *The Formation of the English Common Law: Law and Society in England from the Norman Conquest to Magna Carta*. London, 1996.

———. *Land, Law, and Lordship in Anglo-Norman England*. Oxford, 1994.

———. "Life-Grants of Land and the Development of Inheritance in Anglo-Norman England." *Anglo-Norman Studies* 12 (1989/1990): 67–80.

Huneycutt, Lois L. "'Another Esther in Our Times': Matilda II and the Formulation of a Queenly Ideal in Anglo-Norman England." Ph.D. dissertation, University of California, Santa Barbara, 1992.

———. "The Rise and Fall of the Cult of Queen Matilda II: Politics, Piety and Personality in Anglo-Norman England." Paper given at Kalamazoo, May, 1996.

Hunt, Noreen, ed. *Cluniac Monasticism in the Central Middle Ages*. London, 1971.

Hunter Blair, Peter. "Some Observations on the *Historia Regum* Attributed to Symeon of Durham." In *Celt and Saxon: Studies in the Early English Border*. Ed. Nora K. Chadwick. Cambridge, 1963.

Hurnard, Naomi D. "Local Justice under the Norman Kings." In *England under the Normans and Angevins*. Ed. H. W. C. Davis. 13th edn. London, 1949.

Hurry, Jamieson B. *The Rise and Fall of Reading Abbey*. London, 1906.

Jaeger, C. Stephen. *The Origins of Courtliness: Civilizing Trends and the Formation of Courtly Ideas, 936–1210*. Philadelphia, 1985.

Jared, Lauren Helm. "English Ecclesiastical Vacancies during the Reigns of William II and Henry I." *Journal of Ecclesiastical History* 42 (1991): 362–393.

Jaubert, Anne Nissen. "Fouilles archéologiques du prieuré Saint-Symphorien." *Le Domfront médiéval* 8 (1991): 5–13.

John, Eric. *Orbis Britanniae*. Leicester, 1966.

Johnson, Charles. "The Last Chancellor of Henry I." *English Historical Review* 67 (1952): 392.

Johnson, Charles and H. A. Cronne. "An Interim List of Errata and Addenda to Davis's Regesta Regum Anglo-Normannorum, Volumes I and II." *University of Birmingham Historical Journal* 6 (1958): 176–196.

Jolivet, Jean. *Arts du langage et théologie chez Abélard*. Paris, 1969.

Jolliffe, J. E. A. *The Constitutional History of Medieval England*. 4th edn. London, 1961.

Kantorowicz, Ernst H. *The King's Two Bodies*. Princeton, 1957.

———. *Laudes Regiae: A Study in Liturgical Acclamations and Medieval Ruler Worship*. Berkeley, 1946.

Kealey, Edward J. "Anglo-Norman Policy and the Public Welfare." *Albion* 10 (4) (1978): 341–351.

———. *Roger of Salisbury, Viceroy of England*. Berkeley, 1972.

Keats-Rohan, K. S. B. "The Bretons and Normans of England 1066–1154:

The Family, the Fief, and the Feudal Monarchy." *Nottingham Medieval Studies* 36 (1992): 42–78.

——. "Domesday Book and the Malets." Unpublished paper, 1994.

——. "Two Studies in North French Prosopography." *Journal of Medieval History* 20 (1994): 3–37.

——. ed. *Family Trees and the Roots of Politics.* Woodbridge, Suffolk, 1997.

Keefe, Thomas K. "Counting Those Who Count: A Computer-Assisted Analysis of Charter Witness Lists and the Itinerant Court in the First Year of the Reign of King Richard I." *Haskins Society Journal* 1 (1989): 135–145.

——. *Feudal Assessments and the Political Community under Henry II and His Sons.* Berkeley, 1983.

Keen, Maurice. *Chivalry.* New Haven, 1984.

Ker, N. R. "The Beginnings of Salisbury Cathedral Library." In *Medieval Learning and Literature: Essays Presented to Richard William Hunt.* Ed. J. J. G. Alexander and M. T. Gibson. Oxford, 1976.

Kern, Fritz. *Gottesgnadentum und Widerstandsrecht im früheren Mittelalter zur Entwicklungsgeschichte der Monarchie.* 2nd edn. Munster-Cologne, 1954. Translated by S. B. Chrimes as *Kingship and Law in the Middle Ages.* Oxford, 1939.

King, Edmund. "King Stephen and the Anglo-Norman Aristocracy." *History* 59 (1974): 180–194.

Knowles, David. *The Monastic Order in England, 940–1216.* 2nd edn. Cambridge, 1963.

——. "The Reforming Decrees of Peter the Venerable." In *Petrus Venerabilis, 1156–1956.* Ed. Giles Constable and James Kritzeck. Rome, 1956.

Knowles, David and R. N. Hadcock. *Medieval Religious Houses: England and Wales.* 2nd edn. London, 1971.

Knowles, David, C. N. L. Brooke, and Vera London, eds. *The Heads of Religious Houses, England and Wales, 940–1216.* Cambridge, 1972.

L'Huillier, R. P. Dom A. *Vie de Saint Hugues, abbé de Cluny, 1024–1109.* Paris, 1888.

Lapidge, Michael. "Ealdred of York and MS. Cotton Vitellius E.XII." *Yorkshire Archaeological Journal* 55 (1983): 11–25.

——. "The Origin of CCCC 163." *Transactions of the Cambridge Bibliographical Society* 8 (1981): 18–28.

Latouche, Robert. *Histoire du comté du Maine pendant le Xe et le XIe siècle.* Paris, 1910.

Lawrence, C. H. *Medieval Monasticism: Forms of Religious Life in Western Europe in the Middle Ages.* 2nd edn. London, 1989.

Lawson, M. K. *Cnut: The Danes in England in the Early Eleventh Century.* London, 1993.

——. "Danegeld and Heregeld Once More." *English Historical Review* 105 (1990): 951–961.

——. "'Those Stories Look True': Levels of Taxation in the Reigns of Aethelred II and Cnut." *English Historical Review* 104 (1989): 385–406.

Le Foyer, Jean. *Exposé du droit pénal normand au XIIIe siècle.* Paris, 1931.

Le Patourel, John. *Feudal Empires: Norman and Plantagenet.* Ed. Michael Jones. London, 1984.

——. "Geoffrey of Montbray, Bishop of Coutances, 1049–1093." *English Historical Review* 59 (1944): 129–161.

——. "Norman Barons." Pamphlet published by the Hastings and Bexhill Branch of the Historical Association. 1966. Repr. in Le Patourel, *Feudal Empires: Norman and Plantagenet.*

——. *The Norman Empire.* Oxford, 1976.

——. "The Norman Succession, 996–1135." *English Historical Review* 86 (1971): 225–250.

Le Prévost, Auguste. *Notes pour servir à la topographie et à l'histoire des communes du département de l'Eure au moyen âge.* Evreux, 1849.

Lear, F. D. *Treason in Roman and Germanic Law.* Austin, Texas, 1965.

Leclercq, Jean. "La Collection des lettres d'Yves de Chartres." *Revue bénédictine* 56 (1945–1946): 108–125.

——. "The Monastic Crisis of the Eleventh and Twelfth Centuries." In Noreen Hunt, ed. *Cluniac Monasticism in the Central Middle Ages,* pp. 217–237.

Lemarignier, Jean-François. *Recherches sur l'hommage en marche et les frontières féodales.* Lille, 1945.

Lewis, C. P. "Gruffudd ap Cynan and the Normans." In *Gruffudd ap Cynan: A Collaborative Biography.* Ed. K. L. Maund. Woodbridge, Suffolk, 1996.

——. "The King and Eye: A Study in Anglo-Norman Politics." *English Historical Review* 104 (1989): 569–871.

Leyser, Karl. "The Anglo-Norman Succession 1120–1125." *Anglo-Norman Studies* 13 (1990/1991): 225–241. Repr. in Leyser, *Communications and Power.*

——. *Communications and Power in Medieval Europe: The Gregorian Revolution and Beyond.* Ed. Timothy Reuter. London, 1994.

——. *Medieval Germany and Its Neighbours, 900–1250.* London, 1982.

Lintzel, Martin. "Heinricus natus in aula regali." In *Miszellen zur Geschichte des zehnten Jahrhunderts,* Berichte über die Verhandlungen der Sachsischen Akademie der Wissenschaften zu Leipzig, Philologisch-historische Klasse, 100–102. Berlin, 1953.

Lloyd, John E. *The Welsh Chronicles.* London, 1928.

Lohrmann, Dietrich. "Pierre le Vénérable et Henri Ier, roi d'Angleterre." In *Pierre Abélard/Pierre le Vénérable.*

Lot, Ferdinand. *Fidèles ou vassaux?* Paris, 1904.

Loud, G. A. "The 'Gens Normannorum'—Myth or Reality?" *Anglo-Norman Studies* 4 (1982): 104–116, 204–209.

Louise, Gérard. "Châteaux et pouvoirs dans le Domfrontais médiéval (Xe–XIIIe siècles)." *Le Domfront médiéval* 9 (1993): 15–17.

——. *La Seigneurie de Bellême, Xe–XIIe siècles.* 2 vols, in 3 parts. In *Le Pays Bas-Normand,* nos 1–2 [parts 1–2] (Flers, 1990), nos 3–4 [part 3] (Flers, 1991).

Loyd, Lewis C. *The Origins of Some Anglo-Norman Families.* Leeds, 1951.

Luchaire, Achille. *Études sur les actes de Louis VI.* Paris, 1885.

Martinet, S. "Le Voyage des Laonnais en Angleterre en 1113." *Mémoires de la Fédération des sociétés d'histoire et d'archéologie de l'Aisne* 9 (1963): 81–92.

Mason, Emma. "The King, the Chamberlain and Southwick Priory." *Bulletin of the Institute of Historial Research* 53 (1980): 1–10.

——. Magnates, Curiales, and the Wheel of Fortune: 1066–1154." *Anglo-Norman Studies* 2 (1979/1980): 118–140.

——. "Royal Monastic Patronage, 1066–1154." In *Religion and National Identity*. Ed. Stuart Mews. Studies in Church History 18. Oxford, 1982.

——. "William Rufus and the Historians." *Medieval History* 1 (1) (1991): 6–22.

——. "William Rufus: Myth and Reality." *Journal of Medieval History* 3. (1977): 1–20.

Mason, J. F. A. "Roger de Montgomery and His Sons (1067–1102)." *Transactions of the Royal Historical Society*, 5th ser., 13 (1963): 1–28.

——. "Saint Anselm's Relations with Laymen: Selected Letters." In *Spicilegium beccense*, vol. 1. Paris, 1959.

——. *William the First and the Sussex Rapes*. London, 1966.

Mayer, Hans Eberhard. *The Crusades*. Trans. John Gillingham. 2nd edn. Oxford, 1988.

Ménager, Léon-Robert. "L'Institution monarchique dans les états normands d'Italie." *Cahiers de civilisation médiévale* 2 (1959): 303–331, 445–468.

Metcalf, D. M. "The Taxation of Moneyers under Edward the Confessor." In *Domesday Studies: Papers Read at the Novocentenary Conference of the Royal Historical Society and the Institute of British Geographers*. Ed. J. C. Holt. Woodbridge, Suffolk, 1987.

Molinier, A. *Les Obituaires français au moyen âge*. Paris, 1890.

Mooers, Stephanie L. [also see Christelow, Stephanie Mooers]. "Patronage in the Pipe Roll of 1130." *Speculum* 59 (2) (1984): 282–307.

——. "A Reevaluation of Royal Justice under Henry I of England." *American Historical Review* 93 (1988): 340–358.

Morgan, Marjorie [also see Chibnall, Marjorie]. *The English Lands of the Abbey of Bec*. Oxford, 1946.

Morillo, Stephen. *Warfare under the Anglo-Norman Kings, 1066–1135*. Woodbridge, Suffolk, 1994.

Morris, Colin. *The Papal Monarchy: The Western Church from 1050 to 1250*. Oxford, 1989.

Morris, William A. *The Medieval English Sheriff to 1300*. Manchester, 1927.

Murray, Margaret. *God of the Witches*. 2nd edn. London, 1952.

Musset, Lucien. "Administration et justice dans une grande baronnie normande: Les terres des Bellême sous Roger II et Robert." *Cahiers des annales de Normandie* 17 (Caen, 1985): 129–148.

——. "L'Aristocratie normande au XIe siècle." In *La Noblesse au moyen âge, XIe–XVe siècles: Essais à la mémoire de Robert Boutruche*. Ed. Philippe Contamine. Paris, 1976.

——. "Aux Origines d'une classe dirigeante: Les Tosny, grands barons normands du Xe au XIIIe siècle." *Francia* 5 (1978): 45–80.

——. "Le Mécénat des princes normands au XIe siècle." In *Artistes, artisans, et production artistique au moyen âge*. Vol. 2. Ed. Xavier Barral i Altet. Paris, 1983.

——. "Les Origines et le patrimoine de l'abbaye de Saint-Sever." In *La Normandie bénédictine au temps de Guillaume le Conquérant, XIe siècle*. Lille, 1967.

———, ed. *Normandie romane*. Vol. 1: *La Basse Normandie*. Vol. 2: *La Haute Normandie*. 3rd edn. St Léger-Vauban, 1985–1987.

Nelson, Janet L. "The Rites of the Conqueror." *Anglo-Norman Studies* 4 (1981): 117–132, 210–221. Repr. in Nelson, *Politics and Ritual in Early Medieval Europe*, pp. 371–401, London, 1986.

Nelson, Lynn H. *The Normans in South Wales, 1070–1171*. Austin, Texas, 1966.

Newman, Charlotte. *The Anglo-Norman Nobility in the Reign of Henry I: The Second Generation*. Philadelphia, 1988.

Nicholas, David. *Medieval Flanders*. London, 1992.

Nicholl, Donald. *Thurstan, Archbishop of York, 1114–1140*. York, 1964.

Norgate, Kate. *England under the Angevin Kings*. 2 vols. London, 1887. Repr. New York, 1969.

Offler, H. S. "Hexham and the *Historia Regum.*" *Transactions of the Architectural and Archaeological Society of Durham and Northumberland*, n.s. 2 (1970): 51–62.

———. *Medieval Historians of Durham*. Durham, 1958.

———. "Red Book of Durham." *English Historical Review* 40 (1925): 523–529.

Orme, Nicholas and Margaret Webster. *The English Hospital, 1070–1570*. New Haven, Conn., 1995.

Partner, Nancy F. *Serious Entertainments: The Writing of History in Twelfth-Century England*. Chicago, 1977.

Pierre Abélard/Pierre le Vénérable: Les Courants philosophiques, littéraires, et artistiques en occident au milieu du XIIe siècle. Paris, 1975.

Pignot, J. Henri. *Histoire de l'ordre de Cluny (909–1157)*. 3 vols. Paris, 1868.

Poole, Austin Lane. *From Domesday Book to Magna Carta, 1087–1216*. Oxford, 1951.

Poole, Reginald Lane. *The Exchequer in the Twelfth Century*. Oxford, 1912.

———. *Studies in Chronology and History*. Oxford, 1934.

Porée, André. *Histoire de l'abbaye de Bec*. Vol. 1. Evreux, 1901. Repr. Brussels, 1980.

Potts, Cassandra. "Les Ducs normands et leur nobles: La patronage monastique avant la conquête de l'Angleterre." *Etudes normandes* 3 (1986): 29–37.

Poulle, Béatrice. "Savigny and England." In David Bates and Anne Curry, eds. *England and Normandy in the Middle Ages*.

Powicke, F. M. *The Loss of Normandy, 1189–1204*. 2nd edn. Manchester, 1961.

Prestwich, J. O. "The Military Household of the Norman Kings." *English Historical Review* 96 (1981): 1–35. Repr. in Matthew Strickland, ed. *Anglo-Norman Warfare*.

———. "Military Intelligence under the Norman and Angevin Kings." In George Garnett and John Hudson, eds. *Law and Government*.

Redelius, Gunnar. "Observations architecturales sur Saint-Symphorien." *Le Domfront médiéval* 9 (1993): 6–9.

Reedy, William T. "The Origins of the General Eyre in the Reign of Henry I." *Speculum* 41 (1966): 688–724.

Reilly, Bernard F. *The Kingdom of León-Castilla under King Alfonso VI, 1065–1109*. Princeton, 1988.

Renault, M. "Nouvelles recherches sur les léprosaries el maladeries de Normandie." *Mémoires de la Société des antiquaires de Normandie*, vol. 281. Paris,
1870.

Richardson, H. G. "The Coronation in Medieval England: The Evolution
of the Office and the Oath." *Traditio* 16 (1960): 111–202.

Richardson, H. G. and G. O. Sayles. *The Governance of Mediaeval England
from the Conquest to Magna Carta.* Edinburgh, 1963.

———. *Law and Legislation from Æthelbert to Magna Carta.* Edinburgh, 1966.

Ridyard, Susan J. "*Condigna veneratio*: Post-Conquest Attitudes to the Saints
of the Anglo-Saxons." *Anglo-Norman Studies* 9 (1986/1987): 179–206.

Riley-Smith, Jonathan. *The First Crusade and the Idea of Crusading.* Philadelphia, 1986.

Robert, Ulysse. *Histoire du pape Calixte II.* Paris, 1891.

Robinson, I. S. *The Papacy, 1073–1198: Continuity and Innovation.* Cambridge, 1990.

Robinson, J. Armitage. *Gilbert Crispin, Abbot of Westminster.* Cambridge, 1911.

Rollason, David, ed. *Simeon of Durham, Historian of Durham and the North.*
Stamford, Lincs., 1996.

Round, J. H. *Feudal England.* London, 1895.

———. *Geoffrey de Mandeville: A Study of the Anarchy.* New York, 1892.

———. *The King's Serjeants and Officers of State.* London, 1911.

———. *Studies in Peerage and Family History.* London, 1901.

Rowley, Trevor. *The Norman Heritage: 1066–1200.* London, 1983.

Russell, Josiah C. "The Date of Henry I's Charter to London." In Russell,
Twelfth Century Studies. New York, 1978.

Ruud, Marylou. "Episcopal Reluctance: Lanfranc's Resignation Reconsidered." *Albion* 19 (1987): 163–175.

Sanders, I. J. *English Baronies: A Study of Their Origin and Descent, 1086–1327.*
Oxford, 1960.

Sauvage, R. N. "Des Miracles advenus en l'église de Fécamp." *Mémoires de
la Société des antiquaires de Normandie*, vol. 2. Rouen, 1893.

Sawyer, P. H. "The Wealth of England in the Eleventh Century." *Transactions of the Royal Historical Society*, 5th ser., 15 (1965): 145–164.

Schieffer, Theodor. *Die päpstlichen Legaten in Frankreich vom Vertrag von
Meersen (870) bis zum Schisma von 1130.* Berlin, 1935.

Schmid, Karl. "The Structure of the Nobility in the Earlier Middle Ages."
In Timothy Reuter, ed. *The Medieval Nobility.* Amsterdam, 1978.

Schnürer, Gustav. *Necrologium des Cluniacenser-Priorates Münchenwiler.*
Freiburg, 1909.

Schramm, P. E. *A History of the English Coronation.* Trans. G. Wickham Legg.
Oxford, 1937.

Seaby, P. J. "Henry I Coin Types: Design Characteristics and Chronology."
Yorkshire Numismatist 1 (1988): 27–43.

Searle, Eleanor. *Lordship and Community: Battle Abbey and Its Banlieu,
1066–1538.* Toronto, 1974.

———. *Predatory Kinship and the Creation of Norman Power, 840–1066.*
Berkeley, 1988.

———. "Women and the Legitimisation of Succession at the Norman
Conquest." *Anglo-Norman Studies* 3 (1980/1981): 159–170.

Sharpe, Richard, ed. and trans. "The Prefaces of 'Quadripartitus.'" In George Garnett and John Hudson, eds. *Law and Government in Medieval England and Normandy.*

Short, Ian, ed. "Gaimar's 'Epilogue' and Geoffrey of Monmouth's *Liber vetustissimus.*" *Speculum* 69 (1994): 323–343.

Smalley, Beryl. *Historians in the Middle Ages.* London, 1974.

Southern, R. W. "Aspects of the European Tradition of Historical Writing: 4. The Sense of the Past." *Transactions of the Royal Historical Society,* 5th ser., 23 (1973): 243–263.

——. *Medieval Humanism and Other Studies.* Oxford, 1970.

——. "The Place of Henry I in English History." *Proceedings of the British Academy* 48 (1962): 127–169.

——. *Saint Anselm and His Biographer: A Study in Monastic Life and Thought, 1059–ca. 1130.* Cambridge, 1963.

——. *St Anselm: A Portrait in a Landscape.* Cambridge, 1990.

——. "Sally Vaughn's Anselm: An Examination of the Foundations." *Albion* 20 (1988): 181–204.

Spear, David S. "The Norman Episcopate under Henry I, King of England and Duke of Normandy (1106–1135)." Ph.D. dissertation, University of California, Santa Barbara, 1982.

Spiegel, Gabrielle. *The Chronicle Tradition of Saint-Denis: A Survey.* Brookline, Mass., 1978.

Stafford, Pauline. "*Cherchez la femme:* Queens, Queens' Lands and Nunneries: Missing Links in the Foundation of Reading Abbey." *History* 85 (277) (January 2000): 4–27.

——. *Unification and Conquest: A Political and Social History of England in the Tenth and Eleventh Centuries.* London, 1989.

Staunton, Michael. "Eadmer's *Vita Anselmi:* A Reinterpretation." *Journal of Medieval History* 23 (1997): 1–14.

Stenton, Doris M. *English Justice between the Norman Conquest and the Great Charter, 1066–1215.* Philadelphia, 1964.

Stenton, F. M. *The First Century of English Feudalism, 1066–1166.* 2nd edn. Oxford, 1961.

Stevenson, W. H. "An Inedited Charter of King Henry I, June–July, 1101." *English Historical Review* 21 (1906): 505–509.

Stewart, I. "Coinage and Recoinage after Edgar's Reforms." *Studies in Anglo-Saxon Coinage.* Ed. K. Jonsson, Numismatiska Meddelanden 35. Stockholm, 1990.

Strickland, Matthew, ed. *Anglo-Norman Warfare.* Woodbridge, Suffolk, 1992.

Stubbs, William. *The Constitutional History of England in Its Origin and Development.* 3 vols. Oxford, 1896–1897.

Susong, Gilles. "Notre-Dame-sur-l'Eau à Domfront: Une mise au point." *Le Domfront médiéval* 6 (1988): 9–15.

Tabuteau, Emily Zack. "The Role of Law in the Succession to Normandy and England, 1087." *Haskins Society Journal* 3 (1991): 141–169.

Tait, James. *The Medieval English Borough.* Manchester, 1936.

Takayama, Hiroshi. "*Familiares regis* and the Royal Inner Council in Twelfth-Century Sicily." *English Historical Review* 104 (1989): 357–372.

Tatlock, J. S. P. "The English Journey of the Laon Canons." *Speculum* 8 (1933): 454–465.

——. *The Legendary History of Britain: Geoffrey of Monmouth's "Historia regum Britanniae" and Its Early Vernacular Versions.* Berkeley, 1950.

Taylor, Silas. *The History of Gavel-kind with the Etymology Thereof.* London, 1663.

Tellenbach, Gerd. *The Church in Western Europe from the Tenth to the Early Twelfth Century.* Cambridge, 1993.

——. "Zur Erforschung des hochmittelalterlichen Adels (9.–12. Jahrhundert)." In *XIIe Congrès international des sciences historiques.* Vienna, 1965.

Thompson, James Westfall. *The Literacy of the Laity in the Middle Ages.* Berkeley, 1939.

Thompson, Kathleen. "Family and Influence to the South of Normandy in the Eleventh Century: The Lordship of Bellême." *Journal of Medieval History* 11 (1) (1985): 215–226.

——. "The Lords of Laigle: Ambition and Insecurity on the Borders of Normandy." *Anglo-Norman Studies* 18 (1995/1996): 177–199.

——. "Orderic Vitalis and Robert of Bellême: A Re-Examination and Assessment of the Twelfth-Century Anglo-Norman Magnate as Chronicled by the Norman Monastic." *Journal of Medieval History* 20 (1994): 133–141.

——. "Robert of Bellême Reconsidered." *Anglo-Norman Studies* 13 (1990/1991): 263–284.

——. "William Talvas, Count of Ponthieu, and the Politics of the Anglo-Norman Realm." In David Bates and Anne Curry, eds. *England and Normandy in the Middle Ages.*

Thomson, Rodney. *William of Malmesbury.* Woodbridge, Suffolk, 1987.

Tillmann, Helen. *Die päpstlichen Legaten in England bis zur Beendigung der Legation Gualas (1218).* Bonn, 1926.

Turner, Ralph V. "The *Miles Literatus* in Twelfth- and Thirteenth-Century England: How Rare a Phenomenon?" *American Historical Review* 83 (1978): 928–945.

Van Caenegem, R. C. "Public Prosecution of Crime in Twelfth-Century England." In *Church and Government in the Middle Ages: Essays Presented to C. R. Cheney.* Ed. C. N. L. Brooke et al. Cambridge, 1976.

Van den Eynde, Damien. "Les Principaux voyages de Pierre le Vénérable." *Benedictina* 15 (1) (1968): 58–111.

Van Engen, John. "The 'Crisis of Cenobitism' Reconsidered: Benedictine Monasticism in the Years 1050–1150." *Speculum* 61 (2) (1986): 269–304.

Van Fleteren, Frederick and Joseph C. Schnaubelt, eds. *Twenty-Five Years (1969–1994) of Anselm Studies: A Review and Critique of Recent Scholarly Views.* Lewiston, NY, 1996.

Van Houts, Elisabeth. "The *Gesta Normannorum Ducum*: A History without an End." *Anglo-Norman Studies* 3 (1980/1981): 106–118.

——. "Robert of Torigny as Genealogist." In Christopher Harper-Bill, ed. *Studies in Medieval History Presented to R. Allen Brown.* Woodbridge, Suffolk, 1989.

——. "The Ship List of William the Conqueror." *Anglo-Norman Studies* 10 (1987/1988): 159–183.

Vaughn, Sally N. *The Abbey of Bec and the Anglo-Norman State, 1034–1136*. Woodbridge, Suffolk, 1981.

———. *Anselm of Bec and Robert of Meulan: The Innocence of the Dove and the Wisdom of the Serpent*. Berkeley, 1987.

———. "Anselm: Saint and Statesman." *Albion* 20 (1988): 205–220.

Von Knonau, G. Meyer. *Jahrbücher des deutschen Reichs unter Heinrich IV und Heinrich V*, vol. 7. Leipzig, 1909.

Von Moos, P. *Hildebert von Lavardin*. Stuttgart, 1965.

Von Oppolzer, Theodor R. *Canon of Eclipses [Canon der Finsternisse]*. Trans. Owen Gingerich. New York, 1962.

Voss, Lena. *Heinrich von Blois, Bischof von Winchester (1129–1171)*. Berlin, 1932.

Walker, Barbara M. "King Henry I's 'Old Men.' " *Journal of British Studies* 8 (1) (1968): 1–21.

Warren, W. L. "The Death of William Rufus." *History Today* 9 (1959): 22–29.

———. *The Governance of Norman and Angevin England, 1086–1272*. London, 1987.

———. *Henry II*. London, 1973.

Wauters, A. "Godefroid Ier, comte de Louvain." In *Académie royale des sciences, des lettres et des beaux arts de Belgique: Bibliographie nationale* 7 (Brussels, 1883): 846–847.

Webber, Teresa. *Scribes and Scholars at Salisbury Cathedral, c. 1075–c. 1125*. Oxford, 1992.

Werckmeister, Otto Karl. "Cluny III and the Pilgrimage to Santiago." In *Artistes, artisans, et production artistique au moyen âge*. Ed. Xavier Barral i Altet. Paris, 1983.

Wertheimer, Laura. "Adeliza of Louvain and Anglo-Norman Queenship." *Haskins Society Journal* 7 (1995): 101–115.

White, Graeme H. "The Career of Waleran Count of Meulan and Earl of Worcester, 1104–1166." *Transactions of the Royal Historical Society*, 4th ser., 17 (1934): 19–48.

———. "The Household of the Norman Kings." *Transactions of the Royal Historical Society*, 4th ser., 30 (1948): 127–155.

———. "King Stephen, Duke Henry and Ranulf de Gernons, Earl of Chester." *English Historical Review* 91 (1976): 555–565.

Wightman, W. E. "Henry I and the Foundation of Nostell Priory." *Yorkshire Archaeological Journal* 41 (1963–1966): 57–60.

———. *The Lacy Family in England and Normandy, 1066–1194*. Oxford, 1966.

Williamson, Hugh Ross. *The Arrow and the Sword: An Essay in Detection*. 2nd edn. London, 1955.

Wollasch, Joachim. "A Cluniac Necrology from the Time of St Hugh." In Noreen Hunt, ed. *Cluniac Monasticism in the Central Middle Ages*.

———. *Synopse der Cluniacensischen Necrologien*. 2 vols. Munich, 1982.

Wood, Charles T. *The French Apanages and the Capetian Monarchy, 1224–1328*. Cambridge, Mass., 1966.

Wootten, William. "A Study of Henry I, King of England, 1068–1107." Ph.D. dissertation, University of Minnesota, 1964.

Wormald, Patrick. "*Laga Eadwardi*: The *Textus Roffensis* and Its Context." *Anglo-Norman Studies* 17 (1994/1995): 243–266.

——. "Quadripartitus." In George Garnett and John Hudson, eds. *Law and Government in Medieval England and Normandy.*

Yver, Jean. "Les Châteaux forts en Normandie jusqu'au milieu du XIIe siècle." *Bulletin de la Société des antiquaires de Normandie* 53 (1955–1956): 28–115.

——. "Le Développement du pouvoir ducal en Normandie de l'avènement de Guillaume le Conquérant à la mort d'Henri Ier, 1035–1135." In *Atti del convegno internazionale di studi ruggeriani.* Palermo, 1955.

——. "Les Premières institutions du duché de Normandie." In *I Normanni è la loro espansione in Europa nell'alto medievo.* Settimane di studio del Centro italiano di studi sull'alto medioevo 16. Spoleto, 1969.

INDEX